I0867298

Edited by Sandra Piesik

HABITAT

Vernacular Architecture for a Changing Climate

New Edition

With over 1,000 illustrations

Contents

Page 1 Toposa granary built of grasses, Nyanyagachor, South Sudan.

Pages 2–3 Traditional Zulu *iqhugwane* structures in South Africa's KwaZulu-Natal province.

Pages 4–5 Indigenous solutions to climates globally (clockwise from top left): Banco village of mud homes on Niger River bank, Mopti Region, Mali; favelas of Rio de Janeiro, Brazil; timber and thatch home and restaurant in coastal Crawl Cay, Bocas del Toro region, Panama; earthen and timber Sámi home in Abisko National Park, Lapland, Sweden.

Pages 6–7 Traditional vernacular structures (clockwise from top left): ceremonial home in West Irian, Indonesia, 1909–11; edifice for storing enemy skulls at Battak Kampong, Sumatra, c. 1890; framework of a Bas-Congo house, Democratic Republic of Congo c. 1944–48; pitched roof houses in Sumatra, Indonesia, c. 1890s; Srinagar mosque, Kashmir; decorated Sumatra home, 1877; wooden church, Korely, Russia; conical detail of temple in West Irian, Indonesia, 1908–12.

Pages 8–9 Climatic variations across the planet shape the landscapes and materiality of local habitats (clockwise from top left): view of houses and fields from Highway 35, Saskatchewan, Canada; circular Tulou structures of South China; Shali fortresses of earthen bricks, Siwa Oasis, Egypt; Lake Village of Ganvie, Benin, Africa.

How This Book Works

Köppen–Geiger Map

Equirectangular projection. Scale 1: 70 000 000

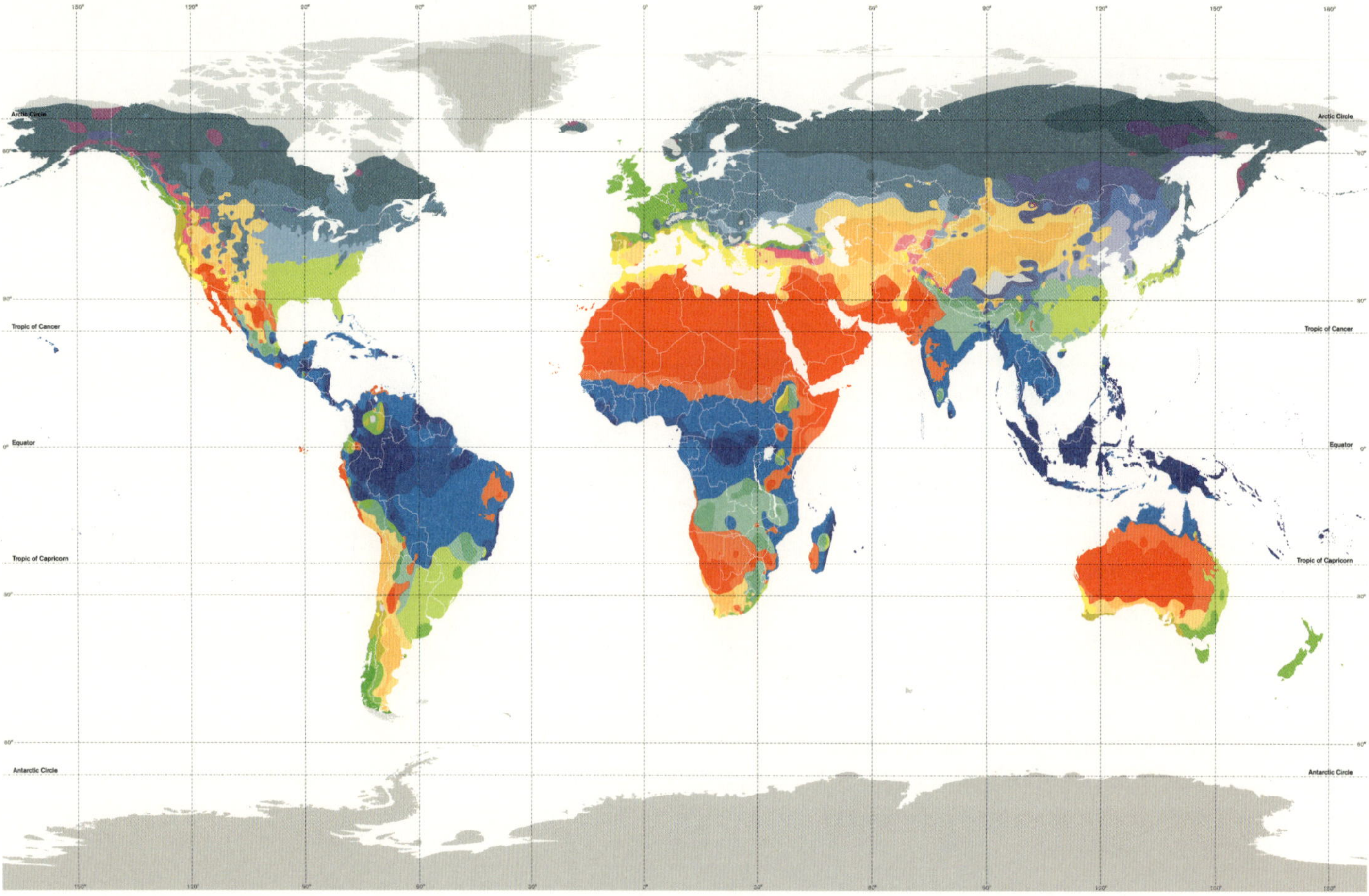

Climate has an enormous influence on both the materials available in a region, and the type of building constructed to ensure adequate shelter. The regionally specific content of *Habitat: Vernacular Architecture for a Changing Climate* is therefore structured in five parts according to the zones established by the Köppen–Geiger system: tropical, dry, temperate, continental and polar.

Within the larger climatic framework of chapters, each region/country entry includes a focused locator map to show the geography of the area discussed, as well as the specific climatic subregions it encompasses.

Entries are also accompanied by two comparative scale bars that chart the Average Temperature and the corresponding Average Rainfall for each season (MAM: March–May; JJA: June–August; SON: September–November; DJF: December–February). The increase or decrease in temperature and rainfall illustrates a meaningful representation of the main climate characteristics of each region and is predominantly based on thirty-year climate normals collated from 1961 to 1990. Note that climate normals for large geographic areas are not included as they cannot give an accurate overview of temperature and rainfall.

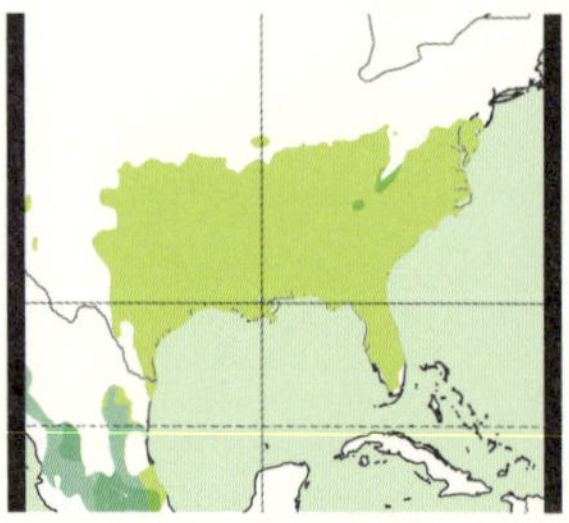

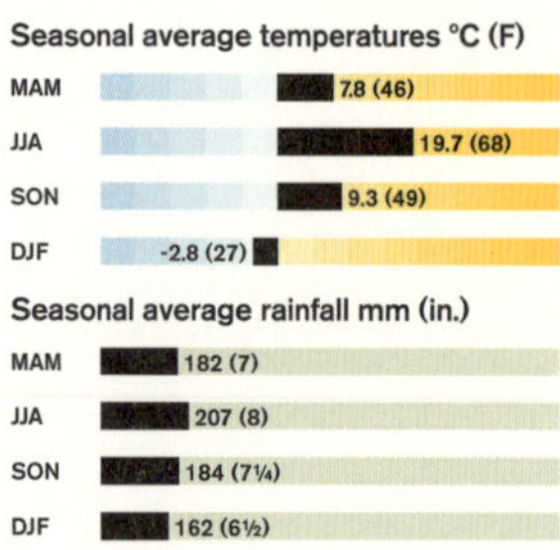

Contributors

Dr Subhi Al-Azzawi
John Amato
Dr Samuel Amos-Abanyie
Dr Iftekhar Ahmed
Barbara J. Anello-Adnani
Professor Anne E. Guernsey Allen
Dr Kjell-Åke Aronsson
Dr Munzifakhon Babadjanova
Peter Zanang-Kazah Barwa
Dr Randall Bird
Dr Ágnes Birtalan
Professor Marcial Blondet
Dr Douglas J. Bolender
Dr Lissant Bolton
Dr Noni Boyd
Professor Ronaldo de Moraes Brilhante
Dr Deidre Brown
Jeanette Budgett
Dr Guglielmo Carra
Dr William R. Chapman
Dr Mounia Chekhab-Abudaya
Professor Don Choi
Professor Jim Coleman
Professor Marjan Colletti
Dr Louise Cooke
Professor Marcos Cruz
Dr Rami Farouk Daher
Dr Hacer Mutlu Danaci
Professor Frederique Darragon
Dr Mark Dike DeLancey
Dr Letizia Dipasquale
Dr Amy Eisenberg
Alessandro Famiglietti
Henry Fletcher
Dr Tammy Gaber
Catherine Gallois
Dr William Galloway
Lucia Garzon
Professor Mark L. Gillem
Nasser Golzari
Yenny Gunawan
Professor Sabina Hajiyeva
Dr Suzanne Harris-Brandts
Dr John Hemming
Denise Heywood
Dr Miriam Ho
Dr Min-Fu Hsu
John Hutchinson
Anna Ietswaart
Isse Israelsson
Gisle Jakhelln
Dr Aldona Jonaitis
Dr Natalia Jorquera Silva
Professor Bashir A. Kazimee
Kirsti Kovanen
Kengo Kuma
U Win Kyaing
Yasmeen Lari
Dr Mike Lawrence
Dr Alice Spencer Leineweber
Professor Ronald Lewcock
Dr Graham Lott
Dr Anna Yu Mainicheva
Alexander Maitland
Dr Olga V. Maltseva
Wolf Mangelsdorf
Larisa Marenco
Professor Saverio Mecca
Professor Paul Memmott
Professor Camilla Mileto
Dr William Milliken
James Morris
Dr Karen Nero
Daw Yin Nyein Aye
Professor Rexford Assasie Oppong
Dr Timothy O'Rourke
Lena Palmqvist
Professor Kyung-Rip Park
Hugo Pereira Gigone
Dr Patrick Pérez
Dr Anna Permilovskaya
Tom Perry
Dr Walter Peters
Dr Sandra Piesik
Professor Suzanne Preston Blier
Dr Beniamino Polimeni
Dr Gray Read
Dr Gregory A. Reinhardt
Dr Laura Rival
Karen Rizvi
Angela Rodríguez de Famiglietti
Sofía Rodríguez-Larraín
Rebecca Roke
Dr Rodolfo Rotondaro
Dr Luis Silvio Rios Cabrera
Graham Saunders
Peter Sheehan
Sigríður Sigurðardóttir
Dr André Singer
Dr Joëlle Smadja
Dr Catherine Souch
Jeffrey Soule
Professor James M. Steele
Dr John M. Steinberg
Professor Matthew Sturm
Professor Su Su
Dr Charmaine 'Ilaiu Talei
Professor Zhu Tan
Professor Gérard Toffin
Dr Jeremy Treadwell
Chris Trott
Professor Michael Turner
Fida Touma
Adriana Useche
Dr Ronald van Oers
Professor Fernando Vegas
Simón Vélez
Rajiv Wanasundera
Dr Debbie Whelan
Dr Ping-Sheng Wu
Aram Yeretzian
Dr Lijun Zhou
Dr María Gabriela Zurita Benavides

Foreword

Tomasz Chruszczow

Having a home – a shelter, a cave, a cottage, a castle, a house – has, as we know, always been a part of humanity's basic needs. It still is today, but one thing that has been changing with time is technology. Its development has resulted in new materials and facilities, which assist everyday life. But nothing has changed as dramatically as the population of this planet. We were around 1 billion at the beginning of the 19th century, 3 billion by the mid-1960s and topped 8 billion towards the end of 2022. Every year there are 75–80 million more of us.

Can all those people live a peaceful and secure life on Earth? How to make this possible within the existing planetary boundaries? Which technologies will help it happen? Which resources will be the most sustainable? How to plan, develop and manage future megacities with 50 million inhabitants – young, ambitious, seeking decent jobs and life standards? What kind of infrastructure will be needed? Future lists of similar questions will certainly be even longer.

Nature, and its resources, has always been a home and a reservoir of materials for humanity and this remains true today. Technologies may have developed, but the basics remain the same: we need fresh and clean air, clean water, energy and food. Since the very early years of humanity, people have been using natural resources to make their lives easier and safer. They have been protecting themselves against various threats: cold; heat; wild animals; bad weather; and, eventually, against other tribes of people. Throughout our entire history, the need to protect the 'group' (nation, tribe, family) and its territory has driven the development of what we now call technology.

Back in 1992, decisions taken at the Rio Earth Summit resulted in the adoption by the United Nations of three major international environmental agreements – the three UN conventions on Biological Diversity (UNCBD), to Combat Desertification (UNCCD), and on Climate Change (UNFCCC). In 2015, another historic landmark treaty – the Paris Agreement – entered into force. It put sustainable, climate-neutral development as the top priority of all countries in the world. Stabilizing the concentration of greenhouse gases in our atmosphere is the ultimate goal of the Climate Change Convention, but poverty eradication, enhancing the resilience of communities to climatic stresses, and food- and water-supply security remain overriding priorities for the majority of developing nations. When planning national policies and actions, all three pillars of sustainability as defined – social, environmental and economic – should be considered equally important.

Human habitat can be described in many ways: by the variety of factors determining living conditions – climate, the surrounding nature, the physical environment; by the design of its buildings; or by the materials and equipment used, for example. When considering habitat, we need to remember that it is a dynamic concept, changing with time as a result of human activity, such as deforestation, damming of rivers or urbanization; natural disasters; and slow, climatic changes. It is always a huge challenge to fully deal with this dynamism and to demonstrate the human ability to adapt and live in a sometimes dramatically changing world.

Humanity now stands at the edge of the great transition from today to the sustainable future. No other option seems to be left, and full implementation of the Paris Agreement will play an instrumental role in setting the new development paradigm. Through this accord, human experiences from all over the world – from every climate zone, and from multiple cultures and traditions – which we now call 'indigenous knowledge' received recognition from the global community. A sustainable future must fully take into account the entire multifaceted treasury of traditional wisdom.

Habitat: Vernacular Architecture for a Changing Climate is an impressive collection of the lessons from millennia of experience, demonstrated as practical examples of ready-to-use solutions – to copy, develop, deploy – for now and for the future. Every climate zone and multiple ecosystems have been included. We are taken for a fascinating trip across our planet, across the richness of wisdom that has developed over the history of thousands of generations and that is available for the generations to come.

Tomasz Chruszczow is Former Chair of the Subsidiary Body for Implementation & Subsidiary Body for Scientific and Technological Advice of the UN Framework Convention on Climate Change. Tomasz was also appointed High-Level Climate Champion for COP24.

Opposite Human habitat is a dynamic concept, changing over time. We now stand at a point of great transition from today to the sustainable future, and our successful inhabitation of the planet relies on implementing climate-neutral goals and acknowledging the importance of indigenous knowledge to achieve this.

Introduction

Sandra Piesik

The history of our relationship, as a species, with this planet is a fascinating one. Ultimately, it is a story shaped by the availability of food and shelter, and the emergence of social structures that make up particular communities and society as a whole. The need to meet the basic demands of human life has been the engine that has driven and moulded our relationship with our environment. Since these needs are the same across the globe, they form a baseline of common experience from which local particularities can be evaluated. Variations in climate from region to region and a non-uniform distribution of resources have led to different strategies and diverse technologies emerging from place to place and according to the specific local conditions and the particular opportunities and threats that accompany them. Geography has significantly shaped our relationship with nature and the decisions that we have made, and continue to make, on questions ranging from how best to build a simple shelter to the organization and development of a city.

Habitat: Vernacular Architecture for a Changing Climate explores this connection between the environment and built form through an examination of five global climate zones: tropical, dry, temperate, continental and polar. These are based on the internationally recognized Köppen–Geiger system, which, broadly speaking, designates five major climate types, each with an identifying letter: tropical (A); dry (B); temperate moist mid-latitude with mild winters (C); continental moist mid-latitude with cold winters (D); and polar (E). The examples in this book are structured in accordance with these Köppen–Geiger zones. In the process, the story unfolds of humanity's capacity to create architecture without jeopardizing the equilibrium of the Earth's ecosystems, upon which human life depends. This story urgently needs to be told if we are to navigate successfully our changing relationship with our planet in the present age.

Below This image from NASA's 'Blue Marble' project is the most detailed overview of the entire Earth's surface to date. Created by compositing a year of monthly imagery captured by satellites, it paints a clear picture of climatic difference across the planet, from deserts to polar regions, as well as tropical, temperate and continental zones.

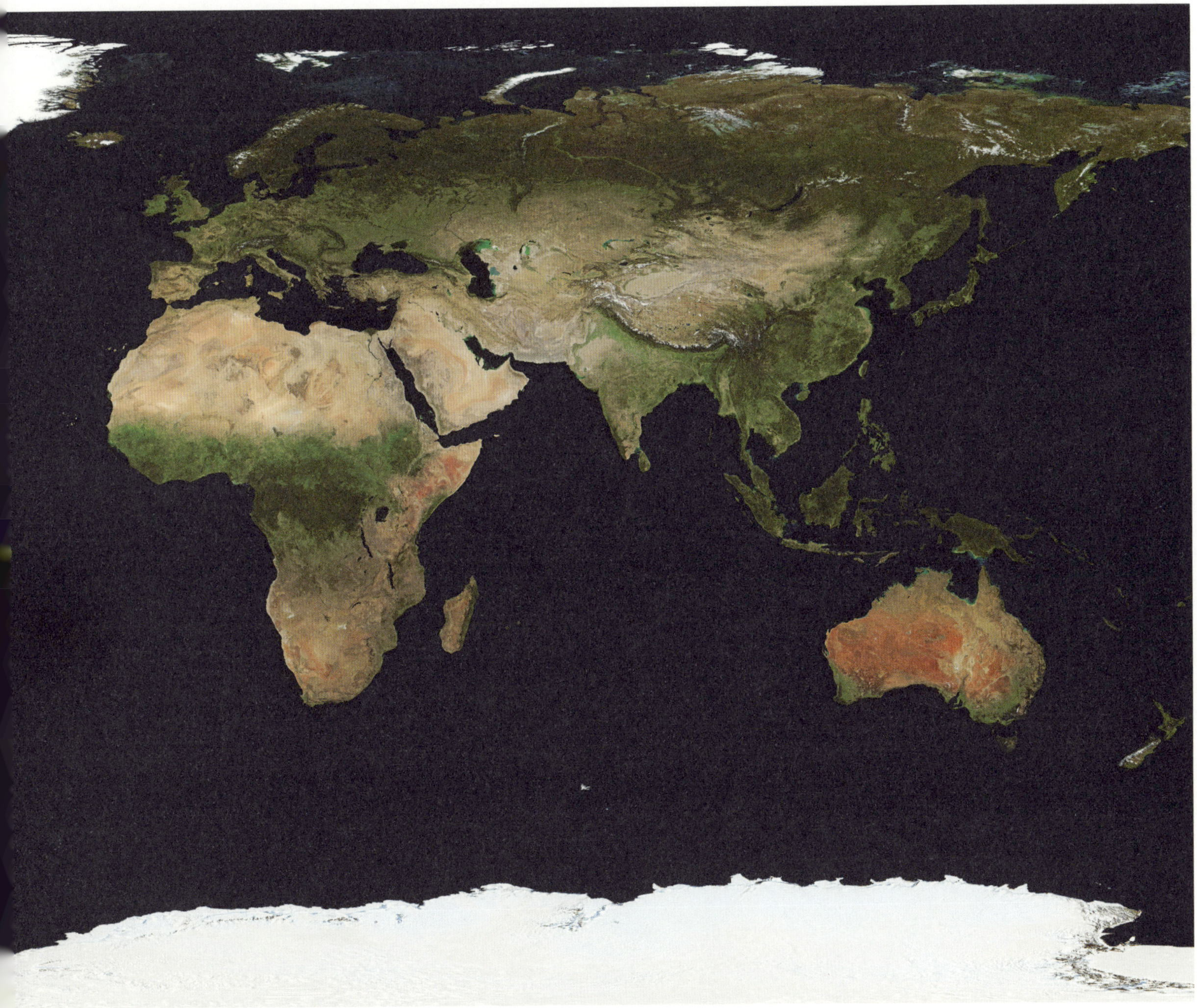

Opposite and below Understanding the authenticity and character of place through built form is paramount in an effort to reclaim a harmonious existence with nature. Traditional dwellings have an inherent logic in their material choice and form – from Dogon mud granaries in Mali (top left) or beehive homes of brick and mud in Syria (below) to structures of grass in the Sudan (middle) or in Sumba, Indonesia (bottom), or homes built of forest materials in Papua New Guinea (top right).

A consensus has emerged among geologists that we have now entered the Anthropocene era, a phase in the Earth's history that is defined by the negative impact of human activity on our climate and our environment. In geological terms, these changes have been observed in an unusually short time-frame, beginning with the Industrial Revolution and the shift to mechanization that has so fundamentally altered our relationship with technology. Since then, the modernization and Westernization of global culture, facilitated by technological advances such as the Internet, has connected us all. In this age of digital interconnectivity, our experience of the unique characteristics of a place can be easily impaired as the world is viewed and interpreted through the lens of Google searches, touch screens and 'big data'. There is a pressing need to rediscover the authenticity and particularity of place. What existed before the advent of modernity? How did we manage to live in harmony with nature before culture was technologized? Are there any lessons to be learned from the adaptation of tested ideas?

Technological confusion is not the only reason for re-examining the tried-and-tested models of sustainable living adopted by our ancestors. Climate change, for example, is posing a genuine threat to the well-being of us all. In addition, there is the problem of reconciling the growing demand for the Earth's resources, as the global population continues to expand, with the brute fact that many of these resources are finite and others are fragile. There are good reasons to attempt to rediscover an equilibrium in our relationship with nature through the sustainable management of our natural resources.

Without romanticizing or 'orientalizing' the past, it is clear that indigenous knowledge systems give us the practical embodiment of centuries of wisdom and experience, which, if properly understood, offers us a masterclass in regional socio-economic resilience. To this end, the section for each climate zone suggests a different package of zero-carbon solutions embedded in local micro-economies, livelihoods, and sustainable, passive architecture.

Although climate zones spread 'horizontally' across latitudes, there are similarities in architectural responses along the 'vertical' longitudes – in all likelihood because the weather conditions and the resources available across each climate belt are similar. The equatorial and southern-equatorial Amazonian rainforest, along with the islands of Southeast Asia, are home to some of the largest plant structures in the world, which even today house communities of up to 100 people. Between the tropics in Africa, we find exquisite grass structures; in Asia, across the same climate zone, we find indigenous communities making imaginative use of plants that recognize people's symbiotic relationship with nature. The largest and most vulnerable climate zone – the desert – exemplifies technologies for construction with earth and stone and all manner of adobe structures. These have addressed heat gain through thermal mass as communities discovered ways to build without timber. Here, the use of plants is limited to palms, imported hardwood and grasses. Livelihoods, economic activities, trading routes and groundwater management were catalysts for development everywhere. In the temperate and continental climates north of the equator, we see – when we trace the history

of the built environment and the use of materials such as timber, stone and brick – an attempt to respond to seasonal changes in weather patterns. Earthquake-resilient buildings in these climate zones have been successfully constructed through lightweight designs that mix timber and earth products. Timber is also used for construction in polar regions, but here – as in the deserts, at the other extreme of the planet's temperature range – earth has also been an important component in construction traditionally.

Nonetheless, the sheer isolation of some communities facilitated the development of unique material cultures and styles of ornamentation. These form a crucial ingredient in maintaining the cultural identity of such remote communities, and as such they are interwoven with traditions of storytelling, art and worship.

Another aspect of contemporary vernacular architecture is presented by the current suburban 'micro-cities', with no infrastructure and millions of people living well below the poverty line. The exponential growth of cities, and the simultaneous high unemployment and lack of technological stimulus in rural areas, has led to a loss of local knowledge and an erosion of regional cultural identities. This remains an unsolved global problem that affects all continents and all climate zones. There are lessons to be learned for modern town planning from traditional cities, indigenous neighbourhoods and historical dwelling-block patterns, which offer alternatives to contemporary 'one size fits all' solutions. Migration from rural areas to cities is another global problem, and examples of agro-forestry, agriculture, groundwater management with a sophisticated knowledge of irrigation, sustainable livelihoods and architecture created from local resources all constitute timeless models of self-sustainable communities. Above all, they create jobs in rural areas and cities alike.

To fully understand rural economies and cultures we need to appreciate that their story is nowadays bound up with the emergence of urban areas. Despite all our technological advances, at the heart of the socio-economic 'DNA' of the city is the climate, and the resources available within it. The influence of climate and resources is particularly apparent in the compact designs of desert cities. These are located not 'in the middle of nowhere', as might be thought at first sight, but adjacent to water sources, oases and trading routes. Historically, such cities have been exemplars of social and religious cohesion that evolved over time in an organic and sustainable way.

All climate zones and continents have also, at some point in their history, experienced some form of colonization and/or foreign influence. Historically, this has meant that European architectural styles have been constructed next to, or instead of, indigenous vernacular architecture – but there are case studies of successful coexistence. However, the advent of globalization and modernism has at times brought with it alien and non-climate-specific typologies that expelled originality and, above all, the use of local, natural materials. Concrete blocks and corrugated iron have all too often replaced imagination, inventiveness, creativity and ornamentation. The history of sustainable ways of living has largely been locked away in museums, heritage villages and architectural theme parks.

However, 'copy and paste' solutions from the past often no longer meet the social aspirations of cultures

Below and opposite Enduring patterns of ornamentation and material culture express the identity of communities. The imagination and creativity of particular, local inventiveness is seen across the globe, in such examples as the distinctive 'Falu Red' homes of Sweden and Scandinavia (below), the profuse interior decoration of an Uzbekistan summer house (top) or the abstract frescoes that decorate the mud homes of the Kassena tribe in the Tiébélé region bordering Burkina Faso and Ghana (bottom).

Hilton
Hilton

Opposite and below Replicated Western 'solutions' to modern living have been adopted ad hoc and are often out of context and overscaled – and adapt poorly to local climates. This contrasting built environment is seen in the Morumbi district of São Paulo, for example (opposite), or in Ulan Bator, Mongolia, where the city centre is incongruent with traditional yurt and timber structures (below).

now. Replicated Western solutions are, in many cases, out of context and overscaled, alienating communities and ignoring not only social structures but also local climatic characteristics. Countries need to establish a new paradigm for the expansion of their built environment – one based on the adaptation of their past and the sensitive use of local resources, as well as meeting modern needs and aspirations. The new generation of hybrid solutions and knowledge may offer a way forward.

Adaptation forms part of Article 7 of the Paris Agreement, a universal, legally binding global climate deal established at the UNFCCC's 21st annual Conference of the Party in December 2015. In this ground-breaking achievement, 197 countries signed up to a climate-change 'roadmap', which included a framework on how to adapt indigenous technologies to modern use at local, subnational, national, regional and international levels. Adaptation is seen as a key component of any long-term climate-change solution that aims to protect people, livelihoods and ecosystems. The Paris Agreement recommends basing this adaptation (as appropriate) on the best available science combined with traditional knowledge systems. The successful integration of socio-economic and environmental actions is linked to the sustainable management of natural resources, and the solutions of the past achieved just such a successful integration.

How, then, might we adapt these solutions for contemporary use? Technology development and transfer (covered by Article 10 of the Paris Agreement) offers recommendations for long-term climate-change resilience

and actions. There is no doubt that the transition from baseline technologies, focused on the deployment of technology with a basic use of tools and local materials, has been the first stage of technological development. Advancement and mechanization led to the next stage of upscaling, known as 'intermediate technology'. The further introduction of high-level mechanization, frontier technologies, science and innovation – as well as research and development – can bring about change, the implementation of developed technologies and a fair distribution of jobs. In this 'win-win' situation, capacity building is paramount. It recognizes the obstacles inhibiting people and organizations while enhancing the abilities that will allow them to achieve sustainable results. This is true not only in developing countries but also in the developed world.

The United Nations' Sustainable Development Goals (SDGs) offer a complementary proposition on global action plans for poverty alleviation, and quite few of them also refer to the built environment – specifically in relation to innovation and infrastructure, sustainable cities, communities, and responsible consumption and production. SDG number 17, 'Partnership for the Goals', is a proposal for a holistic approach to implementation, through multidisciplinary, cross-sector collaborations.

The Paris Agreement recognizes that climate change, and the impacts of the measures taken in response to it, will affect us all.[1] In the words of Ban Ki-moon (UN Secretary-General 2007–16), 'There is no plan B, because we do not have a Planet B.' *Habitat: Vernacular Architecture for A Changing Climate* demonstrates, through a multidisciplinary approach involving more than 100 distinguished contributors, that human ingenuity has developed successful solutions for 'Plan A' that worked for us and our planet for millennia. If properly understood and retrieved, these same solutions can be adapted to our present moment – and see us safely through the next millennium.

Below and opposite To bring about sustainable change it is vital that technological development and knowledge transfer occur. The results of this holistic approach will be necessarily broad and may encompass answers such as construction with plant by-products (below left), a project led by Sandra Piesik that formed palm-leaf food shelters; the increased use of softwood in such buildings as Cullinan Studio's Stonebridge Hillside Hub (below right); or structures built from recyclable materials like Shigeru Ban's cardboard construction for Christchurch Cathedral in New Zealand (opposite).

Overleaf Successfully occupying their territory for generations, the tree houses of the Korowai people in New Guinea are just one of many solutions presented in this volume that illustrate the range of ingenuity and indigenous knowledge that is so important for us to rediscover.

The Influence of Climate on Building Design and Materials

Catherine Souch

Climate has an important influence both on the design of buildings and on the availability of local materials used in their construction. From the earliest human times, shelters have been constructed to provide protection from the intense heat of the sun; hostile temperatures, hot or cold; heavy rain or snow; and winds of varying severity and direction. Building styles, settlement patterns, materials and methods of construction all have been developed and adapted in response to elements of weather and climate in order to provide insulation or shading; to reflect or store as much of the sun's energy as possible; to enhance ventilation; or to protect against intense winds, rainfall, heavy snow or flooding. These practices continue today. However, many modern buildings have become increasingly complex, involving technologically advanced construction materials and mechanical systems for controlling interior air quality, thermal comfort, lighting and acoustics. Often these rely heavily on the use of non-renewable energy, and are costly to install and energy-intensive to operate.

Buildings also create their own microclimates, accentuating or moderating elements of the background climate. Cities, for example, are often warmer than surrounding rural areas because of the additional heat generated by their occupants, along with the greater storage of the sun's energy by dark building materials and the styles of construction of tall buildings, roads, and so on. Recognition of this phenomenon (commonly called the 'Urban Heat Island', or UHI, effect) – and concerns about changing climates at local, regional and global scales – have also served to focus greater attention on climate-sensitive architecture and design, as a strategy for both climate mitigation and adaptation.

Climate Zones

Ultimately, our climate results from seasonally varying patterns of solar energy across the Earth's surface, moderated by the effects of large continents, oceans and their currents, mountain chains, large inland bodies of water and regional patterns of land cover, whether vegetation or snow and ice. The differences in heating levels from the equator to the poles, and the seasonal changes in these in the two hemispheres, drive the atmosphere – creating wind and weather, and zones of rising and sinking air – and thus influence global patterns of rainfall and humidity. These features interact to produce a wide array of different climates. However, the similarities of climate within a given area do allow the Earth to be divided up broadly into climatic zones or regions.

One of the most frequently used climate classifications was developed by Wladimir Köppen (1846–1940). First published in 1884, with modifications by Köppen himself in 1918 and 1936, the system was developed further in collaboration with Rudolf Geiger (the Köppen–Geiger system was first published in 1961).

The Köppen–Geiger system (hereafter: Köppen) rests on the basic idea that native vegetation is the best expression of climate; climate zone boundaries can therefore be defined with vegetation distribution in mind. Typically, Köppen climate zones are defined in terms of average annual and monthly temperatures and precipitation, along with the seasonality of precipitation. Thus, the Köppen scheme is based on 'observed' features: meteorological data or, in its absence, vegetation. Other climate-classification systems may be 'genetic' (based on the causes of climatic conditions, such as solar radiation, air masses or pressure systems) or 'applied' (created for a particular climate-associated problem, for example potential evapotranspiration for agriculture).

At its simplest level, the Köppen system defines five major climatic types: each type is designated with a capital letter – tropical (A), dry (B), moist mid-latitude with mild winters (C), moist mid-latitude with cold winters (D) and polar (E). Each climate type then contains sub-regions, which incorporate special regional characteristics such as seasonal changes in temperature and precipitation. In mountainous regions, where rapid changes in weather conditions bring about sharp changes in climate type, delineating climate regions is particularly problematic. These regions are designated H, for highland climates.

All climate classifications have been subjected to varying degrees of criticism. Köppen's system has been criticized because its sharp boundaries do not correspond to the natural boundaries of climate, which tend to have more gradual transitions. However, as a framework to describe the main patterns of vegetation, temperature and precipitation across the globe, it is a widely used and valuable tool.

Opposite Around the world, dwellings are shaped by the climate in which they occur. Climatic variation affects the degree of shelter required as well as the natural environment and materials available to build with. In New Mexico's Frijoles Canyon, for instance, soft rock walls known as tuff have been extracted for centuries to form cliff dwellings for the ancestral Pueblo people.

Overleaf The Köppen–Geiger climate classification system remains one of the most referenced systems for classifying climate type. The map is formed of five principal zones: tropical (A), dry (B), temperate (C), continental (D) and polar (E). Within each main climate type are variations grouped according to precipitation and temperature.

Köppen–Geiger Map

Equirectangular projection. Scale 1: 70 000 000

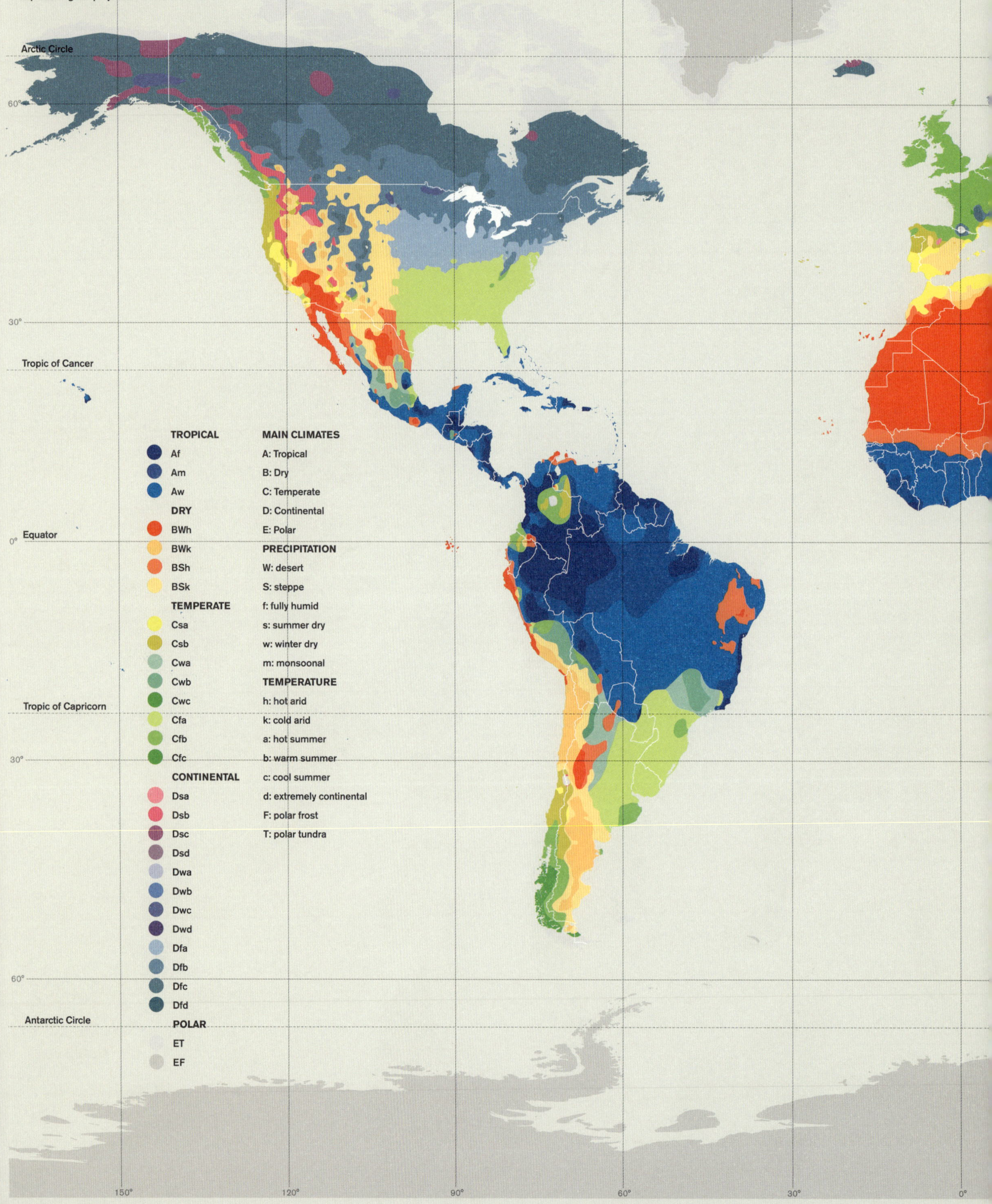

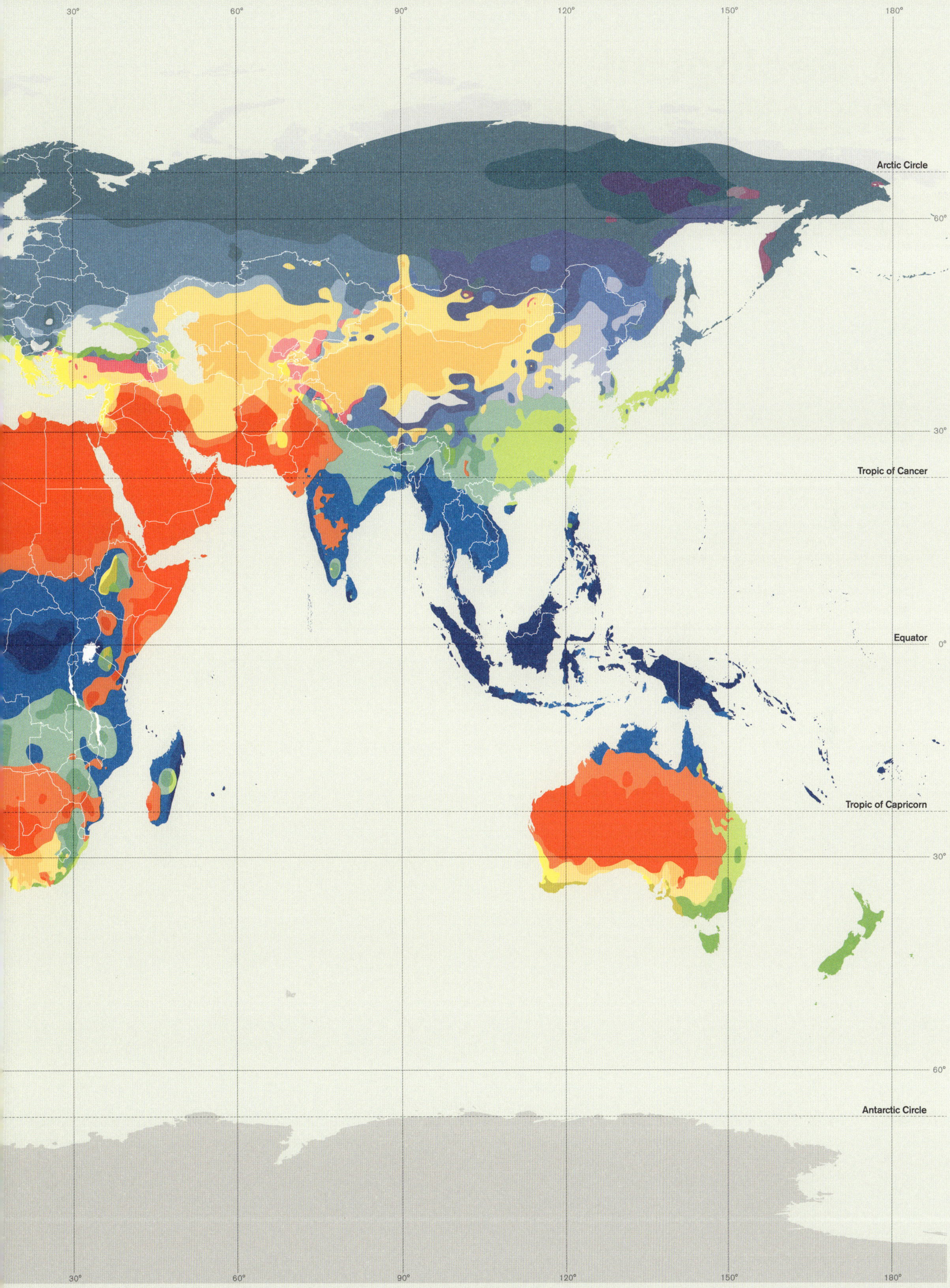

30°
60°
90°
120°
150°
180°
Arctic Circle
60°
30°
Tropic of Cancer
Equator
0°
Tropic of Capricorn
30°
60°
Antarctic Circle
30°
60°
90°
120°
150°
180°

A Geological Classification of Earth Materials in Vernacular Construction

Graham Lott

Classification of the earth materials used in the construction of vernacular buildings on a worldwide basis is a major challenge – particularly in view of the well-documented local and regional geodiversity of the materials available. In general, by definition, the materials used in such indigenous vernacular buildings, including both domestic and non-domestic forms, have been obtained from near their construction site. Consequently, such materials may include not only the full range of geological stone (or rock) types available – including igneous, metamorphic and sedimentary material – but also their highly variable erosion products, created by the natural weathering of such stones under a plethora of different climatic conditions.

'Earth materials' are defined here as natural materials sourced from the rock mass of the Earth's crust. They include stone or rock (igneous, metamorphic and sedimentary) and the weathering products derived from these different stone varieties, in the form of superficial soils, or regolith. The latter comprise clays, muds, silts, sands and gravels or complex, unconsolidated mixtures of several of these components. In a classification scheme, the nature and use of organic materials as binders, such as plant material or manures, would need to be evaluated separately.

Any proposed classification scheme will also need to be flexible enough to evolve over time, as new studies and interpretations are made of the earth materials used in our global vernacular built heritage.

The principal aim of any classification scheme is to provide a reproducible means of communicating information by grouping together those members with similar characteristics into a clearly defined system. As yet, while a number of informal, local schemes for the classification of earth materials exist, no single scheme appears to have gained widespread international acceptance. This may in part be the result of the increasing complexity evident in the wide compositional range of vernacular materials that have already been described from existing sites worldwide.

However, as new information from current research projects around the world is now becoming available on a more regular basis – via publication on the Internet for example – the development of a formal classification of vernacular buildings, based on the composition and geological provenance of the earth materials used in their construction, should now be achievable. Any classification proposed here, however, should be viewed as only a preliminary scheme reflecting our growing, but currently still incomplete, knowledge base.

Some Definitions

Stone and Stone-derived Materials

There are currently numerous different geological rock-classification schemes available, many of which have evolved over decades to meet specific local needs. Consequently, there is no single scheme likely to be currently accepted unequivocally by all researchers on a worldwide basis. Most current schemes, however, use the same basic root names (such as sandstones, limestones, granites, slates) and a range of common descriptive prefixes (quartz or volcaniclastic sandstone, coral or shelly limestone, calcareous clay, silty mud, and so on), but can differ in detail depending on the requirements of the classifier. For instance, the vernacular architecture of most coral-island communities is unlikely to exhibit a wide variety of construction materials, while that of a village or hamlet in Europe or South America can include a great diversity of rock types.

The geological rock classification suggested here is based on schemes generally in use by the geological community, for example the British Geological Survey and its US equivalent, the USGS. While experience tells us it is unlikely that, internationally, users of such schemes will ever agree on a single classification without some local modification, the basic methodology and structure presented in these schemes share much common ground.

The classification of igneous rocks is primarily based on distinguishing those rocks that have crystallized from the cooling of deep-seated magmatic intrusions (slow-cooling, coarsely crystalline fabrics) within the Earth's crust, and those that have been modified by emplacement at shallower depths (rapid-cooling, finely crystalline fabrics) or as the products of subaerial volcanic eruption such as lava flows or volcanic ash.

The classification of metamorphic rocks is based on a number of features, including the identification of the original metamorphosed (altered) protolith – in other words, was it originally an igneous, a metamorphic or a sedimentary rock?

The classification of sediments (natural superficial deposits) and sedimentary rocks (lithified sediments)

Opposite Though various geological schemes for classifying earth materials exist globally, they differ according to local variants and needs. A comprehensive, planet-wide system for classifying basic earth elements, for example coral (top left), agate (top right), quartz (bottom left) or slate (bottom right), would allow for a reproducible, consistent means of sharing and communicating such information.

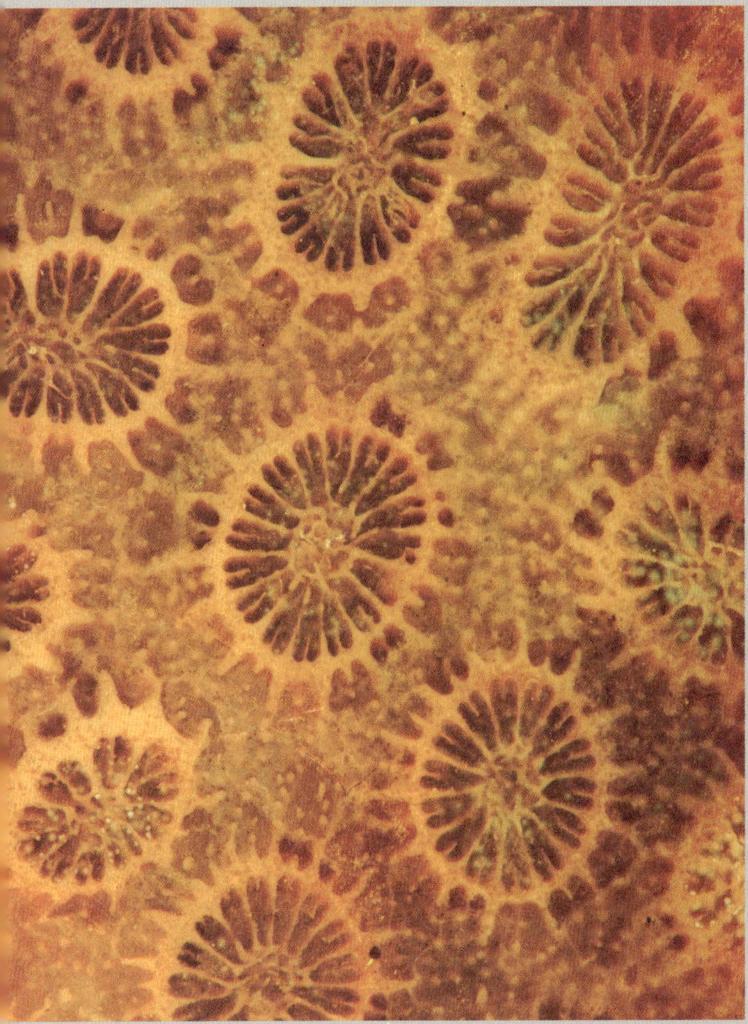
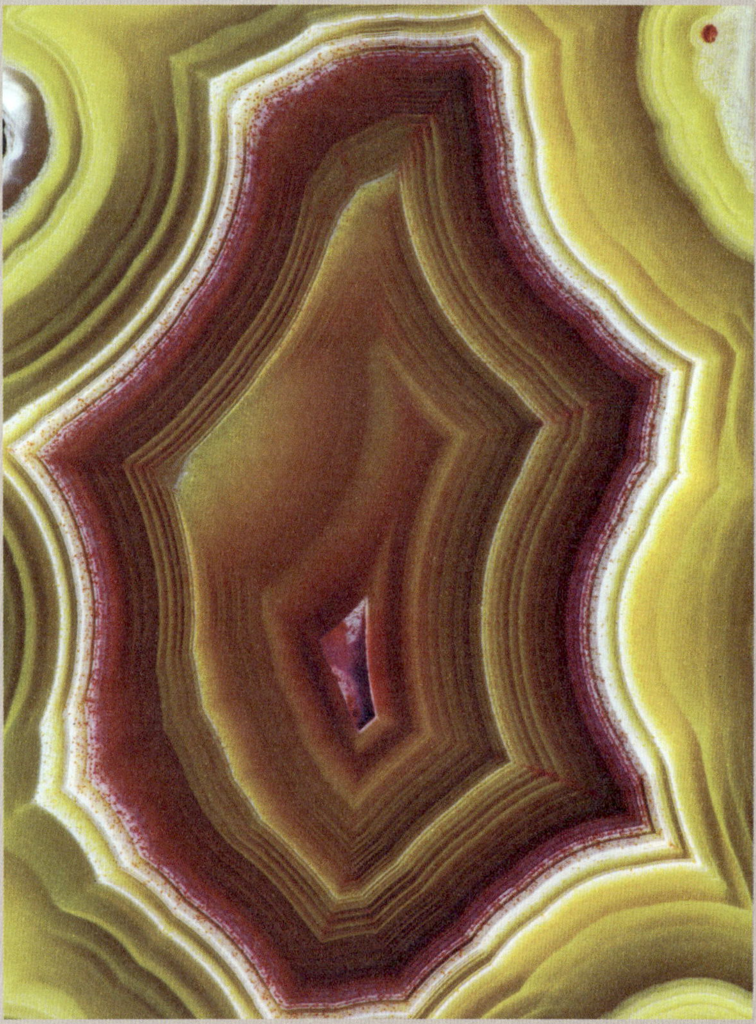

Opposite top and middle Vernacular constructions in many parts of the world are formed of soil-based structures, such as adobe bricks; however, most soils contain additional elements such as (clockwise from top left) sand, grass, salt or sulphur. Therefore, even with an essential base of earth, classifying the use of an exact soil – which has 230 different subdivisions of type – is complicated.

Opposite bottom and below Across the world, adobe is used to build vernacular structures: in the harsh and dry landscape of northwest Namibia, the Himba are nomadic Bantu people who build with materials available locally, such as earth, which is rendered with a mixture of earth and cow dung (opposite bottom left, below right). In the ancient Libyan town of Nalut in Jibal Nafusa, more than 400 chambers were built for storing and protecting grain (opposite bottom right). In the High Atlas Mountains of Morocco traditional adobe homes of the Berber are made from a mix of mud, straw and water (below left).

is based on their environment of deposition, grain size and grain, intergranular cement content and/or their detrital matrix composition.

The classification of man-made products derived from all these stones or sediments is based on their original mineralogical composition and any mineral or organic additives (lime, clays, manure, vegetation, and so on) incorporated before and after production (for example, sun-dried, fired clays for bricks and tiles).

Soils and Unconsolidated Superficial Sediments

In most parts of the world, vernacular buildings are frequently constructed by using weathered materials dug from the unconsolidated soil (earth) or other superficial deposits (regolith) overlying bedrock. Consequently, any proposed classification of vernacular building materials must make reference to current, internationally accepted soil classification schemes. Probably the most comprehensive of many such systems is the FAO UNESCO scheme, which, for example, identifies 10 primary soil subdivisions.[1]

In contrast to most geological rock classifications, which are fundamentally based on their genetic origin (that is, igneous, metamorphic or sedimentary groupings), formal soil classification schemes are generally tied to a mixture of chemical composition and climatic/environmental features. Consequently, soil classification schemes can be highly complex, with more than 230 subdivisions.

A Proposed Geological Classification

In order to develop a suitable scheme to classify vernacular building materials, a combination of two primary aspects of earth materials is required – recognizing first their geological parents and secondly the impact of the climatic zone (current or historic) within which their soils or weathered profile have developed. Six climatic zones have been incorporated into the present proposed classification: dry; dry (deserts); warmer humid (including temperate); cooler humid; tropical humid; and polar. A definition of each of these zones and the soils within would need to be included in any informed classification system.

Building stone

The general term building stone encompasses all naturally occurring rock types used for building purposes, and it includes representatives from each of the primary geological rock groups – igneous, metamorphic and sedimentary.

Igneous rocks are formed by the cooling of molten magma in one of two ways:

A) injected into the Earth's crust to form extensive subsurface intrusions, which are eventually exposed as outcrops at the Earth's surface by weathering and erosion. Slow cooling of these intrusive igneous bodies produces coarsely crystalline rock textures, often characterized by large crystals of feldspar and quartz (e.g. granitic rocks).

B) extruded onto the Earth's surface as lava flows or as explosive volcanic ash falls. Rapid cooling of these extrusive igneous rocks, as they are extruded, produces a much finer-grained, or equicrystalline, rock texture (e.g. basaltic lava flows).

The geological term granite strictly refers to coarse- to very-coarse-grained crystalline igneous rocks in which pale-coloured quartz, feldspar and mica are the dominant mineral components – with only minor proportions of darker coloured minerals, including mica and hornblende.

A sand is an unconsolidated sediment composed of accumulated sand-sized grains (from 63 microns to 2 mm [⅛ in] in diameter) derived from the weathering, decay and erosion of rocks of any pre-existing stone lithology. Sand composition can vary depending on the mineralogical composition of the source material. Sands can form in marine, freshwater and terrestrial environments. A sandstone is a lithified (cemented) sand.

A limestone is a sedimentary rock composed of more than 50 per cent carbonate, usually in the form of fossil fragments (macro- and microfossils) or ooids, embedded in a carbonate matrix (mud) or cement. Limestones include both calcium- and magnesium-rich (dolomitic) carbonate varieties.

Sediments

A mud is an unconsolidated sediment comprising a mixture of clay minerals (less than 2 microns in diameter) and silt-sized grains (2–63 microns). Muds can form in marine, freshwater or terrestrial environments. A mudstone is a lithified (consolidated) mud.

Processed products

The term brick describes a small, rectangular block of fired or sun-dried clay/mud. The term clay brick (clay lump) describes a small, rectangular block of fired or sun-dried clay. The term mud brick describes a small rectangular block of fired or sun-dried mud.

Flagstones and fieldstones

A flagstone is sedimentary rock that can be split along its natural horizontal bedding planes into thin sheet-like slabs. The splitting exhibited by such stones is commonly

termed fissility. Thinly bedded or fissile sandstones and limestones can both provide good sources of flagstones.

Fieldstone is a general term for a durable stone of any rock type, usually collected from near-surface exposures and outcrops, commonly of boulder and/or cobble size, that is used as a general walling material with little or no further dressing or cutting of the stone required.

Mortars

The term mortar is generally used to describe the fine-grained binding/bonding material used as a bed, on which either bricks or stone blocks are set in a building or freestanding wall. In vernacular buildings, the most common mortar mixes have a lime base, using local chalk, limestone or shell fragments. However, the composition of the aggregate present in the mortar can vary widely, and is usually a reflection of the use of locally available materials.

Earth buildings

The general term earth buildings includes all those structures formed of compacted and dried soil, usually sourced from the local area. In addition, some forms include other organic binders such as straw. Consequently, while the construction methods used in such buildings can be intrinsically similar, their compositions can be very variable and are largely dependent on the geology and mineralogy of the local rock outcrops. There are, therefore, many forms of earth buildings, including cob, pisé, rammed earth and adobe.

The principal link between these different types of earth construction is that the material itself provides good thermal insulation and, if properly constructed, protects occupants from the elements and constitutes a very durable building material.

Snow

Snow can be very simply defined as highly porous, frozen water vapour, precipitated as fine, white ice crystals or flakes (crystal aggregates). However, modern atmospheric science has shown that there are many different forms of snow or ice crystals (at least eighty types), some of which are more common than others. Snow accumulates in beds or layers and each snow layer shows markedly different characteristics: crystal size, density and solidity.

Detailed studies of such snow accumulations place a particular reliance on recognizing the general character of the snow crystals present, and the resultant microstructure and microporosity that develops. Such studies have also shown why some snow accumulations are more suitable for the construction of snow dwellings than others.

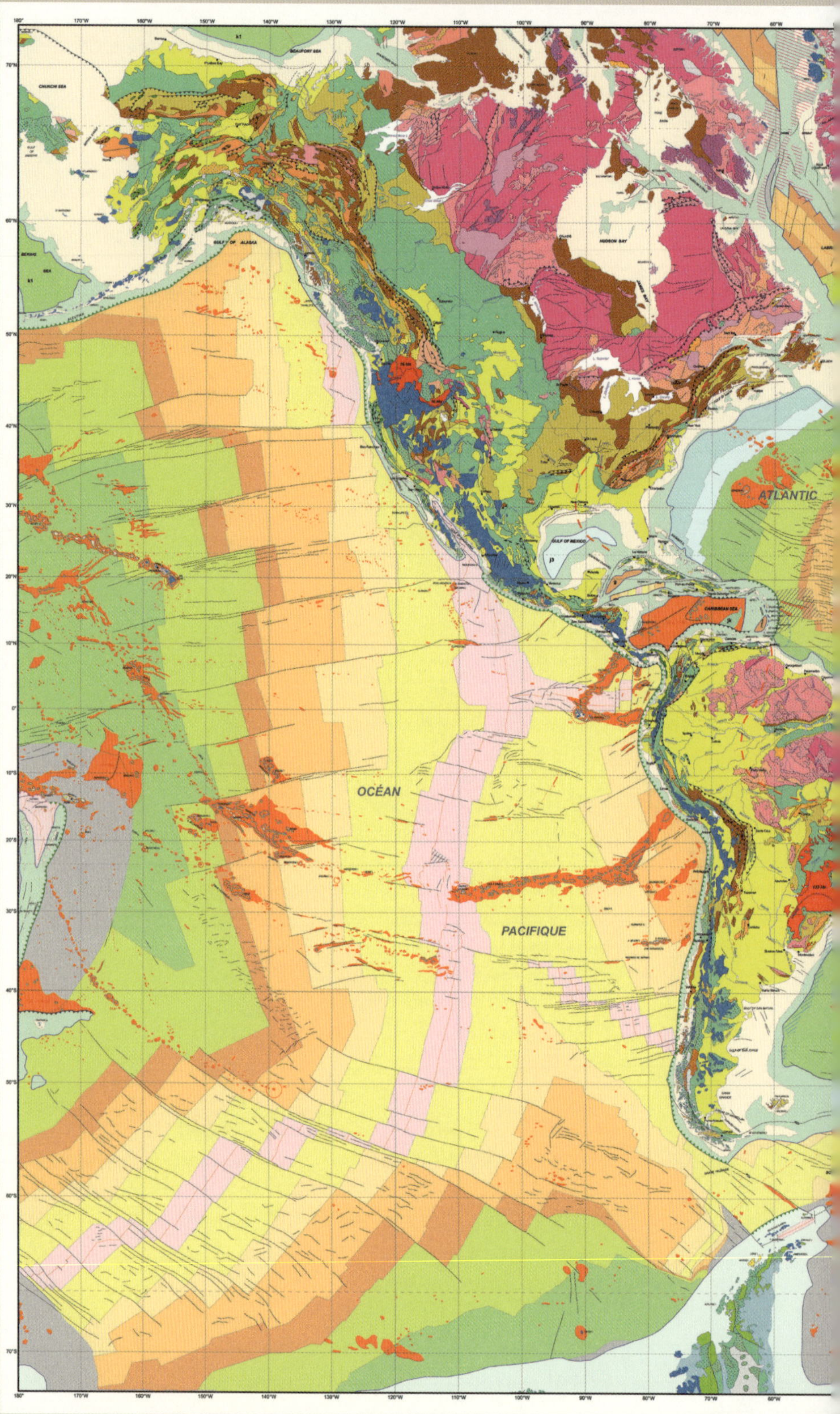

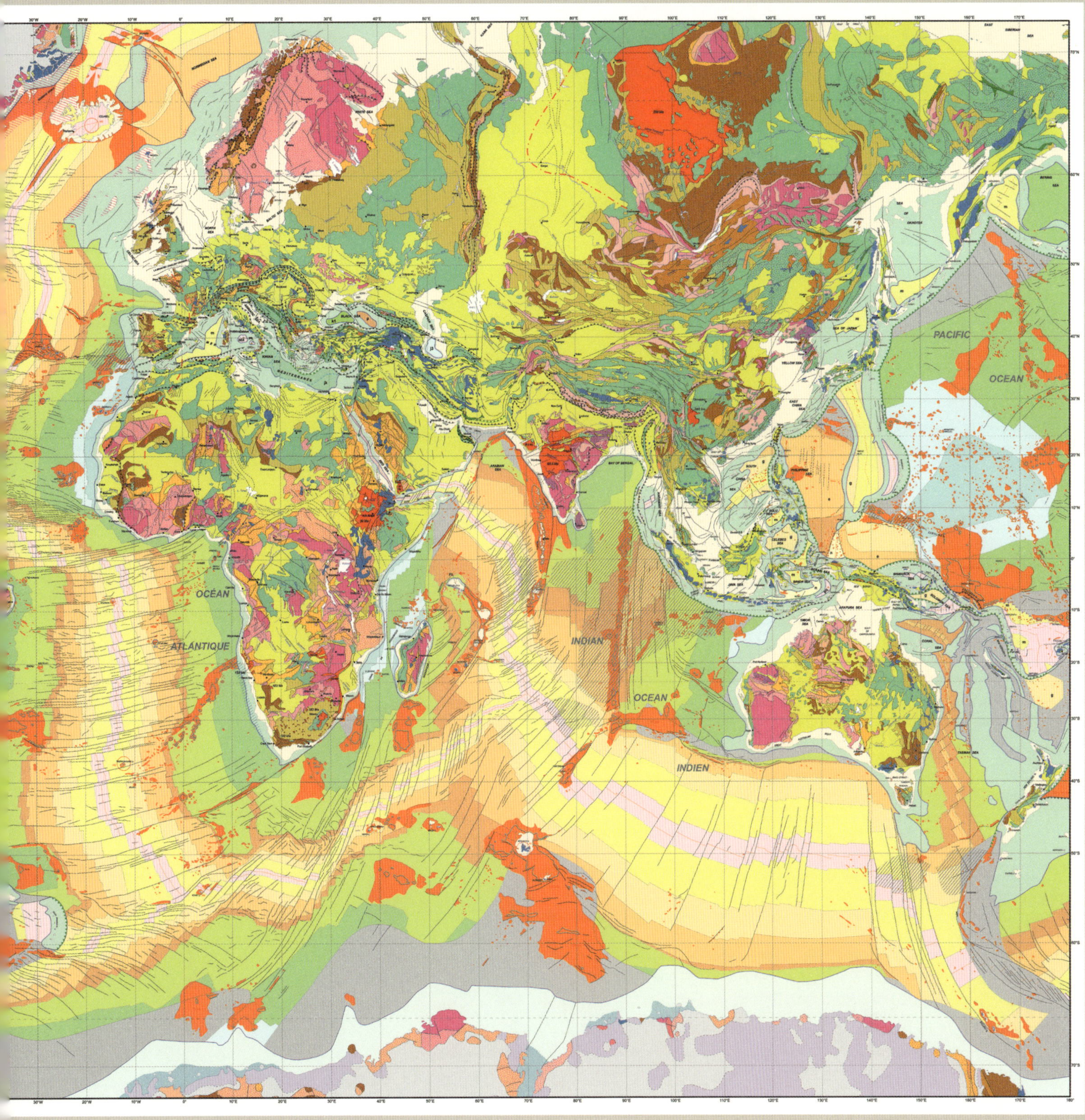

Above The Geological Map of the World by the Commission for the Geological Map of the World (CGMW) illustrates the Earth's geology and structure. It colours key geological interests such as the limits of continental/oceanic crusts (blue lines), the three eras of the Proterozoic Eon (the most recent geological era, before complex life on Earth – oldest in mid-pink to youngest in bright orange) for the continental crust, and the locations of accretionary wedges (red lines), which are wedges of massed sediment that occur at the intersection of plates. The age of the oceanic crust, from the Middle Jurassic to the present, is indicated in pale blue at the edge of the crust through to pale pink at plate intersections.

Plants in the Built Environment

William Milliken

'Living roofs', 'green' walls, garden bridges and overpasses... In an increasingly lifeless world of concrete, glass and brick, we are feverishly inventing ever more imaginative ways to bring chlorophyll into our polluted urban lives. We know that living with plants around us is beneficial for health, mental well-being and the environment. We feel comfortable surrounded by wood, cladding our floors and walls with thin veneers of timber – real or mock – to create the illusion of a more natural space than the one that we actually inhabit. From houses to factories, bridges and railways, we have been exploiting the extraordinary properties of cellulose – of complex natural materials evolved over millions of years to support monumental living structures – since the day we vacated our gloomy ancestral caves.

The structures of plants are to some degree determined by the environment to which they have adapted, but also by their ecological niche and their place in the evolutionary tree of life. The plant world is broken down into numerous hierarchical groups, each of which has its own particular characteristics. Monocotyledonous and dicotyledonous plants are 'built' very differently from each other. For example, the anatomy of the 'wood' in the stem of a palm tree (*Arecaceae*) is entirely different from that of an oak (*Quercus*), and likewise (in consequence) its physical properties. Particular structural characteristics may be common to a family or genus, or they may be scattered across the plant kingdom, reflecting the parallel evolution of features necessary for survival under similar conditions. Cork, for example, whose phenomenal thermal resistance protects trees from fire as well as insulating our homes, occurs in a wide range of species found in combustible habitats.

Humankind's inventiveness and ingenuity in adapting plant materials for construction is impressive. From the 'paper houses' of Japan – resistant to earthquakes yet dangerously susceptible to fire – to the floating reed houses of the Marsh Arabs, humans have taken what is on offer and adapted it to local conditions. We have even incorporated living plants into the structures of our dwellings: some Korowai of New Guinea construct houses in the lofty canopies of emergent rainforest trees.

Many traditional societies continue to build their houses entirely, or very nearly entirely, from plants, using timber and bark for frames and walls, fibres for tying and binding, and leaves and stems for thatch. The myriad variations on this theme are governed by cultural preference, technology, environmental conditions, and the range of species available and their abundance. If you live in a tropical rainforest, you will probably roof your house with palm leaves; by a marsh, with reeds; on a prairie, with grass; and in a temperate forest, with wooden shingles. On the desert coast of Peru, where it never rains at all, a simple structure of reeds and mud provides sufficient shelter, while the winters of the Himalayas demand something much more solid and weatherproof.

Our ability to know which species to use for which task is the product of thousands of years of experimentation and observation. Which timbers are the least palatable to termites or fungi? Which trees have the strongest fibres in their bark? Which thatching leaves will last longest before being consumed by insects, and at what phase of the moon should they be harvested in order to maximize longevity? Durability of building materials is less of an issue for nomadic or semi-nomadic societies than for settled ones: for forest nomads such as the Penan of Borneo, a shelter may not need to last more than a day or two. Long-term occupation, stimulated by a shift from hunting and gathering to agriculture, not only demands more careful selection of species (for example, rot-resistant timber), but also puts increasingly heavy pressure on local resources.

As populations grow and resources come under strain, sustainability frequently becomes an issue. Among some treeless islands of the Scottish Hebrides during the 19th century, for example, the harvesting of marram grass for thatch was made subject to regulation when over-exploitation was found to be causing the destabilization of coastal dunes, resulting in the loss of agricultural land beneath windblown sand. Roofing timbers for cottages on those islands were salvaged from the shore or imported from the mainland: these were scarce resources, carefully guarded and sometimes moved from one house to another. For landowners to evict their tenants in the infamous Highland Clearances, burning the roof timbers was all that was required.

Settlement, and ultimately urbanization, is commonly accompanied by a shift towards inorganic materials in the built environment. Nevertheless it is rare for plants to be completely usurped, though their continuing presence often takes subtle forms. Adobe bricks made from light clay or earth are strengthened by the inclusion of grasses.

Opposite In comparison with settlements of our predecessors – or traditional societies now – our typical contemporary urban environment includes densely built fabric and greatly reduced plant material. Ingenious designs to reintroduce plants into cities include Singapore's Supertrees at Gardens by the Bay by Grant Associates/Atelier One/Atelier Ten (top left) and Patrick Blanc's vertical garden wall at Caixa Forum Foundation in Madrid, Spain (top right and bottom).

GEORGES
MÉLIÈS
Seducidos por el Arte
Obra Social "la Caixa"

Opposite Plants play their own role in the built environment – from the natural resources of trees for construction (top left, bottom), which require sustainable husbandry to protect against decimation of slow-growing species or rainforests, to mosses, lichens or algae that we have come to appreciate and even replicate (top right), and to the form of naturally occurring structures like the giant Amazon water lily (middle) said to have inspired the ironwork of Joseph Paxton's 1851 Crystal Palace in London.

The lime used in mortar and concrete has accumulated over millions of years on the bottom of tropical oceans, formed from the calcareous skeletons of tiny planktonic plants. The pitch that seals roofs is the product of vegetation entombed in primeval swamps, and the amber that once famously furnished the walls of the Catherine Palace in St Petersburg leaked from the trunks of ancient trees. Bamboo (Poaceae), the extraordinary structural properties of which have been exploited throughout its natural range, still furnishes scaffolding for the construction of high-rise buildings in many parts of the world.

And plants, of course, also find their own roles within the built environment. Mosses, lichens and algae colonize our walls and roofs, adding colour and character that we have come to appreciate – and now even to replicate artificially. Vines and ivy adopt our walls as substitutes for trees, softening the impact of harsh artificial structures. Sometimes we encourage them; at other times, we fight them off. In their absence, we frequently incorporate plant-inspired forms or symbolism into the structure or the decorative detail of our buildings. The ironwork of Joseph Paxton's Crystal Palace, for example, was allegedly inspired by veins on the underside of the giant Amazon water lily.

Timber has never left the construction scene, though its use has waxed, waned and evolved over the centuries. As supplies in the industrialized world declined, global trade opened access to seemingly limitless stocks from overseas. New species appeared, and others gradually made their exit. Western red cedar, for example, is now widely used while hardwoods have largely been replaced by faster-growing softwoods, and construction technology has adapted to accommodate their differing physical properties. Thanks to modern lamination techniques, previously inconceivably vast wooden beams can now be stitched together from timbers of modest plantation trees.

We are now well aware that the plunder of the world's forests and the destruction of Earth's natural habitats are far from sustainable activities, threatening not only our natural resource supplies but also the very environment that we live in. Emerging sustainable forest management and certification schemes have made some progress towards better husbandry of the world's forests, but the problem is far from solved. Fifty years from now, the built environment will be substantially different: pressure on land and habitats will be greater than ever. Energy efficiency will be critically important, and renewable plant resources may be playing an increasingly important role in sustainable housing. As the global environment changes, the species that we will still have access to and the climatic conditions that they will be sheltering us from will, likewise, have shifted in many parts of the world. This will, to some extent, be just another chapter in the long evolution of humans' changing relationship with, and dependence on, plants. But it is likely to be a dramatic one.

The structures of plants are to some degree determined by the environment to which they have adapted, but also by their ecological niche and their place in the evolutionary tree of life.

An Anthropological Introduction to Vernacular Architecture

André Singer

The traditional dwelling is not just an isolated element within culture, but is a part of a system of symbolic representations which give it meaning.[1]
– Gérard Toffin

In our age of rapid technological innovation and progress, it is easy to view vernacular architecture as a romantic means of preserving outdated and often impractical forms of habitation. Perhaps anthropology, in its eagerness to be seen in a postmodern era as less in pursuit of indigenous, isolated societies and more as relevant to the larger dynamic community, has not recently engaged itself as sufficiently with the changes in vernacular architecture as it could. Yet anthropologists have never denied its importance; from the communal longhouses of Amazonian forest groups to the substantial yet portable yurts that enable the nomadic herding peoples of Central Asia to move their families across the steppes, cultural life and the space in which it is lived have been viewed as inextricably linked.

This relationship is, however, changing at an increasingly rapid pace. In this volume, we see how the processes and materials of construction – as shown by, among others, architects, planners, historians, scientists, climatologists, geologists, botanists and economists – are reacting to the modern world. Architecture is ubiquitous, whether we acknowledge it or not, and it plays such a vital role in the human condition that it becomes increasingly important to also consider its cultural and societal dimensions. It is imperative for the needs of any society, not merely as a matter of economic necessity, that structures reflecting social, spatial and aesthetic values should be investigated and understood, which in turn makes vernacular architecture especially important.

Anthropology, with its ability to draw upon an understanding derived from field participation, should and must have an increasingly important contribution to make to this dialogue. When researching the Timurid peoples' transition from herding nomads in western Afghanistan to sedentary farmers in eastern Iran for example,[2] the most significant defining feature in the dramatic changes that had impacted throughout their lives was that of cultural space. Moving from portable goat-hair tents to the adopted mud-brick courtyard structures that formed their new dwellings had a major impact on relationships, social groupings and group roles in Timurid society. Clearly, in all cases where the forms of dwelling change and the designs, materials of construction and

Left Recognizing the importance of vernacular architecture as well as of traditional and indigenous materials in contemporary structures can lead to the successful cross-pollination of ideas in our increasingly connected planet.

environmental context alters, we are faced with new social parameters that need our understanding and attention.

More than fifty years ago, Claude Levi-Strauss pointed out how, when the inhabited space of people is threatened, so too will the culture of those people potentially disappear.[3] Now more than ever, as traditional modes of design and construction are being superseded at an unprecedented pace, the importance of understanding those links is essential. If the nature of a dwelling exists as an integral part of social and cultural life, it follows that changing or updating the space of that dwelling cannot be successfully accomplished without consideration of the pre-existing relationships. We live in an era when, as several authors in this volume point out, planners, governments and even United Nations organizations are re-evaluating the importance of not just vernacular design and architecture but also the use of traditional and indigenous materials in contemporary structures. That is where the benefits of a cross-pollination of research and experience from different disciplines will be of enormous value. It is also why this volume is such a welcome contribution to our awareness of the current state of vernacular architecture, and a timely reminder of how, in the future, we will ignore its significance to our cost.

Opposite As forms and designs of dwellings change, and new technologies allow for better adaptation to the surrounding environment, we will face new social and cultural challenges that require our understanding and attention.

If the nature of a dwelling exists as an integral part of social and cultural life, it follows that changing or updating the space of that dwelling cannot be successfully accomplished without consideration of the pre-existing relationships.

The Value of the Vernacular

Jim Coleman and Henry Fletcher

The vernacular builders of the world learn to be true to the types and conditions of the buildings that they not only construct, but also occupy. – Paul Oliver

At the heart of all the processes relating to the production of the built environment, one relationship is key – that between the occupant or user and the constructor. Buildings, cities and managed landscapes provide the most fundamental images of our communities, societies and economies. Within this enormous range of built places and their responses to the underlying natural environments (wherever these may lie on the spectrum from life-giving to hostile), the contractual distance between constructor and inhabitant goes a long way towards determining the degree of locality or regional specificity. Switches from traditional to modern methods of construction are generally accompanied by a shift: from local labour handling local materials to produce housing or other built functions for their own communities, towards non-local labour handling materials with more complex and spread-out supply chains to produce a built environment that is more modular in quality and less regionally and culturally specific. As societies move towards increasingly specialized and leveraged economic models, the accepted comfort and productivity gains from this progression are often accompanied by losses of a less monetized, more intangible nature – sometimes social, sometimes aesthetic or cultural, sometimes in terms of complex risk/comfort trade-offs. This is in addition to possible socio-economic losses associated with the decline of traditional skills and construction knowledge, and the possible demise of associated micro-businesses.

In many ways, the creation of value through the application of human labour to raw materials (in some cases the very ground that lies below us, in others the vegetation that thrives in the water around us) can be considered the oldest manifestation of the core economic model by which economists understand the world. The losses observed as societies leave vernacular construction behind and move towards alternative procurement arrangements may be considered classic examples of market failures, whereby indirect benefits or positive externalities are not taken into account when switching from one system to another. This essay seeks to unpack the economic cases for retaining, reinstating or reinventing locally specific construction methods, or possibly finding a suitable place for them alongside modern construction methods, as well as some of the issues surrounding such initiatives to 'bring back the vernacular'.

Economic justification for the protection or reinstatement of vernacular architecture, or the reintroduction of vernacular construction techniques, can be made in multiple ways at multiple levels. A global-level case can be made for the promotion of low-carbon or low-embodied-energy construction (which is frequently, but not always, a quality of regionally specific approaches), since slowing the rate of climate change is a widely acknowledged global goal. But a low carbon footprint has never been the driving rationale for techniques that emerged over millennia of development. Other global-level cases may be made for specific characteristics where their loss might be considered a loss of universal value or of a global asset.[1] However, where only a global-level case has been made, local populations may very often be sceptical of the validity of this style of argument – perceiving it, at best, as naive romanticism or, at worst, as deliberately anti-development.

Opposite Promoting low-carbon, often locally specific methods of construction makes sense for economic reasons, as well as for the wider worldwide goal of slowing climate change. The grand mud mosques of Djenné, Mali, for instance, require annual maintenance using indigenous techniques to repair and restore the exterior cladding of these great structures. Their preservation is highly desirable – economically, culturally and for our climate.

In many ways, the creation of value through the application of human labour to raw materials can be considered the oldest manifestation of the core economic model by which economists understand the world.

Opposite The successful use of local knowledge, materials and production techniques benefits both supply and demand and is seen throughout the world including (clockwise from top left) thatched fronds for dwellings in the Solomon Islands; earthen bricks on the roof of a home in Ouarzazate Province, Morocco; mud brick construction baking in the sun on Elephantine Island, Aswan, Egypt; repaired mud lintel in Rwanda; construction of composite walls using clay and straw, Southeast Asia; building a hut using vernacular traditions, Shoa Province, Ethiopia.

A stronger and more persuasive case may be made at the local or regional level. Arguments in support of this approach typically revolve around poverty-alleviation or quality-of-life issues. Modern methods of construction, while often cheaper or appearing to require less maintenance than traditional construction techniques, can lead to often unforeseen consequences in terms of health issues or social change. In these situations, the economic impact of switching approaches may not be fully known or could involve a trade-off between benefits in the short term (say, greater disposable income) and longer-term costs (say, greater morbidity rates associated with particular materials or enhanced risk from physical shocks). These choices may be perfectly rational in the given context, so for anyone wishing to drive a reversal of this consensus it will be important to understand in detail what the underlying causes and indirect costs and benefits associated with each approach are. In particular, it should be recalled that societal or, in an increasing number of cases, environmental change may be driven by developments largely external to the community in question. Examples include the shift away from an agrarian model due to urbanization[2] or falling crop prices, the loss of vegetation due to rising temperatures and the lowering of annual rainfall.[3] These changes may exert a strong influence over the decision to switch. Reversing the change from traditional to modern will not address these wider issues, so it will be critical to visualize a hybrid that draws, in an appropriate manner, contemporary benefits from vernacular techniques in a clear response to the current context. A strong case for this more nuanced, local-agenda-driven type of initiative is more likely to arise in partnership with a community than from outside it.

Understanding the context for change is the starting point for any effort to introduce, reintroduce or reinterpret vernacular architecture. Considering this in basic economic terms, the emphasis may be placed on improving the supply side through technical development or the demand side through the creation or stimulation of the market. Very often the choice of approach will be determined by the origins of the promoting group for the intervention and its underlying rationale, but a good strategy will likely target both sides of the economic equation.

On the supply side (frequently favoured by promoting groups from an engineering or architectural design background), additional finance may be made available to communities working with traditional methods, or training may be provided to ensure that techniques previously transferred orally and by apprenticeship systems are protected or spread more widely. In addition, there may be potential to raise the measurable quality of the local construction-skills base by qualifying or 'credentializing' traditional built-environment-related skills. The expectation underlying this approach is that a broader distribution of traditional skills will lead to a greater uptake of these skills (either as they are, or reinterpreted). Focusing exclusively on this approach risks failure if the process does not adequately address the reasons why new techniques or materials are being selected in favour of the old, or if the complex societal traditions that used to accompany and support their deployment are not considered alongside the technical issues.

A demand-side approach (more likely to be selected by a group oriented towards economic development) will draw upon economic levers to 'pull through' the preferred techniques in one way or another. If the protection and promotion of a vernacular environment are known to hold long-term economic benefit in terms of increasing visitor numbers to a town or city, then tax breaks, micro-credit or grants may be offered to those developing buildings in that style. Spending public money, or community-raised finance, in this way could be justified on the basis that it will invigorate the local economy through attracting more and higher-spending visitors as well as retain more of the development spending and revenue in the local community, because both materials and labour will be locally sourced. In locations where the local economy is not likely to be *directly* stimulated by a more attractive environment, then more innovative ways of raising demand will need to be sought – communities may be offered financing or insurance products that remove the perceived barriers to uptake, for example. In some cases, educational or advertising campaigns may be sufficient to raise the perceived value of traditional-based products. The costs of these programmes, though light, could be offset by the increase in the external or long-term benefits to the community of switching back – or, more

Where an aesthetic appreciation may be the starting point for revaluing lost or fading construction methods, this must quickly be accompanied by real and demonstrable benefits if a transition to, or back to, such methods is to be sustainable.

likely, switching to an optimized hybrid approach – so long as the recovery of these costs can be successfully negotiated between the relevant parties. In all cases, and whatever the balance of supply- and demand-side activities, the shape and efficiency of the underlying market should be understood and acknowledged. Most markets are highly imperfect owing to low availability or equity of information or high barriers to communications and transport (which may introduce distorting transaction costs), and these imperfections can often give an advantage to the sorts of large organizations that manage supply chains for modern methods of construction.[4]

This book celebrates the value, the beauty and the collective ingenuity of vernacular architectures. The relationships between societies and the structures that they build around themselves are laid bare for their complexity and their fragility. Where an aesthetic appreciation may be the starting point for revaluing lost or fading construction methods, this must quickly be accompanied by real and demonstrable benefits if a transition to, or back to, such methods is to be sustainable. These benefits must be framed in the contemporary context, a process that will likely feature some difficult truths – but these must be acknowledged, scrutinized and absorbed into any new proposition. Choices made by inhabitants and constructors alike are almost always rational, but they may well be less than optimal. This has been the case in the past and the present, and will likely continue to be so in the future unless all options outlined above are considered.

Below The historic Peacock House in the heart of Kabul, Afghanistan, was one of the first restoration projects achieved by the Turquoise Mountain NGO. Part of a wider initiative to restore Kabul's historic old city and save the Afghan craft industry, the once-crumbling house of mud brick and wooden screens (left) was rebuilt in 2009 (right).

Opposite top An ancient site in the Hunza Valley, Pakistan, the Baltit Fort was abandoned by the Hunza Mirs in 1945, and began to decay. Included on the UNESCO World Heritage Tentative list, the structure was surveyed by the Royal Geographical Society of London and a restoration programme was initiated with the aid of the Aga Khan Trust for Culture, Historic Cities Support Programme. The fort has been fully renovated and is now a museum.

Opposite bottom Also in the Hunza Valley, the Altit Fort was in disrepair, with its structures of stone walls fixed with compacted soil failing. The Aga Khan Trust for Culture, Historic Cities Support Programme and the Norwegian government helped with the recent restoration of the fort using community-based conservation practice. Now, the iconic building is a tourist site and at the same time has allowed villagers to resettle in the surrounding arable lands.

TROPICAL

Equirectangular projection. Scale 1: 70 000 000

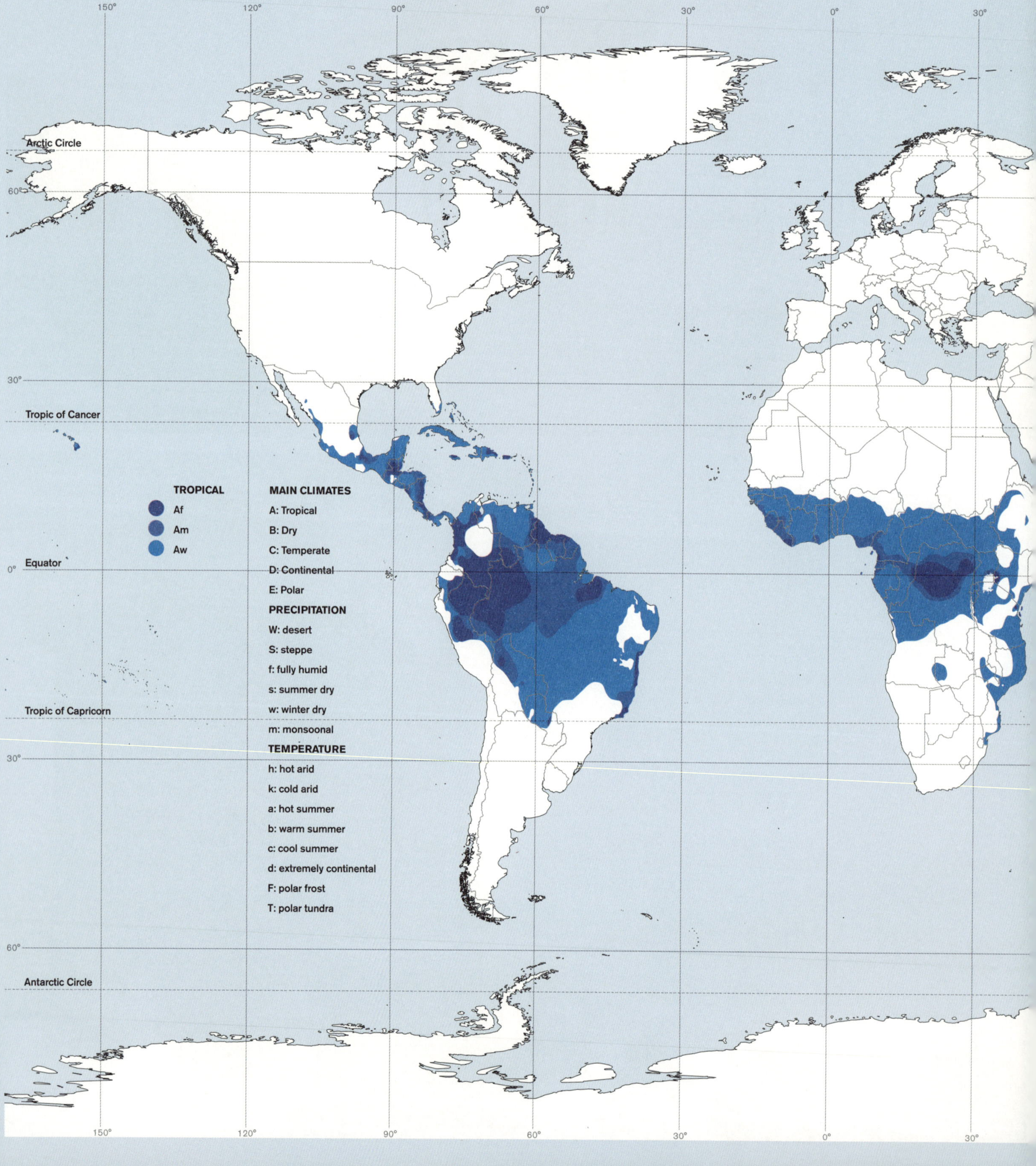

The general characteristics of the tropical climate zone, which extends northward and southward from the equator to about latitude 15–25°, are year-round warm temperatures (all months of the year have average temperatures of 18°C [64°F] or higher) and abundant rainfall (the typical annual average exceeds 1,500 mm [59 in]). The major subregions of this zone are defined in terms of their seasonal distribution of rainfall – tropical wet (Af), tropical monsoon (Am), and tropical wet and dry (Aw).

At low equatorial elevations – particularly the Amazon lowland, the Congo River basin and the East Indies from Sumatra to New Guinea – high temperatures and abundant year-round rainfall combine to produce a dense, broadleaf, evergreen tropical rainforest.

Within the tropical wet climate, diurnal and seasonal temperature variations are small (usually less than 3°C [37°F]), because the noon sun is always high and intense, and the length of daylight is relatively constant. However, there are significant variations in temperature between day (average high about 32°C [89°F]) and night (average low about 22°C [71°F]), with implications for built structures. Daily intense heating and uplift result in towering cumulus clouds and heavy, localized showers. These usually end by evening, and skies clear. Typical annual rainfall totals exceed 1,500 mm (60 in) and in some cases, especially along the windward side of hills and mountains, may surpass 4,000 mm (160 in). High humidity and cloud cover tend to keep maximum temperatures from reaching extremely high values. Cooling at night can result in the air becoming saturated, with occasional fog or dew covering the ground.

Where monthly precipitation totals drop below 60 mm (3 in) for one or two months of the year, the climate is classified as tropical monsoon. Here, yearly rainfall totals are similar to those of the tropical wet climate, because the dry season is brief and large amounts of rain fall during the rest of the year. Soil moisture is sufficient to maintain the tropical rainforest through the short dry period. Such tropical monsoons occur along the coasts of Southeast Asia, India and northeastern South America.

Poleward of the tropical wet region, total rainfall decreases, and there is a gradual transition to the tropical wet and dry climate region, with its distinct dry season. Although annual precipitation usually exceeds 1,000 mm (40 in), the dry season, with rainfall less than 60 mm (3 in), lasts for more than two months. Tropical rainforest cannot survive this 'drought', and the dense evergreen forest gives way to tall savannah grass scattered with low drought-resistant trees. The dry season occurs during winter, when the region is under the influence of a global zone of high pressure (the subtropical highs, or STH). In summer, this zone moves poleward and is replaced by a zone of converging air from the two hemispheres (the intertropical convergence zone, ITCZ), bringing heavy precipitation – usually in the form of showers. This rainfall is enhanced by other weather systems moving through the region.

Tropical wet and dry climates not only receive less rainfall than the tropical wet climate region, but more variable precipitation year-to-year, often associated with variations in the monsoon. In one year, there may be destructive floods; in another, serious droughts. As with the other tropical regions, daily temperature variation usually exceeds the annual range. However, the climate is less monotonous day-to-day. At night, low humidity and clear skies allow for rapid cooling and by morning temperatures drop to 20°C (68°F) or below. The principal such areas lie in western Central America, both north and south of the Amazon Basin; southern, central and eastern Africa; parts of India and Southeast Asia; and northern Australia.

Abundance and Diversity in Tropical Regions

Multiplicity is embedded in the vernacular architecture of tropical climates. It is driven by the distinct geographical characteristics of each region, from the Caribbean in the west to the thousands of Micronesian islands in the east. Latin America and Africa, as well as India and Southeast Asia, are home to the largest rainforests on the planet. The ethno-linguistic richness of these regions is remarkable: there are 240 tribes in Brazil and 370 in Nigeria, and 1,000 languages are spoken in Papua New Guinea. What do these multitudes have in common? They have embraced the environmental conditions of the tropics with great sensitivity to the local ecology and an understanding of plants and the weather, and have embedded this understanding in an architectural language while at the same time responding to the social structure and beliefs of their societies. Belief was part of nature, it was derived from nature; the development of material culture and architecture was a result of community engagement with both. Construction used the abundant local plants, predominantly timber, palms (coconut, raffia and sago), and a variety of grasses, vines and rattans; and, in some areas, mud, clay and stone. Houses on stilts remain a predominant form in many tropical countries.

Building with plants need not mean building at a small scale, however. This is demonstrated by some of the largest plant-based structures in the world – including the community buildings of the Wajãpi people in the Amazonian Upper Xingu region, Yanomami circular settlements, the longhouses of Borneo and the unexpected plant structures of Papua New Guinea's tropical rainforest. These constitute a multitude of forms of architectural virtuosity. The hierarchical structure of these societies was often expressed by internal layouts that offered each family privacy as well as distinguished places for tribal chiefs. One communal building would accommodate around 100 people, roughly twelve families. Interestingly, the typology of Brazilian *malocas* (communal huts) resembles that of traditional meeting-house structures in Micronesia, where, additionally, ornamentation on gables was used to tell stories.

Western Africa, too, boasts remarkable examples of everyday storytelling through ornamentation. Burkina Faso's *bambolse* houses give witness to contemporary decor, transforming fences, clothes and objects into art forms. Tropical countries in Central Africa also see the adaptation of basket-weaving technologies into house construction, with an innovative use of grasses. The 'everyday' is embraced in the rural huts of Myanmar, where the relationship between agriculture and architecture has been refined to perfection. Religious beliefs shaped the typology of houses in Laos, and human body proportions those in Hawaii; the meeting of the spiritual and the natural culminate in the imaginative bamboo structures of Indonesia's Sumbanese people.

Today, however, across many continents, indigenous cultural and often unique ecological heritage is being replaced by concrete blocks, corrugated roofs, and, occasionally still, asbestos sheeting – all in the name of 'modernity'. Alternatives for re-engaging the vernacular in an authentic urban fabric are almost nonexistent, and many of the aforementioned masterpieces may now be glimpsed only in architectural theme parks. Migration from rural areas to cities is real, however – and Brazilian *favelas*, as well as the slums of India and Southeast Asia, demonstrate the pressing and unresolved problem of not only accommodating millions of people in micro-cities without infrastructure but also the lost paradigm of equilibrium: of living in harmony with nature. Climate change, floods and hurricanes, which are affecting communities across tropical climate zones in a dramatic way, serve as a pressing reminder that we urgently need to regain this equilibrium.

Left Stilt houses are a predominant building type in tropical countries, such as these Korowai homes, New Guinea.

Chattel Houses and Timber Architecture of the Caribbean

Below Historical view of traditional thatched huts in Jamaica (left) and a vernacular thatch-roofed hut in Tobago, Caribbean (right).

Opposite top Developed from its simple origins as a portable single-room dwelling, Barbados chattel houses became more elaborate, with additions such as cooling verandas.

Opposite bottom In an effort to control the heat and encourage ventilated interiors, shutters and shades were developed. This elaborate shutter design known as the 'Demerara window' is top-hinged, and named after a province in Guyana.

Ronald van Oers

Geography/Climate and Culture

The Caribbean region, as discussed here,[1] comprises thirty main islands and archipelagos, spread across 4,000 km (2,500 miles) of sea, and includes also the terra firma sovereign states of Belize, Guyana and Suriname and the overseas territory of French Guiana. This relatively small region, according to landmass, has nevertheless an enormous diversity in architectural heritage stemming from European colonial times (Spanish, British, French, Dutch and Scandinavian) and incorporating American, Asian and African influences as well. Yet in spite of this huge diversity, many commonalities exist, making this a fascinating region for the exploration, identification and documentation of vernacular buildings.

While caution should be exercised not to perpetuate colonial myths about Arawaks and Caribs, the general theory is that warring Caribs moved out from the South American mainland across the arc of the Lesser Antilles and carried out successful raids against the more developed civilization of the Tainos, who were living principally in the Greater Antilles – for example, Puerto Rico, Hispaniola and Cuba. Archaeological evidence indicates that sometime after 400 BCE, pottery from mainland South America, horticulture and permanent settlements appeared throughout the Lesser and Greater Antilles as far as the Dominican Republic. In the Greater Antilles around 600 CE, settlement patterns, layout and even house structures all appear to change, which suggests a significant adaptation from the mainland cultural tradition to local insular conditions.[2] When the Spanish arrived in the Greater Antilles, 'they found a complex of allied villages grouped together in related chiefdoms with complex social and political networks'.[3]

Materials

Until well into the 17th century, the vast majority of the towns in the Caribbean were built almost entirely of timber – including their religious and government buildings, and the homes of ordinary and wealthy people alike. Owing to the dominant shipbuilding industry, carpenters were more numerous than masons. Moreover, carpentry tools were more durable than those of masonry, which also were not manufactured locally but imported. With villages gradually growing into towns, and towns into cities, tradesmen and craftsmen such as smiths, carpenters and builders became increasingly more important. This was accompanied by a formal organization and institutionalization of their work:

> No-one could set up a shop or business as he liked; he must obey the rules of his craft. Everyone who was to become a tradesman had to go through seven or more years of training in the service and under the protection and discipline of a master in that trade – the apprenticeship. When he became a master himself, he had to belong to a guild or club, which made all the rules for that particular trade.[4]

Opposite top and below Traditional thatched roofs are still seen in farmhouses in the UNESCO World Heritage Site of the Viñales Valley, Pinar del Rio Province, Cuba. Here, age-old methods of agriculture continue alongside established architectural techniques and materials.

Opposite bottom This tobacco-drying house in the Viñales Valley illustrates elements commonly employed in this region, such as palm thatch and timber-framed construction.

Formal work organization was also the case with regard to the first black settlements. Historian Pieter Emmer writes:

> Many of the dwellings were constructed using a system of labour organization that included *cayapas* or gangs of workers, forms of cooperation which involved communities working together for an individual, who would in turn be obliged to lend his contribution in building houses for the other members of the community. Supervision generally was in the hands of a white overseer and one, or several, black bosses. Some slaves managed to become artisans and craftsmen, plying the trade of carpenter.[5]

Overall, however, very little is known of the local builders and craftsmen, many of whom must have been black.[6]

Together with seasonal hurricanes, a series of fires soon showed the need for an upgrading of building materials, which accelerated the construction of stone dwellings.[7] A general pattern emerged throughout the Caribbean. Emmer comments that:

> Until perhaps the middle of the 16th century, relatively fragile edifices of somewhat precarious durability, and built of relatively humble materials, predominated. These were hut-like constructions of clay-and-wattles, thatch, or similar materials. They were succeeded by wood construction, and in some places, by the 1670s or 1680s, by masonry – with the exception of the stonework and masonry of military fortifications and defensive walls.[8]

Construction Techniques

Within Caribbean Indian villages at the time of Columbus, individual houses in general were arranged around a central square and they were in large part constructed from the royal palm (*Roystonea regia*). They were simple but sturdy structures, constructed of walls of planking from the tree's trunk that was protected from rain by a plaster of hardened mud, and covered by palm-thatched roofs. The majority of houses were circular in design, with a conical roof, commonly referred to as the Amerindian *bohio*.[9] According to historians, 'This type of dwelling was said to be best able to withstand heavy gales'.[10] The *bohio* influenced Caribbean architecture to a large extent over the centuries, as the first houses built by the European settlers were not adequate for the tropical conditions. Quite soon, the incomers adapted the design of their houses according to local traditions so as to take fuller advantage of climate, resources and skills.[11]

By the end of the 16th century, three distinctive architectural trends had emerged. Firstly, the architecture of colonial towns and cities in the Caribbean in general reflected the styles of the European ruling nations of the time. This wide variety of styles included Gothic and Romanesque influences dating from the early 1500s, as well as Baroque of the late 17th and early 18th centuries in the Spanish settlements on the main islands of Cuba, Hispaniola and Puerto Rico. In many of the smaller islands of the eastern Caribbean, the British introduced stately Georgian and Victorian architecture, while the French brought their roof styles and the Dutch and Danish imported their traditional gables. Secondly, next to the colonial towns and cities, the first industrial

architecture relating to technology and mass production was introduced through the plantation system. And thirdly, from the indigenous *bohio* local populations developed a rural style of building. From these three strands evolved a new, Caribbean style of architecture, drawing on this wide variety of local and external influences.[12]

Building Plan/Form

Within the general pattern described above, particular types and characteristics of local timber vernacular architecture developed, of which the chattel house in Barbados and the wooden architecture of Cuba are perhaps the most characteristic.

Chattel Houses

Chattel houses, literally meaning 'movable property',[13] constitute a distinctive Barbados vernacular. Originally they were very simple single-room dwellings, made from clapboard, placed off-ground on piles of coral stone to keep out insects and other pests. As time went by, some of them became slightly more elaborate, being extended by the addition of other units or reconstructed in stone, acquiring gabled roofs and 'jalousie' shutters (from French terminology) for ventilation purposes, and being painted in a variety of colours.[14] When workers moved from one plantation to another, they brought their complete homes along by dismantling, moving and reassembling them in sections. With the exception of those on Barbados, most chattel houses on the Caribbean islands have long disappeared.

Cuban Timber Architecture

Cuba boasts the most extensive and important collection of architectural heritage in the Caribbean, including timber vernacular examples, with well-preserved historic buildings from the 16th, 17th, 18th, 19th and early 20th centuries. This is in part because of its size, but also because of its relative isolation: the US boycott prevented the island's modernization and development, which has wreaked havoc on the other Caribbean islands in terms of the authenticity and integrity of their architectural heritage. One-third of the World Heritage sites in the Caribbean region (seven out of a total of twenty-one, including three in overseas territories, as of June 2014) are to be found in Cuba. These include the historic cities of Havana, Trinidad, Cienfuegos and Camagüey, as well as Viñales Valley – each containing important aspects or ensembles of vernacular architecture expressed in locally sourced materials.

Left Housing on the shores of Cayo Granma in Santiago Bay, Cuba, represent the country's vernacular well, with their wooden shutters and cooling verandas, which moderate the heat.

The first seven villages founded by the Spaniards in Cuba during the first half of the 16th century were almost entirely constructed in timber, taking advantage of the availability of an array of tropical hardwoods and local labour and skills to master this material.[15] The character of Cuba's first cities was defined to a large extent by timber architecture, which remained a pervasive aspect during subsequent stages of development, when urban areas increased in size, construction increased in scale, and functions and techniques changed; 'it evolved and incorporated a formal and technical multiplicity of elements that have allowed it to survive until today'.[16] As such, the wooden vernacular has coexisted for more than five centuries within a plethora of different architectural models and styles used primarily for housing, but also for markets and public buildings such as theatres and churches. Cuba's timber vernacular architecture is well represented in larger urban ensembles in Cayo Granma in Santiago de Cuba Bay and Jagua in Cienfuegos Bay. Perhaps the largest collection of timber vernacular architecture in Cuba is to be found in settlements related to the island's dominant industries – for example, sugar. These settlements were carefully planned, functionally as well as formally, as they were organized around a centre, with an axis that ran from one end with a church to another where the sugar estate's owner lived, usually with a park in between, and all facilities grouped in lateral streets. The residential areas were clearly differentiated between housing for the directors, technical staff and workers on the one hand, and that for immigrants and temporary personnel on the other. This distinction was apparent in the design, spatial organization and quality of the construction materials. However, as Nilson Acosta Reyes has noted, 'as an ensemble these towns maintained a distinctive urban coherence in harmony with the surrounding landscape; [unfortunately] only some neighbourhoods, such as that of the railway men in the city of Camagüey, have maintained their urban design in essence'.[17]

Architectural Features

Next to these specificities, related to certain islands, general features can also be identified that tie the Caribbean vernacular 'family' together. The Caribbean's vernacular architecture, therefore, is like a mosaic – only revealing itself when viewed at the large (in this case, regional) scale.

One such ubiquitous feature is the balcony, which could either run around the entire internal courtyard of a dwelling, as in Spanish designs, or be fitted to the front of the house. In the latter case, it could shade a sidewalk or cover a porch or colonnaded space below. Balconies could be open or completely enclosed, with screens or louvred shutters for privacy.

Porches are also omnipresent throughout the Caribbean, both in urban and rural dwellings, appreciated in particular for sitting outside during the cool evening hours. With the exception of some of the drier islands – such as the Bahamas, or the Dutch Antilles of Aruba, Bonaire and Curaçao – many islands were sources of timber, including precious hardwoods. The local vernacular then consisted of timber frames covered with clapboard or weatherboard, assembled with the use of wooden pegs instead of iron nails, in the traditional shipwright's manner.

Window openings were covered by wooden shutters, or jalousies, which could admit light and cool draughts of air but kept the rain out. These features came in a variety of designs, the simplest form being the storm shutter made of heavy wood planking and often side-hinged. One particularly beautiful and elaborate shutter design was the 'Demerara window', named after a province in (formerly British) Guyana. It is top-hinged with a latticed window box extending from the base of the window.

Last but not least, fretwork ornamentations found on the gables, porches and balconies were commonly known as 'gingerbread', an elaborate form of wooden latticework. Originating as hand-carved designs in timber, they quickly became popular, more intricate and fashionable, and spread across the Caribbean – even to the southern United States.[18]

The Caribbean Today

Now, there is a clear recognition of the vulnerability of the historical vernacular timber architecture remaining in cities and towns of individual Caribbean islands – and of the urgent need to document and preserve this heritage, which is disappearing rapidly due to socio-economic changes, natural disasters, lack of maintenance and neglect. Over the past few decades, several efforts have been made – by the United Nations Educational, Scientific and Cultural Organization (UNESCO), the Organization of American States (OAS) and the Organization of the Wider Caribbean on Monuments and Sites (CARIMOS) among others – to identify and map the various types of timber-built heritage still present in the Caribbean region, and to exchange information on issues of protection and conservation. Overall, these efforts have aimed at debating the role of this heritage in strengthening cultural identity – both of individual islands and of the Caribbean region as a whole – and at identifying opportunities for sustainable development, in particular from tourism.

But valuable time has been lost, and today ever fewer larger ensembles of Caribbean vernacular architecture remain. Many countries and islands in the region have witnessed the large-scale destruction and disappearance of their timber vernacular, either by natural disasters or urban development. Fragmentation and serious alteration of the existing timber building stock are more the norm than the exception. Insufficient resources, both financial and human, are one reason; lack of appreciation of the local vernacular is another, as the wooden houses are still regarded as a social stigma connected to the 'days of enslavement, poverty, and living on someone else's land'.[19]

Few Caribbean cities today retain a critical mass of urban ensembles in timber vernacular, which would allow a full appreciation of the city's foundation and its social and economic development as expressed in urban patterns, streetscapes and architectural history. Perhaps one of the finest remaining examples, Georgetown in Guyana, experiences the loss of several historic wooden buildings a year due to fire, lack of maintenance and wanton destruction. Even Paramaribo in Suriname, the timber inner city of which was registered on the World Heritage List of UNESCO in 2002, recently received an alarming report from UNESCO that its state of conservation has deteriorated to a point where the World Heritage Committee will have to consider putting it on its Danger List. Sadly, what is left on most Caribbean islands are, at best, a few isolated buildings that are lone representatives of a once rich, intricate and traditional pattern of built expressions of cross-cultural exchange and expert craftsmanship in timber, which united the region in diversity.

Opposite top **A typical strategy of colonial Cuban architecture, the wooden shutters on a balcony in Santiago de Cuba provide inhabitants with relief from the heat and protection from rain, while also providing privacy for residents.**

Opposite bottom **Porches provide a sheltered place from sunshine, as illustrated by this historical, dilapidated colonial façade with colonnades in the Centro Habana district of Havana, Cuba.**

ECOA 24

Creole, Carbet, Caboclo and Brasileiro-Caribbean Houses of French Guiana and Brazil

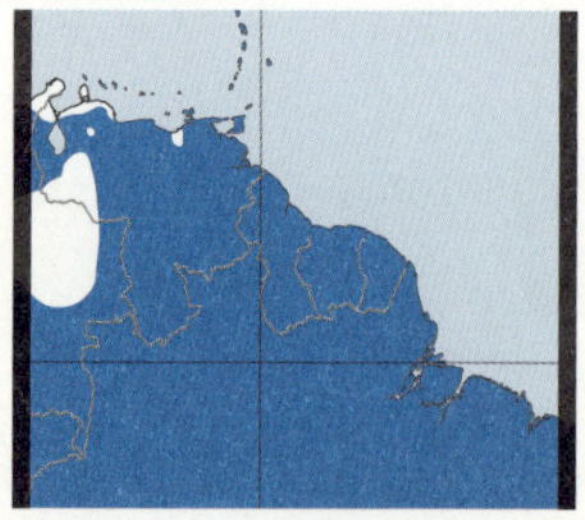

Seasonal average temperatures °C (F)

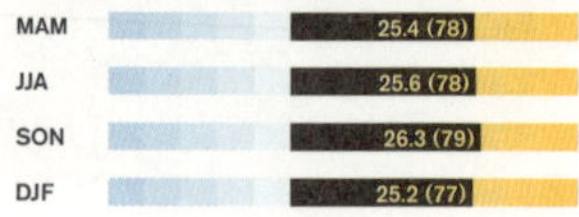

Seasonal average rainfall mm (in.)

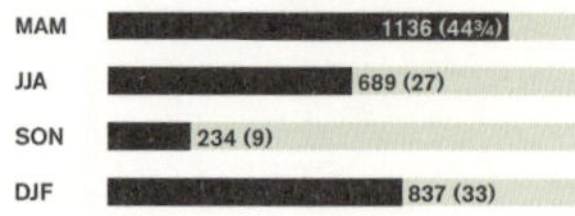

Patrick Pérez

Geography/Climate

Located on the border of Brazil and French Guiana, the lower valley of the Oyapock River is an almost flat territory where river and sea dispute between them stretches of flooded savannah and rainforest. Its fauna and flora are varied and conducive to human settlement, encompassing timber, fertile land, palms and vines, fruits, game and fish.

Construction Techniques and Building Plan/Form

Four architectural types are present in the region.[1] These types are distributed according to their adaptation to biogeographical, social and cultural local constraints: creole and Brasileiro-Caribbean houses are present in towns, in flat and dewatered areas; the Palikur carbet can be seen in villages of Amerindian communities, on cleared areas in the forest; the Brazilian caboclo house is found on river banks.

The creole house (GranCaz in creole) inherits its type from the shipwright techniques of the 18th century. It is a simple, rectangular structure, sitting on stones, formed of hardwood frames (*Dicorynia*, *Qualea* and *Tabebuia*), filled with bricks and lime, and covered with a duopitched tin roof. Openings in the gable ends and window transoms provide ventilation for the internal volume. The decorations are few and modest. Colour plays a role in social distinction. The presentation of the building (whether offering its longitudinal façade or its gable end to the street) indicates either institutional or private status.

The carbet is the traditional home of the Palikur Native Americans. With wide roof coverage and open on all sides, the carbet is entirely made with forest materials, cut with a machete and tied with lianas. The structure is composed of barkless roundwoods: heavy-density timber (*Tabebuia*) for the poles, and light wood for the framing. The roof is covered with palm leaves (*Manicaria*, *Mauritia*, *Euterpe*, *Attalea*, *Geonoma*) arranged vertically on the battens. This community habitat is now mainly devoted to the production of cassava flour, or to ceremonial and institutional functions.

The caboclo house is a riverside structure found in tidal reaches. It is the home of the Caboclo people, who make a living from the river in trades such as fishing or boating. In order to accommodate this riparian existence, a vocabulary of an astonishing richness of forms unfolds around the Caboclo dwelling, and connects to the surrounding neighbourhood – encompassing bridges, pontoons, ramps, canoes, fishing equipment and storerooms. In harmony with its environment, this dwelling creates a strange and beautiful landscape.

The Brasileiro-Caribbean house combines two models: the Anglo-Caribbean bungalow, with its central nucleus surrounded by a gallery and terraces, and the creole house, in a concrete-block version. The aesthetics of the Brasileiro-Caribbean house's openings, with its characteristic arches, proceeds directly from the Brazilian colonial mansion with shutters, balustrades and, sometimes, a tiled roof. This dwelling type is made mostly of imported materials (concrete blocks, steel, bricks and tiles). It owes its success to its aura of 'modernity' and social distinction, but, poorly ventilated and too hot by night, it is not well adapted to the Amazonian environment.

Below left The creole house is characterized by its colourful, rectangular structures of hardwood with a duopitched roof and shutters.

Below right The Brasileiro-Caribbean house combines two styles: the bungalow surrounded by verandas, and elements such as arches, shutters and balustrades that borrow from the style of colonial Brazilian mansions.

Opposite top The open-sided ceremonial carbet of Amerindian communities is formed from local materials: barkless roundwoods form the structural frame, tied with liana and waterproofed by vertically arranged rows of palm leaves.

Opposite bottom Caboclo housing with shaded verandas is found along the riverside and provides shelter for Caboclo peoples, who have adapted the typology to include additions such as ramps, bridges and canoes, in harmony with their riverside existence.

Indigenous and Colonial Structures in Venezuela

Alessandro Famiglietti, Angela Rodríguez de Famiglietti and Adriana Useche

Geography/Climate

The Venezuelan climate is usually classified as tropical, even though it is also possible to find desert and temperate regions within the country's borders. There is, therefore, no unique way in which to examine 'the vernacular' in Venezuela. In architectural terms, three main groups could summarize the country's traditional building stock: its indigenous architecture, its earthen architecture, and foreign-influenced buildings. These are linked by the syncretism that characterizes Venezuelan culture.

Construction Techniques and Building Plan/Form

Venezuela's indigenous people generated two types of housing, collective and single-family, with variations according to their location on or in land, water, forest, moorland or plains. Structures with a provisional character, often mere windbreaks, such as the Yanomami's *shabono* huts, sheltered complex family groups. The most common types of these structures, or 'land roofs' as they are known, are the Bari hut or the Piaroa cabin, both large-scale constructions with a roof that extends down into the soil. Their construction was largely similar from region to region in the way that the vegetation-based materials adopted were used – even up to the scale of the Warao *palafitte*, a small single-family housing unit found on lakes and lagoons, with roofs of Temiche palm (*Manicaria saccifera* Gaertn.) that are supported on mangrove wood.

In terms of land architecture, *bahareque*, adobe and *tapial* (rammed earth) formed the construction of rural landscape enclosures and early Venezuelan cities alike. *Bahareque* is the most economic and widespread technique, with a framework of wooden posts, interwoven with cane and bamboo and covered in clay. The adobe provided by clay blocks was fabricated in moulds. *Tapial* was the wall structure that characterized the country's colonial period, when a house built with this method attracted much prestige. The *tapial* was placed on a solid rock base, with timber formwork forming an enormous crate for the compaction of the earth.

European colonizers brought a clear urban structure to the Americas that is seen in newly founded settlements, which were based on the scheme of a central square surrounded by important buildings, leading out from it. At the scale of private, domestic spaces, however, the building forms worked well with their tropical environment; they 'owned' the locality and yet were also protected from it. The colonial house therefore became the ideal in Venezuelan cities for more than two centuries, according to the imported Spanish tradition. *Tapial* and adobe walls, coloured-tiled roofs, austere and pale friezes and airy patios were crucial components of the form – supplemented in some cases by balconies, blinds and coloured-glass windows. In urban houses, façades with ironwork and plaster mouldings denoted prestige and economic strength. In rural houses, the lack of ornamentation and detail testified to the relative austerity experienced by small-town families.

A vernacular architectural approach is now most often seen in formal and spatial elements rather than in construction materials. These buildings respond to the control of light, wind and tropical weather and, especially, to research into passive strategies for cooling and heating.

Below The Piaroa hut, a communal dwelling with a roof that extends to the ground, is one of Venezuela's most typical indigenous forms of architecture (left). In contrast, the Warao *palafitte* of the region is an open-sided, single-family unit of palm thatch found on lakes and lagoons, such as this in the country's eastern regions of the Orinoco Delta (right).

Opposite Three construction techniques commonly seen in Venezuela's land architecture include adobe blocks (middle right), *bahareque* techniques using framed wooden posts, cane, bamboo and clay (top and middle), and *tapial* or rammed earth (bottom right). Later colonial Spanish influences included ornamental plaster mouldings (bottom left) as seen in this historical house in Coro old town, Falcón state.

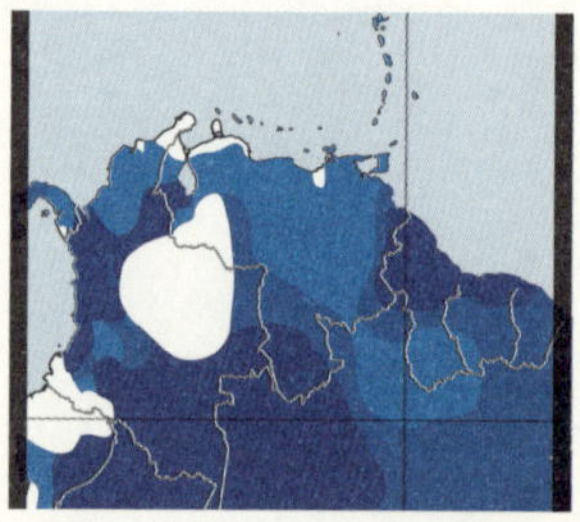

Seasonal average temperatures °C (F)

MAM	25.9 (79)
JJA	24.9 (77)
SON	25.4 (78)
DJF	25.1 (77)

Seasonal average rainfall mm (in.)

MAM	394 (15)
JJA	811 (32)
SON	490 (19)
DJF	180 (7)

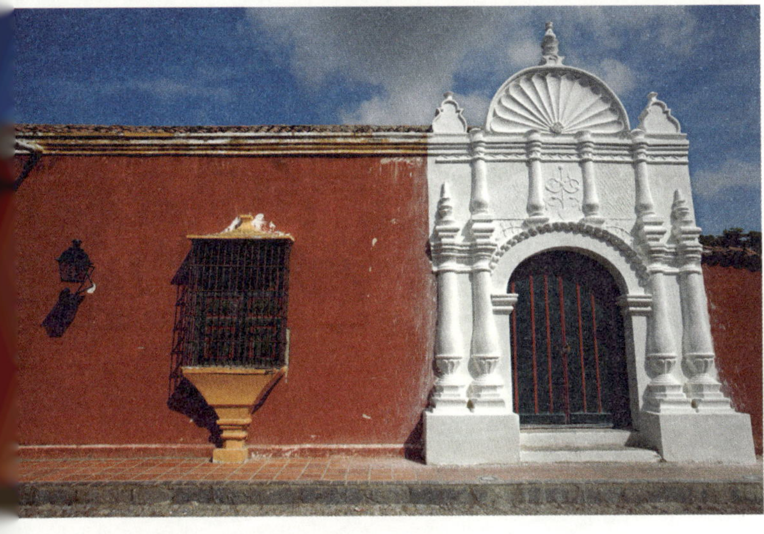

Traditional Waorani Houses of the Ecuadorian Amazon

María Gabriela Zurita Benavides and Laura Rival

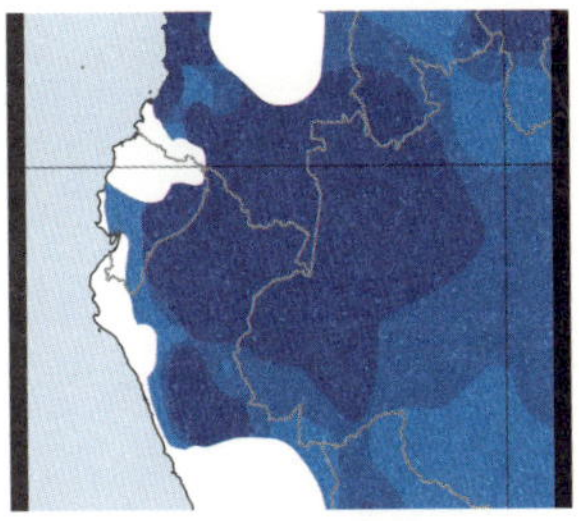

Seasonal average temperatures °C (F)

Seasonal average rainfall mm (in.)

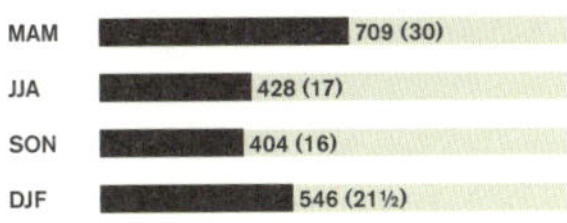

Opposite top and right Displaying the key characteristics of a Waorani longhouse, these images show the rectangular planned homes with roofs that reach the ground. Such buildings house multiple families and engender close connection.

Opposite bottom Built of a range of hardwood species of the Amazon, the A-frame structures of the Waorani are woven with palm and secured by vines, all of which are harvested locally.

Geography/Climate and Culture

The Amazonian region of Ecuador is home to the Amerindian Waorani people. Waorani society has been transformed following the first sustained contact with the outside world in 1958, and this process has resulted in changes in natural habitat and dwelling forms. Before deciding to organize themselves in villages, the Waorani used to live along the slopes of the region's interfluvial area – the southern tributaries of the middle Napo River – where they built rectangular longhouses. Following their 'pacification' by evangelical missionaries in the late 1950s, they started establishing semi-permanent villages along rivers and roads, where longhouses coexist with walled houses on stilts. The spatial configuration of their contemporary sedentary villages testifies to new social strategies as well as to the adaptation to modern, urbanized ways of living. Currently, the Waorani population numbers roughly 3,200 (as estimated in 2011 by Nacionalidad Waodani del Ecuador, Ecuador's official ethnic organization); the largest of their villages is inhabited by 280 people, and the smallest by ten people.

Materials and Construction Techniques

A thatched palm roof, reaching to the ground and woven with palm fronds, covers the A-frame structure of traditional Waorani longhouses. The poles are made of various hardwood species and plants that are common in the interfluvial area, where their abundance traditionally informed the choice of dwelling site. Before the Waorani 'pacification', longhouses formed multifamily matrilocal residences, sheltering a mother with her husband(s), unmarried children and married daughters. Each married woman had her own hearth and hammock. In Waorani society, kinship is created through acts of sharing, and the longhouse is the privileged place for this activity.

Building Plan/Form

In today's smaller communities (ten to fifty people), villagers still trace their lineage through the female side of their families and that of their direct kin, while unrelated families now live together as neighbours in the larger villages. Everywhere, the nuclear family takes precedence as the pervasive new social unit. In both small and large villages, 'traditional' longhouses, or *nanikabos* (their Waorani name means literally 'houses like those of our forebears'), are found side by side with 'modern' houses, built in the style of the Waorani's former enemy, the Runa-Kichua. Houses found along rivers are sometimes built over a 6 m by 9 m (20 x 30 ft) platform, which provides protection from flooding and snakes. Such river locations are new adaptations; in the past, longhouses were located on hilltops, where people could easily monitor the movements of intruders.

The Runa-Kichua architectural model features square stilt houses (4 m x 3 m in extent; 13 x 10 ft) with vertical walls and platforms of palm trunk, a semi-opaque cladding technique that allows residents to watch what is happening outside their homes. Stilt houses are practical innovations for people who no longer sleep in hammocks, and for families who spend the night on a blanket (or sometimes a mattress) laid directly on the bare floor. The thatched roof of the Runa-Kichua house, adopted by some of today's Waorani families, has the advantage of requiring fewer palm fronds than the traditional longhouse. Moreover, it can be woven with *Carludovica palmata* leaves, a common species that grows abundantly in cultivated gardens and fallows. These palms are always at hand when needed, and they are easy to transport, which allows people to change the thatch of their houses as often as needed (typically, two or three times a year). Each nuclear family owns two buildings: one, thatched, used as a kitchen; the other, covered with metal roofing sheets, used as a dormitory. The constant smoke from the kitchen's hearth protects the waterproof qualities of the thatch.

The coexistence of these different types of building and architectural models well illustrates the ways in which Waorani people have adapted to foreign influences and integrated into modern society, while maintaining a privileged space for their traditional kinship relations.

Below Runa-Kichua models of housing borrow from the eponymous tribe and are formed of raised, square-planned homes with straight sides built primarily with timber. This gives the advantage of distance from floods or snakes, as well as requiring far fewer palm fronds to construct.

Opposite top Now centred around nuclear family units, contemporary Waorani villages continue to include versions of the traditional longhouse, or *nanikabos*. This reflects their ongoing reverence for the shared relations the structure engenders.

Opposite bottom Retaining the floor-to-ceiling structure of the ancient Waorani longhouse, more recent examples are now built alongside rivers and at lower levels, in contrast to earlier, more defensive settlements built on the top of hills.

Upper Xingu and Wajãpi Vernacular of Brazil

Catherine Gallois

Below As illustrated by these historical photographs, Upper Xingu dwellings constructed solely of forest-based plant materials have long existed in the Brazilian Amazon.

Opposite The Amazon rainforest is occupied by the complex networks and territories of indigenous peoples, although these are invisible from the air.

Geography/Climate and Culture

The study of Brazilian indigenous architectures is challenging, as this vast country has an enormous cultural richness thanks to its various social, historical and territorial contexts. Its varied construction techniques reflect the cultural diversity of its 247 indigenous groups, spread all over the country and speaking more than 150 different languages.

Territorial areas occupied by indigenous peoples are not 'great human voids' – an idea that has been a widespread and long-held belief in Brazil, in relation to territorial planning of the Amazon. The forms of territorial occupation displayed by many indigenous peoples in Amazonian forests, for example, constitute real and complex 'webs' of numerous paths, although they are invisible in aerial photographs.

Materials and Construction Techniques

The indigenous dwellings cited here are exclusively built with materials of plant origin, natural resources taken mostly from the deep forest. The construction of these traditional houses is a collective work, and each part has its specific name – either referring to the plant species and its structural function or alluding to the name of a body part. Today, the management of the plant species used for artefacts, handicrafts and building is a challenge faced by many indigenous peoples such as the Wajãpi of Amapá and other groups living in the Upper Xingu region of central Brazil.

The construction techniques employed by these people are based on deep knowledge of a wide variety of natural materials and plant species, and are still employed by the Wajãpi and the Upper Xingu groups. Similar building techniques are also still currently being used by many other native groups in Brazil. But all these unique traditional building techniques, which permit the formal and spatial richness of indigenous architectures, depend on environmental management and the strengthening of local control over natural resources. Also fundamental are the official recognition of native territories, demarcation and protection of indigenous lands, and the implementation of cultural inventories, which are absolutely crucial in order to extend contemporary appreciation of Brazilian indigenous architectures.

Opposite Forming the elliptical base envelope of a traditional family house, or oca, Xingu construction techniques are still practised (top). Combining traditional culture and new technologies, this oca is supplemented by a bicycle, satellite dish and motorbike (bottom).

Above Though ethnographically diverse, peoples of the Upper Xingu region share an architectural language, as exemplified by this village of oca family houses that encircle a central circular plaza.

Upper Xingu Indigenous Architecture

The Upper Xingu region comprises the basin formed on the northern flank of the central Brazilian plateau. It is located north of Mato Grosso, a floristic transition zone between the central highlands and the Amazon rainforest. The Xingu Indigenous Park is home to a variety of native groups, who speak Arawak languages (the Wauja, Mahinaku and Yawalapiti), Karib languages (the Kuikuro, Kalapalo and Nahukwa), Tupian languages (the Kamayurá and Aweti), and a further, isolated tongue: Trumai. They constitute part of an ethnographically complex regional and historical system. Although they are all part of the Upper Xinguan multilingual society, these groups share the same spatial organization and housing architecture. Villages are organized around large, elliptical dwellings, which are situated along the circumference of a circle surrounding a central plaza. These houses shelter several families each.

According to anthropologist Michael J. Heckenberger, a beautiful Xinguano village must have the following:

> a large, open plaza and wide, straight roads extending to the horizon in one or two directions. The local landscape expands into a broad countryside of manioc gardens; groves of piquí fruit trees; wide open fields of sapé, an invasive grass that is critical as house thatch; diverse areas of secondary forest growth, which is graded from low to medium-sized.[1]

Kuikuro and Yawalapiti houses share very similar shapes and building techniques. Their dwellings have two entrances: a main doorway that faces the village plaza, and another that gives on to spaces for preparing manioc and to the gardens. In the Kuikuro language, the house is known as *üne*, and is supported on three thick central posts (*agahagu*). These have stability thanks to cross-bracing (*uhaku*). The walls are made of logs forming an ellipse-shaped base envelope (*üngita*). Long vertical rods, which run from floor to outer edges, are tied at the top, fulfilling the function of main rafters (*isitisu*), with their finer end placed highest in order to facilitate mooring along the ridge tie beams. These are accompanied by small rafters comprising thin rods (*isitisu kusügü*). The *sapé* grass (*inhe*) covering is tied to horizontal small sticks (*üngau*), and has to be replaced several times a year with fresh grass collected from the surroundings. Two diagonal, crossed rafters (*is-isogoko-gu*) are situated inside the house – on one side of the grass cover.

Wajãpi Indigenous Architecture

The Wajãpi live in northern Amazonia, in Brazil's Amapá state. The Wajãpi ethnic group comprises various local groups, each of which holds political autonomy that is formed by the association of several nuclear families through a network of relationships. A local group will not necessarily be confined to a single village, with its attendant spatial organization, but might encompass a set of such settlements. Wajãpi villages (*taa*) are composed of one or more courtyards (*okary*), which are connected by paths. These spaces do not necessarily have a particular geometrical shape, and are surrounded by deep forest (*kaa*) and by gardens (*koo*). Like the indigenous peoples of the Upper Xingu, the Wajãpi practise swidden (slash-and-burn) agriculture; the Wajãpi, however, display a higher degree of territorial mobility (*jisyrysyry*). The latter feature is seen in their practice of changing the location of the *okary* to another place – either near to or far from the place previously occupied by it.

Wajãpi vernacular architecture basically encompasses three types of house, all of which are built by their owners: *jura*, the biggest house type, with an upper floor; *yvy'o*, a single-storey house type; and *tapaina*, a kind of temporary dwelling. *Tapaina* are small structures that may comprise simply kitchens with a low loft for roasting or for grating manioc, or temporary houses in new villages, prior to the construction of a larger *jura* or *yvy'o*. Wajãpi homes have many construction features in common but, since they are built by their owners, each of them may have individual particularities. Their proportions, for instance, might vary greatly. In a *jura*, the roof might end up almost meeting the floor level – or, as with the *yvy'o*, it may be very low in relation to the dirt floor.

These houses are covered with straw and palm leaves (*ubim*). They have two walls, but sometimes one of the extremities of these is rounded, forming a semicircle – an arrangement called *javi revikwarã*, which means 'the buttock of the tortoise'. In August 2001, four Wajãpi men built a *jura* house in the gardens of Rio de Janeiro's Indian Museum. It could be considered a genuine Wajãpi residence, as it was constructed at full scale with a floor area of 82 sq m (880 sq ft) and used approximately twenty different plant species, all of which came from Amapá.

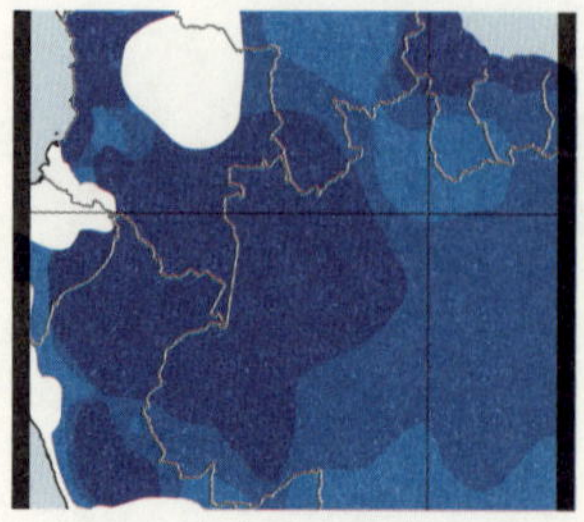

Seasonal average temperatures °C (F)

MAM	26.8 (80)
JJA	27.2 (81)
SON	28.1 (82)
DJF	27.2 (81)

Seasonal average rainfall mm (in.)

MAM	128 (5)
JJA	80.3 (3)
SON	106 (4)
DJF	82.7 (3)

Opposite top left and top right All houses are built by Wajãpi owners, giving rise to local variation in shape, proportions and materials. Drawing on materials readily available from the forest, homes typically include roofs of straw and palm leaves, which are collected by hand and stitched into place.

Opposite middle left and bottom left Open-sided Wajãpi *jura* are the largest houses constructed by this ethnic group, in Amapá state. Houses built by this group range in size, from *jura* to the single-storey *yvy'o*.

Opposite middle right and bottom right Straw and palm leaves form the basis of the roof. They provide water resistance for the open-sided structures without reducing cross ventilation.

Yanomami Vernacular of the Brazilian Amazon

William Milliken

Geography/Climate and Building Plan/Form

Like many other indigenous groups in the Amazon, the Yanomami build large, circular wooden dwellings, thatched with palm leaves, that house the entire community. Smaller roundhouses (*yanos*) have an opening in the centre of the roof to allow smoke to escape, while larger ones comprise a central courtyard surrounded by a ring-shaped dwelling, walled on the outside and open to the centre.

The timber species used in their construction are determined partly by availability: the Yanomami occupy a large territory spanning the Brazilian–Venezuelan border in the northern Amazon; it includes both highland and lowland areas, and the forest composition varies considerably between these zones. Nevertheless, closer examination shows recurring botanical themes that are common not only to the Yanomami but to many other Amazonian peoples.

Materials and Construction Techniques

In 1994, a joint botanical–anthropological survey carried out a detailed inventory of construction materials in a single large (approximately 80 m [260 ft] diameter) lowland roundhouse, known as the Watoriki theri, which had been built the previous year. At least fifty-two

Below A distinctive circular Yanomami village seen from the air in the Catrimani Valley, northern Brazil.

Opposite The communal Yanomami roundhouse (*yano*), principally composed of buried posts, tie-beams and rafters with a thatch of *Geonoma* palm leaves, is effectively a series of conjoined family dwellings, each built by its occupiers.

plant species were recorded and over 1,600 structural components enumerated for this one structure. The Yanomami are traditionally a semi-nomadic people, spending up to half the year trekking through the forest (staying in makeshift temporary shelters) and the rest of the time in their villages. Every few years they will abandon their *yano*, migrate to a different area and build a new one. The *yano* at Watoriki, while structurally similar to traditional Yanomami houses, was strategically established close to a health post and airstrip, and was built to accommodate an unusually large and increasingly sedentary population. It therefore needed to last longer than normal.

The components most likely to fail in Amazonian forest dwellings are thatch and buried posts. There is not much that can be done about the former – the best thatching leaves in the region are cut from a small *Geonoma* palm and inevitably need replacing after a few years. This is a time-consuming business: the *yano* at Watoriki was thatched with about 500,000 such leaves (about 50 per sq m), each carefully woven onto supporting slats made from the split trunks of *Socratea* palms, which are then tied to the rafters to form a waterproof roof. Nevertheless, it is common knowledge among many indigenous groups that durability of thatch is influenced by the phase of the moon in which the leaves are cut, probably reflecting nutrient changes associated with the lunar cycle.

With regard to the latter component – buried posts – certain timber species are much more resistant to rot and termite attack than others. It is not hard to see how such knowledge would be acquired, as the Yanomami inevitably observe decomposition rates of different trees in the forest and, after felling, in their swidden (slash-and-burn) gardens. The majority (72 per cent) of the three rings of main supporting posts in the Watoriki *yano* were cut from just two species: *Manilkara huberi* (also known as *maçaranduba*) and *Centrolobium paraense*. Both are commonly used for house posts elsewhere in Amazonia, and are highly valued in the timber trade for their durability. Minor, less structurally important posts showed a more varied composition, although certain families and genera again predominated.

The main requirements for *yano* rafters are length, narrowness and straightness, with a high strength-to-weight ratio favoured. Rotting is less of an issue than might be assumed, as smoke from the constantly burning hearths protects them. Two related families of Amazonian trees, the *Annonaceae* (custard apple family) and *Myristicaceae* (nutmeg family), commonly exhibit this combination of properties, and made up 81 per cent of the 867 rafters at Watoriki – with one species of *Xylopia* (*Annonaceae*) accounting for more than 50 per cent of the rafters.

The components of the house were lashed together, principally with the aerial roots of an epiphytic aroid (*Heteropsis flexuosa*) commonly known in Brazil as *cipo titica*. Tough, flexible and relatively abundant in the forest, these roots are widely used for this purpose and also supply the Yanomami's main basketry material. Strips of fibrous bark from the trunks of *Lecythidaceae* (Brazil nut family) trees, and occasionally selected forest vines, were also used for lashing, but to a lesser degree.

The larger the *yano*, the more significant the issue of resource availability becomes. A small *yano* may be constructed entirely from the 'ideal' species, while a

Above left Open-sided structures and closed-style dwellings are both found in Yanomami villages. Traditionally occupied for approximately half of the year while their (semi-nomadic) occupiers trek in the forest, the dwellings are eventually abandoned every few years or so for a newly made structure.

Above right and opposite The Yanomami live in one of the most inaccessible regions of the Amazon. Repairs to structures were originally undertaken with self-made tools for working timber. Roofs are maintained by replacing sections of *Geonoma* palm thatch when required.

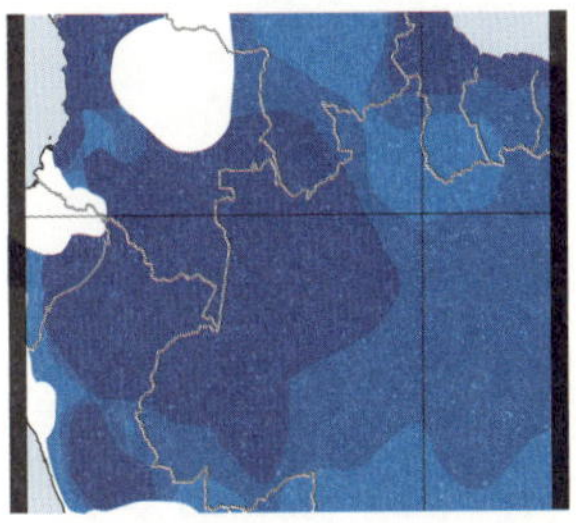

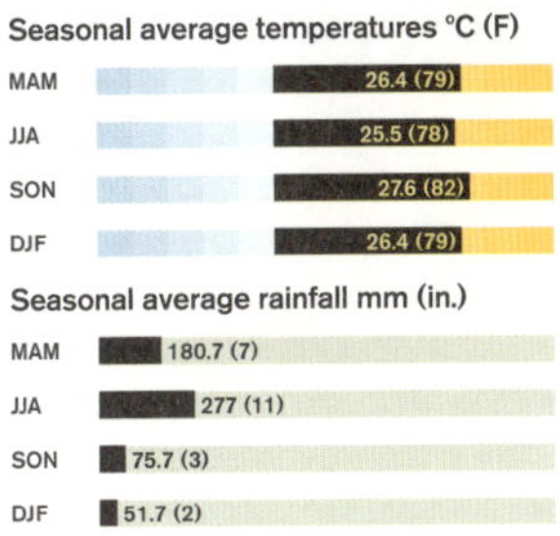

construction the size of the Watoriki theri requires a greater level of compromise. All the materials must be cut and carried by hand, and there is a limit to how far it is worth dragging a tree through the forest. Thus, for example, while the 'ideal' *Xylopia* accounted for 73 per cent of the rafters in the main outer ring of the roof (which was built first) it only made up 26 per cent of the (later) inner ring. This was apparently because the supply in the vicinity of the village was exhausted.

However, selection of materials is also influenced by personal preference. Ostensibly a single communal structure, the *yano* is actually a series of conjoined family dwellings built primarily by the families that will occupy them. The outer wall at Watoriki ranged from flimsy sections of vertical thatch to solid walls of split *Socratea* palm, which probably reflected the fact that older members of the community had direct experience of the attacks of raiding parties, and of the former need for defensive walls and palisades, while younger ones did not.

When the new *yano* was surveyed in 1994, it already incorporated adaptations to the 'traditional' Yanomami house, including an innovative inner-roof design borrowed from the Shamatari (western Yanomami) village of Kapirota u. The people at Watoriki had migrated from the highlands to the lowlands, and in doing so gained access to a better species of thatching palm (*Geonoma baculifera*). The technique that they used for roofing was said to have been learned from workers employed at an SPI (Indian Protection Service) post on the upper Demini River established in the early 1940s. The fact that these leaves last only a few years was not a significant problem in the past, but at Watoriki – where the community planned to stay considerably longer than was customary, and where they were aware that the resource had been significantly depleted in the construction of their house – it was a concern.

When the surveying team returned to the village in 2014, new influences were visible in the materials that had been used to repair it during the intervening two decades. In addition to the factors mentioned above, the selection of materials is partly influenced by technology. Prior to the advent of metal tools, which initially arrived through trade with neighbouring indigenous groups, the Yanomami were limited in their choice of trees for construction. The Watoriki theri of 1997 was built with machetes and axes, but by 2014 the community had gained access to chainsaws. Timber species that would previously have been unrealistic to work were suddenly accessible, and some use of sawn timber could be seen around the building. Sections of the outer wall had been repaired with *Mauritia* palm, using a technique that was said to have been learned from visiting Carib Indians.

Influences on the selection and manner of use of construction materials by the Yanomami are similar to those experienced not only by other Amazonian communities but by people around the world. They reflect a complex interaction of emerging ideas and preferences, developing technology, social and environmental change, and related changes in resource availability. This is by no means a new phenomenon. What may nowadays be considered 'traditional' indigenous architecture is no more than a snapshot in an evolutionary process that has been running for millennia, and will doubtless continue to do so for many more.

Indigenous *Malocas* of Amazonia

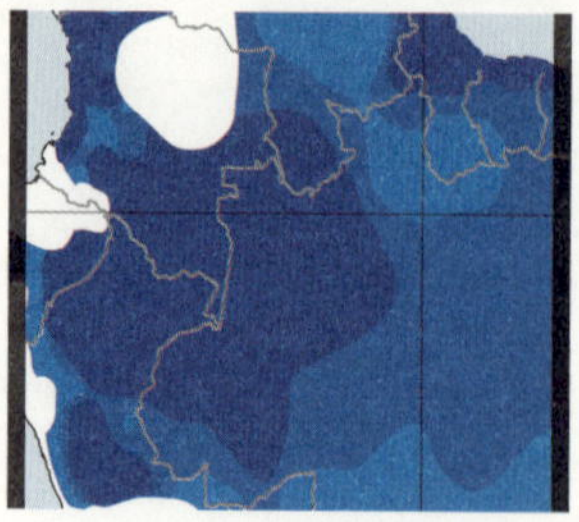

Seasonal average temperatures °C (F)

MAM	26.4 (79)
JJA	26.8 (80)
SON	27.5 (81)
DJF	26.5 (80)

Seasonal average rainfall mm (in.)

MAM	271.7 (10¾)
JJA	58.4 (2¼)
SON	65 (2½)
DJF	252.4 (10)

John Hemming

Geography/Climate and Culture

The Uaupés River (spelled Vaupés in Spanish) is an Amazonian headwater that flows from the tropical rainforests of southeastern Colombia into northwestern Brazil, towards the Rio Negro and the main Amazon. In recent millennia, a dozen indigenous peoples on this river and its tributaries have come to resemble one another in almost every aspect of their societies. Most of these tribes speak Tukanoan (notably the Tukano, Tariana, Cubeo and Wanana), but the Desana speak Arawak.

Building Plan/Form

One common trait of these peoples comprises the magnificent communal huts, or *malocas*, which are unlike dwellings anywhere else in Amazonia. At first sight, these houses resemble early Christian basilicas or Paraguayan Jesuit churches. They have a rectangular plan – about 30 by 12 m (100 x 40 ft) in extent. A central roof beam, probably of *buriti* palm (*Mauritia flexuosa*), runs the length of the building, and is supported by two rows of straight and smooth tree-trunk columns over 9 m (30 ft) high.

Below Rectangular *maloca* with straight, closed sides of the Vaupés River people (top left) and the Tukano (bottom left and below) in the Brazilian Amazon.

Opposite top A feature of the indigenous *maloca* (seen here in the background) is its striking roof, which almost reaches the ground.

Opposite bottom The renowned Maloca Ipanoré in Mitu, Uaupés region, is noted for its size and is decorated with characteristic bright geometric patterns.

Where these *malocas* resemble early churches is in their straight, rectangular roof planes, which slope almost to the ground on either side. Their triangular façades are of woven trellis covered in bark cloth, decorated with bright geometric patterns. The principal elevation contains a large door – the main source of light for the interior. The gables are of woven palm fronds, expertly tied to a trellis of straight beams and rafters by cords of split liana. The roof is totally watertight – a *maloca* remains bone dry, even in tropical downpours – and the low side walls are tough enough to resist arrows or even gunshot.

A Uaupés *maloca* will typically hold about 100 people from a dozen families. Each family has a private compartment, with palm-thatch partitioning, for its hammocks, cooking fire and few utensils – manioc graters, bows and arrows, fishing tackle, baskets and gourds, and feather ornaments – which often hang from rafters. The chief's family are accommodated at the closed far end. The wide central aisle comprises communal space – for children to play; for women to prepare food and drink; and, above all, for frequent ceremonies with ritual dances and much consumption of mildly alcoholic and hallucinogenic beverages. It is all kept spotlessly clean.

Historically, outside observers were struck by the social harmony and comfort of these great *malocas*. They were the symbol and bulwark of each tribe's tradition, beliefs and independence. For this reason, every *maloca* was demolished during the 20th century by missionary zealots determined to impose Christianity. But some are now being rebuilt, by indigenous people seeking to recover their rich heritage.

Favelas of Brazil's Urban Periphery

Ronaldo de Moraes Brilhante

Building Plan/Form

From a formal point of view, favelas are characterized by a high density of irregularly distributed dwellings resulting from spontaneous occupation patterns. These settlements can be arranged on flat areas or on hillsides, invariably in regions that hold no real interest for the property market. Although fragile, the sites may present environmental risks. The access to these settlements usually consists of narrow and uneven streets. In many cases, the irregularity of the building plots gives rise to clusters of homes that lack any kind of formal arrangement.

Favelas are the result of urbanization and industrialization processes linked to a lack of infrastructure, as well as the lack of a consistent housing policy designed to help impoverished parts of the population that sought a means of subsisting in Brazil's cities. In the late 19th century, the main Brazilian cities adopted modernizing urban policies, which were responsible for the eradication of tenements – architectural forms that originally housed the workers in these urban centres. Thus, a large contingent of the population was expelled from the central cores of the nation's cities and forced to improvise ways to meet the growing housing demand, which intensified throughout the 20th century.

Materials and Construction Techniques

Favela dwellings are usually composed of small rooms with low levels of lighting and ventilation, high humidity, structural problems and poor accessibility. Owing to their occupants' scarcity of resources, these structures are characterized by poor-quality building materials, poor workmanship and a relatively limited lifespan – all because they are built of 'leftovers' available from the formal city. Since the late 1980s, temporary slum huts – built with pieces of wood, metal cans and other rudiments – have increasingly been replaced by buildings constructed with clay bricks – albeit still usually without external finishing. As these settlements are illegal, most favela dwellers do not own their homes, which limits their access to basic civil rights, contributing to social vulnerability in relation to healthcare, education, violence, work and income.

Since the origins of the Brazilian republic until the mid-1980s onwards, the slums were recognized as urban pathologies to be exterminated. The attempted removal of such settlements from Rio de Janeiro city between 1968 and 1975, and more recently with the World Cup Soccer (2014) and the Olympics Games (2016), represented the most violent periods of government-imposed exclusion and repression in the history of these settlements in Rio de Janeiro. Exclusion and repression were imposed by governmental actions with the aim to segregate the most impoverished parts of the population into the city's distant peripheries. Their inhabitants, the *favelados*, became major political actors in the nation's urban realm. Insisting on equal recognition and rights to the land, they formed the People's Assembly (Assembléia do Povo) in 1979 and gained a network of public support.[1] Their actions enhanced the legitimacy of their previously marginal forms of housing.

In fact, the adaptations of favelas to Brazil's varied urban landscape has contributed to the formation of a rich and diverse use of space. The lack of sanitation and drinking-water supply systems – and of basic public services relating to health, transport, education and leisure – has, in recent years, been countered by a process of urbanization that has sought to improve the quality of life of those living in favelas. These interventions have aimed, in most cases, at improving the urban structure of public spaces and constructing new housing units for residents who occupy areas with a high risk of landslides. Recent Brazilian legislation has encouraged the issuing of land titles to slum residents, thereby legitimizing further legal steps towards the establishment of so-called Zones of Special Social Interest (ZEIS), which lay down new architectural parameters for such 'popular' dwellings. In practice, there have, unfortunately, been chronic difficulties in the fair and democratic promotion of these new rights by government.

Today, despite the social, political and economic factors that continue to marginalize the issue of poverty in Brazil, the favelas are part of the culture and way of life of the contemporary Brazilian metropolis.

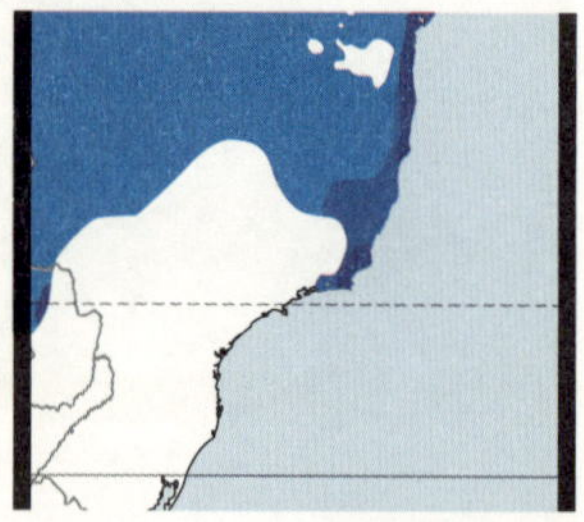

Seasonal average temperatures °C (F)

MAM	25.3 (77)
JJA	21.7 (71)
SON	23.1 (73)
DJF	26.3 (79)

Seasonal average rainfall mm (in.)

MAM	123.3 (5)
JJA	57.3 (2¼)
SON	98.3 (4)
DJF	147 (5¾)

Opposite The dense hillside development of Rocinha in Rio de Janeiro is Brazil's largest favela, with a population of between 100,000 and 200,000 people. Favelas are an inherent part of the city's contemporary character.

Emidio do Badalo
12012
Emidio do Badalo
12012

Guarani 'Big Houses' of Paraguay

Luis Silvio Rios Cabrera

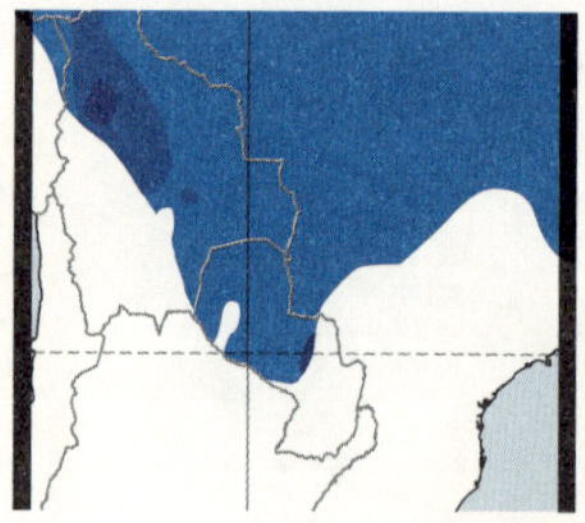

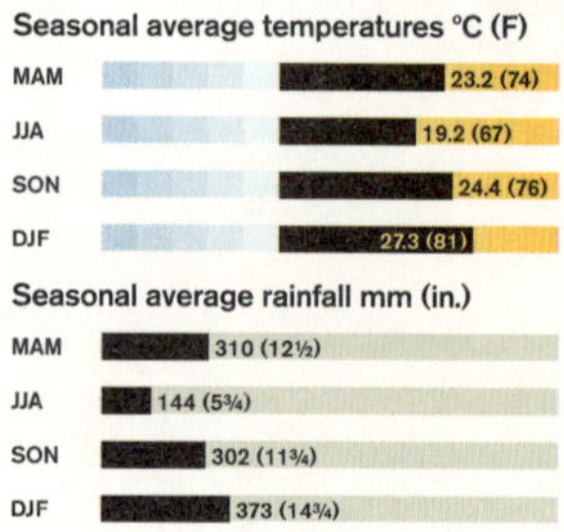

Opposite The tent-like and insect-proof 'big house' of Guarani natives in Paraguay provides a large collective dwelling, which stands approximately 15 m (50 ft) high and up to 50 m (165 ft) in length. Bamboo structural frames with intermediate hardwood columns are clad with straw and readily available forest materials.

Geography/Climate and Materials

Paraguay is located near the tropics. Its climate can be considered 'composite', with higher (monsoon-season) humidity levels than those experienced in hot and dry zones. Otherwise, most of its climatic characteristics are similar to those in the latter region types. The design criteria for its vernacular buildings are therefore roughly the same as for those in hot and dry climates – except that the maximization of cross ventilation is highly desirable during the monsoon period.

Paraguay's eastern region of the country is warm and humid with plenty of water, and was heavily forested throughout most of its history – from the Spanish conquest of around 1500 to the mid-20th century. From the latter point onwards, its territory began to be converted to large-scale livestock and agricultural use. As a result, much of its wooded area, along with the associated traditional construction materials, has been dramatically reduced.

Building Plan/Form and Construction Techniques

The Guarani natives of eastern Paraguay traditionally constructed a collective type of dwelling known locally as *oga guasu*, or 'big house'. It typically had a roof around 15 m (50 ft) wide and high, and a variable length ranging from 25 to 50 m (80 x 165 ft) – and sometimes even longer, depending on the number of families accommodated in its collective space. This typology was already noted in the first chronicles of the era of the colonies, and it was still evident at the beginning of the 20th century.

The aforementioned house layout was typical of dwellings in the Amazon region; it allowed between forty and seventy or more families to live inside, keep their cooking fires burning throughout the day and regulate the levels of smoke escaping through a hole in the highest part of the roof. Nineteenth-century Swiss doctor Johan Rudolf Rengger commented: 'This form of construction is necessary inside the jungle, where it would be almost impossible to live in an open hut because of the countless numbers of insects.'[1] To erect these dwellings, the natives used bamboo (*Bambusoideae*), which was pinned to the ground and, with the support of an intermediate beam and hardwood columns, joined over the centre of the building, where a space was located to vent the fumes. This roof, with its tent-like form, was then covered with straw and sheets of other materials available from the forest. Each family occupied the space between a pair of timber columns.

Structures erected for religious purposes in the village, or *tava*, subtly responded to this residential format. Their roofs did not reach the floor, but the same column formations could be observed in the galleries that they presented to the street. As in the communal residences, these marked the site of each family 'room' in the subdivided internal space.

The Spanish colonization of South America involved processes of forcible resettlement known as 'indigenous reductions'. These were facilitated with Franciscan and – in the case of the then 'Province of Paraguay' in particular – Jesuit assistance. The 'reductions' comprised orthogonally ordered camps modelled on the forms of traditional Iberian rural towns with which the Spanish conquerors were familiar.

Homes based on orthogonal proportions are still to be found in Paraguay's urban environment, where, in an extension of this colonial typology, they incorporate exterior decks with structured shading that protect pedestrian walkways from the sun and rain. For example, the city of Luque in central Paraguay retains a block with strip-housing characteristics, which is today protected as a historic monument.

Vernacular and Colonial Structures of Sierra Leone, Liberia, Guinea and Guinea Bissau

Tom Perry

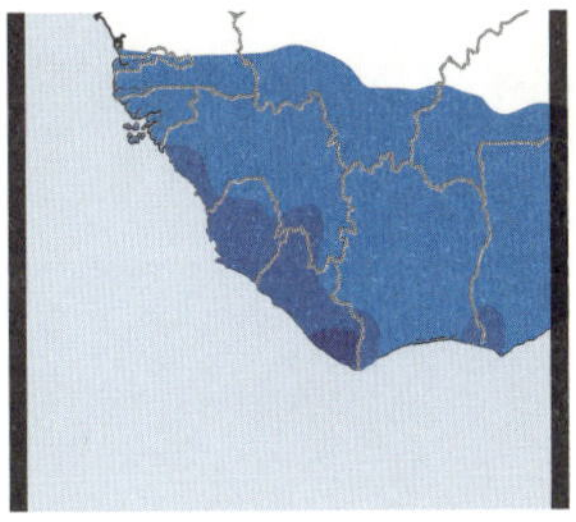

Geography/Climate

Western Africa is hot and equatorial, with significant rainfall from May to October when the African monsoon brings water north from the equator and discharges it over the lush forests of Sierra Leone, Liberia, Guinea and Guinea Bissau. While the winter months bring hot, dry winds south from the Sahara, much of the coastal region of Sierra Leone, Liberia and Guinea remains green and verdant.

Materials and Construction Techniques

Local architecture has formed as a response to this climate, as well as social and domestic traditions and the availability of materials and skills in the region. For much of western Africa, this has traditionally meant mud-brick construction and layered thatch roofs that provide a lightweight, waterproof skin that also insulates against the sun.

Colonial settlers in the region brought with them their tropical experience, and architectural styles with open verandas and overhanging roofs to keep the torrential rain out. Buildings were increasingly lifted off the ground to catch the sea breeze – styles that were played out in colonial houses from Southeast Asia to the Americas.

These new inhabitants from Europe and the Americas also brought an elevation in skill levels, and the ability to work in a wider variety of materials – from the use of local stone to anchor a building in strong winds to timber boarding, a style exported first from Europe to what were then the North American colonies, and subsequently to the settlements of Freetown, Sierra Leone and beyond.

Opposite Contrasting traditional thatch-roofed huts and modern tin-roofed houses Port Loko, Sierra Leone, West Africa.

Right The lush landscape of the rainforest region above Freetown, Sierra Leone, remains verdant throughout the year, giving an abundance of natural building materials.

Building Plan/Form

This new style is best seen in the buildings of Hill Station, sitting above Freetown, where the British colonial authorities relocated from their stifling coastal flats.

In a modernizing and turbulent world, the cities of western Africa have changed beyond recognition and the old styles and skills have in many places been lost. The major cities of the region, many established as small but important ports by the colonial powers, have faced significant periods of growth – first through the independence process in the mid-20th century, and then again through periods of unrest associated with the brutal civil wars that have raged across the region from the end of the 20th century.

This series of civil conflicts, most notably in Sierra Leone from 1991 to 2002, brought instability to the region as people fled to the relative safety of major cities such as Freetown. Transient populations now occupy swathes of fast-disappearing pristine natural landscape, placing unprecedented pressure on natural resources and urban infrastructure, and contributing to cities such as Freetown and Conakry, Guinea, expanding well beyond their limits.

With increasing development and infrastructure demands has come greater displacement of people. There is an urgent need to plan for growth and to involve communities in their own future. Where architecture once responded to climate, local landscape and culture, in many urban communities there is now an aspiration to 'modernize', importing systems and materials from developed nations. This 'quick fix' solution has brought about improvements in living conditions for some, but remains out of reach to the urban poor, who continue to build with whatever materials and skills are at hand.

A recent project undertaken by the UK's Prince's Foundation worked with people on the northern edge of Freetown to design a building that fulfilled the community's needs while also seeking to respond to environmental pressures. First, the existing community's neighbourhood was mapped in order to understand how it worked and what infrastructure was needed to improve the lives of the 2,000 people who live under the shady palms of this former market garden. A visiting clinic, study and training rooms were proposed alongside key facilities such as toilets, which the community could manage in order to provide income for maintenance.

Following training in carpentry, masonry and metalwork skills – alongside the basics of site management, health and safety and the operation of both modern and traditional tools – a thirty-strong local team built the Coconut Farm Community Centre. The building responds to its immediate environment, sitting within the palms that give the farm its name and incorporating the existing large boulders that the children use for play. Construction utilized locally made Hydraform interlocking blocks in order to minimize the use of concrete and mortar and reduce the need for external finishing.

Covered decking incorporated around and between the buildings ensures that there is usable space even in the wettest downpours. Windows are fully operable, to promote air flow despite heavy rainfall. Roof vents along the ridge draw the hot and humid air through and away from the interior; the overhangs keep these spaces dry even with windows fully open, ensuring minimum solar heating to the walls, keeping them cool through hot days.

Above Traditional building techniques such as the layered thatch of these open-sided huts in Guinea, West Africa, respond to local conditions, providing a lightweight, waterproof skin that protects against solar gain.

Opposite top left and right The elevated Hill Station buildings in Freetown, with deep roof overhangs and covered, open ground floor, exemplify the colonial settlers' influence on the region – as do the weatherboard houses known locally as *bod ose*.

Opposite middle The Coconut Farm Community Centre in Freetown offers a building that responds to its environment. It was built by the local community and is designed for its specific needs.

Opposite bottom Uncontrolled urban growth in Freetown has created slums, many of which are built from imported materials and systems that do not respond well to the conditions of the local environment.

Gurensi Mud-based Vernacular of Burkina Faso and Ghana

James Morris

Above The quarters of one of the wives of the chief of Tiébélé, situated within his compound in Tiébélé, Burkina Faso. Villages within 'Gurensi' culture are made up of many extended polygamous-family compounds such as this one.

Geography/Climate and Culture

On the border of Burkina Faso and Ghana, a group of people variously called Gurensi, Kassena, Nankanse or Frafra have evolved an expressive, intricate, highly decorative and intensely beautiful mud-based vernacular architectural style that is entirely unique. Within the ninety or so villages that make up this small region lie more than one different ethnicity, three distinct language groups and a colonial dividing line that now forms the international border. Though not a single 'people', such is the extent of their cultural homogeneity that we can reasonably think of them as such.

Within this 'Gurensi' culture, social structures and religious practice influence the architectural aesthetic. Before the colonial era, soothsayers were the principal authority figures; there is, therefore, little 'elite' architecture to speak of. Villages still consist of numerous extended polygamous-family compounds, themselves made up of multiple individual, interlinked structures; each family comprises a head, his wives, his married sons and their wives, and his grandchildren. A new wife takes up residence in the husband's compound. The ritual head of the family, the oldest living male, confers with the soothsayer, who consults the ancestral spirits on all-important family decisions, including marriage. The majority of people are animist; even those who are Christians or Muslims adhere to some traditional practices – especially at funerals, as upon death the ancestral world is entered.

Materials and Building Plan/Form

Historically, the Gurensi had no concept of 'art', but they did have, and still do possess, an understanding of *bambolse*; the word implies embellishment, or to beautify. Generally speaking, the men are the constructors of Gurensi buildings and the women make them beautiful. A traditional compound consists of a number of round and rectilinear structures, each a living quarter or granary, joined by high exterior walls and both high and low interior ones. Standalone circular rooms are intended for young men, rectangular houses for newly wedded couples, and so forth – although recently, the more easily constructed rectangular buildings have come to predominate. New rooms are added as the family grows; when someone dies, their quarters are left to collapse. The raw materials remain in place for reuse by a future generation. At the main entrance to the compound are two conical mounds,

homes for the spirits of male ancestors, for whom senior men serve as priests; inside are comparable shrines for women.

The compound entrance door typically faces west or southwest, and the space just outside is the male domain. The compound interior, with the exception of the cattle pen, is the women's space. Each wife has her own suite of rooms for life, made up of two adjoined circular buildings: a living room and a kitchen with a linking stoop door between. This is where she brings up her children and receives her husband; whose responsibility it is to visit his wives and keep them contented. On the interior walls, intricately moulded polished-mud 'dressers' are formed, supporting stacks of decorated calabash pots, cups, bowls and other kitchenware – as striking a 'fitted kitchen' as can be found anywhere.

On the exterior, this sculptural theme extends to include mud-moulded staircases and stepped ladders carved out of forked branches that allow access to flat roofs where clothes and vegetables can safely be dried. Doorways, especial to the circular buildings, are so low that incomers have to stoop almost to the ground; they then immediately face a wall that has to be climbed over. This defensive system means that an intruder can be hacked with an axe while his or her head is in the perfect position, arrows cannot reach the interior and evil spirits and wild animals are kept at bay. Roofs can be accessed from the inside, in order to prevent attackers gaining the advantage of height.

Wall plastering and painting is a female activity, completed in the dry season of March and April. Typically, houses are redecorated every four or five years, the

Above top Detailed view of the mud-moulded quarters of one of the wives within the Tiébélé compound of the chief of Tiébélé, Burkina Faso.

Above A women's pair of rooms within a family compound in Sirigu, Ghana, showing stoop doorways, elaborate decoration and ancestral shrines.

Opposite Detail from a rectangular male room with hanging amulet within a Sirigu compound, Ghana – the shape of the door and the abstract patterning are subtly different from the women's rooms.

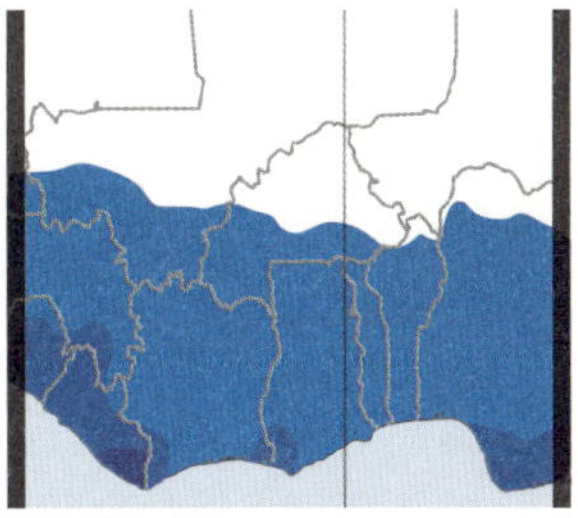

Seasonal average temperatures °C (F)

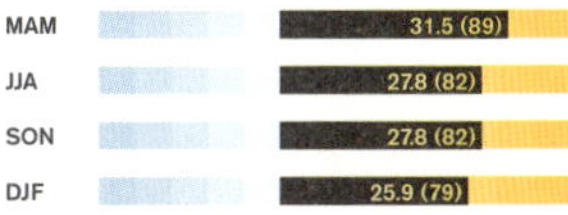

Seasonal average rainfall mm (in.)

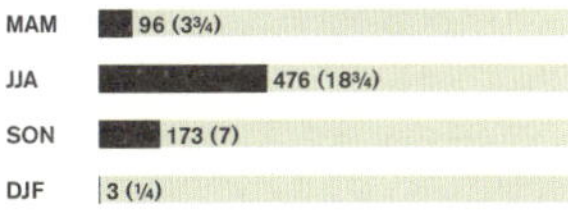

decision to *bambolse* depending on the availability – financially, environmentally or otherwise – of mud, water, pigments, helping hands, time and motivation. The walls are sanded down with a flat stone, and the building is then re-rendered with mud in preparation. Colours are traditionally from red soil, black pulverized rocks and a white chalk-like stone. Nowadays, cement render, bitumen and white paint are commonly used, and the customary varnish-like fixative made from the seed of the locust-bean tree is becoming increasingly expensive to access.

Traditionally, decorative styles differ within the region; individual creativity is also a component. Wall paintings are largely nonfigurative and geometric. Seemingly abstract patterns, complicated to decipher, make reference to the immediate environment – the woven narrow strips on a man's shirt, the rows in a cultivated field or the sticks on the bottom of a woman's basket. Symbols related to male prestige adorn the exterior walls: walking sticks, drums, triangular amulets holding potent medicines, and hunting implements. The women's spaces reflect their more domestic orientation, most specifically a representation of the fibre net that holds their calabash vessels. Also present are the much admired mosquito-eating bats, the sacred boa constrictors that hold a grandmother's spirit, and the lizards that 'christen' a new house by running across it. Often these depictions take the form of raised reliefs, and are consequently more evident in certain lights. More recent additions reflecting contemporary influences are often figurative, but always the guiding motivation remains to beautify.

This, however, is a picture of a culture that is slipping away – it relies on traditional skills and a traditional way of life. In more affluent Ghana, such traditional houses are harder to find as larger concrete-block and tin-roofed dwellings have obvious benefits with respect to contemporary life. If the walls of traditional dwellings are cement rendered, they cannot breathe and so rot from the inside, leading to collapse. In villages such as Tiébélé, in Burkina Faso, the mastery required to build the intricate shape of the low stoop doorways on circular buildings has now been lost entirely; the local young men try to rediscover the method, realizing too late its value as a tourist lure. Additionally, Christian missionaries entice their converts away from buildings associated with a perceived despicable way of life, to the cemented purity of the modern world. Limited international conservation programmes are in place, but they risk creating architectural 'theme parks' designed to attract the tourist dollar. True preservation is a complex conundrum to resolve.

Vernacular Settlements of Côte d'Ivoire, Ghana, Togo, Benin and Cameroon

Rexford Assasie Oppong and Samuel Amos-Abanyie

Opposite This mountainous landscape with family compound of adobe cabins and straw roofs of the Matakam tribe ('Mafa' or 'Kirdi') in the Mandara Mountains, North Cameroon, which illustrates the identifiable conical-shaped building forms found in traditional settlements of Benin, Cameroon, Ghana, Côte d'Ivoire and Togo.

Below Shaded houses of the Holi tribe in Onigbolo Isaba, Benin (left) and the spectacular roof overhangs at the village of the Wenohian in Ghana (right). Though formally different, both illustrate shelters that adapt to the arid local environment using materials at hand.

Geography/Climate and Culture

In the remote past, the effect of geographical environments on history was greater than it is today.[1] Nonetheless, even though it is not the only factor shaping their history, geographically favoured areas continue to present many advantages to a people. The varying opportunities presented by geographical conditions across the West African subregion have given rise to a number of 'life zones' with distinctive terrain, climate and natural vegetation as well as culture.[2] Ghana, Togo, Benin, Côte d'Ivoire and Cameroon fall within three of these zones: the coastal strip, the forest, and the savannah of the Guinea Coast.[3] Within each of these areas, people obtain their livelihoods in similar ways, their social customs being broadly alike. Their forms of political institution also follow the same pattern, and their religions have much in common.

Traditional political and social bonds existed in West Africa until the 18th century. Chiefdoms with strong kinship relationships greatly influenced political organization and religious activities in most of the region's small states. With increasing sizes and numbers of communities, laws of succession were created for the appointment of one man as the 'chief executive' who governed an area containing a number of settlements. Traditionally, West Africans believed that supernatural beings and forces had enormous influence both in their natural environments – in the form of sudden storms and catastrophic epidemics – and in their social relationships. Religious beliefs provided an explanation of such unpleasant events, and buttressed the authority of chiefdoms.

Materials and Building Plan/Form

West African societies have, over many thousands of years, tackled the basic problem of providing shelter in a wide variety of ways. According to Maurice Mitchell and Andy Bevan, the most basic motive for building has been to provide shelter for a defined kinship group, often within a clearly marked protected area.[4] However, the underlying approach has been to adapt shelter to the natural environment, for protection from extremes of climate, and to use local materials such as earth, stones, thatch, bamboo, palm frond, raffia palm and wood saplings/poles for building construction. Beyond the construction of dwellings for individual kinship groups, shelter also provided for social amenities – such as education, health and community facilities – that yielded productive roles for society at large.

The settlement patterns and traditional building forms of Benin, Cameroon, Ghana, Côte d'Ivoire and Togo bear many similarities. These vernacular dwellings were mainly comprised of conical or rectangular units built around a common space. Now, modern building materials, such as sand-cement blocks and glass, as well as corrugated metal roof covering, are gradually finding their way into the vernacular and organic settlements and architecture. The Ganvie lakeside village in Benin, for example, is similar to the Nzulezu lakeside village in Ghana.

Generally, the planning and building practices employed by colonial administrations – especially in West African urban areas – incorporated very little adaptation for tropical climates.[5] Traditional building in this region was chiefly the product of an agrarian society, and one that required a very limited range of materials.

Contemporary Application

Over the years, the provision of vernacular forms of shelter,[6] and the steps taken by West African societies to meet the scale of their housing need, have changed – especially in the last quarter of the 20th century.[7] The key challenges facing the vernacular today go beyond changes in methods of housing provision; the availability of traditional materials; the population increase resulting from urbanization, planning controls, changing expectations and taste; and political expediency. They provoke, perhaps, a deeper intellectual reflection that may in the end reject any association with the term 'vernacular' at all.

Arguably, the adoption of traditional building approaches to address the current housing problem in West Africa would depend on the availability of more of the traditional building materials and skills to the younger generation, who instead have a strong affinity with modernity. This is despite the fact that modernity should, ideally, influence vernacular architecture in a positive way.

West Africa today is home to an impressive array of visual cultural-heritage producers, including artists, fashion designers, non-professional building designers and professional architects. They all derive inspiration from the traditional visual cultural heritage of the region, and utilize a variety of modern materials to meet the demands and requirements of the diverse works of architecture generated by the sophisticated needs of consumers. Unfortunately, although responses by these cultural-heritage producers have shown a wide range of skills in their work – both personally creative and commissioned – the positive impact on vernacular architecture has been limited. Modern styles, aesthetic expressions and taste preferences have emerged that are at odds with the traditional vernacular architecture of West Africa.

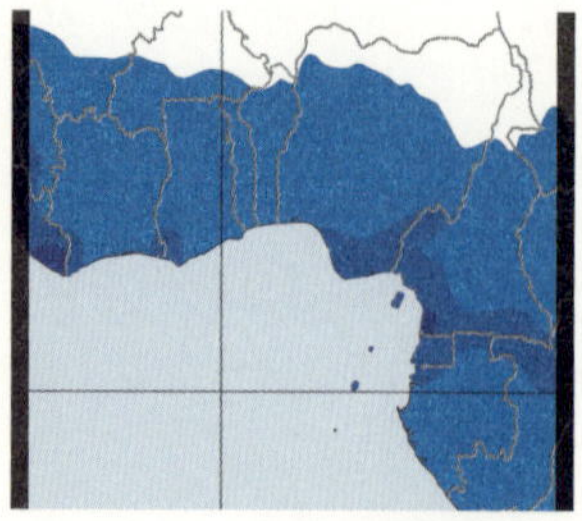

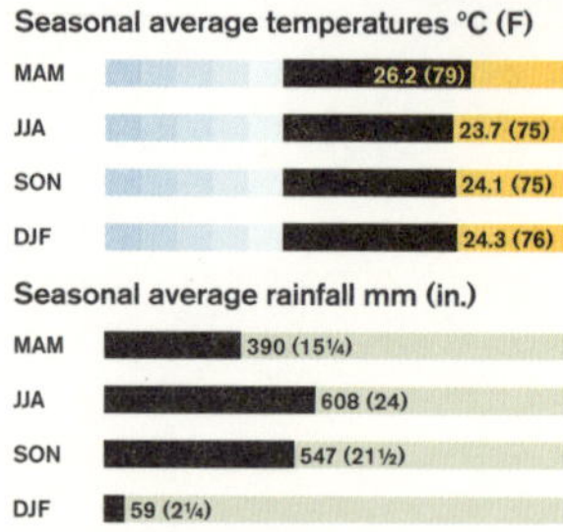

Below and opposite Modern buildings of sand-cement blocks, glass and corrugated metal coverings are slowly superseding vernacular precedents. From areas such as Cape Coast beach (below) to the Ganvie lake village (opposite), West Africa is changing its relationship towards materials and building methods.

Hausa, Yoruba and Igbo Vernacular of Nigeria

Peter Zanang-Kazah Barwa

Geography/Climate and Materials
Vernacular architecture in Nigeria is as varied as the nation's many tribes, which number over 370; however, as the country has a clear majority and minority faction, this factor is also reflected in its built vernacular. While some tribes have lost their arts, crafts and construction skills by adopting completely modern materials and techniques, others have managed to preserve a good deal of their traditional architecture. This is most evident in the motifs and murals of some modern Hausa residences in Zaria city in the north of the country.

The three major Nigerian tribes with an influential vernacular architecture are the Hausa of the north, the Yoruba of the southwest and the Igbo of the east.

Hausa Vernacular
Hausas are located within northern Nigeria. The climate here is tropical dry and the rainy season runs from June to September; the rest of the year comprises the dry season. The region's vernacular architecture is characterized in terms of building materials by the use of adobe blocks for walls, with straw, rice husk and other vegetable materials being used as aggregates and binding media; a hay of dried elephant grass (*Pennistum purpureum*) for roof thatch; laterite for foundation bases; and the cut stems of the deleb palm (*Borassus aethiopum*) as structural timber.

Hausa dwellings have established systems, with spatial arrangements emphasizing privacy for the womenfolk of the household. Both circular and square-based plans may be adopted – along with roofs of rib-vaulted, conical thatched or flat mud construction. All, however, display small doors and windows, and the use of wall motifs and murals by embossing, bevelling, engraving and sometimes direct painting. This latter decorative aspect is the one of the important elements of Hausa vernacular architecture still surviving in some modern homes.

Major cities still boasting Hausa vernacular buildings include Kano, Zaria, Katsina and Sokoto. In recent times, however, relatively few households have incorporated vernacular techniques into their designs. When they do it is visually pleasing and a captivating means of cultural preservation.

Yoruba Vernacular
In the south of Nigeria, the climate is more akin to that of tropical rainforest regions. It is characterized by long and heavy rainfall – in fact, there are actually two wet and two dry seasons per year. The first rainy season runs from March to July and is followed by a short dry August break lasting two to three weeks. After this, a short rainy season starts around early September and lasts until mid-October. This is then followed by a long dry season: late October to early March.

A typical Yoruba compound is orthogonal (either rectangular or square-shaped). There is a clearly defined entrance into the compound, with another, rear exit that leads to spaces for cooking and ablution. Walling systems are of cured earth blocks, monolithic cob or wattle-and-daub infill to simple structural frames. *Gbodogi* leaves (*Sarcophrynium*) are used for roofing, placed above hardy, termite-resistant timber (from any of a number of palm trees). Roofs are usually steeply pitched, with either a hip or a gable – or a mixture of both forms – in order to throw off the maximum amount of rainfall.

Igbo Vernacular
Igbo vernacular architecture bears certain commonalities with that of the Yoruba tribe in terms of available materials, construction methods and techniques. This is attributed to the similarities in climate across their respective regions. Yet in terms of design characteristics there are many differences between the two.

The spatial arrangements typical of Igbo vernacular are, in fact, closer to those of the northern Hausa tribe. Nonetheless, a particular emphasis is placed on the special hierarchy favoured by the Igbo in their location of rooms. These are typically positioned according to the relationship of the room's owner to the *obi*, the hut belonging to the head of the compound.

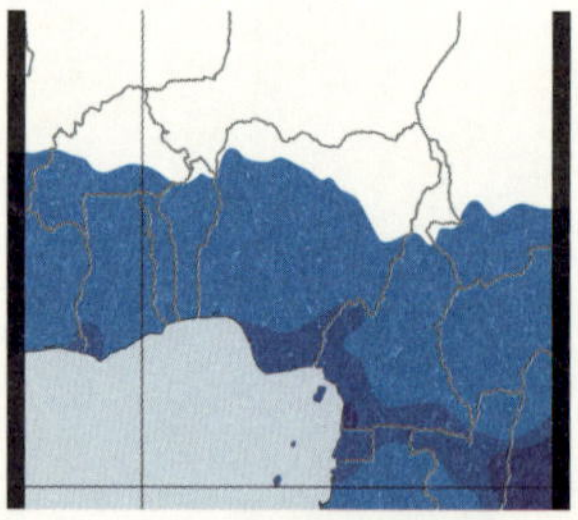

Seasonal average temperatures °C (F)

MAM	29.3 (85)
JJA	26.2 (79)
SON	26.2 (79)
DJF	25.3 (77)

Seasonal average rainfall mm (in.)

MAM	220 (8¾)
JJA	599 (23½)
SON	309 (12¼)
DJF	22 (1)

Opposite top, middle, bottom right Like all buildings of the Hausa type, thick adobe walls and small windows and doors help regulate against heat gain. In contrast to the simple earthen Hausa homes (top), decorative detailing as seen on domestic exteriors (middle) and at the emir's palace in Zaria (bottom) shows a modern variation, made by embossing, painting, bevelling and engraving the building's surface.

Opposite middle left and right The tall thatched roof and adobe walls of traditional Igbo houses are seen in the Umuajatta village meeting house (left) and a smaller home in the province of Anambra (right).

Opposite bottom left A view of early 20th-century decorated panels inside an Igbo house, part of the traditional elaborate artistic complexes.

MALADU BI DAKIN

Sooro Residences of Northern Cameroon

Mark Dike DeLancey

Materials and Construction Techniques

In the Cameroon grasslands, a hilly region to the west of the country, residences are generally square in plan and built of lashed raffia-palm ribs with flat, circular ceilings. The overhangs of these create eaves that, in the houses of the wealthy, might be extended further and supported on wooden uprights to create a porch. The right to decorate the wooden porch and rectangular doorways with anthropomorphic imagery is reserved for royalty. The roof is composed of an internal pyramidal construction of palm ribs placed atop the circular ceiling and supported by the walls of the structure beneath. Circular platforms connect this internal structure to an external, conical roof frame thatched with grass, the base of which follows the circumference of the circular ceiling. The resulting structure unites the square plan of the living space below with the circular plan of the conical roof above. The walls of the building may be elaborated with geometric designs by lashing additional layers of raffia-palm timbers to the structure of verticals and horizontals, in particular employing interwoven diagonals. The multiple layers of palm ribs may be left exposed, or the outermost pattern might be highlighted by packing the spaces between with earth.

In the Adamawa region to the north, residences may be either square or circular in plan. However, they are generally constructed with earth walls laid in a series of courses, and with conical roofs thatched with a particularly long, thin grass. When attached by the base of the grass stalks, the roof is much sturdier, but the tufted ends of the grass do not lie smoothly. When attached by the tuft of the grass, the long ends create a sleek exterior surface, but the fragile ends break off easily, forcing the homeowner to renew the thatching more frequently. It is only the wealthy who are able to afford the latter approach. The roof is finished by adding a small conical cap, a miniature version of the roof as a whole, to protect the apex.

Wealthier patrons throughout northern Cameroon, particularly those with noble titles, may emphasize their status by constructing buildings of the type known as a *sooro*. Historically the prerogative only of political elites in the Fulbe-ruled Islamic states founded in the early 19th century, this type has become more widespread over the course of the 20th century. The *sooro* is characterized by

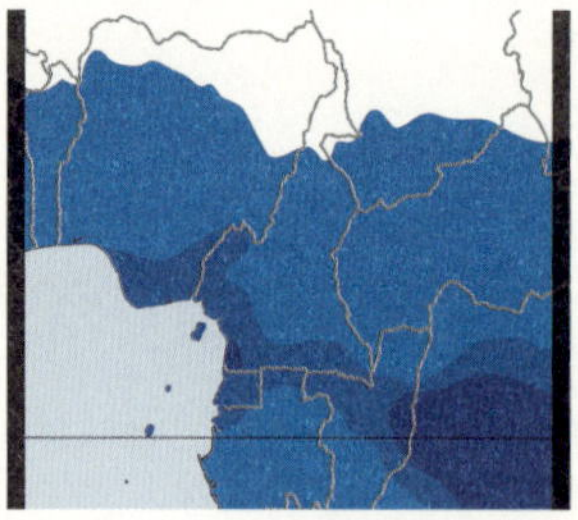

Seasonal average temperatures °C (F)

MAM	26.2 (79)
JJA	23.7 (75)
SON	24.1 (75)
DJF	24.3 (75)

Seasonal average rainfall mm (in.)

MAM	390 (15¼)
JJA	608 (24)
SON	547 (21½)
DJF	59 (2¾)

Left Grass-thatched residences of the Matakam people, between Maroua and Mokolo, in Cameroon's Far North Province. Created using long, thin grass, the conical roofs sit atop walls constructed of earth.

Above left A local woman outside a traditional dwelling with square plan and conical roof, Ngaoundéré, Adamawa Region.

Above right Wealthier northern Cameroon peoples construct traditional *sooroji*, which stand out for their sweeping roof overhang formed of thatch overlaid on earth, atop timber framing, as in this building known as Jawleeru Nja in the palace of Ngaoundéré, Adamawa Region.

the incorporation of a ceiling supported by earthen pillars. This ceiling is composed of layers of progressively smaller lengths of timber, laid in alternating directions and sealed with a layer of earth. A thatched roof may then be raised above this ceiling, or – in more northern, drier climates – the roof may be omitted altogether, creating a terrace. The *sooro* has the virtues of incorporating an attic storage space for grain; giving added protection against fire; and, particularly on the cooler Adamawa Plateau, reducing the amount of interior space needing to be heated. The *sooro* is now found among other cultural groups of Cameroon, such as the Mboum and Di'i. Modern versions created in the major cities employ cement walls, plywood ceilings and conical corrugated zinc roofs.

Numerous small communities inhabit the Mandara and Atlantika mountain ranges along northern Cameroon's western border with Nigeria. The terrain here furnishes plentiful granite for building purposes. This might be laid dry or with mud mortar, on a circular plan with conical roofs thatched with grass or millet stalks, although government-encouraged modernization and the hegemony of Islamic groups have pushed many towards building rectilinear-planned residences. Individual units are joined by stone walls, and the material is likewise employed for the terracing of agricultural land. In extreme cases, entire mountainsides may be treated in such a way.

Small agricultural communities are the norm, with the basic 'unit' comprising the compound of a man, his wife or wives, and possibly extended relations. In all cases, entrance is through the male head of the compound's residence, to which may be attached a room where a ritual cow has been raised since birth for eventual sacrifice – possibly a memory of an ancient pastoralist past on the plains below. Quarters for the wife, or wives, follow. The residences of wives may be built of less permanent materials, indicating the precariousness of their place in the family (divorce is not uncommon). Three basic patterns of compound planning exist, from which a variety of permutations may be derived. In the first model, each wife may have her own bedroom, granary and kitchen. In the second, each may have her own bedroom, with incorporated granary, but share a common kitchen. In the third model, the wives may have a communal bedroom, but each have her own granary and kitchen. The individual granaries, however, may be grouped together in a single room. In these last two models, the granaries are silo-like in form, their tops projecting through a flat ceiling into an attic space. Access is achieved by climbing through a hole in the ceiling via a ladder. In all cases, the male granary devoted to holding the family's millet – a staple food and 'male' crop, in contrast to the legumes and vegetables raised by the women – is located in the women's quarters. Sacrificial offerings to the male's protective ancestors are made at the compound entrance and the male granary, in the male and female areas of the compound respectively.

As urbanization proceeds at a precipitous rate in much of Africa, housing options such as the traditional *rugo* (compound) are largely relegated to the countryside owing to the dense urban fabric. Nevertheless, examples such as the cement-walled corrugated zinc-roofed *sooro* of northern Cameroon show that traditional forms can be expressed in industrial materials; the desire to do so suggests the continued importance of expressing local identities.

Beehive-style and Palm-timber Dwellings of the Democratic Republic of Congo and South Sudan

Below View of conical thatched residences with enclosing verandas, Democratic Republic of Congo (left). Conical-roofed building of the Mangbetu people, DR Congo, painted with geometric decorations in the 1930s (right).

Opposite top Dwellings of conical roofs set atop circular-planned walls in a valley near Uriva, DR Congo.

Opposite bottom A typical closed-sided home in the vicinity of Mt Nyiragongo, eastern DR Congo, shows a wall frame composed of lashed vertical and horizontal palm timbers packed with earth. In this region, Kuba homes may include roofs woven of palm thatch.

Mark Dike DeLancey

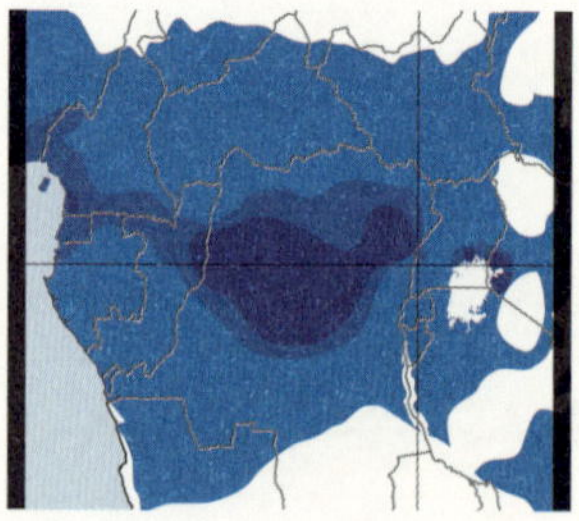

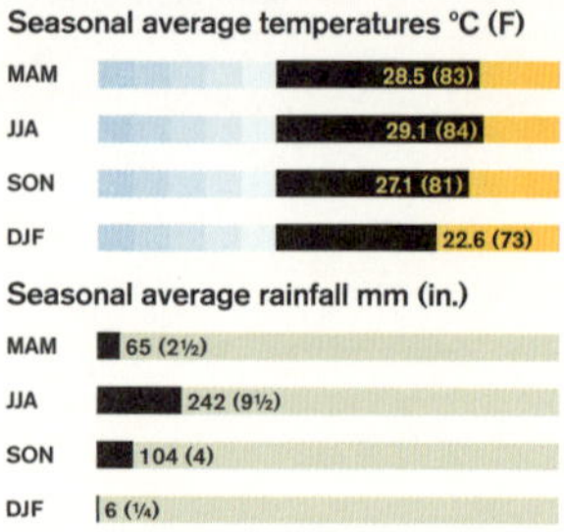

Materials and Construction Techniques

The Azande and Mangbetu populations of the northeastern Democratic Republic of Congo and southeastern South Sudan have historically built a variety of residence types. Northern groups of these populations erected circular structures with walls of earth or woven mats. Southern populations tended towards rectangular houses of palm ribs, sealed with plantain leaves between their palm-rib frameworks. Fairly lightweight materials were employed perhaps in part because villages, as was historically common in Central Africa, moved approximately every ten years as agricultural soil became depleted or to mark the accession of a new ruler. Beginning in the early 20th century, however, along with peoples in many other areas of Africa, the Azande and Mangbetu shifted towards earthen-walled roundhouses with conical thatched roofs and to increasingly permanent settlements.

These later dwellings were often decorated on their exterior wall surfaces, and possibly in their interiors as well, with elaborately painted geometric designs that recalled the motifs that one might have once found woven into raffia-fibre mats – suggesting a sort of vernacular architectural memory. By the mid-20th century, representational designs on the exteriors of houses became more common, and frequently depicted the changing social environment. Residential mural painting was, in fact, quite widespread throughout the Democratic Republic of Congo, and some of the first Congolese painters to work on paper in the southern city of Lubumbashi, such as Albert Lubaki and Djilitendo, were either originally mural painters or appear to have been impacted by that medium.

In contrast to the circular-plan beehive-style houses of the eastern areas of Central Africa, and having more in common with southern Mangbetu and Azande practices, the Kuba in the Democratic Republic of Congo create rectangular-plan residences of palm timbers with pitched, thatched roofs and high thresholds that emphasize the distinction between interior and exterior space. So, too, do the Kongo people of the Democratic Republic of Congo and of the neighbouring Republic of Congo and Angola. These plans are marked out with vertical palm timbers, after which horizontal ones are lashed to the exterior with vines. The vines may also be used to create decorative patterns on the exterior of these buildings. Derived ultimately from raffia-fibre mats and cloth, for which the Kuba are renowned, the designs employed are often named after the formal qualities of the patterns themselves or after their original creators. Some designs may also carry more abstract meanings, while certain motifs are reserved exclusively for the houses of the nobility and royalty. High-status architecture in the region follows the same essential form as that of the vernacular, the main distinctions being the degree of external decoration and size.

Beehive Structures of Rwanda, Burundi, South Sudan and Kenya

Mark Dike DeLancey

Geography/Climate and Culture

Most of the Central African region is subject to heavy annual rainfall, and much of it is blanketed in thick forest, surrounded by grasslands to the north, east and south. The main nomadic groups in the heavily forested areas are the various so-called Pygmy cultures, who prefer generally to identify with their specific group such as the Baka, Efe or Mbuti.

Materials

These groups may move settlements periodically in order to most efficiently exploit the available forest resources. Their residences are created by women of the group from the long, slender stems of the *Heisteria parvifolia* plant. These stems are lashed together into a domical framework that is then covered with freshly cut, broad leaves of the *Maranthaceae* family.

Construction Techniques

Many cultures throughout this region construct residences with poles inserted in the ground in a circular plan and then gathered at the apex, in what is commonly referred to as a 'beehive' type of construction. Horizontal poles are lashed to these verticals in order to create a frame, which is then entirely thatched. The thick and continuous thatching is perhaps a response to the often heavy rainfall during the wet season.

Rwanda and Burundi

The populations of Rwanda and Burundi have taken the 'beehive' building form to its greatest heights – creating beehive-type houses of a grand size. Unsurprisingly, this development necessitates construction by a group, including the extended family and friends of the future occupants.

The flexible vertical poles of these circular residences are interwoven with supple horizontal lengths of bound papyrus reeds (*Cyperus papyrus*), in a technique that ultimately recalls the virtuosity of basket weaving in the area. Indeed, mats woven with geometric patterns, matched by similar designs on furnishings constructed of earth – such as beds and benches – may be used to segregate internal spaces within the dwelling. A separate, internal ceiling is lashed to the lower walls, over which the vertical poles are gathered at the apex. The entirety of the exterior is then thatched, creating a domical form with a projecting entry porch. The interior space of these houses, which may be 6 m (20 ft) or more in diameter, necessitates multiple support poles.

Such a residence would be part of a larger compound, or *rugo*, composed of three courtyards enclosed with bamboo palisades. The large central enclosure, serving as a cattle corral, incorporates the residence on one side lying opposite the main compound entrance on the other. A forecourt encloses this main entrance, while a secondary courtyard encloses the rear of the residence. This private rear court might incorporate subsidiary residences for additional family members, an ancestral shrine, latrines or granaries. While Rwanda and Burundi both boast a high population density, *rugo* tend nevertheless to be dispersed, enabling close proximity to the occupants' fields and grazing lands.

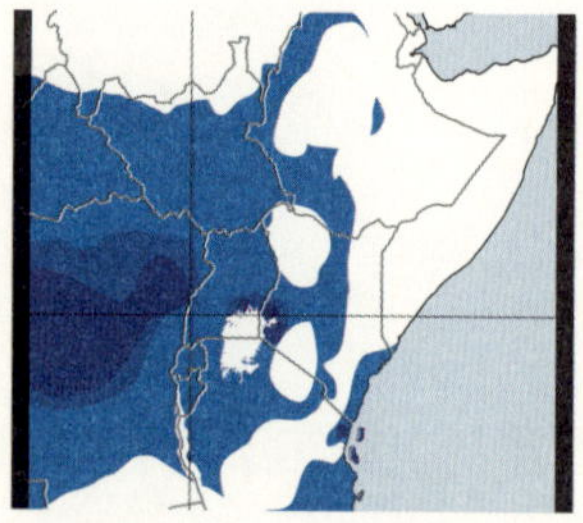

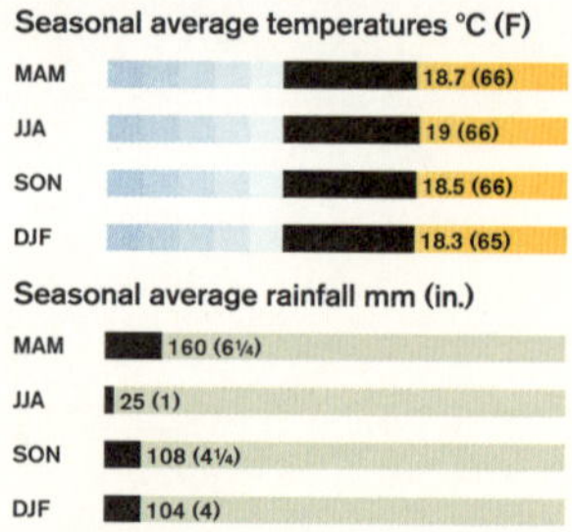

Opposite top Nomadic Baka people constructing 'beehive' huts from forest materials in Central Africa.

Opposite bottom Baka women of Central Africa use *ngongo* leaves to erect huts known as *mongolu* made from plant stems and vegetation.

Opposite This royal building in Nyanza, Rwanda, is reminiscent of local basket-weaving techniques (top). In contrast to its large size, conical-shaped structures in fields of the Virunga volcano area, Rwanda, are small and earthbound (bottom).

Top left Aerial view of traditional housing with *rugo* (courtyards), scattered on a hillside in the Mugongomanga region, Burundi.

Above and top right Construction of a building in a Toposa village, Nyanyagachor, South Sudan. This nomadic culture builds elevated granary and 'beehive' dwellings (bottom left and right).

South Sudan and Kenya

Permutations of the beehive type may be seen among the Murle and Toposa of South Sudan, as well as the Pokomo and Kamba in neighbouring Kenya. The grand size of Murle houses necessitates internal supports, while a front porch attached at a 90° angle protects the privacy of the interior. Construction is generally undertaken by women, a cultural characteristic usually associated with nomadic cultures. The Toposa of southeastern South Sudan build a type of house similar to that of the Murle, with whom they also share a tradition of transhumant pastoralism. The exteriors of Toposa dwellings are given a distinct character, however, by thatching with shorter-length grass or reeds, giving the appearance of numerous sharply defined, overlapping registers.

Wooden Palaces of Madagascar

Randall Bird

Geography/Climate

Madagascar has several climatic zones, including a dry, wooded savannah in the northwest, wet montane rainforests along the east coast, temperate grasslands with dramatic rock outcroppings in the central highlands, and an expansive desert in its southern region.

Materials

The island's vernacular architecture encompasses an array of building types and construction materials, ranging from timber royal architecture, impressive stone tombs and brick houses in the highlands, to small-scale houses made of local vegetal materials in the arid northwest and south.

Construction Techniques

A prime example of Malagasy vernacular is the type of wooden palace or house known as a *tranokotona*. It was constructed by the Merina, the people who inhabit the central highlands of Madagascar and who ruled over two-thirds of the island throughout most of the 19th century. In the Malagasy language, *trano* signifies any dwelling and the suffix *kotona* denotes a more specialized variant – namely, a Merina house whose walls are constructed from vertical wooden planks. A fundamental sign of elite status was the various species of hardwoods used to construct *tranokotona* – only elite Merina were allowed to possess these prestigious timbers.

Tranokotona were located in hilltop fortresses, known as *rova*. As an outstanding example of a *tranokotona*, a mid-20th-century reconstruction located in the *rova* of Merina King Andrianampoinimerina (reigned c. 1785–1809) at Ambohimanga, survives today as one of the chief symbols of Merina kingship. The palace's dimensions (approximately 6 by 7.5 m [20 x 25 ft] in plan, and 9 m [30 ft] high) and its exaggerated verticality are determined by the importance of height as a key architectural feature

Below left Besakana, one of the residences of King Andrianampoinimerina, in the *rova* (fortified complex) of Antananarivo, Madagascar, is built in the traditional style with tall, pitched roofs reserved for Merina aristocrats.

Below right Traditional timber-and-raffia structures signify the *tranokotona* (residence) of a king, chief or tribal leader, such as this example of the Antaimoro people in Manakara.

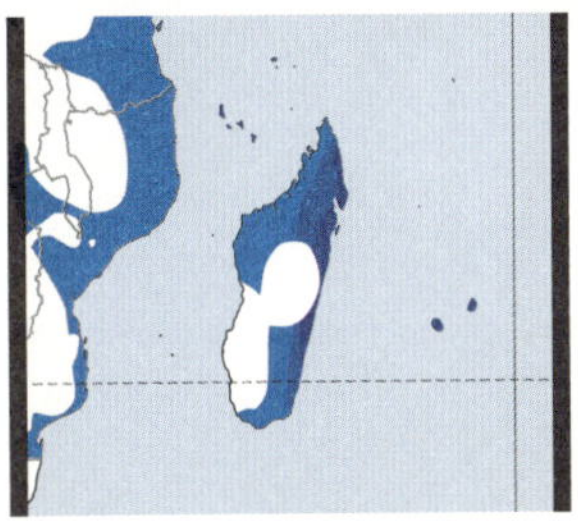

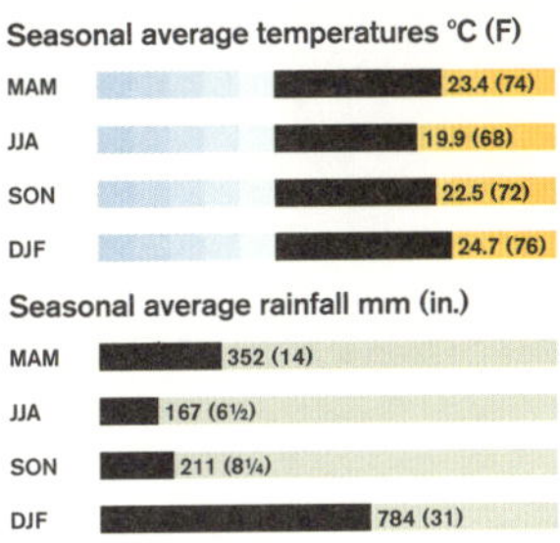

Above **Village houses set in the landscape of Madagascar's central highlands represent the region's more humble built expression. These small-scale agricultural homes share the basic pitched-roof form, but do not have the height, materials and associated prestige of the Merina *tranokotona*.**

used to visualize elite status. This connection between building height and elevated social standing in royal Merina society served as an enduring precedent throughout the 19th and 20th centuries for Merina houses, whether they were constructed from wood or brick. The combination of scale, verticality and rare materials, together with the long *tandrotrano* ('horns of the house') feature along the edges of the gables beyond the ridgeline, set the palace apart from any other surrounding building. They were also signifiers, for many Merina, of their historical and cultural heritage stemming from Southeast Asia, where similar architectural features are ubiquitous, and from where the Merina had migrated more than 1,000 years ago.

Building Plan/Form

The single entrance on the palace's western façade is in keeping with a Malagasy construction practice involving the sole placement of openings on the north- and west-facing walls of dwellings (entrances to Merina tombs also face west). For a variety of symbolic reasons (for example, the northeast corner of the house being its most sacred space, and associated with royalty and esteemed ancestors) and functional explanations (the main winds originate from the southeast), the east façade is treated as a solid wall without portals or fenestration – a tradition that continues to this day in some rural areas of the highlands. The sense of arrival at the *tranokotona* is heightened by the verticality of the interior space, which is further enhanced by the three tall pillars (*andry*) that extend more than 7.5 m (25 ft) to either the tie beams or the ridge. Symbolically, the *andry* represent the still point of the house, where all things begin and end.

Kachha, Pukka and *Semi-pukka* Houses of India

Karen Rizvi

Geography/Climate
The essence of Indian vernacular is resilience and adaptation. India's diverse traditional styles have evolved in harmony with its broad landscape. Driven by climate, culture and available materials, local craftspeople forge the shape of a roof or girth of walls with skill and acquired knowledge. Together, the cultural values of a community and the elements of nature compose an intimate dialogue of life that has survived for countless generations.

Materials
The issue of sustainability looms large in the 21st century – particularly with regard to available materials. The push for environmental sensitivity is on the rise as cities grow, populations expand and resources decline. Vernacular communities are a model of sustainable living: little is wasted in traditional settlements. Structures degrade naturally and materials are adapted, recycled and reused. Vernacular houses have a simple beauty, and are cheap to construct and rebuild. In India, these buildings fall into three categories: *kachha* (crude, temporary), *pukka* (finished, proper) and *semi-pukka*, a combination of the two.

Construction Techniques and Building Plan/Form
The Kachha House
The *kachha* house of thatch, grass, mud or bamboo must be rigorously maintained year round. According to the Hindu *vastu shastra* (sacred text on building forms and layouts), the spiritual force of a home is enhanced by auspicious alignment with the cardinal points and natural features such as rivers, hills and vegetation. Three main features of Indian domestic dwellings are the courtyard, the threshold and the hearth. The courtyard is the house's equilibrium point, where home meets sky. The threshold marks the public-to-private transition, and the hearth (*chulha*) is the primary locus of family activity.

In the western desert region of Rajasthan and Gujarat, elegant shapes sculpted in mud rise from the desert floor. Village layouts are rectangular or circular, with building types ranging from individual family dwellings to grain stores, enclosures for animals and small shrines. Huts are made with thick mud or clay walls, decorated with abstract painted motifs. Grass and timber roofs create thatched verandas to shelter work areas above clay floors.

In the fertile lands of central India, between Gujarat and Orissa, several tribes – including the Gonds, Agaria

Above Compounds of thatch, mud or grass homes are known as *kachha* (temporary) homes. Varying in materials and shape across the country, the *kacha* in the Gagadi village of Rajasthan take the form typical of western India and are sculpted from mud.

Opposite left. The shape and materiality of these barrel-like huts at a Toda mund (village), Ootacamund in the Nilgiri Hills of Tamil Nadu c. 1865 are typical of a *kacha* settlement in southern India.

Opposite right Another variant of southern Indian *kachha* is seen in the fishing village of Appikonda near Kakinad, Andhra Pradesh. Like many *bangla* or 'bungalow' of this region, homes are circular in plan with conical roofs.

and Saora – combine Hindu traditions with older tribal beliefs. Single-storey dwellings are made of mud and interwoven sticks, covered with roofs of thatch or clay tile. A typical two-room home is built on a plinth in order to protect against flooding. A series of posts support beams that extend to form a veranda. The larger room is divided by a screen, and shelters animals and accommodates family activities. The second, smaller room contains both the hearth and the storehouse for grain.

Eastward to Bengal, the rainy landscape flattens into a moist lattice of rice fields. Amid groves of fruit trees, the traditional *bangla* house consists of sturdy bamboo-post walls supporting a curved roof over a raised floor of rammed earth. The space is divided into zones that respect privacy and allow for family growth. The *bangla*, or 'bungalow', was popular with British settlers, and became the archetype of British homes in colonial times.

The monsoon culminates in India's northeastern hills, delivering the highest annual rainfall in the world. Earthquakes are a common occurrence in the region. The matriarchal Khasi people of Meghalaya orient their homes towards the rising sun and avoid the west, considered to be the domain of the dead. Houses here are framed in light timber or bamboo posts, sunk into rubble foundations that allow flexible movement. Sturdy tin sheets have superseded the traditional straw roof.

Southern *kachha* forms vary from circular homes with conical thatched roofs in Andhra Pradesh to houseboats made of woven palm in Kerala. In Tamil Nadu, the Toda tribe builds a beehive-like mud dwelling with an arched grass roof.

The Pukka House

The *pukka* house is more expensive to build than the *kachha*, and is made of more durable materials – including fired brick, timber and clay tiles. In northern India, the *haveli* (mansion) is designed to contain a large family of multiple generations. Roofs are most often pitched and clad in stone tile. The building is raised on a plinth, and approached by steps leading to a colonnaded walkway surrounding a central courtyard. Public spaces for men are separated from private spaces for women.

European colonial influence spread to both civic and domestic structures. *Havelis* fused Indian with Western classical or Gothic architectural elements. Under Portuguese rule, classical and Baroque colonial church forms emerged in Goa and Madras. The Mughal influence on northern Indian Islamic architecture yielded masterpieces such as the Taj Mahal and the city of Fatehpur Sikri. The dome, arch and *jali* (lattice screen) are widely used elements in provincial mosques and houses. Affluent merchants in Punjab and Uttar Pradesh blended *jali* windows, carved and arched gateways and intricate calligraphy into their *havelis*.

The Himalayan region north of the Gangetic Plain offers a splendid variety of *pukka* buildings constructed by the Hindus of Punjab, the Muslims of the Kashmir Valley and Tibetan Buddhists from Ladakh. Houses have pitched slate roofs over robust wooden beams and walls of mud-mortared boulders. The *gompa* (monastery) and *lhakhang* (temple) have mud-plastered, whitewashed rock walls and flat roofs, with interior pillars of intricately carved and brightly painted timber.

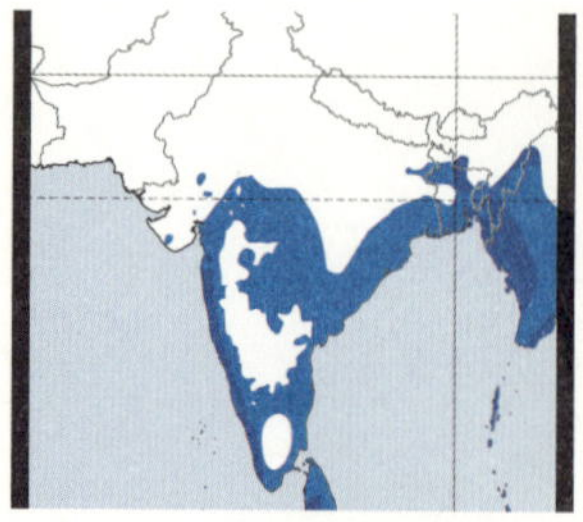

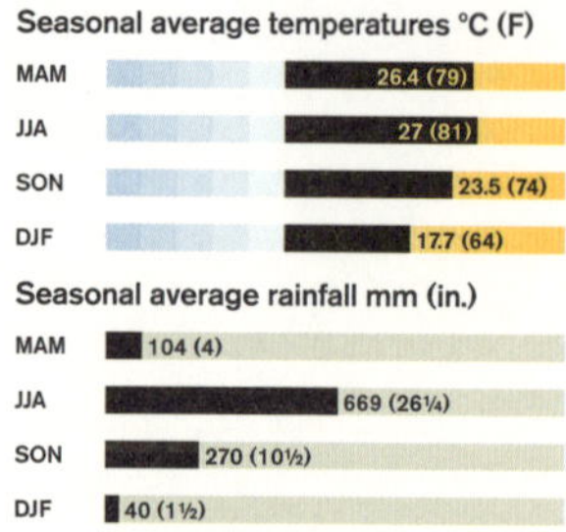

Below More costly than the *kachha*, the *pukka* house and its larger variants such as public buildings are made of durable materials such as fired brick, timber and clay tiles. The Jama Masjid (Friday Mosque), to the rear of Delhi's Red Fort, illustrates an example of colonial and Indian fusion in a civic *pukka* structure.

Tall palm trees and rainforests dominate the Dravidian south. Temples in Kerala are made of stone or brick, with *gopura* (gateways) at each cardinal point. At Kailashnath, the *garbhagriha* (inner sanctum) is set within an ornamented tower (*vimana*) carved from rock. The *nalukettu*, a traditional *pukka* home in Kerala, follows the *vastu* configuration of a central courtyard surrounded by four blocks for domestic life. Elegant wooden columns set into a paved stone floor support a deep veranda and steeply angled tile roofs.

Urbanization and Informal Settlements

Across India, vernacular buildings share a common connection to the environment, climate and culture. The sustainable lifestyles that they represent are under pressure from new forces – among them climate change, modernization and urbanization. Today, villagers aspire to own cars, air conditioners and durable concrete houses. Higher sea levels threaten coastal settlements, erratic weather patterns disrupt farming, and landslides and soil erosion strip the hills of trees. Rising mountain temperatures cause river flooding, while other regions suffer droughts. Towns spread into farmland and disturb wildlife habitats. New commercial and industrial enterprises generate waste and pollution.

Around the world, urbanization brings multiple challenges. Mass migration will raise urban populations from 47 per cent of the global total in 1999 to 61 per cent, roughly 5 billion people, by 2030. Expansion is highest in developing countries, with more than 90 per cent of the rise occurring in Asia. Between 2008 and 2030, India's urban population will rise as a proportion of the total from 28 per cent to over 40 per cent.

More than 93 million people reside in informal settlements, or slums, within Indian cities. The results of this phenomenon are accelerating urban poverty, strains on water and energy resources, overextended infrastructure and widespread disease. Yet, deprived of clean water, sanitation and medical care, slum residents have created thriving micro-cities. The informal settlement of Dharavi in Mumbai has a population of nearly 1 million coexisting families of Christians, Muslims and Hindus from all over the country. A bustling economy emerges from a dense mosaic of shacks overlaid with acres of corrugated metal. Pottery and textile manufacturers export goods from here around the world. Recycling centres process tonnes of waste, including computers and machine parts. Craftspeople prepare leather and assemble furniture and clothing. Though beset by infrastructural problems, Dharavi persists as a self-sustaining community.

A complex picture emerges for sustainability in India in the 21st century. Innovations in vernacular conservation, urban planning policies and 'green' development bring hope. Derelict stepwells are being restored in order to provide clean water and communal spaces. In Mumbai, abandoned textile mills are being adaptively reused for housing. Kolkata residents have united to preserve the East Kolkata Wetlands, an ecosystem of fishponds that uses sunlight to break down garbage and sewage into fertilizer and irrigation for fish and vegetable farmers. These small-scale efforts can be part of a larger strategy to set a positive course for modern India while protecting its traditional lifestyles.

Below **Colourful, decorative and substantial, the variety of *pukka* structures range in expression across India. Here, Rajasthani examples include the blue village of Jodhpur (top left) and the ornately tiled interior of the Juna Mahal palace in Dungarpur (bottom right). Colonial influences on the *pukka* are seen in the arched façades in Mathura, Uttar Pradesh (top right) and Varanasi (bottom left).**

Opposite top Strongly affected by its two monsoon seasons, the northeast and southwest quarters of Sri Lanka are typically verdant, such as this central highlands area of Maskeliya Lake and Adam's Peak.

Opposite bottom In hot and humid regions along the country's coast, villagers often employ thatched leaves of coconut or palm to create closed-sided huts that allow cooling breezes to pass through the structure.

Below Historical examples of Sri Lankan villages illustrating open- and closed-sided huts, the latter typically seen in fishing villages.

Vernacular and Colonial Structures in Sri Lanka

Rajiv Wanasundera

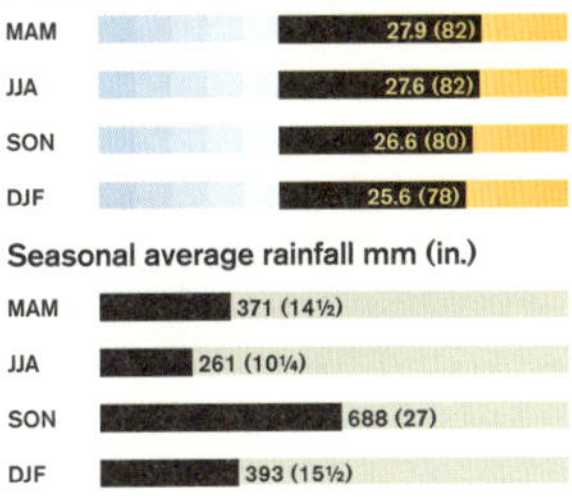

Geography/Climate and Culture

Sri Lanka is a teardrop-shaped island 430 km (270 miles) long and 225 km (140 miles) wide. Twenty-three kilometres of the shallow Palk Strait separates it from India – leading it to be strongly influenced by, but remain culturally distinct and fiercely independent from, its larger neighbour. Many cultures have left their imprint on the country – from Arab and Chinese traders in the first millennium CE to a succession of colonial powers from the 16th century onwards. This was due to its important location at the centre of the Indian Ocean, midway between East and West, at the crossroads of the maritime spice trade.

The climate of Sri Lanka is tropical and strongly affected by the two monsoons that bring rain to the northeast and southwest quadrants of the country for four months of the year. The southwestern quarter is warm and humid, while the plains in the north-central region of the island are relatively arid. The central mountains, which rise to a height of 2,400 m (7,870 ft), boast a more temperate climate.

Its population of 21 million people consists of the majority Sinhalese community (75 per cent) and minority Tamil and Muslim communities (8 and 7 per cent respectively).[1] While the Sinhalese are mostly Buddhist and the Tamils mostly Hindu, there are significant Protestant and Catholic minorities in each community. These racial and religious differences are, in turn, reflected in the vernacular architecture of Sri Lanka.

Materials and Construction Techniques

Sri Lanka has a long and distinguished building tradition dating back to 250 BCE. However, only the monumental religious and civic buildings were constructed of stone and other masonry; their ruins are still visible in the ancient cities of Anuradhapura and Polonnaruwa. Domestic buildings were made out of perishable materials, of which little archaeological evidence remains.

Robert Knox, an English sailor who landed in Sri Lanka in 1659, was held prisoner for nineteen years by the king of Kandy, the inland city that served as the island's capital at that time. He wrote an account of his years on the island, which contains one of the earliest descriptions of its vernacular architecture:

> Their Houses are small, low, thatched Cottages, built with sticks, daubed with clay, the walls made very smooth... They employ no Carpenters or house-builders, unless some few noble-men, but each one buildeth his own dwelling. In building whereof there is not so much as a nail used; but instead of them everything which might be nailed, is tied with *rattans* and other strings, which grow in the woods in abundance; whence the builder hath his timber for cutting. The Country being warm, many of them will not take to pains to clay their walls, but make them of boughs and leaves of Trees... The great people have

handsom [sic] and commodious houses. They have commonly two buildings one opposite to the other, joined together on each side with a wall, which makes a square *Court-yard* in the middle. Round about against the walls of their houses are banks of clay to sit on; which they often daub over with soft *Cow-dung*, to keep them smooth and clean.[2]

The floor levels of buildings were raised, typically by 600 mm (24 in) or more, since foundations were built directly on the ground. This also helped to take advantage of breezes and to provide security against animals. Most domestic buildings feature courtyards to allow for ventilation in every room. Overhanging roofs provide protection from the sun and the rain.

The building materials used vary by climatic region within the country. In the hot and humid coastal areas, thatched coconut (*Cocos nucifera*) or palmyra (*Borassus flabellifer*) leaf is used for both walls and roofs, which allows the easy passage of cooling breezes. Where insulation is needed to protect from the heat, walls are either made of mud (rammed earth or wattle-and-daub, as described by Knox) or with sun-dried clay bricks with an additional finish coat of lime plaster for protection. Roofs are constructed of coconut or palm-leaf thatch, or clay tile in the form of a flat shingle for grander buildings. Window openings in pre-colonial buildings were generally small in size or nonexistent.

Above and right In areas such as the tropical temperate central hill country of Sri Lanka with its tea plantations, typical British colonial influences can be seen. The bungalow expresses the popular single-storey house style of the region, with a tiled hipped roof and veranda in a garden setting.

Below right The close relationship between landscape and vernacular Sri Lankan architecture is seen in the open-sided, shaded *ambalama*, which was historically used as a roadside resting place for pilgrims, such as this noted example in Karagahagedara.

Above Today, Sri Lanka's Hindu population is almost exclusively comprised of Tamils, and is expressed architecturally in colourful, decorative forms, such as this temple in the northern Jaffna district, Keerimalai. The layout of Tamil homes and buildings follows a strict logic that sees the separation of purified and non-purified areas.

Building Plan/Form

Differences in plan can be determined between Sinhalese and Tamil vernacular houses, even though they share common characteristics such as the courtyard. There is a greater openness in the typical Sinhalese house form, given the non-hierarchical nature of Buddhism. Tamil houses, on the other hand, follow a much more prescriptive layout owing to caste considerations and the need to separate purified and non-purified zones.[3]

Exposure to Western colonial powers from the 16th century onwards enriched Sri Lanka's vernacular architecture. Starting in 1505, the Portuguese occupied coastal areas and are credited with introducing elements of classical architecture to the building vocabulary, such as Tuscan columns, arches, large window openings and timber shutters. The Dutch, who ousted the Portuguese in 1658, left a legacy of town houses, built to the extent of their plot lines with deep front verandas and rear courtyards. The British, who replaced the Dutch in 1796, introduced the bungalow to Sri Lanka – the single-storey house with front and rear verandas set in the middle of a garden.

Overall, Sri Lankan vernacular architecture is characterized by a direct and sympathetic relationship with the landscape, and a straightforward and elegant use of building materials. No building type reflects this better than the *ambalama*, a traditional roadside resting hall for travellers, built along the main highways in the medieval period. A few, such as the *ambalama* at Karagahagedera, survive to this day. Located on a granite outcrop, resting on four boulders that protect the timber structure from the damp and termites, its large overhanging roof affords shelter from the sun and rain while the raised platform provides a resting place for weary travellers.

In modern Sri Lanka, vernacular building materials, despite their climatic suitability, have fallen out of favour. Concrete masonry units or mass-produced brick in conjunction with Portland cement mortar are the default options. Roofs are primarily constructed out of corrugated, galvanized metal or asbestos sheeting. When tiles are used, they are more likely to be the interlocking Mangalore-type roof tile, a 20th-century Indian import. However, starting in the 1960s, pioneering Sri Lankan architects, such as Geoffrey Bawa and his collaborator Ulrik Plesner, drew inspiration from local building traditions. They reintroduced vernacular typologies like the courtyard house and popularized traditional materials, such as the half-round roof tile. As a result, certain vernacular building types have seen a resurgence in popularity and have been utilized as an elegant solution for getting access to light and air when building in tight urban spaces.

Vernacular Traditions of Bangladesh

Barbara J. Anello-Adnani

Geography/Climate

The Sundarbans, one of the world's largest mangrove swamps, supports exceptional biodiversity, buffering Bangladesh against cyclones and rising seas. This low, flat delta – much of it still rice paddy – where the Ganges, Brahmaputra, Jamuna and Meghna rivers spill from the Himalayas to pour into the Indian Ocean at the Bay of Bengal, is at the fulcrum of complex change. Sea levels, expected to rise more than a metre (3 ft) by 2100, will displace millions. Chittagong, for centuries a vital port, is now choked by pollution.

Materials and Construction Techniques

The weaving and dyeing of silk and cotton, which made ancient Bengal a centre of textile arts, now accounts for nearly 80 per cent of Bangladesh's current exports. This industry is centred on Dhaka, the capital, which supports more than 15 million residents in an urban sprawl; concrete high-rises and slums encircle a crumbling, traffic-choked historic city core. The nation is ranked eighth in world population tables, and Bangladesh faces challenges in dealing with coastal reforestation, providing flood shelters and re-envisioning its cityscape on a 'green' footing – one that admits water but that also buffers the city with strategic replanting. Using its vernacular traditions of boat building and pile construction with renewable materials, and incorporating state-of-the-art design strategies, Bangladesh is poised to develop a new tropical, urban architecture.

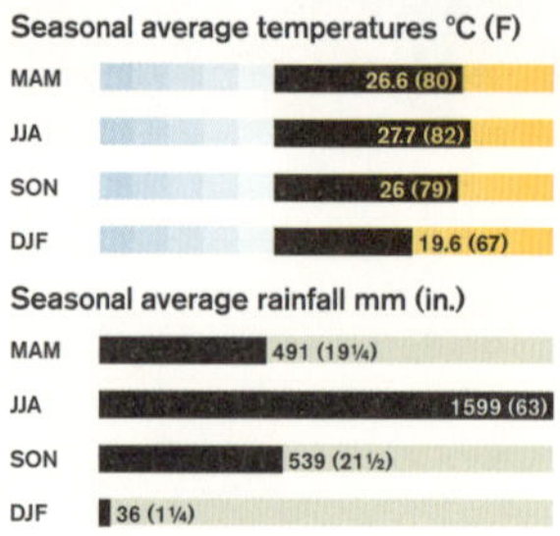

Right Traditionally constructed dwellings on bamboo stilts contrast with modern, high-rise concrete buildings, as seen in this view of Dhaka.

Traditional Farm Dwellings of Myanmar

Su Su, U Win Kyaing and Daw Yin Nyein Aye

Below Once typical, this increasingly rare example of a vernacular *laalyar tell* (farm hut) in Sri Ksetra Pyu, Bago Region, is built of tree trunks, bamboo matting, slats and thatch, all drawn from the local surroundings.

Geography/Climate

Farmers in Myanmar traditionally built shelters within the area of their cultivated lands for their own convenience during the planting or harvesting seasons. These farm huts (*laalyar tell*) were carefully constructed in a naturally sustainable way. Nowadays, with the introduction of modern materials and techniques, vernacular building expertise and habits are becoming rare – and these traditional structures are objects of preservation and study.

A prime example is the *laalyar tell* found within the city of Sri Ksetra Pyu in Pyay township, in Myanmar's south-central Bago Region. It is of a type once common in surrounding areas of Pyay as well as generally in central Myanmar. This region has a cold season, during which temperatures drop to around 16°C (61°F), a wet season with heavy wind and rain, and a hot season with temperatures as high as 42°C (107°F).

Materials and Building Plan/Form

The hut at Sri Ksetra Pyu is aligned, as was customary, with its gables facing east and west – a primarily climatic decision, which reduces its exposure to direct solar radiation. It takes a rectangular form, with a veranda

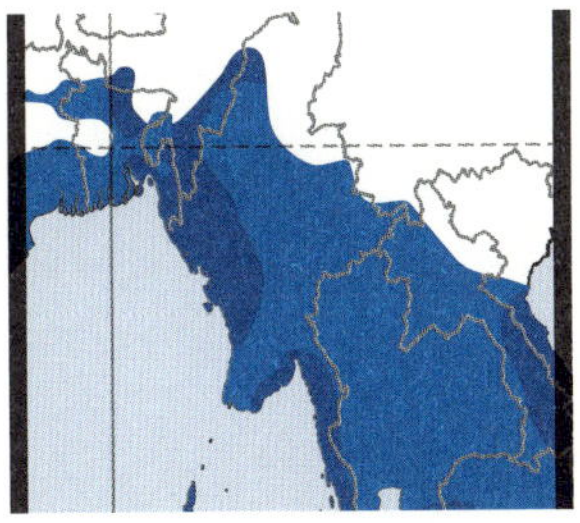

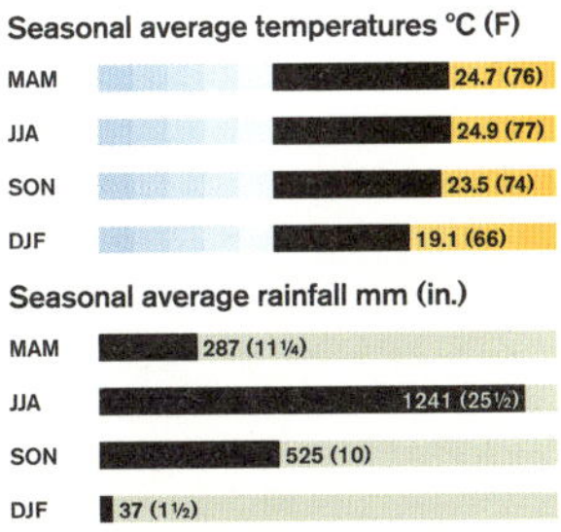

Below Plans and section of the Sri Ksetra Pyu *laalyar tell*: its sheltered veranda to the front minimizes exposure to the sun, as do the gables, facing in the customary east–west direction.

at the front. The building materials, selected from the natural surroundings, have a low thermal capacity and high insulation values. Tree trunks are used for posts and beams, bamboo mats for walls, bamboo slats for floors, and bamboo and thatch for the roof.

Its roof resembles a traditional Myanmar hat (*ka mauk*), which protects the head from the extreme heat. The building is raised on stilts, which provide an open 'undercroft' that allows breezes to enter between the bamboo slats of the floor. Solar radiation is effectively controlled by the extensive thatched roof with its large overhangs. The hut's walls are low, thereby effectively reducing the vertical areas exposed to the hot sun and making the task of shading easier – in order to provide a cooler microclimate within and around the building. The large overhangs also provide protection against driving rain.

The farm hut has a hovel for cattle and bullock carts; room for ducks and pigs, and for the breeding of chickens; and space for circular bamboo baskets containing rice and beans. The eastern portion of the dwelling forms a shrine, the southern part of which is the *nat* (village guardian) shrine. Beside the dwelling, red pepper, chilli and tomato plants are grown, irrigated with waste water from the kitchen. In front of the hut, there is a space to clean paddy and beans after the harvest.

The farm around the hut is heavily cultivated with paddy, beans and vegetables. This sets the building in a cooler environment, as the vegetation absorbs the sun's heat. A farmer and up to five family members will remain in the hut from June to January, returning to their permanent village house at least once a week.

The various spaces of the hut are differentiated according to social, cultural and religious issues, structural forms, and behaviour patterns, in order to fulfil all the occupants' needs. The typical Myanmar farm hut thereby offers a fine example of the use of space, time, materials, climate, orientation and knowledge in order to meet the requirements of its inhabitants.

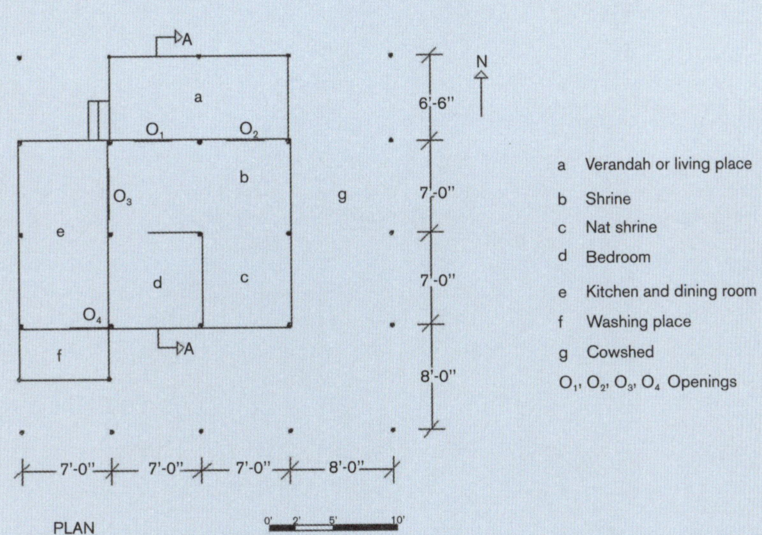

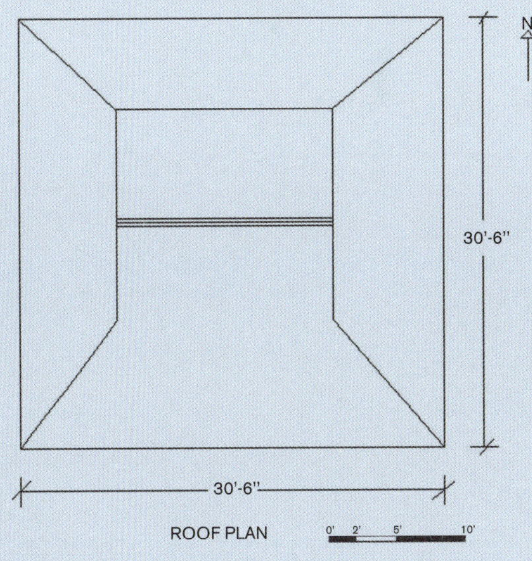

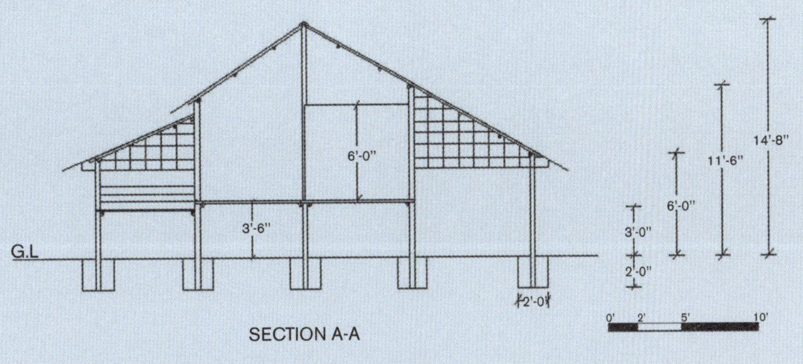

Southeast Asian Adaptation to Migration, Mobility and Monsoons

Barbara J. Anello-Adnani

Geography/Climate

Southeast Asia shares one of the earliest and longest histories of built form. Between the tropics of Cancer and Capricorn, the equatorial region's hot, moist weather and seasonal monsoons support rainforests with remarkable biodiversity. Sufficient water and lush nature provided sustenance and shelter to early human migrations out of Africa to South Asia. Sea levels were much lower than they now are; today's archipelagos were then linked by land, making it possible to walk from Thailand to Java. Today, these waters connect much of the world's maritime trade, with sea routes as important as the land.

Materials and Construction Techniques

Vernacular architecture, marked by themes of migration and mobility – often by boat – was shaped and transformed by the exchange of ideas, technology and goods between India, China, mainland Southeast Asia, the Malay Peninsula, Indonesia and the Philippines. Architectural forms shared characteristics: elevated pile construction; the use of renewable natural materials such as rattan (*Calameae*), bamboo, coconut fibre, *alang-alang* (*Imperata cylindrica* grass) thatch and tropical woods; a tripartite plan; and a generous, sloping roof with a prominent ridge pole. The tensile strength,

Below Though their built expression varies, the vernacular of Southeast Asia shares architectural elements such as constructions on raised piles, the use of natural materials and generous sloping roofs with marked ridge poles. Examples such as the *tulak sumba* of Indonesia (left) and the longhouse of Papua New Guinea (right) both display these features, despite their geographic distance.

Opposite United by its abundance of water and lush natural materials, Southeast Asian vernacular architecture has many raw elements in common: bamboo (above left, right, centre below, centre right below), coconut fibre (centre above left, centre below left), rattan (bottom right), cogon grass (bottom left) and straw. This rich diversity is seen in examples from a thatched cottage in Lombok, Indonesia (centre above) to bamboo leaf-and-straw roof construction in Thailand (centre above right).

Opposite Located in a tropical, monsoonal band, vernacular Southeast Asian examples such as these from Indonesia illustrate the close relationship between traditional built development, culture and the local climate. The *tongkonan* or ancestral house of the Toraja people in South Sulawesi (top and bottom right) is a collectively built dwelling with distinctive boat-shaped roofs and deep upswept gables, set on a platform raised on stilts. Its elevated form encourages cooling breezes to enter the house and protects against flooding and moisture, while the steeply pitched roofs and deep eaves quickly cast off rain and prevent it penetrating the interior. Within Indonesia, and even the same island, similar climatic strategies can be seen but are reflected in varied forms – from the *rumah baru* in Kampung (middle left) to the dwellings of the Ngada (bottom left), both on Flores Island.

pliability and abundance of bamboo make it valuable in construction. Woven, tied, pegged or notched, traditional structures used no metal. The sloping roof, often ornamented with horned gables, was designed to repel hard rains and equipped with triangular openings or a central circular aperture for ventilation. Sheltered space beneath the elevated house kept it safe from weather and predators; it also increased air circulation, sheltered domestic animals and shaded working space. Materials included red clay or mud brick, tile, stone, stucco, and vines and grasses from rainforests. The traditional house was largely prefabricated, renewable and movable.

In a tropical environment, the relatively short life of domestic structures belies the continuity of forms and motifs, and the conscious efforts by those who build and use these structures to ensure the preservation of traditional forms.[1] Spiritual beliefs were not segregated from, but rather found expression in, all aspects of material culture, ritual, performance and architecture. *Feng shui*, now a popularized notion, existed in principle throughout the region; construction was planned and proceeded with both pragmatic and esoteric considerations, requiring rituals and offerings on an auspicious schedule. The house, its site, landscape, village plan and burials were all designed to align the living with ancestors, Earth and cosmos. Not simply a dwelling, the house was situated so as to hold its inhabitants in a harmonious balance with universal forces, both natural and spiritual. Roxana Waterson explored the anthropology of the Southeast Asian house as an institution central to understanding kinship systems and the organization of social relations.[2] Dorothy Pelzer's photographic documentary of the vernacular architecture of Southeast Asia provides an unparalleled reference.[3]

The Austronesian architectural vocabulary was enriched by trade between Southeast Asia, China, Vietnam, India and the Arabian Peninsula. Archaeological and epigraphic evidence, including bronzes and ceramics recovered from shipwrecks, documents exchange between the 'mandala-states' of early Southeast Asia through the Strait of Malacca connecting the Pacific and Indian oceans. Stone sculpture and the ruins of walled cities and temples from Bengal to Java remain from the 'golden age' (5th–14th centuries CE) of syncretic Hindu/Buddhist polities. In Bangladesh's northern hills, ruins remain of a 9th-century Mahayana Buddhist *vihara* (a large, terraced monastic complex), sculpted and carved to instruct the faithful. Recent excavations in central Vietnam added another Cham site to the no fewer than thirty towers belonging to this intriguing civilization (8th–12th centuries); these Hindu/Buddhist monuments include the World Heritage Site of My Son (600–700 CE), damaged by 20th-century bombs.

The later spread of Islam brought different architectural forms and motifs from the Bay of Bengal as far as the Philippines and Brunei, where Magellan's voyages (1519–22) initiated the period of European colonization. Spanish, Portuguese, French, British and Dutch interests divided the region well into the 20th century, transforming regional architecture into a diverse modernity. Nationalist anti-colonial movements of the early 20th century were interrupted by war. The Philippines gained independence in 1946; the Federation of Malaya, in 1957. Since 1963, the nation of Malaysia incorporates both the peninsula and the states of Sabah and Sarawak (Borneo). Singapore achieved nationhood in 1965; Bangladesh, in 1972; and Brunei, 1984. Vietnam reunited north and south in 1975.

Architectural historian Anthony Tung notes that the 20th century was dramatically destructive of traditional architecture through war, political upheaval, population growth and industrialization.[4] Destruction, often deliberate and planned as part of modernization efforts, also resulted from unregulated urban development, neglect, poverty and limited initiative. Presently in Southeast Asia, traditional villages and the longest-surviving domestic structures

Right Po Klong Garai, a brick-built Cham temple at Phan Rang Thap Cham, southern Vietnam, is one of at least thirty Hindu/Buddhist towers that represent the reigning style of the 8th–12th centuries in this region of Southeast Asia.

are, by their very nature, in the keeping of the poorest, oldest citizens. Modernization is often synonymous with air-conditioned steel-and-glass high-rises – and relentless urbanization is its defining process. However, efforts to reinvent a sustainable urban model while preserving architectural traditions are under way at local and international levels, strengthened by the recognition of the value of both material and intangible cultural diversity.

The Mekong Delta, like the Bay of Bengal, is severely threatened by pollution and rising seas. Hanoi, Ho Chi Minh City, Dhaka, Chittagong and Manila share the problems of expanding populations, traffic snarled in inner-city streets designed for pedestrians, polluted waterways, crumbling housing, and inadequate infrastructure and public transportation. Yet their traditions hold promise for a new, green architecture. The presence of garden-pavilion houses, interior courts, water palaces, irrigation, canals, boats and bicycles all suggests a revitalized urban design connecting history, landscape and city to a sustainable future.

The key to forging an innovative new paradigm that fuses architecture, urbanism and environmentalism depends on reversing the trend of rampant environmental destruction; developing a contemporary, green architecture while preserving historic structures and neighbourhoods; and establishing the long-term conservation of natural and built habitats. By considering geology and ecology along with contemporary needs and uses, designers can reconfigure habitats using recycled materials, solar orientation, natural ventilation and power, and siting that enhances rather than destroys the landscape. With a dynamism informed by the methods of vernacular architecture as well as by cutting-edge technology, and learning from the sustainability of its past, Southeast Asia can lead in developing a new tropical architecture that joins urban and agricultural, natural and built, creating homes that shelter while conserving and renewing resources. This, in fact, is what true vernacular architecture has always done.

Right Drawing on local knowledge and materials, the architecture of Southeast Asia today can develop its sustainable vernacular forms. Time-honoured materials include bamboo, which is durable and readily grown and can be used for a variety of building applications, including thatch for roofs (top left and centre) and woven walls of bamboo-strip (top right).

Bamboo Stilt Houses of Laos

Denise Heywood

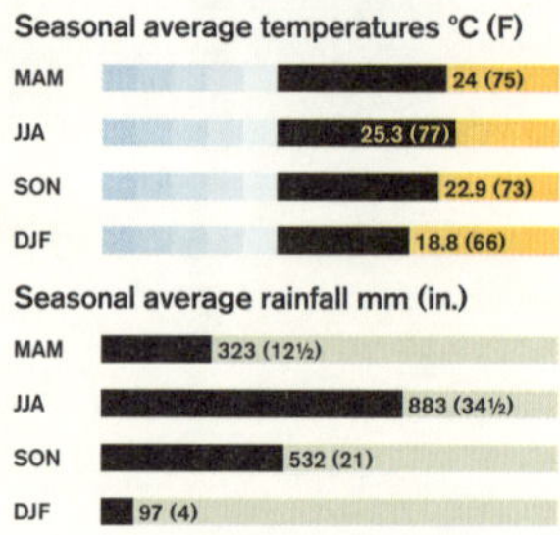

Right Elevated homes made of bamboo typify the Laos vernacular. Here a village of the Khmu ethnic group near Luang Prabang illustrates the duopitched roofs, which aid in chanelling heavy rains away.

Geography/Climate and Culture

Vernacular architecture in Laos is based on local needs and traditions, and has evolved over time to reflect indigenous beliefs and social structures. Houses are at the centre of the customs, laws, taboos, myths and religion that bind Laotian villagers together. However, religious and secular architecture overlap in Laos, and comparable styles of vernacular building can be used to house Buddhist monks or laypeople. Local aesthetic preferences govern the design as much as architectural principles, and the resulting structures are an integral part of the community.

The Lao, whose population encompasses great ethno-linguistic diversity within a geographical region of steep mountains and broad rivers, believe that their lives are ruled by natural and supernatural forces, and many ancient animistic ideas are incorporated into their houses. Siting is important and dwellings are oriented auspiciously, usually towards water, according to ancestral lore handed down through generations. Villagers hold that the landscape and its elements, and the energies with which they are charged, will influence patterns of habitation. At the commencement of construction, an astrologer is consulted in order to prevent disturbance of the spirit guardians of the land; and a propitious period is chosen for felling trees and preparing the frame of the house.

Materials

The Laotian vernacular house is made of tropical hardwood or bamboo (*Bambusoideae*), often built on stilts, with a steep duopitched roof covered in bamboo, wood, daub or tiles. Some residences have a carved veranda on one side. Raising a house on stilts is eminently practical in this climate. It affords ventilation in the tropical heat and protection from animals, insects and flooding in the monsoon season. The area underneath provides a sheltered space for cooking, family life and activities such as weaving textiles. These pitched-roof houses have high gables or hipped roofs with extended eaves to allow the tropical rains to run off.

Building Plan/Form

Bedrooms are arranged so that a sleeping person's head, in accordance with superstitious beliefs, points towards the south. The feet should never be over the head of another sleeping occupant. Lying with the head towards the west is taboo, as the setting sun symbolizes death.

The assembled structure, decorated with intricately carved fretwork and delicate floral or geometric patterns, is covered with terracotta tiles or palm leaves. The transom above the door is usually ornately carved, according to historical scriptures and symbolism, to signify the threshold, ward off evil spirits and welcome visitors, who remove their shoes.

Prayers are said at the start and finish of construction, with candles, incense and chanting Buddhist monks attending each stage. Prior to occupation, the owner will ensure that a house is blessed by monks, accompanied by flowers and holy water.

An altar with a Buddha image and family relics is present inside every home. Outside, a small spirit house is placed in front of the dwelling: this is a miniature structure resembling a house, often quite simple, raised on a pole. They are held to contain the spiritual guardian, or *phi*, of the home, and belong to early animistic beliefs. Offerings of rice, flowers and incense are brought to the spirit house every day.

Finally, auspicious trees are planted around the house bringing both shade and beauty, and resulting in a harmonious environment

Regional Adaptations of Thailand's Vernacular

Below An abundance of water informs much of the Thai vernacular. Examples from the late 19th century include a family outside their steep-roofed 'floating' house on the Chao Phraya River near Bangkok (left); and a view of a Thai floating market with steep-roofed structures and corn cob vendors (right).

Opposite top Houses on the Klong Plu River of Klong Prao village in Mu Koh Chang National Park, Trat Province, illustrate typically elevated Thai housing, which allows for rising water levels.

Opposite bottom The *ruen Thai derm* house type is a closed-sided dwelling beside the water with a raised living area enclosed by timber panels and sheltered storage underneath.

William R. Chapman

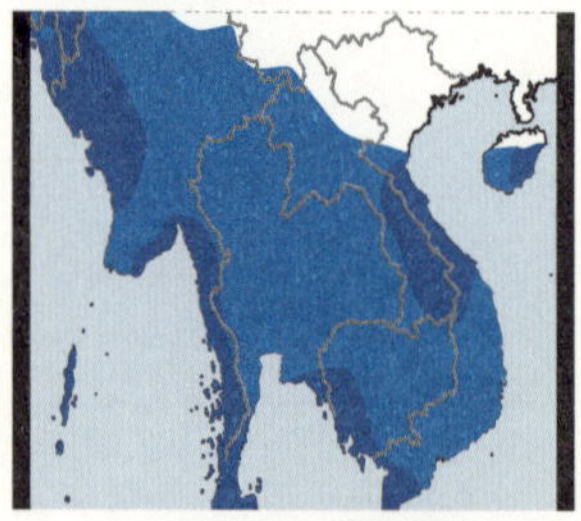

Seasonal average temperatures °C (F)

MAM	28.1 (82)
JJA	27.2 (81)
SON	25.9 (79)
DJF	23.9 (75)

Seasonal average rainfall mm (in.)

MAM	315 (12½)
JJA	870 (34¼)
SON	598 (23½)
DJF	82 (3¼)

Geography/Climate

Thai vernacular architecture was traditionally a response to both cultural preferences and environmental conditions. With much of the country subject to periodic flooding, Thai traditional houses were typically elevated a full storey above ground level; noted contemporary architect Sumet Jumsai has argued that ancient inhabitants of the region, including what is now modern Thailand, were increasingly subject to the encroachment of seas and flooding by major river systems. A cosmology dominated by mythical river and sea creatures was an important legacy of the water-based societies of an early period, and continued into recent times.

As with other Southeast Asian countries, Thailand's climate is dominated by a monsoonal pattern. The winter months are dry and initially cool, but end with several weeks of extreme heat and humidity. The summer, beginning in June, is marked by torrential rains, which often lead to flooding late in the calendar year. Thailand's traditional new year (*Songkran*) is in April, and it marks the peak of the hot season; the Thais greet this time of year with rituals involving cleansing and anointing, a practice that has more recently evolved into a week-long water-fest.

Building Plan/Form

Scholars have historically emphasized the regional character of Thai vernacular house types. There are also variants within regions and innumerable specialized houses and other building types, ranging from *kuti*, homes for monks, to storage buildings and 'floating' houses typically associated with urban water-based markets. The notion of vernacular architecture also embraces religious structures and Western-influenced utilitarian and elite houses – notably, in this case, the many workers' dwellings developed by the Thai railroads in the early 20th century, and the numerous shophouses and mansions constructed by an increasingly Western-oriented elite from the late 19th century onwards.

The most celebrated Thai dwelling form is the *ruen Thai derm* house common to the central Thai plains and the Chao Phraya River watershed. With its steeply pitched roof and panelled construction, the central Thai house fits perfectly with its environment, placing the living area on a platform above the flood-prone ground level and providing a storage and utilitarian area – as well as a recreation zone – beneath the sheltering timber building above. *Ruen Thai derm* houses range from larger multi-unit 'cluster' dwellings (*ruen krueng sab*) through smaller single- or double-unit platform houses down to simple bamboo or combined timber-and-bamboo shelters (*ruen kreng pook*).

Opposite top Known as 'Lanna' houses, this raised northern house type has an extensive veranda and is formed from timber and other materials found locally.

Opposite bottom A closed-sided southern house type sits lower to the ground than many other Thai dwellings and is typically crowned with gabled or hipped roofs and decorated with elaborate sawn-work.

Below Simple, steep-roofed, raised northeastern house types tend to be less decorative and smaller than their northern counterparts, though both variations include undercroft space for storage.

Northern Thai houses, located in the area corresponding to the ancient kingdom of Lanna, are also raised above ground and rely, as do central Thai houses, on local timber and other natural materials. Unlike central Thai examples, however, the 'Lanna' house features a terrace or balcony deck at one end, not at the centre of the building. The roofs are usually gables, albeit typically without the curved bargeboard common in the central plain. A signature element is the *kalae*, stylized flame- or wing-like crossed boards placed at the apex of the gable ends. Of relatively modest size, northern Thai houses are nonetheless notable for their intricate carved and sawn timber ornaments and their spacious interiors.

The drier northeastern section of the country – an area called Isan or, alternatively, Isarn – is notable for its simple, rectangular houses, constructed of timber, thatch and sheet metal (the last-named material introduced largely after the Second World War). Reflective of the modest economy of the region and its cooler, drier climate, these houses lack the decorative displays of their northern and central counterparts and tend to be far smaller. Their undercrofts serve as resting areas and sites for looms. Occupants also stored – and still store – agricultural equipment under these houses, sometimes also utilizing the lower spaces as animal shelters.

Southern Thai houses demonstrate that region's heterogeneous population, with its influences of Malay, Chinese, Indian and European architectural traditions. Houses here typically have gabled or hipped roofs with cross vents (or sometimes 'gablet' – gable-on-hip, or 'Dutch gable' – forms). Many southern houses feature elaborate sawn-work decoration suggestive of Indian or Islamic designs. As with other Thai houses, southern dwellings are typically elevated above ground level, with the more urban examples being enclosed by timber panels or masonry walls at the lower level.

In addition to houses, Thai vernacular architecture encompasses rice and other storage buildings, primitive rural rice mills and variations on Thai religious architecture. Detailed studies, by Professor Woroj Srisuro of Khon Kaen University, of northeastern Thai temple forms, known as *sim*, brought attention to these important building types and also helped to encourage new designs based on traditional forms. The southern part of the country also features traditional mosques, in keeping with the high number of Muslim residents; mosques also feature in Bangkok and other central Thai areas, though typically of more recent design.

Thatch, Wood, *Keng* and Khmer Houses of Cambodia

William R. Chapman

Geography/Climate

Cambodia is a hot and humid country, characterized by monsoonal weather and the periodic flooding of lowland areas. Rice production and fishing have long been mainstays of its economy, and Cambodian settlements still reflect these traditional activities.

Building Plan/Form

Urban houses in Cambodia follow the conventions of combined Chinese and European building types, notably two- to three-storey timber dwellings and two-storey masonry shophouses. These have historically been interspersed with colonial-era villas and institutional buildings. However, timber houses in both urban and rural settings best exemplify Cambodian ideals and traditions.

Rural Cambodian dwellings are well adapted to the prevailing conditions of flooding near riverbanks. Many are raised on timber stilts; in some instances, stilts can reach 10 m (33 ft) or more in height. They also provide security for occupants, and work and storage spaces beneath. As in neighbouring Thailand, Cambodia has a tradition of floating 'raft houses', now largely confined to the Tonlé Sap Lake area near the ancient Angkor Thom site.

Thatch Houses

The most basic dwelling form in Cambodia is the woven palm-and-grass, or 'thatch', house, supported on bamboo or simple timber platforms. This building type ranges from small shelters situated at ground-floor level to larger, raised dwellings. Its wall-cladding and roofing material typically comprises sugar palm (*Borassus flabellifer*) leaves, which are tied to longer rattans (*Calameae*), forming individual 'courses' that are attached to the building in layers.

Wood Houses

Cambodian wood houses feature substantial timber uprights and horizontal supports, and timber-framed roofs. Typically, the supporting posts extend from ground level to the wall-plate height of the buildings. These posts are set out in a grid pattern, their number and distribution depending upon the form and size of the dwelling. Posts are notched to receive horizontal members. Roof rafters, in turn, are set onto the horizontal wall plates and reinforced by tie beams linked to the main supporting posts.

Wall-cladding materials for these wood houses include palm leaves, grass and, in wealthier houses, both vertical and horizontal timber boarding. Roofing materials vary, and include traditional grass and palm-leaf sheathing, ceramic tiles and, more recently, sheet metal.

Cambodia's traditional wood houses are still valued for their expression of national heritage and for their comfort. High and open roofs, extended elevations above ground level, and timber cladding are all environmentally advantageous in the country's hot and wet climate. They also have a social and touristic appeal that makes them desirable as restaurants, coffee houses and galleries.

Keng and Khmer Houses

Two further Cambodian dwelling types are the *keng* house and a form known as the 'Khmer' house. Both of these are associated with religious complexes, typically as monks' residences. The *keng* house, with its telescoping gable roofs and elaborate cresting and other gable treatments, suggests both religious architecture and Chinese influences. The hipped-roof Khmer house has similar connections to religious architecture, and is relatively rare.

The most common form of Khmer dwelling is the *roong daul* house. This is a gable-roofed building with full or half-gable returns on the narrow ends (the latter form reminiscent of the Western 'Dutch gable'). A variation of this type is the *roong duong* dwelling, which has only a single side hip or 'shed'-type roof. Another widespread form is the *bet* house, a hipped-roof dwelling sometimes associated with Chinese settlements. A further common type is the *kondaing* (also spelled *kantiang*) house, a gable-roofed structure with narrow returns and prominent, exposed gable ends. Both the *bet* house and the *kondaing* or *kantiang* dwelling may be built up in units, with multiple roofs – generally two parallel roofs, but in some cases three or even four, with intervening valleys.

During the colonial period, and particularly after 1900, Khmer house types became important symbols of Cambodian culture. Indigenous Khmer residents in both provincial towns and the capital, Phnom Penh, favoured large timber houses of a traditional type into the 1950s, typically incorporating French and Chinese features such as tiled ground floors and elaborate tiled roofs. In 1965, the noted Khmer architect Vann Molyvann designed a complex of '100 houses' based on the country's traditional forms as a project for the National Bank of Cambodia. This project represented efforts to extol Cambodian traditions in the context of independence after 1953.

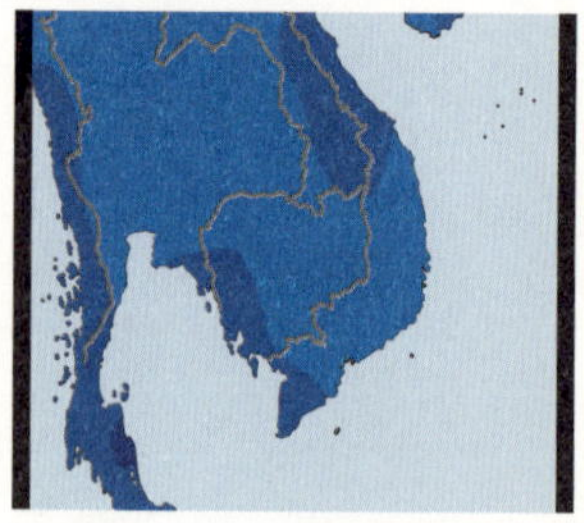

Seasonal average temperatures °C (F)

MAM	28.3 (83)
JJA	27.3 (81)
SON	26.4 (79)
DJF	25.2 (77)

Seasonal average rainfall mm (in.)

MAM	311 (12½)
JJA	860 (34)
SON	664 (26¼)
DJF	68 (2½)

Opposite top Adapted to survive vast rains and flooding, rural dwellings are often raised on stilts, which give security and create undercroft storage spaces.

Opposite bottom Rare Khmer houses share a connection to the forms of religious architecture and are seen in a range of variations, including (left to right) *kondaing*, *bet*, Khmer, *roong daul*.

Vietnam's Regional Eclectic Vernacular

Below The mixed heritage of Vietnamese architecture has been shaped as much by location as by culture. Buildings in the World Heritage Site of Hoi An city, Quang Nam Province (left) for example, contrast with an elaborate, raised, Nguyen-era imperial citadel of Ngo Mon (Noon Gate) further north in Hué (right), which was influenced by Chinese and French styles.

Opposite Raised, steep-roofed traditional houses known as *rong*, of the Konjori ethnic minority in the Kontum Province of Vietnam's highlands, provide communal halls for shared receptions, ceremonies and housing guests. Though decorative features vary between groups, the *rong* commonly feature a base formed of eight large wooden posts and thatched roofs.

Barbara J. Anello-Adnani

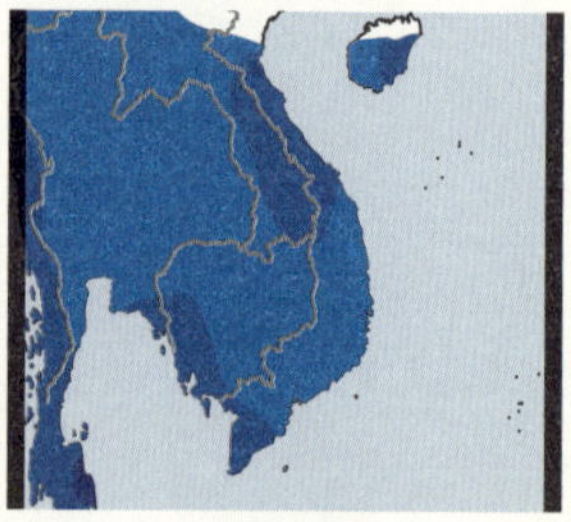

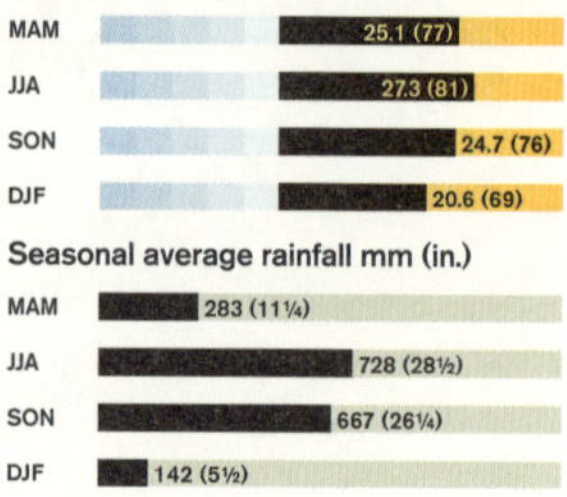

Geography/Climate and Culture

Regionally divided by geography as much as by historical developments, Vietnam's architectural history developed differently in the country's north, centre and south. Dongson bronze drums (c. 1000 BCE–500 CE) – found as far afield as Alor, East Nusa Tenggara, Indonesia, Sumatra and Borneo – attest to early maritime trade from the northern Vietnamese coast. On the central coast, Hoi An, a trading entrepôt at its height from the 15th until the early 19th century, handled Chinese and Vietnamese porcelain, silk and other goods. Now a UNESCO World Heritage Site, noted for the preservation of its timber architecture, Hoi An's built heritage includes Chinese, Japanese and Vietnamese styles. French Catholic monks first came to Vietnam through this port in the 17th century.

Construction Techniques and Building Plan/Form

Vietnam shares Austronesian traditions through its central-highland ethnic-minority *rong* houses. These communal longhouses on stilts, with sloping thatch or woven-bamboo roofs, were largely destroyed during the 20th century wars for independence, and their inhabitants dispersed. In recent decades, however, *rong* community houses have been rebuilt around Kontum, Pleiku and Buon Ma Thuot – in some cases using original beams that had been buried for safekeeping.

The north of Vietnam, influenced by Chinese Tang dynasty architecture (618–906 CE) also required shelter from a colder climate, while its central and southern regions incorporated Hindu/Buddhist cultural built forms, with structures more open to the environment. The capital, palaces and citadel at Hué, central Vietnam, belonging to the Nguyen dynasty (1802–1945) were influenced in their design by Sébastian Le Prestre Vauban (1633–1707), the renowned French master of siegecraft; their plan refers to Beijing's Forbidden City (Ming and Qing Palace, built 1406–20). Severely damaged by French and US bombs (in 1947 and 1968 respectively) and now a UNESCO World Heritage Monument, Hué is undergoing restoration.

Colonial architecture with unique French, Chinese and Vietnamese elements distinguishes District 1 of Ho Chi Minh City, formerly Saigon. A sophisticated network of canals supporting the Mekong Delta's agricultural irrigation facilitated trade between the interior and the coast, linking the waterways between Funan (the earliest known state of Southeast Asia, 100–550 CE), Angkor Borei (Funan's capital, 70 km [40 miles] south of Phnom Phen) and Angkor Wat (the famed building of the temple complex at Angkor). Now choked with pollution, these ancient waterways, once so successful, present a challenge to be met by the 21st-century paradigm of water management and urban design.

Multicultural Identities of Malay Vernacular

Barbara J. Anello-Adnani

Geography/Climate and Culture
Kuala Lumpur's Petronas Towers, the world's highest 'twin towers' today, reflect Malaysia's affluence from gas, oil, rubber and tin, while archaeology in the country's northwestern Lenggong Valley reveals hominid history over a period of almost two million years – longer than in any place outside Africa. Between these extremes lie centuries of human habitation.

Building Plan/Form
Early Malay architectural forms, influenced by Hindu/Buddhist prototypes, included the Javanese *pendopo* (pillared pavilion) with a triple, sloping roof, supported by columns. Roofs are important in the tropics, where open walls join building interiors with the landscape, making the garden a vital design element. Local hardwoods, bamboo and palm used to construct the Malay house also shaded and cooled it. Intricate timber carving, in foliate and geometric patterns of Chinese or Islamic origin, traditionally decorated both humble Malay houses and rich palaces. Few humble structures in the country predate the colonial era, however, because of the use of these perishable materials.

The southern seaport of Malacca, a World Heritage City, retains its unique multicultural architectural identity – encompassing Malay, Sumatran, Chinese, Tamil, Arab, Portuguese, Dutch and British influences. Founded by a Sumatran prince, Malacca was a thriving 15th-century port; the Minangkabau people brought to it their boat-like decorative timber architectural style from central Sumatra. Generations of Straits-born Chinese (*Peranakan*, or *Baba-Nyonya* in the native Malay) developed a colourful fusion of culture, cuisine and design. Carved teak (*Tectona grandis*), ebony (*Diospyros*) or rosewood (*Dalbergia*) decorated wealthy homes, combining geometric and floral motifs with dragon and phoenix images. Established in 1786 by the British and administered by the Bengal-based East India Company, Georgetown was the capital of the island of Penang. Its colonial administrative buildings incorporated local designs with the Mughal-influenced and Palladian styles of the Raj.

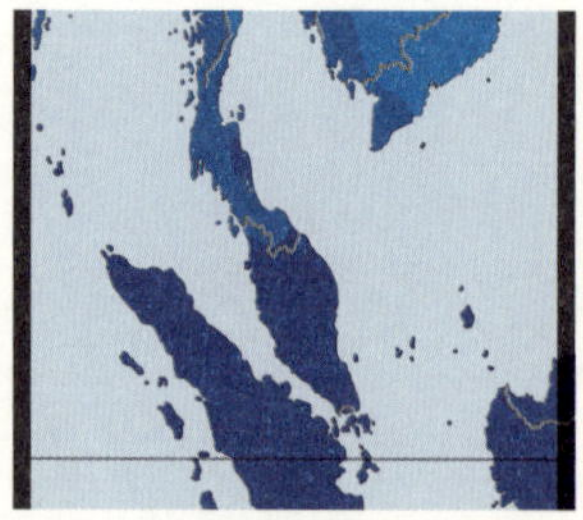

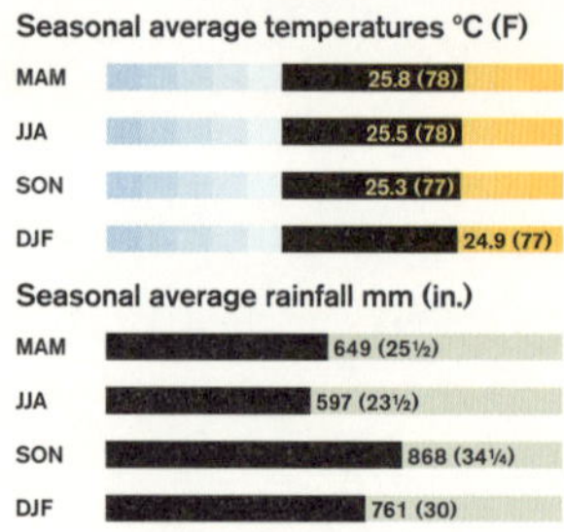

Left The city of Malacca reflects the diversity of this seaport's history as a trading base and includes different cultural influences, from Japanese, Chinese and Islamic to Dutch, Portuguese and British.

Opposite The colonial era of Malacca is reflected through its masonry housing with arcades and shuttered timber screens (top), while the influence of the Mughal Palladian style can be seen in the Kapitan Keling Mosque, built in the 19th century by Indian Muslim traders in George Town, Penang, Malaysia (bottom).

隴西

Vernacular and Colonial Structures of Singapore

Barbara J. Anello-Adnani

Materials and Building Plan/Form

A thriving port in the 14th–16th centuries, known as Temasek, Singapore was claimed in 1819 by Sir Thomas Stamford Raffles as a base for British operations in Asia.[1] Immigrant Chinese, Tamils and Arabs developed the distinctive Malay styles of vernacular architecture. Open verandas, tall shutters, decorative tiles and pastel-hued stucco were all distinguishing features of the style – as were curved and vented roofs, which mitigated the effects of the heat, allowing buildings to breathe. Neoclassical details were incorporated into *Peranakan* buildings (those belonging to Straits-born Chinese-Malay communities), as ethnically distinct neighbourhoods developed in a landscape of orchids and palms. Rows of narrow, two-storey shophouses opened onto the street, with living spaces extending the full depth of the building. Arcades sheltered residents from sun and rain; shop fronts were faced with hand-painted decorative tiles and painted, pastel stucco.

Seasonal average temperatures °C (F)

MAM	26.9 (80)
JJA	26.5 (80)
SON	26.3 (79)
DJF	25.9 (79)

Seasonal average rainfall mm (in.)

MAM	609 (24)
JJA	471 (18½)
SON	642 (25¼)
DJF	774 (30½)

Opposite Typical of Singapore's vernacular, these historical views illustrate open-fronted timber properties (top); a boat quay, c. 1890, bordered by colonial structures (middle); and colonial-era arcades – a feature of the British influence on Singaporean architecture (bottom).

Below Traditional *Peranakan*, or *Baba-Nyonya*, style shophouses in Singapore. Both are Malay terms that refer to the descendants of the early Chinese-Malay settlers in Singapore.

Singapore's rational, disciplined development, under Prime Minister Lee Kwan Yew (served 1959–90), provided healthcare, education and good-quality housing for all citizens, making Singapore a high-tech global centre. With modernization, many historical structures and neighbourhoods were destroyed; however, Singapore's current goal of having 80 per cent of all new buildings certified by Green Mark standards (the country's building rating system for environmental assessment of structures) by 2030 inspires its architects to explore local traditions for contemporary energy-efficient solutions.

Since the nineteenth century, the highlands, tropical rainforests, plantations and gardens of Singapore and Malaysia have played a significant role in botanical research, contributing to advances in horticulture, medicine, pharmacology, science and industry. The 74-hectare (183-acre) Singapore Botanic Gardens, established in 1859, in the heart of what is now a very urban Singapore, preserve the extraordinary biodiversity of tropical flora at a time when the rainforest is most imperiled.

Rainforest Longhouses of Brunei Darussalam

Barbara J. Anello-Adnani

Geography/Climate

One of the world's smallest, wealthiest nations, Brunei Darussalam – an Islamic monarchy – shares the island of Borneo with Malaysia and Indonesia. Its oil wealth supports a state-of-the-art urban lifestyle. Kampung Air, a water village on stilts in the Brunei River, stands adjacent to Bandar Seri Begawan, the modern capital that replaced it. With an extraordinarily rich ecology, many of Borneo's tropical rainforest species are still unidentified. However, the island's ecological habitats are threatened by logging at an unprecedented rate, replacing forest with oil-palm (*Elaeis guineensis*) plantations. National parks protect what remains of ecological diversity, including threatened and vulnerable species, but the deliberate destruction of Borneo's rainforest portends the death of one of the world's richest ecological environments.

Building Plan/Form

Borneo's traditional longhouse is as much a social as an architectural form. Sited parallel to water or at the fork of two rivers, the longhouse was prefabricated, built all at once, and rebuilt every decade or two. Housing ten or more families, longhouses were raised, reached by notched log or ladder, with a veranda the length of the building under a long, ridged roof. The interior was divided for privacy: tools hung outside; valuables inside, under the roof. While some longhouses are still used, the destruction of Borneo's environment threatens their ancient lifestyle. Protecting Borneo's biodiversity is essential to revitalizing a vernacular architecture sustained by the natural environment.

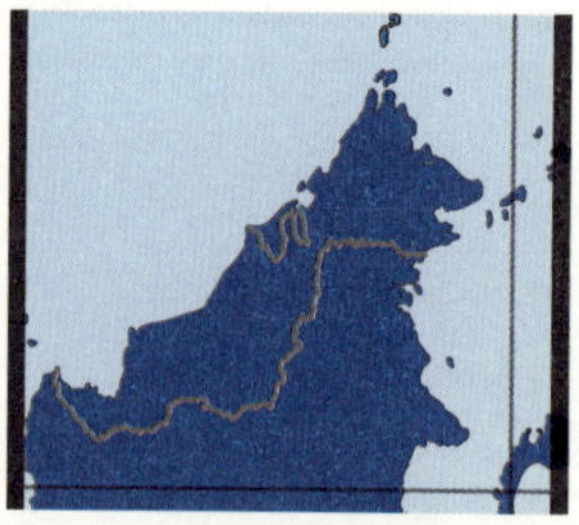

Seasonal average temperatures °C (F)

MAM	27.2 (81)
JJA	27.2 (81)
SON	26.8 (80)
DJF	26.2 (79)

Seasonal average rainfall mm (in.)

MAM	571 (22½)
JJA	652 (25¼)
SON	823 (32¾)
DJF	676 (26½)

Below Traditional longhouses of Brunei Darussalam were built from prefabricated elements sourced from the rainforest.

Right Logging threatens the future of Borneo's rainforest and vernacular traditions are endangered by the introduction of modern materials that are easy to build with.

Opposite Known as *kubo* and raised on stilts, with split-bamboo floors and thatched roofs, the traditional rural houses are either closed-sided – shown here at Sitio Bato Ili village near San Jose, Occidental Mindoro province (top), or open-sided as seen in Batad village, northern Luzon Island (bottom).

Below left Notched tree trunks provide access to a thatched-roof house, or *balé*, of the Ilongot people, Luzon Island.

Below right Against a background of raised, stilted homes in central Luzon Island, Ifugao villagers perform the essential task of husking rice.

Kubo and *Balé* Homes of the Philippines

Barbara J. Anello-Adnani

Seasonal average temperatures °C (F)

MAM	26.4 (79)
JJA	26.2 (79)
SON	25.8 (78)
DJF	24.7 (76)

Seasonal average rainfall mm (in.)

MAM	343 (13½)
JJA	796 (31½)
SON	783 (31)
DJF	426 (16¾)

Geography/Climate

Much of life in the Philippines is lived on or around water, with the boat more essential than the wheel. Dugout canoes, bentwood houseboats and double riggers show a range of creative responses to the environment – all constructed using natural, local materials. Experience gleaned from dealing effectively over centuries with the rise and fall of waters, flooded paddy and silting rivers enriches the range of solutions to the 21st-century challenges of rising sea levels, clean water supply and the preservation of natural habitat and species. The question is: what can designers take from traditional methods and materials to inform a vocabulary of renewable, movable, and flood- and earthquake-safe design ideas?

Construction Techniques

The humble *kubo* has sheltered rice farmers for millennia. The most basic Filipino structure found in rural areas, it comprises a simple shelter on stilts – sometimes using living trees – with a split-bamboo floor and thatched roof. The Ifugao *balé* (pavilion), found in that region on the northernmost island of Luzon, is made of local hardwood, layered shingles or thatch, and bamboo and stone. The *balé* uses post-and-beam construction, with flat, stone footings supporting its columns. Elevated above ground and reached by ladder or notched plank, its thatched roof slopes down to floor level. Contemporary Filipino architects are returning to bamboo as a viable material for 'green' design: it is cheap and flexible, with great tensile strength. Some varietals of bamboo can even grow to maturity within three to four months.

Rumah Adat and *Marapu* of Indonesia's Sumbanese Vernacular

Yenny Gunawan

Geography/Climate and Culture

In the case of an indigenous people such as the Sumbanese of the island of Sumba in eastern Indonesia, one must first understand their belief system before extracting the ecological knowledge from it.

Such knowledge is embodied in the belief system of indigenous societies; as the natural and social scientist Fikret Berkes writes, traditional ecological knowledge is 'a cumulative body of knowledge and beliefs, handed down through generations by cultural transmission, about the relationship of living beings (including humans) with one another and with their environment'.[1]

The Sumbanese belief system is known as *marapu* – a term with several meanings, including 'the respected', 'the deified', 'the hidden', 'the crystallized' and 'the accomplished'.[2] Sumba's traditional leaders understand it as the hidden and the sacred, but its many diverse meanings are connected to the way in which *marapu* perceives everything in the world: humans, animals, plants, earth, material/matter, water, and so on. *Marapu* does not focus on one deity but identifies the sacred quality of a thing, and its goal is to keep that sacred characteristic as it is by managing human attitudes and behaviours. These attitudes materialize in, for instance, prohibitions on felling trees in certain forests; restrictions on burning certain fields; and regulations forbidding defecation and urination in the sea, lakes and rivers but allowing them in forests.[3] In following this system, the Sumbanese believe that they will gain happiness and prevent misfortune or disaster.

These attitudes and behaviour lead – simultaneously yet unconsciously – to a balanced and harmonious state between humans and their environment.[4] Wildlife may therefore live undisturbed, cattle may eat the grasses, the water stays pure and effluent becomes fertilizer in the forest. Apparently, the ecological knowledge contained in *marapu* emphasizes appreciation and respect towards Sumba island's environment with its dry tropical climate, three- to four-month average rainy season, temperatures ranging from 29 to 31°C (84 to 88°F) and its deeply riven plateaus covering an area of 11,500 sq km (4,400 sq miles).

Below Ratenggaro village in the Kodi district of western Sumba has a three-layered concentric arrangement, with houses in the outer ring, tombstones in the middle and an open central field for rituals.

Opposite Not yet clad with thatch, this view of a *rumah adat* reveals its principal structure of bamboo. This fast-growing and easily accessible building material is ideal for constructing Sumba's precipitous vernacular dwellings.

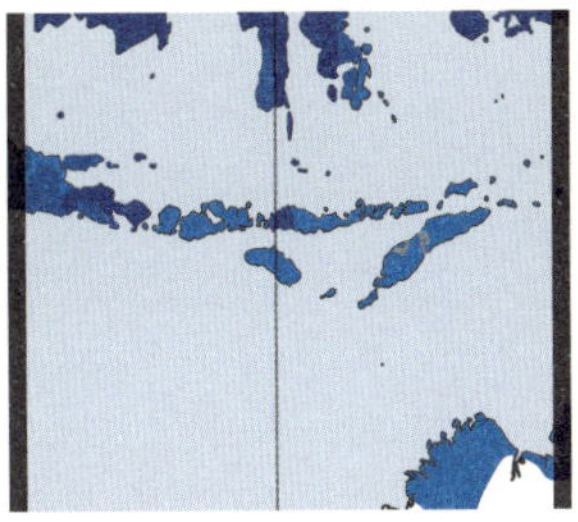

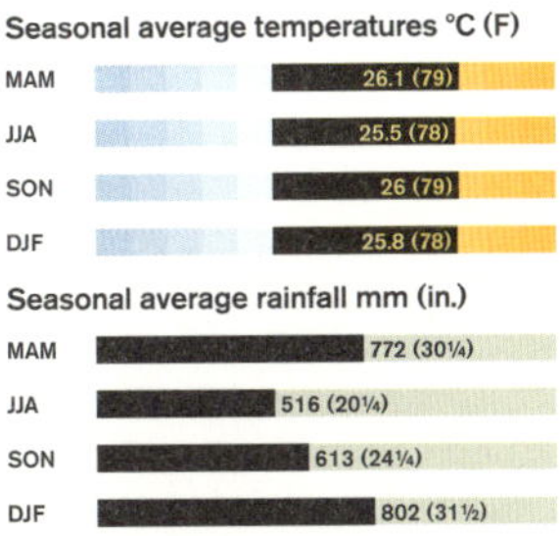

Opposite Though structurally similar to the *rumah adat* of Sumba's coast, wall structures in mountain homes have more closely spaced bamboo rods to prevent wind penetration.

Right The central tower-like roofs of the *rumah adat* – here seen in Sodan village, Sumba island – allow the evacuation of smoke and heat from the constantly burning fire beneath it.

Materials and Building Plan/Form

Certain attitudes and behaviours indicate traditional ecological knowledge in the Sumbanese vernacular house, the *rumah adat*, with its tower-like roof form. The first apparent suggestion of this is the slight difference in its bamboo walls depending on the location of the village in question. Houses in coastal villages, such as Ratenggaro in the northwest, have fewer walls than those in hill settlements, such as Sodan, central Indonesia. Although all these dwelling walls are made from bamboo rods, those in Sodan's houses have a denser arrangement of those rods in order to prevent the cold wind from entering the house. In Ratenggaro, by contrast, wall arrangements are more open on two sides of the house, allowing the wind to move freely.

The second such indication lies in the choice of materials with regard to their availability and regeneration. On Sumba, bamboo, grass and reeds are plentiful. The Sumbanese therefore choose to use the most abundant and fast-growing materials: bamboo for the majority of building components, from roof structures to walls and floors; and reeds for the roof thatch. The use of nails is forbidden, so the bamboo is bundled together using thin roots or rattan (*Calameae*). This way, any dilapidated bamboo or thatch is easily removed (typically, every five to seven years) without affecting the adjacent good material. Large trees (of *kalimbi* wood – *Carissa carandus*), which are rarer and take longer to grow than bamboo, are used only for main structures: the posts and beams. In some coastal villages – Ratenggaro included – most beams are of coconut wood (*Cocos nucifera*) because the larger trees common in hill villages are rarer here. These structural timbers are also jointed without nails, which likewise facilitates occasional change of components. Other materials used include limestone, for foundations and tombs. Limestone is available all over Sumba, since the island is made up of deep plateaus 'composed primarily of sandstone and mudstone with some igneous intrusions overlain by recent limestone'.[5] Unlike the more ephemeral bamboos and timbers, stone is typically only used once in the life of a building, which can be handed down from one generation to another. This attitude towards materials, combined with the Sumbanese habit of cattle rearing but not hunting, and only rarely fishing for food, contributes to the island's protected ecosystem.

The third attitude is related to the Sumbanese convention that a fire in the dwelling should be lit at all times, and should be neither too big nor too small. The fire is located in the kitchen, in the centre of the house, directly below its tower-like roof form; a timber box, for storing and preserving food, hangs above the fire. The lit fire creates hot air in the kitchen, which vents through the tower roof and is replaced by cooler air from other parts of the house. This process continues throughout the day, creating good-quality ventilation inside the dwelling. Living spaces surround the kitchen, and are raised approximately a metre (3 ft) above ground level. They are divided into several rooms, which are distinguished by the further variation of floor levels for different activities. Lower floors are for receiving guests and youngsters; higher floors are for private activities, such as the daily household round of eating, sleeping (with different areas for female and male occupants), and meetings of elders and leaders – as well as for ancestral *marapu* spirits. These raised floors are made of bamboo rods arranged with a 10 mm (⅜ in) gap between them, allowing occupants to see their livestock (cattle, pigs and chickens) below as well as letting the wind penetrate, keeping the bamboo dry. The wall and floor construction combined with the arrangement of the tower-like roof form, the living spaces and the kitchen with its lit fire therefore contribute to the creation of a permanent, comfortable breeze. Temperatures inside the *rumah adat* are typically around 22–24°C (71–75°F), 6–7°C (42–44°F) lower than those outside the house.

The Sumbanese *rumah adat* produced by the aforementioned traditional ecological knowledge is therefore both adaptive to and sustainable within Sumba's natural environment. This knowledge constitutes an 'intuitive wisdom in which life was organized around a highly refined awareness of the environment'.[6] It is therefore essential that the traditional ecological knowledge that existed in many vernacular societies' belief systems is handed down in this changing and developing world – not necessarily as belief systems in themselves, but as an enduring way of seeing and respecting nature.

Aboriginal Structures of Tropical Australia

Timothy O'Rourke

Geography/Climate and Culture

Aboriginal people in the wet tropics region of Australia developed a distinctive vernacular architecture influenced by the climate and the materials sourced from their diverse rainforest environments. Located along 360 km (220 miles) of the northeastern Queensland coast, the region is defined by its mosaic of tropical ecosystems and a contiguous range of mountains that rise abruptly from the narrow coastal plain and contribute to the region's high and intense rainfall.

Prior to European colonization in the late 19th century, the relatively dense population of Aboriginal groups identified by their clan and dialect: linguists estimated at least twenty-seven dialects for the region. Across the landscape, a network of walking tracks connected campsites, ceremonial sites and economic resources. Habitual campsites were located near watercourses on the edges of clearings that were maintained by Aboriginal fire regimes. People changed camp locations and moved between camps for economic, climatic and sociocultural reasons, with clan groups owning well-defined estates. Their shelters varied in form and size, but the semi-permanent wet-season dwelling was a domical type made from flexible hardwood saplings.

Construction Techniques

The primary structure of these shelters was based on two or more semicircular arches made from pairs of thin, carefully selected saplings, 15 to 20 mm (⅝ to ¾ in) in diameter. The opposing saplings, sharpened at the basal end, were driven into pre-dug holes, bent into an arched form, intertwined and lashed. Lashings were preferably heat-treated split rattan (*Calamus caryotoides*), but could also be bark twine (*Ficus* spp. for example), leaves (*Lomandra* spp.) or vines. Starting at the rear, single saplings were driven into the holes made around the elliptical or circular plan, and bent over and lashed to the parallel arches. Additional diagonal bracing and secondary framing members (for which purposes rattan canes were also used) created a pre-tensioned rigid lattice structure.

This structural system and the flexibility of the claddings allowed for considerable variation in building plan shape and size, as attested by archival records. Larger dwellings were above head height at the apex (about 1.8 m [6 ft] tall) and, by extending the number of arches, a longer vaulted form could house larger groups – up to twenty people according to historical accounts. These residences could be extended to accommodate household changes, and records describe closely spaced dwellings connected by passages. The historical evidence suggests that these structures were occupied throughout the extended wet season, and perhaps reoccupied over several years. Enclosed dwellings all contained at least one fire, which kept the interior dry and improved the longevity of the building fabric. A permanent wet-season dwelling would take a couple of people one or two days to build, but smaller, more transient shelters could be erected in a matter of hours using the same structural system.

Materials

Cladding varied according to the availability and proximity of material to campsites. Different types of palm leaves, bark, grasses and reeds were used as thatch. Leaves of the rattan *C. moti* – a climbing palm widespread in the rainforest – shared the same name, *mija*, as the generic word for shelter and camp in one rainforest language. Fan palm (*Licuala ramsayi* subsp. *ramsayi*) and *C. moti* leaves were used in overlapping layers and tied to the structural frame. Blady grass (*Imperata cylindrica*), which grew in the rainforest clearings, was sorted into bundles and tied to the frame in order to produce a weatherproof thatch. Used in thick layers, palm leaves and blady grass were noted for their capacity to insulate dwellings in cold weather. Sheets of myrtle bark (*Melaleuca* spp.) were stripped from the larger trees on coastal plains and formed a durable and weathertight cladding, which could be reused for several seasons. Other types of palm leaves, barks and reeds were also used as cladding.

For disparate Aboriginal groups living in more rural areas, customary building practices persisted throughout the 20th century, with traditional dwellings still in use in the 1960s. In the 21st century, a relatively small number of people maintain the knowledge and building skills required to reconstruct traditional domical structures, which are used in cultural representations across the region.

Research and experimentation may yield further applications for some of these traditional building materials and technologies. Underexplored materials include many species of Australian rattan, which are abundant and grow quickly, and which may adapt well to climate change.

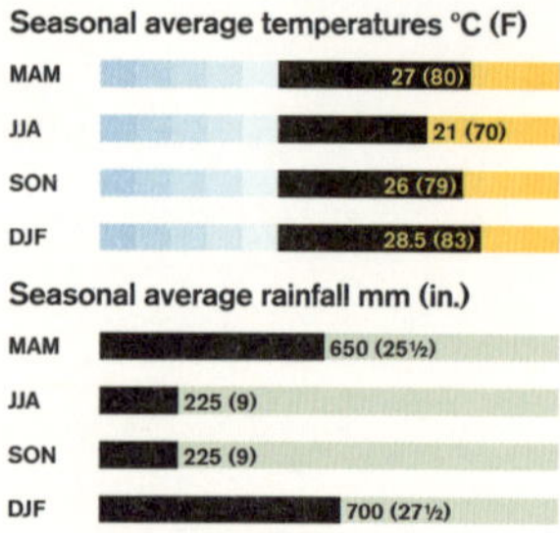

Opposite top left Historical image of Aboriginals erecting shelter from forest materials, Australia. The shelters varied in height and girth depending on the type and availability of plants nearby.

Opposite Drawing on readily available natural materials from the rainforests of northeastern Queensland, the envelope of Aboriginal shelters was principally formed of leaves, such as fan palms, blady grass, or less frequently, myrtle tree bark. These coverings sat above a framework of saplings to produce a weatherproof thatch.

Longhouses and Korowai Treehouses of New Guinea

Below Photographer and adventurer Frank Hurley's image of Dubu Daima longhouse in Kaimare, c. 1921 (left). Hurley described the houses as having 'superior workmanship'; the structures he observed are clearly seen in this arched construction, raised off the ground and built with timbers lashed with cane and vine (right).

Opposite top Papuan longhouses are enclosed by a thatched roof of sago palm leaves, as seen in this 1920s photograph.

Opposite bottom Interior of an Abelam men's cult house in Abangai village, East Sepik Province (left). The façade is composed of paintings on palm spathes, which are joined together on the ground and then raised and fastened to the front of the house (right).

Seasonal average temperatures °C (F)

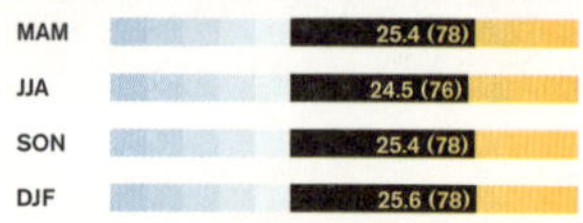

Seasonal average rainfall mm (in.)

Lissant Bolton

Geography/Climate

People have lived on the island of New Guinea for around 55,000 years.[1] The island's linguistic complexity (around 1,000 languages are spoken) is matched by its environmental and cultural diversity. With a spine of high mountains, large rivers, coastal plains, grasslands, swamps and rainforests, there is a wide variety of different environmental contexts in which people have developed different ways of living and building. Since the late 20th century, the island has been divided politically into the independent nation of Papua New Guinea in the east, and the easternmost provinces of Indonesia (often called West Papua) in the west.

Materials

Before colonial and post-colonial times – which brought corrugated iron, concrete and other materials – the peoples of New Guinea utilized bush materials such as wood, leaves and cane in order to produce a great diversity of vernacular architectural forms. These include many different kinds of domestic structures, articulated alongside other buildings in diverse village and hamlet layouts. In a country where people spend a lot of time out of doors (or on verandas or in roofed shelters), these village buildings are sometimes arranged together like rooms in a large house. Kinship relationships as well as land ownership may determine where each dwelling is sited. Inland, especially in the hills, houses are often built directly on the ground. On the coast, they may be built on stilts, in some cases over water or tidal areas, so that people move from house to house in canoes. Some have enclosing walls; others are open, with oversailing roofs that sweep down to the earth.

Construction Techniques

The diversity encountered in New Guinea's vernacular architecture is as much a function of social and cultural arrangements as of the environment. In the Gulf of Papua, whole Gogodala communities used to live together in a longhouse 100 m (330 ft) or more in length, each built on a rise of land in the swamps at the mouth of the Aramaia River. Structurally, each longhouse consisted of an arched roof set over a platform, the platform itself being nearly 2 m (6 ft) above the ground. It was built from timbers lashed with cane and vines, and thatched with sago-palm (*Cycas revoluta*) leaves – the roofing material commonly used throughout New Guinea. Internally, it was divided into a long central chamber for the men and boys (with sleeping platforms above the central hall) and a series of two-storey cubicles to the sides, which were occupied by the women and young children. Fireplaces were set on mud slabs on the floor, the smoke helping to drive away mosquitoes. Photographer Frank Hurley, visiting a longhouse at Uladu village in 1922, recorded that 'everywhere superior worksmanship was evident. . .uprights plumb and joists level. The floor, which was made of slats of goru palm overlaying close joists, was as solid as earth.' Hurley added that views from the door of the house 'were beyond beautiful'.[2]

Building Plan/Form

In small-scale societies where everyone is known to one another, people often create differences between themselves and mark them by restrictions on relationships and on movement. Commonly, New Guinea societies emphasize the distinction between genders, and certain buildings are restricted to certain categories of men or women. In some villages, dwellings are arranged around a large ceremonial house of some kind – often a cult or spirit house, which only initiated men can enter. Men might sleep in the ceremonial houses, while women and children live in the domestic structures. These ceremonial houses are often decorated inside and out with carvings and painting. Along the Gulf of Papua coastline, for example, large ceremonial houses consisting of an arched roof enclosing a platform stored painted boards, and were hung with large, painted masks. The men of the community sat and slept in the cool darkness inside the house, among these spiritually powerful objects.

By contrast, the Abelam in the hills north of the Sepik River decorate the soaring triangular façade of their ceremonial or spirit house with red-, yellow-, black- and white-painted bark panels, fitted together. These buildings are set directly on the ground. The ridge pole of the house supports the roof from the apex of the house front to the ground at the back, and the roof, clad with sago-palm thatching, slopes from the ridge to the ground on either side. The façade is painted and constructed on the ground, and then lifted as a single unit to fit the front of the house. The building is used in a series of male initiation rituals; inside, carved and painted figures and bark paintings line the walls. The spirit houses are built on the central plaza of a village, itself set on a ridge in the hills. Around the plaza are the smaller, domestic structures of the villagers.

Below and opposite A Korowai family's tree house located in a small, isolated clearing, West Papua. The lofty dwelling usually lasts for around one year and is accessed by a ladder; its height is believed to provide the family with protection from spirits of the forest.

New Guinea stilt houses or tree houses have often captured the popular imagination. They used to be made by the Koiari people on the south coast of Papua New Guinea, and are still made by the Korowai in West Papua. The Koiari built their tree houses high above ordinary dwellings, at least in part for protection in warfare. While the Korowai sometimes erect very high tree houses, their dwellings are generally built 8 to 12 m (26 to 39 ft) above ground level in a cleared area of forest. The house platform is supported by a base of cropped trees, and the walls and a roof are built on that base. The Korowai rarely build houses together; rather, they build a family dwelling in a clearing apart from other homes. They fear spiritual horrors that inhabit the forest, and the houses provide elevated protection for them. These houses rarely last more than a year, so that each household will build a new one annually. The history of people's lives is recorded through the sequence of houses in which they have lived, each dwelling being named and remembered by the species of tree that served as its main support.[3]

If people nowadays incorporate introduced materials in their buildings, they also still make substantial use of traditional bush materials. The single most significant introduction, apart from the use of imported tools, is that of nails: traditional bindings are now rarely used in construction. In urban contexts, people often create dwellings from any kind of material that is available – including corrugated iron and plastic sheeting. Ceremonial houses no longer tend to be built, while churches are often constructed from concrete, corrugated iron and glass. But a great diversity of largely local dwelling houses are still built across the island, and arranged together in the light of kinship and other social arrangements.

Micronesia's *Bai*, *Ulitao*, *Pebaye*, Katelu and Stone Constructions

Karen Nero

Geography/Climate

The more than 2,000 small islands of Micronesia form a series of chained island groups, with highly humid temperatures averaging 27°C (80°F) and reaching roughly 36°C (97°F). All lie within the 'West Pacific Warm Pool', and according to marine biologist Sylvia Earle, surface temperatures in this region that are greater than 28°C (82°F) affect planetary circulation patterns.[1] The Northwest Pacific is the most active region of the pool, forming tropical cyclones in the northern summer.[2] The high continental Marianas and Palau were settled from Island South East Asia (ISEA) by at least c. 1500 until 1250 BCE; the remaining high, volcanic islands were settled from offshore Near Oceania (c. 100–200 CE); and the predominantly coral atolls as late as 1000 CE.[3] All are vulnerable to droughts, typhoons and changing sea levels, and Micronesians have long relied upon mutual aid from neighbouring islanders, thereby forging a cultural area.[4]

Construction Techniques and Building Plan/Form

The Palauan *Bai*

One form of Micronesian vernacular – and a monumental one at that – can be seen in the earth-and-stone architecture of Palau's meeting houses. Erected on stone or coral platforms, these community structures are usually used by men. Earthwork terraces and platforms covered 20 per cent of Palau's main island by 750 BCE, when Palauans began to build massive and elaborate stone architecture on coastal step-terrace foundations. These were indicative of increased sociopolitical hierarchies and warfare.[5]

When the British East Indian packet ship *Antelope* was wrecked on Koror's outer reef in 1783, the village of Koror was already well established, with stone piers, docks, paths and large stone platforms on which highly decorated chiefly meeting houses (*bai*) were constructed. These were documented by the ship's officers and illustrators during their three-month stay.[6] The central village of Koror is one of two paramount chieftaincies that were then solidifying their power. Today's main roads follow Koror's early stone pathways, which are depicted in historical views leading to the dock and allied villages visible in the background. Watercolours from 1783, and from a return visit in 1790, also documented ornate meeting houses.[7]

We know that Palauan village councils contracted other village's men's clubs to construct large buildings for them – off-site, in order to protect from insect damage – using precise carpentry techniques with shell tools.[8] The high gables and internal beams are decorated with black, white, red and yellow bas-relief paintings. This style was a late arrival, 'brought by the gods from under the sea', that shows ongoing links to Toraja and Batak decoration and design.[9] After assembly of the *bai* on its stone platform, its thatched roof and sides are lashed together only at the ridgeline. In the event of a typhoon, these lashings are cut, causing the sides to slide down; the rafter poles, which are embedded in the ground serve to protect the decorated building. Openings at the apexes of the gables permit the residing deity (and hot air) to depart.

Of these traditional meeting houses, only the ancient Bai-ra-Irrai (near the centre of Irrai village on the island) survived the Second World War and recent typhoons – and that only by being disassembled and hidden in a cave. Nonetheless, *bai* continue to provide the design and some principles of indigenous construction for innovative community and national buildings. In the 1950s, an unprecedented nationwide 'twin' *bai*, with four gables representing Palau's senior villages, was designed and built by national elders, with an enclosed museum and open meeting area. Destroyed by a major typhoon, it was followed by a gabled cement 'national' *bai* and then the Belau National Museum example.

Traditional *bai* are still being constructed, such as the prestigious example recently assembled on the traditional hillside stone platform of the Melekeok paramount chieftaincy on Babeldaob Island.

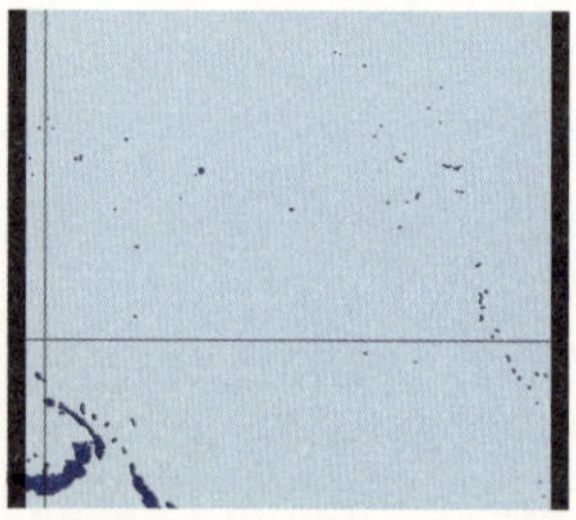

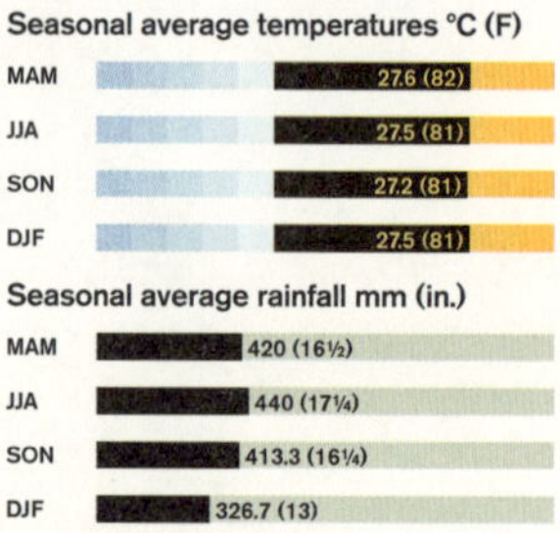

Opposite top Exterior of the steep-roofed council house, or *bai*, of chiefs on Koror, Republic of Palau, 1921 (left). Painted murals on the façades are a significant feature and tell mythical narratives (right).

Opposite bottom Meeting houses form the heart of villages, such as this sole surviving example, Bai-ra-Irrai, a sacred 200-year-old *bai* in southern Babeldaob, Palau. Its thatched roof and sides are pre-assembled and secured with lashing along the ridge, which can be simply cut, releasing the thatch from the structure in the event of a typhoon.

The *Ulitao* of the Mariana Islands

By around 1200 CE, the Chamorros of the Mariana Islands also developed monumental stone architecture.[10] This fact is well known from the ruins of two embedded parallel lines of limestone or volcanic stone pillars, with hemispherical capstones, that once supported the roof of their large *ulitao* houses – used for meetings and to protect their fast sailing canoes. Today, only these stone fragments remain,[11] after disastrous depopulation and lengthy colonial transformations. Long-term phosphate mining has also played a part in destroying the built heritage of Nauru and the Banaba Islands.

The *Pebaye* of the Yap Islands

The high-gabled *pebaye* meeting houses of the Yap Island group are supported by massive turmeric-painted wooden pillars. These are lashed together and decorated with intricate patterns that encode their histories in a similar way to the paintings of Palau, with which these islands have always had close relationships. Stately dances are performed on the large stone platforms of the house, where stone money is displayed.

The Meeting Houses and Canoe Houses of the Outer Islands

The Katelu sacred men's meeting house is ancient, built on rock posts and the only such example still existing on the Outer Islands (the collective term for the inhabited nine atolls and two islands of Yap). The decline in these sacred houses may be attributed to increasing storms and to the local rise of the Catholic Church.[12]

Throughout the Micronesian atolls, much of the cultural focus is on these islands' long-distance voyagers and their deep V-shaped asymmetrical canoes with aerodynamically designed outriggers. These were traditionally housed in a series of high thatched canoe houses along the shore, which now serve as male community centres.

Canoe houses, built right on the shoreline, are very vulnerable to high tides and typhoons. Traditionally, they would be tied to the ground with strong ropes, in case the need arose for 'putting down' the entire house to provide the least resistance while sheltering the occupants inside from devastating winds. A small door or escape hatchway would be built into the gable end at high level in case the waves generated by a typhoon threatened to trap and drown the occupants inside.[13]

Clockwise from top left Ancient columns preserved at House of Taga archaeological site, Guam; turmeric-painted wooden pillars support a traditional *pebaye* meeting house at Yap Island, Yap State; traditional items of Yap stone currency were historically displayed on stone ceremonial platforms; an example of the vernacular tall thatched structure for canoe storage in Micronesia; traditional closed-sided, thatch-roofed sacred houses such as this example in Yap Island have become increasingly rare.

Above The ancient city of Nan Madol, Pohnpei, was built upon flat, man-made islets and served as the ceremonial and political centre for the upper echelons of society.

Left and far left Columns of prismatic basalt form the ramparts of Nan Madol, such as this altar or tomb in the ruined Sun Temple (right).

The Stone Vernacular of Pohnpei and Kosrae

Another example of Micronesia's masonry vernacular, the Nan Madol site on the island of Pohnpei includes ninety-two man-made islets that were built up on the reef flat with large basalt borders and 'logs' in an enclosed area 1.5 x 0.5 km (1 x 0.3 miles) in extent.[14] Nan Madol was constructed mainly after 1100, and was, until roughly 1500, the ritual and residential centre of Pohnpei for society's highest-ranking members, including special islands for dancing and preparing *sakau* (a kind of kava).[15] The largest island enclosure is Nan Douwas, a ritual centre that nowadays is covered by fruiting breadfruit trees and medicinal trees and plants.

Pohnpei is also home to monumental subterranean earthworks, including trenches, mounds, stone walls and hilltop features – all of which are recorded in the island's oral histories. The trenches are now used to store disaster resources in case of major droughts or destructive typhoons. Two of these trenches, at the Salapwuk Settlement in Kiti, one of Pohnpei's five municipalities, measured roughly 23 m (75 ft) long by 5–15 m (15–50 ft) wide by 1 m (3 ft) deep. A second, Y-shaped trench measured roughly 20 m (65 ft) long by 10 m (33 ft) wide at the Y-juncture, with a variable depth reaching 1.5 m (5 ft).[16] A series of earthworks and stone features have also been identified throughout the surrounding area, the features of which appear to parallel examples found on other Micronesian islands such as Chuuk.

To the southeast of Pohnpei, a further monumental city is to be found at Lelu in the state of Kosrae. Lelu is similar to Nan Madol to the north, and both cities are currently under consideration for World Heritage Serial Cultural Site status. A watercolour based on Jules LeJeune's drawing during French explorer Louis Isidore Duperrey's visit to Kosrae in 1824 gives a rare view of the spectacular, tall meeting houses of this reef-flat man-made city, and a few of its inhabitants and visitors. Dense series of similar meeting houses would have adorned many of the impressive, but currently bare, stone platforms.

A traditional Kosraean meeting house has recently been constructed close to the high school and the Kosrae Historic Preservation Office and Kosrae Museum.

Chiefly Dwellings of the Marshall Islands

In the early 20th century, and presumably earlier, the dwelling of the highest ranking *iroij* (chief) of a Marshall Islands atoll served as the community meeting area, where people would gather outside to 'bring gifts and request favours, including healing' and receive food.[17]

The Meeting Houses of Kiribati

The traditional meeting houses of the island chains of Kiribati are found on each of the atolls today, albeit smaller than the *maneaba* (meeting houses) recorded by the artists on the Wilkes US Exploring Expedition.[18] The image shown appears to represent a much taller and more elaborately gabled roof construction than normal, but otherwise a typical (current or traditional) meeting house. Sizes vary by period and location.

Micronesian meeting houses have an affinity with Island Southeast Asian roof styles, and cognate words (*marae*, *bai*, *pebaye* – Oceanic and Micronesian words each meaning 'meeting house') demonstrate the deeply shared heritage of the Pacific region.

Right Residents gather before a steep-roofed, thatched village meeting house, or *maneaba*, to greet a British official, Gilbert Islands, Kiribati. Such meeting houses still exist but vary according to place and age; most are less elaborate and built at a smaller scale than this ceremonial example.

Navala and Lau *Bure* of Fiji

Charmaine 'Ilaiū Talei

Materials and Building Plan/Form

The 19th-century missionary Thomas Williams wrote, 'the form of the houses in Fiji is so varied, that a description of a building in one of the windward islands would give a very imperfect idea of those to leeward'.[1] Certainly, unlike that of other South Pacific societies, Fiji's vernacular architecture varies in form and materials from region to region – but it is epitomized in the *bure*, a typical wood and thatched home. Two earlier *bure* types remain prevalent as contemporary forms, and now apply new building materials. Firstly, there is the hipped-roof *bure*, as represented by Navala village in Ba province, Viti Levu. Secondly, there is the *bure* with rounded end walls and a curvaceous roof form, which is found in the Lau Islands and the southeastern islands of Fiji, and which was inspired by Tongan architecture.

Navala is a unique village because its inhabitants choose to build and live in *bure* in order to retain, among other things, their indigenous way of construction and living. The village consists of a chiefly *bure*; ordinary *bure*; a school; and a *rara*, or open communal area planned in a cross formation. It is home to approximately 1,000 people. Traditional builders from Navala are often requested at tourist resorts for rethatching or lashing internal furnishings. Normally they are subcontracted to rethatch the roof with local vegetation and lash the internal roof structure with coconut sennit, or *magimagi*, after certified modern builders have constructed a building's shell using contemporary materials.

A *bure* in this region is usually rectangular in plan with a central post supporting a hipped-roof structure. A particular decorative feature of Fijian vernacular architecture is the pair of ornamental fern trunks projecting from the ridge beam. The thatching is thick, and insulates the residents against both the heat and the cold of this mountainous area. Notwithstanding regional variations, the houses of Fiji normally sit on a *yavu*, or raised platform, made from compacted soil and dressed with local stones or boulders.

Opposite top Steep-roofed, enclosed wood and thatch huts, or *bure*, of the Navala village Viti Levu (left). Woven walls such as this (right) form a traditional Navala house, which sits on a raised platform of stone, *yavu*, upon compacted earth.

Right Fiji's vernacular varies according to the island's topography, but houses of Navala village are still built using traditional methods. This includes a thickly thatched roof that protects from both hot and cool temperatures in the mountainous region.

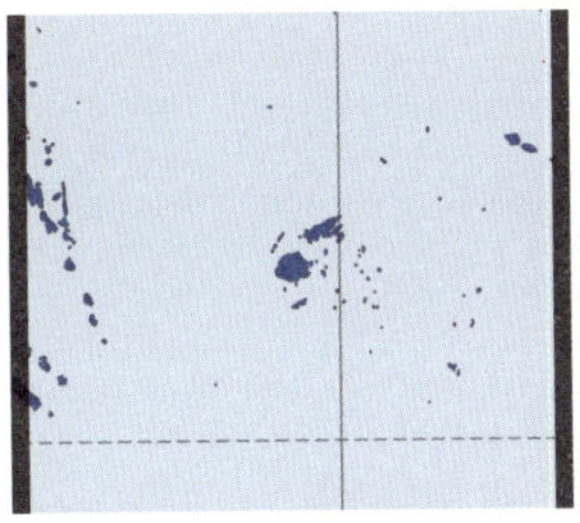

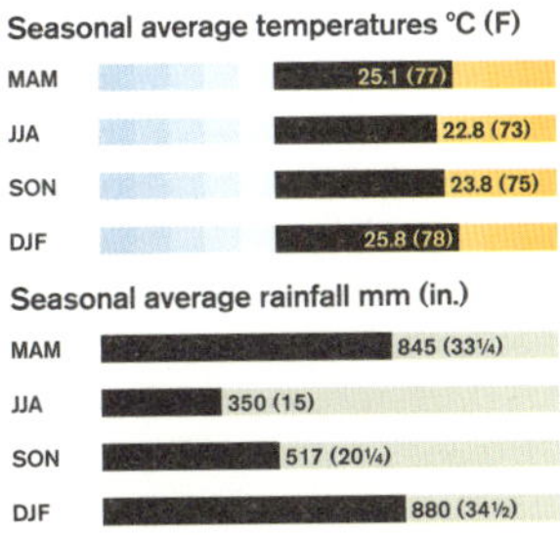

Opposite On the Lau group of islands, the Fijian *bure* is seen in its variation with rounded ends.

Below Despite the introduction of synthetic thatch, traditional methods of thatching are maintained thanks to high tourist demand; Lau people are here engaged in the vernacular technique at Lakeba Island.

The Lau group of Fijian islands constitutes a region influenced culturally by neighbouring Tongans, who arrived in the late 18th century and settled on various islands, including the chiefly Lakeba Island. For this reason, the form and material technology of the Tongan *fale* were appropriated by the Lauan people. (The *fale* is a traditional building with rounded ends and a curved roof.) Like its Tongan equivalent, the Lauan *bure* today uses contemporary building materials, such as corrugated iron as a roofing material and various modern wall claddings.

The establishment and success of tourism in Fiji have continued to perpetuate these two vernacular building forms. The contemporary tourist *bure* expands the original's architectural canon in its form, function, material palette and linguistic meaning. More than any other traditional material and technology, thatching and *magimagi* continue to adorn these contemporary *bure* – thereby perpetuating traditional craftsmanship and providing an avenue for learning and training for younger Fijian men. However, when replanting of thatching materials, such as the sago palm (*Cycas revolute*), is not factored into the *bure*'s maintenance, the raw plants can become non-renewable; a good plant management strategy is crucial.

Synthetic thatching, available locally, provides an alternative and appears 'traditional'. However, since synthetic thatching materials require different installation specifications and less maintenance, it can be anticipated that traditional *bure* craftsmanship and technologies will inevitably fade with the introduction of such innovations. Certainly, Fiji's *bure* is an evolving architecture, and one that has grown from village traditions to local contemporary architects' treatments; and depending on where one is in Fiji, one can witness its various stages of transformation.

Timber and Palm Vernacular of Tonga

Below The *fale* floor finishes and coverings are made from *Pandanus*, and call on the ancient knowledge of harvest, preparation and weaving techniques. The fale wall coverings are evident in historical photographs like this one.

Opposite top *Fale* share the principal base construction of four posts but roof structures vary: sections show the *faka-Manuka* type (left) and the *faka-Tonga* (right).

Opposite bottom A contemporary Tongan landscape with vernacular *fale* built from modern housing materials; this approach is becoming more prevalent.

Charmaine 'Ilaiū Talei

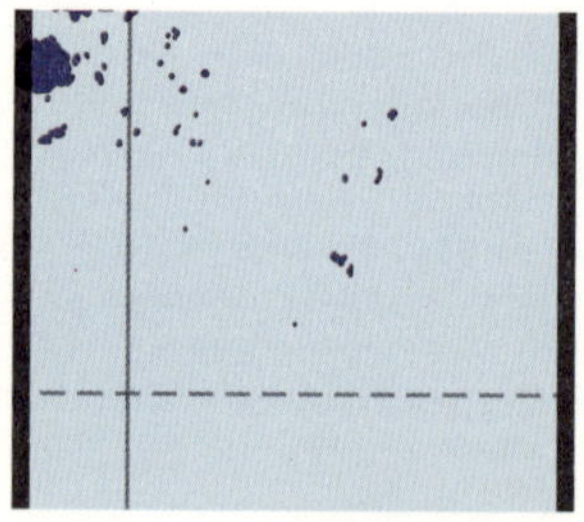

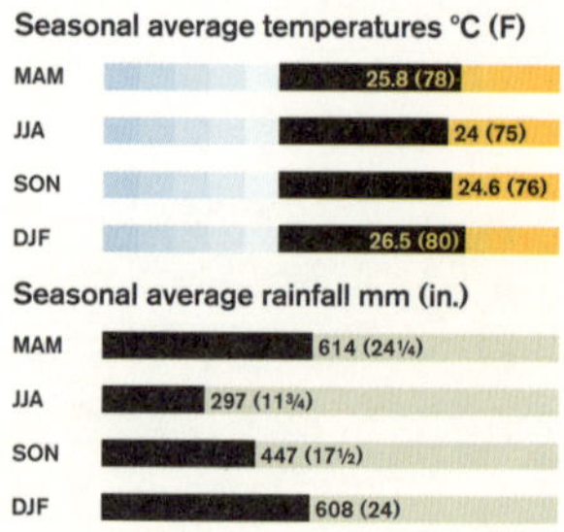

Geography/Climate and Culture

The Kingdom of Tonga is one of the remaining monarchies in the South Pacific, with an archipelago that spreads 360,000 sq km (140,000 sq miles) across the Pacific Ocean. Its vernacular architecture is typically understood as the *fale* Tonga. According to early engravings of Tonga there were several *fale* forms. However, explorers such as Captain James Cook contributed to the idealized descriptions of early residential *fale* as a building usually with rounded ends and a curved roof. Up until the 1970s, this traditional *fale* Tonga constituted the kingdom's homogeneous vernacular, and was found across its entire island chain.

Materials

Such buildings have traditionally used local materials: coconut-palm (*Cocos nucifera*) fronds for thatching and various floor coverings; coconut wood for small and flexible roof members; other, stronger local timbers, like 'ironwood', for structural posts and beams; and *Pandanus* for floor finishes and coverings. *Sennit* lashings tied the roof junctions, which portrayed genealogies and mythology important to resident families.

Construction Techniques

The idealized *fale* Tonga displayed two main structural roof configurations, the *fale faka-Tonga* and the *fale faka-Manuka*. The latter had three angled struts, while the former had a vertical post supported along a beam. In earlier times, the chiefly families built their homes in the distinguished style of the *fale faka-Manuka*.

A *fale* Tonga was enclosed by three types of thatching, using an assortment of braiding and weaving techniques of coconut fronds. The *pola* thatch was woven for wall linings and roofing. The *pola faka-tefisi* was plaited and then applied on the ridge capping like a type of flashing, pinned down to the roof members. The coverings over door and window openings were woven as *pola faka-ha 'atuia*. These thatching techniques – particularly the first- and last-named – are still seen today on temporary buildings in the bush, or on outdoor kitchens. Tongans who have lived in a traditional fibrous *fale* Tonga remember that the *fale*'s interior was cool when it was hot outside and warm when cold – highlighting the climatic prospects of the *fale*'s original thatching methods.

Building Plan/Form

The oval floor plan of the *fale* Tonga was often divided into three sections – the rounded ends being private sleeping spaces, called *leke* by locals, and the centre forming a multifunctional sitting space for more public occasions. The curvaceous roof proved aerodynamic during cyclones and strong windy seasons. People recall huddling together under their curved roof, which would be unlashed and pulled down from its posts by the men of the family, and held down around the edges while the women and children bunkered inside. Today, elements of the traditional *fale* Tonga are expressed in a range of contemporary

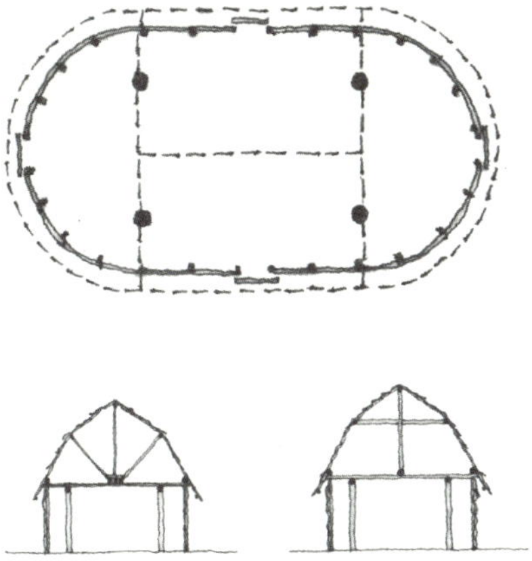

structures, from churches and school halls to government and commercial buildings. Sometimes the form of the building is maintained and imported materials replace the earlier fibrous thatchings and floor coverings. Regardless of such evolutions, Tongans continue to live and treat these new spaces like the traditional *fale*.

There are environmental features of the traditional *fale* Tonga that suggest potential sustainable features for Tongan contemporary *fale*. For example, the use of locally sourced materials is a project explored by the Queensland government's 'Cocowood' research project, which aims to harvest ageing palms in South Pacific countries in order to produce veneers and timber for architectural purposes. In recent years, Tonga has continued to be devastated by cyclones and strong winds, which have destroyed homes, crops and livelihoods. Perhaps the traditional *fale*'s curvaceous roof provides a historically tested architectural form that can help to address such modern concerns.

The 'Big Roof' of the Cook Islands

Opposite top left Lofty 'big roof' architecture is a motif of vernacular Cook buildings and is culturally and environmentally important. Decorative roof timbers, such as this detail at Titikaveka, Rarotonga, are prevalent.

Opposite middle and right The hillside town of Avarua in Rarotonga was a site of colonial expansion. In the hot and wet climate, the most usable part of the imported bungalow form was the sheltered, cool veranda.

Opposite bottom The oldest remaining buildings in the Cook Islands are formed of lime-plastered coral constructions, such as this example of the Oneroa Sunday School, Mangaia.

Jeanette Budgett and Jeremy Treadwell

Geography/Climate and Culture

The Cook Islands, a scene of British colonial expansion throughout the 19th century, experienced the loss of its vernacular architectural traditions almost immediately upon contact with the European incomers. In an architectural technique introduced by British missionaries, and flourishing from the 1820s to the 1890s, coral was collected from the islands' reefs and used as rubble stone or burned to make lime plaster. The missionaries, most without any formal architectural training, attempted to recreate images of 19th-century Britain. Their early buildings often failed, their efforts for controlled order frequently undone by torrential tropical downpours. Traditional carving and the use of *sennit* (coconut-fibre) lashings found their way into mission-period architecture, and the resulting buildings were compelling hybrids of Cook Island and colonial influence. Today the remaining handful of coral churches, Sunday schools and cottages are the oldest buildings in the Cook Islands.[1]

Materials and Construction Techniques

With the arrival of the British Protectorate in 1891, a shift to timber-frame construction overtook coral techniques and further displaced traditional Cook Island building practices. Timber-framed bungalows, which housed the British and New Zealand colonial agents, had their architectural origins within the wider British Empire. In the Cook Islands, they constituted a form of second-tier colonial vernacular. With the extension and elongation of the veranda, the formal interior rooms of these early houses became progressively enclosed and dysfunctional. The resulting darkness and heat were not relieved by the fanlight windows that adorned every opening. Meanwhile, the veranda, shadowed and open to the breeze, was ultimately to provide the main living space of the house. This type of housing, while problematic in many ways, persisted in part because of the durability of its materials and – eventually – because of its re-imaging within a touristic and historical iconography.

Coral is no longer used as a building material in the Cook Islands, and there are sound arguments against erecting massive-walled structures in this part of the world. With regard to environmental performance, the climate is hot and wet, making ventilation of prime importance. Traditionally, cooling (and drying out) was achieved by sea breezes, which filtered through woven walls of reed. By contrast, the old coral churches achieved coolness by virtue of their spacious interior volumes and thickly thatched roofs.

In the 1990s and early years of the 21st century, the Cook Islands have continued to be prone to a form of 'globalized' architecture. Indicators of this condition include a preoccupation with the familiar tropes of Modernism. A minimalist approach can be seen in many contemporary alterations to existing historical churches: flush, suspended ceilings close in their airy roof spaces and smooth, white surfaces replace the carved and painted timbers. Most recently, 'gifts' of glassy air-conditioned buildings by the Chinese government are appearing in the Cooks. They offer little from an environmentally sustainable perspective, and in terms of larger economic and political relations the sustainability discussion becomes complex.

Building Plan/Form

A noticeable feature of much Pacific architecture is the 'big roof'. In hotter places, the Pacific vernacular dispensed with walls altogether – as may be seen in the example of the Samoan *fale tele*. Both structural and ornamental detail proliferated in the interior roof spaces of the historical Cook Island churches. Crossing timbers, *sennit* lashing and carved surfaces affirmed the cultural significance of this vaulted space. The lofty roof – important in architectural, cultural and environmental terms – suggests a very different architectural preoccupation from the flat roof and ceiling that have become fashionable in the late 20th and early 21st centuries.

The pitched roof was famously suppressed in iconic Modernist architecture for most of the 20th century. It was regarded not just neutrally, but with an active suspicion. As Austrian-born Modernist architect Josef Frank once commented,

> it [the flat roof] ends the house at its top exactly where its functions end, without the addition of the unclear, irrational attic with its mysticism.[2]

Modernism thereby rejected the spatial roof, believing its shadowy ceiling void to be functionally superfluous. Yet fortunately, in the outer reaches of the Pacific, the pitched roof retains a persistent logic in the oceanic climate. In fact, in the last throes of Modernism, in the extremes of the tropical Pacific, the expansive pitched roof was made to work not as a simple reservoir for excess heat but as an active component for cooling in the schools built by New Zealand architects Angus, Flood and Griffiths between 1969 and 1976.[3]

Tourist accommodation in the islands frequently resorts to the air-conditioned chalet with sealed interiors, missing both architectural expression and the sensuousness of a tropical climate. While ample opportunities exist to explore the potential of coconut-frond roof thatch, coconut-husk lashings and woven *Pandanus* for interior linings, they are seemingly hampered by a preoccupation with the 'architecture of elsewhere'. The architectural culture of the Cook Islands continues to be largely run from New Zealand design offices, and it can be argued that locally relevant architecture will only develop here from Pacific architects trained to draw on their local and historical contexts.

The perceptually rich, formal possibilities of the big roof, which juxtapose exterior form and mass with interior volume, not only evoke a poetic history of tectonic association in the Pacific, but also promise a potential future of passively ventilated sustainable buildings, constructed under the expansive 'social roof' of a true Pacific vernacular architecture.

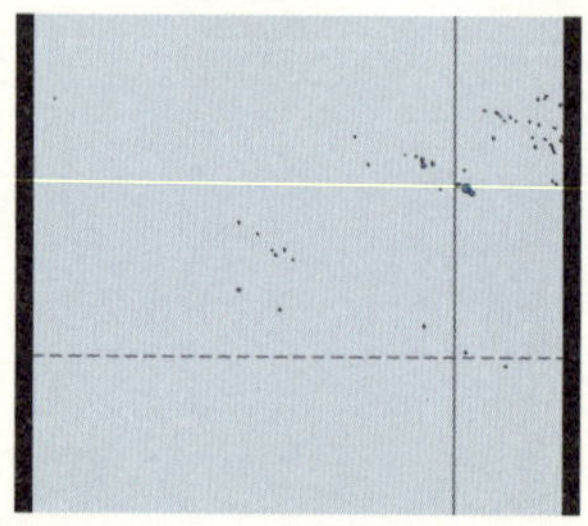

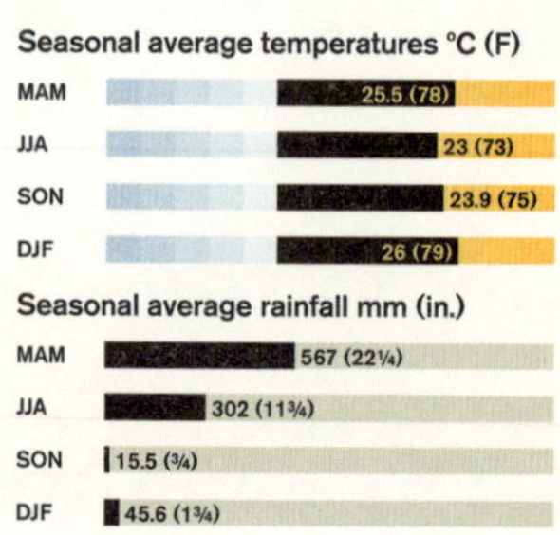

Fare and *Marae* Structures of French Polynesia

Anne E. Guernsey Allen

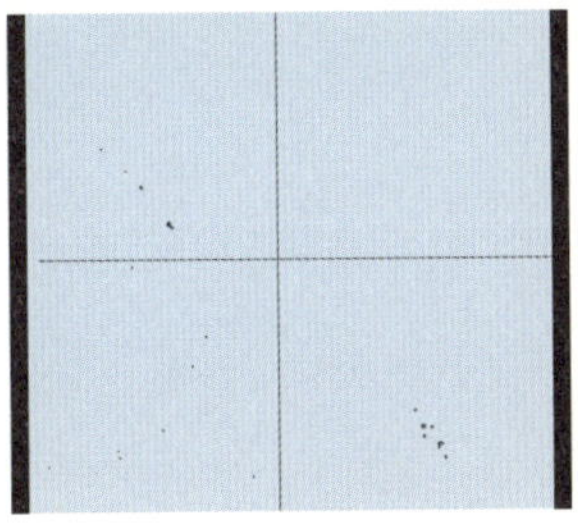

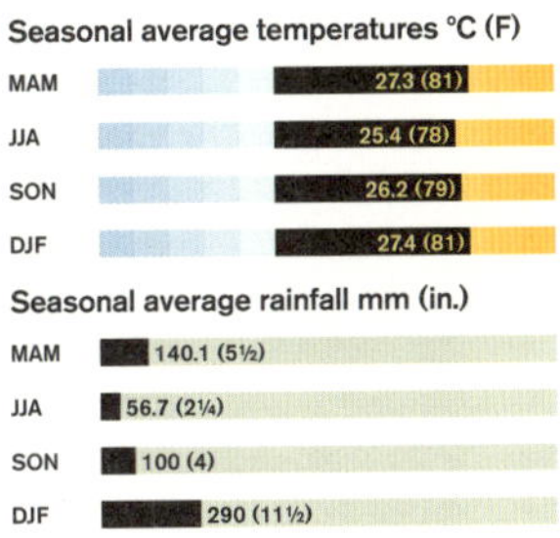

Opposite top Often single-room structures with curved ends, Tahitian *fare* were usually built with bamboo frames and thatched roofs of coconut leaf, *Pandanus* or grass.

Opposite middle Stone ceremonial platforms, or *marae*, and deeply thatched, raised houses, or *fare*, on the shore of Lake Fauna Nui, Maeva, Huahine Island.

Opposite bottom *Marae* at Kamuihei, Nuku Hiva (left) and Tahiti Nui (right) illustrate key principles of the construction. Built of stone particular to the local area – basalt, limestone, tuff, and sometimes coral – the open rectangular courts served political and religious purposes.

Materials and Construction Techniques

In Tahitian, *fare* means building. The island's pre-contact builders utilized local materials in their built vernacular: breadfruit (*Artocarpus altilis*), coconut (*Cocos nucifera*) and ironwood, among others – and sometimes bamboo (*Bambusoideae*) – which commonly formed the *fare* (house) and other structures. Coconut leaf, *Pandanus* or grass thatching were used to make up roof finishes. Although some mortise-work existed, most architectural members were lashed together using coconut-husk twine or bast strips. Builders used post-and-lintel technology, with a series of central posts in the Windward Islands to the east, and tie beams in the Leeward. Most structures sat directly on the ground, although a small number in hilly areas had stone platforms (*paepae*).

Building Plan/Form and Culture

Houses were generally single-room rectangular structures, most with rounded ends. Plaited coconut-leaf blinds provided protection from the elements. Movable bamboo latticework walls existed in the Leeward Islands, but were not common.

In contrast to *fare*, *marae* were constructed of local stone. These more permanent structures served various political–religious purposes. A *marae* comprises an open rectangular court, averaging 7.5 by 20 m (25 x 65 ft), faced with stones, and sometimes terraced. American anthropologist Kenneth Emory found that in the Windward Islands, these facings were made of small limestone, tuff and basalt pieces. In the west, squared, upright slabs of coral limestone were used, in part because of their ready availability. There were also upright stone backrests set into the pavement. At one end would be the *ahu*, a place reserved for the gods; only the priests, sanctified chiefs or carriers of the sculpted 'god-objects' were allowed to tread here. Stone or timber uprights marked the front and rear of this area. Nearby would be the *avaa*, or 'bed of the god', where sculptures were placed during ceremonies. Depending upon the size of the complex, there might be other small platforms or enclosures.

In the Society Islands, *marae* were linked to specific gods and chiefly families. In the late 18th century, they became more elaborate – a development that corresponded with increased social stratification and religious change. On Mo'orea, the oldest temples were relatively small and used only raw corals as facings. Later, the cutting and dressing of blocks becomes evident. *Marae* also began to increase in size, and a stepped variant of the *ahu* appeared. Builders began to use even-sized worked basalt cobbles in their walls. These changes appear to be connected to the rise of the 'Oro (god of war) cult that took root on the island of Ra'iatea, and which introduced new forms of sacred objects and rituals. Meanwhile the islands of Mo'orea and Tahiti were waging war for complete control of the archipelago. Large temples were first constructed on Mo'orea, starting around 1743. The *marae* of Maha'iatea on Tahiti, with its *ahu* of eleven *paepae*, was created just before the arrival of British sea captain James Cook in 1769. Local elites used these huge complexes in order to gain the support of divinities in their bid for absolute political power.

On visiting the Society Islands in 1769, Cook remarked: 'The houses or dwellings of these people are admirably calculated for the continual warmth of the climate, they do not build them in Towns or Villages but separate from each other and always in the woods and are without walls so that the air coold [sic] by the shade of the trees has free access in whatever directions it happens to blow.'[1]

Hawaiian Dwellings of Thatched *Hale*

Alice Spencer Leineweber

Building Plan/Form and Culture

The shape and form of the Hawaiian house has intrigued observers since first Western contact with the islands in 1778. John Webber, artist on Captain James Cook's third expedition in the Pacific, recorded the first Western view of a *kauhale* (community of houses) grouped around an open workspace. Each *hale pili* (grass house) had a high, gabled roof with a continuous line of grass thatching for both roof and wall. Later artists observed distinctions between the houses of *ali'i* (high chiefs) and those of *maka'inana* (commoners). Chiefs had larger houses with articulated ridges of special grasses; all, however, were still grouped around a central open space. Despite the abolition of the era of native religion, *āikapu* (literally, 'sacred eating'), chiefs retained distinct buildings separated by function well past the mid-1850s: the *hale mua* (men's meeting house), *hale noa* (mingling house for men and women), *hale o papa* (women's house) and *hale pe'a* (menstrual hut).

As in many cultures, the proportions of the human body related directly to the layout and construction of traditional Hawaiian space. The basic unit of construction was the *anana* (outstretched arms, fingertip to fingertip): this indicated the close relationship between bodily need and the space created. All layouts of columns, posts and thatching purlins reflected the ratios of the personal *anana* of the builder. The *kuhikuhipu'uone* ('architect') often set columns approximately 1.5 m (5 ft) apart; this was the dimension of *moku*, or the length from the tightly bent outstretched elbow to the opposite fingertip. The centre of the body, or *piko* (navel), set the height of the wall top – except in the case of the king's *hale mua*, which had taller proportions.

Materials and Construction Techniques

Traditional construction materials included *'ōhi'a* (*Metrosideros macropus* – a eucalyptus species) for primary and secondary timber posts, and *'ilima* (*Sida fallax* – a hibiscus species) for roof purlins. Posts and purlins were tied with *'ie 'ie* (*Freycinetia arborea*) vine or *'uki'uku* (*Dianella sandwicensis*) braided into long lengths. Joinery consisted of male and female parts notched together and then lashed. Thatching was of *ke pili* (*Heteropogon contortus*), a tussock grass, or *kī* (*Cordyline terminalis*) leaves – each gathered into bundles the size of a circle made by the touching of the thumb and index figure, or plaited into panels for walls.

Various rituals accompanied the building of these vernacular structures. Red fish were set at the bottom of the holes that held the main posts, white *kapa* (native cloth) was laid across the threshold, and the final cutting of the piko grass over the doorway blessed the completed building. The trimming of the doorway was considered the final act of construction. The interior floor was levelled with dirt, and then finally set with smooth stones; upon these were laid coarse mats of several layers, and then mats made with grasses – some grass as fine as a single hair. The interior was typically devoid of furniture except for a large, raised platform at one end for communal sleeping.

The Hawaiian grass house was transformed over time with the addition of timber-framed windows and doors, and *lānai* (a type of covered porch), but the traditional form vanished by 1900 when a house was moved from the Napali coast of Kaua'i to the Bishop Museum on the island of O'ahu. On display in the Hawai'i Hall, the house has been re-thatched three times – the most recent being in 2009. The first plantation-worker housing, allied with the rise of plantation farming in the 17th century, used the thatched house for labourers, in a combination of Hawaiian and Japanese farmhouse forms. Many of the island's building departments now allow for the construction of grass houses for public use in tourist areas, with a special provision for them recently included in the building code.

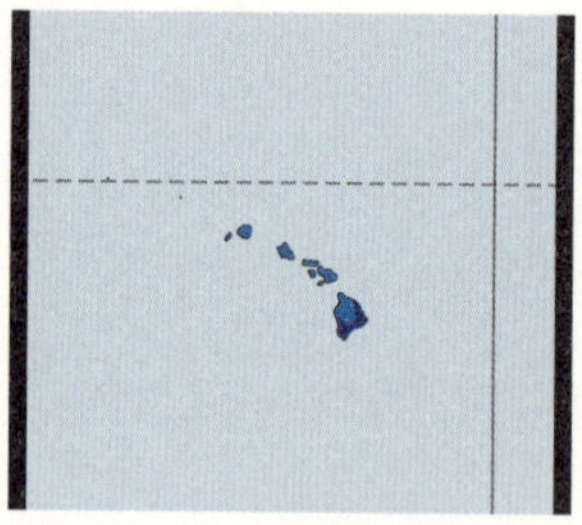

Seasonal average temperatures °C (F)

Seasonal average rainfall mm (in.)

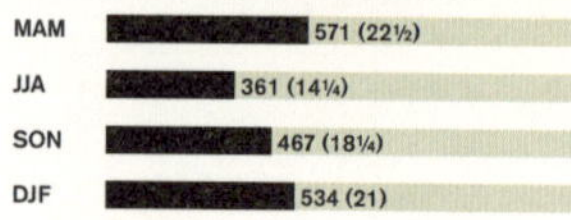

Opposite top left Engraving of the village of Waimea, on the island of Kauai, showing steep-sided huts at low and high levels.

Opposite top right All vernacular houses were grouped around a central open space, as illustrated in this etching of a missionary preaching to native people in a palm-roofed enclosure flanked by traditional structures, c. 1826.

Opposite Traditional Hawaiian temples notable for their size and articulated ridges of grass are increasingly rare; this example is protected by walls of timber and lava-rock at Pu'uhonua o Honaunau National Historical Park in Hawaii's South Kona district, Big Island.

DRY

Equirectangular projection. Scale 1: 70 000 000

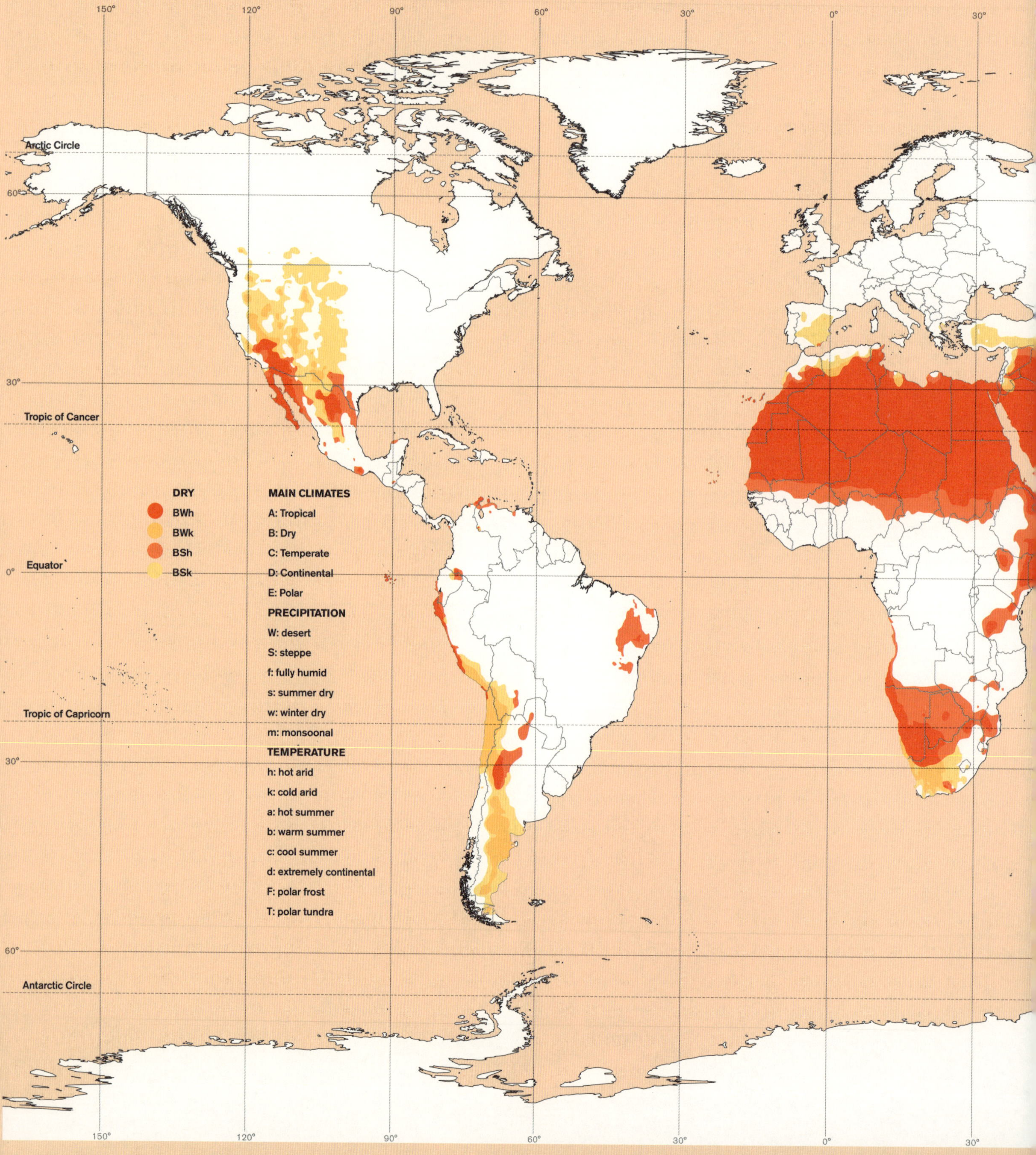

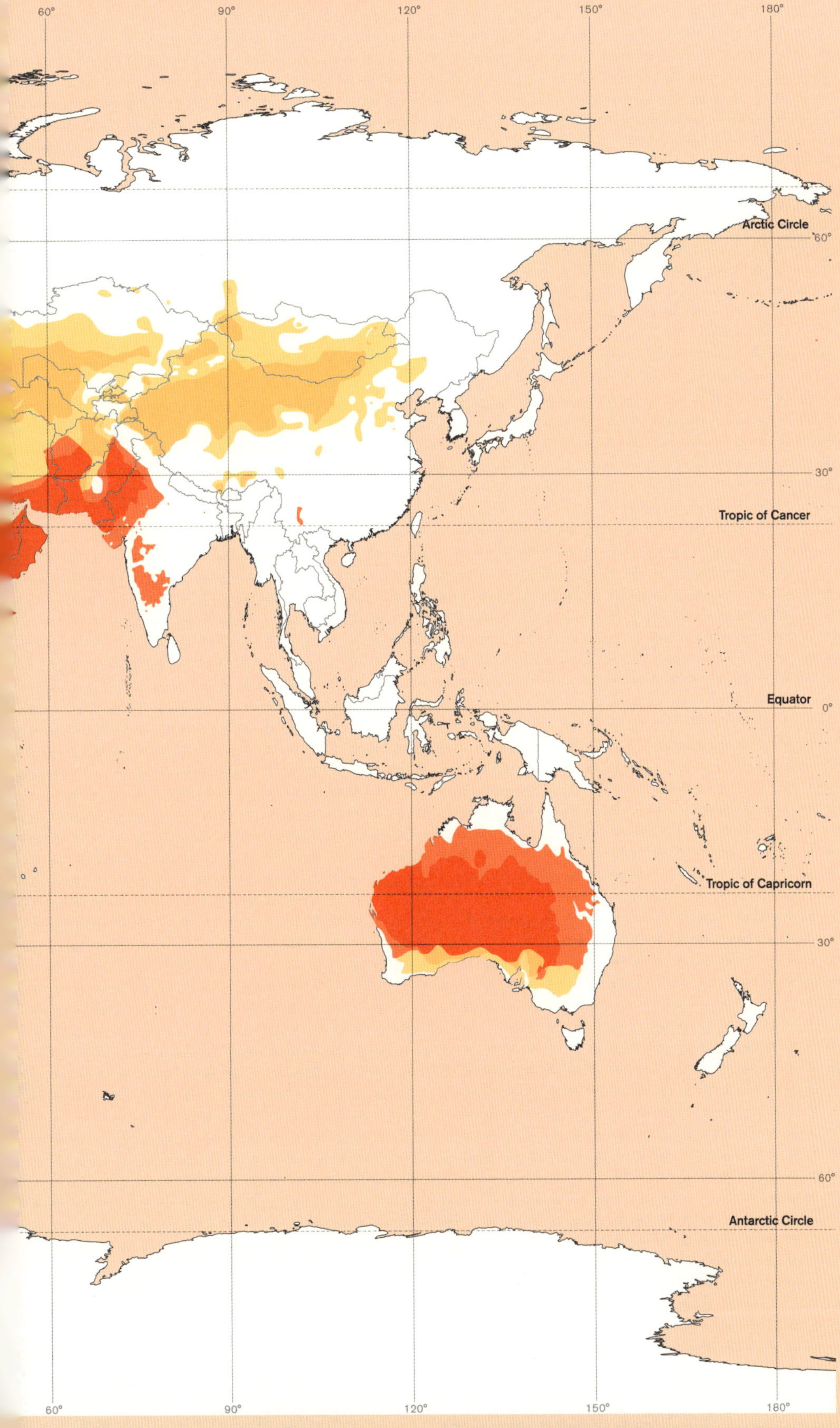

Precipitation (water gain) in the dry climate zone is less than potential evaporation and transpiration – the amount that would occur if a sufficient water source were available (water loss). These subtropical deserts extend from roughly 20 to 30° latitude, in large continental regions, often surrounded by mountains. According to Köppen, the dry regions of the world cover more land area than any other major climatic type (about 26 per cent). Clumps of trees are more isolated than elsewhere, and grasses dominate the landscape.

These regions depend not only on precipitation totals but also on temperature, which greatly affects evapotranspiration. Regions are more likely to be classified as dry if most of the precipitation is concentrated in warm, summer months when evapotranspiration rates are greater. Precipitation in a dry climate is both low and irregular – typically, the lower the amount, the greater the variability.

The major dry regions of the world can be divided into two primary categories. The first includes the subtropics, between latitudes 15 and 30°, where the sinking air associated with the subtropical high-pressure zones produces generally clear skies. The second is in the continental interiors of the middle latitudes. Here, far from sources of moisture, areas are deprived of precipitation. This continental dryness is often accentuated by mountain ranges that produce a rain-shadow effect.

The Köppen system captures these two climate types based on dryness: the arid and the semi-arid, or steppe. These can be divided further, based on temperature: hot and dry, with a mean annual temperature above 18°C (64°F); or cold (in winter) and dry, with a mean annual temperature below this value.

Arid climates are found along the west coast of South America and Africa, and across much of the interior of Australia. Although meagre, vegetation that needs little water (xerophytes) exists in these regions, reliant on infrequent rains and capable of surviving long periods of drought. Such vegetation includes various forms of cacti and short-lived plants that grow during rainy periods.

In low-latitude deserts, intense sunlight and clear skies result in high daytime temperatures; maxima can exceed 50°C (164°F), although 40–45°C (104–113°F) is more common. At night, the air's low vapour content (relative humidity is usually less than 25 per cent) allows for rapid cooling, and minimum temperatures drop below 25°C (77°F). Arid climates have a very large daily temperature range. During the winter, temperatures are more moderate, and minima may drop below freezing. Other effects on temperature and humidity may be superimposed on this pattern – for example, those due to the effects of monsoonal circulations.

In middle-latitude deserts, average annual temperatures are lower than in their low-latitude counterparts. Summers are typically warm to hot, with afternoon temperatures frequently reaching 40°C (104°F). Winters are usually extremely cold, with minimum temperatures sometimes dropping below -35°C (-31°F). Many of these deserts lie in the rain shadow of extensive mountain systems, such as the Sierra Nevada and Cascades in North America, the Himalayas in Asia and the Andes in South America. Their small amounts of precipitation tend to come from the occasional summer showers of mid-latitude storm systems.

Around the margins of these areas, where the rainfall is a little higher, the climate gradually changes to semi-arid. This steppe region typically displays short grasses and scattered low bushes, trees or sagebrush (*Artemisia*). More poleward regions experience colder temperatures, and rainfall is replaced by snowfall in winter. Annual precipitation is generally between 200 and 400 mm (8 and 16 in).

Solutions to Climatic Extremes in Desert Regions

Spread across five continents, desert is the largest, most vulnerable and probably the most diverse climate on the planet. It comprises hot and cold deserts as well as semi-arid hot and cold steppes. Arid environments are extreme; they range from the large temperature difference between day and night in Mexican and American southwestern deserts to the hottest places in the world – the recorded temperature of the sand in the Sahara and Rub Al Khali deserts has reached 71°C (159°F). The colder semi-arid steppe climates of Asia are, additionally, prone to earthquakes. Nonetheless, the expression of architectural forms found in these unforgiving regions, the use of local materials and their working with the local geography are breathtaking. The key environmental requirements to be accommodated in such climates are: the need for shade; the provision of thermal mass through the building envelope; and, of the utmost necessity for survival, the successful management of water.

Desert regions traditionally developed typologies comprising compact cities, narrow streets and dense building-block patterns, which provided a livable environment for their inhabitants. The social and tribal structures of society play a vital role in construction of a city: urban planning in desert regions is intimately related to tribal neighbourhoods. The model of North African and Arabian Peninsula oasis cities – with their *medinas* (walled towns), palm groves and an organizational structure that at times would accommodate sub-Saharan trading routes – can become an exemplar of sustainable settlements for modern-day planners. The Caucasus and other regions further east give witness to sensitively executed earthquake-resistant settlements, elements of which could also be appropriated for contemporary use.

The palette of available building materials is common across many continents and desert types, ranging from stone, limestone, earth, mud and salt bricks and clay to wattle-and-daub. A prevailing characteristic across these regions is the construction of thick walls, up to 2 m (6 ft) in width, to ensure thermal mass. Hot deserts have a shortage of hardwood; the species used there often comprised palms, date-palm leaves and a large variety of grasses. The lack of high-quality timber impacted on the evolution of their architectural language of domes and conical shapes, which perform best in compression, offer a reduced area of solar radiation (in comparison to flat roofs) and can be constructed without timber. This attractive architectural form was present not only in the traditional earth structures of Latin America and the Near East but also in the grass structures of Africa. We also find similarities along the Tropic of Capricorn in the kind of materials used by, for example, the South African Zulu in their immaculate 'beehive' grass houses. They offer a brilliant model for an environmentally responsive and biodegradable architecture.

The inventiveness of desert housing solutions is inspiring, and ranges from the cave and cliff settlements created by the Ancestral Puebloan culture in the southwestern United States to Cappadocia's picturesque houses in Turkey. In the Sahel, beautifully ornamented mud houses raise architectural form into the realm of art and sculpture while embracing a community spirit in the annual rebuilding of these dwellings.

Links between architecture and nature are expressed in materials as well as through land management and agriculture. The Bolivian Chipaya masters and oasis-city builders of the deserts offer timeless case studies of sustainable development and land-management principles developed over 1,000 years ago.

Left In unforgiving desert regions, inventiveness is a necessity: nomadic tent communities of the Tuareg offer one such example.

Pueblo and Mesa Developments of the American Southwest and Mexico

Opposite Positioned on the edge of escarpments, or mesa, settlements in Mexico and the American Southwest drew on materials to hand to create shaded villages and defensive structures, such as this watchtower on Arizona's North Grand Canyon rim.

Below left Historical view of Acoma Pueblo, New Mexico, c. 1883, recognized as the oldest inhabited settlement in America.

Below right Aerial photograph of a Mexican pueblo c. 1900, illustrating their relatively low building heights and characteristically thick walls.

Mark L. Gillem

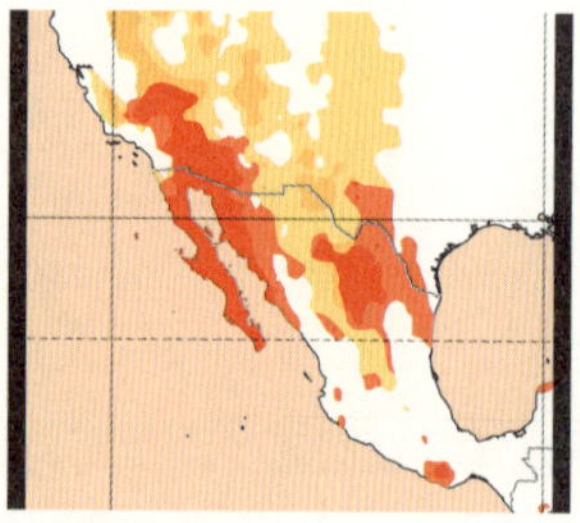

Geography/Climate

The majestic landscapes of the southwestern United States and northern Mexico consist of towering peaks, protected valleys and dramatic escarpments. During the day, the sun beats down on this arid landscape, but at night the desert-like setting cools off dramatically. This climatic rhythm has influenced the region's vernacular architecture for centuries.

Author Lisa Heschong suggests that 'In the desert the characteristic problem is extremely high daytime temperatures coupled with uncomfortably low temperatures at night.'[1] In fact, temperature swings in the region of 17–20°C (62–68°F) in one day are common, and temperatures across the year range from record lows of -45°C (-49°F) to highs of over 48°C (118°F). Additionally, the region is quite dry, with low rainfall and an average annual humidity of between 30 and 40 per cent. Moreover, with more than 350 sunny days per year, it is blessed with the sun as a natural heater if appropriately accounted for in the design of buildings.

In his seminal work, titled *House Form and Culture*, Amos Rapoport argues that the most enlightening architectural solutions, at least in terms of climatic response, are often found in areas with the most severe temperatures and weather patterns, which include the mud and stone houses of desert belts encountered around the world.[2] This certainly applies to the American Southwest and northern Mexico, where, prior to the advent of air conditioning, climate was a major determinant of building typology. However, material availability also has a major impact on the characteristic traits of traditional buildings in this region.

Materials

Simply put, buildings were made of local materials. As architect Christopher Alexander notes, in traditional societies buildings were made of 'hand-processed materials like wood, brick, mud, straw [and] plaster, which are easily modified by hand by the inhabitants themselves'.[3] While the historical material distinction between functional uses in vernacular architecture was not as pronounced as it is today, when steel- and concrete-framed commercial buildings contrast with timber- and metal-framed dwellings, different areas within the region used unique, locally accessible materials to construct climatically responsive buildings. Given the fact that traditional building scales were similar regardless of use – vernacular buildings rarely exceeded three storeys, for example – the material differences between a commercial, residential or ceremonial structure were minimal.

Opposite top and bottom Sited at the base of a mesa – a steep, flat-topped hill – the remains of an Ancestral Puebloan settlement at Pueblo Bonito, Chaco Canyon National Park, New Mexico, communicate the plan and materials of vernacular villages. Although large by Ancestral Puebloan standards, the interior rooms of Pueblo Bonito do not have immediate external access or window ventilation, but link to a large central courtyard.

Below Thick walls absorb heat and create shade, such as this one in New Mexico made from stone, mud and wood. Layered stone is an efficient and widespread vernacular building material used in the architecture of the American Southwest and northern Mexico.

Construction Techniques

Given the nature of these local materials, perhaps one of the most characteristic attributes of vernacular buildings in this region is the thickness of their walls. Building sites across the region have readily available soil and rock that inhabitants converted into walls in the form of adobe bricks, earthen blocks or layered stones bedded in with rudimentary mortar. Given the densities of these loadbearing materials, the walls assumed a thickness that is unusual today, but that thickness had non-structural benefits as well. Its thermal mass absorbed the sun's heat during winter days and radiated it back into the living spaces in the evenings. And, if adequately shaded during the summer, the thick walls kept the interiors as cool as possible.

Architect Marc Treib describes how these walls work: 'Throughout the day the walls, particularly those facing south and west, receive considerable radiant heat from sunlight, which is absorbed by the adobe. But some time is required for this heat to penetrate through the wall mass. All throughout the cool night the heat in the walls radiates into the room, keeping it warm, until by morning the heat has dissipated and the cycle begins anew, with the room remaining cool throughout the day.'[4]

In addition to the climatic advantages, these walls had another practical benefit. As Alexander notes, handmade thick walls can be carved out to create alcoves and niches that add a personal character to the spaces.[5] In vernacular dwellings of the region, these became places for important cultural markers or served as much-needed storage areas.

Another common feature of many vernacular buildings in the region is some type of deep overhang that shades the walls and window openings from the high summer sun. While the overhanging cliffs of the Ancestral Puebloans (discussed below) serve this function, a more common approach was to extend the roof, add balconies or arcades, or set the windows back deeply in the thick walls. The goal was to stop the sun's light from transforming into heat as it passed into the building or through glazing. When overhangs were absent, operable shutters were frequently used to block the sun (and wind) from entering the building.

Consistent daytime ventilation is not as critical in hot arid climates as elsewhere, given the fact that there is no need to bring hot air into rooms that have been cooled throughout the night. The traditional approach was to keep the hot air of the day out of buildings, then use night ventilation strategies to cool the interior spaces. Hence, windows need not be as large or as frequent as is the case in more humid locations with less of a temperature swing throughout the diurnal cycle. Just a few strategically placed windows aligned to the wind direction can be enough to funnel cooling evening breezes into the building.

Building Plan/Form

While individual buildings clearly respond to the region's unique climate patterns, the layouts of traditional settlements also respond appropriately in ways that create compact, walkable areas. Some common themes are evident across the region, and these gave shape to settlements large and small.

Left As with Native American houses, this church on top of a mesa in the Acoma Indian Reservation, New Mexico, rotates the use of its external veranda depending on the season: it is occupied during the day in cooler months, and at night when the days are hot.

Opposite top The compact, connected buildings several storeys high at Acoma Pueblo, New Mexico, are typical of building patterns in hot arid climates, which provide shade for neighbouring dwellings and streets.

Opposite bottom Crafted from the sides of mesas, Ancestral Puebloan cliff settlements illustrate ingenious vernacular strategies for regulating heat loss and gain. Such villages were established in sites that gave the advantage of shade in summer but were open to full winter light. As well as giving protection from climatic variation, they provided defence from Navajo and Apache hostilities.

Compact Layouts

As G. Z. Brown notes, 'In hot arid climates, which rely less on cross ventilation cooling strategies, buildings are placed very close together. . .to shade each other and adjacent streets.'[6] The Acoma Pueblo in present-day New Mexico, which according to tribal accounts has been occupied for over 2,000 years, is a representative example. Connected buildings define and shade its pedestrian-scaled streets, and these multi-storey buildings support significant population density within a very small area. Communal squares and plazas are carved out of the building fabric, and form the social spaces of the pueblo.

Another compact pattern of development in the region called for building under the mesas (steep-sided, flat-topped hills) rather than on top of them. This approach was mastered by the Ancestral Puebloan culture – a group of Native Americans who lived roughly between the 1st and 14th centuries in what is now the southwestern United States. They built impressive roads that linked discrete villages across the desert landscape. Some of these settlements were indeed set atop mesas, but others were eventually tucked under deep, overhanging cliffs. According to Heschong, the Ancestral Puebloans were shrewd judges of the climatic possibilities of their desert sites. For their cliff dwellings, they selected places afforded summer shade from overhanging ledges yet open to the full winter sun: 'With their backs to the cliff, the dwellings were protected from the winter winds and also took advantage of the thermal mass of the earth to moderate the temperature flux.'[7]

While the climatic advantage of these dwelling sites is obvious, one cannot discount the additional defensive value of the locations, given frequent raids on their more exposed settlements by the Navajo and Apaches. It is likely that in their selection of the cliff dwelling as a type, the Ancestral Puebloans prioritized protection both from the climate and from their competitors. While the basic siting approach under an overhanging cliff was consistently adopted, the actual size of these settlements varied from just a few rooms to full 'villages' with more than 100 rooms. While there are nearly 600 documented cliff dwellings within the present-day Mesa Verde National Park alone, what the US National Park Service refers to as the 'Cliff Palace' is perhaps the most well known today. It comprises a complex of 150 living rooms with twenty-three ceremonial chambers known as *kivas*, which originally supported an overall population of roughly 100 people. To create these structures, the Ancestral Puebloan builders used readily available wood for beams, sandstone for walls, and a mortar fashioned from ash, soil and water. Like the more conventional adobe structures found above ground, the dense, thick walls of these cave dwellings performed the same solar-absorption and re-radiating function described previously. Openings in the walls were equally minimal but optimally placed – in this case, to capture the breezes that moved up the face of the cliff.

The configuration and use of individual traditional dwellings also responded to climatic needs. For example, it would not have been unusual in the cliff dwellings for occupants to vary their use patterns according to seasonal temperature changes. This is similar to the way residents of Acoma Pueblo near Albuquerque, New Mexico, would alter the way they inhabited their homes. As Brown notes, the pueblo 'is an example of a two-zone residence in which the time of day that each zone is used changes dramatically from season to season'.[8] External terraces are assigned daytime uses during cooler times of the year, while internal spaces are used at night; in the warmer seasons, this use pattern is transposed.

Shaded Courtyards

Another traditional design model of this region integrated shaded courtyards within buildings. Rapoport argues that this model dates back at least 9,000 years, and he refers to settlements using courtyard housing as 'the inside-out city' wherein buildings focus inward to a central courtyard rather than outward towards a street.

A key goal of this vernacular type was to provide privacy within dense settlement patterns, in which the exterior walls of buildings frequently abutted the edge of the street. Small windows and entry doors may be carved into these walls, but the general focus was on the interior. While some scholars have made the case for the climatic advantages of courtyards, Rapoport suggests that these benefits may not be as significant as the social processes supported by such spaces.[9] Courtyards can mitigate the kind of noise levels that would be intrusive in more compact developments, and they can provide a great degree of privacy for building occupants.

As an element, the courtyard was a common feature in buildings across the region, but perhaps its most common application came in the traditional housing found throughout Mexico. These homes often doubled as workplaces – and included storage rooms, workrooms and even areas for animals. The courtyard, or *placita*, served multiple purposes, and evolved into one of the most essential elements of these multifunctional dwellings. At times, these traditional buildings even had two courts – one for the family and one for work.

Arcades

Covered walkways are also part of the historical pattern in many settlements across the region. These arcades not only protected the building's walls but made walking much more comfortable during the hot summer months. Although they are old models, arcades continue to serve a purpose today. Alexander argues that 'arcades – covered walkways at the edge of buildings, which are partly inside, partly outside – play a vital role in the way people interact with buildings'.[10]

Conclusion

Lessons from the traditional dwellings and settlements of the American Southwest and Mexico are still relevant today. While construction methods have changed and utilities of all sorts now need to be incorporated into building designs, the fundamental principles of the vernacular remain valid.

At the scale of the individual building, the ability to use local materials appropriate for the region is as valid now as it was in the time of the Ancestral Pueblo people – particularly bearing in mind the increasing present-day focus on local sourcing. Given the current approach to maximizing energy efficiency in buildings, the tactic of using thicker walls to increase insulation values and reduce heat transfer is also gaining popularity – especially with the interest in Passive House technologies. When these approaches are coupled with the use of deep overhangs and suitable windows, energy use can drop dramatically. This focus on 'energy reduction first' is a key element in the drive to achieve more energy-efficient buildings. What reduction cannot account for, recovery of energy through renewable resources like the sun and wind can make up the energy difference. In many cases, properly designed buildings, especially in the American Southwest, can be energy independent.

At the urban scale, the focus on more compact layouts has received widespread attention from planners and architects in the last two decades. Such layouts – which support walkability, transit and cars – are seen as viable replacements for the low-density automobile-dominated suburbs found throughout the United States. Similarly, shaded courtyards and arcades are elements that can continue to make urban living desirable, efficient and functional. While not all-inclusive, when taken together, these attributes of climate-responsive design can serve as a 'roadmap' for today's architects interested in anchoring their designs to the region's unique cultural and climatic context.

Below Covered walkways are commonly found in vernacular architecture of the region. The shaded zone they create gives longevity to the lifespan of building walls and makes pleasant passages for walking in the height of the summer.

Opposite top Courtyards are a typical feature of building plans in hot, arid climates. The courtyard, or *placita*, became a vital component of housing: a site for work, storage and even housing animals. This example in rural Mexico includes traditional ovens for baking.

Opposite bottom Courtyards and arcades continue to be relevant for their effective climatic regulation, as seen in the Palacio Clavijero in Mexico's Michoacán state. Protecting from heat gain while allowing cooling breezes, this spatial typology creates a shared social centre that is protected from the street.

Colombian Boyacá and Guajira Dwellings

Lucia Garzon

Geography/Climate

Colombia contains several relatively dry regions, particularly in the north, near the country's border with Venezuela.

The Guajira, for instance, is an area with a warm, dry and hospitable climate. It is a peninsula on Colombia's Caribbean coast, with mountains not exceeding 900 m (3,000 ft) high, which extends into the Gulf of Venezuela. Rains there are scarce and poorly distributed; annual rainfall is between 125 and 400 mm (5 and 16 in). The strong sunshine, with average annual temperatures of 28°C (82°F), constant winds, high evaporation and quite distinct seasons create a well-defined vernacular architecture for the region.

Another dry zone is the semi-desert area in the Andean region of Boyacá. The Villa de Leyva municipality, for example, has an elevation 2,143 m (7,030 ft) above sea level and its temperature varies little throughout the year: between 17 and 18°C (62 and 64°F). The region has several mountain climates ranging across three rugged landscapes – one with a semi-desert microclimate and rainfall between 700 and 1,000 mm (28 and 40 in) a year. This landscape also has eroded sections, where fossils preserved from the Cretaceous period (roughly 146 to 65 million years ago) can be found.

Materials

This dry climate facilitates the growth of thorny bushes and cactus, with a high proportion of trees of the genera *Stenocereuscacti*, *Cereus*, *Pereskia*, *Opuntia* and *Pilosocereus*. There are also leguminous bushes such as *Prosopis juliflora* (a kind of mesquite), *Pithecellobium dulce* (also known as Madras thorn), *Haematoxylum brasiletto* (or Mexican logwood), *Diphysa cartaghenensis* and *Parkinsonia praecox*.

One of the most common local species is *Stenocereus griseus* (also known as the dagger cactus). The indigenous Wayuu people recognize this cactus by its size, its long and sharp thorns, its eight to nine ribs and the length and straightness of its branches. Its local classification is based on the life cycle of the plant: in the juvenile stage, it is called *yosú* in Wayuunaiki (the native language); once the stems have died, the 'wood' (xylem) is called *yotojoro*; the fruits are called *iguaraya*.

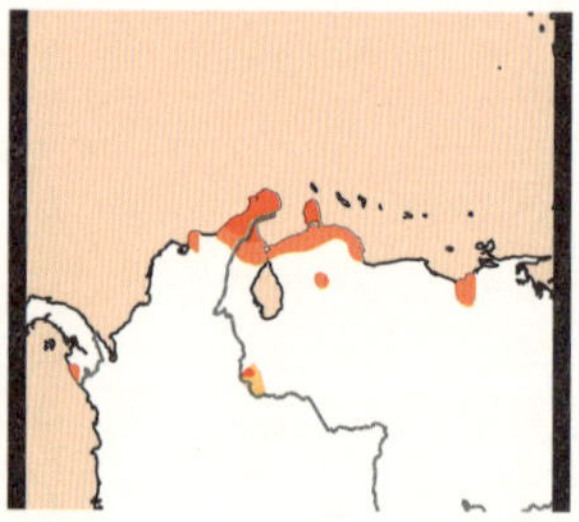

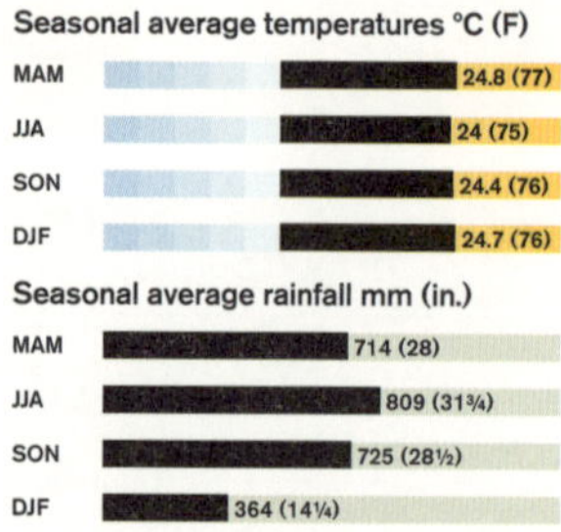

Left Arid landscapes of Colombia are mostly found in the north, such as Villa de Leyva in the Andean region of Boyacá.

Opposite Houses in dry Colombian climates use readily available local materials, such as wood, palm, adobe and *yotojoro* (dried cactus stems) to build lightweight structures that give shade while allowing cooling breezes to pass through. In such arid regions, the limited materials available are applied to various building types, from homes to animal shelters.

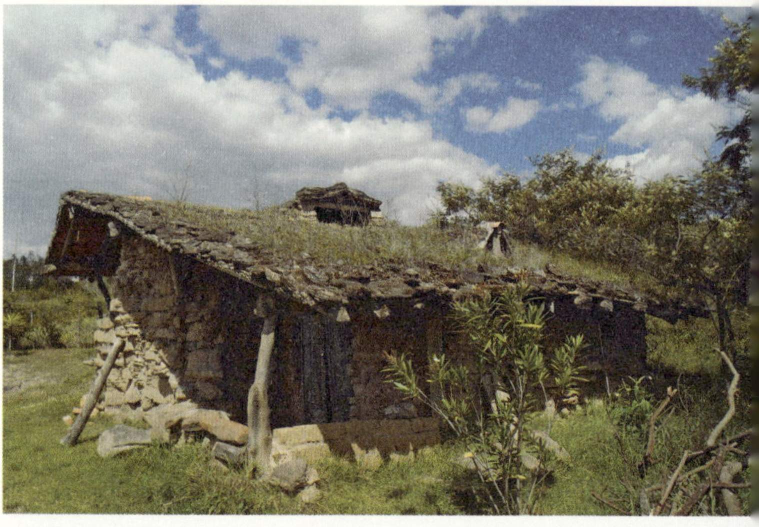

Left Colombia's relatively dry regions include the Guajira Peninsula. Scant rainfall and strong sunshine shape this environment, which is arid and populated by thorny bushes and cacti. The relatively limited materials mean buildings are typically modest, such as this settlement of Wayuu indigenous people in Punta Gallinas.

Opposite bottom left Unstable, sandy soils in the hilly Boyacá region give rise to partially submerged structures, formed from earth and stone.

Opposite bottom right Overhanging eaves on houses in Colombia's arid regions are essential for shade. Monopitched or pitched roofs, such as on this dwelling in Villa de Leyva, extend beyond the perimeter walls, supported by columns of native timber.

Below Locally available bamboo-like grass known as 'wild cane' forms the primary roof enclosure, lashed to the wooden frame by rope made from a grass also sourced nearby.

Building Plan/Form and Construction Techniques

The typical house of the Guajira region is a modest structure – a so-called *piichi* or *miichi*. It is generally divided into two sets of living quarters: a sleeping area, where hammocks are hung, and an area for rucksacks, where the family clothing is kept. (Precious water is stored in narrow-necked mud jars buried in the earthen floor.) Outside, timber tree trunks may be fixed in the soil, in which are kept hollow gourds full of seeds for future sowing. These dwellings generally have a rectangular structure, although in some places they might be semicircular in plan. Their walls are sometimes covered with *bahareque* (a wattle-and-daub type finish), at other times with *yotojoro*. Their roofs are typically pitched – either monopitch 'lean-to' style or duopitch – and often also clad with *yotojoro*. In modern times, there has been a great increase in the number of zinc roofs; the arrival of modernity has influenced the population, who have tended to abandon local materials.

Near the principal house of the Guajira settlement can be found the traditional arbour. This consists of a roof with a flat ceiling, which rests on six columns. The arbour is an important place: the communal activities of the day take place there, and it is the place in which the community receives guests. Its construction is fundamentally carried out using *yotojoro*, but this may be combined with other types of plants, timber or – nowadays – even steel.

The buildings of the mountainous Boyacá region are located on unstable, sandy soils, and are usually partially buried. Their structure can be classified as a 'mixed media' earth-building technique, supported by columns and beams in native timbers. The walls and heavy roofs are built with flagstones approximately 400 mm (16 in) square, the walls comprising stones bonded with a mortar of clay soil. The finished, 'suspended' ceiling is made from *Gynerium sagittatum*, a local bamboo-like grass known as 'wild cane', placed between the roof beams at about 500 mm (20 in) centres.

The 'mooring' structures of these buildings are composed of natural fibres, fastened with plant fibre sourced locally and known as *how*. This material is extracted from a grass-like plant called *iche*, which, twisted once, forms a durable rope. This resource has been used in the region since pre-Columbian times; it is also employed in other crafts, such as basket weaving and mat making.

Totora and Adobe Homes of Peru

Marcial Blondet and Sofía Rodríguez-Larraín

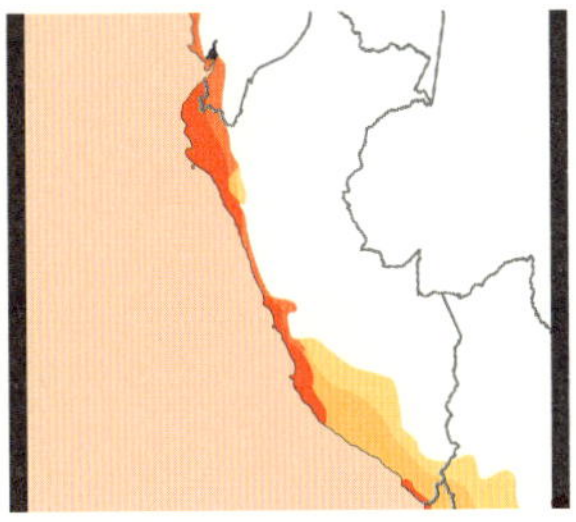

Seasonal average temperatures °C (F)

MAM	19.8 (67)
JJA	18.4 (65)
SON	19.8 (67)
DJF	20.3 (7)

Seasonal average rainfall mm (in.)

MAM	427 (16¾)
JJA	228 (9)
SON	348 (13¾)
DJF	490 (19¼)

Opposite Enormous variation in Peru's geography and inhabitation creates great differences in landscape and resources, including (clockwise from top left) the desert coast of Paracas National Reserve; a terraced hillside near Lake Titicaca; Inca terraces in the Colca Canyon Chivay; historic Machu Picchu site in the Andes.

Right Common to the Peruvian vernacular, homes are usually low-lying and formed of adobe or *quincha*, a composite of cane or reed, and mud.

Geography/Climate

Peru boasts great geographical, natural and cultural diversity – and its vernacular construction is different in each of its main regions: the coast, the Andes and the Amazon jungle. The Peruvian coast is a desert strip crossed by several valleys. The Andes mountains are rich in stone, and home to the famous interlocking masonry of the Incas. The Amazonian region is covered by lowland tropical rainforest.

Materials and Building Plan/Form

Since pre-Hispanic times, ceremonial terraced pyramids were built in Peru with adobe (mud bricks) and *quincha* (timber frames, covered with mud). Today, most vernacular construction employs the same architectural expression: that of single- or two-storey houses made of adobe or *quincha*.

Another vital material, *totora* reed, forms the basis for life in the Uros islands of Lake Titicaca. This perennial herbaceous plant (*Schoenoplectus californicus*) flourishes in water, and its roots (*kile*), which grow roughly 2 m (6 ft) deep, allowed for the construction of islands for the pre-Inca Uro people.

In the country's Andean region, houses of up to three storeys are built with adobe, with roofs consisting of eucalyptus tree trunks covered with *ichu*, a highland wild grass, or clay tiles. At high altitudes, most Peruvian vernacular dwellings are made of stones bedded in mud mortar, with *ichu* roofs. Since the 1970s however, tin corrugated sheets (*calamina*) have become a common roof cover.

Construction Techniques

The vernacular houses of Peru's coastal region have walls of sun-baked adobe bricks or wattle-and-daub, with lintels of *algarroba* wood (of the *Prosopis* genus) and flat roofs made from cane trellis. Rain is not expected – the emphasis is rather on shade and cooling, and these buildings are used for little more than sleeping. In the past, the elite and priesthood occupied more elaborate palaces and temples, but these edifices used the same materials as the humbler dwellings. These elite structures would have had painted stucco walls, geometrical mud fretwork, pyramidal roofs, courtyards, ramps and staircases.[1]

Thanks to its great thermal mass, earthen construction is particularly suited to the cold winter weather. Examples of earthen Andean construction include houses in the community of Cotos, located at 3,800 m (12,500 ft) above sea level. Because of its proximity to Lake Titicaca, the weather is relatively mild there, and frosting does not occur. Its traditional adobe dwellings are distributed around a courtyard and surrounded by low stone walls for wind protection and to enclose cattle. Most roofs are covered by two layers of fibres held together by straw or leather ropes. The thick upper layer is made of wheat or barley straw; the lower is made of *totora* reed resting on wooden branches. *Totora* is an excellent insulating material thanks to its hollow stem. In order to conserve heat, most walls have no windows; as a consequence, lighting and ventilation are poor. No chimney is provided in the kitchen and therefore the air is highly polluted, often causing respiratory illnesses. Some rooms have been 'modernized' with *calamina* roofs, thus reducing the thermal insulation provided by the traditional *ichu* roofs; these are very cold in winter.

As mentioned above, the Uro of Lake Titicaca also employ *totora* for their island homes. Each family group builds its own island, cutting the plant to the required size and covering the island's surface with cut reeds. Each individual family has a single-room house (mainly used for sleeping); these are placed around a common central space where all communal activities take place. They use *totora* to fashion houses, boats, mattresses and seats – and as cooking fuel and as a food rich in iodine for both animals and people. Because it has a high resistance to extreme temperature, it was used to cover the walls in winter in the ancient houses of Puno city, which is adjacent to Lake Titicaca. Today *totora* is being studied for new thermal applications, as well as to reinforce the houses of the highland Andes that are facing the effects of global climate change.

In contrast to Peru's dry regions, vernacular construction in the tropical Amazon jungle – where the climate is hot, humid and rainy – predominantly uses timber, bamboo and palm fibres. The region's timber-framed houses have few walls, in order to facilitate ventilation, and have roofs covered with palm fibres.

Below **Because of their high altitude, homes in the Cotos region require some protection from cold Andean weather. Stout, deep walls are made from locally available adobe bricks; roofs are formed of thick layers of barley or wheat straw above highly insulating *totora* reed.**

Opposite **The *totora* island vernacular is peculiar to the resources and needs of its Uro villagers. The *totora* reed is essential for all aspects of life – from the construction of each family home, to the furnishing of its seating and mattresses – and is even used for boat making.**

Chilean Structures of *Quincha*, Adobe and Guayaquil Cane

Hugo Pereira Gigone

Geography/Climate

Northern Chile has two climatic zones: the littoral north, along and up to 50 km (30 miles) inland from the coast; and the desert north in the interior, rising to 3,000 m (9,800 ft) above sea level. Both zones are dry and sparse in vegetation. However, the former, influenced by the presence of the Pacific Ocean, experiences lesser temperature fluctuations than the latter, which is additionally very windy. Both zones also fall into climate type BWk under the Köppen–Geiger system.

Materials and Construction Techniques

An excellent example of this climate type, and of the use of local materials, is seen at Tulor, a village of approximately 700 inhabitants in the northern Norte Grande area. From ancient times, this region's original inhabitants – a people named the Atacameños – built circular earthen structures to house their communal activities. These buildings, known as *ayllus*, best afforded the protection required in the face of such an extreme climate. Accordingly, Tulor's buildings have massive earth walls, typically 300 mm (12 in) thick, which stabilize the internal temperature of their rooms. Thermal comfort is also aided by the use of a mud covering, laid over roof structures made of rustic timber joined by dried animal skins; and by the minimal numbers and sizes of window and door openings.

The vernacular construction solution conceived by the Atacameños was subsequently applied for several centuries, until this region underwent the process of modernization that accompanied the establishment of Chile's 'nitrate towns' in the 19th and 20th centuries. At this time, Chile was the only place in the world with naturally occurring sodium nitrate, the lucrative basis for both fertilizer and explosives. One extraordinary example of a modernized town is Chacabuco, a 'factory' settlement of 4,000 people that was not much smaller than the nearest city, San Pedro de Atacama, which had 5,000 inhabitants. All the residential workers' areas of the immense Chacabuco complex were housed in adobe structures with the same 300 mm (12 in) thick walls and mud-covered timber roofs.

Further up in the Chilean Andes, the absence of wood gave rise to rustic stone constructions that use mud to bind the rocks together. These buildings also used straw roof coverings to protect against the cold climate. The ancient peoples sometimes applied mud over this covering. Churches, tall, defensive structures called *pukaras*, and even entire villages were built according to these principles.

The Incas introduced an ancient construction system into this region. Named *quincha*, it comprises a timber frame covered with mud. This vernacular technique persisted into the colonial period, and can be found in different types of buildings all over the country. Historical testimonies mention it particularly in the context of churches, military infrastructure, housing and railway stations along the northern coast. This is because it responds better to earthquakes than the monolithic construction systems, such as adobe or rammed earth, that are used in the interior desert zone.

During the 19th century, new building techniques combining earth and wood were adopted. The reason for this altered construction method stemmed from trade between Chile and the United States: ships taking sodium nitrate to North America used as ballast for the return journey both pine (*Pinus*) wood from Oregon and strong sugar cane (*Saccharum*) from the Ecuadorian port of Guayaquil. The new building system became known as 'Guayaquil cane', and the resulting structures offered greater seismic protection. Compared with adobe techniques, the less rigid composite construction of Guayaquil cane yielded better to earthquake shocks.

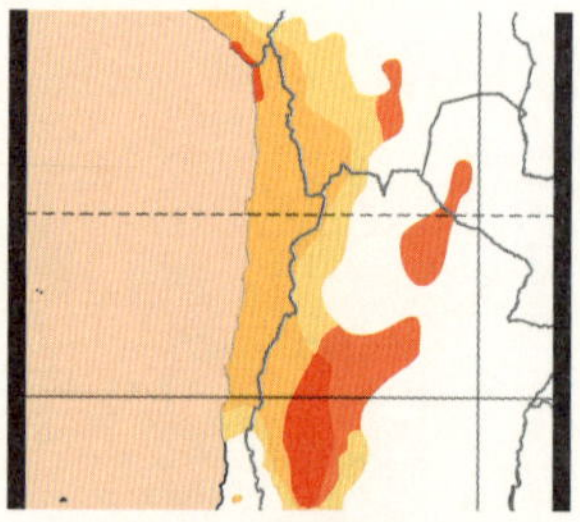

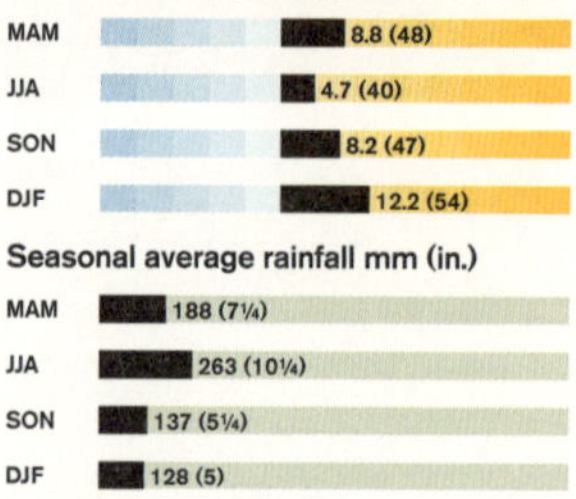

Opposite top The workers' quarters of the Chacabuco factory settlement typify the structure of this region, formed of 300 mm (12 in) adobe walls.

Opposite middle left Circular earthen ruins of the ancient city of Tulor, home of the Atacameños peoples.

Opposite middle right and bottom left Details of *quincha* construction, showing the horizontal and vertical assembly of canes, which are set in place by mud or earth.

Opposite middle and bottom right Vernacular architecture of Chile's northern reaches uses the materials to hand: stone, rather than wood, is plentiful and is bound with mud and covered with straw roofs.

Conical Chipaya Homes of Bolivia

Natalia Jorquera Silva

Geography/Climate and Culture

On the Andean plateau, located among the high peaks of the Andes in South America, indigenous people subsist thanks to intricate territorial management systems undertaken in a hostile territory with an average altitude of 4,000 m (13,000 ft) above sea level and a mostly tropical dry and cold climate. The Chipaya culture, part of the Uru Nation is one of Bolivia's many indigenous Andean cultures. It is considered to be one of the oldest in the Americas, originating in roughly 2000 BCE.

Chipaya is located in the Bolivian region of Oruro, on an immense plateau to the north of the Coipasa Lake and salt flats, and is traversed by the Lauca River. The cold-arid climate has extreme temperature fluctuations during day and night, in both summer and winter, with strong winds and hot sun. The climate is accorded a place in the local religion, where natural elements such as water, rain, fire and wind are represented by deities (including Mother Earth, or *Pachamama*) that are revered and respected in order to ensure survival.

Materials

The only available natural resources are the highly saline soil, pastures and water, which have been cleverly managed to provide for the cultivation of quinoa cereal and grazing for sheep, llamas and pigs. This scarcity of resources, along with the region's geographical isolation and a strong local identity, have maintained the unique culture of the Chipaya community. This is expressed in its language, its organizational and productive system, its beliefs, its clothing and its vernacular architecture.

The Chipaya control the territory to make it habitable and fertile using a specific land management system. Their command of water from the Lauca River makes survival possible, and has given them the name of 'water men', or *qhas qut suñi'.* In fact, three techniques of water management are combined in the territory: first, the *Pikhi*, to take water from the Lauca River through channels; second, the *Pikh*, to contain and hold water using a system of dikes made from soil and grass; third, the *Lamea*, a practice of flooding salt flats during the winter in order to extract soil, leaving the land available for arable activity. These three measures are carried out along with a religious ceremony called *Lauca Arunta* or *Mallku Lauca*, in the course of which animal sacrifices and libations are offered to the river in order to secure its continued flow, ensuring food production and the continuity of life.

Construction Techniques and Building Plan/Form

The traditional Chipaya house, the *walucha* or *wallichi koya*, is conical and has a circular floor plan. It is small, only 3–4 m (10–13 ft) in diameter, and as with most Andean homes, the majority of domestic activities are performed outdoors. Each dwelling has a single door to the east, where the sun rises; they all have a northwest–southeast orientation and can be grouped in clusters of four to five units. This ensemble also includes smaller structures, called *phutucu*, which have the same conical shape and are used as barns or for food storage.

Chipaya building culture is based on the use of *tepes*, blocks cut directly from the salty soil, with which a circular perimeter wall is constructed that tapers as it rises, ending in a cone. *Walucha* and *phutucu* differ in that the former has a thatched roof, which is made from the scarce grass available, while the second is made entirely of *tepes*. Conical dwellings do not need timber for beams, which is useful in a region with a scarcity of tree cover. Additionally, the conical form has less surface exposure to the sun than more orthogonal profiles and it has better strength against strong winds, which provides improved temperature conditions in the interior.

Today, most of the region's population lives in the town of Santa Ana de Chipaya, and traditional houses and dwellings are used only sporadically for rural activities. Nonetheless, the vernacular architecture and planning of the Chipaya provide lessons through their strategies for land management in regions with infertile soils and scarce resources.

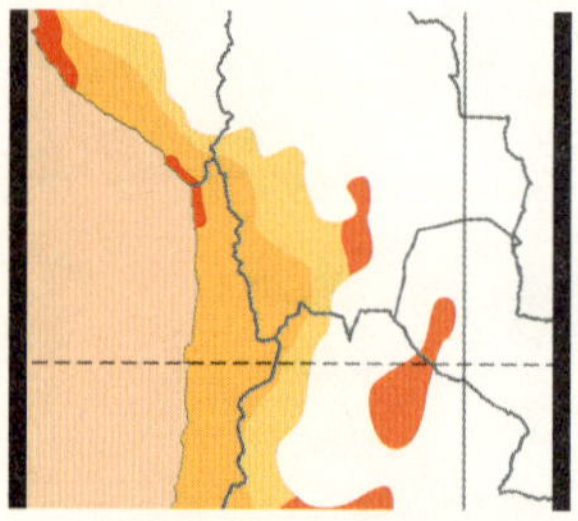

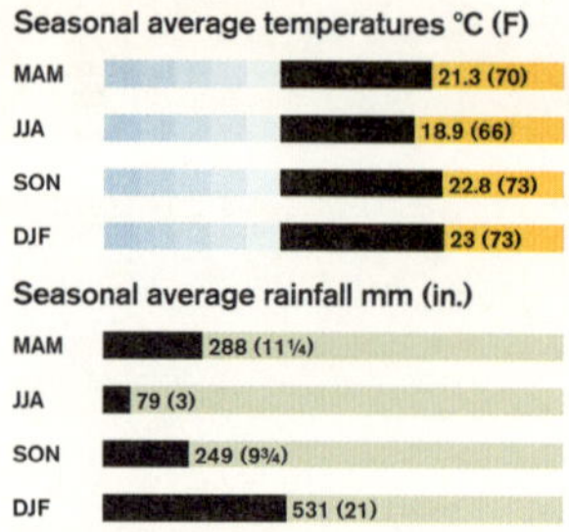

Below Judicious harvesting and cultivation of grass on the Andean plateau allows for the *walucha* thatch roofs. Simpler structures for storage or barns, known as *phutucu*, are built solely of soil blocks.

Opposite top and middle Relative isolation and the highly saline environment inform traditional Chipaya people's lives.

Opposite bottom Chipaya homes (*walucha* or *wallichi koya*) are distinctive cone-shaped structures formed of salty earthen blocks.

Argentina's Altiplano Vernacular of Adobe Brick, Stone and Mud

Rodolfo Rotondaro

Geography/Climate

Argentina is 3 million sq km (1.2 million sq miles) in area, with altitudes ranging from 7,000 m (23,000 ft) in the Andes in the west, down to sea level in the east. Its diverse 'vertical' and 'horizontal' biogeographical regions is therefore of extraordinary magnitude. About two-thirds of this vast territory is associated with arid and semi-arid ecosystems.

The altiplano is an extensive arid region in the northwest of Argentina. It is singular, and characterized by vernacular Andean high settlements. The climate is semi-arid with temperatures that range from 21°C (70°F) in summer to -18°C (-0.4°F) in winter. The resulting structures respond to the great variation in temperature, with thick adobe walls to protect against fluctuating heat loss or gain. This contrasts with the forested region of Misiones province in the northeast of the country, for instance, which has a humid climate with tropical characteristics, and typical temperatures of 38°C (100°F) in summer and 18°C (64°F) in winter.

Materials and Construction Techniques

An example of altiplano vernacular may be found in Rodero, a town lying 3,230 m (10,590 ft) above sea level in the Quebrada de Humahuaca Valley in the arid northwest. Rodero's chapel is a popular building serving the local community of shepherds and the surrounding rural population. Its architectural morphology is simple, and very similar to that of the colonial churches of the region. The three elements of its nave, sacristy and tower (*campanary*) are arranged in line. Its roofs are duopitched except for that of the tower, which boasts an adobe dome. The entrance door leading to the nave is oriented to the east. There are very few window openings: only one in the sacristy and one on each side of the tower at belfry level.

Rodero chapel was constructed using the vernacular technology that is used throughout the valley, which is characterized by popular knowledge and originated with the area's indigenous people. The building's foundations are shallow, and built with local stones bedded in a mortar made of mud. The adobe-brick walls, forming a structural masonry envelope, were assembled in successive horizontal layers using mud mortar and artisanal methods. The building's plasters are made of mud and straw. Its various roof forms rest on triangular wooden trusses made from trunks of *cardón* (*Tillandsia* spp.) supported directly off the walls. The roof beams are covered with three layers: narrower boards of *cardón*, a fine coat of mud and a final coat of straw fastened with fine wires.

The Rodero shepherds were, in today's parlance, 'self-builders', and they conserved the region's vernacular building techniques and its architectural patterns. The chapel shows a clear example of the persistence of these traditions in the vernacular architecture of northwestern Argentina.

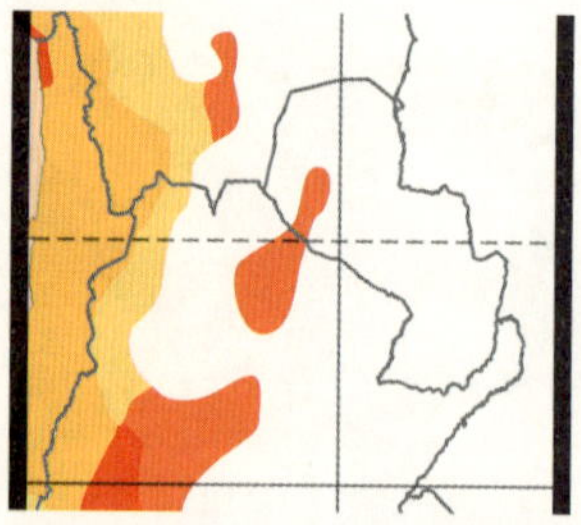

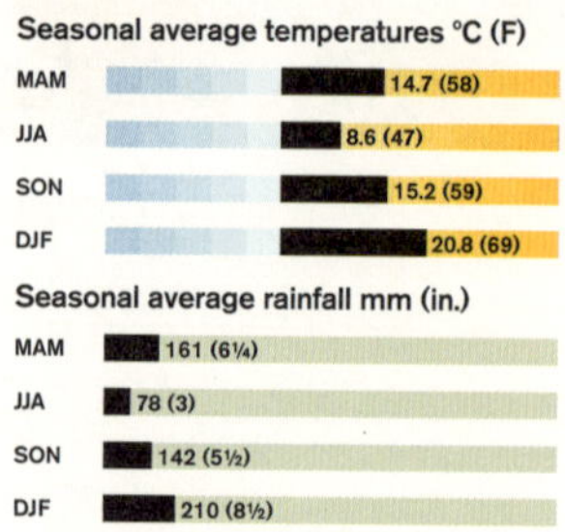

Opposite The church of Rodero town in the country's northwest valley of Quebrada de Humahuaca was built by local members of the community. Its structure typifies architecture of the region, with adobe brick secured by mud and straw plaster, set atop foundations of stone.

Climate, Resources and Cultural Adaptations of African Vernacular

Suzanne Preston Blier

Opposite top Dogon granaries or storage buildings in Ireli village, Dogon Country, Mali, exemplify the use of earth in the African vernacular. Capped by straw thatch and raised on stone bases, the structures resist entry from water or insects.

Opposite bottom With a base material of earth, but following a striking variation, the *tata somba* of the Atakora region in Benin take the form of circular-planned fortresses. Providing protection from animals or intruders, the distinctive (usually) multi-storey structures create shelter below and platforms for drying grain above.

Geography/Climate and Culture

Traditional building materials, technologies and practices have made it possible for African populations historically both to address an array of changes and to do so in a manner that draws on key societal values. While individual strategies of engagement vary, broader conceptual frameworks emphasize how buildings need to be adaptable to changing family size and community population and other changes over the course of history.

Earth is a particularly important building material in many parts of Africa, not only because it is widely available and, in essence, 'free', but also because over a structure's lifespan, sections of a building or compound can be taken down and rebuilt to meet new needs. Earth can last several hundred years, provided that it is a carefully selected and reworked mix and it is roofed and regularly plastered to safeguard against water damage. Equally importantly, earth displays considerable tensile strength: 3,100–5,500 kilopascals, increasing to 6,600 kPa with the addition of small amounts of cement. Earth also has good thermal properties, which keep structures cool through the heat of the day and warm at night when the temperatures fall. Other widely available building materials such as bamboo are also employed to great effect. Sometimes vegetal walls are packed with earth in a manner similar to the wattle-and-daub technology long used in Europe – finding use not only in rural African residences but also in palaces.

Building Plan/Form

In the same fashion that earth and vegetal materials are adopted in myriad ways (each society often employing its own unique technologies and styles of building), so too are vitally important design strategies. Some structures are built around an open courtyard that not only allows light into rooms but also serves to collect rainwater in large terracotta vessels positioned beneath roof eaves. Shade from roof overhangs provides shelter from the harsh sun and from the sometimes torrential rains, enabling family members to socialize and work in this central, open area throughout the year in both domestic and religious structures. In nomadic communities – where the lives of inhabitants are determined by the needs of cattle herding, fishing, hunting and other activities – portable structures are made from an adaptable set of flexible poles, vegetal lashing strips and various coverings (textiles, leather, broad leaves or thatch). These enable entire communities to move with ease, and to reshape family and other social relations each time that these residences are set up in a new settlement. The direction of doorways may reflect political status, prevailing winds, the position of the rising or setting sun, or new friendships that have formed between residents. African vernacular architecture has, in such ways, historically addressed vital factors of both climate and local resources; adaptability and sustainability are two of its most important and enduring qualities. As Africa and other continents face the impact of global climate change and increasing population growth, long-standing vernacular forms may prove to be important models for the future.

Moroccan, Tunisian and Egyptian Dwellings of Tents or Mud Brick

James M. Steele

There is a wide variety of regional microclimates across the dry and often arid arc of northern Africa, which stretches from Morocco in the west through Tunisia in the middle to Egypt in the east. Each of these regions is differentiated by the confluence of an extraordinary set of geological features, including the Atlantic Ocean, the Atlas Mountains, the Sahara, the Mediterranean Sea and the Libyan desert. In addition, Islam has created an overarching religious tradition throughout this region, which has historically interacted in an integrated way with these geographic factors to shape the many different vernacular typologies that have evolved there.

Morocco

The middle and western reaches of the Sahara, which are inarguably the most extreme of these regions, have been the formidable home of the Tuareg for centuries. They demonstrate some of the most ingenious environmental adaptations, configured to conform to the *tinariwan* ('the deserts'), divided among salt flats, rocky moraine or mountains of sand. These nomads have survived, as the Bedouin have elsewhere, by creating long, narrow tents, woven from the hair of their camels and sheep using a small portable loom. The tent fabrics are stretched out on easily transported short poles, with the long, open sides of the tent facing east and west to catch whatever prevailing wind is generated during the diurnal cycle; the dark hair of the weave absorbs the sun's heat, which accelerates the captured breezes.

The Sahara Occidental eventually confronts the Atlantic coast on the west, and Rabat, the capital of Morocco, is located where the Bou Regreg River flows into the sea. It originated as the fortress, or *ribaat*, of the much older city of Salé, founded across the river in 1146 by the Almohad Caliph Abd al-Mu'min. It was his base for the invasion of Spain, and Caliph Yaqub al-Mansur subsequently made Rabat the Almohad capital. He expanded its walls, and commissioned the building of the Kasbah of the Udayas, as well as a large mosque, where the Tower of Hassan stands today. Almohad authority declined after Yaqub's death, construction of the kasbah and mosque stopped and power shifted eastward to Fez. The monumental walls of Rabat remain largely intact, but most of the vernacular houses inside them have been destroyed. However, the remains indicate a uniform sequence of interrelationships between public markets, mosques and private houses found elsewhere in the region.

Previous analysis of these patterns has typically concentrated on superficial formal similarities rather than on deeper issues. The latter might include the process of land demarcation and subdivision, including the allocation of land for public and private use; the principles, and operation, of land allotment (*iqta*); the reconciliation of territorial claims on land (*ikhtitat*); the impact of various types of tenure and ownership of land and buildings, such as the *waqf* (religious endowment), on growth and change; the institution of jurisprudence (*hisba*); and a comparison of legal solutions and customs.

Below left Urban Moroccan vernacular responses to climate, as well as to cultural and legal customs, have shaped the predominant use of shared walls with few or no windows, and internal courtyards.

Below right and opposite top Communities of nomadic Tuareg in the Sahara, Morocco, make tents using fabric woven from camel and sheep hair, which are pitched with long sides facing the prevailing east–west breeze.

Opposite bottom The established built response of blank outer walls and inner courtyards is seen in this aerial view of Fez, Morocco.

Most recently, scholars have been factoring these important aspects of Islamic jurisprudence into considerations of how Morocco's vernacular houses – with their shared, windowless mud-brick walls and internal courtyards – were formed and amalgamated to create the unique urban context of the region. Such social considerations have been combined with the buildings' architectural responses to ensure privacy as well as slow heat transmission and the night-time containment of cooler air that rises by convection during the heat of the day.

This ubiquitous urban pattern and house type is even more evident in Fez, which is arguably the most characteristically Arab city in the region because it was formed by an unprecedented confluence of immigrations. These began with an influx of Berbers during the early period of Islam, followed by refugees from Andalusia thanks to rebellions in Umayyad Cordoba in 817, and others from Kairouan, Tunisia, in 824.

Tunisia

Comparisons between houses in Fez and the original dwellings of the 9th-century refugees from Tunisia, such as those in Sidi Bou Said and other coastal villages, reveal the variety possible within the basic courtyard typology. Originally called Jabal el-Menar (Tower Mountain), Sidi Bou Said was renamed after the religious leader Abou Said ibn Kalef ibn Yahia Ettamini el Beji, who was buried there in 1231. The village attracted outside settlers during the time of the Ottoman Empire (c. 1299–1922/23), and the wealthy French artist and Arabic musicologist Baron d'Erlanger built his home, 'Ennejma Ezzahra', there in 1909. The latter has an arcaded and domed exterior; blue doors and *mashrabiya* (screens or grilles of turned wood); and a sequential, horizontal series of internal open courtyards, which bisect the dwelling from east to west to provide convective cooling. It also houses a large *hammam* (bath) and clear division between public and private space. It served as a model for the much more modest houses that followed in this picturesque village.

The mud-brick houses on the island of Djerba, in the Gulf of Gabès, 580 km (360 miles) south of Sidi Bou Said, further challenge the commonplace image of the typical Arab house. Like Fez, this Tunisian island has also been a crossroads of many different faiths and cultural influences in the past; it remains a centre both of the Ibadi school of Islam and of a small Jewish community that traces its origins back to Aaron (the brother of Moses). The local residential forms of massive, whitewashed mud-brick walls and arcaded central courtyards are echoed in the venerable Ghriba Synagogue in Hara Sehira on Djerba itself. Other local mud-brick houses, called *menzels*, have domed roofs and share party walls; additionally, they are not whitewashed, which gives them a more 'ceramic' look.

Above top left Variations on the Moroccan courtyard typology are seen throughout Tunisia, such as at Sidi Bou Said, with its foreign influences and distinct blue and white colour.

Above right and bottom left Mud-brick constructions on the Tunisian island of Djerba are finished with whitewash and often include central colonnaded courtyards. These adaptations are seen in homes as well as public buildings, such as the El Ghriba Synagogue (right) and the mosque (left).

Opposite Hassan Fathy's approach brought together the mud-brick building techniques of Nubian architecture and traditional Egyptian convection devices, such as vaulted, open halls, or iwans. His development at New Gourna aimed to provide an exemplary town built from inexpensive materials available locally, with buildings that were cool in the summer and retained heat in the winter.

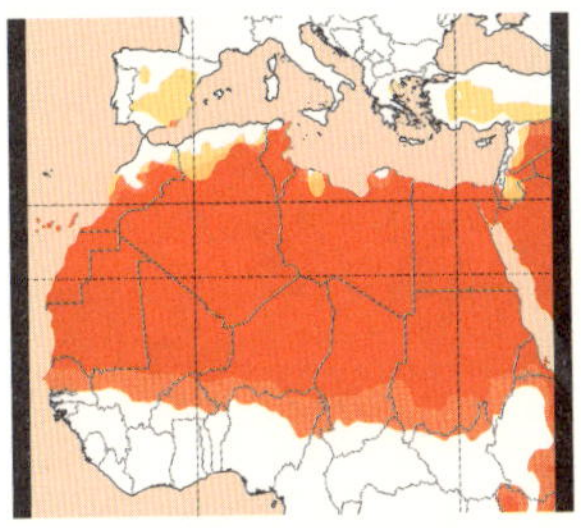

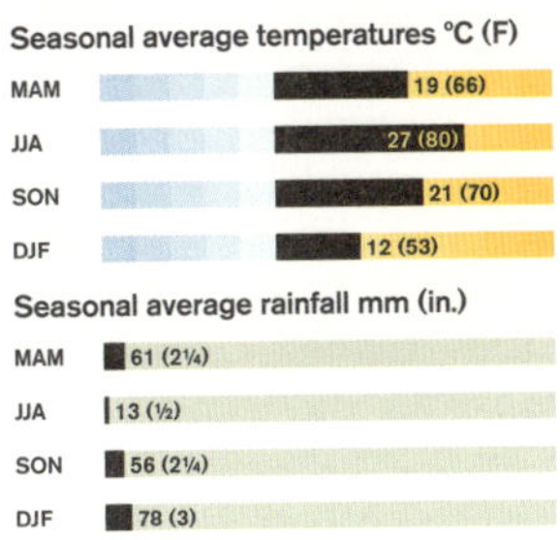

Egypt

In 969, the fourth Fatimid caliph, al-Mu'izz Li-Dinillah, and his general, Jawhar as-Siqilli, led an army from their Tunisian capital of Al-Mansuriyah, into Egypt – establishing Al-Qahira, or Cairo, that same year. The Fatimids adopted local residential forms, and the Qa'a (hall) of Dardir is one of the rare surviving examples of this type of accommodation. It is an axial reception room, flanked by vaulted halls open at one end (known as iwans) and facing into a central court covered by a high *shuksheika* (tower) that expelled hot air by convection. His investigations of this building inspired noted Egyptian architect Hassan Fathy to establish a national architecture, free of Western influence. He traced the Qa'a back to the Abbasid Palace of Al-Ukaider in Iraq, built by Isa ibn Musa in 775, thence to Fustat (the precursor of Cairo), Egypt after the Muslim conquest and subsequently to Fatimid Cairo. Fathy is best known for his New Gourna village near Luxor, described in his 1969 book *Architecture for the Poor*, where he used this configuration, along with other Cairene typologies in combination with Nubian mud-brick building techniques and promoted the result as authentic Egyptian architecture.

However, Fathy's lesser-known New Baris project, near Kharga Oasis in central Egypt, begun in 1964 and curtailed by the Six-Day War in 1967, more emphatically demonstrates the mature development of his principles. Commissioned by the Organization for Desert Development after a large aquifer was discovered, it was intended as an agricultural village for 250 initial settlers, with a view towards expansion to 5,000 residents. Lack of soil cohesion made it necessary to adapt sand for construction. The market, which was the only building completed, is characterized by soaring wind towers that funnel the cool, laminar flow of desert air down into storage chambers below ground level, to keep perishables cool in the 50°C (122°F) heat until they could be shipped to Cairo and Luxor. Despite its partial realization, New Baris is a stunning testimony to Fathy's achievement in repurposing Egypt's traditional vernacular.

Defensive *Qsur* of Algeria

Mounia Chekhab-Abudaya

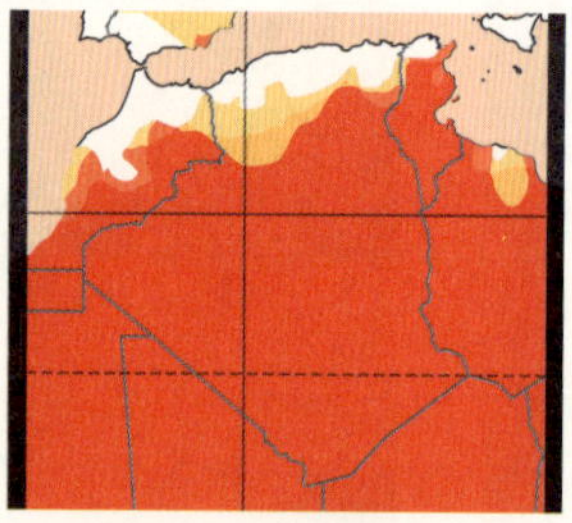

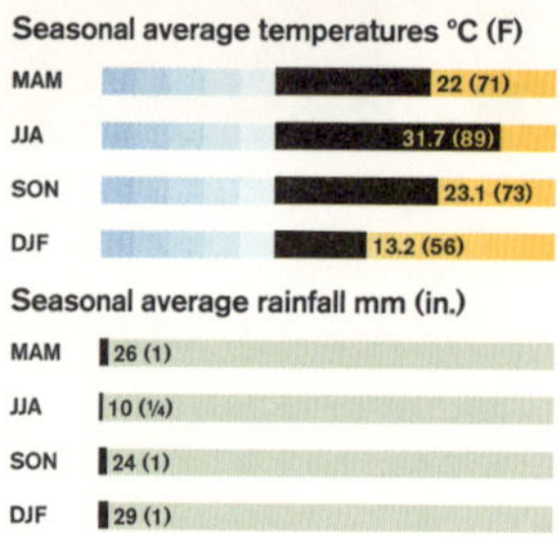

Geography/Climate

The *qsar* (plural: *qsur*) is a type of human settlement widely distributed across the Sahara Desert, including many examples located today not only in Algeria but also in southern Morocco, southern Tunisia, Libya, Mauritania and Mali. It is characterized by its use over a wide-ranging time span – probably since the early first millennium BCE, according to ancient structures recorded by the archaeologist D. J. Mattingly in the Libyan Fezzan (the southwest region of that country).[1] Mattingly's model might have given the scale for the construction of other edifices that were adapted to the desert. This phenomenon has its origin not only in long-distance exchanges between the populations of the Maghreb and the Bilad al-Sudan, but also between Africa and the Mashreq (the Arab countries lying to the east of Egypt). A further influence is the Islamization of this geographical area during the medieval period – in particular, the diffusion of the Ibadism movement.[3] This type of settlement also directly reflects a merging of the lifestyles of sedentary and nomadic populations.

The establishment of populations in this area of the Sahara appears to significantly predate the medieval period, and the *qsar* is certainly not a creation *ex nihilo* of the modern era. The numerous modifications and extensions that the *qsur* have undergone over several centuries complicates their accurate dating. However, a comparison of this settlement type's main components encourages the development of a typology to identify some common characteristics that would help position the *qsar* within the urban planning of the Islamic world.

Materials

The primary construction materials of Algeria, and of this region in general, are limestone, used with a local mortar (*timchent*), and date-palm trunks (*Phoenix dactylifera*), which are adopted for structural elements such as roofs, arches and domes, as well as door openings. Adobe bricks (*ṭub*) are used in housing and defensive structures, which are punctuated by towers and doors.

Above Found throughout Algeria, and in other parts of the Sahara Desert, fortified villages known as *qsur* are built of adobe bricks and sited on rocky promontories that allow for surveillance. This example of El Meniaa (ancient El Golea), dates from around the 10th century.

Right and far right Readily available building materials include limestone, date palms – which are used for structural elements – and mud or adobe bricks that enclose the structure. The latter provide low-cost walls and roofs with effective insulation against the heat.

Building Plan/Form

The systematic analysis and comparison of some *qsur* of southeastern Algeria (the Righ, the Mzab and the Miya areas and El Meniaa) reveal shared architectural features that can be used to identify a common type for this region. The *qsar* can be defined as a fortified village, generally ovoid in plan, built at height on a rocky promontory (*gâra*) and near a ravine (*wâdî*). The general urban plan of the observed sites shows firstly a strong relationship with the morphology of the land as well as the immediate natural environment, which may encompass the palm grove, depression or rocky plateau. This environment directly influences the building materials used in construction and how the spaces are distributed within the city. Thus, the proximity to a source of water forced people to adapt to the topography of the sites on which they were settled. In addition, altitude occupies a crucial place in the organization of the village's plan. The *qsur* of the Righ and the Mya (except for Gara Krima) were relatively low lying, while those of the Mzab, El Meniaa and Gara Krima cling to the summits of high, isolated mounds (*gûr*), only sometimes extending below the ridge.

Whereas the great mosque of the *qsar* is located at the centre of town and is accessible only to urban residents, the market is typically situated at the periphery, revealing the wider role of the *qsar* as a relay on trans-Saharan trade routes. Spaces inside the *qsar* are organized according to a tribal hierarchy, with specific districts and a complex lane network. Its regional architectural features include a pyramidal capping for watchtowers and minarets; the absence of either a *minbar* (pulpit) or decoration in prayer halls in the region; and the brick decorations and domes encountered in the Righ, which incorporate the architectural features of the Souf and the Tunisian Djerid – both of which came under Ibadi influence during the medieval period.

Most of the *qsur* are now abandoned, although some have been reoccupied by poor or marginalized populations. As in the medinas (walled cities) of some major metropolises in the Arab world, a noticeable poverty is observable nowadays in the *qsur*. They are relegated to the background in favour of a new form of urbanism, contiguous with the old. Some completely abandoned sites, such as Temacin, are the result of multiple causes of damage (lack of maintenance, partly due to progressive privatization of the lands, or floods) and have sometimes suffered massive destruction coordinated by the local authorities, as was the case for the *qsar* of Mestaoua, in present day Tuggur. Some inhabited *qsur*, like those in the region of Wargla, have experienced a densification of their populations, with equally destructive urban-planning consequences because their architectural 'rescue' has only recently been countenanced.

Above Often organized in an ovoid plan, the spatial organization of *qsur* responds to tribal hierarchy within. Markets are usually located at the periphery to allow for trade between villagers and outsiders on trans-Saharan trade routes.

Opposite Without proper upkeep, and with increasing popularity of new types of urban arrangements, most *qsur* have lost favour and are now only occupied by poor inhabitants, or have fallen into disrepair, such as these ancient sites near Temacin (top) and the ruins of Tindjillet Ksar (bottom).

Libya's Vernacular of Berber *Taddart*

Beniamino Polimeni

Above In Libya's Nafusa Mountains, the concept of environmental sustainability and the rational use of natural resources play an emblematic role.

Geography/Climate

The oasis towns of Libya's desert regions provide perhaps the most celebrated examples of the country's traditional architecture – particularly the cities of Ghadames and Ghat, located in the Tripolitania and Fezzan regions respectively. Once vital to the trans-Saharan trade route, they form just one part of an extended and little-known vernacular heritage scattered throughout the country.

Another geographical area, the Nafusa Mountains, is home to dwellings that provide perhaps the most significant 'window' on to the lives and traditions of the indigenous people of this region. Although similar situations can be found in different parts of North Africa, in this particular geographical area the concept of environmental sustainability and the rational use of natural resources play an emblematic role. The northern boundaries of a plateau that extends from the Matmata region in Tunisia to the coast not far from Misurata in Tripolitania contains many surviving settlements in which the scarcity of natural resources has led to customs and construction traditions that closely follow economic principles. All these traditions can be found in the shape of introverted urban forms, in landscape transformations, in the structure of fortified granaries and in traditional dwellings.

Building Plan/Form and Construction Techniques

Housing is the main constituent of these villages, and is the element that best allows examination of the close connections between cultural identity and adaptation to the environment. The house is the most basic urban unit – the element that develops, through successive articulations, into complex systems that proceed from the human to the territorial scale.

The *taddart* – which literally means 'the place where I live' – is the traditional Berber dwelling. In its simplest form, it consists of a rectangular room with a ratio of the lengths of its two sides of 1:2; a single vertical opening simultaneously serves to ventilate, illuminate and provide access. The room is covered by a vault or, less frequently, by a flat roof. This type of house is generally constructed from roughly worked limestone boulders bound together by gypsum mortar. The walls that form the rectangular rooms are relatively thick in order to provide a cool indoor environment in hot weather; sometimes these walls consist of rows of niches and small arches, creating a structure that is the base for vaulted spaces, or *kamur*.

Basic houses with flat roofs, or *mirì*, are generally built with a repetitive series of small, parallel beams made of olive or palm wood, which support several layers of a waterproofing mortar called *zimzà*. The initial modification of these basic units is the transition from the mono-cellular to the bi-cellular type, based on increased housing needs. This transition takes place vertically, horizontally or in cross-section, and separates work-related activities (stables or storage areas called *tamidalt*) from domestic activities. The simplest way of achieving this double cell is by mirroring the basic quadrangular room along its short side – adding a space that is generally used as a small granary. A vertical duplication of the initial room is also often carried out by adding an upper space – vaulted or covered by a flat roof, and accessible by external stairs made of olive wood (*derji*).

Courtyard houses are the final stage of a typological process that originates in the fusion of basic units around a central space. Primitive examples of this transformation process can be found in instances of a small open space added to the front of a mono-cellular unit and delineated by a wall, defining an open courtyard, or *ammas n taddart*. This aggregative process eventually creates a totally enclosed space.

The simplest example of this process of growth is a square cell with an external, rectangular courtyard that has an area equal to a quarter of the dwelling space. This configuration is generally located in a favourable location – either perpendicular to the secondary road of a village, or parallel to the northern border of the plateau on which the settlement sits. Another type consists of the connection of two quadrangular cells to another unit, so creating an open courtyard. This building type is delimited by a wall containing the main door. Its windows are generally symmetrical and open inwards, providing privacy and bioclimatic comfort. A third category encompasses many examples in which a rectangular cell is duplicated vertically. This type usually has an external courtyard with the same area as that of the cell itself. A variation of this two-storey type consists of three square rooms that create a right angle between them, with a resulting reduction of possible courtyard surface. Both of these two-storey cases have windows and doors facing the courtyard, although some small square windows may also be located facing towards the road or northern border.

Materials

The materials used across all the aforementioned building variants are olive or palm wood for door frames, floors and staircases; limestone boulders and rubble for walls, arches and vaults; and various kinds of gypsum mortar and plaster for binding the rubble stone, and as a traditional finish for the external walls. Modern materials and technologies such as Portland cement mortar and reinforced-concrete roofs can be found in some isolated examples, in which different transformations – dating back probably more than half a century – have modified the original types, creating a new typological sequence.

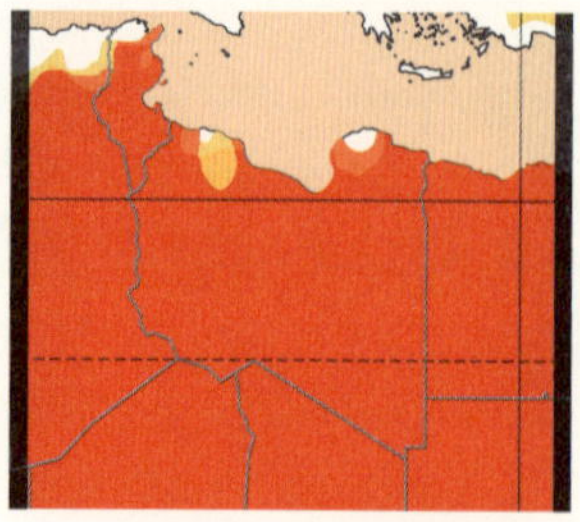

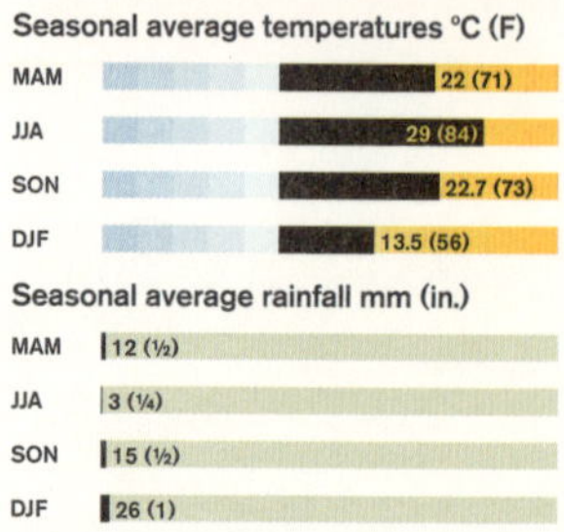

Below and opposite top, second and bottom rows Vaulted spaces of traditional Berber dwellings and granaries are formed from thick slabs of limestone boulders joined with gypsum mortar. Their deep walls give protection from solar gain and their staircases and door and window frames are made from olive or palm wood.

Opposite third row Flat-roofed houses are based on a single-cell structure that can be increased, cell by cell, as required. Elaborate courtyard variants have multiple cells separated by a central cell-wide court.

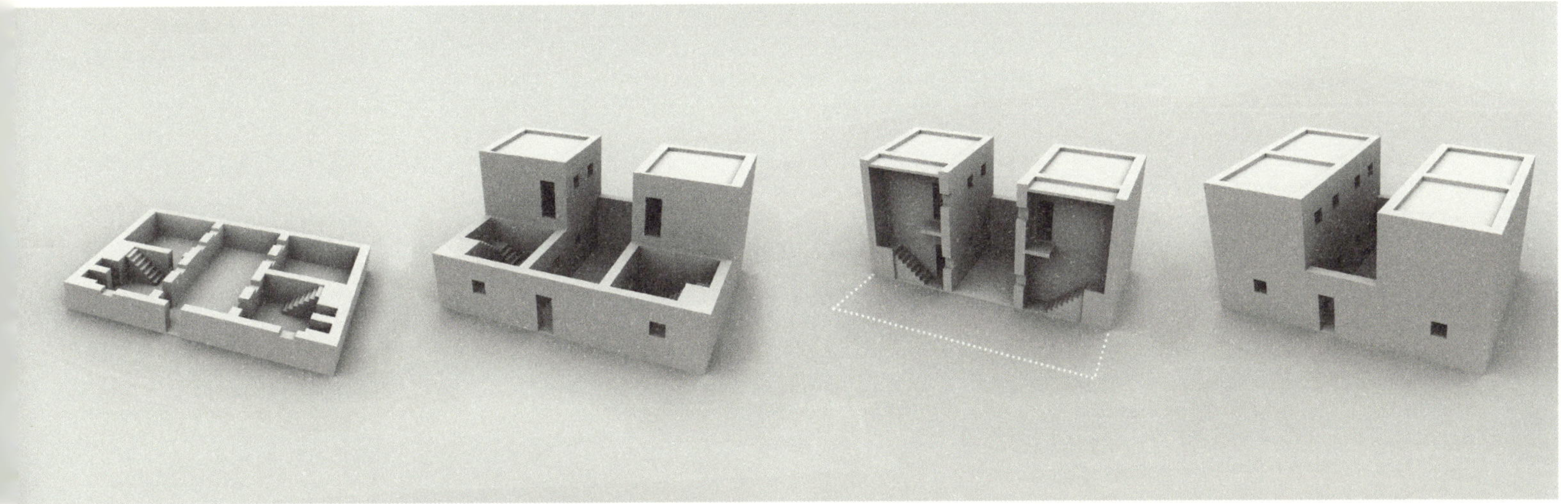

Khayma and Mud-brick Dwellings of Mauritania and the Sahel

Mark Dike DeLancey

Geography/Climate and Culture

Until the 1970s, the vast majority of Mauritanians were nomadic, living in tents. Drought drove most to the cities – in particular the capital, Nouakchott. Nonetheless, their nomadic heritage remains central to Mauritanian identity, and their vernacular architectural heritage is acknowledged in contemporary references to the nomadic tent in the urban environment. A much smaller population historically lived in the oases of Mauritania, scratching a living from the earth, as well as profiting as stops on the trans-Saharan trade routes and as centres of Islamic scholarship.

Construction Techniques and Building Plan/Form

A Mauritanian tent – or *khayma*, a term also used to denote the family – is usually pitched facing southwest to avoid strong opposing winds. Historically, its goat-hair velum (membranous structure) was woven by women in strips that were then stitched together; nowadays, white cloth purchased in the markets is more often employed. The velum is stretched taut over two long wooden poles, arranged such that their round club-shaped bases are placed just inside the entrance and at the back of the tent. They rise towards the centre of the structure, where their thin tips are fitted into the underside of the *hammar*, a wood block shaped like an upturned ink blotter.

The *hammar* protects the velum from the pointed ends of the poles, a function further effected by inserting a long, thin piece of cloth between *hammar* and velum. The sides of the tent may be raised on shorter wooden props to provide for light and breezes, or dropped at night against the wind and cold. In poor weather, the space between the central poles may be widened so that the velum falls on the ground. Sand will then eventually seal the edges of the tent.

More permanent residences are constructed of unbaked mud brick or, in mountainous areas, of stone masonry, often with a protective coating of mud plaster. This stone masonry may be arranged with thin courses of flat schist alternating with thicker courses of sandstone. Entrance from the street is through a vestibule with off-axis doors to obstruct visual access. Exterior walls present long, undecorated surfaces, relieved only by the entrance with its high sill to protect against sand ingress.

The heart of the residence is a square courtyard, within which most daily activities occur. Kitchen, guest rooms, sleeping chambers, storage rooms and shops surround the courtyard. Opposite the vestibule is a long, rectangular building, often two storeys high, in which guests are received. Roofs are supported by palm timbers or various types of acacia, above which are laid crosswise branches, mats and, finally, an earthen terrace. Such roof terraces, often employed for sleeping in the hotter periods of the year, may be accessed by staircases formed from broad slabs of stone corbelled out from a wall. Decoration of wall surfaces consists of single triangular recesses, created with flat stones, or multiple recesses stacked in pyramidal compositions, to create relieving arches above the doorways.

In the far southeastern city of Oualata, a unique heritage of architectural ornamentation produced by women involves low-relief earthen arabesque decorations painted with white and red clay. It has been suggested that these embellishments, placed around the entrance and on internal courtyard walls, are abstracted from Arabic calligraphy, thereby emphasizing women's roles in educating children and possibly referencing Islamic protective devices.

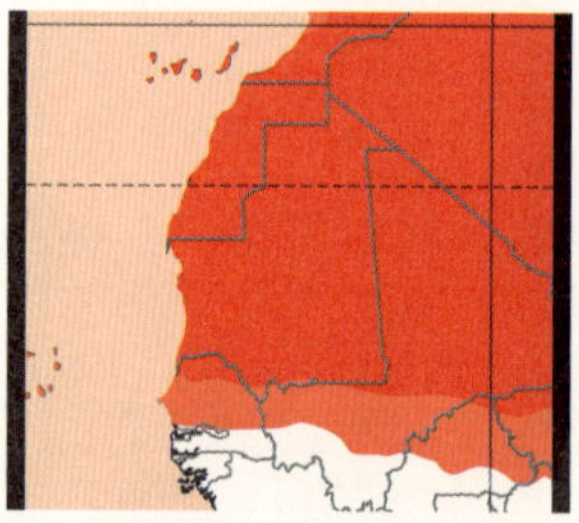

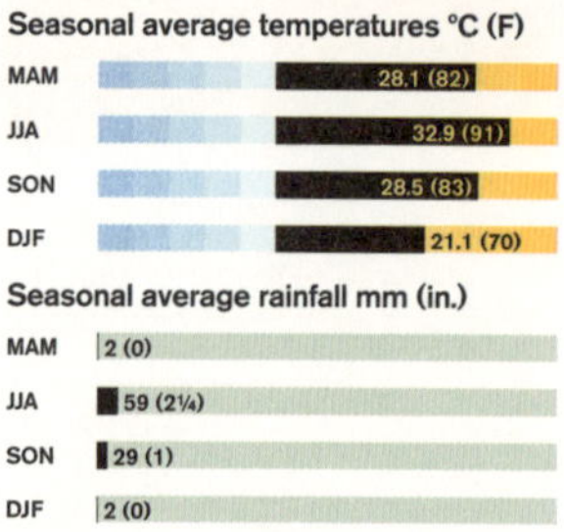

Opposite top Although they were once a highly nomadic population, drought and the increasing preference for urban living mean many Mauritanians now lead sedentary lives in towns and cities.

Opposite bottom Despite the altered pattern of use from traditional nomadic life, tents or *khayma* remain an essential part of the architecture of the region and sit side-by-side with permanent dwellings of mud brick, schist and sandstone.

Adobe Architecture of Mali and Niger

James Morris

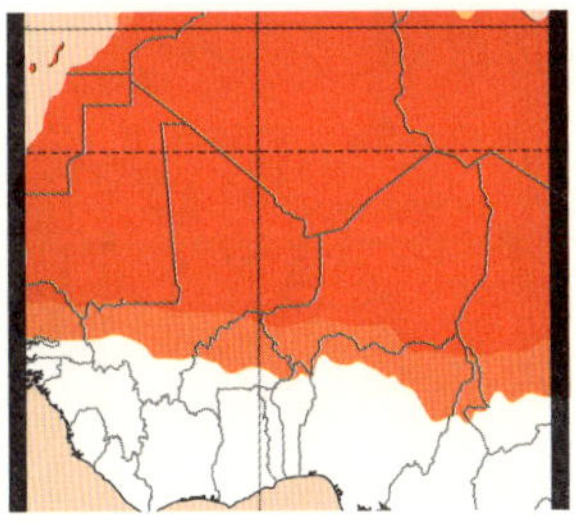

Seasonal average temperatures °C (F)

	°C (F)
MAM	30 (86)
JJA	32 (89)
SON	28 (82)
DJF	21 (70)

Seasonal average rainfall mm (in.)

	mm (in.)
MAM	14 (½)
JJA	159 (6½)
SON	43 (1¾)
DJF	1 (0)

Opposite Conical and rectangular granaries built of mud in the Dogan village of Ireli under the Bandiagara escarpment, Mali.

Right A mosque in Kossa, Niger, which was recently designed and constructed by one of the students of the architect Falke Barmou.

Geography/Climate

The word 'Sahel' in Arabic means coast or shore, and in the Sahel region of West Africa the 'sea' lapping this shore is the Sahara Desert. The region's towns and cities are historic trading ports from which camel trains would have journeyed, carrying the riches of Africa to the greater Islamic world. This trans-Saharan economy went into decline when 15th-century Portuguese merchants opened new sea-bound Atlantic trading routes. What emerged from this history were extraordinary and unique architectural landscapes, still largely extant within the modern nations of Mali and Niger.

Materials and Construction Techniques

Built around a core of sun-baked clay bricks, pierced through and reinforced with wooden struts, then rendered with a mud paste, the traditional buildings of Mali and Niger show that from the most basic of materials and in the harshest of conditions, creative people can develop highly expressive and visually enchanting architectural styles, striking in their sculptural form. The bold, monolithic masterpieces of once-wealthy cities such as Ségou, Mopti, Djenné, Gao, Agadez and Timbuktu play with the sunlight and the inherent properties of the mud itself to emphasize shadow, texture, silhouette, profile and form. With each annual re-rendering, the shape of a building is subtly altered; change and movement are ever present. As each render coat dries, the surface is covered in a web of cracks before it slowly starts to peel off. The material is therefore tactile, warm and vulnerable, and these buildings demand and receive an engaged relationship with their users. Their maintenance and resurfacing is part of the rhythm of life; there is an ongoing, active participation in their continuing existence.

These buildings are commonly perceived as being 'architecture without architects' – and by implication are ascribed a primitive purity missing in the modern world. However, in reality the structural engineers and creative minds behind both historic and contemporary buildings in the Sahel are known people. Operating in a manner comparable to a medieval European guild of masons, groups, castes or families of master builders exist in differing forms throughout the region. Some individuals have achieved considerable influence, and some have been attributed with supernatural powers. The royal architect of Mansa (Lord) Musa, a man of Berber origin called al-Sahili, oversaw Musa's sizable building programme. At Timbuktu c. 1325, he built the still-extant

Opposite top The Friday Mosque, Djenné, built around 1906, is the largest surviving mud building in the world.

Opposite bottom and above left Dwellings of chiefs and merchants are elaborate structures of Mali and Niger's mud-timber typology. The contrast between the ornate finishes of high-status houses and the more simple rendered shape and finish of typical homes can be seen in the House of the Chief in Djenné (opposite) and a more typical Djenné townhouse (above).

Above right Mosques in the cities of Mopti, Djenné, Timbuktu and Agadez are renowned for their decorative interpretation of the regional style. Examples such as the Friday Mosque in Agadez include minarets spiked with timber sticks that give a distinctive appearance. Additionally they act to regulate the internal temperature and assist with annual re-rendering.

Mosque of Djinguereber. During the 1960s, in the Niger village of Yaama, the architect Falke Barmou designed the striking and award-winning Friday Mosque, having been inspired by God in a dream. His apprentices went on to become recognized architects in their own right, building inventive structures that draw on their shared Hausa heritage while incorporating their own architectural innovations – all working with the same basic materials of mud, water and timber reinforcements.

Building Plan/Form

This perceived indigenous culture is also not so purely indigenous. Influences within the region can been traced from the wider Islamic world, Berber traders, neighbouring African cultures and the colonial French, who were keen to promote the notion of a 'Soudanese' style and identity of their own making. The early 20th-century French governor of Djenné became particularly involved in the reconstruction of the town's Friday Mosque – its third known incarnation, which made it the largest mud-brick building in the world.

Within the historic towns and cities, the principal buildings are places of government and worship, and the houses of chiefs and merchants. Additionally, the countryside is adorned with granaries that extend the range of sculptural form. In rural Hausa areas of Niger, huge upturned ceramic pots spread across the landscape, each filled with the season's agricultural produce. In Mali, the cliff villages of the Dogon – some still animist, some Muslim – resemble from above a complex puzzle of geometric shapes. Combinations of square, rectangular and circular interwoven granaries, pathways, living quarters and *togu-na* (great shelters), together make up the village whole.

The most famous buildings of this region are the great mosques of Mopti, Djenné, Timbuktu and Agadez, but its truly individual monuments are less well known. The 12th-century Dougouba Mosque sits like a piece of singular sculpture in its village landscape, its minaret a sliced cone with sticks protruding seemingly at random from the curved façade. Lacking the more evolved and formal appearance of the later Malian mosques, this is perhaps from where the style originated. The functional purpose of these projecting branches is to help regulate the building's moisture content and aid the annual re-rendering, but their striking visual impact and dynamic presence, which would come to define the region's unique aesthetic, are more significant still. Another example, Nando Mosque, was reputedly built overnight by a giant, in perhaps the mid-19th century. Its supernatural origins seem to have influenced its free-form 'Gaudí-esque' shape and abstract decorative patterns. Perhaps that famous Catalan architect saw early photographs of the mosque brought back by the European explorers who were first penetrating these African heartlands in the 1870s and 80s. The mosque's raison d'être may have resulted from incursions by Fulani Islamic fundamentalists intent on converting the animist Dogon heartlands a few decades earlier (not unlike those taking place in northern Mail and Niger today). Their jihadist mission to convert and eradicate un-Islamic practices possibly failed, as female-breast motifs and other animist Dogon symbols remain, just evident, in the near-complete darkness of the interior.

Nomadic and Sedentary Structures of the Sahel from Chad to Somalia

Mark Dike DeLancey

Geography/Climate

Encompassing the Somali coast and the mountainous highlands of Ethiopia, this region of the Sahel merges with the Sahara in the north. Within this area, dry and rainy seasons alternate, creating geographical diversity that is reflected in the local vernacular.

Materials

Given the variation of climate and culture in the Sahel, available building materials differ from region to region.

The nomads of Chad, central-northern Sudan and Somalia utilize tent forms for their dwellings, fashioned from varied materials that include camel velum and types of acacia fibre. As in most nomadic societies, all of these tents are owned, created, raised and struck by women.

The inhabitants of the Somali coast share the coral vernacular architecture of the Swahili-speaking regions of Africa's eastern seaboard. Rubble stone is adopted in the rocky Ethiopian interior. The settled architecture of Sudan and South Sudan uses earth construction – a technique that reaches its regional apotheosis in the vernacular of northern Cameroon and southwestern Chad.

Construction Techniques and Building Plan/Form

Chad

Many nomadic populations across the Sahel employ a variety of tent forms, which enable transhumant animal husbandry. The Tubu of Chad use a frame tent with a rectangular plan and three rows of support poles. These poles are bound together with flexible acacia roots, and the central ones are longer than the sides – creating a rounded roof, which is covered with woven *dum* palm mats. Tubu tents are pitched with the rear end – supported within by the occupants' saddle, saddlebags and bedframe – oriented towards the wind, which blows alternately from the northeast and the southwest. The entrance, at the opposite end, opens into a small vestibule screened from the main area of the tent to protect privacy. The tent wall behind the bed is adorned with a broad leather wall hanging decorated with cowry shells arranged in geometric patterns, created for the marriage of the woman of the tent by her mother and female relatives.

Notwithstanding its use in central Sudan (for which, see below), the ultimate regional exploitation of earth as a building material is to be found in southwestern Chad, as well as in neighbouring northern Cameroon. It is the parabolic domed residential structure called a *teleuk*, built by the Mousgoum people of those localities. Its form stretches the structural possibilities of mud to their maximum in a concept similar to the coil-pottery method. The *teleuk* is built of progressively constricting rings of earth without the use of the kind of centring typically employed for building arch-like structures. Its exterior is decorated with mud reliefs in the form of vertical half-cylinders or nested, inverted 'V' forms that provide footholds for those engaged in the construction and maintenance of the upper reaches of the structure. These buildings are constructed by specialized masons, usually male, while their interiors are typically ornamented by their female occupants with moulded or incised abstract decorations. A compound might incorporate a *teleuk* for the husband and each wife in this potentially polygamous society, arranged in a circular plan. Mousgoum settlements range from villages composed of multiple compounds to larger towns. Currently, the *teleuk*, which fell out of favour during the 20th century owing to expense and the specialized knowledge required, is being revived as a symbol of Mousgoum identity.

Sudan/South Sudan

The Kababish of central-northern Sudan also employ a rectangular-plan tent, but, unlike those of the Chadian nomads, its structural elements are held in place by tension. Oriented towards the east, the direction of both Mecca and the rising sun, the Kababish tent employs three rows of poles arranged north–south, with the central row rising higher than the outer ones. These poles support, and are in turn held in place by, a velum composed of strips of camel hair sewn together at the selvage.

Although distinct from the Swahili-style coral architecture encountered in Somalia discussed below, the vernacular of Sudan's Red Sea coast also historically employed coral as a building material. This can perhaps best be seen at Suakin, a city that came into its own as a major port under Ottoman control in the 17th century, until superseded by nearby Port Sudan in the early 20th century. Multi-storey buildings with turned-wood *mashrabiya* lattice windows that protect the interiors from the hot sun and prying eyes indicate the close relationship with the nearby Arabian Peninsula, as well as the impact of Ottoman Egyptian architecture. New building types, such as the recently restored three-storey *caravanserai* (travellers' or merchants' inn) constructed in 1881 by Shenawi Bey, also indicate the impact of external patronage on the city.

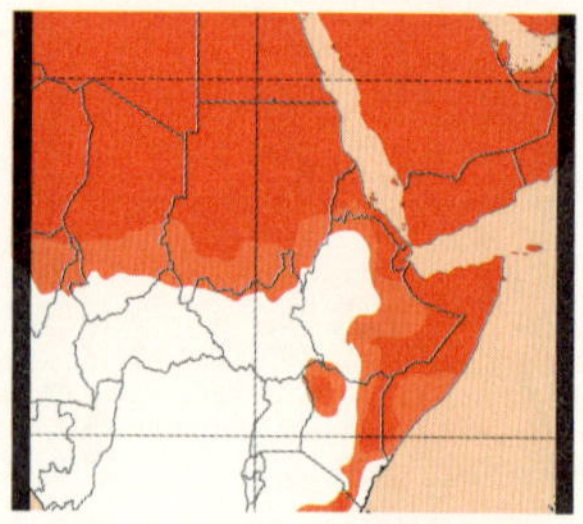

Seasonal average temperatures °C (F)

MAM	28 (82)
JJA	28 (82)
SON	27 (80)
DJF	24 (75)

Seasonal average rainfall mm (in.)

MAM	78 (3)
JJA	135 (5½)
SON	79 (3)
DJF	11 (½)

Opposite top and middle Tents are seen in various typologies across the Sahel region of Central and East Africa. In Chad, tents are often of Tubu origin: framed in a rectangular plan, their apex poles are taller than the peripheral ones, creating a barrel-shaped roof, which is clad with palm mats.

Opposite bottom left In contrast to Tubu tents, the Kababish of central-northern Sudan create tents of camel velum secured in tension and facing east, towards Mecca and the rising sun.

Opposite right The *teleuk* in southwestern Chad is built by the Mousgoum people and displays the decorative and insulating properties of earth. The exterior protuberances form footholds for creating and maintaining the structure, which is made of progressively smaller earth coils.

Opposite top Structures of Sudanese sedentary peoples in the early 20th century were primarily built using earth. They added decorative façades, such as the El-Geyf Mosque built of coral masonry, in Suakin, a port city in the Sudan.

Opposite bottom right Two-storey, circular churches in Ethiopia built since the 17th century are modelled on residences for the wealthy made of sandstone masonry. This centrally planned church in the process of being roofed is near Lalibella, Ethiopia.

Opposite bottom left and middle Somali nomads utilize tents but, unlike their counterparts in Chad, these are constructed with circular frames known as *aqil*, made of acacia timber arcs and enclosed by woven grass and fibres also of acacia.

Below Colonial and post-colonial effects on the Sahel are seen in the historical fabric of Mogadishu on the Somali coast. Incorporating Chinese, Indian and Italian influences, the whitewashed surfaces recall the coral architecture of Africa's eastern seaboard.

The vernacular of the sedentary peoples of the Sudanese interior is largely built of earth. An extraordinary tradition of architectural decoration employing representational and geometric reliefs and paintings, as well as embedded ceramics, was practised by the Nubian population of southern Egypt and northern Sudan in the first half of the 20th century. Although largely focused on the exterior entrance façade, interior decoration was common as well – and consisted largely of woven mats and basket lids used in wedding ceremonies. Ceramic plates produced contrast with the matt earthen walls, identified employment, and deflected the evil eye. Painted and relief ornamentation reflected the contemporary environment and abstract designs potentially derived from the female-dominated pottery tradition. Animal skulls such as those of bulls, sheep and crocodiles were attached to the façade and served as protective devices with an ancient pedigree. Most decoration was created by household members, although professional decorators were more common in northern Sudan. Professionally executed decorations were much more likely to incorporate architectural references such as domes and minarets. Much of this architecture and its decoration was financed through a combination of wide-scale employment of Nubian men in the hospitality industry in major cities such as Luxor, as well as by government compensation for land lost to the gradual raising of the Aswan Dam. The demise of the tradition corresponded with the completion of the dam in 1970 and the subsequent dispersal of the Nubian population. Echoes may be found, however, in the much more widespread practice of ornamenting exterior surfaces of contemporary residential buildings to honour those who have made pilgrimage to Mecca.

Ethiopia and Eritrea

To the east of Sudan and South Sudan lie the mountainous highlands of Ethiopia. In northern Ethiopia and southern Eritrea, rectangular-plan rural farmhouses are built of stone rubble, its courses alternating with timbers in a method reminiscent of the ancient Aksumite tradition most famously seen in the 6th-century church of Debre Damo. (This method also characterized the Kaaba [sacred shrine] in Mecca in the lifetime of the Prophet Muhammad.) A wall of granaries divides these farmhouses into a frontal living area and a rear cooking and storage area. Peripheral benches and beds are integral with the walls, while storage shelving consists of wall recesses.

In contrast, two-storey circular-plan residences for the wealthy are built exclusively of sandstone masonry. An inner, square plan, formed by four corner pillars on the ground floor and arches on the first, is surrounded by a circular outer wall. The roofs of these dwellings are conical, with the pillars raising the centre higher than the exterior circular walls. Such residences provided the prototype for circular churches built since the 17th century, in which a central square space containing the altar is surrounded by circular ambulatories.

Somalia

As opposed to the aforementioned rectangular nomadic plans of Sudan and Chad, Somali nomads employ a circular frame tent, or *aqil*, composed of intersecting arcs of acacia roots covered with mats. Exterior mats are woven of grass and acacia fibres, while communally woven decorative interior mats are made exclusively of acacia fibres dyed to create geometric designs.

The Somali coast is home to the northernmost extension of the Swahili-style coral architecture of the east coast of Africa. However, close connections can be also seen with the architecture of the Middle East and South Asia – witness the 13th-century mosque of Fakhr al-Din in Mogadishu, incorporating several domes, one of which is topped with a Chinese celadon vessel, and a complex interplay of spaces atypical of Swahili architecture, which tends to favour a hypostyle plan. The elaborately carved white-marble *mihrab* (arched niche oriented towards the direction of Mecca) and portal facing have been identified as the work of Gujarati artists from Khambhat (formerly Cambay), India. Historic Mogadishu, one of the numerous city-states established along the East African coast, was dramatically expanded and provided with broad connecting avenues under Italian colonial rule. The whitewashed surfaces of its colonial and postcolonial public buildings recall the heritage of coral architecture.

Southern Africa's Vernacular Diversity

Debbie Whelan and Walter Peters

Geography/Climate

The climate of the eastern seaboard of Africa ranges from temperate to subtropical and tropical. Areas inland of the Drakensberg escarpment are subject to very hot summers and cold winters, but owing to local climatic generators they cannot be classified as 'hot and dry' as they are well watered and fertile and have lush vegetation. The vegetation itself is also vital in providing varying 'toolkits' of material, with which both indigenous peoples and white settlers build their houses. This complexity provides for a vast array of architectural responses, allowing for different interpretations of space, form and texture.

Furthermore, the eastern seaboard of Africa is overlain with multiple influences: early travellers, traders and the like brought with them new technologies and ways of seeing space, while at the same time local people contributed to the development of white settler vernaculars, creating a richness and whimsy in the extant vernacular landscape. Considerations of space and gender provide important abstract layers to the tradition of the construction and form of the buildings of the Zulu, for example, while the secluded homesteads of the Tembe–Tsonga people in northern KwaZulu-Natal and southern Mozambique have vastly different layouts from the prescribed form of their close neighbours, the Zulu.

West of the Drakensberg, the largely flat inland plateau gradually slopes towards the Atlantic Ocean – a route also followed by the region's rivers (ultimately via the Orange River). The east, with its higher elevation (Highveld) enjoys decidedly more rainfall; the southwestern, semi-arid steppe is known as the Great Karoo; while the northwest is characterized by a hot, arid desert. The southwestern cape of the region enjoys a dry summer and a subtropical climate, also known as 'Mediterranean', with the majority of the rainfall occurring in winter.

Right The range of materials and climatic differences shaping South Africa's eastern landscape gives rise to a fascinating variety of regional and tribal structures. In this view of the uKhahlamba-Drakensberg Park – an area of KwaZulu-Natal – conical-roofed thatched Hlubi buildings sit alongside modern equivalents.

Opposite top left and middle left two Using materials available locally, the interpretation of woven dwellings in South Africa includes grasses, used in the Zulu beehives (top), and the reeds and palm fronds of the basket-like homes built by the Tembe–Tsonga (middle images).

Opposite top right and bottom left Coral rag homes along the eastern coast vary in the construction of their walls: from stone in inner regions, such as the Inyanga Plateau (top) to limestone rubble formed from fossilized coral nearer the coast (bottom). All are crowned with a conical thatched roof.

Opposite bottom right and below The homes of Tembe–Tsonga people rely on locally available reeds and palm fronds to form their distinctive stepped roofs of thatch, which are constructed separately and then hoisted atop the walls.

Materials, Construction Techniques and Building Plan/Form

There are myriad material options available to people living on the African east coast. This abundance points to the emergence and continual development of a series of vernacular architectures heavily embedded in tradition and belief – yet which, by employing different materials, have departed from the rigours of tradition, showing that the idea and interpretation of vernacular architecture cannot be subject to a static analysis.

Coral Rag and Palm-leaf Construction: Coastal Region

Travelling down the African east coast, one finds coral rag constructions (buildings of rubbly limestone blocks formed mostly from petrified coral) in the dense townscapes of the Swahili coast. These buildings are a resultant combination of indigenous materials and the strong overtones of centuries of trade, particularly Omani. Many of the local indigenous residents practise Islam, while their neighbours may be Christian or follow indigenous religions involving ancestor worship. The more formal buildings in their vernacular often sit side-by-side with those more modest and of palm-leaf (*makuti*) construction, which respond to the tropical climate and the requirements of mitigating heavy rainfall as well as allowing for natural ventilation in the hot and humid conditions. Away from the coast, a greater reliance on stone – particularly at foundation level – and timber is seen, usually topped off with a thatched grass roof. These are found in both the archaeological record and contemporary constructions such as those located on the Nyangani Plateau of eastern Zimbabwe.

Basket Houses: Tembe–Tsonga Region

Further south, the Tembe–Tsonga people in southern Mozambique and northern KwaZulu-Natal, South Africa, build basket-like houses out of reeds and palm fronds. In these buildings, the roof is constructed separately and then lifted onto the wall construction once completed. Tembe–Tsonga thatching is often overlapping, a feature that distinguishes it in landscapes occupied by multiple tribal groups. In the past, the internal spaces of these buildings were highly decorated, in that the palm fronds that formed the roofing were interwoven into patterns.[1]

Grass-dome Building: KwaZulu-Natal

The Tembe–Tsonga are neighbours to the Zulu, a previously pastoralist people who, in the KwaZulu-Natal grasslands, perpetuated a grass 'beehive' building tradition, in which the circular structure, or *iqhugwane*, was constructed of withies of the sickle bush (*Dichrostachys cineraria*). The dome itself sometimes consisted of over ten different types of grass, each with a different and specific function.[2] Resolution of the final covering with regard to elaboration is limited: the more prestigious homesteads in the past had a covering of grass mats over the dome, while historical examples show some decoration in the form of grass ropes, which were woven into geometrical shapes. Importantly, this thatched tradition was an ideal climatic response: not only were the grasslands of the coastal littoral formerly abundant in different varieties of building material, but as a building component grass is climatically appropriate as it keeps spaces cool in summer; insulates during winter; shrinks in hot, dry periods, allowing for limited release of heat; and swells in the rainy season, thereby shutting out the rain.

The grass building tradition was well recorded by early white travellers, and was an integral part of a strongly defined cultural and traditional landscape that also incorporated metaphysical meanings and gender roles.

Broadly speaking, the grass dome was part of a greater construct, namely the Central Cattle Pattern, in which the cattle acted as both a physical and a cognitive centre of the lifeway of the Zulu.[3] Cattle ownership has connotations of wealth; allows for marriage, through the *lobola* system of bride-price contribution; and separates men from women, in that keeping cattle is a man's occupation and women traditionally have scant access to livestock.

The Zulu homestead is ideally circular, with a central fenced-off space containing the cattle byre, or *isibaya*, the domain of the men. Entrance is from below, and one passes the bachelors' and visitors' houses at the entrance before moving up the hill past the dwellings of children, arranged into units containing those of the same age and sex, the wives' houses and the kitchen buildings, until one reaches the house of the *umnumzane* (the head of the homestead), which is known as the *indlunkulu*.

The space of the house is gendered, with a basic division between men on the right and women on the left in a building in which the entrance typically faces east. The divisions within this generality are based on age and status: a mix of men and women may be found on both sides, indicative of hierarchies within the homestead as well as of different generations.

Importantly, the houses are circular. They will also have a religious space at the rear, the *umsamo*, which is the place in which consultation with the ancestors will occur. Ancestors have a strong relationship with the thatching grass of the roof – even for contemporary Zulu people living in suburban homes, most buildings inviting congress with the ancestors will have a thatched roof.

Below Located in the grasslands of KwaZulu-Natal, the *iqhugwane* structures of the Zulu are circular in plan and in their arrangement around each homestead's central shared space.

Opposite Woven in a dome shape from up to ten different types of grass and secured with grass ropes that are both decorative and functional, the Zulu 'beehives' work in synergy with their climatic context. In summer, the dried material shrinks and creates gaps that allow for the cooling release of warm air; winter rains cause the grass to swell, becoming an impermeable membrane.

2

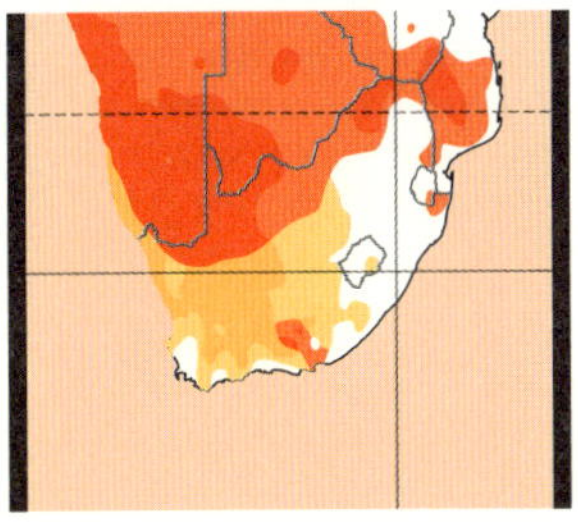

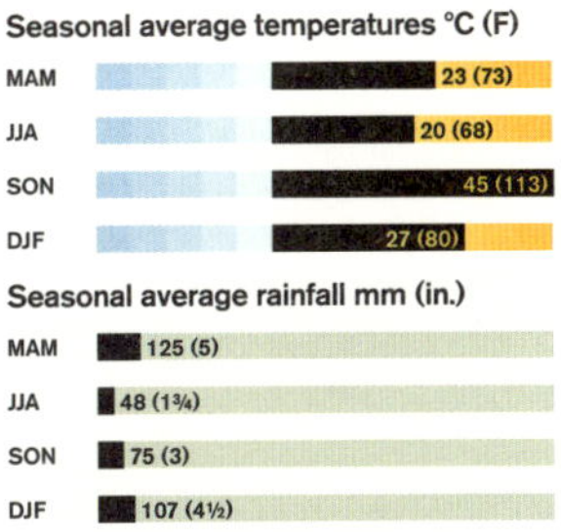

Opposite top ***Rondawel*** **or round dwellings in the rural KwaZulu-Natal district of Msinga have become more prevalent since the 1970s. Formed of thatched roofs and rendered stone and timber walls, the homes are distinctive for their external decorative bands of plaster at the entrance.**

Opposite bottom Known as ***isimodeni*** **style, decoration of** ***rondawel*** **has become increasingly exuberant. The painted effects are used to mark the (largely female-occupied) dwellings and include entry aprons, stairs and sometimes 'blind' windows in bas-relief.**

Thatched-dome Building: Msinga

Msinga is a central district of KwaZulu-Natal, focused on the confluence of the Tugela and Mzinyathi rivers. It is a deeply traditional area, in that men from the cities will travel here to find 'good, traditional' wives who subscribe to the old value systems. It also is an area from which, since the late 19th century, men would travel to work in the mines in Johannesburg, leaving their wives behind. For more than a century, therefore, Msinga has been a place dominated by womenfolk, waiting for their men to return from the mines at Christmas time.

While this lifestyle of interstitial existence between urban centres and the rural district of Msinga prevailed for many decades, its buildings remained quintessentially traditional in format and construction. Msinga is one of the few areas in which thatched domes existed until recently, their popularity declining because of a number of factors such as fire and the limited availability of the material. Certainly by the 1970s, the prevalence of thatch had begun to decline, leading to an increasing reliance on the thatched cone-on-cylinder, or *rondawel*. These buildings tended to be constructed around a timber frame densely packed with stone, and were characterized by decorated plastered bands to each side of the entrance.

The earliest of these decorations appeared in the 1980s, and were known by the name *isimodeni* (literally, 'modern') after beadwork with similar patterns. This is significant, as the Zulu are well known as decorators (their ceramics and beadwork, for instance, have an international reputation), but Zulu homestead decoration is not widely documented, perhaps owing to the pragmatic restrictions on decorating grass buildings.

It is also significant that the *isimodeni* style of decoration was not a singular event. From the late 1990s through to the present time, the possibilities of wall decoration have expanded, to the extent that some houses are decorated in their entirety. There is also a strong platform for experiment: original *isimodeni* homesteads were decorated simply, in that paint was applied to a plastered surface. More contemporary structures are entirely covered in a thick plaster, which is literally carved out with objects such as teaspoons, creating a strong bas-relief. These forms are then painted. This decoration is not limited to a mere application of chevrons and pastiche decoration; some buildings have developed the decorative aesthetic further.

As noted earlier, the retention of strong traditions with respect to gender, space and form is a marker of buildings in the Msinga district. 'Real' buildings are circular, have thatched roofs and are also windowless. In order to transcend this hiatus, there are a number of examples of houses in which windows, with all their descriptive paraphernalia, are represented as part of the whole of the decoration of the house – including air ventilators, window sills, mullions, transoms and frames. The only part that is missing is the glass. These 'blind' windows perhaps recognize an architecture of cultural liminality – one that is deeply entrenched in the traditions of what buildings 'ought' to be – and at the same time are products of families in which the men have been working in urban centres for generations. This interfamilial acculturation is manifest in the attempted replication of the city in rural areas (the homes) while at the same time, the stasis of tradition (the value system of Msinga) remains intact.

Space around the Msinga building is also strongly defined; an apron surrounding the *rondawel* may be lined with white-painted stones, an impractical solution that heightens the decorative and perhaps the metaphysical aspect of its execution. The entrance steps themselves may also have a variety of different resolutions, celebrating the idea of entrance and the transience of threshold between outside and inside. In traditional homesteads, the entrance to the beehive dome is often embellished with a variety of medicine containers as well as other ritual objects. Furthermore, the horns of animals that have undergone ritual slaughter will also be found in this space.[4]

The prescribed format of the homestead is also challenged. The landscape in Msinga has steep gradients, meaning that a literal transcription of the Central Cattle Pattern is compromised. This is resolved through the use of a series of terraces, still centred on the cattle byre. Houses for the women, both kitchen units and dwelling spaces, remain circular. Occasionally, in a homestead in which a man has returned from his time in the city, the main house will be an articulated version of an orthogonal dwelling, in Western style with cascading roofs – what local architect Rodney Harber refers to as the 'American flat'.[5] More importantly, in many cases in Msinga the house at the bottom, the entrance to the homestead in the area usually occupied by visitors and bachelors, will be square. This form of building, imported by immigrant settlers, has been an architectural reference point in most areas of southern Africa for many decades: certainly, the first example of a square building among the Zulu was noted in the time of the Zulu king Cetshwayo (1826–84), at his Ondini homestead. The adoption of such forms in other parts of South Africa is evident,[6] but the wholesale acceptance of these has been slow in KwaZulu-Natal. In conservative, rural areas, these building forms were certainly frowned upon until quite recently, in much the same manner as a tiled roof or a circular building with windows would be.

Within a process of continual change, the examples in Msinga show that vernacular architecture may remain with its roots firmly entrenched in a traditional abstract framework without totally departing from the main requirements of the provision of a space called home. This heightens the idea of vernacular architecture as being a very present practice, and at the same time being able to draw on external influence without having to fully subscribe to the architectures that produced it.

The Cape Dutch Style

The southwestern tip of the continent was settled by Dutch and other northern Europeans in the mid-17th century. Here, Cape Dutch developed – a settler vernacular indigenous to South Africa. This architecture is characterized by thick walls of random rubble or unbaked bricks and double-pitched thatch roofs with end gables; the façade of the front gable, placed centrally in transverse, is often elaborate. Usually whitewashed, the entrance elevation is offset by deep-green sash or casement windows, often with shutters. It is symmetrically arranged about the central stable door with a fanlight, and the whole is fronted with a *stoep*, a narrow raised platform, sometimes with built-in end seats. The fanlight serves to illuminate the hallway, which gives access to multifunctional rooms in T-, U- or H-shaped plans, with clay-tile or slate floors and high, boarded ceilings.

To prevent conflagration, a decree was issued early on prohibiting the use of thatch in Cape Town. This led to the development of a flat-roofed variant with a layer of bricks or clay, known as a *brandsolder*, a fire-proof ceiling to catch burning thatch in the event of fire. The chimney was built against a side gable. Sometimes, external stairs gave access to the attic on the other gable.

Dutch-speaking people migrated inland in large numbers from 1830 onwards, in an event known as the *Groot Trek*, taking with them the Cape Dutch typology, which was adapted to the semi-arid conditions of the Karoo. The hallmark of this variant was the *brakdak*, a flat roof consisting of a thick layer of earth on reed mats and poles, which in the dry environment required no waterproofing but was invariably covered and rendered impervious with corrugated sheet iron as this became available. While sashes with shutters disposed symmetrically about the entrance door and its fanlight still marked the front elevation, the gable of the *Karoohuis* was reduced to a pediment with a cornice or string course, or sometimes stepped. However, more often than not, in time the *brakdak* became concealed below a hipped or gabled roof of corrugated iron sheeting. Similarly, the *stoep* was covered with a roof of the same material with lean-to, catenary, bullnose or bell-cast profile to become a veranda, and enclosed with timber posts and trellises, rows of which dignify the streetscapes of many a Karoo *dorp* (village).

Namibian Vernacular

Northwest of South Africa across the Orange River lies Namibia, characterized geographically by the Namib Desert along the Atlantic and a wide, flat central highland plateau with high diurnal temperature ranges and sparse rainfall. In this environment, not surprisingly, the first missionaries with their following from South Africa in the 19th century adopted the *Karoohuis* or *matjieshuis* typologies (for the latter, see below). *Boer Dorsland* trekkers, South Africans who explored or settled in northern regions during the late 17th century, opted for *hardbieshuise*, with their walls and flat roofs of firm or hard reeds plastered with clay and dung – often with stable door and shuttered windows (probably legacies of the Cape Dutch style).

The south of Namibia has traditionally been occupied by the Nama, a formerly nomadic people who accommodated themselves in dwellings consisting of a hemispherical subframe of saplings sheathed in woven rush matting. The Nama required accommodation that was light, portable and capable of being erected and dismantled easily, a feat accomplished by rolling up the reed mats, bundling the saplings and loading the oxen. Such *matjieshuise* can still be found in Namaqualand, just south of the Namibian border, where for extra protection the mats are covered in a layer of sacking.

The pastoralist Herero of central Namibia use saplings and poles for wall and roof constructions, historically of beehive structure but now almost exclusively flat-roofed and rectangular. These are plastered with a thick mixture of clay and dung.

The savannah of northern Namibia is the habitat of the Ovambo, agriculturalists and herdsmen. Thanks to the higher rainfall here, the shedding of torrential rain away from the roof and walls becomes an important design factor. It is addressed by using steeply pitched roofs of thatch, usually conical and oversailing, on cylindrical walls – essentially the ubiquitous *rondawel*, as referred to in the section on the eastern coast, above.

Contemporary South African Vernacular

The *rondawel* has largely replaced earlier forms of traditional housing yet has been superseded by the 'four-corner', a house with a monopitched, corrugated iron roof, walls of concrete block and steel or timber windows that offer only basic thermal control.

However environmentally unconvincing and inappropriate for urban living, informal settlements of 'shacks' (*iminjondolo*) are an emerging built vernacular in the region. Despite their 'random' arrangement, they follow an innate urban logic, observing contours and providing for footpaths – in essence, the kernel of vernacular villages.

To provide sustainable and relevant housing in post-apartheid South Africa, authorities would benefit from examining extant vernacular layout, forms and materials.

Below left The Cape Dutch style introduced by European settlers to Africa's southwestern cape is typically formed of thick walls rendered white, with double-pitched thatched roofs and a centrally arranged façade.

Below right The previously nomadic Nama people of southern Namibia create lightweight, portable structures of hemispherical shape, built from saplings and enclosed by reed mats. Sacking is sometimes added for extra protection.

Opposite top Southern Namibian dwellings of the Nama people traditionally matched their nomadic existence. Made of a light, movable sapling frame with woven rush matting, the domed structures could be easily transported by oxen.

Opposite bottom Despite the rich cultural and material heritage of South African vernacular structures, the *rondawel* has largely replaced the variety of regional and climatic responses that once marked different regional contexts.

Earthen and Date-palm Structures in the Arabian Peninsula

Peter Sheehan

Geography/Climate

The Arabian Peninsula covers an area of just over 3 million sq km (1.1 million sq miles), and is composed of seven countries: Saudi Arabia, Yemen, Oman, the United Arab Emirates, Qatar, Bahrain and Kuwait (Yemen will be covered in a separate entry). Altogether, it is home to some 80 million people. The peninsula forms part of Asia but geologically is actually a subcontinent, the Arabian Plate, created by the rifting of the Red Sea in the Eocene Period (56–33.9 million years ago). To the north it merges with the deserts of Syria and Iraq, but its other limits are largely defined by the rich tropical waters of the Red Sea, the Gulf and the Indian Ocean.

Just as its geology has provided the huge reserves of oil and natural gas that have dramatically influenced its rapid development and the growth of its cities in modern times, so the range of its topography has also contributed to its past economies, vernacular architecture and ways of life. More than two-thirds of the peninsula is taken up by the wilderness of the Arabian Desert, visited sporadically by pastoral nomads. Settlement is found along the western and southern edges of the peninsula, where the narrow coastal strip and its coral reefs are fringed by the high mountains of the Hejaz, Yemen and Oman. Away from the coast rainfall over the mountains allowed settlement on the piedmont plains, along seasonal river beds or in oases fed by groundwater. The central upland plateau of the Najd is framed by the vast sandy deserts of the Nafud in the north and the Rub al Khali, or Empty Quarter, in the south, while to the east it slopes into the *sabkha* salt flats and shallow waters of the Gulf with its islands and coastal settlements.

The climate of the peninsula is generally extremely hot and arid, with high levels of relative humidity along the coasts. The southern edge is touched by summer monsoon rains. Protection from the sun is one of the major requirements of vernacular buildings, although seasonal rainfall – particularly in the mountains – is sufficiently heavy to require weatherproofing. Climatic conditions make the extraction and economical use of water a priority, and the wider region is home to the ingenious underground channels, or *aflaj*, that tap deep aquifers. The cultural landscapes of the oases and the vernacular traditions that they preserve have recently been recognized by UNESCO as having outstanding universal value. A shared water supply produced a requirement for cooperation and a complex, customary law for the regulation of water use in the oases, with timings based on astronomical observations. Modern demand for water has also put the area at the forefront of advances in desalinization technology.

Economy/Culture

The traditional economic life of Arabia was based on a range of activities including date production and goat, sheep and camel husbandry. Grain and coffee are grown in the valleys and terraces of the Hejaz and Yemen, while the climate and groundwater are ideal for the tolerant and ubiquitous date palm (*Phoenix dactylifera*), which forms an integral part of the region's history, culture and way of life. Some 14 million palm trees[1] on the peninsula produce more than 30 per cent of the world's dates: a high-energy and easily transportable food product supporting an ecosystem in its shade and providing a range of by-products for use in construction and daily life. Date farming has even produced a specific regional vernacular construction in the form of the *madbasa*, or date press, known from the second millennium BCE onwards, where layers of dates would be stored in a sealed room for their juice (*al- dibs*) to trickle through a network of plaster channels set into the floor and collected in an earthen jar.

Historically, the Red Sea and the Gulf have always been major crossroads for trade and new ideas. The similar climate and a long history of trade, conquest and shared cultural and religious life have produced a close relationship with vernacular construction in neighbouring areas – Mesopotamia, Persia, Egypt, the Horn of Africa and the Indian subcontinent – that were separated by water but linked by the seaborne trade of maritime empires in which the materials and technology of shipbuilding was closely linked to the vernacular. The continued importance of ancient port cities like Jeddah, Aden and Muscat has been supplemented in modern times by the transformation of small coastal settlements, once dependent on fishing or pearling, and of inland oasis towns into large metropolitan cities such as Riyadh, Dammam, Abu Dhabi and Dubai – the last-named being one of the fastest-growing cities in the world. Archaeological work continues to demonstrate the interaction of the vernacular across this wider region and the continuity of its forms, materials and techniques over more than 5,000 years, while the importance of trade and merchants is reflected in the enduring form of the covered *souq*, or market.

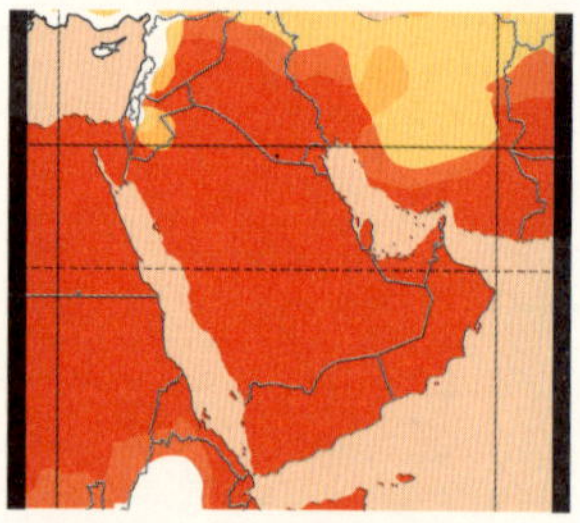

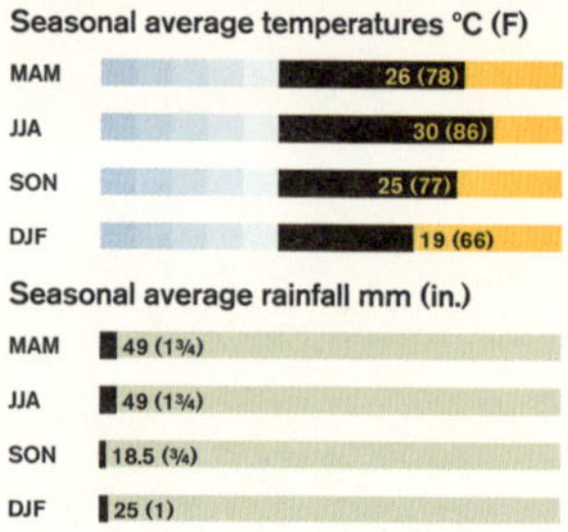

Opposite top Historically based on natural resources such as fishing, pearls and date palms, many settlements of the Arabian Peninsula, such as Dubai (seen here c. 1940), relied on the controlled use of desalinated water to allow development in the hot and arid climate.

Opposite middle In the high mountainous reaches of Oman, buildings of earth are commonly found. Their dense walls with limited openings are a tool for thermal control, relying on convection to force warm air out of upper windows at night while cool air is introduced through lower openings.

Opposite bottom Also built of earth, the Al Ain fort in Abu Dhabi was established in the late 19th century as a means to protect the city and its palm groves.

The Arabian Peninsula is also the birthplace of Islam; the site of its holy cities of Mecca and Medina; and, over the past 300 years, the heartland of its most conservative form. Its countries share a spoken and written language, as well as a language of construction that Islam has played a special role in disseminating from the creation of its early empire in the 7th century onwards. Architecturally, this influence finds its major expression in the form of the mosque and the open prayer space, or *musalla*, oriented to Mecca and providing a location for communal prayer and the focus of community life. Other significant cultural factors affecting vernacular forms include reconciling the need for reception rooms with the requirements for modesty and the separation of male and family quarters, often provided with a bent-axis entrance preventing views into the house from outside. The existence of large family groups and the tribal structure of society provided opportunities for communal building, particularly for the nomadic component of the population needing to produce temporary or seasonal accommodation.

Materials and Construction Techniques

Coastal Vernacular

The materials available for construction vary with the distinct environments and economies of the peninsula. The rich fishing and pearling in the surrounding tropical seas, coupled with the presence of coral and seastone, created in the Gulf countries a distinct coastal vernacular (now mostly vanished) of courtyard houses with ground-floor rooms for winter use and upper rooms or roof terraces accessed by stairs in the summer. A frame of stone piers and palm tie beams was used to produce rooms with a maximum width of about 3 m (10 ft), a dimension based on the length of the mangrove roofing poles brought from the Malabar Coast or East Africa along ancient trade routes. The arrangement of narrow rooms helped cooling, while buildings were positioned close to each other in order to provide shade and oriented to minimize heat gain. The prevailing northwest wind was utilized in the ingenious forms of wind towers and wind ventilators, or *badgir*, as well as by creating double-height spaces between blocks of rooms. Gypsum and lime, sometimes supplemented by shell, was burnt to produce the *juss* mortar and plaster used both in construction and for carved decorative panels and mouldings.

Inland Settlements

Away from the coast, earth buildings predominate in the mountains and the oasis settlements on the outwash plain or next to seasonal river beds (*wadis*). These buildings include forts, defensive towers and fortified houses erected to protect the inhabitants of the oases and their produce from inter-tribal raids. They all demonstrate traditional building techniques, using the thermal qualities provided by thick mud walls with limited small openings for light and air, with a structure of palm logs and with palm-mat roofs. Floors and walls are finished in waterproof *sarooj* plaster made from a mixture of clay and manure. Summer cooling is achieved by opening windows at ground-floor level to the night breezes and then closing them during the day to let hot air rise and escape through small vents set into the upper part of the walls.

Below left and right Stout, thick walls of earth and stone seen at Bin Biduwa Al Darmaki (left) and in Sharjah (right) illustrate the robust construction techniques that include mouldings and sculpted exterior niches.

Opposite top Tall, narrow buildings reduce solar gain and create shading below. Ventilation of such buildings often includes shuttered windows that give control over the admission or evacuation of air, as well as of views into and out from the dwellings.

Opposite bottom Traditional villages near oases or *wadis* (seasonal river beds) are usually formed of earth. This building technique includes roofs constructed of palm logs with palm-mat roofing, with walls finished in waterproof plaster made from clay and manure.

ورشه للتبريد

Date-palm-leaf Architecture in the Arabian Peninsula

Sandra Piesik

Materials and Construction Techniques

Arish Typologies

As well as the *bayt al-shaar*, a large portable tent made from animal hair, permanent dwellings in the Arabian Peninsula are often supplemented by temporary structures using a range of palm-leaf *arish* typologies, a type of agricultural waste from date palm cultivation that is frequently used in arid areas with a shortage of resources. The materials and construction techniques using palm fronds are generally known as *arish*, although the diversity of their architectural forms, scale, locations, functions and ethnic groups contribute to various different names for such structures.

Elements of sustainable design are evident in various *arish* architectural forms. Simple yet innovative techniques respond to the three main microclimates of the region: desert, mountains and coastal areas. *Arish* typologies in the desert areas are characterized by a thermal mass and relatively thick walls that enabled cooling of the interiors by up to 23°C (73°F), with structural life spans of up to twenty-five years. Mountainous areas near the coast with a prevailing wind close to the ground aided the development of wall systems that enabled internal cooling of houses at floor level. In populated urban areas the additional cooling device of wind towers, also built of palm leaves, resulted from Persian influences on sea-trading cities.

Contemporary Application

Since the Second World War, within the space of a single human lifetime, the wealth created by the global oil and gas industries has utterly transformed vernacular architecture and urban forms throughout the Arabian Peninsula, along with much of its traditional economy and cultural habitat. The United Arab Emirates, for example, now has the highest environmental footprint per capita in the world. As in other regions, the depletion of non-renewable resources and significant environmental and social challenges have led to a growing recognition of the contribution that a deeper understanding of past cultural landscapes in general, and vernacular architecture in particular, can make to sustainable development and quality of life.

This can be seen in the demise of *arish* structures: in 1950, Dubai still had around 4,000 palm-leaf houses, yet today, traditional palm-leaf technologies are almost absent from everyday life in modern society on the Arabian Peninsula. With Saudi Arabia and the UAE leading the global production of dates, there is an opportunity to re-contextualize ancient palm-leaf technologies to a modern use.

A window of opportunity remains to reconnect with traditional knowledge and put it to practical use, developing new tools related to food, energy and climate control.

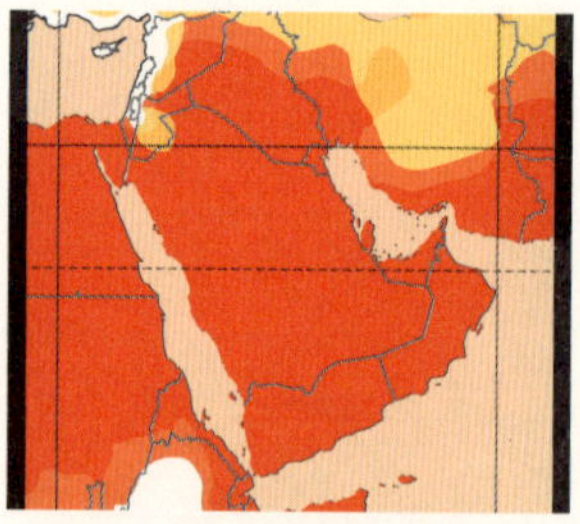

Seasonal average temperatures °C (F)

MAM	26 (78)
JJA	30 (86)
SON	25 (77)
DJF	19 (66)

Seasonal average rainfall mm (in.)

MAM	49 (1¾)
JJA	49 (1¾)
SON	18.5 (¾)
DJF	25 (1)

Below and opposite Temporary structures built from date-palm leaves, known as *arish*, supplement permanent dwellings in the Arabian Peninsula. Though the same basic rectilinear form is used to build the homes, variations occur dependent on the local micro-climate, whether desert, mountainous, wasted or urban.

Tower Houses and Courtyard Dwellings of Yemen

Ronald Lewcock

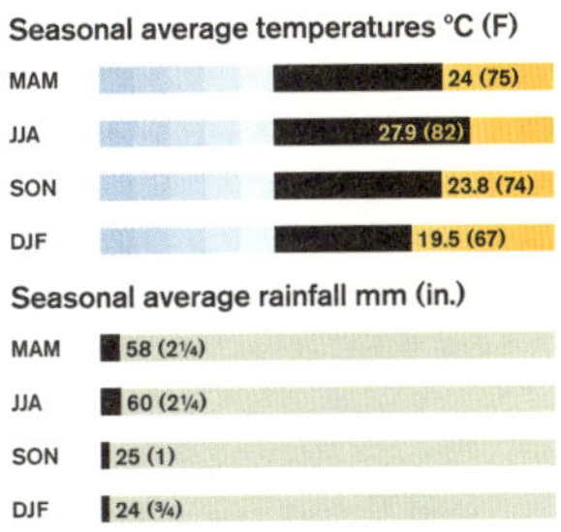

Opposite top The city of Shibam exemplifies the 'tower houses' found in mountainous areas of Yemen. These multi-storey dwellings are often made of sun-dried mud brick, or stone, and are based on vertical construction principles that minimize a building's footprint.

Opposite bottom Aerial view of the Old City of Sana'a, Yemen. The city is one of the country's urban centres that include spacious green gardens. These areas separate tribal neighbourhoods, continuing an ancient Middle Eastern pattern of settlement.

Geography/Climate

In the steep mountains of Yemen, monsoon rains from the Indian Ocean provided enough water twice a year for irrigation, but were of little use for agriculture. This meant that what water there was had to be supplemented by terracing on the mountainsides. Here, little horizontal space could be spared for buildings, so courtyards were out of the question. Instead, houses were developed with a minimum size of 'footprint' – and were often sited on steep slopes. The tall, narrow homes that resulted were usually six to eight storeys high, and sometimes as much as ten storeys.

On the narrow western coastal plains, however, a tradition of simple courtyard houses that are richly decorated in flat plaster patterns survives.

Construction Techniques

Construction of the high houses was of sand/clay sun-dried brick – where these materials were available. More prestigious buildings in mountain areas had their lower storeys built in stone and upper storeys in baked brick. Walls would often be a metre (3 ft) thick at the bottom and grow progressively thinner as the building rose.

Building Plan/Form

The ground floor of the tall houses was traditionally for animals, the mezzanine above for farm produce and mills, with residential use beginning only at the third floor level, which contained the main reception room of the house (the *diwan*). Above this were communal rooms for family living and cooking. Larger houses had relaxing rooms at the top for entertaining during the afternoon siestas; these had splendid views.

Within the courtyard typology seen in houses on the coastal plains, Yemen has a number of hypostyle courtyard mosques (*apadana*) of very early type, three of them known to have been originally built by companions of the Prophet. Some were rebuilt by the Umayyads. Other mosques include early buildings of the *apadana* type, and medieval mosques with early Turkish, Egyptian or Afghan/Indian influence.

Cities and towns followed an ancient Middle Eastern pattern of segregated tribal neighbourhoods. In the capital, Sana'a, and some of the other conurbations, the market gardens that separated the neighbourhoods can still be seen. Each neighbourhood, or quarter, had a main street running through it and dead-end side streets leading to private houses. Each also had at least one mosque and its own public hot baths. The Friday mosque would be built adjoining the market in one of the gardens. Market buildings were kept low for security; there were no houses or accommodation there. Around the market were the stables for camels and caravan animals, generally located beneath warehouse storerooms with inns for visitors on top. These alternated with camel mills for grinding grain and salt, often with *waqf* (religious endowment) accommodation for poor widows and students situated above them.

Right Markets like San'a in Yemen were commercial and cultural centres. The market buildings included stables for draught animals but no permanent accommodation. Inns for visitors to the market were situated above the stables.

Architecture of Stone and Clay in Israel and the Levant

Below Villages in the dry region of Galilee and Judea were mostly located according to proximity to water. Their successful establishment relied on intricate systems for water harvesting, crop cultivation and soil management.

Opposite Throughout the region, stone was preferred for buildings: it was more abundant than timber, and a more enduring material. At higher levels, such as the Golan Heights (bottom), terraced settlements were built. They benefited from greater defence than low-level villages and allowed for better supervision over orchards and fields.

Michael Turner

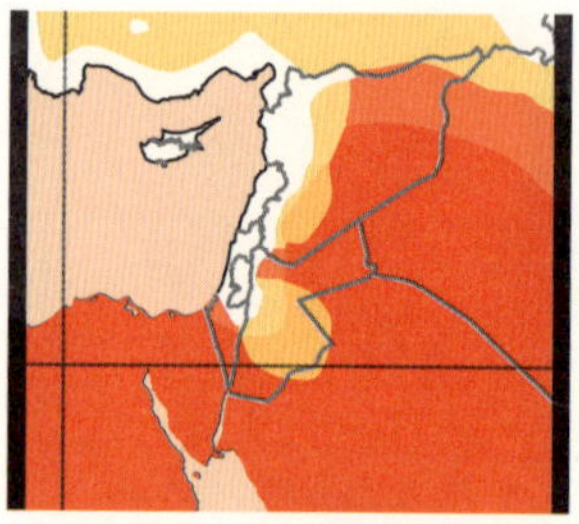

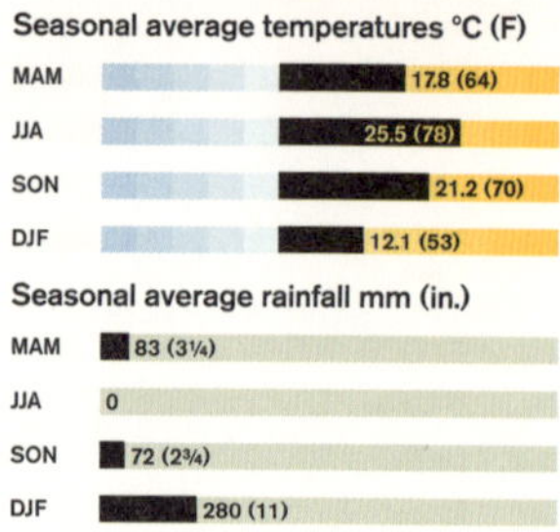

Geography/Climate

Situated at the southwest extremity of the Fertile Crescent, the Levant lies on one of the crossroads of civilizations, where ancient Egypt and Assyria, the Hebrew Kingdoms, the Greek, Roman and Byzantine empires, and the later Muslim caliphates all contributed to the creation of a complex, layered landscape representing ever-changing values. Moreover, this historical microcosm is overlaid by four biomes – Mediterranean, Irano-Turanean, Saharo-Arabian and Sudanic – within a narrow corridor of some 80 km (50 miles) from the Mediterranean to the Dead Sea and the Jordan Rift Valley.

These biomes follow a formula of social structures based on family kinship, maintaining agricultural and industrial patterns of life such as those found in the Islamic *hima* (a system of environmental protection), with areas designated for the welfare of the community and modus operandi for sharing natural resources – especially water. With this level of bio-cultural intensity, vernacular building knowledge permeated all local traditions and was often syncretistic.

Poorer country dwellers chose to situate their homes on higher ground, at either the top of a hill or on a hillside in order to protect against flooding and allow better supervision over orchards and fields. This also provided a natural defence – as in the Palestinian throne villages, each of which was dominated by a semi-feudal family. Proximity to water sources was a deciding factor in village location, as was the possibility for expansion developed alongside a system of cisterns, wells, springs, aqueducts and *q'anats* (underground drainage channels).

The agricultural terraces cross-cutting these biomes can be examined from the viewpoint of the successive waves of civilizations that have recreated this landscape of terraces, comprising millions of stones over a three-millennia period.

Buildings and terraces in Galilee and Judea – including the lowlands, hills and desert – incorporate an intense and intricate system for cultivation and water harvesting. This evolving cultural landscape integrates many installations for soil management, together with presses, shelters and summer huts (locally named *'ariseh* or *shomera*), which were designed as circular structures and built with dry stonework often topped with branches.

The vernacular of the Negev Desert region is evidence of five centuries of Nabatean technology, ending in the 2nd century CE. The towns, forts, watchtowers, caravanserais (inns), milestones and sophisticated agricultural systems incorporating water conservation dispersed along the Incense Route are an outstanding response to a hostile desert environment.[1] This significant trading network, in operation from the 3rd century BCE to the 2nd century CE, facilitated not only the distribution of frankincense and myrrh from the Arabian Peninsula to the Mediterranean but also the transmission of traditional knowledge and cultures.

This ancient technology lives alongside the dramatic changes that are taking place within the semi-nomadic

Opposite Locally available materials are the key factor in determining the forms of villages and urban buildings. In contrast to clay-based buildings near the Mediterranean plain, houses in hilly regions were built with broad stone bases rising to vaulted stone roofs, with small windows and entrances.

Below This schematic sketch illustrates the construction method for creating a vaulted stone roof. Rising from a rectilinear plan formed of broad composite walls, the vault is supported by beams that fit into sockets within the wall structure.

Below right Middle-class town houses, such as these in Jerusalem's Old City quarter, were typically based on simple, square-shaped family units with stone vaults, organized around an internal courtyard.

tribes of the region, as families settle into permanent dwellings. Tents become caves, caves become rooms, and rooms become houses – thus creating organic village forms supported by new social patterns.

Materials

The different geomorphologies and materials encountered in each biome have traditionally been key factors in determining urban and village form. Tawfiq Can'aan recorded the region's vernacular construction in his 1933 seminal booklet *The Palestinian Arab House: Its Architecture and Folklore*, describing the architecture of stone, clay and the now extinct reed-mat buildings of the Hula Valley. Stone houses were constructed in the hill country where quarries were readily available, while the Mediterranean plain and Sudanic region relied on bricks based solely on clay. Early traditions at the Temple in Jerusalem recorded the high priest's plea on the Day of Atonement: 'For those who lived in the region of Sharon… do not let their homes become their graves.'[2] The residents of this coastal Mediterranean plain then constructed their homes from bricks with a high sand content. These structures required frequent renovation, continuing the subregional tradition, and, as the prayer suggests, were the source of tragic events caused by their collapse.

Stone houses tended to be built with broad composite walls up to 1 m (3 ft) thick and a vaulted stone roof. Alternatively, they could have thinner walls and a timber roof, similar to the technology applied in the construction of the clay houses with wooden-truss roofs consisting of *sawarit* (long tree trunks) or *mahruq* (imported beams). Timber was often a scarce resource, and where possible stone was sought – the more resilient material also indicating a higher socio-economic status.

Building Plan/Form

The town houses of the middle class followed a number of urban typologies based on the *beit* or family unit, about 5 to 6 m (16 to 20 ft) square, with a stone vault. These units created the *hosh*, or central courtyard, a significant feature with an accompanying water cistern and belonging to a single *hamula* (extended-family unit). Individual houses of wealthier families were based on a grid including a *liwan* or *iwan*, a central hall surrounded by living rooms.

Little change occurred during the near half-millennium of the Ottoman Empire until 1840, when the advent of the *Tanzimat* reorganization programme in the Levant brought feudal land reform and the beginning of modern urbanization processes. As railways extended their network, new materials were brought to areas in this hinterland; steel, and then modern concrete, provided options and additions that began to blur the familiar typologies comprising the local vernacular language – although hill regions and extensive nomadic areas remained unaffected by these external influences. Subsequent changes in society, family kinship and gender norms rendered many traditional urban forms anachronistic, and attempts at their adaptive reuse have created a plethora of discordant additions.

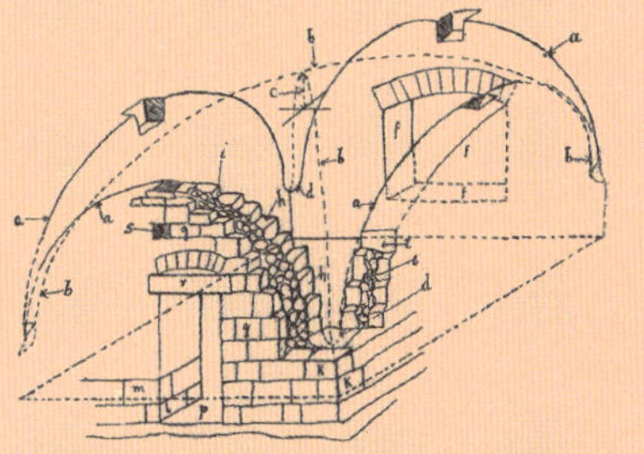

Fig. 5. Schematic sketch of the *hlālāt* of an unvaulted room. a. Future lines of penetration between walls and vault. b. Future lines of diagonal ribs to groined vault. c. Difference in height between wall arches and diagonal arches. d. Bracket stone at springing line of arches. e. Sockets to receive beams for the *tûbār* of the vault. f. *markas*, *rakseh*; g. outer facing; h. inner facing. i. *dabš* layer; k. *zāwieh* (corner stone). l. *kalb*; m. *'aragah*; p. *burtāšeh*; r. *šāšiyeh*: s. opening for ventilation (a small *tāgah*); t. *musmār* stone.

Throne Villages of Palestine's Central Highlands

Fida Touma

Geography/Climate and Culture

Although historical Palestine is small in area (around 27,000 sq km [10,400 sq miles]), it is quite diverse in terms of topography, which naturally affects the typologies and materials of its vernacular architecture. For example, in the Jordan Valley to the east, with its lowest point of 408 m (1,338 ft) below sea level and with fertile and readily available earth, one finds mud-brick and mud architecture. In the southern desert, and en route to the southernmost, dry parts of the country – as well as the western and northern lowlands – Bedouins roamed and controlled the landscape; their dwellings were tents and caves. In the western coastal plains and central highlands, sandstone and limestone provided the main building material. This allowed for variations in built style and structure, including single cross-vaulted homes, simple rural houses with flat straw roofs carried by stone arches, and more complex interconnected buildings. Overall, the climate of the area and the availability of agricultural land dictated the orientation, location and composition of individual dwellings and of the village or town as whole.

Three different modes of production and, hence, three types of human settlements and architecture, may be seen to result from these conditions: urban, rural and nomadic. While historically most urban settlements in Palestine were located in coastal areas, the majority of its villages were located in the central highlands. Al-Naqab Desert, the Jordan Valley and other lowlands such as al-Hulah, Gaza and Asqalan were predominantly the domains of Bedouin tribes but also included some villages. Up until the British Mandate of 1922, the settlement types were quite distinct.

The central highlands of the country are the focus here. This area featured the main characteristics of the region's vernacular peasant architecture and a more sophisticated form that developed during the rule of the *shuyoukh al nawahi*, or district lords. During the 18th and 19th centuries, the central highlands (today's West Bank) were divided into three main areas: Jabal Nablus, Jabal al-Quds (Jerusalem) and Jabal al-Khalil (Hebron). Each of these areas was in turn divided into different administrative districts named *nawahi* or *mashaiyyekh*. Every district formed an independent administrative and economic entity: in effect, a taxation unit. The sheik of the district was the tax collector on behalf of the Ottoman central government. These sheikhs and their families resided in settlements known as 'throne villages' (*qura al-karasi*) – of which there were about twenty-four in total.

Building Plan/Form

Throne-village vernacular formed a hybrid typology between urban and peasant architecture. It combined the basic features of peasant homes and peasant family quarters with a more sophisticated style in terms of decoration, size and function. As with many vernacular buildings in Palestine, these castles or palaces were informed by the need for a defensive location – one that did not encroach on the agricultural lands, social relationships or social status of the inhabitants – and by climatic concerns. The castles themselves were of a monumental size and scale; they were prominently situated, inward-looking buildings arranged around a courtyard, with majestic main entrances, decorated wooden gates, and a bent L-shaped entrance lobby (which provided maximum privacy for the inhabitants – particularly for the women of the sheikhs' families). Unlike peasant women, who worked in the fields, those belonging to the families of feudal sheikhs were restricted to the domain of their palaces.

The basic building unit in the majority of these palaces was the simple peasant house. This comprised a single cross-vaulted room (around 5 x 7 m [16 x 23 ft] in size) with thick double-faced limestone walls (reaching up to 1,200 mm [47 in] in depth). Suad Amiry and Vera Tamari's description of these units makes clear that they were divided into three main areas reflecting their occupants' social and practical needs: the lower portion, the *qa' el-beit*, housed livestock and farm tools; the middle part, *al mastabeh* ('platform'), formed the principal family living and sleeping area; and an upper level, the *rawiyeh*, was used as a larder. No walls subdivided the space, but several tall clay-and-straw storage containers (*khawabi*) separated the *mastabeh* from the *rawiyeh*. The stone hearth – *al Mawqid* or *al Wijaq* – formed the main focus of the *mastabeh* and occupied the same wall as the main door; the sole heat source of the dwelling, it was used chiefly on cold, wet days when activities moved indoors. The house also had arched niches (*taqah*) set into its walls; foremost among these would be the *qos* or *mirkaz*: a large, deep, arched recess reserved for mattresses and bedding.[1]

Construction Techniques

Generally speaking, these vernacular buildings would have had few and small exterior openings in order to sustain privacy and maintain a defensive status. Larger openings were to be found on the upper levels, to monitor the

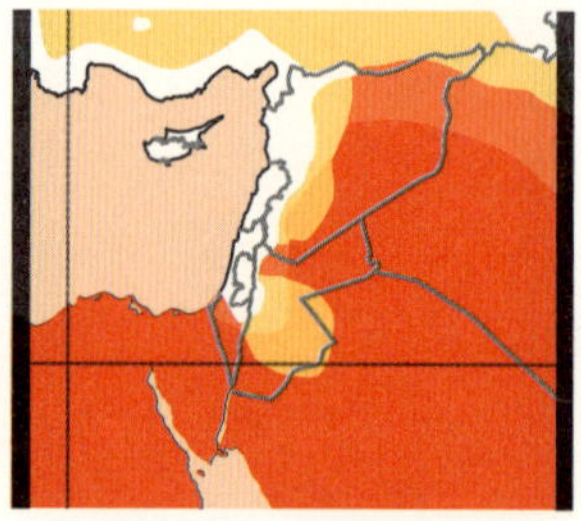

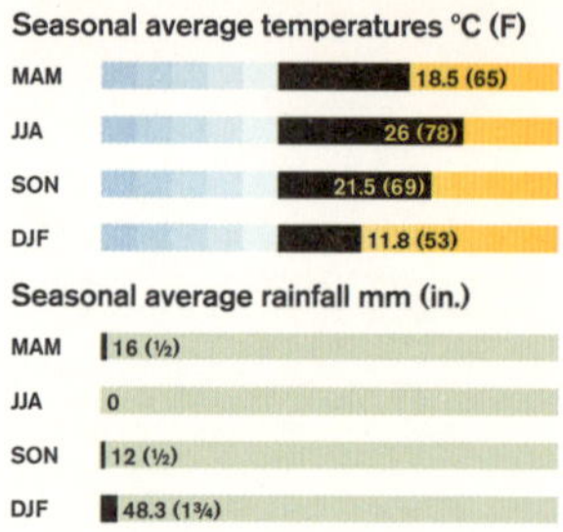

Below and opposite Characteristics of Palestine's regional vernacular are seen in the hybrid typology of the throne village. Though based on the simple building unit of peasant houses, these defensive castles were more sophisticated in decoration and use, and on a much larger scale. Typical elements include dense, high walls with small windows enclosing a central internal courtyard that leads to three separate levels for livestock, living/sleeping, and food storage.

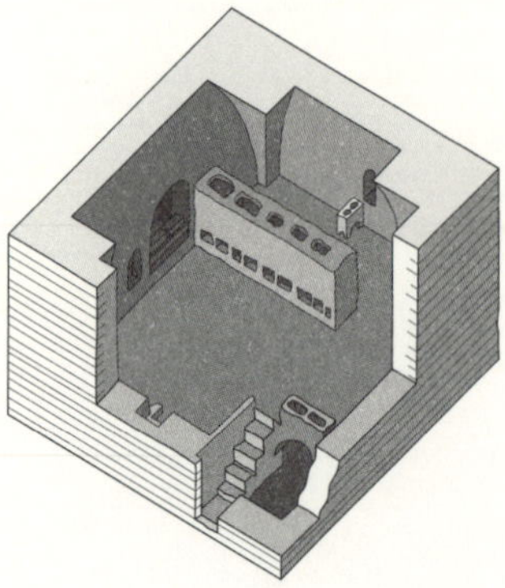

surroundings and to provide the needed air circulation. In the case of peasant dwellings, only the latter function was required; for wealthier families, large upper windows also allowed in more sunlight and, with carefully crafted ornamentation, reflected their higher social status. The main courtyard was the heart of the castle, where all activity took place and on to which all doors would open either directly or indirectly. The thickness of the walls provided the optimum thermal mass and insulation to cool indoor spaces and provide the required level of humidity in the summer, and to keep them warm in the winter. The central courtyard also provided shelter from the wind, which blew strongly from the west and brought dust from the east during season changes. Work spaces were located close to the main façades of the houses, affording additional shading during the day. Water, a rare commodity, was collected from the roofs through a system of holes and pipes, and all was channelled through the courtyards to either one or two wells that served the castle and allowed it to survive the summer and any potential siege.

This type of construction is no longer practised in Palestine. The Second World War and the 1948 colonization and occupation were a turning point in social and economic relationships in the country, and peasant life as it had previously been known changed forever. Concrete structures and cement-based blockwork now dominate the landscape, with stone serving only as a cladding material and being excavated extensively throughout the country.

Agrarian, Urban and Nomadic Vernacular of Jordan

Rami Farouk Daher

Geography/Climate

Jordan is located in the east Mediterranean region of western Asia, and is classified into four main bio-climatological regions: subhumid Mediterranean in the high mountains, as in the capital, Amman, and the northern city of Ajlun; semi-arid Mediterranean in most cities, for instance Madaba and Irbid; arid Mediterranean, as in Mafraq and Zarqa; and Saharan Mediterranean, as in the towns of Azraq and Ma'an and the desert region of Wadi Araba. Therefore, the country's regions range between dry, humid temperate and dry desert climates.

Building Plan/Form

Jordan's cultural regions could be divided into three categories in terms of lifestyle and vernacular architecture: the agrarian village setting, the town and urban setting, and the steppe and desert setting. Such diversity within a small geographical area has created various typologies in terms of building plans and forms.

Peasant Housing

One particular vernacular/agrarian architectural type exists in the many agricultural villages all over northern and central Jordan – in places such as Mkies, Salt, Hartha and Samad. It has produced various models including the single-space peasant house, the courtyard (*hosh*) house (composed of several single-space rooms organized around a courtyard), and the *liwan* house (composed of two rooms with an exposed central space that opens into the natural surroundings).

These peasant dwellings are strongly linked to an agrarian lifestyle in which the majority of food drying, processing or storage activities are carried out in the courtyards or on rooftops. Most courtyards included water wells and various low-lying structures, such as the *tabun* oven for baking bread or an outbuilding used as a bathroom. These vernacular/agrarian houses were usually built collectively, with many village residents participating in the construction process – especially the raising of roofs for the single-space dwellings. These took the form of cross vaults or repetitive arches that supported a flat roof.

Three-bay Houses

Another type, prevailing mostly in urban areas and the product of master builders' techniques, was the three-bay house with its strong indoor–outdoor relationship. This type, which is also termed the 'central-hallway dwelling', flourished not just in Jordanian cities and towns but also in urban Lebanon, Palestine and Syria. The emergence of the 'Ammani three-bay house' during the first decades of the 20th century is linked to the arrival of various migrants from Lebanon, Syria and Palestine into Jordan's capital, Amman, and other Jordanian towns. These incomers included master builders, who brought a certain tradition of building that was subsequently moulded in the Ammani context to produce humble urban dwellings built with local stone. These residences contributed to the creation of a middle class in many Jordanian cities, and to a special relationship of the dwelling with place and open space.

The central hallway was the heart of the house and its main living space, and in many cases extended into the frontal set-back garden in the form of a porch or simply an extended open space where one would find many produce trees including lemon, fig and pomegranate. The main material of construction was rough stone in regular courses, but concrete could also be used as a supporting structure behind the stone. Roofs were mostly spanned using steel I-beams, with a thin slab of concrete.

Bedouin Tents

Towards the south and east of Jordan, the prevailing vernacular type is the traditional Bedouin tent, known as the *bayt ash-sha'ar*, a long, horizontal black tent made of goat- and camel-hair cloth. It prevails in the eastern part of Jordan towards the steppe (*al Badiya al Sharqiya*) and in southern desert areas such as Wadi Araba, Wadi Rum and Petra. The tent is easily dismantled and reassembled to suit the nomadic lifestyle.

The *bayt ash-sha'ar* is classified, in terms of the use of its spaces, into the *mahram* (women's quarters) and the *madheif* (the area for adult males and for receiving guests). Both are provided with simple furniture, such as rugs and pillows. Furthermore, it can be classified spatially in terms of the number of main central posts (*wassit*) used in the structure, and the spaces (*raba'h*) created accordingly. For example, the *gatbah* is built with one post and two spaces, while the *mkhoumas* has five posts and six spaces. The Bedouin tent is well adapted to environmental factors – for example, its front elevation usually faces east in order to receive the winter sun and avoid the western wind.

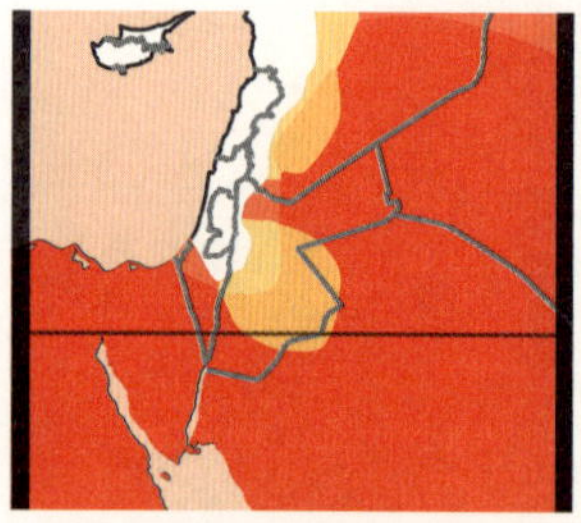

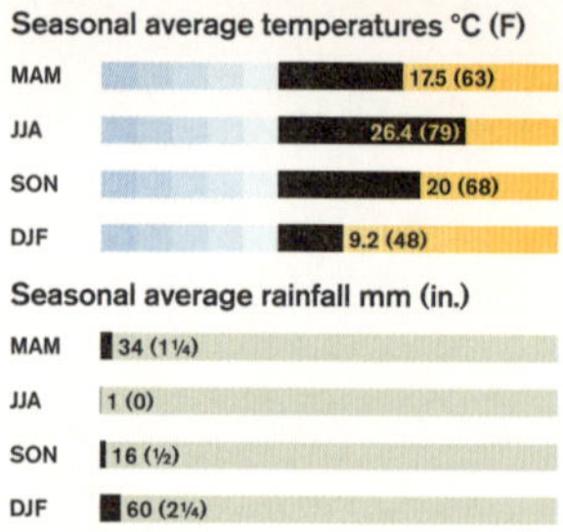

Opposite top left and top right The predominant Jordanian urban typology of stone or concrete housing provides indoor–outdoor living, seen in this view of Amman's outskirts. Homes such as this three-bay variant (right) are shaped around a central hallway, which forms the main living space and is a conduit between the street and the rear garden.

Opposite middle Housing found in rural regions usually focuses on simple spaces built of stone with an internal or protected central space in which to dry or process crops.

Opposite bottom Jordan's traditional nomadic Bedouin communities live in dark-coloured tents of goat or camel hair that are easily dismantled, and readily oriented in response to sun direction and prevailing winds.

Stone and Sustainability in Lebanese Dwellings

Aram Yeretzian

Geography/Climate

The geography of Lebanon is characterized by three regions – namely, the coast, the mountains and an inland plateau known as the Bekaa Valley. These regions are distinguished by four distinct climatic zones, designated as coastal-Mediterranean (mostly warm and humid), mid-mountain (cold and humid winters), high-mountain (colder winters and dry summers) and the inland plateau (also with cold winters and dry summers).

Materials

With the exception of a few mud-brick houses built in the Bekaa, the notable feature of vernacular architecture in Lebanon is stone construction, manifested in several typological applications including rectangular houses.

Building Plan/Form and Construction Techniques

Traditional villages and towns were an assembly of closely built stone dwellings. The 'negative' spaces between these houses encouraged social interaction, while the orientation of the streets allowed summer and mid-seasonal wind flow that made them cooler. The narrow spaces between buildings, which served as walkways and meeting places, were shaded during hot summer months.

The rectangular dwelling, built by its owners from natural materials such as stone, earth and timber, using handmade tools, was considered to be the basic type in the mid- to late-19th century. The builders, familiar with the prevailing climatic conditions, constructed houses in a way that would ensure their harmony with the natural environment.

A typical dwelling consisted of two levels; the lower served as shelter for livestock, while the upper level comprised a large space intended for sitting, cooking, dining, sleeping and storing goods. During the day, mattresses were rolled up and stored in an internal thick wall called the *yuke*, which also served as storage space for grains that were replenished in summer. Small windows and doors (defined by the length of the stone lintels available) were made by the village carpenter from solid timber sections. Terraces, located adjacent to the dwelling, were covered with grape vines whose foliage provided shading in the summer and which in winter, thanks to the falling leaves, allowed sunlight to enter, thus contributing to indoor and outdoor comfort. For sanitary services, a very basic toilet was located in the garden.

Water was transported in clay pots from the village well, and rainwater was harvested from the roof.

The lower storey was vaulted to provide the necessary support to the earth surrounding the house, as well as to the dwelling on the upper level. On the upper level, the 900 mm (35 in) thick walls consisted of two skins with rubble between them. The walls, hand plastered on the inside with mud chaff of a white colour, had a natural character and were rounded at the edges.

In summer and in the mid-seasons, open windows allowed cooling by natural wind flow. The thick walls prevented solar heat from warming the interiors and shaded the deep-set windows, thus helping to reduce entry of the sun's rays and achieving a comfortable indoor environment. In winter, household activities took place around the fireplace, which served for both cooking and heating. For fuel, wood, brushwood and dried manure were gathered from the vicinity of the house. The internal space was kept warm because the thick walls and small windows prevented heat from dissipating. Small openings at the top of the walls extracted the smoke and fumes from the fireplace.

Dwellings had external loadbearing walls and a timber roof structure. Tree trunks were used for posts and beams, their lengths defining the depth of the spaces. Above the wooden beams, small branches were laid out and covered with 50 mm (2 in) of dry shrubs. On top of that, about 250 mm (10 in) of earth was finished with a thin layer of stone chips covered with a lime–chaff screed. The built-up roof surface was compacted with a hand-operated stone roller. This type of maintenance was important to close the cracks that resulted from inclement weather. The roof was used as a working area for drying tomatoes, wheat, cereals, fruits and pine cones.

Around the end of the 19th and the beginning of the 20th century, this form of vernacular construction evolved into a 'traditional Lebanese architecture' with buildings that exhibited components imported from Italy and France, among other countries, such as red roof tiles, metal water pipes and wrought-iron decorative features.

The vernacular architecture of Lebanon was adapted to, and sat in harmony with, its natural context in terms of response to climate, integration to site and construction materials. The concepts applied in this type of architecture are valuable in informing the process of contemporary architectural design and planning.

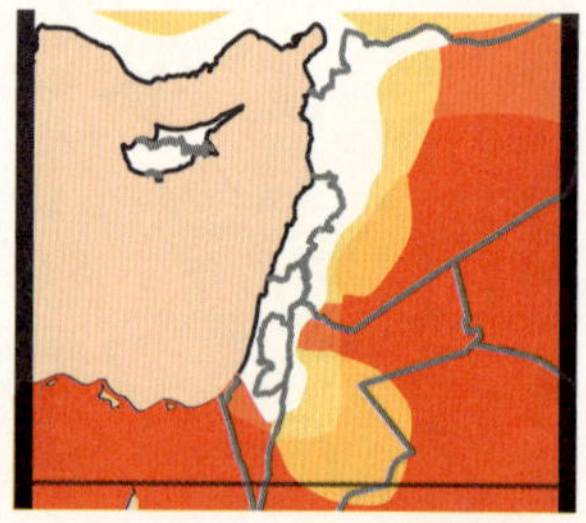

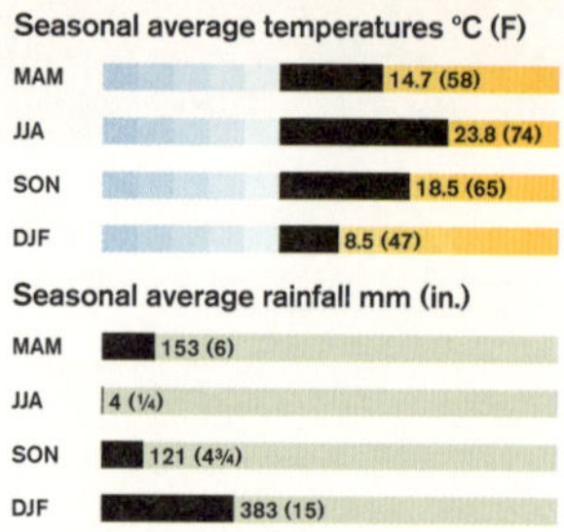

Opposite Usually several storeys in height, the houses of the traditional villages of Lebanon, such as Arnun viewed here from Beaufort Castle, South Lebanon, were most often built of stone and in close proximity. This method of construction helped to control the local environment by channeling wind currents and creating shade.

Syria's Villages of Earthen Domes

Saverio Mecca and Letizia Dipasquale

Geography/Climate

The region south and east of Aleppo, from the Euphrates to Salamiya, has been inhabited since Neolithic times by both sedentary and nomadic peoples, who have alternately dominated the area.

The so-called 'arid margins' region corresponds to the limits of Syria's steppe zone, whose extent can be estimated as covering 55 per cent of the country's territory. The diversity of habitats, in relation to the uses of the land for agriculture and stockbreeding, are linked to the dry climate and soil of the area. In these arid margins can be found a population 'mosaic' comprising varied cultural groups: Ismailis, Alawites and Christians; Kurdish or Circassian refugees; and tribal nomads. Despite this cultural and social diversity, great homogeneity exists in the architectural and building culture, based on an adaptive approach to the available materials: clay, earth, limestone and basalt – or even materials recovered from previous settlements of the Byzantine era.

Construction Techniques

Vaulting technology appears to have been quickly mastered in the ancient Near East. Domed roofing started in Tell Halaf c. 5100 BCE, and has been in use for centuries in traditional Syrian rural architecture. The earthen-domed house evolved over time, stemming from a willingness to apply and develop the most appropriate solutions to meet human needs in relation to the available environmental resources.

Earthen domes are superior to flat roofs because their shapes are cheaper to build in a region scarce in timber. They better resist rain leakage and they expose less surface to the summer sun, reducing solar radiation and achieving generally good climatic conditions in their interior spaces.

Opposite Domed structures in Syria form the strongest possible structure that can be built with the readily available materials of clay, earth, limestone and basalt. The superior waterproofing and reduced radiation of this building type ensures its widespread use.

The corbelled dome is realized by laying earthen bricks according to a continuous helicoidal spiral, tapered and often tilted towards the centre. The mason would lay the bricks, perched on the ring of the dome, in an anti-clockwise direction in order to favour the use of his right hand. This allowed the construction process to proceed more efficiently, without any scaffolding or need to adjust the bricks.

Generally, the base thickness of Syrian earthen domes depends on the single adobe-brick dimension, between 350 and 500 mm (14 and 20 in); it is slimmer at the top, between 150 and 200 mm (6 and 8 in).

Building Plan/Form

The distribution and use of the spaces in this housing type correspond somewhat to those of nomadic camps, and the shape of the dome could be seen as symbolically evoking the tent.

The house's basic element is a double unit made up of two square cells, with an internal length of about 4 m (13 ft) each side, each cell covered by a dome and communicating through an arch called a *qantara*, or a *nhit* if made with stones.

The different heights of the dwellings' perimeter walls may help to distinguish more clearly two main types in the vernacular landscape of the domed villages of Syria. Firstly, there are the so-called domes of the Sultanya or 'Sultan dome' – *Qubba Sultanya* – with a perimeter base that rises up to the height of the door lintel, creating a wall spanned by the dome roof. Secondly, there are simple domes with a very low base. Between the two are other variants that alter according to the height of the perimeter base. Both complete pointed domes and truncated domes have been found – the latter where the availability of wooden branches has cut short the construction of the dome and diverted it into a flat roof.

A typical living unit (or *dar*) was based on the combination of several earthen-dome cells or blocks, which are arranged around a central courtyard, creating a sheltered and enclosed space. The elements of a basic earthen house may comprise one or more main rooms about 4 m (13 ft) square with various functions (living, sleeping or for visitors), a kitchen, a bath (*hammam*), a store, a stable, a toilet, and fences, a garden and a small store for hens and pigeons; as well as an earthen traditional bakery (*tannur*), a stage (*mastaba*) and a well.

The earthen-dome villages of northern Syria display several main urban-morphology types. Spontaneous villages have no shaped streets, squares or precise, limited urban spaces. Semi-regular villages have a general public space, semi-private spaces, main streets and more narrow streets (*zuqaq*), as well as a mosque. Regular villages have a principal square, small squares (semi-private space), perimeter roads, interior main streets and *zuqaq*, a mosque, and an open market or bazaar.

Contemporary Applications

The conservation of the region's corbelled-dome buildings has always been part of a natural process, developed over the decades by the population of northeastern Syria. They have passed on the knowledge associated with this type of building construction from generation to generation, ensuring regular maintenance in order to prolong the buildings' useful life.

The cultural and architectural heritage of northern Syrian villages is nowadays subject to natural and sociopolitical threats. The endemically difficult conditions in the area due to its harsh climate, scarcity of resources and isolation have grown worse because of the conflict affecting the country since 2011.

The use of earthen corbelled domes may be seen as an affordable and appropriate solution in a future reconstruction process following the enormous damage suffered by Syria and its built heritage. From functional, constructive and climatic aspects, corbelled domes represent an excellent architectural solution, which could also assist the development of local economies.

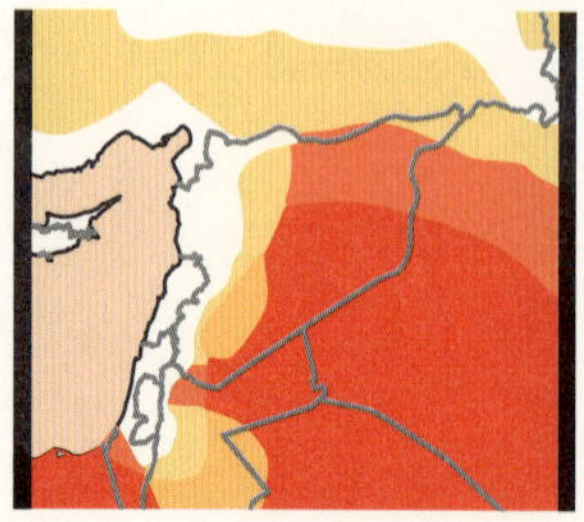

Seasonal average temperatures °C (F)

MAM	16.4 (61)
JJA	28 (82)
SON	19.2 (66)
DJF	7.2 (45)

Seasonal average rainfall mm (in.)

MAM	33 (1¼)
JJA	1 (0)
SON	17.6 (¾)
DJF	61 (2¼)

Below Symbolically evoking a tent, domed housing settlements are arranged with a correlation to nomadic camps. Typically, living units are composed of a cluster of domed structures, with a shared, protective central courtyard.

Opposite top left Varied heights of cells are determined by their construction logic: Sultan domes are the tallest, formed of four walls capped by a dome; lower domes are built up directly from ground level.

Opposite top right The basic unit of domed houses or *dar* is formed of two cells linked by an arched doorway.

Opposite middle and bottom The basic two-cell typology of Syrian domes provides living and sleeping spaces. Often, they are expanded to include a larger settlement with separate corbelled structures. These are used for cooking, bathing and storage, as well as baking and housing animals.

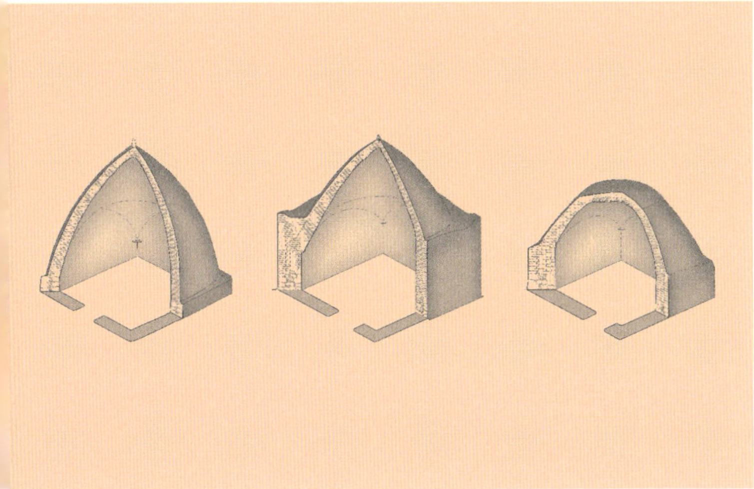
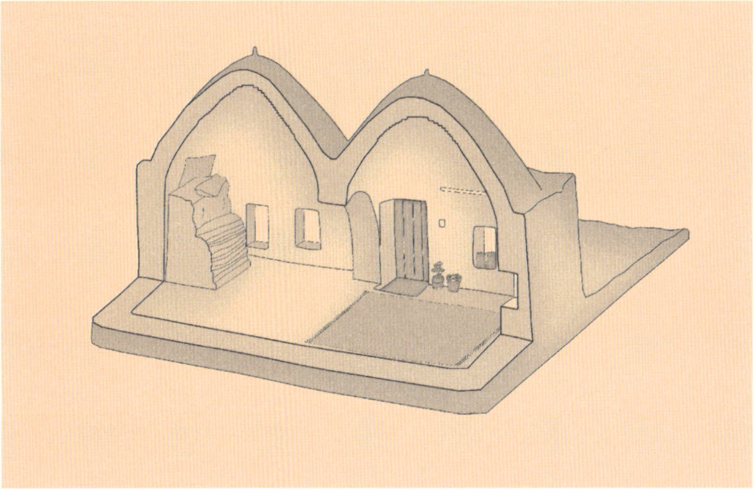

Troglodyte and Timber Dwellings of Turkey

Tammy Gaber

Geography/Climate

Turkey is situated in a unique 'cusp' condition: it bridges the continents of Europe and Asia, and – more importantly with respect to vernacular construction – is home to three climatic regions, including arid and semi-arid, temperate and continental climate zones. The political boundaries of the contemporary nation therefore encompass more than a singular cultural tradition, and the multiple climatic regions and layers of historical rule and habitation have ensured diverse and particular approaches to its vernacular design.

Materials

Timber is the main vernacular material in urban centres such as Istanbul, whose historical wooden villas are world-renowned. By contrast, in remote regions such as Cappadocia, the equally famous cave dwellings make use of volcanic rock for their unique forms.

Construction Techniques and Building Plan/Form

The Traditional Wooden Houses of Istanbul

The ancient city of Constantinople boasted the famed Hagia Sophia and other great Byzantine structures. Subsequently, when captured and converted into the Ottoman capital, renamed Istanbul, it also became home to hundreds of Ottoman monuments. Many mosques were constructed and, from small to grand, all were elaborately decorated. Their shallow domes and 'pencil' minarets still frame the skyline of this city, which is the gateway to two continents.

The common construction method for Istanbul houses from the 16th century onward was timber frame. Some 18th- and 19th-century wooden dwellings can still be found in the city, such as those in the cobblestoned neighbourhoods of Sultan Ahmet district, Balat Fener and Soğukçeşme Sokagi. Their many types include waterfront structures built along the Bosporus; the *kosk*, or pavilion structure; the *yali*, or vacation home; and the wooden houses, usually three storeys high, that were built closely together in the urban core.

These last-named dense, urban structures, like their waterfront counterparts, have a stone ground-floor level with first and second floors constructed in heavy timber framing. Occasionally some may incorporate brickwork for the upper walls, but the structure remains predominantly timber. Each closely built dwelling occupies a vertical volume, with the more public spaces – reception room, storage, kitchen and dining – located on the ground floor. Upper storeys contain the more private bedrooms and family sitting rooms. In most of these houses a projecting space (*çikma*), enclosed in timber, cantilevers out over the street, no more than a metre. These spaces developed from traditional balconies that were either wholly or partially covered depending on the climate of the region. A *çikma* was completely enclosed, and sometimes its windows would be covered with a wooden lattice called a *kafesler*, which allowed views outward only and which permitted air and light to flow freely without revealing the private interiors. This arrangement is similar to that of the timber-lattice *mashrabiya* cantilevered balconies commonly found in Ottoman Egypt and the Middle East.

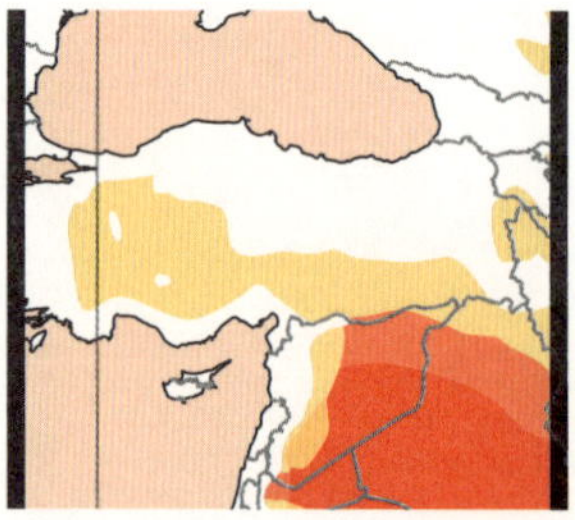

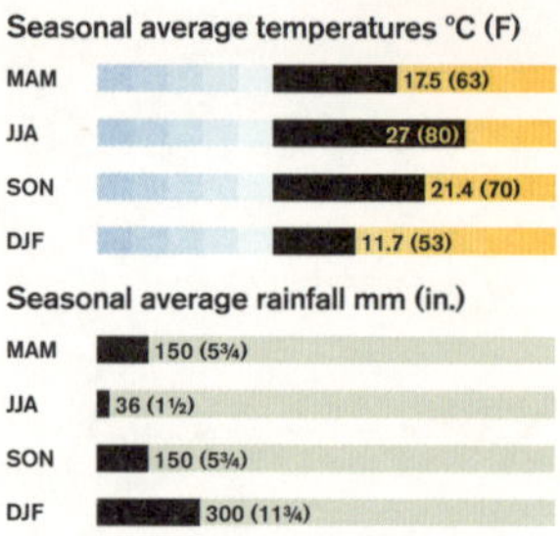

Below Because of its diverse geographical conditions, dwellings in Turkey range from caves in the Anatolia region to timber structures in Istanbul with Ottoman and Byzantine influences.

Opposite In Istanbul neighbourhoods such as Balat Fener and Soğukçeşme Sokağı some 16th–19th-century timber homes survive. Densely clustered, these homes are often three storeys high, with projecting and sometimes enclosed balcony areas, similar to Arabic *mashrabiya*, at upper, private levels.

KEMAL CAPRAZ EVİ
OSMAN BATUR HAN KÖŞKÜ

The Cave Homes and *Peri Bacalari* of Cappadocia

Located in central Anatolia and bounded by mountains on nearly all sides, Cappadocia's 1,000 m (3,300 ft) high plateau encompasses numerous towns and spans an area of 400 sq km (150 sq miles). The region's location, in combination with its unique sedimentary deposits of tufa created by formerly active volcanoes and subsequent erosion, has inspired habitation of some sort or another within the carved-out cavities of the landscape since at least the 4th century CE.

The troglodyte homes (as well as monasteries) of Cappadocia demonstrate a remarkable, unique approach to creating spaces in a continental climate; however, as the region also borders two further climate zones – arid and semi-arid – the area has hot, dry summers and cold, snowy winters. The stone mass surrounding their internal spaces demonstrates particular thermal qualities, making habitation in this relatively harsh climate possible.

The cave dwellings are carved laterally out of the sides of larger formations of volcanic rock or from tall, freestanding rock formations – locally called *peri bacalari*, or 'fairy chimneys' – in which the spaces are carved out vertically, over several internal storeys. Out of the mass of this monolithic material, apartment-like units are created.

Similar spatial configurations are to be found in the nearly 400 churches, monasteries and chapels in the Cappadocia region, the troglodyte retreat thereby creating a safe haven for thousands of Christians during Muslim Seljuk and Ottoman control of neighbouring regions. The extraordinary ancient city of Derinkuyu, one of several such urban agglomerations, is carved between seven and eight storeys below ground, with living quarters for 2,000 families along with spaces for worship, education, stables, storage and other necessary community activities. Such 'subtractive' spaces, carved from rock throughout the Cappadocia region, also accommodate contemporary functions, including restaurants, shops and workshops such as the ceramics centre in the town of Avanos.

The sequence of rooms in the cave dwellings is organized with public areas for living and dining near the front and private quarters for sleeping towards the rear, with doors between some of the private spaces. The rear of the home is mostly inhabited in the winter, when the 'thermal lag' provided by the rock mass makes for warmer interior space. The cave home is fronted with a house-type construction, and often a courtyard to allow for more comfortable living and outdoor activities in the warmer summer months. This attached structure also incorporates various types of storage and stable rooms.

The primary construction technique of these cave dwellings is therefore one of subtraction of material from the soft volcanic rock. This is largely tufa, but there is also limestone and sandstone in the area. Internal and external staircases are also carved out of the soft stone. The additively built home that fronts the cave dwelling, and the rooms surrounding the courtyard, use fired brick and mortar for their walls and are vaulted with timber, which is also used for doors and framing.

Right Known locally as *peri bacalari*, cave dwellings in central Anatolia make use of existing eroded volcanic rock of the region. Whole villages are enclosed by the tufa rock: carved laterally into the formations, homes have public functions towards the entry and warmer, more private areas for sleeping at the rear.

Beehive Structures of South Anatolia

Hacer Mutlu Danaci

Geography/Climate

The 'beehives' of the county of Elmali, in Turkey's southern Antalya province – which are known locally as bee *seren*, meaning 'bee stile' – are rare and unique vernacular architectural structures set within a distinct geographical and cultural landscape, situated on the western side of the Toros Mountains and the Bay of Antalya, and in the centre of the Teke Peninsula in Turkey's Mediterranean region. This has been an important centre of population throughout human history because it possesses ample water sources and fertile soil, and because it lies on several trade routes that connect Anatolia to the Mediterranean.

Materials and Construction Techniques

Individual *serens* are typically positioned on a timber platform built over a high rectangular prism, and can be found among the farms and grasslands, such as in the villages of Büyüksöğle and Küçüksöğle. They were constructed from stone masonry by erecting dry-stone walls with closely placed reinforcing elements over a square base, and were topped by trunks of Mediterranean cedar (*Cedrus libani*), called hemlock locally, with a length of around 1.40 m (4 ft). These trunks, known as *kara kovan*, were hollowed out by carving and piled up in a rough triangle on the flat timber platform over the bee *seren*, which has the appearance of a tower. The adoption of cedar exemplifies a use of local materials, while the overall architectural characteristics of these structures are reminiscent of ancient Lycian mausoleums.

Building Plan/Form

The height of *seren* roofs varies from 5 to 10 m (16 to 33 ft), but the hive is always constructed at a level that is difficult to reach so that the honey can be protected from bears and non-flying insects. The platform consists of timber girders spread over four corners. Access is gained through a high window by way of, typically, three timber foothold 'steps' that project from the main structure. An internal platform with a height of approximately 2.4 m (8 ft) can be reached via this window, which is only large enough to permit a single person to crawl through it. Honey can be extracted through a roof opening, which has approximate dimensions of 650 x 650 mm (25 x 25 in).

Seasonal average temperatures °C (F)

MAM	16.5 (61)
JJA	30.3 (86)
SON	20.6 (69)
DJF	6.3 (43)

Seasonal average rainfall mm (in.)

MAM	200 (7¾)
JJA	25 (1)
SON	50 (2)
DJF	200 (7¾)

Right Particular to the fertile region of Elmalı, local bee towers or *seren* rise up to 10 m (33 ft) in height and contain honey pots protected from bears and flightless insects. Enclosed by timber and dry-stone walls, the structures have just enough room to be accessed through a single high window.

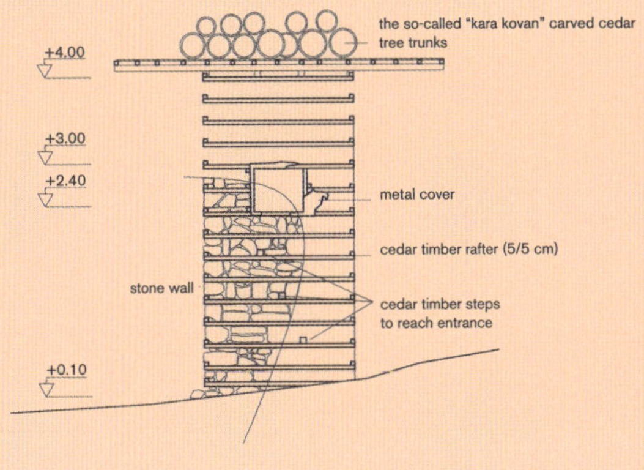

SOUTH FACADE

Iraq's Microclimatic Courtyard Dwellings

Subhi Al-Azzawi

Geography/Climate

The greater part of Iraq lies in the hot and dry climatic region of the subtropics. The average daily maximum temperature in the shade in summer (mid-May to mid-October) in Baghdad, for example, is about 45°C (113°F) with a diurnal range of 20°C (68°F); the minimum relative humidity varies between 15 and 20 per cent.

As a result, the great majority of the vernacular housing stock in Baghdad and other Iraqi cities up to the middle of the 20th century consisted of indigenous or traditional courtyard dwellings.

The indigenous courtyard houses of Iraq belong to a type of dwelling that began its development between 2750 and 2500 BCE in the Diyala region to the northeast of Baghdad. This type underwent continual development in Mesopotamia during the Sumerian, Akkadian, Babylonian and Assyrian civilizations – and further development during the various periods of Islamic civilization. Towards the middle of the 19th century, they seem to have reached their ultimate degree of improvement in microclimatic and environmental design, as well as in meeting the socio-religious demands placed on them and in achieving technical expertise within the limitations of contemporary building technology.

Building Plan/Form

In 762 CE, the region of Baghdad, where the Tigris and the Euphrates are only 60 km (40 miles) apart, was chosen by Caliph al-Mansūr as the site for the new capital city of the Abbasid Dynasty. It became known as 'the Round City' because of its perfectly circular form comprising three concentric walls and an outer moat. It had four radial gateways dividing it into four equal quadrants, but with an unequal number of radial streets in each. In 768, the capital began to expand to the east of the Tigris, and later became the main city of the region.

In 1853–54, the first accurate survey of Baghdad was carried out by Commander Felix Jones and Midshipman Collingwood (then of the British Indian Navy). It showed a city comprising two parts: the larger (Rusafa) on the eastern bank and the smaller (Karkh) on the western. The former was enclosed by an earthen dyke on the outside and a brick wall on the inside with a moat between them along three sides, as well as a wall alongside the river bank, to protect it from flooding by the Tigris. The western part, the level of which was slightly higher, was also enclosed by an earthen dyke – in this case, to protect it from inundation by the Euphrates.

In 1950, the historic city centre of Baghdad comprised seventy-six traditional neighbourhoods, fifty-four in Rusafa and twenty-two in Karkh. These have expanded incrementally and organically (but also harmoniously), and have formed the essence of the city, with all the important public buildings located along the river front in

Below Indigenous courtyard dwellings comprise the vast majority of Baghdad's buildings – a typology that has slowly been adapted and improved since its incarnation in the Diyala region, northeast of the city, more than forty-five centuries ago.

Opposite top Incremental and organic expansion of Baghdad's historic centre is primarily based on the growth of the larger eastern sector of Rusafa and the smaller western settlement of Karkh, divided by the Tigris River.

Opposite bottom Neighbourhoods usually consisted of homes, alleyways, markets, schools and mosques – the Al-Kazimiyyah Shrine is the city's most famous – with a consistent pattern of two-storey courtyard-based structures.

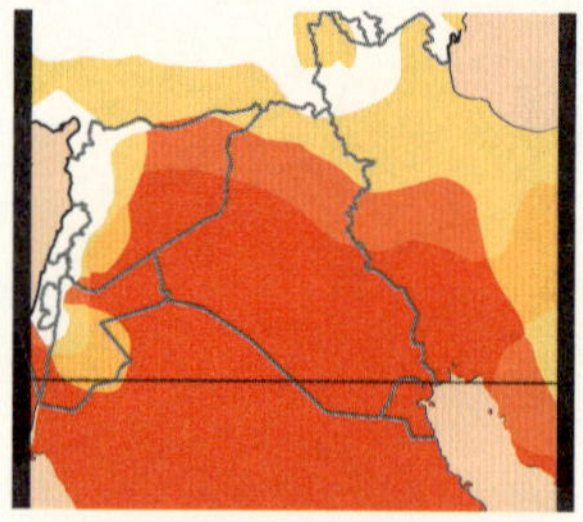

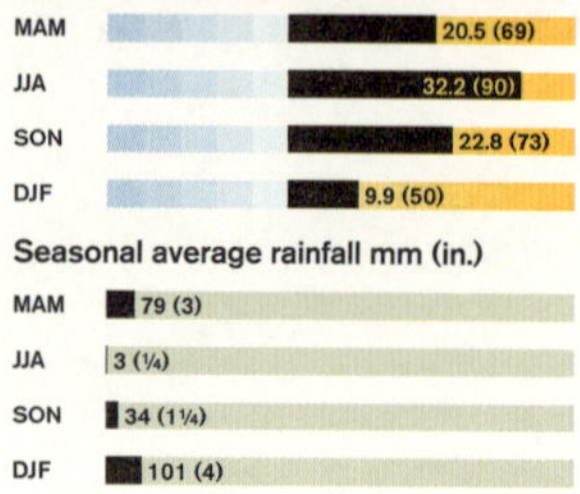

Rusafa. A neighbourhood usually consisted of houses, alleyways, a mosque, a madrasa (later replaced by separate state schools for boys and girls, each in a large courtyard house), a bazaar (or *souq*) that may be shared with adjacent neighbourhoods, corner shops (*'attarin*), an inn (*khan* or *caravanserai*), a tea house (*chay-khana*), and separate public baths (*hammam*) for men and women.

In such severe climatic conditions, traditional master builders adopted and adapted the two-storey courtyard house, with habitable rooms and spaces looking inwards towards the court (*hawsh* or *housh*). This gave inhabitants sunlight, daylight, natural ventilation, contact with the weather and a view of the sky – as well as physical, visual and aural communication between storeys: directly on the ground floor and indirectly through the access balcony (*mamsha*) at first-floor level. The internal courtyard became an oasis of shade and thermal comfort as well as of visual and aural relief, with fountains and water channels feeding fruit trees and shrubs that provided welcome shade and evaporative cooling. Such a fierce climate also necessitated mutual protection for the dwellings from the scorching heat of the sun. Courtyard houses were therefore built contiguously, back-to-back and side-to-side, thereby reducing the overall surface area exposed to solar radiation.

To protect the city's inhabitants further from the heat of the sun within the courtyard-house form, master builders also resorted to the use of habitable semi-cellars (*nim sard-ab*) at part-subterranean level, and even to incorporating fully subterranean habitable cellars (*sard-ab*). In this way, they took advantage of the thermal inertia of the cellars' thick retaining walls as well as that of the ground beyond them. These basements were used during the summer afternoon siesta (*qaylula*). In contrast to these subterranean spaces, the flat roof terrace (*satih*) was fully exposed to the sky and was used as an outdoor sleeping area in summer, losing desirable out-going radiation that rose up from the structure and the inhabitants, giving comfortable conditions. The dwelling is essentially two houses in one climatically and environmentally: the ground floor, lower than the first, restricts incoming sun and overheating in summer; the first floor, positioned high up, allows sun and heat gain in winter. Only the first floor is used in winter, because of rising dampness and the low altitude of the sun; the rest of the house is used in summer.

Additionally, the inhospitable climatic conditions necessitated shaded external pedestrian circulation space, which here took the form of narrow, meandering alleyways. This shading effect was further enhanced by the outward projection both of oriel windows (*shah-nashin*) and of flat roof terraces at eaves level (*sachagh*) from the buildings towards the centre of the alley. When such a vertically staggered façade profile is mirrored on both sides of an alleyway, this results in a substantially sheltered cross-section. The lane is adequately wide for pedestrian circulation at ground-floor level, narrow enough to allow cross ventilation at first floor, and with a minimal gap at roof terrace to permit direct solar radiation to penetrate.

The courtyard became a design tool for the individual house, with a potential for habitable floor levels incorporated into dwellings. Smaller four-level types included a *nim sard-ab* at semi-subterranean level; five-level types included a mezzanine (*kabsh-kan*) at first-floor level; six-level types included a *sard-ab* located under the floor of the courtyard. All multi-level homes included a flat roof terrace, or *satih*.

Since the houses do not incorporate external windows on their non-street façades, they could be built contiguously along three sides, thereby helping to reduce the size of building plots. Party walls between dwellings receive no direct solar radiation, and are therefore ideal elements for incorporating air scoops (*bad-girat*), which direct hot, dry air from roof-terrace level through inlet openings incorporated in the high parapet walls to outlet openings at ground-floor and semi-subterranean level. In descending through these vertical shafts, the air is cooled through inversion (the opposite effect of convection) by coming in contact with the cold internal surfaces of the *bad-girat*. It is further cooled and humidified through evaporative measures by passing across a porous water jug placed on the sill of the outlet opening in the *talār* (habitable colonnaded recess) at ground-floor level and in the *nim sard-ab* at semi-subterranean level. Sometimes, the outlet opening takes the form of a cooling pit (*zam-bur* or *zan-bur*) set into the floor of the latter.

The use of an internal courtyard for climatic reasons also coincided with socio-religious demands for absolute privacy of the interior, especially for areas reserved for its female inhabitants, from overlooking (*sharafiya*) by neighbours and passers-by.

Construction Techniques

The thick retaining and party walls of these buildings are constructed of masonry comprising two skins of fair-faced bricks with a central core filled with broken bricks of varying types and sizes. They are all bedded in a mortar of lime and sand or lime and ash up to a height of 1 m (3 ft) from ground level; above that, they are bedded in gypsum mortar. Every sixth course is a binding layer of paving bricks extending over the whole width of the wall, which is reduced in thickness from one floor level to the other by narrowing the width of the core. Internal partition walls between rooms use a composite construction of vertical timber studs with brick infill panels, the whole being plastered on both sides. The fired brick, of various shapes and sizes, is produced using locally available clay.

The windowed wall of characteristic *shah-nashin* overlooking the alleyway at first-floor level is built of timber studs with vertically sliding sash windows (without counter-weights) at lower level and fixed lights at high level, as well as a spandrel panel next to the floor and another next to the ceiling. The windowed wall of habitable rooms (*jam-khana* and *ursi/ardhi*) overlooking the courtyard at ground- and first-floor levels respectively are similarly constructed. However, such walls in the *ursi* of large courtyard houses of well-to-do families, which were built between 1850 and 1900, are double-glazed.

The floor at first-floor level and that of the roof terrace are similarly built with a composite structure. They use pole beams of poplar (*Populus* – known locally as *qawagh*) with rough timber boards (*lawh ragum*) nailed to them, topped by mats of split-and-plaited reeds and mud (as well as earth for levelling), and are finished with paving brick bedded in gypsum mortar.

Contemporary Application

These indigenous courtyard houses form an important vernacular architectural heritage. Through the centuries they have fulfilled the functional needs and living aspirations of their inhabitants, respected religious demands and social customs, complied with community traditions, expressed aesthetic values, visual proportions and geometric patterns of local crafts and artists, and been built within their owner-occupiers' financial means.

Opposite top A cross-section of a typical Iraq courtyard house with its multiple levels that work with seasonal solar gain. Semi-cellars away from the sun are cool in summer, while upper rooms admit sunshine and give warmth in winter. The dwellings' principal inward focus is towards the courtyard, which provides visual and aural relief, as well as shade for thermal comfort.

Opposite bottom Scenes of Baghdad's old quarters illustrate many of the defining architectural features of Iraq's courtyard homes. Circumscribed by narrow shaded streets, houses are built of masonry and share party walls. Openings to the street are protected by *shah-nashin* (oriel windows with screens) that provide both privacy and solar protection.

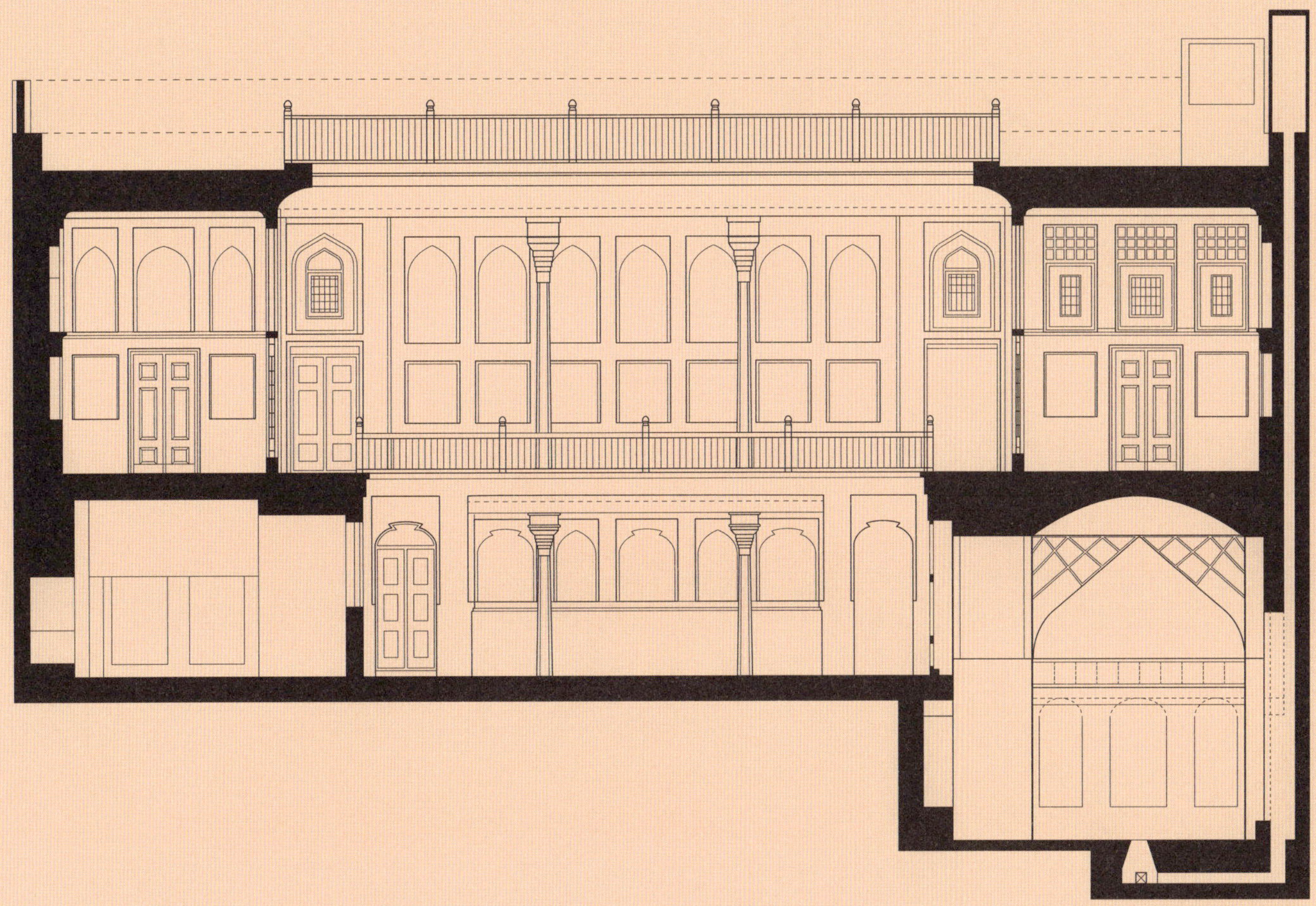

Reed Constructions of Iraq Marsh Arabs

Alexander Maitland

Opposite Giant reeds form the basis of life for Iraqi Marsh Arabs. Used for buildings, animal sustenance and boat-making, the reeds grow up to 7.5 m (25 ft) in height and form walls, floors, ceilings and the structural framework of traditional guest houses or *mudhifs*.

Below Documented by the early English explorer Wilfred Thesiger, the buildings and homes of Marsh Arabs once housed the entire population of 400,000. These views by Thesiger illustrate the weaving of mats by a Suaid man and boy (left) and the partially completed structure of a *mudhif* with supporting arches formed of giant reed bundles (right).

Geography/Climate

The marshes of southern Iraq, covering roughly 15,000 sq km (6,000 sq miles), were once believed by historians to have been the site of the Garden of Eden. The twin rivers, Tigris and Euphrates, that formed these vast wetlands unite as the Shatt al Arab and flow southeast past Basra, into the Arabian Gulf.

Materials

Reeds are of enormous importance in the daily lives of the Marsh Arabs, or Ma'dan, whose remote wilderness had remained virtually unchanged for 5,000 years.

The Ma'dan traditionally fed their buffaloes tender reed shoots; they harvested reeds to build coracles, houses and house foundations, and used split reed stalks to weave mats as a covering for floors, roofs and walls. Reed dwellings built by the Marsh Arabs were traditionally durable and well-ventilated and gave protection from the weather. In the hot, humid marsh summers they were infinitely preferable to buildings constructed of mud brick or concrete.

Construction Techniques

The giant reeds used for house building, *Phragmites communis*, also known as qasab, grow to a height of 7.5 m (25 ft). A typical *mudhif*, or guest house, on the Tigris measured 18 m (59 ft) long, 6 m (20 ft) wide and 5.5 m (18 ft) high. The horseshoe arches supporting the roof were made from giant reed stems bound closely together. From a 3 m (10 ft) circumference at their base, the arches narrowed to a 750 mm (30 in) circumference at the apex. Bundles of reeds, like 50 mm (2 in) cables, were lashed, one above another, the entire length of the huge barrel-vaulted building. This horizontal ribbing contrasted effectively with the *mudhif*'s arches. Layers of overlapping reed mats, similar to those used on the floor, covered the roof. The reeds used for arches and walls retained their natural pale-gold colour whereas the ceiling reeds, darkened by smoke, would grow to look as if they had been varnished a deep reddish-brown.

Mudhifs on the Tigris were constructed with nine or eleven arches. Others, documented on the Euphrates, had as many as fifteen, seventeen or even nineteen arches, but were never more than 4.5 m (15 ft) high and 4.5 m (15 ft) wide. The principal arches were sunk 600 mm (24 in) deep below floor level. When it became necessary to repair them, the occupants dug a trench alongside the *mudhif* and cut away the rotted arch bases. The shortened arches were then allowed to settle. Depending on its surroundings a *mudhif* might last for ten years or more before it had to be demolished.

Building Plan/Form

The *sarifa* – a smaller, rectangular building, with trellised walls – had a pitched roof covered with matting, supported on two reed pillars. The ridge pole was made either from a single palm trunk or from bundles of reeds. Another building type, known as a *raba*, served as both a guest house and a private dwelling. The *sitra*, a reed-built extension to a house, was used by nomadic Ma'dan to shelter their precious buffaloes in winter.

Contemporary Application

Although schemes for draining areas of the marshes for cultivation were already being planned in the 1950s, after the revolution in 1958 drainage was delayed by military incursions from Iran and, later still, by the Gulf War of 1991. In the wake of an uprising soon after that conflict, villages were destroyed, lagoons were poisoned and thousands of Marsh Arabs were tortured and killed. The population, estimated at 400,000 in 1960, had shrunk thirty-five years later to well under 40,000. It remains to be seen how far efforts to re-flood and repopulate these magnificent wetlands can restore their wild habitat, unique architectural heritage and traditional way of life.

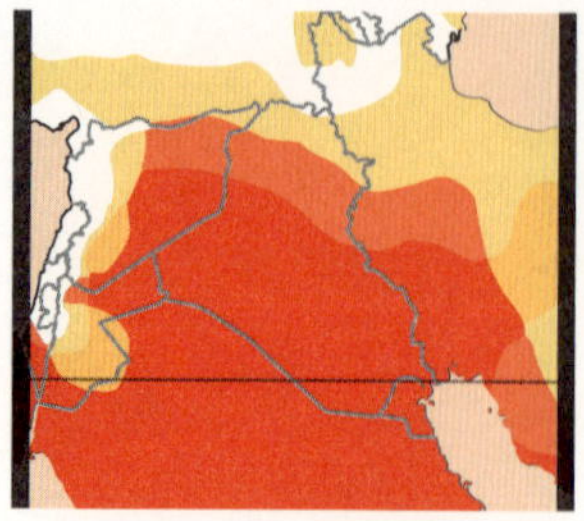

Seasonal average temperatures °C (F)

Season	Temperature
MAM	23.5 (74)
JJA	33.7 (92)
SON	25.6 (78)
DJF	12.7 (54)

Seasonal average rainfall mm (in.)

Season	Rainfall
MAM	11 (½)
JJA	0
SON	4.3 (¼)
DJF	17.3 (¾)

Left and opposite top Supported by reed bundles that taper from a circumference of 3 m (10 ft) at the base to an apex of 750 mm (30 in), the *mudhif* ribbing creates a huge barrel-vaulted structure.

Opposite middle Traditionally, the durable, well-ventilated *mudhif* gave protection from the hot, humid environment of the marshes and would generally last up to a decade, depending on location and exact local conditions.

Opposite bottom Dismantled, the components of smaller structures known as *raba* could be moved by boat, creating an adaptable building type that is responsive to environmental changes, such as rising water levels in spring.

Variety, Locality and Western Influence in Iran

Nasser Golzari

Geography/Climate

Iran's climate – with its extensive variation in temperature, rain- and snowfall, and both dry and humid conditions – can offer, in mid-spring, swimming in the sea to the south or skiing in the northwest. Iran is divided into six distinct climatic regions, and this rich variety has resulted in an impressive array of particular local architectural forms with specific spatial organizations, construction techniques, and habitation and cultural practices.

Some of these distinct typologies can be seen in the 'stepping' villages of the north and west of Iran, in the provinces of Gilan, Kurdistan and Azerbaijan. Another, more universally familiar local vernacular comprises the courtyard houses with walled gardens and serene public spaces in the central desert towns and the southern provinces of Yazd, Fars, Esfahan and Khuzestan. The local vernacular has evolved in these typologies, celebrating the topography and the climate while responding to the social narratives and contemporary cultural practices of the region.

Construction Techniques and Building Plan/Form

Northern Vernacular

The vernacular typologies of Iran are mostly evident outside its main urban centres. Although these towns and villages form an important part of the country's heritage, they are disappearing owing to the lack of government investment and the dominance of the large cities.

The significant forms of the villages in the provinces of Gilan, Mazanderan and Kurdistan step down the hill in response to the steep topography while reflecting local collective lifestyles and sociocultural practices.

In the same region – in such cities as Rasht, Anzali, Amol, Sari, Sefeed and Rood – there are other vernacular forms that respond to the prevailing heavy rain and high humidity. They have steeply pitched roofs, either of thatch or corrugated metal, with verandas (*aivan*), raised ground floors on stone bases, and continuous balconies all around their upper-floor levels. Their thin, long building forms offer effective cross ventilation and extensive daylight on either side of each room. The buildings of this region use elegant wooden structures with tapered timber posts supporting their thatched roofs – or, more recently roofs made of corrugated galvanized aluminium or Corten steel sheeting.

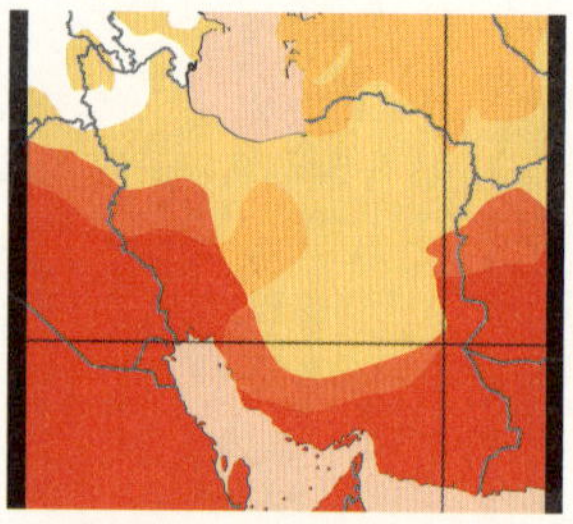

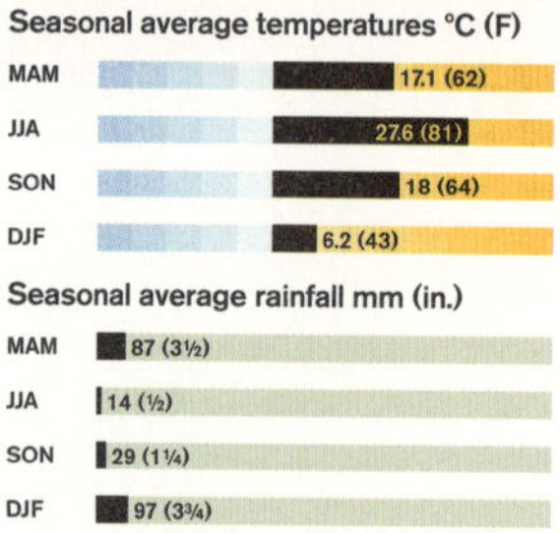

Right Iran's wide range of climatic conditions shape the country's great diversity in building types. Examples such as the stepped villages seen in the north and west are just one response to the local context: provincial settlements on steep hillsides with little rainfall.

رستوران
مدرسه
راهنمایی
دبیرستان

Southern and Eastern Vernacular

The building typology of the eastern and southern provinces of Yazd, Khuzestan and Baluchistan, and of the Persian Gulf region, have had limited coverage in Iran and are even less known abroad. The cities close to Iran's borders with Iraq and Pakistan display a rich mixture of Arabic and Pakistani/Indian cultural practices, which to some extent have influenced the local architecture. The combination of heat, humidity and dust with such cultural specificities as seasonal living has influenced a fascinating local architecture, with its spatial arrangements of walled gardens and habitable roofs, varieties of wind catchers and earth-building construction.

Importantly, the urban character of this region consists of narrow, zigzagging, interconnected alleyways with tall earthen walls to protect the passer-by from the sun and the desert wind. The zigzag nature of these alleyways reduces the wind velocity as well as creating an engaging spatial form. The urban public spaces here are concentrated around central courtyards with ponds and vegetation, and some have tall colonnades and multiple levels for seasonal occupation. Like the alleyways, they too are interconnected, influencing the townscape and forming the cultural landscape of these cities; their earthen materials form a 'roofscape', with domes over bazaar/market areas. These features are best seen in the provinces of Yazd, Shusgtar and Dezful.

The Terraced House: a New Hybrid Vernacular

The other, more common, building typology that has come to dominate most of Iran's modern cities is the terraced house. These very ordinary buildings – mostly 'architecture without architects' – show how social, cultural and environmental practices have been embraced and integrated, with their spatial organization generating new vernacular forms.

In 1892, the British statesman Lord Curzon declared of Tehran, 'We are in a city which was born and nurtured in the East but is beginning to clothe itself at a West-End Tailors.' This statement still reflects a particular view of Tehran's process of Westernization, dating from the 19th century. The impact of Western influences became more visible during the period of the Pahlavi dynasty in the mid-20th century. Then, new Western features and characteristics borrowed – and, at times, enforced – by the Iranian regime started to replace the traditional architectural fabric of Iran's main cities. Ironically, this 'Western cloth', as Curzon saw it, could not entirely ignore or wipe out the Middle Eastern characteristics of these cities. They have managed to maintain a strong imprint of Iranian architecture, appropriating and at many junctures clinging to their identity in this process of change.

The typical Iranian terraced house is just one of the local building typologies that has managed to hold on to its Middle Eastern quality while being clearly influenced by European styles. It first emerged in the 1960s, yet remains a key feature of the city in the form of two- or three-storey blocks with a single courtyard, known as a *hayat* (garden wall) in Farsi. Its distinctive form hosts mostly lower- and middle-income families.

In analysing the transition from public to private thresholds in this terraced house, there is clarity in the arrangement of the elements from outside to inside and from the ground level to the upper floors. Each element – such as the *hayat*, the raised terrace or the position of the pond or staircase – plays an important role in setting up transitional spaces from the public realm of the street to the private realm of the dwelling interior. Unfortunately, even though these terraced houses reflect a strong local identity within contemporary Tehran, they have been fast disappearing in order to be replaced with high-rise apartment blocks. Quite probably, in the future they will be argued to be Iran's vernacular heritage.

Below Tehran's once-thriving fusion of Iranian–Western elements – such as terraced homes with gardens – is now dominated by high-rise apartment blocks built in the Western style, which largely ignore adaptations to the local context.

Opposite Cities in Iran's eastern and southern provinces occupy hot, humid and dusty territory. Local buildings utilize closely arranged earthen structures organized according to a zigzag plan that creates shade and mitigates the speed of desert winds. Flat roofs allow for seasonal inhabitation; many dwellings in the region include wind catchers (bottom right) that ventilate the interior.

Afghan Yurts, Terraces and *Qala*

Below The northern regions of Afghanistan are home to the yurt: structures of woven felt or mats that are highly portable and used widely by nomadic communities in Central Asia.

Opposite Highly mountainous and wooded, the northeast alpine region of Afghanistan gives rise to terraced villages built from timber post-and-beam structures. Arranged over three levels, the village is structurally and socially interconnected: a roof of one dwelling forms the patio for its neighbour above.

Bashir A. Kazimee

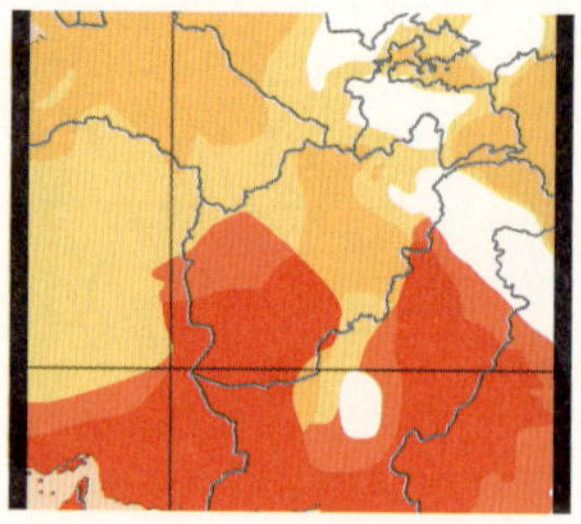

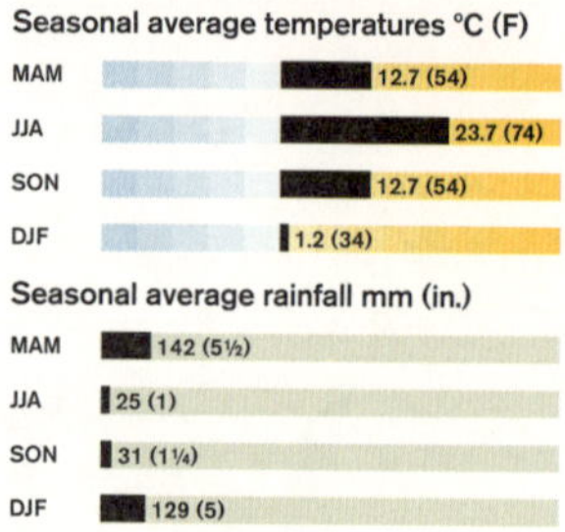

Geography/Climate

Afghanistan's diverse geographical regions are distinguished by the elevated and rugged mountain ranges of the Hindu Kush, which penetrates the country from the northeast at Pamir. The terrain then fans out into the central and southwestern highlands, gradually spreading to the flatter, lowland desert plains of the west and southwest regions of the country. The ensuing topographical features and the availability of local materials allowed for the development of numerous settlement forms and shelter types, which reflected the terrain and suited the specific environmental and cultural needs of its population.

Materials

In mountainous areas, timber for house construction is obtained from coniferous forests adjoining the villages. Timber-frame construction is particularly suitable for its earthquake-resistant properties; tremors are occasionally observed in Afghanistan's mountain regions. Mud-based adobe-type construction is used in the central and eastern tribal areas, as well as in the arid western and southwestern lowlands. In the northern regions of the country, nomadic communities use felt or woven-mat yurts – a portable shelter type encountered from Mongolia across Central Asia and as far west as Turkey.

Construction Techniques and Building Plan/Form

The picturesque, clustered, terraced villages of Nuristan, located in the country's wooded, alpine northeast region, are skillfully framed with layers of alternating timber and stone infill construction. The houses themselves are of post-and-beam timber construction. Their interiors are embellished with sophisticated wood-carved artwork, perfected by *buri* artisans that celebrate their unique local charm. Nuristan is inhabited by a distinctive native population in relatively isolated villages dispersed through deep, narrow mountain valleys. The main village in Nuristan is Kamdesh, at an altitude of about 1,800 m (6,000 ft) above sea level. Homes here are generally two or three storeys in height; the lower levels contain storage rooms and stables, with the upper floor is occupied by a large communal room in which the family cooks, sleeps and receives guests. The roofs of the dwellings are constructed directly above and alongside each other, so that one household's flat roof serves as a patio for their neighbours above.

The fortress-farmhouse, or *qala*, is native to the country's eastern and central tribal areas, where security and farming requirements are the necessities. This building type, with its massive high outer walls, is constructed skillfully by using chunks of mud (*pakhsa*) obtained from the site and by adopting adobe building materials. *Qala* may have elaborate watchtowers at all corners, with perhaps more along their peripheral walls; these were used for security in an area where tribal feuds

were once a common threat. Their size and architectural treatment varies according to the status and wealth of the family concerned. A *qala* may house the families of tenant farmers employed by a landowner, in which case it will have a utilitarian design dictated by agricultural needs. A more elaborate *qala* might be constructed to meet the standard and prestige of wealthy inhabitants, and is often provided with ornamentation on the outer walls as well as the customary watchtowers. Larger *qala* may contain several courtyard houses in order to accommodate the extended families of a wealthy landowner; these often also include a guest house with notable architectural features, which stands above the entry gateway.

Settlement patterns and building forms in the hot, arid regions of Afghanistan's west and southwest lowland belt, with its meagre precipitation and scarcity of timber, evolved compact clusters of courtyard houses, constructed of thick adobe walls, roofed with a vaulted or domed construction. This courtyard architecture plays a conscious role in the moderation of the climate, providing desirable living conditions for the comfort of families in this region. In a large urban aristocratic house, the courtyard may contain elaborate sitting rooms augmented by an attached wind tower for air circulation and opening to a portal (*aiwan*) facing the central court. Some dwellings are provided with a cool basement (*zirkhana*), where the family can retire for an afternoon siesta. Commonly, such courtyards are provided with fountains and water pools (*hauz*), and ornamented with trees, edible plants and flowers that help to moderate the high temperatures and provide a pleasant home environment.

Between the aforementioned zones may be encountered seasonal migratory nomads with their livestock, seeking fertile pastures and using portable tents and yurts, which can be readily assembled and installed for their temporary inhabitation. The Afghan yurt is a sophisticated portable dwelling employing sections of latticed wooden frames, which are assembled into a circular enclosure with a timber-framed domical roof. The side wall and roof is then enclosed by felt panels or woven reed mat for insulation. Yurt dwellings are found in the north and northeastern regions of the country.

Contemporary Application

The above observation of the indigenous architecture of Afghanistan characterizes varying degrees of interaction between the compelling constraints of geography and culture. This relationship, which is mediated through accumulated knowledge and experience, has produced enduring building typologies and design techniques that form a 'close fit' with the ecology of place and regional identity. In view of the post-war reconstruction efforts in Afghanistan, the application of vernacular knowledge and architecture principles seems essential and timely in order to address the challenges of housing provision, affordability and economic equality.

Left **Giving security from once-common tribal threats, the *qala* of Afghanistan's east and central regions are bounded by weighty walls of mud and marked by watchtowers. Their size and decorative treatment increases according to the resident family's resources and status.**

Chaura, Earth, Timber and Stone Dwellings of Pakistan

Yasmeen Lari

Geography/Climate

Bordering the Arabian Sea, between India to the east, Iran and Afghanistan to the west and China in the north, Pakistan covers around 800,000 sq km (300,000 sq miles) and has diverse climatic conditions. Though the country is formed of three major geographic areas – the northern highlands, the Indus River plain and the Balochistan Plateau – its two predominant climates are humid subtropical, and hot desert. The latter regions experience virtually no rain annually, and average summer and winter temperatures range from 35°C (95°F) to 15°C (59°F) respectively. Comparable with other desert regions that share these characteristics, local buildings found in the Pakistani desert climate usually take advantage of readily available construction materials, including clay, adobe and cob/wattle and cob. The advantage of the construction method using these materials is its ability to mediate external temperature difference and to more successfully survive seismic activity, which occurs most often in northern Pakistan because of the convergence of the Indian–Eurasian plates.

Materials

In many areas of Pakistan, stone masonry and timber framing and bracing are used in vernacular wall construction along with filling materials. However, the country's predominant construction material is unfired clay, which utilizes diverse earth-construction techniques. A range of adobe/sun-dried mud brick, large lumps of clay similar to Western cob, layered mud and mud-filled wattle and cob is applied from the mountainous north to the plains of southern Pakistan. In some areas, skilled artisans' tribes rely on mud construction for their livelihood. Whatever the form of earth construction adopted, roofs invariably use heavy, often oversized wooden logs or joists.

Right **Though Pakistan's climatic range creates local variation in buildings, many areas draw on constructions that incorporate timber and stone, such as can be seen here in the Phander Valley near Chitral in the north.**

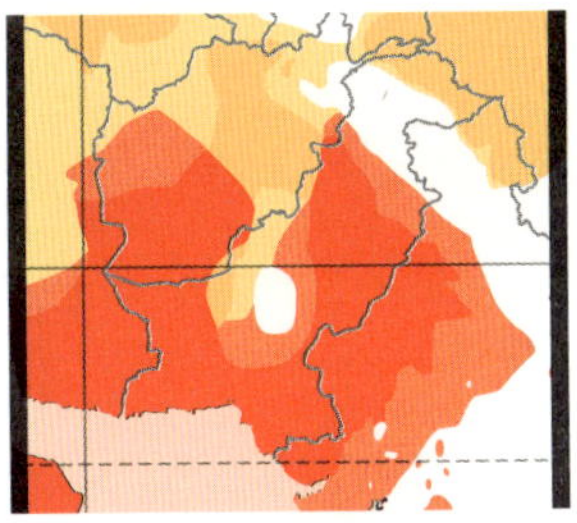

Seasonal average temperatures °C (F)

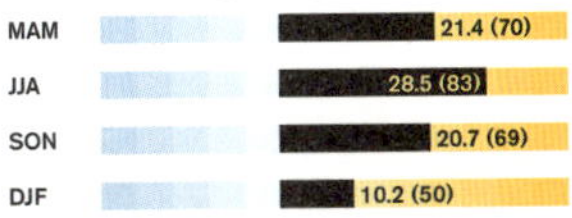

Seasonal average rainfall mm (in.)

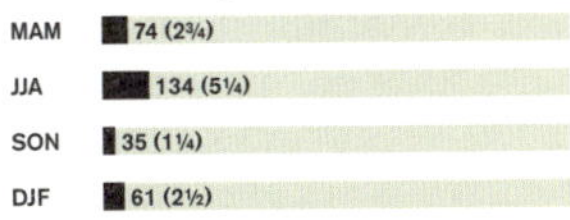

Opposite top left and right Formed in a simple square plan, homes and mosques are often built of thick mud that gives thermal protection.

Opposite middle left and right Structures cross-braced with timber are found in the northern region of the country and offer improved seismic resistance.

Opposite bottom left and right Traditional conical *chaura* homes in Sindh province are a distinctive Pakistani feature. Built with reinforced mud walls and thatched roofs, they provide good seismic protection.

However, in Pakistan, as in many other parts of the world, adobe/unfired clay construction has long been regarded as synonymous with 'backward' cultures.[1] The pursuit of modernity has inhibited attention to vernacular forms and techniques by contemporary architects and engineers. The connection between non-industrial materials and local skills, leading to sustainable construction, remains largely unheeded more than half a century after Egypt's Hassan Fathy created the community of New Gourna near Luxor.[2] Although extremely sustainable and eminently suitable for the redevelopment of disaster-affected communities, only a handful of vernacular methodologies have received official patronage for large-scale application by governments or international aid agencies.[3]

The region's vernacular construction has promoted social cohesion, fostering pride and a sense of ownership through community participation. However, the participation of women in 'self-build' in Pakistani construction has not been quantified or studied in any depth.[4] Women in almost all communities in the country's rural areas are accomplished in the art of earth building, and continue to play a significant role in realizing shelter during post-disaster rehabilitation. In fact, the best kind of earthen plaster found in the subcontinent is one that is applied by women. They mix earth with dung and straw, knead it and roll small portions in their hands before applying it, later adorning the façades with folk patterns and artwork, signifying pride and ownership.

Construction Techniques

Cob/Adobe Construction

The rectangular plan form and flat roof are among the most popular dwelling forms all over the country. Flat roofs are used as an extension of the house, including for sleeping during the hottest seasons. Thick mud walls provide thermal mass, keeping interiors cool or warm depending on the weather. Roofs are normally built with thick logs, with branches or bamboo used as purlins, and covered with layers of mud. While the walls are usually well constructed, these roofs are highly vulnerable and often cause the collapse of the entire structure. Poor roof construction can allow extensive rainwater ingress into the rooms and seepage into the core of mud walls.

In order to make structures flood resistant, various methodologies have been devised by the Heritage Foundation of Pakistan (HF), which include providing protection at the base and overhanging eaves, as well as the use of lime in the base and in external renders.[5]

Timber Framing and Cross Bracing

The technique of cross bracing using timber elements has been practised for centuries in the northern part of Pakistan. This methodology provides seismic-resistant structures, many of which withstood the massive Kashmir earthquake of 2005. The wall consists of vertical and horizontal timber members tied together with diagonal struts, providing not only strength but also resilience. This 'skeleton', with its cross bracing, is usually filled with mud or stone masonry bedded in mud mortar. The traditional roof consists of heavy wooden logs covered with layers of mud plaster. Known as *dhajjidewari* or *dhajji*, it has been considered 'a valid form of construction in seismic areas',[6] as long as its joints are carefully crafted.[7]

Building Plan/Form

Wind Catchers and Atria – Cooling Strategies

Where unfired clay and other vernacular techniques provide insulation from intense heat or cold in the region, it is the innovative wind catcher, rising high above the roof, that forms the most effective device in areas with prevailing breezes. The wind is channelled through a vertical chute into various rooms, where openings are provided in order to direct the breeze to create a cooling draught. The resulting roofscape, with its proliferation of wind catchers, lends Thatta town (located close to the World Heritage Site of Makli Necropolis) a picturesque character. The walls of wind catchers are normally constructed with vertical posts and interlacing branches, covered internally and externally with mud plaster and finished with stucco tracery and ornamentation.[8]

Another traditional spatial methodology for regulating internal microclimates is the enclosed atrium form, which has long been used successfully in dry, hot regions of the country. The introverted character of the resulting house also provides privacy for women and protects the interiors from the hot sun. The air collected during the night keeps the rooms surrounding the courtyard cool for most of the day, thus providing comfortable living conditions without the use of mechanical devices.

The *Chaura*

A particularly picturesque Pakistani building form is the circular unit known as the *chaura*, which is identified with the rustic desert culture of Sindh province. Built with vertical wooden log posts, with an infill of sunflower stems or reeds, and capped with a thatched, pointed roof, these have been found to be the strongest vernacular construction type for seismic and flood resistance. The distinctive conical roof is also used with circular earth walls. The thatch treatment (without any tarpaulin barrier) allows the roof to breathe, while the insulated walls of mud or breathable reed construction create a cool interior during hot weather.[9]

Azerbaijan's Structures of Embellished Brick

Saverio Mecca and Sabina Hajiyeva

Geography/Climate

The geography of Azerbaijan varies from semi-desert and dry steppes to moderate regions with mild and dry winters.

The Sheki-Zagatala region is one of the oldest inhabited areas of the country. It is renowned not only for its moderate climate, with mild and dry winters, and its landscape, but also for its architectural heritage – both monumental and vernacular. The dwelling houses of this region are among the most interesting in Azerbaijan.

Materials

Vernacular buildings in Azerbaijan have always used a variety of materials because of the diversity of climatic conditions in the country's different areas. In the Baku-Absheron region, buildings were erected of limestone and traditionally had flat roofs. The vernacular of the country's southern regions employed brick. In the mountainous Sheki-Zagatala region, rich in rivers and forests, buildings are characterized by cobblestone in combination with brick and timber. These mixed brick/cobblestone walls, using various laying techniques, testify to the skill of the master masons in using local building materials and incorporating architectural qualities, thereby providing both the necessary durability and the desired decorative effect.

The brickwork walls included friezes, and such wall ornamentation showed great originality: they might consist of a fir-tree pattern or a stepped device, occasionally close in form to a Western-style classical meander. Sometimes the figured laying comprised alternating vertical and horizontal bricks, to create diagonal patterns.

Adobe-type brickwork was traditionally bedded in a clay mortar. The thinnest possible ornamental patterning of brick was used in various arch details, in interiors and on façades, and was traditionally achieved using a white clay plaster-like mortar (consisting of gypsum and lime) – known locally as *gyaj* or *gyaja*. This was also good for stucco moulding and decorations, as it is uniform and has a mirror-smooth surface finish.

Building Plan/Form

Very few ancient or medieval dwellings have been preserved in Azerbaijan; those that do exist were uncovered during archaeological excavations. Among these, there is a large variety of types but the range is most clearly shown in the Sheki-Zagatala region of the country.

The houses of Sheki-Zagatala – all of which have a masonry structure, mostly of two storeys – are characterized by rich architectural detailing and natural stone and brick construction. Arcades comprising open, deep verandas (or *eyvan*); wooden balconies; walls incorporating brickwork, fragmentary masonry and cobbles (from grey-green stone to dark-red brick); and tile roofs all generate the characteristics of this region's typical cityscapes.

In many cases, the basic element of the dwelling façade is a spacious veranda with wooden profiled columns, or a masonry arcade – either of which can be as wide as the premises themselves. The temperate climate allows this space to be used for most of year, and its importance is emphasized by the richness of its decorative treatment. These deeply shaded spaces – often with an openwork, carved fence and a soffit of exposed ceiling beams in combination with the smoothly plastered, light wall surfaces – lends an intimacy appropriate to the dwelling's needs.

The traditional, richly decorated fireplace (or *bukhary*), underlining either the longitudinal or cross axis of a room, is the main ornament of the principal-room interiors. Small wall niches, intended for fixtures and the storage or display of fine household goods, are symmetrically placed on both sides of the *bukhary*. The larger niches found on longitudinal walls were used to store bedding during the day.

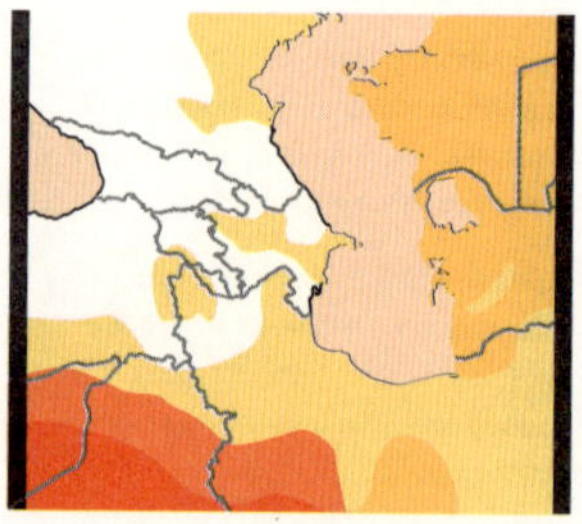

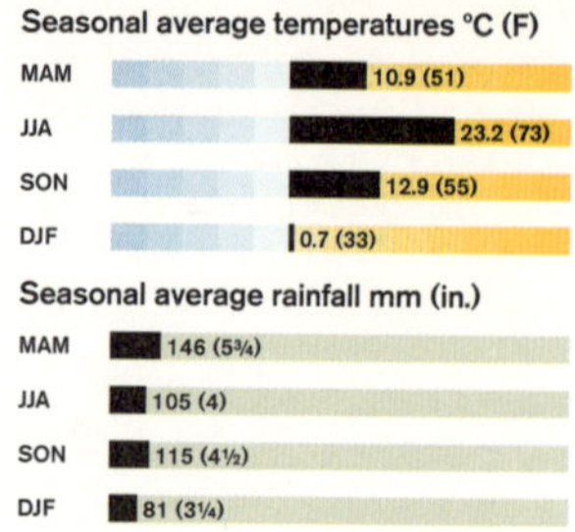

Opposite top left The Sheki-Zagatala region is one of the country's few that show instances of preserved traditional homes.

Opposite top right and bottom Rich architectural detailing is the immediate characteristic of Azerbaijan's masonry structures. Most dwellings are two storeys and incorporate intricate brickwork façades, tiled roofs, wooden balconies and verandas that become an informal extension of the living space.

Şəki şəhər
Ömər Əfəndi
MƏSCİDİ

Summer and Winter Homes of Uzbekistan

Anna Ietswaart

Geography/Climate

Situated in the heart of Central Asia, Uzbekistan is located between the vast steppes of Kazakhstan to the north and the Pamir Mountains to the south. Its continental climate is marked by extremes; temperatures can exceed 45°C (113°F) in summer and drop to -20°C (-4°F) in winter. Rainfall is rare. Water runs from the mountains and down into the plains through two major rivers. Since ancient times, major irrigation systems have transformed some of these desert regions into fertile oases. The main cities of ancient Transoxiana (the 'land beyond the Oxus') – Samarkand, Bukhara, Khiva and Tashkent – prospered from their location at the crossroads of trade routes until the 16th century.

Heat, earthquakes and sandstorms are facts of life in Central Asia. Storms continuously sweep through the region's towns and cities, carrying sand and dust. The narrow and winding streets act as windbreaks and produce shade. The area's traditional housing provides an extremely effective response to this environment.

Materials and Construction Techniques

The traditional Uzbek house is built with a wooden frame on a foundation of mud bricks. Mud brick is considered ideal for this purpose as it absorbs seismic vibrations. For the same reason, diagonal beams are incorporated into the wall structure. The timber frame is then filled with mud bricks and covered with clay and plaster. To improve insulation, the walls exposed to the sun are deep, and contain cavities that are used as shelves. The roof is composed of layers of timber, straw and soil, up to 800 mm (32 in) thick, to absorb the large differences in temperature. Both walls and roof require thorough annual maintenance.

Over the centuries, some imported building materials were required, including essentials such as wood. Timber was procured by river from neighbouring Tajikistan. With the supply of birch (*Betula*) and plane (*Platanus*) dwindling historically, timber has also been imported from Kazakhstan. Sole plates were made from local hardwood, such as apricot (*Prunus armeniaca*) or mulberry (*Moraceae*).

Stone is also rare in Uzbekistan. Traditionally, baked brick constituted the building material for madrasas, mosques and caravanserais. Mud brick, consisting of a mixture of clay, straw and water, is considered a more humble masonry option, and is used for domestic construction.

Building Plan/Form

Although every region of the country has its varieties, a common characteristic of the traditional urban dwelling of Uzbekistan is its orientation regarding sun and wind. Archaeological excavations tracing back to the 9th and 10th centuries show that the heliotropic orientation of the Uzbek house has existed for millennia. Though this habitat existed well before the Islamization of the region, because the layout of the vernacular house readily accommodated the precepts of Islam the new faith contributed to the fixity of the architectural typology. The only discernible change was that as a result of the prohibition of figurative art under Islam, decoration tended towards the depiction of geometric ornaments and plants.

The dimensions of a plot may vary according to the wealth of the occupying family, but its proportions are fixed. The living rooms are constructed around an open courtyard; this acts as a central space, from which all rooms can be reached and can derive their light.

The two main rooms face each other on either side of this court. The larger of the two, the *mekhmonkhona* (guest room), will be orientated towards the north. Two rows of windows provide natural ventilation: the upper row of openings lets warm air leave the room, while cooler air is taken in through the lower row. This main room is not only high – varying from 3.5 m (12 ft) to as much as 8 m (26 ft) in height in very wealthy households – but also elevated in order to allow for breezes to easily pass through. Conversely, the 'winter' room faces south, opposite the *mekhmonkhona*. Its low ceiling allows heat to easily fill the space. All the windows of the winter room can be secured with wooden shutters. In winter, the 'summer' room is used for storage – and vice versa.

The guest room can be reached via a stairway to an elevated terrace, the *soufa*, which is covered by the *iwan*, a canopy supported by carved wooden columns. Underneath the terrace, semi-buried in the naturally cool soil, are the service spaces, such as the basement (*podval*) for storage, domestic animals and poultry. The kitchen either adjoins the *iwan* or sits, detached, in the courtyard.

Contrary to the country's religious structures, with their colourful façades, Uzbek domestic buildings hide their riches on the inside. Whether rich or poor, the façade of each house is plastered with adobe in keeping with the Islamic virtue of humility. Whoever has the good fortune to be invited inside, however, may encounter a treasure trove.

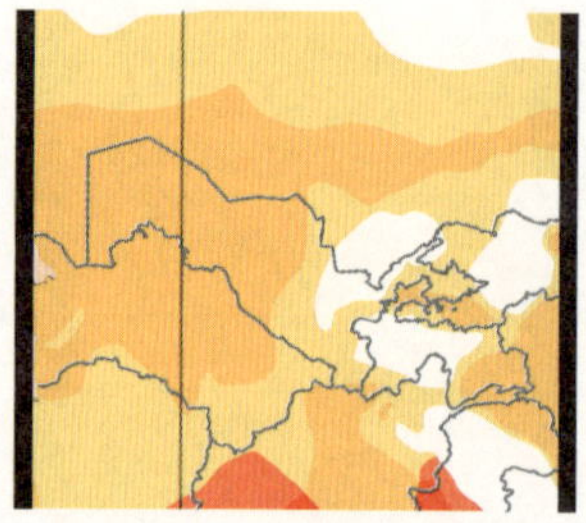

Seasonal average temperatures °C (F)

MAM	12.9 (55)
JJA	25.8 (78)
SON	11.7 (53)
DJF	-2.1 (28)

Seasonal average rainfall mm (in.)

MAM	87 (3½)
JJA	11 (½)
SON	31 (1¼)
DJF	67 (2½)

Opposite In keeping with Islamic tradition, decoration of the traditional Uzbek home is limited to the interior. The walls of these guest rooms known as *mekhmonkhona* are traditionally divided into panels with niches that are profusely patterned with geometries, stars, knots or floral motifs.

الهی تا قیامت باد آباد

Opposite top right and diagram below Traditional structures of Uzbek houses centre around a courtyard from which all areas are accessed. The court is used to divide the home into two rooms – a large, raised *mekhmonkhona* room facing north for summer living, and a smaller south-facing winter room.

Opposite top left The summer room is almost twice the height of its winter counterpart and includes pairs of double windows to introduce cool air and allow warm air to escape.

Opposite bottom and below Junctions between walls and ceilings are decorated with honeycomb-style *muqarnas*, finished in bright colours and gold paint, as with the rest of the interior.

To begin with, the walls of the *mekhmonkhona* are traditionally divided into panels and niches decorated with geometric shapes or floral themes, stars and knots, and quotes from the Quran. Extensive tea sets are kept on carved plaster shelves (*tokcha*). Where wall and ceiling meet, decorative *muqarnas* (honeycomb-style ornamentation) bridge the junctions. Everything is executed in bright colours and gold paint; these colours historically bore great significance, as they did in European medieval iconography.

In pre-Soviet Central Asia, the decorative arts were very highly regarded. Master craftsmen (*usto*) were linked to their work. They took great pride in never reproducing a design in another house, and even within a dwelling it was taken for granted that all panels should be different. Other *ustos* would be hired for wood and plaster carving. The woodwork of the ceiling beams, the front door and the columns of the *iwan* were embellished with carvings. Geometric patterns, *panjara*, carved from panels of plaster filter the light coming in through the windows while letting stale air out. Such houses also used to be almost devoid of furniture; the family would sit and sleep on *courpatcha*, foldable mattresses, that were stowed during the day.

For the sake of equality, the Soviet regime sometimes divided large houses into two – leaving one family with a winter and the other with a summer room – or installed a wall dividing both the *mekhmonkhona* and the winter room in two. While the house owners were banished to a small flat, the newly installed families did not feel the same responsibility towards the house and its maintenance as the original owners, and were unfamiliar with the tradition of living in a courtyard house. Hence, the traditional structures of Uzbek towns deteriorated. Recently, the law on private ownership, nullified since the collectivization of the 1930s, was reinstated. Lawful owners can now claim their property, walls can be torn down and rooms united. However, the majority of bourgeois houses had already been turned into estates for public functions such as hospitals and schools.

Turkmenistan's Earthen Structures

Louise Cooke

Geography/Climate

Turkmenistan is characterized by its Köppen–Geiger classification of cold desert climates, with very little rainfall annually and extreme desert temperatures of up to 50°C (164°F) in summer and -10°C (14°F) in winter. Almost 80 per cent of the country is formed by the Kara-Kum (Black Sand) Desert.

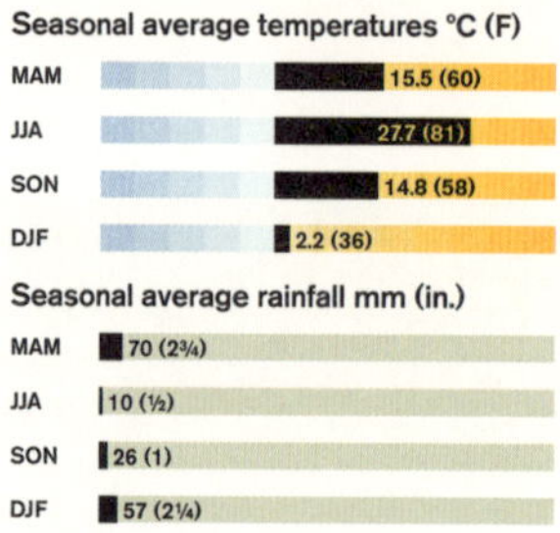

Right Accommodating a range of applications – from rammed earth and cob constructions to earthen mortars, plasters and renders – the ancient remains of Merv illustrate the diverse breadth of wholly earthen buildings, such as this grand, fortress-like residence of Great Kyz Kala.

Materials and Construction Techniques

The vernacular architecture of Turkmenistan is immensely diverse, with structures ranging from traditional earth buildings and desert-dwelling yurts to those constructed under the influence of imperial Russian and later Soviet developments, through to a range of developments in independent Turkmenistan that utilize broadly postmodernist design and materials in a similar pattern to that seen from the Middle East through to Central Asia.

The World Heritage Site of Ancient Merv in the Mary region comprises a consecutive series of discrete walled cities that gradually developed on adjacent virgin sites. Within the core area of the archaeological park of Ancient Merv, the cities of Erk Kala and Gyuar Kala date from the Parthian and Sasanian periods, Sultan Kala from the Seljuk period, and Abdullah Khan Kala and Bairam Ali Khan Kala from the Timurid period. This pattern of urban development and growth was responsible for the creation of a vast cultural landscape, and is common throughout much of Central Asia. It is associated with the successive and varying power structures and dynasties that rose and then declined throughout this immense region.

Ancient Merv demonstrates the rich diversity and history of building with earth in the region. Earth is used for both loadbearing and non-loadbearing construction. The construction techniques associated with it range from mud brick to various monolithic forms (rammed earth and cob), earthen mortars, plasters and renders. Earthen building materials were used in addition to fired bricks from the Seljuk period onwards, at a time when fired bricks were used primarily for damp-proof coursing (and for higher-status building types than the humble dwelling). Nonetheless, even after the introduction of fired bricks many structures continued to be constructed wholly from earthen building materials.

Using earth in these different forms enabled the realization of a variety of different building types. For example, the surviving structures at Merv represent defensive, monumental and religious architecture, working buildings, and monuments connected with funerary practice, while the below-ground archaeological material represents the rest of the abandoned cities.[1] A number of these structures are particularly impressive, including the Great Kyz Kala and Little Kyz Kala – elite rural residences built like fortresses and known as *köshk*.

Traditional Turkmen settlements were primarily composed of single-storey structures; historically, these had flat earth roofs, but now much more commonly display inverted V-shaped roofs formed of various corrugated materials.[2] The majority of the contemporary mud-brick dwellings have fired-brick exteriors, an approach utilizing the thermal characteristics of the mud bricks alongside the perceived benefits of reduced maintenance associated with fired bricks. In contrast to the dwellings, many of the contemporary storage structures are made from mud brick and/or *paksha* (cob), with the *paksha* building tending not to be plastered.

Tajik Courtyard Houses and Kyrgyzstan Yurts

Below The Tien Shan mountains form parts of both Tajikistan and Kyrgyzstan. Its dry and continental climate is suitable for nomadic summer settlement in the upper alpine region, as captured in these historical views.

Opposite Layers of sedimentary clay are found on the Tajik plains. This readily available building material has meant the predominance of adobe bricks, which are used widely to make the traditional courtyard home. In contrast, dwellings in the Pamir Mountains use stone to make windowless rectangular homes (middle and top right).

Munzifakhon Babadjanova

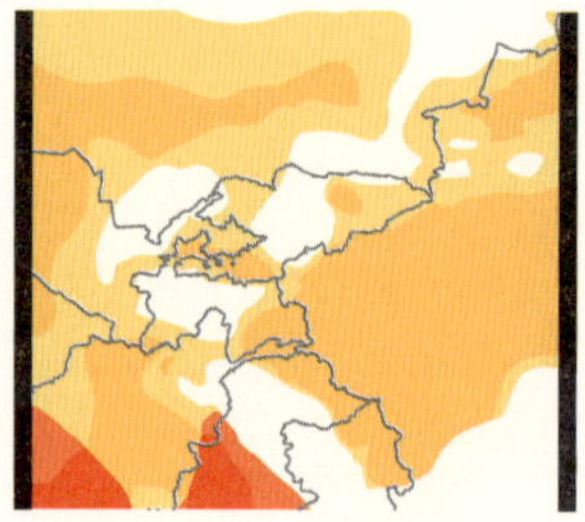

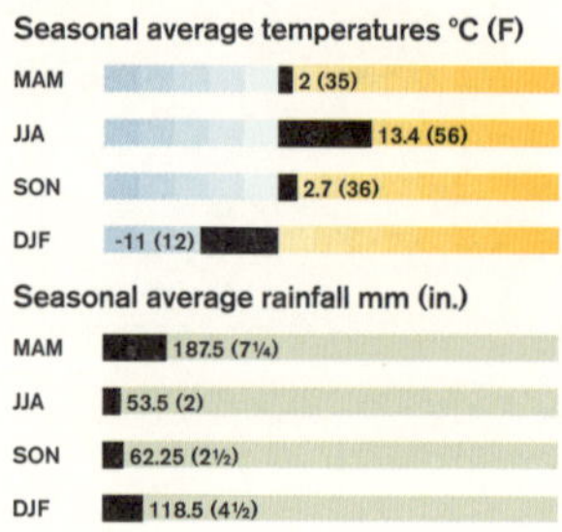

Geography/Climate

Tajik territory includes both lowlands and mountainous regions. Nearly half the country is situated at an altitude of 3,000 m (10,000 ft) above sea level, and its many mountain ranges rise to a height of 7,000 m (23,000 ft). Overall, 93 per cent of Tajikistan is mountainous, with the highest peaks lying in the Tien Shan and Pamir ranges. The climate is mainly dry and continental – with short winters and hot summers. Its territory varies in typology according to elevation – from subtropical desert plains and steppe foothills to freezing massif areas.

Kyrghyz territory shares the Tien Shan mountains, and also encompasses the Eastern Pamir range. Its nomadic population winters in the valleys, and in the summer occupies its highland alpine meadows.

Materials

Thick layers of loess deposits on the plains provide Tajik builders with a simple and highly suitable material to work with: clay, which is widely used. Adobe brick was the main material for masonry walls in the country up until the time of Alexander the Great's campaigns in Central Asia (4th century BCE), since when this type of construction method began to be superseded.

Natural stone was used sparingly, in more monumental work and in cities, typically for the bases and capitals of columns and hellenized pilasters. However, it was also adopted in particularly mountainous areas, such as the Pamir region.

Construction Techniques and Building Plan/Form

Tajikistan

Knowledge of vernacular construction techniques was passed on from generation to generation among the Tajik people, who adapted their expertise to the prevailing climatic conditions. The country's traditional courtyard homes provide an example of close adaptation to climate. The cool night air lingers throughout the following hot day in their windowless rooms – and a small pond in the centre of the yard, along with strategically placed planting, serves to 'soften' the harsh, dry air.

Traditional Tajik houses were usually decorated internally: carved ceilings were colourfully painted with various patterns, and walls contained carved built-in cabinets, which stored household items including dishes and clothes. Such methods also applied to Tajikistan's renowned traditional decorated teahouses, which today are built by the country's master craftspeople – often for export to other countries.

The Pamir Mountains area – with its stone cliffs, secluded groves in river basins, clear water from mountain streams and seemingly boundless sky – is often called 'the Roof of the World'. The folk houses of the western Pamir Tajiks used stone; they were rectangular in plan with no windows, and had a flat roof supported on wooden pillars, as in ancient times.

Opposite Kyrgyz people use yurts constructed with a modular four-part structure, including a door frame, lattice walls, and an upper/lower circular rim. Tensioned bands secure the construction, which is enclosed by a *guise* (felt covering).

Below Like many traditional dwellings in Central Asian countries, in Kyrgyzstan a yurt is an ancient way to survive the varying climatic extremes and to accommodate a nomadic way of life.

Kyrgyzstan

Since antiquity, the traditional dwelling of Kyrgyzstan has been the yurt – a masterpiece of vernacular architecture, and an outstanding achievement of nomadic civilization. Its structure is generally similar among the nomadic peoples of Central Asia; its local distinctiveness is shown through its exterior and interior decor. Kyrgyz yurts display a variety of manufacturing methods, and their ornamentation competes with the bright mountain colours.

For transportation, this relatively compact and light dwelling requires only two or three camels or three or four horses. Its wooden frame is erected in four stages. First, the door frame is assembled; then, sliding lattice walls are attached to it; next, an honoured and respected elder raises its round rim, whose members are inserted into the slots in the upper ends of the dome poles; finally, the lower edges of the rim are tied to the upper edge of the walls. This basic frame construction is secured with many tensioned bands, known as *ormok*, and then enclosed by a *guise* (large felt covering), usually composed of two large sections – one for the vertical walls, and one for the roof – both of which are formed of stitched pieces of felt. The house is then ready for use.

The oldest type of door on a Kyrgyz yurt comprised a curtain of felt or mats; it was subsequently replaced with a timber-framed assembly. In either instance, the door was decorated with special designs intended to magically protect the house from evil forces and orient it towards good outcomes: numerous offspring, an abundance of livestock and good health.

Traditional dwellings across all Central Asian countries have much in common: 'Tajik'-style homes can also be found in Uzbekistan, and yurts in Kyrgyzstan, Kazakhstan, Tajikistan and Mongolia – all nowadays different countries, each with their own borders. Nonetheless, the architecture and culture of a people have no boundaries, only their own specific elements and fragments.

Ger Dwellings of Inner Asian Mongolia

Ágnes Birtalan

Geography/Climate

The *ger* (tent, or house) or the *esgii ger* (the round felt tent, or felt house) is considered an appropriate type of dwelling in the Inner Asian zone, of which Mongolia forms a part. Widespread in the steppe zone and the semi-desert of the Gobi, the *ger* – as a type of dwelling – responds to the climatic challenges of Inner Asia. Its construction is suited to the extremes of the continental climate: during the winter, several layers of felt, comprising inner and outer covers, are put onto a wooden frame; in summer, the covering material (not necessarily felt) can be turned up in order to provide ventilation. To protect the construction from the prevailing winds, the *ger* door in Mongolia is positioned to the south or, in some areas, to the east.

The *ger* is used by various groups of the Mongols as well as by some Turkic peoples (including the Kazak, Kyrgyz and Kapakalpak) in Central Asia. The felt house is commonly known as a 'yurt', a term of Turkic origin that covers a wide semantic field, denoting in addition the closer parts of a pastoral territory.

Materials

The *ger* is constructed from lightweight materials (wood and felt), which are suitable for transportation – and it can be erected and dismantled in as little as an hour, depending on the manpower available. Its materials are either sourced from the natural environment, like the wooden components used in the frame, or are harvested from livestock – like the felt, which is generally fabricated from sheep wool, and the ropes, which are spun from the hair of various kinds of cattle.

Materials for the *ger*'s timber frame (*yas mod*)[1] traditionally varied according to the availability of tree species. The most frequently used were willow (*Salix*) or larch (*Larix sibirica*), these supplied the roof ring, or 'crown' (*toono*), the roof pole (*uni*), the lattice wall (*khana*), supporting columns (*bagana*), doors (*khaalga*), and – especially in winter – the floor (*shal*). The various parts of the felt covering (*esgii bürees*) were traditionally manufactured by the nomads themselves, and included the felt cover for the crown (*örkh*), for the roof (*deewer*) and for the side walls (*tuurga*), as well as the felt door (*esgii üüd*). The lower edge of the circular tent (*khayaawch*) might also be of felt, or alternatively of canvas (*tsawag*). These felt components are fastened by internal and external ropes: the main rope (*chagtaga*), the girth (*khoshlon*), the 'belt' (*büslüür*), and various fixing ropes (*daruulga*).

Construction Techniques

The size of the *ger* depends on the number of its walls (usually between four and eight – although sometimes even more lattice walls were fixed together, using leather straps). With regard to floor-to-ceiling height, present-day Mongolian *gers* are relatively low (usually 2–3 m [6–10 ft] high) compared with Central Asian Turkic yurts (approximately 3–4 m [10–13 ft] high), because longer, bent-roof poles are used in the construction of the latter. The framework of an ordinary *ger* can be richly decorated with motifs from Mongolian art, including symbolic Buddhist ornaments. The felt parts are usually undecorated; however, *gers* erected for festive or tourism purposes can have a coloured felt cover, embellished with traditional motifs.

Building Plan/Form

There are several theories on the genesis of the *ger*. One school of thought holds that its roof structure evolved from the form of a traditional pit dwelling, while another identifies its origins in the wall structure used in the *tipi*-like tent of reindeer breeders from Siberia (which are also still used by other groups, such as the Tsaatan of northern Mongolia). The earliest evidence of the *ger* can be found among prehistoric petroglyphs and also in early Chinese sources, which describe the dwellings of Inner Asian nomads. Sources from the time of the Great Mongolian Empire (13–14th centuries CE) inform about the use of *gers* constructed for the families of the ruling elite, which were transported by ox cart.

The *ger*'s portability is essential for cattle-breeding nomads, who have to move several times in a year to reach fresh pastures (traditionally in every season, but in recent times usually with less frequency). When they migrate to another pasture, the *ger* is transported by camel, cattle-drawn cart or truck. The roof ring, believed to be the passageway between the human world and the spirits' realm, is an object of veneration; it is always placed at the top of the dismantled structure. While moving to the next pasture, only temporary dwellings were erected, for example, from the roof poles and some felt parts of the main *ger*. In forested territories, the *ger*'s wooden frame might be covered with bark instead of felt. In southern Siberia, wooden houses were even built imitating the *ger* structure.

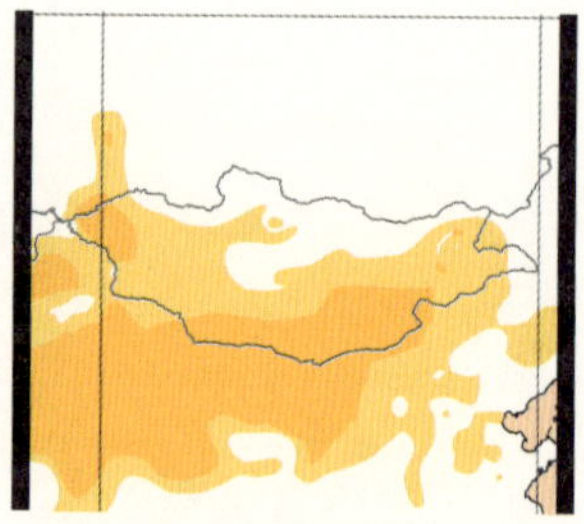

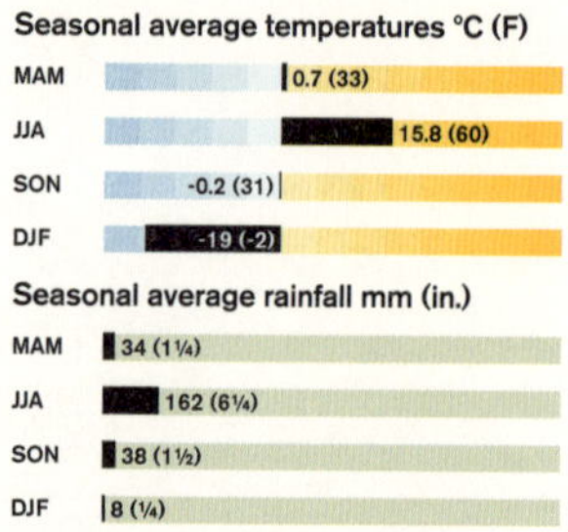

Opposite Components of the Mongol tent-house, or *ger*, include timber frames, felt enclosures and home-spun rope. Traditionally the homes were made of elements sourced from the natural environment or harvested from livestock.

In addition to the circular *ger*, various other types of tent with square bases are used by the Mongols for specialized work activities (hunting or collecting fodder) or for festivities. The *maikhan* tent, for instance – at its most simple, a length of cloth supported by a ridgepole atop two vertical posts – can be erected and dismantled more easily than the standard *ger*. Of all these variations, however, the *ger* has the largest internal dimensions, commensurate with the overall requirements of nomadic social life.

Several generations may live in one *ger*, but newly-weds usually receive a brand-new *ger* near to the husband's parents' dwelling. The furnishings of a *ger* serve for daily activities, for night rest and for everyday and festive occasions. The allocation and arrangement of space reflect the social status of the inhabitants and their guests: the western half of the inner space belongs to the menfolk. Distinguished guests are also seated here, close to the home altar (which will be opposite the door). The eastern part of the internal space is assigned to the women and includes the kitchen, located just to the right-hand side of the door, as well as a space designated for small children; female guests are also seated here. The *ger* contains several sacral and proscribed places, for example the fire brazier, the door threshold, the altar and the spaces between the columns. A complex system of taboos and prohibitions regulates both the inhabitants' and visitors' behaviour. Tending the fire (the main fuel is cattle droppings) and its equipment is done with particular care in order to prevent fire disasters in the surrounding grassland.

The *ger* is comprehended as a world model, with an imagined *axis mundi* in the middle of the tent (from the fire brazier to the roof ring). Conversely, the macro-cosmos is also conceived of as a huge *ger*, floating above humanity. The *ger* figures in Mongolian folklore both as reality and as metaphor. There is a special sub-genre of Mongolian literature devoted to the appraisal of the *ger*: the *geriin yörööl* – a catalogue-like enumeration and laudation of the particular parts of the *ger* and of its whole, which ends with a formula that blesses the inhabitants and asks for good fortune in life.

The probable use of the *ger* over several millennia, and its present-day popularity for economic and tourism purposes, testifies to the suitability of this wooden/felt structure for the Inner Asian climatic environment. Today, nomadic families still maintain and manufacture for themselves some components of the *ger*. However, many now also choose the products of the *ger* factory (and several private workshops) operating in the capital, Ulan Bator, where all the necessary parts can be ordered.

The *ger* is not merely a dwelling designed to accommodate the sociocultural activity of the nomads; it also belongs to the most honoured symbols of Mongolian national pride, and as such figures prominently in national festivities.

Right **Though variations of the yurt or *ger* dwelling are seen across Central Asia, the Mongolian version is usually lower than its Turkish counterpart. The lightweight components suit the traditional pattern of inhabitation of nomadic cattle-breeders, who would move seasonally to fresh pastures.**

TEMPERATE

Equirectangular projection. Scale 1: 70 000 000

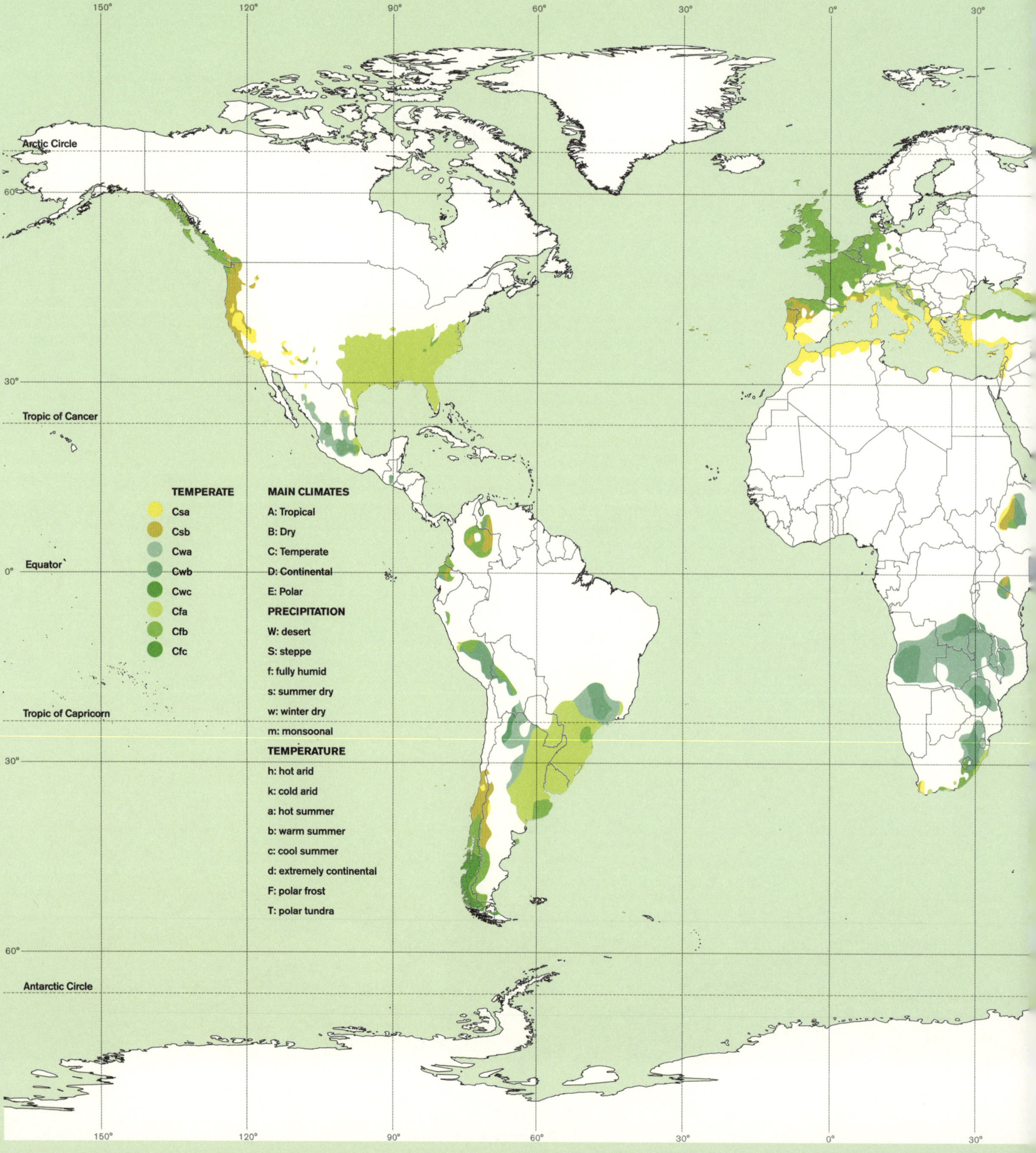

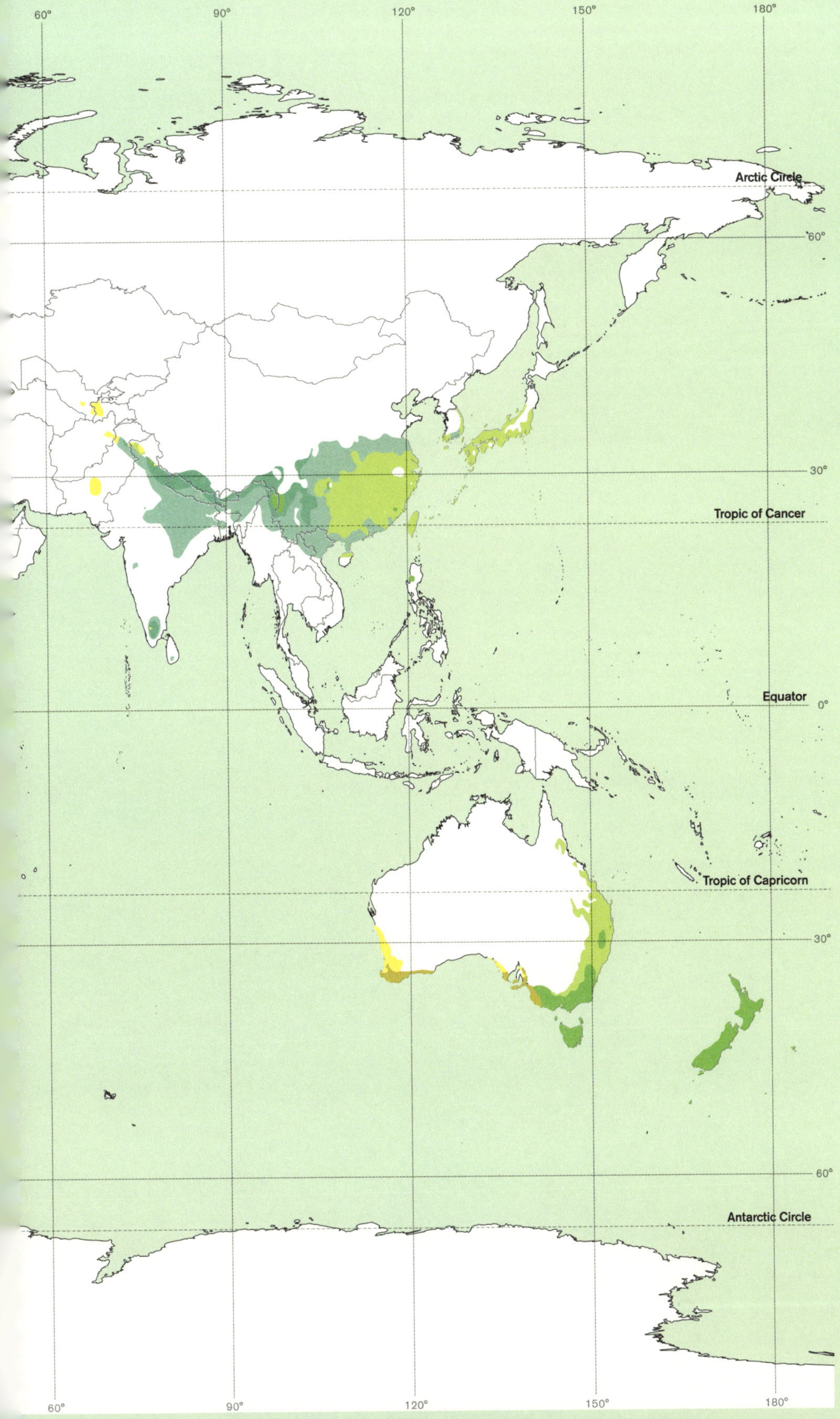

The general characteristics of the moist subtropical mid-latitude climates, type C, are distinct summer and winter seasons, and humid, mild winters with average temperatures of the coldest month below 18°C (64°F) but above -3°C (26°F). Such regions tend to be found on the eastern and western regions of most continents, from about 25 to 40° latitude, and can be subdivided into humid subtropical (Cwa) and dry summer subtropical, or Mediterranean (Csa).

Humid subtropical climates are found principally along the southeast coasts of continents. They dominate eastern China, the southeastern United States and South America, and the southeastern coasts of Africa and Australia, generally between latitudes 25° and 40°. A common trait is hot, humid summers as warm, humid air flows poleward in these regions from subtropical high-pressure systems. This results in high temperatures and high humidity. Rainfall often shows a summer peak, especially where monsoons are well developed, as in Southeast Asia. In other regions, weak summer fronts may bring occasional relief. However, devastating heatwaves, sometimes lasting weeks, can occur if an upper-level ridge of high pressure moves over the area.

Winters tend to be relatively mild – especially in the lower latitudes, where air temperatures rarely drop below freezing. Poleward regions experience colder, harsher winters and more common frost, snow and ice storms, but heavy snowfalls are rare. Winter weather can be changeable, as mid-latitude storms bring wind and cold rain fronts through the region. However, many subtropical climates such as Southeast Asia or Florida have very dry winters, with frequent brush fires and water shortages.

Humid subtropical climates experience precipitation throughout the year, with typical averages between 800 and 1,650 mm (32 and 65 in). In summertime, when thunderstorms are common, much of this precipitation falls as afternoon showers. Tropical storms entering this region can add substantially to summer and autumn totals. Winter precipitation most often occurs with eastward-moving middle-latitude storms. On the western sides of many continents, the temperatures in these regions are moderated by prevailing winds from the ocean, keeping winter substantially warmer than at locations inland. Moving equatorward of these marine climates, the influence of the subtropical highs becomes greater and the summer dry period becomes more pronounced. Gradually, the climate changes from marine (Cfb) to dry-summer subtropical, or Mediterranean (Csa): mild to wet winters and mild to hot, dry summers.

As its name suggests, a Mediterranean climate is typical of that region of the world. Characterized by dry summers and mild, moist winters, the majority of this climate zone has relatively mild winters and very warm temperatures. Commonly occurring on the west coasts of continents, these climates are experienced by much of California, parts of Western and South Australia, Central Asia, southwestern South Africa, and Chile. The seasonality of rainfall is driven by the shift of the subtropical high-pressure cells north/south in response to the annual cycle of solar heating. During summer the regions are dominated by subtropical high-pressure cells with dry sinking air. This makes rainfall unlikely except for occasional thunderstorms. This summer period without significant rainfall may last for four to six months. In winter, when the subtropical highs shift equatorward, the polar jet stream and associated periodic storms reach into the lower latitudes of the Mediterranean climate zone bringing rain, with snow at higher elevations.

Materials, Buildings and Adaptations for Temperate Climates

Spread across several continents, including southeastern regions of North and Latin America, Europe, East and Southeast Asia as well as the North Pacific Islands, temperate climates are often located on geographic borders of desert and rainforest climates. Classified as C in the Köppen–Geiger's system, temperate climates have shaped architectural solutions that provide cooling and shading during summer and thermal mass for autumn and winter. Vegetation of temperate climates is similar across continents; hardwood, mud, brick, straw and agricultural by-products for thatching are most commonly used materials.

Architectural solutions in a temperate climate share passive methods of cooling and use of materials. However, the differences are apparent in the builders themselves – from native indigenous peoples to the later arrival of other cultures. Both North and Latin America have case studies of early constructions as well as modified colonial architecture that was adapted to fit local conditions. In North America, the construction of an indigenous 'chickee' house originally built by Seminole tribes with cypress log structures and thatched roofs of palm fronds sits alongside colonial architecture in the form of the Charleston House and shotgun house typologies.

The temperate climate of Latin America produced a similar pattern of indigenous and colonial architecture across Paraguay, Uruguay and Chile. Rural areas are characterized by pre-Columbian indigenous architecture adapted to Hispanic and Portuguese styles. These two types of native and colonial architecture demonstrate porous cultural boundaries and the mutual influence of cultures while also embracing local climatic conditions and resources.

Cultural diversities are highly apparent in Europe, where the presence of diverse ethnic groups produced vernacular architecture in response to equally diverse microclimates. Materials such as timber, stone, earth, clay, brick, mortars and wattle-and-daub have been shared across the continent. Environmental elements such as wind, rainfall, exposure or protection from the sun as well as differing settlement densities shaped the European vernacular.

Eastern and Southeast Asia, as well as the North Pacific Islands, offer exceptional examples of timber construction and technologies; Chinese, Korean and Japanese vernacular is synonymous with this material. In China, for example, wooden courtyard houses oriented in response to climatic conditions were arranged to form compounds and uniform urban systems that also reflected the social structure of Chinese society. Round *tulou* typically seen in the Fujian Province of coastal southern China epitomize communal architecture that may provide a solution for neighbourhoods of densely populated cities today. Kam architecture in China's Guizhou Province demonstrates another type of communal self-sustainable living based on agroforestry. The use of local timber by highly skilled carpenters has created magnificent drum tower structures that are central to Kam living.

Rare examples of South Korean *neowa* houses with bark-shingle roofs and predominantly red pine construction engage with rural living in mountainous areas. Different timber species were used for different *neowa* building elements, which demonstrate the sophisticated adaptation of architectural form in response to different plant species. The ancient history of Taiwanese vernacular is best represented in settlements that belong to one social group of a single clan. Their architectural form of settlements accommodates houses for immediate and distant families of one social group. Meanwhile, Japanese *minka* houses offer an archetype of 'houses for the people' and a masterclass in the diverse use of plant-based materials for both rural and urban areas.

Left In temperate climates, such as southern China, buildings offer cooling in summer and thermal mass in winter.

Chickee, Charleston and Shotgun Housing in the American South

Gray Read and Larisa Marenco

Geography/Climate
The Southern vernacular of the United States comprises three main building types within three distinct cultural building traditions, which responded specifically to the temperate climate of the region: the palm-thatch 'chickee' built by Native Americans in Florida; the 'single house' characteristic of Charleston, South Carolina, based on a classical European type; and the shotgun house, ubiquitous in the 19th century and said to have origins in Africa and Haiti.

Building Plan/Form
All three types adopt similar climate strategies, yet in strikingly different architectural forms. All include porches and shaded yards as principal areas for work and social life, creating an urban pattern that allows breezes to penetrate even compact cities. And all offer high ceilings and strategic openings to induce ventilation by drawing hot air up and out.

The Chickee
Among the diverse building traditions of the native peoples of the region, an iconic example is still built as garden structures by members of the Seminole tribe of Florida using traditional, local materials. The 'chickee' consists of a structural frame of rot-resistant cypress (*Cupressaceae*) logs covered by a thatch roof made of palmetto (*Sabal*) fronds. Historically, chickees often had a raised platform of small, split cypress branches to provide working or social space – whether in a village or constructed remotely as a hunting or fishing camp in the exposed Florida Everglades.

This raised platform catches the breezes and provides some defence against insects, while the high-pitched, dense roof of the chickee shades and insulates from the sun and sheds rain while allowing heat to rise up and out. Chickees can be built quickly from common wetland trees joined or lashed together – and they can be disassembled just as rapidly, leaving behind no non-organic waste.

The Charleston Single House
The English and French settlers who arrived in the southeastern region of the United States brought with them a very different idea of architectural form from those of the indigenous population – building boxy, symmetrical houses based on Renaissance principles of proportion. The implicit model for a colonial house had a central stair hall with flanking rooms on two or three levels, and presented a formal façade to approaching visitors. In the warm, humid climates of many colonies – including those of India, South Africa and the Bahamas – wide roofs and porches surrounded a square house.[1] In the American colonies, the manor houses of southern plantations had sweeping verandas, sometimes on two levels, supported by tall, classical columns, creating a portico that almost engulfed the house. These elegant houses oversaw vast plantations worked by slaves brought from Africa, until the mid-19th-century Civil War abolished the practice.

Below Garden structures known as 'chickees' are built in Florida by Seminole tribes and draw on local materials for their construction. The raised, open-sided platforms for socializing and work admit cooling breezes that provide shade from the sun, mitigating the heat.

Opposite Formed of a timber frame and thatched with palm fronds, the simple chickee structure shades and insulates its inhabitants. Its breathable roof allows heat to release and it can be disassembled as quickly as it is made, leaving no inorganic waste.

832

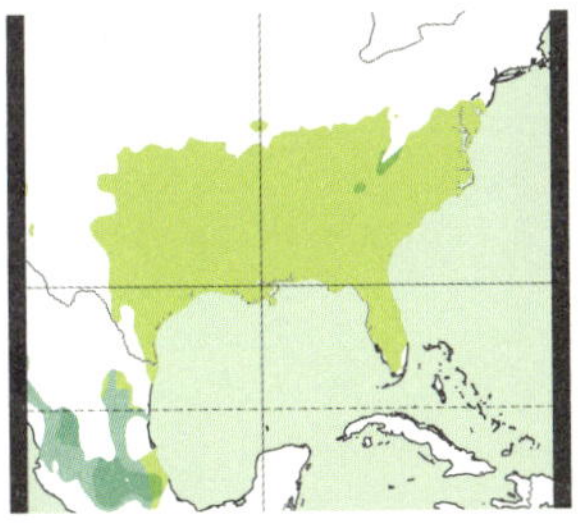

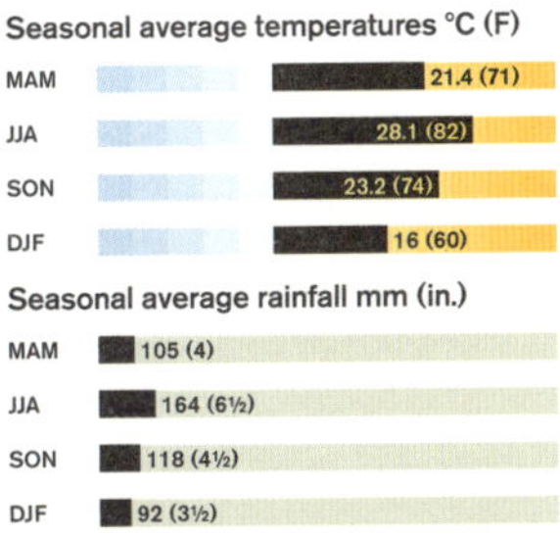

Opposite top Colonial settlers' homes such as this Louisiana plantation house were based on Renaissance proportion and presented a colonnaded façade.

Opposite bottom The characteristic single-storey, gabled shotgun houses built by Americans of African descent were adapted to suit the climate, with high ceilings and covered porches.

Below Urban lots are usually about 9–15 m (30–50 ft) wide and streets were built in a grid, seen in this aerial view of Charleston.

Quarters for these labourers would usually mean bunkhouses arrayed behind the main residence, along with kitchens, shops, stables and work yards.

Further modification of the plantation house characterizes the vernacular fabric of the port city of Charleston, South Carolina. There, these adapted mansions housed middle-class artisans and wealthy traders. The 'Charleston single house', arguably originating on the Caribbean island of Barbados, reduced the classical prototype to a single room in depth, which was turned 90° to fit on a narrow urban lot.[2] The gable end of the house faces the street, and the formal façade with a front porch, or 'piazza', faces a side yard or garden to the south or west depending on the orientation of the lot. From the pavement, visitors enter through a doorway to the piazza, walk past a front parlour, then turn to enter the formal front door leading to a central stair hall. The kitchen and servants' quarters stretched out behind the house, where they could be overseen by the owners.[3]

Architecturally, Charleston's single houses are narrow, and the main storey is elevated 600–1200 mm (24–48 in) off the ground. Every room opens to the piazza and garden, sometimes with triple-sash windows extending from the floor to a high ceiling, so they can be opened fully to allow the occupants to step out. Windows may have interior shutters, which can be closed in the heat of the day to block bright light and contain cooler air. Houses of the wealthy were built in masonry rather than wood, thereby affording a degree of thermal mass to moderate the temperature.[4] The central hall also acts as a 'stack' to draw warm air from the rooms upwards, and attic spaces are ventilated with grilles in the house gable ends.

Piazzas were mostly used at night, when families sat outside and the house windows were opened to cool down the interior. On very warm days, the two-storey central stair hall could become a living space, and on hot nights beds might be dragged out to the piazza. Gardens also offer respite from the heat, and were often surrounded by brick walls, which were shaded by trees and flowering vines, keeping the space cool and pleasant.[5]

The gracious life of Charleston was, of course, built on slavery, which supported both the plantations and the trade of the city. The stark divide between classes at that time is apparent in the differences between the main house and the quarters of the servants or slaves. The small houses behind the 'mansions' are low and mean – with no piazza, and little shade or ventilation.

Shotgun Houses

In contrast, when Americans of African descent built dwellings for themselves, they developed a characteristic house type with roots in Africa and the Caribbean, which was already adapted to warm, humid conditions. The 'shotgun house' is a long, narrow wood-framed structure, one room wide, with a porch entry on the gable end facing the street. Its rooms open in sequence from front to back, with windows on both sides for cross ventilation and no hallway. Shotgun houses generally had high ceilings and covered porch space that made a sociable working space in all weathers. In cities such as New Orleans, shotgun and 'double-shotgun' houses, which were made up of two attached single shotguns, were built on narrow urban lots with as little as 1 m (3 ft) between them, creating the vernacular fabric of the town.[6]

Quincha, Adobe and Stone Structures of South America

Natalia Jorquera Silva

Geography/Climate

Within the area classified as a temperate warm-humid climate in South America, there are many variations and sub-climates. This vast territory covers almost 18 million sq km (7 million sq miles) and its diverse geography creates many local microclimates, which supply a variety of natural resources.

The many 'micro-environments' of its temperate, warmer humid areas alone vary from the subtropical jungle in southern Brazil and parts of Paraguay to the temperate oceanic climes in the plains of Uruguay, the semi-desert valleys in the central-north of Chile and Argentina, and the Mediterranean climate in central Chile. However, common features of all these environments are four well-defined seasons and precipitation, to a greater or lesser extent, depending on the exact location. The presence of rainfall promoted the growth of vegetation and the use of timber as a basic element of indigenous construction. This was then supplemented by adobe, brick and stone masonry with the arrival of Spanish and Portuguese settlers from the late 15th century onwards.

Opposite clockwise from top left Encompassing a range of microclimates, the temperate regions of South America include areas as diverse as Brazilian jungles, the verdant plains of Uruguay, semi-desert valleys of northern Chile and Argentina, and the Mediterranean climate of central Chile.

Above This adobe house in Pumanque, Chile, includes a shade-giving veranda to provide relief from the intense heat. Such adaptations typify colonial Spanish and Portuguese influence on South America's vernacular.

Materials

Despite the existing climatic and cultural differences across this vast area, some constants remain in its vernacular architecture. This can be seen despite the many cultures from which this vernacular originates – indigenous, Spanish or Portuguese, African or *mestizo* (mixed race or ethnicity – often Spanish/Native American). Both the 'informal' indigenous and the 'established' colonial architecture used local materials and responded optimally to the environment in which they found themselves, serving as examples for sustainable architecture today.

Construction Techniques

Throughout the southern part of the continent, two main types of vernacular architecture can be distinguished: that of indigenous pre-Columbian origin and that of the Hispanic and Portuguese colonial period. The latter was adapted to the local environmental and cultural conditions, and its construction techniques were influenced by pre-existing technologies.

The indigenous architecture of these temperate and humid areas of the continent is characterized by its informality; by its sporadic (temporary or seasonal) nature; and by the fact that it was limited to basic activities such as eating and sleeping, while the remaining domestic activities were undertaken outdoors. The houses comprised half-timbered structures, which were either left open or infilled with a mixture of light vegetable matter or raw earth mixed with vegetable matter. The wetter and warmer the climate, the more open were the dwellings in order to improve natural cross ventilation. However, in places with a greater diurnal temperature variation, external walls made of raw earth and thatch were the preferred method of enclosing interior space. Nowadays, many examples of Latin American indigenous vernacular architecture still exist in rural and remote areas.

The region's colonial 'vernacular' followed a formal well-defined architectural and constructional pattern, and therefore might not be considered as a true vernacular. However, with the passage of time this architecture was adapted to various local environmental realities: the different climates of each country and region, available natural resources, prevailing local techniques, and, in the case of Chile, seismic activity. These local differences had an impact on the otherwise uniform architectural typology – for example, on the colonial haciendas, which are widespread in Chile, Argentina, Paraguay, Uruguay and Brazil but which vary greatly in their construction techniques.

Building Plan/Form

Paraguay

Paraguay's traditional architecture retains the strong legacy of the Guaraní people, mixed with the influence of the Spanish conquest. This architecture is now most evident in rural areas, and it is characterized by the combination of a couple of enclosed spaces with one or more semi-open spaces, which ensure natural ventilation to deal with the heat and humidity. This type of building is considered a 'big roof', which is open-sided and which can be adapted for different functions. The local materials used are timber, palm, straw and leather – with the straw-thatched roof being a very typical characteristic of the country's indigenous architecture.

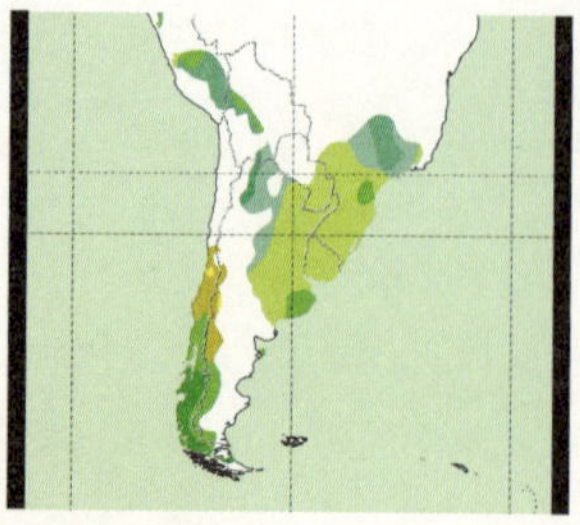

Uruguay

In Uruguay, indigenous architecture from various ethnic groups (the Charrúas, Guenoas, Minuanes and Chaná-timbúes) also centres around the sporadically inhabited house made of wood, leather and vegetable matter. With the arrival of the first Portuguese settlers in 1680, stone began to be used as a construction material. The best-known examples of this technique are the architecture of the city of Colonia del Sacramento, now a UNESCO World Heritage Site, and some colonial buildings in the historic district of the capital, Montevideo. Rural housing, as in Paraguay, combined both indigenous and colonial traditions, and was built mainly on raw earth – especially when adopting the technique known as terron (a block cut directly from the soil) with a timber frame covered with rough straw.

Chile

The various indigenous ethnic groups that inhabited Chile's central, temperate zone left a legacy of temporary architecture built with vegetation and raw-earth elements, known locally as quincha. This technology is particularly common in the north-central region of the country known as Norte chico ('Little north'). In this area, there are still many rural towns whose architecture is a product of both adaptation to various environments and a symbiosis between indigenous traditions and the Hispanic legacy. The buildings there maintain some colonial features but the technology is indigenous, with the predominance of half-timbered and earth-daubed walls with thatched roofs.

In the central region of Chile, which has a Mediterranean climate, the most important traditional and recognized architecture is of Spanish colonial origin. It is characterized by the use of adobe as the main building technique, a product of the local abundance of clay soil. This provides thermal mass, with large, thick walls – an important response to the significant variations in diurnal temperature. This architecture is encountered in hundreds of villages throughout five regions in Chile, and its predominant features are formal, closed, introspective buildings, organized around central courtyards and closely linked to agricultural activities. However, there are many variations of this type, depending on latitude: further north, where the climate is dry and temperate, the architecture is more compact; further south, where the rains are more abundant, an exterior veranda appears as an important element. This last-named feature allows people to walk outdoors while protected from rain, and it also shields otherwise vulnerable adobe walls from rainfall.

The main challenge that the Spanish settlers faced in Chile was that of adapting their architecture to the seismic conditions of the country. Thus, original colonial architecture had to be modified – lowering heights, decreasing the slenderness of walls and incorporating timber elements in order to reinforce adobe masonry walls. All these actions constitute valuable vernacular earthquake-resistance strategies.

Brazil

In Brazil, as in Paraguay, there still exists colonial-Portuguese architecture with similar characteristics to that found in the rest of Latin America. Some of the most notable examples are the vernacular buildings of the gold-mining settlements of Almas, Portos and Natividade in the northern Tocantins area of the country, and Serro, which is located along the old road of Estrada Real in the southeastern Minas Gerais region. Alongside this heritage, there exists a rich indigenous vernacular architecture – especially in the Amazon forest, where it has remained intact owing to its geographical isolation.

Opposite Thatched vegetation and timber construction are basic elements of indigenous buildings in the Latin American region. Spanish and Portuguese settlers supplemented these earlier materials and methods with adobe, brick and stone masonry. The thermal mass these materials provide mitigates variation of diurnal temperature changes.

Vernacular Responses to Climate across the European Continent

Fernando Vegas and Camilla Mileto

Geography/Climate

The European continent has three predominant climates: the oceanic climate that covers a large part of its central territory, characterized by abundant rainfall, temperate winters and cool summers; the Mediterranean climate, on the shores of the Mediterranean Sea, characterized by mild, wet winters, dry, hot summers and variable autumns and springs, regarding both temperature and rainfall; and the continental climate, with scant rainfall and extreme temperatures, and great differences between summer and winter.

The availability of traditional construction materials in each place on the European continent determines the built substance of its vernacular architecture, which – depending also on the climatology, the temperature and the rainfall – determines the configuration of floor plans, with the possible presence of an outdoor 'room' such as a patio; building shape, especially the roof; and the relationship between the interior and exterior space through the existence, dimensions and types of porches, bays, openings and filters in the façade.

Water

The presence of a larger or smaller amount of water, its state and the frequency with which it appears often determine not only the shape of dwellings but also the way in which they are grouped.

Wind

The European continent is traversed by various wind patterns. The westerlies are constant winds that blow from west to east in latitudes of between 30 and 60°; they have a moderate effect on the climate of western European coasts, which are also influenced by the Gulf Stream. They are at their strongest between 40 and 50°, which are known to British sailors as the 'roaring forties'.[1] Besides this forceful current, which circulates at a great height, there are thermally generated local winds created by the difference in temperature between the variable warm and cool zones (day- and night-time breezes between the sea and the land), and those created by dynamic means due to the accumulation of air in a particular spot because of the existence of a mountain chain.

Opposite The hill town of Montilla in Spain's south typifies a response to the warm, temperate environment, with its dense central township surrounded by verdant vineyards and farm housing. Thick building walls are typically rendered in gypsum and punctuated with small openings to protect against strong summer sunlight and cooler temperatures in winter.

Right Alpine huts were devised as a strategy to protect against the roaring gales and scant sunlight that typify northern and central European regions. Logs were a logical building material based on the abundance of timber in the Alps.

Besides their influence on the climate, these winds have also fashioned European vernacular architecture, generating scattered or collective urban solutions and configurations of dwellings. Indeed, the layout of many European rural settlements can still be interpreted as a strategy of sheltering from unwanted strong winds while, conversely, facilitating the circulation of pleasant breezes.

The predominant wind direction in each place also affects the interior layout of that locality's vernacular houses, wherein trial and error has been used to create a horizontal route for currents of air that permits or prevents cross ventilation between the different rooms on each level, and a vertical route in which the staircases or the fireplace location contribute to the dwelling's internal ventilation.[2] In cold climates, these dwellings customarily have their bedrooms placed at the rear of the interior space in order to ensure greater thermal comfort, whereas in the warmer, Mediterranean zones each room can mediate heat gain through at least one window – although this may look on to an inner courtyard, which also acts as a chimney in the building's cross-ventilation strategy. In both types of dwelling, different types of curtains were generally used. In cold-region dwellings, beds themselves often had a curtained canopy, which could be pulled closed to keep the sleeping place warm. In warm-climate dwellings, internal doors were often replaced by hanging, light curtains or lines of beads that would not stop air from circulating from room to room.

Fire

Fire is present in different ways in vernacular buildings, fulfilling one or more functions and helping to configure the dwelling depending on the climate. In traditional vernacular architecture in warm European climates, fire has been used mainly for cooking and only occasionally in winter for heating, whereas in cold climates, fire has generally been used not only for cooking but also for heating and even for illuminating the rooms during the dark winter nights. The European geographic 'frontier' regarding the use of fire only for cooking or for cooking and heating lies approximately at latitude 40° N.[3] Since the European continent lies in a strip running from latitude 36° N to 70° N, it is clear that only the vernacular architecture of the south of Spain, Italy and Greece – along with the majority of Mediterranean islands – could dispense with fire as a source of heat, while most vernacular European architecture traditionally depended on the presence of fire as a means of heating in order to survive. Furthermore, traditional European vernacular architecture located above 55° N, which implies six or fewer hours of light a day in winter, has especially needed fire for lighting.[4]

The forms that fire takes in vernacular dwellings at different latitudes range from simple, traditional wood or coal fires on which the kitchenware is placed directly, to open ranges, with tripods sitting on the fire, or hanging pots, which at the same time provide heat for the room. In the transition area between latitude 40° N and the zones immediately to the north of it, braziers are quite commonly used not only for portable heating but also as a cooking tool. In central Europe, built-in majolica-tiled stoves are common (the Russian *pechka*, or German *Kachelofen*), and are used for cooking, heating and even lighting.[5]

It is important to point out, too, the presence of the sauna (*Rauchsauna*, *thermae*, *bastu*, *banya* or steam baths) all over the European continent, even since pre-Roman times;[6] this device was conceived not so much as a heating system as an aid to personal hygiene, and it was usually located in constructions independent from the main dwelling.

Finally, it is interesting to mention the existence of *glorias*, a traditional vernacular subfloor heating system in the architecture of the north of Castile (Spain), probably developed from the heating mechanisms used in Roman or Arab baths. These, however, are also found in distant lands like Korea (where they are known as *ondol*) or China (*kang*),[7] where they provide heating for dwellings in cold continental climates where no firewood is available, using straw as their only fuel.

Below left To manage heat gain in warmer Mediterranean zones, rooms often have at least one window that overlooks an inner courtyard, which also acts as a flue in the building's cross-ventilation strategy.

Below right Cave dwellings draw on the inherent properties of the natural surroundings as a means to mediate heat in warm climates. Troglodyte homes provide an immediate respite from high summer temperatures and are to be found all over the Mediterranean region and the Rhône Valley.

Opposite top The form of European vernacular townships and dwellings is often configured in response to the prevailing wind direction. The Spanish village of Riglos nestles below a huge sandstone outcrop – a strategy used by its settlers to protect against strong winds.

Opposite bottom In more temperate European climates, such as the township of Guadix in southern Spain, wind direction also shapes the interior plan of vernacular housing. Frequently, staircases or chimneys are positioned to enable a vertical route with which to evacuate warm internal air.

Above Differing latitudes across the European continent create varied intensities of sunlight, which directly shape the architectural responses. Characteristically, the strong solar gain in southern regions is reflected in external shading devices such as shutters, curtains, lattices and blinds. Interstitial areas between street façade and interior, such as patios, create sheltered, open areas that extend an individual's living space. These often laid with stone or tiles.

Sun

The varying degree of sunlight that reaches the different latitudes of the European continent has a great influence on the configuration of its vernacular architecture and especially on buildings' relationships with the exterior. The scant sunlight in the centre and north of Europe – in addition to other conditions, such as the height of the location and its exposure to the wind – has traditionally given rise to very compact vernacular dwellings with bays of limited size, built close to the ground or even embedded in it, in an attempt to minimize the loss of heat from the interior of the house. More frequent sunlight in these places was always very welcome but not to the extent that large bays were inserted, because the loss of heat involved would not be compensated for. The transition between indoors and outdoors in such structures is always rather abrupt: merely through a door – or, at best, though a small hall for robing and disrobing, usually without any intermediate spaces.

The intense sunlight characteristic of the Mediterranean Basin generates a similar exterior compactness in vernacular architecture, with bays perhaps larger but still limited in size – this time in order to prevent too much heat from penetrating indoors. The indoor–outdoor relationship is richer than in northern climes, with a great variety of 'in-between' spaces or places located on the borderline between indoors and outdoors,[8] and with an abundance of shading and cooling systems.

Such in-between spaces include terraces, porches, raised platforms, pergolas, pavilions, half-open sheds, porticoes and colonnades – in other words, places partially exposed to the open air and partially sheltered by the building. They arise when the threshold of the building expands and stretches, becoming large enough to create a space that can accommodate living. Patios deserve a special mention as they are to be found all over the Mediterranean area. The tradition of the patio dates back to the distant past, with Greek or Roman houses as prime examples, although they are by no means the oldest. Patios have proved useful in many of this region's buildings, not only to provide light and ventilation but also as an element articulating communication and life within the house.

Shading systems may comprise lattices (fixed or openable), louvred shutters, net curtains, solid timber shutters, roller shutters, Roman blinds, internal or external Venetian blinds, curtains or roller blinds. Blinds can also be used to hang down vertically or at an angle over the handrail of a balcony for the purpose of offering light, shade, breeze and side views and, at the same time, safeguarding privacy from the front.[9] This warm part of Europe also boasts street-shading strategies to allow people to walk along public thoroughfares protected from the sun, such as generous eaves and cornices running along narrow, winding streets; whitewash finishes that partially avoid the absorption of heat; and street porticoes offering shelter from both the sun and the rain. Other individual shading elements include parasols; awnings or textiles stretching from a street façade to the one opposite; trees with large crowns, or the shade of palms or grapevines and other climbing plants; wooden pergolas; trellised wooden roofs; and canopies intermittently scattered over the streets.[10]

In this warm-climate European vernacular, cooling systems have traditionally been used based on height (the presence of tall rooms with draughts passing overhead

Above Colonnades to the building exterior and to internal courtyards are frequently used in the Mediterranean Basin as a shield from the extreme summer heat that is typical of the region. Other architectural means that provide cool, shaded places to walk typically include porticoes, generous eaves, narrow streets and individual shading elements, such as parasols or pergolas.

in order to favour convection), mass (the use of thick walls with great thermal inertia), air (the promotion of cross ventilation between façades with different thermal gradients due to the different exposure to sunlight or the dissipation of heat in stair wells or chimney flues), and the presence of water and vegetation, which accentuate the effect of the strategies enumerated above. Apart from the overall design, which takes into account the circulation of local winds and the creation of shading systems permeable to wind, other natural cooling systems have been devised in the urban areas of these warm European regions. These include the presence of vegetation, utilizing its capacity to evaporate and hold water in its foliage, and the incorporation of water in the form of fountains, ponds, street wetting, and so on.

Materials and Construction Techniques

As is the case with traditional constructions in the rest of the world, European vernacular architecture is mainly the result of a balanced combination between the dominant climate in each place, the construction materials available in the immediate surroundings – arising partly from the climatic conditions – and the use of space and the system of social relations established in a particular place – again, both partly as a result of climatic conditions. The construction techniques used to build with these materials in each climatic and social context evolved over the centuries, based on old currents of technological transference and a process of trial and error, seeking to adapt in the best possible manner to the physical conditions of each location.

Vernacular architecture is conceived on the basis of taking advantage of the resources available at a reasonable price considering the functional needs of the building. In places with an abundance of stone, it is natural to use stone for building enclosures, shelters or stepped terraces; it is also a way of clearing fields in order to facilitate ploughing and crop production. In alluvial valleys, earth is commonly used: it is an extraordinarily cheap raw construction material. Where water was scarce, rammed earth was more usual because it requires a water component of only 5 per cent for construction purposes, provided that the appropriate formwork techniques were available. On the other hand, if enough water and straw was available to produce sun-dried bricks during a dry season, adobes were more commonly found. In some areas, the lack of basic means, constant rain or even simply greater urgency led to the construction of cob walls. If timber was available too, mixed solutions were adopted, such as half-timber or post-and-beam structures with a cob or wattle-and-daub filling. Brick manufacture was much more expensive than the aforementioned methods because more fuel was consumed in the process. Brick factories therefore required a certain amount of organization and the coordination of the various crafts involved. They also depended crucially on the level of local economic development, the presence of suitable clay and timber (or scrubland) for the kilns, and the procurement of mortar, which could be made from, among other things, earth, lime or gypsum depending on the availability in the area and the owner's financial means.

Walls

The most common structural systems in Europe are based on loadbearing walls made of stone, brick, earth or timber, bonded variously with earth or lime or gypsum mortars – the last-named also possibly used for interior and exterior rendering. Stone is used throughout the continent, but less frequently north of the Rhine and Danube basins where it alternates with brick (commonly found all over Europe). The presence of stone and brick in these places also permits the erection of pillars, whose use endows interior spaces with greater functionality but simultaneously requires the availability of sizable timber beams to bridge the gap between pillars in order to erect joisted upper floors.

Horizontal log construction – in its three main variants of double-saddle notch log, double 'V' notch log and double square notch log – is limited to places with abundant timber, principally the Alps and the heavily forested areas of eastern and northern Europe. Log houses were exported by European migrants in several waves, beginning in the 17th century, to North America across the Atlantic Ocean, to the North American Pacific Coast across the Bering Strait, to Paraná in Brazil, to Argentinian Patagonia and to Australia.[11]

Earthen walls can be encountered all over Europe, although mainly in plains and alluvial areas. Special mention should be made of those examples located in the Iberian Peninsula, which are found both in monumental and in residential architecture,[12] and in particular in the Pannonian (or Carpathian) Basin of east-central Europe. In the latter case, earthen architecture in more than forty building variants and techniques became very popular following the 18th-century publication of fire edicts for the vast Austro-Hungarian Empire, which prohibited log houses and favoured earth constructions.[13]

Rammed earth walls are to be found mainly in four specific areas of Europe: the Iberian Peninsula, the area comprising southeast France and northwest Italy,[14] the Pannonian Basin, and the Baltic countries. Adobe walls, whose production additionally needs straw and more water than rammed earth walls, were mainly spread over the northern half of the Iberian Peninsula, eastern France, the Padanian Plain (Italy) and the Pannonian Basin. Cob walls are rare, and scattered throughout the continent – mainly in humid areas with plentiful supplies of straw and water.[15]

Until the 19th century, half-timbered construction – based on the combination of box-framed walling with either close studding or square panels filled with adobe, cob, wattle and daub, and so on – was a very widespread and popular traditional construction technique in areas with an oceanic climate, although it could also be found in some parts of the Mediterranean in medieval times. This type of building was exported during the 17th, 18th and 19th centuries by European migrants to the east coast of North America, Brazil and southeast Australia.[16]

Below Loadbearing stone, brick and earthen walls form the most consistent elements of building construction throughout the European continent. The enduring and fire-resistant qualities of these materials ensured their popular use and eventually superseded other methods, such as half-timbered construction, which declined from the 19th century onward.

Opposite top With stone locally available, this detail of a typical wall in southern Spain illustrates how the building's solid thermal mass, its minimal and shuttered apertures, and its terracotta roof tiles form a carefully considered answer to the need to moderate heat.

Opposite bottom In cooler European regions, such as in northern Germany, more substantial and well-insulated building envelopes have always been necessary. This historic façade in Überlingen, near Lake Constance, shows architectural variation, its timber-framed wall adjacent to solid constructions of render and stone.

Opposite Roofs and interiors of vernacular structures on the continent often draw on timber as a base element. Wood was widely available and typically used to create loadbearing structures. Upon this sturdy framework, timber or stone shingles, or thatch, enclosed the building. Inside, raw floor surfaces were laid with wooden board, flagstone paving, or tiles of ceramic or concrete, all of which provided additional thermal protection.

Floors

Floor and roof structures in European vernacular construction are formed mainly by the use of wooden beams and joists, with bays infilled with whatever materials were freely available in the region. These could be wooden planks, bricks, stone slabs, gypsum or wattle – or a combination of earth with any of the above. Depending on the availability of timber and sawmills in the area, beams and joists could either be simple logs, without bark, or could have sawn, squared profiles. The availability of timber also dictated the infill material, and wooden planks were most commonly used in Europe – especially in relatively forested areas – with wattle being often adopted in wetlands and marshy areas. In drier, rural regions with less sophisticated means, stone slabs were often employed to bridge the (normally short) bay spans that lay between the joists.

In areas with a relatively scant amount of timber and possibly many gypsum deposits, jack-arch (or 'flat-arch') floors with either gypsum-poured or flat tile vaults were developed. These became widespread from the 16th century onwards, along the Mediterranean coast from the south of Spain, with some gaps, to the island of Sicily.[17] At the end of the 18th century, this solution was exported to Britain and other parts of Europe, where it was often put into practice until the early 20th century. It was particularly used in dwellings and industrial plants or warehouses with metal joists and brick vaults, fundamentally because the brick vaults were fireproof – especially if the bottom part of the metal joists was protected or covered to avoid exposure in case of fire.

On this horizontal floor, composed of different materials depending on availability in the vicinity and functionality in each case, it was common to spread a layer of earth, lime mortar or gypsum in order to provide a certain amount of thermal and acoustic insulation between the various floors of the building. In the past, this layer was used directly as the surface of the floor, as in the traditional case of simple tamped earth or earth-and-lime floors found in many parts of central and eastern Europe; *massetti* in northern Italy; and *Anhydritestrich*, or anhydrite flooring, in German-speaking regions of central Europe. Alternatively, a surface of oiled gypsum might be adopted in areas with abundant gypsum deposits, for example in the east of the Iberian Peninsula.[18] In most cases, as soon as the owners of the dwellings could afford them, these raw surfaces were limited exclusively to acting as an insulating layer and were progressively covered with a second layer of floorboards, flagstone paving or ceramic tiles (either earthenware or glazed) in ceramic-producing areas. In the late 19th century, other much more economical options, such as colourful cement tiles, became extremely popular all over Europe.

Roofs

The supporting structure of the roof, formed by timber joists and an upper board to serve as a base for waterproofing, repeats many of the patterns described for floor solutions above – especially those made with wooden boards, stone slabs or wattle. Roofs in buildings with jack-arch floors made use of a range of constructional possibilities, comprised of an upper board made of timber, woven wattle or flat tiles.

Waterproofing techniques for such roof structures depended on availability of materials – employing stone slabs, slate, shingles, in timber-rich log-house areas, or ceramic tiles, which became common in large parts of Europe. Slate roofs are found throughout Europe – in almost all regions of France and Switzerland, in the western half of the British Isles, as well as in parts of Spain, Germany, Greece and eastern Europe. Shingle roofs can currently be found in eastern and central Europe, although they were once widely used in other timber-rich European regions from the Roman era onwards. Ceramic tiles, introduced into Europe also during Roman times, adopted many shapes, ranging from simple, rectangular plain tiles and Dutch S-shaped pantiles to Spanish half-truncated cones.[19] Slates, shingles and clay tiles have also been used occasionally to clad walls, offering extra waterproofing and even (in the case of shingles) enhanced insulation – particularly in areas where walls were exposed to damp, wind and rain.

The traditional thatched roof – historically the region's most popular vernacular solution, used in every European country without exception, with different local species – can still be found in many corners of the continent, although it is not used very frequently nowadays.[20] Several types of straw and reeds in bundles, tied or nailed together, are normally applied, either directly to the roof structure or to an intermediate cane mat.

Other structural roofing and waterproofing systems, such as corbelled domes, are mainly associated with Mediterranean dry-stone construction methods, although they can also be found in the British Isles and Iceland. These may be used for isolated farmers' or herdsmen's cabins to shelter their occupants from inclement weather, or may even generate a whole, fascinating village, as in the case of Alberobello (Italy), Village des Bories (Gordes, France) or Cabanes du Breuil (Saint-André-d'Allas, France). A special case of corbelled domes, without any equivalent in Europe and which can only be compared to the beehive structures of Syria,[21] are the domed huts of Castile, which are made of adobe rather than stone masonry.[22]

Another interesting roofing system is provided by the example of excavated architecture, where the terrain itself fulfils waterproofing and run-off functions, examples of which can be found principally all over the Mediterranean region and the Rhône Valley, and which became especially popular in the 19th century with the increase of demographic density in Europe.[23] Most of the underground architecture to be found in these European regions comprised newly excavated caves or, at least, significantly modified natural caves or cavities.[24] There are also examples of the remains of semi-subterranean winter dwellings in southeastern Europe and around the Danube Basin, made of timber poles and logs covered with wood, brush and earth.

Finishes

The finishes of vernacular architecture in Europe range from exposed stone or brick to formwork whose finished surface derives from contact with its boarding, to renderings made of diverse materials. There are no set rules regarding the location in Europe of exposed or rendered fabrics, a decision that depends ultimately on a combination of the friability of the material used (for example, an unrendered adobe finish lasts less longer than a brick one) and its exposure to weathering. As is often the case in vernacular architecture, however, there does exist a close relationship between the availability of a specific material in situ and its application in local architecture. Traditionally, three exterior renderings have been used on the European continent: earth, lime mortar and gypsum.

Mud rendering is common in areas where earth is usually used as a construction material – especially to protect adobe, cob, half-timbered and wattle-and-daub fabrics. Rammed-earth building fabrics have a smooth finish because of their formwork, and in principle this resists weathering better than alternatives. There are, however, also cases of mud renderings protecting rammed earth, or even lime-crusted rammed earth that is applied inside the formwork while building. Earth architecture, along with brick or stone masonry fabrics, can also be rendered with lime mortar, which is more expensive than mud – so its adoption often depends on a building owner's financial standing. There are also cases all over the Mediterranean, not necessarily in dry zones, where gypsum has been used historically as the outer rendering of buildings with excellent results.[25]

Above From exposed stone or brick, to rendered or exposed adobe, the materials used to finish structures in Europe are as much dependent on locally available materials as on tried and tested techniques. Mud, gypsum and lime mortar are the three traditional renders that can be traced across this region; to a lesser extent limewash and rammed earth also feature.

Below The extent and manner in which land surrounding a dwelling is used varies immensely throughout Europe owing to the climatic range – from cool northern regions to the intense heat of the south. For the latter, while most rural areas are more dispersed, in towns and cities the population density forces alternative occupation of spaces such as balconies, roofs and the street.

This is a specific phenomenon associated with areas rich in gypsum. External gypsum renderings can be found, for instance, in buildings in Sicily (Caltanissetta, Enna, Agrigento and Trapani); in Abruzzo (Gissi, Gessopalena) in Italy;[26] in Valencia, Játiva, Cuenca, Teruel and even Madrid in Spain;[27] and in the city of Paris and its environs,[28] thanks to the fabulous historic quarries of Montmartre.

Finally, despite recently falling into disuse, limewash is another type of finish traditionally present in European vernacular. It can be found in the south of Spain, some parts of the British Isles, Holland, Belgium and the surrounding area, the south of Scandinavia, the Czech Republic and some areas of Poland, among other places.

Building Plan/Form

The space of pertinence of a dwelling,[29] understood as the free plot of land surrounding it, varies enormously all over Europe – especially and ultimately due to the climatic conditions mentioned above. This domestic space, originally intended to be used for livestock and crops, is generous in damp climates and much less so in dry climes. People's need to live close to a supply of water became smaller and smaller in urban areas thanks to the progressive densification of buildings and the scarcity of free space. In some cases, it reached its minimum expression as simple balcony, which architectural scholar Gianfranco Caniggia defined as 'what remains of the space of pertinence'.[30]

The various forms of this space of pertinence are often the arenas in which social events, cultural manifestations or production processes take place. In Mediterranean Europe, the private inner patio, carved out of the volume of the traditional building, is the space of pertinence. In colder and wetter areas of the European climate, the vernacular architecture in rural areas created more open and scattered spaces of pertinence, made up of separate buildings erected around the threshing floor or open spaces used for livestock or crops. This is the case of the English yard, the *corte* of the Veneto region, the Germanic *Bauernhof*, the Finnish *piha* and the Polish *podwórze*.

However, especially in the European Mediterranean countries, the lack of this space of pertinence because of the dense development of rural and urban nuclei was compensated for, in a way, by the appropriation by their inhabitants of the streets as spaces of pertinence, as an exterior extension of the dwelling. So people took chairs and tables outdoors, turning the street into an open-air living room. This catalysed social relationships among city dwellers,[31] and was a process 'hosted' by the traditional cityscape and architecture, manufactured by neighbouring craftsmen with local materials and created at the human scale of these historical settlements.

Cob, Stone, Clay, Thatch and Timbered Buildings of the British Isles

Mike Lawrence

Geography/Climate

The built heritage of the British Isles has a history dating back many thousands of years, to the stone-and-turf buildings of Scotland from 3700 BCE. Its building typologies and styles are very varied. This can be directly linked to the wide range of landscape and geology that is characteristic of the British Isles, as well as to the variable weather conditions associated with an island on the edge of the Atlantic Ocean, which generates powerful weather systems.

Materials

Vernacular architecture is generally constructed from readily available local materials. Where stone predominates, buildings use rubble-stone walls, which developed with the advent of technology into masonry and massive ashlar buildings. In wooded areas, timber was used for structural elements, originally infilled with wattle and daub, and later – again, as technology developed – with fired-clay bricks. In areas with a paucity of both stone and wood, earth buildings were constructed.

As with the walls of the building, so with the roof. Where thin slabs of stone were available, they were quarried to be used as stone slates – for example, in the Cotswolds of the southwest of England. Metamorphic stone such as slate, found in various parts of the UK, could be split into thin sheets, which could be used to form an impervious protection against rainfall. Where neither of these were available, other local materials such as reeds, heather or even turf were used.

Where limestone was locally available, this was burned to form lime, the preferred binder for masonry since pre-Roman times. The burnt stone was 'slaked' with water, and the resultant sticky lime putty was mixed with sand and grit to form a mortar. This could be used to bind stones together, or to daub on the surface of walls to form an airtight, moisture-resistant coating: lime plasters and renders.

Construction Techniques

Early settlements were formed where manual labour was available. As such, fishermen would build in sheltered seaside spots; farmers in hollows in the landscape, protected from the elements but close to fields. Increasing populations and demand for tradesmen meant that small villages and towns developed. In all cases, the architecture was defined by the availability of local materials.

The enormous variety of geology and landscape in the British Isles therefore inspired, of necessity, an equally broad variety of construction typologies. Up to the 17th century, it would have been possible to look at a building and be able to place it in its locality within a few tens of kilometres, such were the peculiarities of the individual construction details and use of materials. An earth building in Norfolk used very different techniques from an earth building in Devon or in Scotland. Each construction technology was informed by the local materials, their availability and the traditional manner of constructing with them, which was passed on from master to apprentice.

The advent of industrialization, and the mass production of building materials – starting with bricks and steel, and moving on to concrete, transported cheaply by canal and rail – resulted in the ready availability of non-local materials. These were uniform in dimension with predictable performance, and often cheaper than locally available equivalents. In addition, the skill set required by builders using such materials was more generic than before. As a result, cheaper labour could be imported from other parts of the country – or even further afield. This meant that builders no longer had a local or regional tradition, and building styles lost their individuality. Where previously construction technology informed architectural design, the advent of uniformity in construction materials allowed architectural design to come to the fore, requiring the technology to adapt in order to meet the demands of the design.

Vernacular architectural style and detail had developed over time to respond to local conditions – for example, in rainy areas, roof overhangs were larger; in areas subjected to flooding, waterproof plinths were used; in windy areas, openings were positioned in the lee of buildings. The development of robust, durable materials allowed architects to design buildings without any reference to local conditions. This resulted in the construction of buildings that no longer responded to the local vernacular, but rather reflected the individual aesthetic of an architect or client.

This journey can be seen in the development of the British townscape from individual properties sharing a common vernacular style, through the grand architectural visions of the Georgian period, to the industrial cityscape of the 19th century.

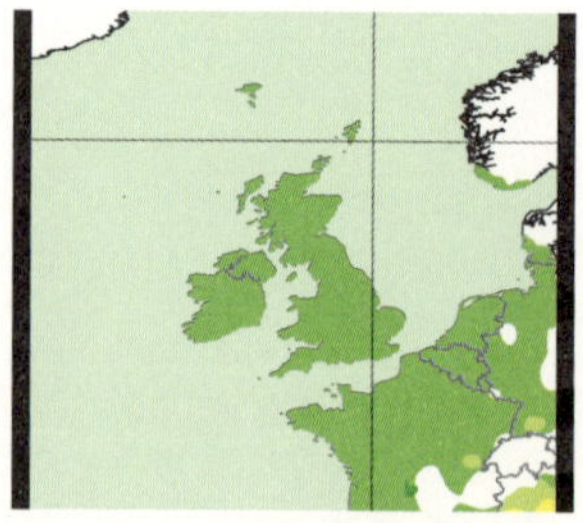

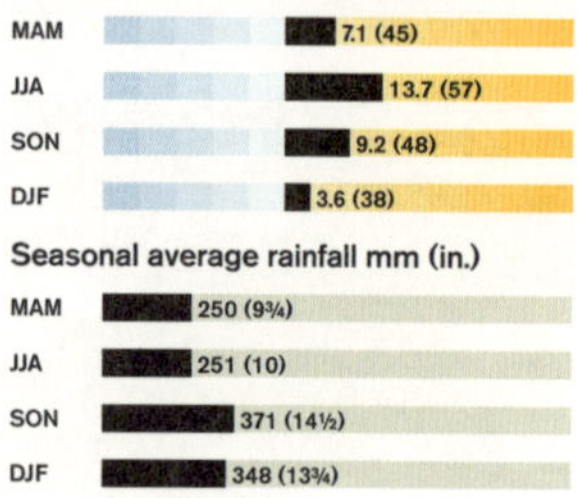

Opposite Great diversity in the geology and landscape of the British Isles inspired an equally broad variety of construction typologies until the advent of industrialization. The peculiarities of individual details and materials were locally specific and easily traced, and included thatch (top right), cob (bottom left), stone (bottom right), slate (middle right), as well as brick, and wattle and daub (both top left), all of which were often used throughout Britain to create waterproof building envelopes.

Opposite **The British vernacular typically includes materials and techniques based on raw materials that have been shaped by processes that change over time. Buildings formed from brickwork (top right), stone, metalwork (middle left), timber (middle) and thatched straw (middle right), as well as half-timbered buildings (top left, bottom right) are identifiable tropes of the British regions.**

Clay

In the southwestern county of Devon, stone was in short supply and the vernacular tradition was to use cob, which is a mixture of mud and straw. In other regions 'clunch' (rammed chalk) or clay blocks were used according to local tradition.

A typical Devon cob building was composed of foundations and plinth made from fieldstone, mortared with lime. The walls were typically 'battered', which is to say they are thicker at the bottom than at the top, and were constructed from a mixture of mud and straw that was cut back with a sharp spade after being formed, in order to create a flat surface. This surface was then coated with a lime render, and finally painted with a limewash (lime putty watered down to a paint-like consistency). This 'breathable' outer layer is essential for the health of earth-based buildings; if it is replaced with a modern cement render, painted with a modern masonry paint, moisture levels inside the wall increase – resulting in often catastrophic failure. The roof of a Devon cottage was thatched using wheat straw from the local fields. The covering can be up to 450 mm (18 in) thick, and needs replacing every twenty to fifty years.

Stone and Stone Slate

A typical farmer's cottage was made from fieldstone walls, mortared with a lime mortar. The roof was made from natural stone slates. These were quarried from 'delves' a metre (3 ft) or so below the surface of stone-slate-bearing fields in the area. The 'as dug' stone was shaped with a hammer, and hung on the roof using oak pegs driven through holes drilled in the slate. The lengths of these slates decreased from around 750 mm (in historical units, around 30 in) at the eaves to 250 mm (10 in) at the ridge.

Because stone slates will decay and delaminate over time, this type of house is usually reroofed every hundred years or more depending on the quality of the stone.

Timber-frame and Infill

In some parts of the British Isles, timber was the most readily available material for construction. The preferred technique was to construct a structural frame from massive oak, with the members attached to each other using pegged mortise-and-tenon joints – a simple interlocking connection in which a mortice (recess) accepts a tenon (protruding prong). The gaps between the members were filled with woven laths, which were then plastered with mud or a lime plaster to create a weathertight envelope. Once fired bricks became more readily available, this 'wattle-and-daub' coating was superseded by a more durable brick-and-mortar infill.

Brickwork Masonry

Buildings of the 19th century made increasing use of industrially produced, fired red-clay brick – especially for mass housing in order to meet the needs of a rapidly growing population. Such brick construction used solid walls in the 19th century, until the cavity wall was developed at the turn of the 20th century in order to significantly reduce water penetration. The middle of that century saw the introduction of the inner loadbearing cavity-wall 'skin', constructed out of concrete blocks, retaining the bricks as an external skin for visual effect. More recently, this type of construction is being replaced with a timber frame, aimed at improving energy efficiency and reducing environmental impact – and in many ways bringing building practices back to earlier, vernacular models.

Alteration and Addition in Vernacular Georgian Dwellings

Suzanne Harris-Brandts

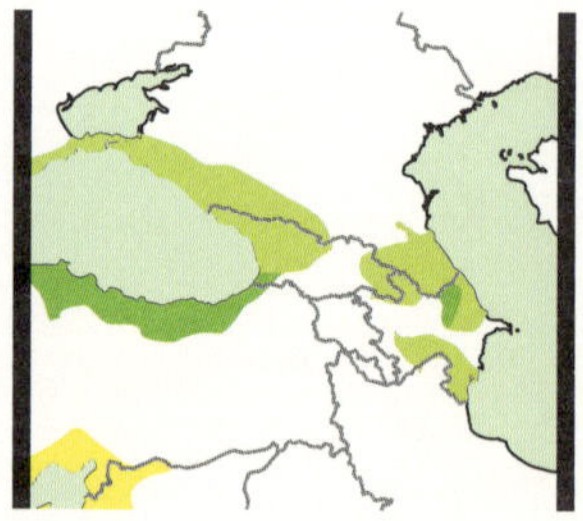

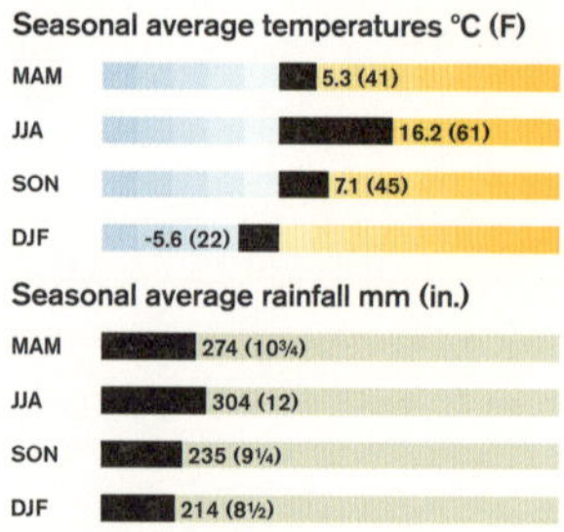

Opposite Traditional large, privately owned houses in Tbilisi were required to alter in response to reduced living quarters imposed during the Soviet regime. This change was accompanied by eclectic local-level alterations, including structures cantilevered from the façade, to alleviate the cramped conditions inside.

Geography/Climate

For centuries, the southern Caucasus has been a hub of global transition, serving as a thoroughfare for historical trading routes and a regional arena of both collaboration and conflict between Europe and Asia. As 'capital' of the Transcaucasus at the beginning of the 19th century, Tbilisi displays a vernacular character indicative of various architectural styles also found throughout neighbouring Azerbaijan and Armenia – owing in part to the Armenian merchants who inhabited the urban centres of the South Caucasus at the time.

Building Plan/Form

Despite being one of the world's oldest continually inhabited locations, present-day Tbilisi has emerged less as a place of deeply rooted architectural tradition than as one of perpetual urban adaptation and transformation. The original city, for instance, lay in ruins following the devastating Persian raid of 1795. More recently, the buildings of old Tbilisi have remarkably braved the transition from Soviet to post-Soviet and thence to capitalist society in the 21st century.

Tbilisi's traditional residential buildings display three core external elements: balconies, courtyards and stairs. Cantilevered balconies (both open and enclosed) project from the street line, and interrupt what would otherwise be rather monotonous private façades. Given these balconies' autonomous protruding construction, their forms were amenable to embellishments that frequently showcased local craftsmanship. The eclectic ornamentation found on such structures – delicately crafted in either timber or metal – covers an impressive breadth of aesthetic styles, ranging from Ottoman to Oriental and from Gothic to Art Deco.

In contrast to their street façades, the courtyard elevations of such buildings are typically more open, offering cross ventilation and a series of semi-exterior dwelling spaces via their large, glazed galleries. Such courtyard colonnades were also able to tie the interior domestic sphere socially to its exterior public realm, engaging the dwelling areas with the active atmosphere of Tbilisi's streets.

During the dramatic shifts of the Soviet era, the traditional gallery spaces of old Tbilisi's courtyard buildings were transformed. In order to provide an alternative means of building circulation and access into newly subdivided interior units, exterior staircases and entrance doors were inserted into the existing façades. The transformation of large, private flats (*dokhodyje dome*) into communal living spaces (*komunalkas*) during the Soviet era followed a 1927 piece of legislation that defined the norm for living space as 8 sq m (85 sq ft) per person. Retrofitting the city's built fabric to comply with such standards meant both the alteration of existing building stock and the introduction of new Soviet building typologies in undeveloped areas. At times taking on impossible feats of acrobatics, stair additions were usually improvised and displayed little consideration for the original building aesthetic. Nevertheless, their layering contributed to the existing vernacular, underscoring a historical language of eclectic embellishments and juxtaposed aesthetic styles.

In keeping with such a vernacular tradition of façade additions and building alterations that resulted from shifts in government policy, it was perhaps predictable that the city's Soviet-era towers would also be transformed in a similar fashion following the collapse of the Soviet Union. Such concrete buildings – many with poor insulation and ventilation – underwent dramatic transformations in the 1990s. They too acquired makeshift semi-outdoor add-ons in the form of precariously cantilevered structures jutting out of their existing façades, conveying a pastiche-like effect of multiple overlaid building materials and textures. The primary purpose of such additions, or *prostrojikas*, was to provide more living space for the tightly packed inhabitants. Yet as with their traditional predecessors, such spaces also worked to capitalize on the Caucasus's warm climate by offering a natural means of ventilation and a new semi-private domestic sphere engaging with the street activity.

Although typically no longer the shining examples of craftsmanship found in old Tbilisi, in essence these self-directed constructs carried through the functionality of earlier Georgian vernacular dwellings. Built from readily available local materials and directly responding to the inhabitants' spatial needs, this new vernacular reflected Georgia's transition from a post-Soviet to a capitalist society and addressed the overarching question of what was to become of such monolithic structures.

HOTEL

Vernacular Diversity of the Himalayas

Joëlle Smadja and Gérard Toffin

Geography/Climate

The Himalayas cover a vast array of environments, ranging from an altitude of 100 (300 ft) to more than 8,000 m (26,000 ft), stretching over a distance of 2,500 km (1,500 miles) and watered by a humid, tropical monsoon flow that decreases from east to west and is blocked by the high range in the north. Contrasting ecosystems provide varied renewable natural resources, which have long been widely used by populations in their domestic architecture.

Materials

At an altitude belt situated between 3,500 and 1,800 m (11,500 and 6,000 ft) above sea level, tree species such as *Abies spectabilis*, *Quercus glauca* (known as ring-cupped oak), and *Pinus excelsa* and *roxburghii* (the latter known as chir pine) in the central and eastern Himalayas, *Cedrus deodara* (Himalayan cedar) in the western Himalayas and various sorts of bamboo play a particularly important role in the region's palette of construction materials. At a lower elevation in the foothills (the Curiya and Tarai areas, for example), *Shorea robusta* (*sal* in the local language) and various *Graminae* (grasses) and reeds are also of central importance in making buildings.

Away from timber-rich areas, stone, earth-walled and wattle-and-daub dwellings are found; roof materials are mainly made of stone.

Construction Techniques

Up to an elevation of about 4,500 m (15,000 ft), the Himalayan region is home to numerous kinds of dwellings that are determined by the availability of natural resources and by climate conditions. The dominant forms in high-altitude Tibet and Tibetanized arid areas, which are characterized by a mineral landscape, are those of stone and/or rammed-earth houses organized around a courtyard. They have few openings, in order to protect their occupants from the cold, and terraced roofs suitable for drying grain and combustible materials. Their walls are thick (typically 450 mm [18 in]). In Nepal's densely wooded middle mountains, the timber facades of certain Tamang houses, for example, with their shingled roofs weighed down with stones, differ markedly from the wattle-and-daub walls and thatch roofs of the houses inhabited by the multi-caste and multi-ethnic hill populations. In some cases (among the Gurung ethnic group and Bahun caste) houses are not of a rectangular shape but have an elliptical or circular form – which is held to be warmer

Right Ethnic diversity and vast changes in altitude mean Himalayan structures vary greatly. At upper mountainous altitudes, villages in the Himalayas tend to favour construction with stone or rammed earth.

Opposite top Traditional mountain houses such as this stone example in the Tibetan highlands are arranged around a courtyard and have limited openings to protect against heat loss.

and stronger – and are covered by conical thatched roofs.

Newar houses in the Kathmandu Valley, for their part, have heavy sloping roofs covered in tiles, with highly decorated, overhanging eaves. In the eastern middle hills (Arun Valley) and Terai (Jhapa district) of Nepal, houses are often built on stilts and their walls are woven out of bamboo and reeds. In addition, all over the Nepalese mountains, roofing stone or shingles cover fixed shelters for herdsmen. At lower altitudes, mobile shelters for shepherds (in Nepali: *goth*) with mat-top covers are a ubiquitous sight. These temporary structures characterize an economy in which livestock roams all year round over the fields, fertilizing them. In the western Tarai plains, the walls of Tharu houses are made of ochre-coloured mud and clay (wattle and daub), and are covered by a large, sloping thatched roof supported by several rows of wooden poles. The roof extends out over the low outer walls. These houses are very dark because there are only a few small openings, in order to protect the occupants from the heat.

In far-eastern humid Arunachal Pradesh (India), where subtropical rainforest covers more than 70 per cent of the land area and where the population practises shifting cultivation, villages occupy clearings in the middle of the forest. Houses here are made of bamboo and wood – with sloping roofs of banana, palm leaf or thatch – and can be transported when the village is displaced. To protect against humidity and wild animals, houses and granaries are built on stilts.

Building Plan/Form

Despite numerous contacts between groups over the course of history, the vast ethnic diversity of the Himalayan region is still reflected in its architecture and spatial patterns. Social and cultural elements play a crucial role in most geographical regions and within most populations. For instance, from the western to the eastern part of the Himalayas, Tibetan and Tibetanized houses present common architectural features. They normally comprise at least a ground floor for keeping animals and for food storage, and a first floor that is used as a kitchen-cum-living room, oratory and grain store. The more affluent family dwellings have an additional storey and servants' quarters. In most cases, the local tripartite religious structure of the world – divided between the gods of the upper regions, the deities of the intermediate realm and the *klu* spirits of the underworld – is often also applied to the house. This provides a cosmological aspect to the dwelling, and reinforces its vertical dimension.

The tent of the Tibetan nomadic herder, who wanders over the Tibetan Plateau, is made of good-quality yak overhair, which is taken from the sides of the animal in the month of June. The tent is of a rectangular shape and consists of two halves; the right side is for male occupants, the left side for female. It covers an area ranging between 12 and 28 sq m (130 and 300 sq ft).

The unique houses of the Newars, inhabitants of the Kathmandu Valley who have also settled in many small towns throughout Nepal, display a distinct structure and compartmentalization of vertical space, reflecting their social patterns. The polarity between 'pure' and 'impure' is a central feature. Newar dwellings are tall – several storeys high – and each storey has its own function. The ground floor is used as a stable or shop, the first floor as a bedroom and granary; the second floor is traditionally a large open living room with no dividing partitions, and the third floor (attic) is used as a kitchen and oratory for the household deities. These houses used to be famous for their carved wooden windows, a feature now on the verge of extinction. The most opulent ones were greatly influenced in the early 20th century by the neoclassical, or *Rana* style, brought to Nepal by Rana rulers from the mid-19th century onwards. Their façades incorporate neoclassical Western decorative elements such as pilasters, stucco figurations, volutes, meander designs, rocaille decor, capitals with angels, caryatides, mascarons (sculpted faces) and painted stucco plaques.

In the West Kameng district (Arunachal Pradesh), within the Nyishi polygamous tribal society, the length of the house represents the number of hearths, which itself depends on the number of wives a man has. It is said that in the past this tally could reach twenty-five, yet a house with five to ten hearths is not a rare sight today. At the front of the dwelling, a veranda and a platform always face eastward – an auspicious orientation since the sun, which is venerated, thereby enters the house directly. Major rituals are performed here. A smaller veranda is built on the opposite side, facing west. This is where the grinding of grain as well as husking or other activities are done, and it is the place through which foreigners enter or leave the dwelling. Dead bodies are also taken out on this side.

In the western Tarai plains (Dang-Deukhuri District), Tharu villages are mostly oriented along a north–south axis. The houses were traditionally built side by side in two rectilinear rows facing each other, on a level piece of ground that forms the dwellings' floors. In the past, Tharus lived in large joint-family households, some of which could include eighty or ninety people. Their inner rooms, occupied by nuclear families, were separated by partitions consisting of large grain storage containers. The kitchen and the deity room are the innermost part of the house. The outer walls (and in some cases, the inside walls as well) are still decorated with moulding in relief, incorporating flower designs, paintings and animal figures, and with engravings.

In most of the vernacular types described above, the main supporting roof post and the fireplace are of great religious significance. They are often associated with the household's ancestors and with prosperity. In all cases, the threshold between the inner and the outer part of the house is always clearly marked, and is the place where important rituals are performed.

Since the 1970s and 1980s, significant socio-economic transformations owing to the opening of this region to the outside world, to forest protection and to restricted access to resources have led to several architectural changes. There has been an individualization of housing, thanks to children leaving their large family houses and to changes in building materials – especially those for roofs. In the hills, straw used for roofing now competes with the need to use it as fodder for cattle, while in the middle mountains fir trees for making shingles now have to be purchased. Today, the roofs of these dwelling types are often replaced with slate, corrugated iron or even flattened tin cans. In the Kathmandu Valley, traditional bricks that are moulded using local earth are being increasingly replaced by concrete. In this region as in other urbanized areas, the traditional architectural heritage is in decline. By and large, throughout the range, Westernized modern houses tend to be built in a chaotic fashion, with no organic relation to the land or to each other.

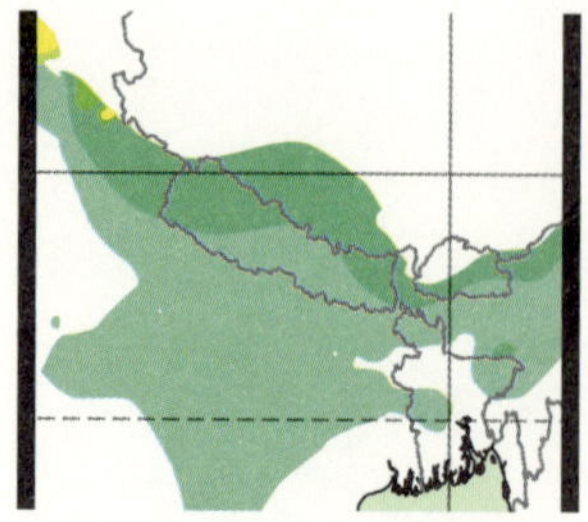

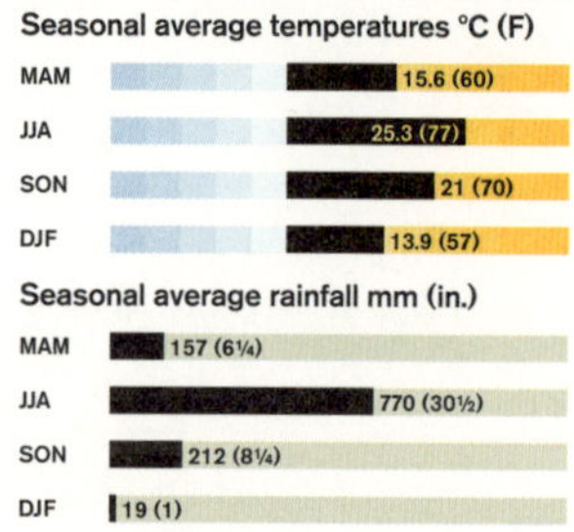

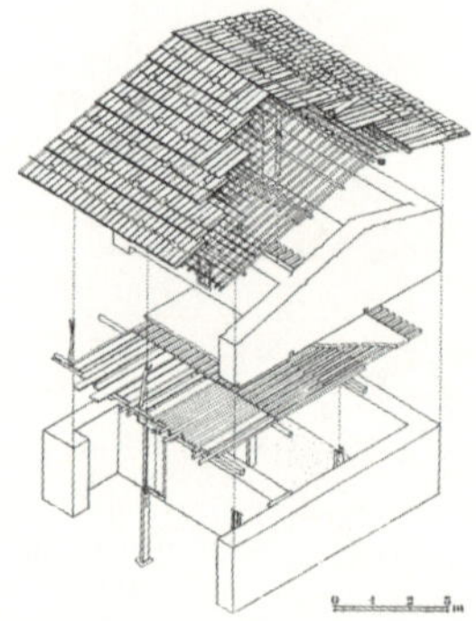

Above and opposite top left Traditional Tamang villages in the Nepalese middle mountains use local materials: stone walls with decorative timber façades are capped by shingle roofs weighed down with stones.

Opposite top right, middle and bottom Niyishi villages in the Arunachal Pradesh region reflect materials found locally and the society's polygamous structure. Built of timber, bamboo and leaves, and with straw roofs, the principal dwelling is the longhouse, which can contain up to seventy people with a separate fireplace for each conjugal family. The entrance of every building is oriented towards the sun in the auspicious eastward direction.

Towers of the Sino-Tibetan Marches

Frederique Darragon

Geography/Climate

The Sino-Tibetan Marches are an earthquake-prone succession of well-watered and well-forested picturesque valleys separated by towering peaks and raging rivers. The region harbours some of the most interesting examples of Himalayan stone architecture, which always also includes earth and timber in varying proportions depending on the local conditions. This geographical corridor, a large part of which is called Kham, was, since time immemorial, a region of mingling, trade and invasion caught between the growing civilizations of Tibet and China. Small kingdoms prospered in fertile pockets, many of them enduring until the 20th century.

Materials and Construction Techniques

Illiterate indigenous populations living between 1,500 and 4,000 m (5,000 and 13,000 ft) above sea level must have long experimented with local building materials before conceiving a sophisticated construction technique that allowed them to build towering, freestanding monuments – now the only surviving testimony to their past grandeur. These amazing structures are made of vertical interlocking stone masonry pillars, strengthened by embedded, unpegged, horizontal wooden beams: an earthquake-resistant architectural technology unique to this region, and one still used in contemporary traditional-style houses.

Around 1,000 such towers still stand today, but at the height of this construction type they must have numbered many thousand. Sadly, this flamboyant tower building ceased in the late 17th century.

Left The distinctive towers of the Sino-Tibetan Marches area are constructed of stone pillars strengthened by embedded horizontal wooden beams.

Opposite Based on variations o f star-shaped plans with between five and thirteen points, the function of the freestanding towers varied in different areas – from defensive structures to storage facilities or trading posts.

Above The corridor of the Sino-Tibetan Marches is a seismically unstable succession of picturesque valleys in which the dramatic, earthquake-resistant towers still survive.

Right Though the flamboyant building type of the star-shaped forms ceased from around the 17th century, there are approximately 1,000 towers that remain standing.

Opposite top The towers are built of interlocking stone with components of earth and timber; the proportional use of each material varies in relation to local availability.

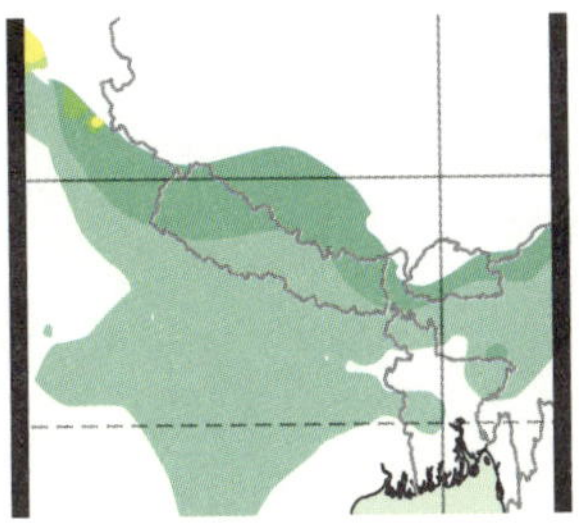

Seasonal average temperatures °C (F)

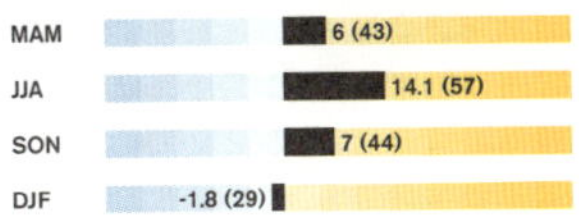

Seasonal average rainfall mm (in.)

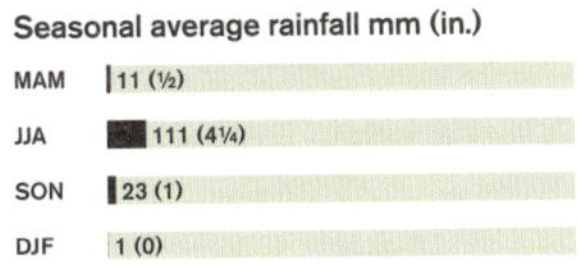

Building Plan/Form

As proven by limited mentions in Chinese annals and by the carbon dating of eighty-two of these structures, the towers of the Sino-Tibetan Marches predate by nearly a millennium both the famous square towers of Tuscany and the oldest ridged towers of Islamic Iran and Afghanistan – the last-named built following a different architectural concept of round towers with ribs or buttresses.

These star-shaped Sino-Tibetan towers all have slightly different configurations, and can be classified into four groups according to their architectural characteristics. Each of these groups corresponds to the traditional lands of a different age-old tribe, most of them descendants of the ancient Qiang people. Although some of these populations took up Buddhism after falling under the sway of the Tibetan Empire of the 7th to 9th centuries, many have held on to their own Qiangic languages and specific customs until today.

As with ancient vernacular towers in other parts of the world, the functions of the Sino-Tibetan Marches towers varied depending on each building's location and architectural characteristics. These functions include their use as status symbols, defensive structures, storage facilities, beacons/landmarks and trading posts.

From 2008 to 2013, the Kham towers and those of the Qiang Minority region and those of the Gyalrong Danba County were added to the UNESCO World Heritage 'Tentative' List inventory of locations under consideration for World Heritage Site status.

Courtyard Dwellings of Central and Eastern Coastal China

Zhu Tan

Geography/Climate

In cultural-geography terms, China's current territory can be roughly divided into agricultural and nomadic regions. The country's eastern part includes plains and hills below 2,000 m (6,500 ft) above sea level; with its prevailing monsoon climate, this forms the main agricultural region. China's western hinterland comprises mainly grasslands, deserts, mountains and plateaus; it forms the country's nomadic region. The bulk of ancient China's population resided – as it does today – in the agricultural zone: the central and eastern coastal areas whose northern boundary was the Great Wall. These were (and remain) the ethnic Han Chinese, who still constitute the majority (more than 90 per cent) of the Chinese population.

The central Qinling Mountains–Huaihe River line forms a natural boundary between northern and southern China. It divides the country's warm temperate zone from its subtropical zone, its semi-humid from its humid region, the Yellow River from the Yangtze River basin. To its north, the rivers generally freeze during winter months and there is mainly dry land on which to grow wheat; to its south, the rivers flow year-round, and there is mainly paddy field in which to grow rice.

Below In central and eastern coastal areas of China, the bulk of the country's population resides in courtyard houses that suit the mild climate of this agricultural zone.

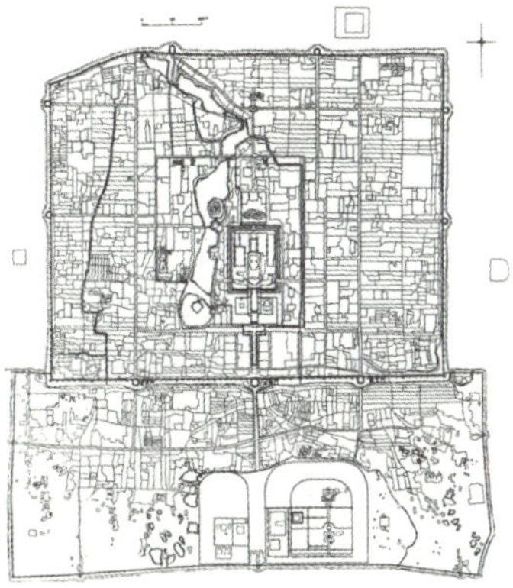

Above and below From a single courtyard to a compound and then to a village, town or city, the whole courtyard system resembles a large, organic, unified building. This pattern is exemplified by the ancient city of Beijing seen in plan (above). Modern buildings are now taking over the skyline (below) and the courtyard system is now mainly found in the old city and the countryside.

Materials and Construction Techniques

China's basic construction material was always timber. Traditionally, it was chosen not because the country was particularly rich in timber resources but because people believed that wood could form the most 'reasonable' structure. The ancient Chinese grasped the technology of these structures and could easily prepare modular, prefabricated components from cut timber. A durable structure could then be assembled very quickly, without using nails or adhesives. Therefore, building with wood, especially as a structural element, became synonymous with traditional Chinese architecture. The chosen timbers were mainly China fir (*Cunninghamia*), Chinese chestnut (*Castanea mollissima* Blume), beech (*Zelkova schneideriana* Hand-Mazz) and zhennan (*Phoebe zhennan* S. Lee).

The ancestors of the Han Chinese inhabited the Yellow River basin, in the northern, agricultural part of China, for thousands of years. Between 25 and 220 CE, they began to migrate to the southern part of Chinese territory. Entire families relocated, and spread their culture – including production technologies and living customs – to the new settlements. They also brought with them their way of constructing houses.

Building Plan and Form

The courtyard house, which forms the principal residential type of the Han, is a typical Chinese vernacular building found predominantly in central and eastern coastal areas of China and based on the agricultural economy. Its inhabitants' lives depended on their relationship to nature, and the way its single-courtyard form is arranged responds to the prevailing climatic conditions. The buildings surrounding its central yard share similar construction methods and have relatively generic, 'empty' main interior spaces; their actual functions are decided by their position and orientation. In order to take advantage of sunlight and warm winds, the key spaces are usually located on the main axis of the house and face south. Least important and functional rooms are located at lower levels and oriented towards the north – the cooler and more shaded side of the building. The dwelling's secondary buildings are located on the courtyard's two long sides. In this way, the buildings surrounding the single, rectangular yard constitute a hierarchical unit, which mirrors the hierarchical form of traditional Han society.

At a larger scale, these single-courtyard dwellings could be easily combined to form a sizable compound, with the individual courtyard building being flexible enough to accommodate other uses – not just a residence but government offices, a school or even a temple. From a single courtyard to a compound and then to a city (or village or town), the whole system therefore resembles a large, organic, unified building. This pattern is perhaps best exemplified by the ancient city of Beijing.

As a result of the migration of the Han Chinese people, the courtyard building was diffused from the centre of the country to the surrounding regions, its form varying according to local natural conditions. Timber was chosen for the primary structure, while the building envelopes were generally made from other local materials. These varied according to climate and geographical conditions, but the most common ones were earth (in the form of bricks) and stone.

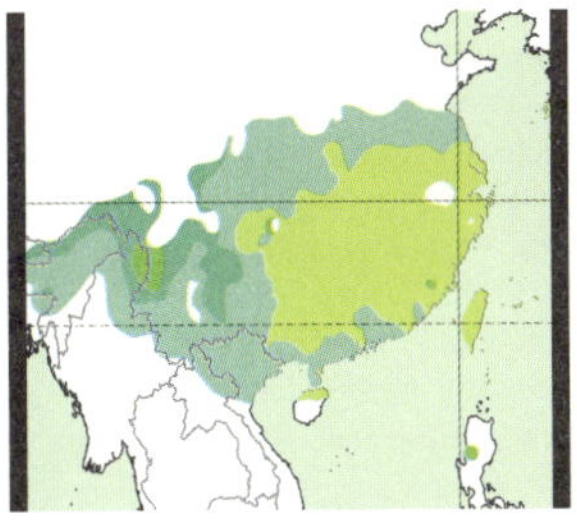

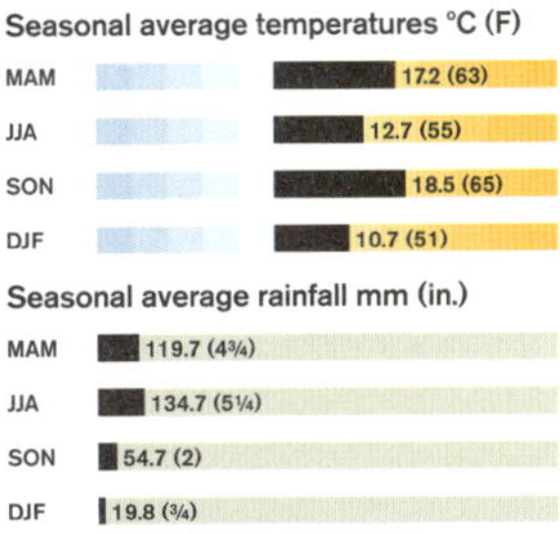

Opposite Though China's warm temperate areas encompass four disparate regions, they share a similar basic pattern of single-courtyard housing, which differs slightly according to local materials and the composition of courtyard spaces.

Below In contrast to the more usual Chinese housing of a courtyard typology in warm temperate zones, the inhabited loess plateau area encourages architectural adaptations, such as narrow, windproof courtyards with an economical footprint in densely populated cities, or the adobe cave houses seen below, which are carved out from the hillside.

The central and eastern coastal part of China is generally held to encompass four disparate regions: the North China Plain; a loess plateau; the middle and lower reaches of the Yangtze River; and the southerly, coastal zone. In each region, the single-courtyard building unit shows distinct attributes – although they all conform to a similar basic pattern. Aside from varying local materials, different shapes of courtyard could adjust the building interiors, and the different compositions of courtyard represent different methods of social organization.

North China Plain

The North China Plain lies in the warm temperate and subhumid climate zone. It is dry and cold in winter, hot and rainy in summer. The area is mainly low-lying and flat, with a general altitude of less than 50 m (165 ft) above sea level. The land is fertile because it comprises the alluvial plain of three significant watercourses: the Yellow, Huai and Hai rivers. It is China's key agricultural base, and one of the most ancient settlement areas of Chinese primitive tribes (from around 5000 BCE). The available construction materials include timber (for structural frameworks) and clay brick (for wall envelopes). This area does not have an abundance of trees, but there is plenty of earth to hand. Insulating against the cold is a vital task of houses in this region, and their brick walls are solid enough for the job. Courtyards are spacious because the built density of the area is low, and because more sunlight is necessary for living quarters than in hotter regions. Furthermore, these larger yard spaces could be used for additional domestic activities, such as drying food and cultivation.

Loess Plateau

The loess plateau region sits on the boundary of China's warm-temperate monsoon climate zone. Its winter is dry, cold and lengthy; its summer is muggy, hot and brief. The total precipitation is small, and concentrated in the summer months. The area lies between 1,000 and 2,000 m (3,280 and 6,500 ft) above sea level, and is covered with up to 200 m (650 ft) of friable, alkaline loess soil. The vegetation is sparse, with a forest-coverage rate of only 5 per cent. The area generally suffers from serious soil erosion, which produces 'gully' landforms. As with the northern plain, construction materials include timber; earth, with adobe being the material of choice in hilly areas; and clay – this region was the principle source of bricks and tiles in ancient times, and some of its villages have produced high-quality clay brick since the Ming dynasty (1368–1644).

This region occupies the same latitude as the North China Plain, so cold-proofing is also an important task of the houses here. It is also very crowded, because large numbers of people have traditionally settled on its limited territory. Dwellings in its plain-cities are therefore constructed with the customary timber frame and (in this area) high-quality brick infill – but their courtyard spaces are relatively narrow, with long sides in a north–south direction in order to defend against the cold wind while economizing on land use. Some buildings have adopted a two-storey format to increase available floor area. In hill areas, earth and adobe have been used more frequently – especially in the cave houses. These distinctive dwellings incorporate 'holes' carved out of the loess hills, which become part of their courtyards.

Middle and Lower Yangtze River Region

The middle and lower regions of the Yangtze River lie in the subtropical monsoon climate zone. The annual minimum temperature generally remains above 0°C (32°F). Spring and summer have substantial rainfall – especially June and July, when the air humidity is also extremely high. The general altitude of the area is less than 50 m (165 ft) above sea level. Surrounded by hills, a series of plains makes up the middle and lower Yangtze Valley plain, on which there is an abundance of lakes and small rivers. The plain is an important agricultural area in south China, which has been called 'a fertile land of fish and rice'. It is also a crowded area, having a relatively large number of inhabitants for its size.

Its chief construction materials are timber, stone and brick. With its heat and humidity, good ventilation and defending against damp and excessive sunlight are the principal tasks of houses in this region. Dwellings are generally tall, with two storeys surrounding a central mini-courtyard. Timber was traditionally used to construct the structural 'skeleton' and the inner walls and floors of these houses, with stone adopted for paving and the lower part of the envelope wall in order to defend against damp. The upper part of the envelope wall was made with a form of brick cavity, with an empty core – a light and economical option that could be insulated if desired. The outside surface of these walls was painted white to reflect the sunlight. The mini-courtyard could bring light and ventilation into the heart of the house, while also collecting rainwater from the surrounding roofs.

Coastal Southern China

China's southern coastal region also belongs to the country's subtropical monsoon climate zone. It is hot and rainy in summer, and warm and dry in winter. The area is mountainous, with taller peaks in the north than in the south, and its percentage of forest cover is very high. There are many valleys and rivers in the area, which are suitable for cultivating crops such as rice, sugar and tea. Its common construction materials include timber; earth, with external walls being in adobe, clay, earth or a mixture of lime, clay and sand); and stone.

Typical of the vernacular in this region is the *tulou*. These large-scale collective residences, of which the circular types are most famous, could accommodate an entire, extended family living together and were mainly located in the valleys of southern Fujian Province. The round *tulou* is enclosed, the buildings inside it arranged around its perimeter and facing inward to a central space that functions as either public realm or the family temple. It is multilayered: the lower floor holds service functions such as the kitchen; the first floor comprises storage space; and the upper floors house the private rooms. Its individual buildings are constructed mainly of timber (for both framework and infill walls), while the external wall enclosure is built of dense, compacted earth. It is a defensive form of architecture, and the archetype for shaping a collective community. The Hakka people (the migrated Han Chinese) adopted *tulou* as their shelter when they first migrated to this region.

Meanwhile, in the western part of this region, the 'four-angle' walled house was developed according to the same defensive logic as the *tulou* but inherited more ideas from the courtyard building prototype. Its external wall was made of hardened earth, and its inner buildings were organized in a layout of regular courtyards reflecting the preceding Han Chinese tradition. The inner buildings of the four-angle walled house often have only ground floors, formed by using either a wood–earth or wood–brick structure.

Below Dwellings in China's coastal southern region are typically either *tulou* or 'four-angle' walled housing as seen below. Sharing the same defensive logic, the four-angled dwellings borrow from the courtyard typology. The hardened external walls were built of earth, with interiors forming a regular courtyard pattern.

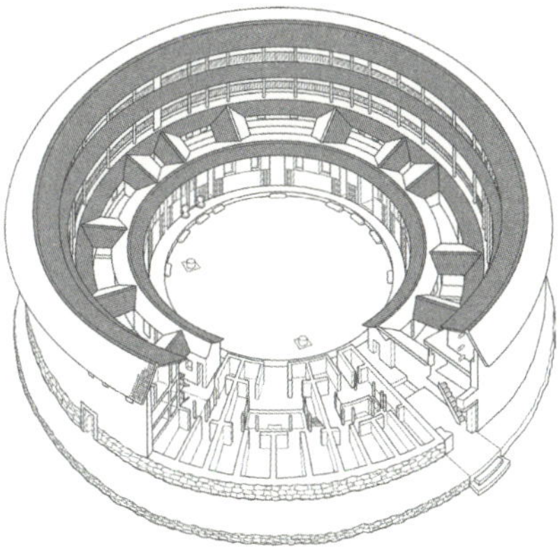

Above Distinctive for its cylindrical form the *tulou* vernacular in southern coastal China is a carefully composed response to the subtropical monsoon climate. An entire extended family can be accommodated in the fortress-like structure, which is oriented towards the central public space.

Right Principally constructed from timber and enclosed by dense compacted earth, the multi-storey *tulou* house has progressively more private spaces at upper levels, with shared common functions at ground level.

Adobe and Rammed-earth Homes of North China

Lijun Zhou

Geography/Climate

The region of northern China is defined as the territory running from the Great Wall to the northern borders, and mainly comprises what are known as the northeast and northwest areas along with the provinces of Inner Mongolia and Xinjiang. In this vast area reside the Han, Manchu, Mongol and Uighur peoples. Owing to the varying characteristics and traditional customs of northern China, its vernacular architecture generally presents a variety of forms. However, the traditional residences of the region display many common characteristics, albeit modified by climatic adaptations to rain, wind and temperature.

Building Plan/Form and Construction Techniques

China's average rainfall distribution for the northern region is below 400 mm (15 in) per year, which places it in an arid and semi-arid zone. In light of this scant rainfall, the roof treatments of the region's residential buildings include vaults, shallow monopitches and flat roofs, which are best suited to the dry drought-prone characteristics of the locality. Rammed earth or earth mixed with grass is frequently employed for these roofs, while walls are mostly adobe with little regard for waterproofing measures.

In most of the region, the maximum wind pressure is above 150 N/m² in winter and north-westerly winds are prevailing and powerful. The gently sloping or flat roofs often seen in residential buildings are built to resist the impact of the cold winds. At the same time, a kind of streamlined vault is employed in Inner Mongolia in the form of the traditional yurt. In some mountainous areas, buildings are constructed on the southern sides of peaks and erected so that the northern, windward face of the dwelling is as small as possible. Openings are designed to mitigate heat loss; in addition, windows are not usually set in north walls. An alternative wind-resistance method used in northern residential buildings is the adoption of the courtyard-house form, which buffers winds with thick walls that define the perimeter.

The average temperature of the region in January is around -20°C (-4°F), necessitating a high degree of thermal insulation. In order to conserve available heat, the residential buildings exhibit simple, rectangular shapes, relatively low eaves heights, and, generally, a relatively low surface-to-volume ratio. All these methods have one goal: that of keeping the amount of building surface exposed to the air as small as possible. Only in this way can the heat-dissipating capacity of the building surfaces be minimized, the indoor temperature retained and its heating-energy requirements reduced. Apart from the Mongolian yurt, which mainly uses cotton matting, walls are constructed from dense rammed earth, brick or adobe – all with thicknesses greater than 400 mm (15 in) in order to improve heat retention. The typical northern Chinese vernacular building is oriented north–south, with large south-facing window areas to maximize illumination levels. Fireplace hearths are also introduced for warmth.

No matter what the internal layout, the arid climate characteristic of northern China makes for distinctive roof forms and relatively fixed wind-resisting external enclosures. Characteristically low temperatures ensure that residential buildings are usually simple in shape and low in height, as well as having a long floorplan. These factors contribute to the unique forms of vernacular residential buildings found in China's north.

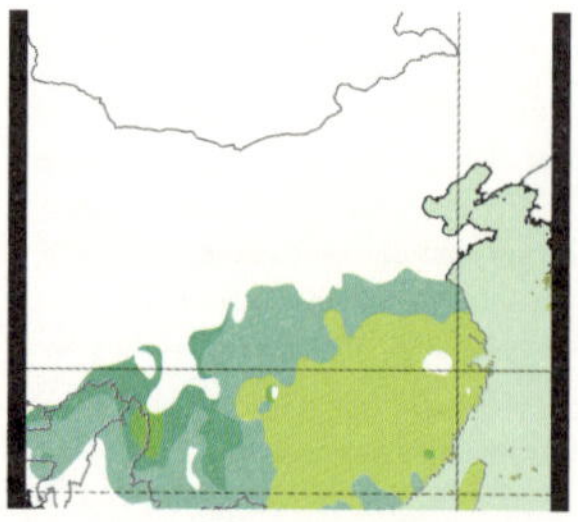

Opposite **Despite differences due to cultural and climatic variation, one of the most common building types in northern China is low, flat-roofed homes – an adaptation to the scant rainfall and the cold winds in winter.**

Settlements and Drum Towers of the Kam People of China

Amy Eisenberg and John Amato

Geography/Climate and Culture

Historically, the Kam people were forcibly displaced from China's best agricultural land by the Han Chinese. Today, the Kam cultural landscape largely encompasses the provinces of Guizhou, Hunan and Guangxi, in which lie verdant riverine mountains and valleys with broadleaf and evergreen forests typical of the humid subtropical montane ecosystem.

The Kam have dwelled in this diverse environment for approximately 2,000 years, developing unique livelihood strategies of harvesting fish and grain from paddy fields, integrating agroforestry and agriculture on mountain slopes, and applying specialized knowledge and skills in utilizing local natural resources.

Kam vernacular architecture is a cultural amalgam that reflects the spiritual and cosmological forces of Kam life. The Kam have held fast to their heritage as a people, and in their architecture they express the significance of their past, present and future. According to China's recent national census, the Kam population today is approximately 3 million, making them the eleventh largest of the fifty-six ethnic minorities of mainland China.

Materials

The Kam are primarily rice farmers, pisciculturists, agro-foresters and carpenters. Professional carpentry is often intergenerational within families, and it takes many years to master it well. China fir (*Cunninghamia lanceolata* [Lamb.] Hook.) in the Cupressaceae family provides the most familiar wood for Kam carpenters, who are paid for their work with money, rice or labour.

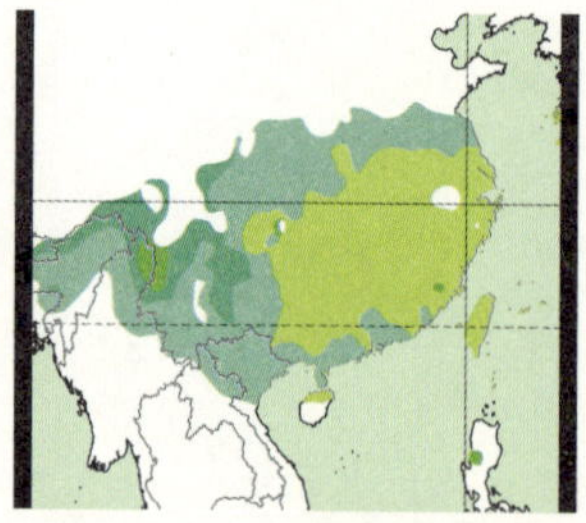

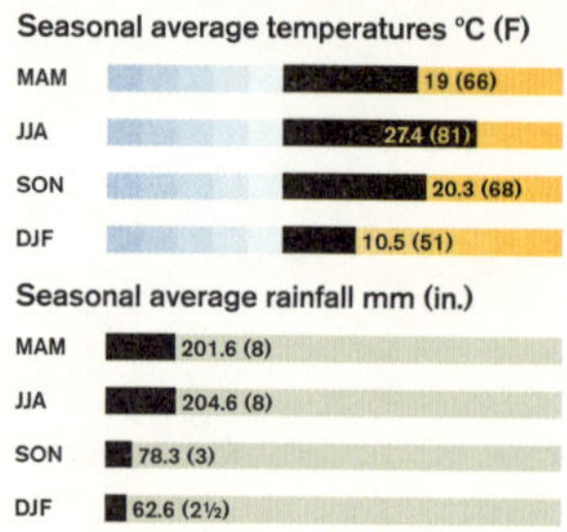

Left Inhabiting the provinces of Guizhou, Hunan and Guangxi, Kam people utilize materials from the mountainous and verdant humid subtropics in which they live, creating structures that are mostly built of evergreen trees.

Opposite top Kam settlements tend to be organized as a cluster of individual groups. As seen here, in Gao Xiu village in Guangxi Province, the dwellings step down the hillside.

Opposite bottom Drum towers are present in almost all Kam villages, such as the women's drum tower in Gao Xiu village seen here. The focal gathering place of Kam life, the towers are the first buildings to be completed when establishing a village and originally housed wooden drums, to warn villagers in the event of danger.

Opposite top Mortise-and-tenon construction is employed in many traditional Kam building and woodworking techniques. Iron stays are used to secure logs and beams, which are most often hewn from *Cunninghamia* wood.

Opposite bottom Bark used for roofing and cladding is harvested from the *Cunninghamia* evergreen, a fast-growing conifer that is fairly resistant to decay. Once dry, the sheets of bark are used to seal buildings. They provide robust protection for approximately five years.

Right top While the drum towers are partly defensive structures, they are also an integral, shared community space in which to sing, dance and play the *lusheng*, a traditional Kam instrument.

Right, bottom Marked by multi-tiered roofs, the drum tower emulates the branching of the *Cunninghamia* tree, which has long been of import to the Kam for its building quality, as well as in economic and spiritual systems. The Kam revere ancient and sacred trees, believing that they embody spirits: it is held that the more healthy and strong trees are, the more prosperous and harmonious the village and its residents will be.

Building Plan/Form

Kam homes are arranged in individual groups within a village, and often the people living in a grouping of houses bear the same surname. These groups or clans often congregate in the drum tower of their respective clan. These drum towers are the highest and most outstanding architectural feature of Kam villages, which also feature schools and public buildings in self-sustainable communities. They – like all Kam building and woodwork – are constructed employing the mortice-and-tenon system, in which two pieces of wood join together securely so that nails are not required.

When establishing a village, the drum tower was the first structure to be built. Originally erected within, and intrinsic to, these edifices was a large wooden drum that served as a signal for alerting villagers in the event of an intruder. This drum was also used to gather the community, and to warn of danger or the impending approach of an enemy's army. Sounding the drum drew the community to the drum tower, where plans were made in response to any threatening situation.

During Mao Zedong's Cultural Revolution, which seriously impacted on all the ethnic-minority peoples of China, Kam cultural relics disappeared. Many drum towers and temples were destroyed in an attempt to extinguish Kam cultural heritage and identity. Since they were removable, almost all drums were burned. Fortunately, some Kam communities have repaired and rebuilt their drum towers and temples, without assistance from the government. Today, there is a resurgence of drum towers, and Kam communities are attempting to reinvigorate the construction and use of these important historical and present-day cultural markers.

Drum towers are a focus of cultural expression and community for the Kam people. Some have a fire pit in the centre, often kept burning with coals with which to light tobacco in a ceramic pipe; some towers have wooden floors. Most Kam houses and drum towers have clay-fired tile roofs, which are fairly easy to repair as the material is held in place by a combination of self-weight and a notch upon which the tiles catch.

The unique architectural design of the Kam drum tower is its multi-tiered, odd number of roofs that are built to resemble the invaluable *Cunninghamia* tree.

Neowa and *Gulpi* Houses of South Korea

Kyung-Rip Park

Geography/Climate

The location of Korea's *neowa* (shingle-roofed) houses of red pine corresponds with the areas where slash-and-burn farmers once lived: the Gaema Plateau and the mountain regions of Hamgyoung and Pyoungan provinces, Gangwon Province and around the Taebaek mountain range.

The mountain villages in this area on the eastern side of the Korean Peninsula have been among the growing number of slash-and-burn farming settlements founded in the country since the 18th century. However, since the 1960s, when the government prohibited slash-and-burn agriculture, most of these houses have disappeared. Fortunately, some of the vernacular residences were recognized as cultural assets, and have been preserved.

Materials

In these mountain villages where flat land is scarce, most people lived by dryland farming. They produced potatoes, corn, rye, oats, beans and wheat. Living at around 1,000 m (3,280 ft) above sea level, villagers had to build their own houses with materials that were readily obtained close by. The features of *neowa* houses, including their distinctive bark-shingle roofs, are intimately bound up with their surrounding natural environment. The houses were erected in the lee of tall mountains, but at a sufficient distance from the peaks to avoid any landslides. *Neowa* houses were also built near sunlit streams, raised high enough to avoid any damage during floods.

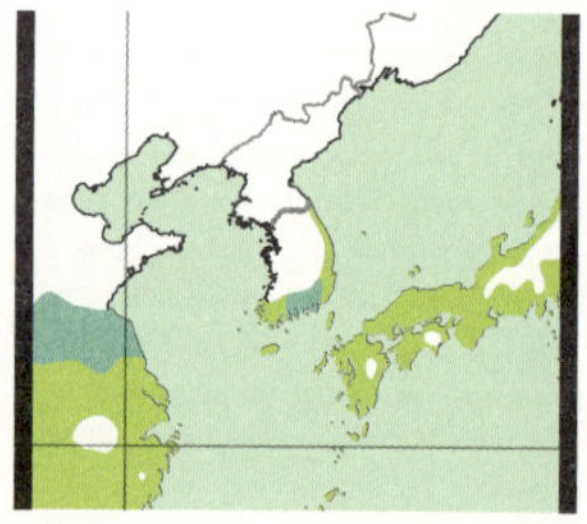

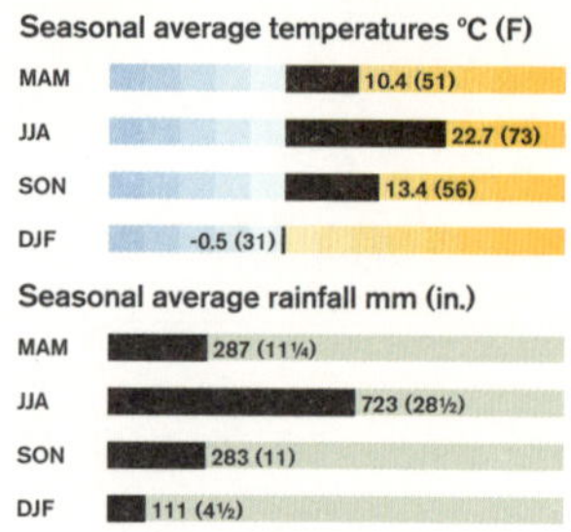

Left Found in the mountainous areas of Korea's Gaema Plateau, Hamgyoung and Pyoungan provinces and the Taebaek range, the *neowa* typology is usually constructed in the lee of valleys at around 1,000 m (3,280 ft) above sea level.

Opposite An extension of their natural surroundings, the *neowa* built by villagers draw on readily available materials, in particular the red pine, which is seen in the bark-shingle roofs.

Opposite top and bottom right Formed of 30–50 mm (1–2 in) thick pine or fir boards woven with ash twigs or kudzu vines, the *neowa* houses also include a variation known as *gulpi*, which uses oak bark rather than pine. Both types have the same internal structure, with clay and hay serving as insulation between gaps in logs for walls and ceilings.

Opposite bottom left Roofs of *neowa* employ timber shingles, which are held down by angular stones. Made by hand, the individual shingles vary in size, and may change shape or shrink according to the temperature. The resulting gaps in roofs allow for natural ventilation, admitting cool air in summer and extracting smoke in winter.

Right Mountain villages in the Taebaek range were among the slash-and-burn farming settlements founded from the 18th century. Since the 1960s prohibition of slash-and-burn agriculture, many *neowa* houses have disappeared in favour of regular town settlements, such as this early example, with its mixture of tile and thatch housing.

Construction Techniques

The *neowa* houses themselves are made with 30–50 mm (1–2 in) thick boards of pine (*Pinus*) or fir (Pinaceae) trees and are woven with ash (*Fraxinus*) twigs or kudzu (*Pueraria*) vines, placed on top of wooden rafters. Angular stones are strategically placed in order to hold down this roof covering. The walls of the houses are built with logs and filled with a mixture of clay and hay in the gaps between. Ceilings are made using same technique. As the structures are built with materials easily obtained from the mountainous locale, *neowa* houses may endure for ten to twenty years and old ones can be partially repaired and replaced.

When fashioning *neowa* houses, axes are used instead of saws to split the material in the direction of the timber, preventing the bark fibres from splitting. As *neowa* are handmade, their size varies and their shape may change with the shrinkage of the wood bark. Consequently, there may be gaps in *neowa* roofs; however, this permits natural ventilation – allowing cool air in during summer, and smoke from indoor fires out in winter. In the summer rainy season, the *neowa* houses expand owing to their internal moisture levels and prevent rainwater from leaking into the house. In winter, the weight of the snow covering the roof keeps the warmth inside. During heavy snowfall, remote houses were often isolated and the outdoor court located in the centre of the dwelling was especially useful.

Building Plan/Form

Since Korea has four distinct seasons, its *neowa* houses are equipped with the proper combination of *maru* (the traditional wooden-floored living areas of these houses) and *ondol* (a traditional Korean floor-heating system). The dwellings are usually laid out in a 'three-by-three' square formation, with an enclosed central court or an additional barn attached on one side. They are usually built so that they are closed to the outside. The guest room, master bedroom, other rooms and barn are centred around the *maru*. This layout is designed to protect livestock from wild animals, and to maximize heat retention. Even within this dense layout, some movable walls and openings of wooden boards or clay allow separated spaces between men and women. A 'cockle', or stove is installed on the wall of the *ondol* room between the kitchen and the *maru*, providing a source of lighting and warmth. In the same region as the *neowa* houses there are also *gulpi* houses, which utilize *gulpi* oak bark instead of the red pine of *neowa* but follow the same internal plan.

Taiwan's Traditional Han Minnan Family Villages

Below The best-preserved example of a traditional Han Minnan settlement is Tainan's Lutaoyang Jiang village, which sits approximately 90 m (300 ft) above sea level. Houses are arranged along streets that run east–west, allowing breezes to pass through the village and cool the dwellings in the annual hot season.

Opposite top Built with a frame of timber, bamboo or concrete, buildings are mostly clad in brick and many are arranged around courtyards, which capture the prevailing wind flow.

Ping-Sheng Wu and Min-Fu Hsu

Geography/Climate and Culture

Taiwan is an Asian-Pacific island located between the Ryukyu Islands to the north and the Philippine archipelago to the south. It is about 36,000 sq km (14,000 sq miles) in area, 70 per cent of which comprises mountains or hills. Its main mountain range runs northeast–southwest, and the plains are chiefly concentrated in the west and east of the island's main, longitudinal valley. The island's climate is divided into a subtropical monsoon zone in the north-central region and a tropical monsoon zone in the south. The rainy season occupies spring and early summer, the typhoon season arrives in late summer and early autumn, and the northeast monsoon blows in during winter.

Taiwan is mainly inhabited by Austronesian aborigines, who settled there roughly 8,000 years ago, and Han Chinese, who migrated gradually from China from the 17th century onwards. Over the past four centuries, it has been ruled in part by the Netherlands (1624–62), Spain (1626–42) and the Kingdom of Tungning (1661–83), then by the Chinese Qing Dynasty (1683–1895), Japan (1895–1945) and the Republic of China on Taiwan (1945–present). The resulting diverse cultural landscapes are evident in the style and design of the island's buildings.

Building Plan/Form

Located in Tainan, southern Taiwan, the Lutaoyang Jiang Family Village is currently the largest and best-preserved traditional Han Minnan (South Fukien) settlement belonging to a single clan. Geographically, the village's building complex is located at an altitude of 82–93 m (270–305 ft) above sea level in Nansi Township. In line with Chinese feng shui concepts, the site overlooks the Youche River and perches on the slopes of Lutaoyang Mountain. In its layout, this long, axial settlement with perpendicular streets runs east to west. The Ancestral Hall of the Jiang Family, located in the centre of the settlement, is a complex of four buildings with three courtyards. The worship pavilion, public hall, shrine and ancestral hall are arrayed along the central axis from front to back. The hall is flanked by six smaller rooms on the left side and seven on the right. In front of the buildings lies a crescent-shaped lotus pond, more than 200 years old, that was used as an essential storage tank for the farm.

The annual hot season in Tainan can last up to eight months, so an important consideration to create a livable and comfortable environment was how to allow breezes to pass through settlements smoothly. As long as air can flow through each house, these dwellings can be effectively cooled. In this region, the westerly wind has the highest wind frequency in the hottest period, so it can effectively flow into squares and alleyways positioned east–west. Furthermore, the alleys, which are about 1 to 2 m (3 to 6 ft) wide, can serve to cast helpful shade in summer, enhancing the cooling effect. Most of the buildings orient themselves to the left or right of the axial Ancestral Hall of the Jiang Family, forming an overall north–south orientation for the village. Openings in their northern and southern walls – as well as underneath the roof – significantly reduce the effects of solar radiation on the living environment.

Materials

Today, about thirty households, totalling more than 100 people, live in more than 130 houses at the family village – each with three rooms. Around 60 per cent of the houses have a timber frame as their main structure; the rest have bamboo frames or concrete structures. Overall, about 81 per cent of buildings are clad in brick; the remainder chiefly comprises bamboo, mud, adobe, stucco-washed finish and concrete.

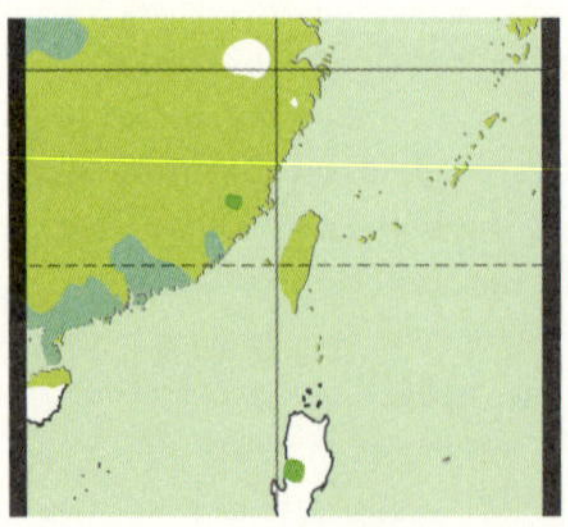

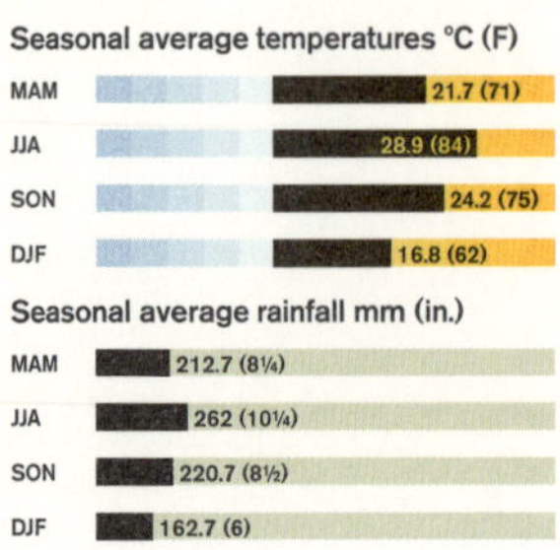

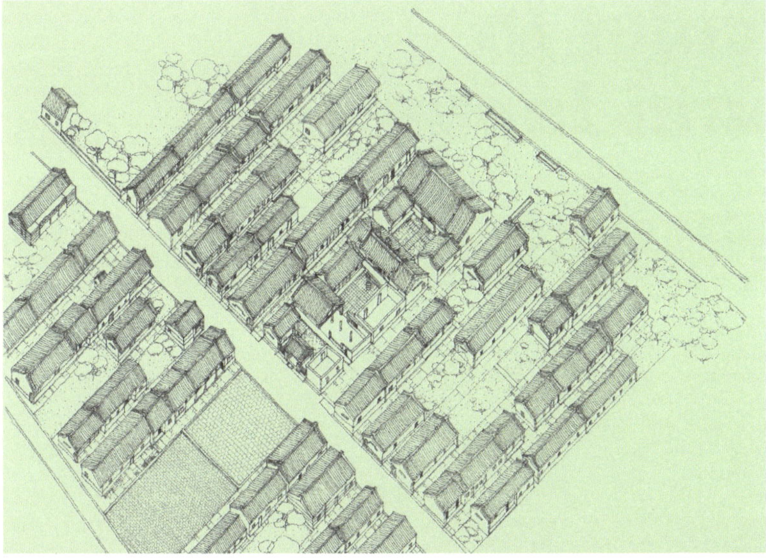

Minka Vernacular in Urban and Rural Japan

Don Choi

Building Plan/Form

Although Japan boasts many types of vernacular buildings, for architects the most important genre has been *minka*, meaning 'folk houses' or 'houses of the people'. The Japanese architect Wajiro Kon coined the term in the early 20th century in his pioneering study of ordinary Japanese houses; since then, *minka* have dominated studies of Japanese vernacular, becoming a major academic subject of their own. Built all over Japan in countless variations reflecting different climatic, cultural and economic conditions, *minka* were the houses of commoners – farmers, merchants and artisans – rather than nobles or elite warriors. Today, numerous outdoor museums, such as Shikokumura in Takamatsu City, display examples of *minka* from all over the country, attesting to the continuing popularity of these dwellings.

The great variety of *minka makes* it impossible to define a strict archetype, but most of these more ordinary dwellings shared several basic characteristics. Firstly, like almost all other Japanese buildings prior to the Meiji period (1868–1912), *minka* relied on post-and-lintel timber structural frames. The universal use of wood stemmed in part from Japan's natural environment; even today, forests cover about two-thirds of the country. Other plant materials provided architectural elements such as straw *tatami* mats and thatched roofs. The walls, which did not bear loads, usually consisted of mud plaster over bamboo (*Poaceae*) laths, although board-and-batten walls were not uncommon in mountainous regions. Secondly, *minka* generally included both raised-floor living spaces and earthen-floor workspaces. In houses built by more prosperous owners, *tatami* covered the floors of much of the raised area. Thirdly, doors in *minka* typically were sliding partitions such as *shoji*, which are lattice screens covered with paper (typically made from the pulp of *kozo*, a paper mulberry [*Morus*] tree); pivoted doors existed, but were less common. Fourthly, most *minka* included an *engawa*, or veranda, on at least one side of the house. This space could be used for both work and recreation, its projecting eaves providing protection from sun and rain. Finally – as in palaces, temples and other types of Japanese buildings – most activities inside *minka* were conducted while sitting on the floor, rather than on chairs. For example, women sewed on the floor, laying down the long swaths of cloth used in traditional kimono. Because each space could be used for multiple activities throughout the day, bedding and furniture were often kept in storage areas and brought out only when needed. This flexibility in the use of spaces has informed more recent efforts to create small, efficient residences in high-density cities such as Tokyo.

Minka can be broadly classified into rural and urban categories. Unfortunately, fires and redevelopment have destroyed the vast majority of urban *minka*, but examples from the Edo period (1603–1868) survive in small numbers in many cities. One of the largest extant groups stands in the district of Imai-cho in Kashiwara city, Nara Prefecture. Imai-cho flourished as a commercial city – first as a

Below Traditional vernacular Japanese houses, or *minka*, are seen throughout the country. Countless variations developed based on climatic, cultural and economic conditions, but all were based on post-and-lintel timber construction.

Opposite Historical *minka* found in villages such as Shirakawa-go and Gokayama, shown here, illustrate many rural *minka* features, including thatched roofing, projecting eaves, *engawa* (verandas) on at least one side of the house, and mud-plaster or board-and-batten walls. The pronounced sloping roofs seen in this village are a response to snowfall in the area.

rare independent trading town from 1575 until 1679, and then as a territory controlled directly by the Tokugawa government. The Otomura House, built for a prosperous merchant and thought to date to the second half of the 17th century, serves as a representative example of an urban *minka*. The interior comprises three zones: the wooden-floored shop area at the front, the *tatami*-floor living quarters behind the shop area and the earthen-floor workspace/kitchen. This combination of shop and dwelling was typical in the dense working-class areas of Japanese cities.

Merchant houses in Imai-cho present unpretentious but varied fronts to the street; their low eaves and relative lack of ornamentation belie the former wealth of the city. In fact, because merchants were considered to be an inferior social class, the military government of the Edo period restricted the size and decoration of their dwellings; more generally, social conventions called for restraint rather than extravagance. In response, merchants often expressed their wealth and taste through seemingly humble architectural elements. The plastered, barred windows (*mushikomado*) of the upper floor, for instance, vary in shape and detail from house to house, as do the wooden grilles (*koshi*) of the ground floor. Used in front of the translucent *shoji*, these grilles provided privacy and protection while allowing light to penetrate to the interior.

The tile roof, which provided protection against fire, also served as decoration: the patterns on the tiles and the shaping of the plaster under the eaves distinguished the Otomura House from its neighbours. Variations in secondary elements such as tiles and grilles allowed architectural expression without violating sumptuary regulations or disrupting the cohesiveness of the street. This strategy in some ways parallels the architectural codes used in some New Urbanist developments in the United States – for instance, Seaside in Florida – which allow design freedom within strict boundaries.

Rural *minka*, like their urban counterparts, developed throughout Japan in response to their climatic, economic and social contexts. Certain elements of *minka* developed in parallel in different regions, while other aspects were unique to a given place. Two examples from mountainous areas, the Shimoki House from Tokushima Prefecture and the Murakami House from Toyama Prefecture, show both underlying similarities and distinct variations. The Shimoki House, originally built in 1781 in the village of Itchuson Kijiya, is a sizable but austere example of a farmhouse from an isolated area of the island of Shikoku. In contrast, the Murakami House in the village of Kaminashi is a relatively grand example of the famous *gassho-zukuri minka* from the villages of Shirakawa-go and Gokayama in Gifu and Toyama prefectures. The term *gassho* refers to the shape of two hands brought together for prayer; Anglophones might describe the steep gables of this style as 'A-frames'. The extreme slope of the roof is a response to the heavy snowfall of the area – while most of Japan except for Hokkaido falls under the Köppen–Geiger classification for warm temperate, fully humid, hot summer, the Gokayama region is classed as snow, fully humid, warm summer. The number of extant houses and their unique qualities prompted UNESCO to designate this area as a World Heritage Site in 1995. The Shimoki House and the Murakami House, both designated Important Cultural Properties by the Japanese government, share certain basic principles of planning, materials and adaptation to their remote locations. At the same time, the latter house in particular shows distinctive features unique to its political and social context.

Perhaps the most striking general characteristic of the *gassho-zukuri minka* is the multi-storey space beneath its steep gable roof. The Shimoki House and most other rural *minka* have only one storey, which is open to the underside of the roof. In contrast, the Murakami House and other dwellings in the area boast three to five upper floors, which were used for raising silkworms. The heavy snowfall and the scarcity of agricultural land in places like Shirakawa-go and Gokayama meant that agriculture alone was often insufficient to support a household, and residents turned to sericulture for additional income. The large scale of many of the *gassho-zukuri* dwellings demonstrates the success of this strategy – silk was traded for farming implements and other non-local goods, and even provided rare cash income. The multiple upper levels also create the most distinctive aesthetic element of *gassho-zukuri* houses – the extremely tall gable with several rows of windows that modulate light and air for the silkworms. This combination of residential, agricultural and industrial functions would seem surprising in many 21st-century settings – for instance North American suburbs, where housing tends to be segregated from other types of buildings. However, the growing population of people who work at home – in particular, as a response to the coronavirus pandemic – suggests that the demand for multi-function dwellings may be increasing.

In terms of planning, both of these houses demonstrate similar principles, although the Murakami House is larger and more complex. Earthen-floor areas were used for cooking, agricultural work and storage, while raised-floor

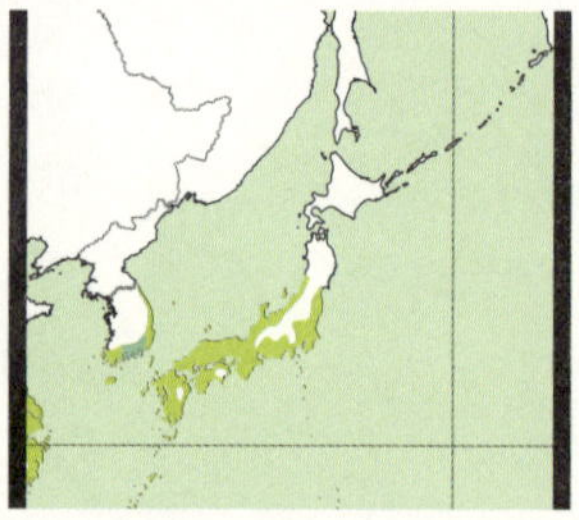

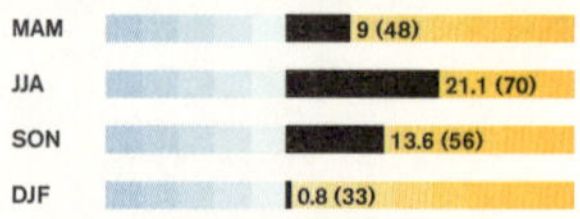

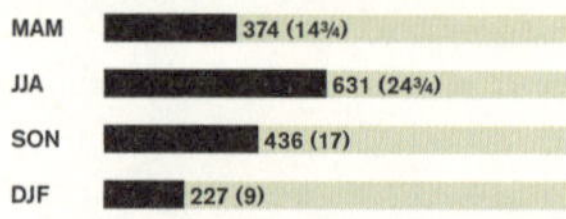

Above Having escaped fires and other dangers of the city, the Otomura House in the Imai-cho district of Kashiwara city is an exceptionally well-preserved example of an urban *minka*.

Opposite *Minka* generally included both raised-floor living spaces and earthen-floor workspaces. In houses built by more prosperous owners, *tatami* covered the floors of much of the raised area. Doors in *minka* typically were sliding partitions such as *shoji* (lattice screens covered with paper).

Opposite top Connections between *minka* roof joints were made with ropes and cords, as seen here. Vines and saplings found locally were used for cords, and straw and linden (*Tilia*) bark for ropes.

Opposite bottom left *Minka* roofs are thatched using locally available materials. Thatch is a good roofing material in temperate climates because it provides effective insulation, is lightweight and can be readily harvested.

Opposite bottom right Massive overhead beams retain the contours of the trees from which they are hewn and allow builders to take advantage of 'imperfect' timber. These irregularities carry through to the interior effect, as seen in this *minka* farmhouse.

sections were used for living spaces. The comparative wealth of the owners of the Murakami House is indicated by the large number of rooms, the extensive use of *tatami* and the presence of a formal *shoin*-style room (drawing room). In contrast, the Shimoki House contains only two raised-floor areas, both floored in wood rather than *tatami*. In both dwellings, sliding screens separate interior rooms from each other, and sliding *shoji* and *amado* (solid wooden shutters) close openings to the exterior. Both houses also feature an *engawa*, which adjoins major interior spaces on the south side for light and warmth.

Materials and Construction Techniques

In both the Shimoki and the Murakami houses, several characteristics of the structure and roof demonstrate adaptations to local conditions. Firstly, except for the columns, many of the wooden structural members are only roughly finished. For example, the massive overhead beams retain the contours of the original trees. This reduced the need for skilled carpenters, who were scarce in remote regions, and allowed builders to take advantage of 'imperfect' timber. A pine tree growing on a mountainside will typically curve, as the trunk emerges perpendicular to the slope and then bends towards the vertical. In many rural *minka*, these curved beams, called *chona-bari*, create an arch-like effect as they curve upward from the exterior wall.

Today, the unique shape of each beam is particularly striking within the modern context of standardized milled lumber. In fact, as designers seek ecologically sound and architecturally expressive materials, they often choose to reuse wooden beams and columns; there is a growing market for material recycled from dismantled *minka*.

In comparison with the massive *chona-bari*, the members of the steeply sloped roof structures in the Shimoki House and Murakami House are surprisingly small. In fact, in remote settlements such as Itchuson Kijiya and Gokayama, trained carpenters often constructed only the ground-floor structure, leaving the roof to the occupants and local residents. Small rafters were far easier to obtain than the large ground-floor beams, and could be found without difficulty from the surrounding forest. In addition, although the ground-floor framework relies on precisely cut joinery, connections between roof members are made with ropes and cords, allowing almost anyone to participate in construction and repair. Vines and saplings were used for cords, and straw and linden (*Tilia*) bark for ropes. Both the Shimoki and Murakami houses were roofed in thatch, a lightweight material that provides good insulation; *susuki*, or *Miscanthus sinensis*, was the most common type. Thatch requires frequent replacement, and historically reroofing was a communal task: the village would gather to quickly dismantle, repair and replace the small roof timbers and the thick layers of thatch.

This use of unskilled labour suggests an alternative to the conventional roles of architect and user. Architects in developed nations generally see buildings as products to be designed and constructed for a client; the building owner typically has little role in the actual construction of a house. In contrast, many *minka* were maintained and partially constructed by their occupants using low-tech methods.

The basic principles of planning and structure seen in the Shimoki and Murakami houses can be seen all over Japan. However, the Murakami House and other buildings within the Gokayama UNESCO World Heritage Site show unique responses to the social, economic and political situation. For example, the Murakami House includes a highly unusual addition: a pit for producing saltpetre (potassium nitrate), one of the components of gunpowder. In Japan at the time, the method for producing gunpowder was a jealously guarded secret; in order to keep its activities hidden from rival clans, the Kaga Clan chose the isolated villages of Gokayama as its production site. The relative lack of arable land also made saltpetre production attractive to local farmers hoping to supplement their income.

Like vernacular buildings in many other places, the rural *minka* of Japan offer general lessons about how builders and occupants can exploit limited resources. For example, the use of local, 'imperfect' materials such as the curved *chona-bari* beams now resonates with architects who wish to create expressive buildings that speak of their unique location. The involvement of the occupants and local residents in the building and maintenance of rural *minka* also suggests an alternative model of design and construction that positions each building not as an independent entity but as part of a shared environment. At a time when many cities are becoming increasingly privatized, these farmhouses are reminders that architecture can engage communities in many ways.

In recent decades, many of Japan's vernacular buildings have continued to offer inspiration for architects looking for alternatives to modern, industrial materials. Kengo Kuma, for instance, adopted forms and materials from farmhouses in his 2000 Takayanagi Community Center, as did Hiroshi Naito for his 1992 Sea Folk Museum in Toba city. Other architects, such as Terunobu Fujimori, use techniques and forms inspired by the vernacular in new construction. For example, the cracked and roughly finished forked column in the Coal House (2008) suggests the aged and irregular timbers of rural *minka*.

CONTINENTAL

Equirectangular projection. Scale 1: 70 000 000

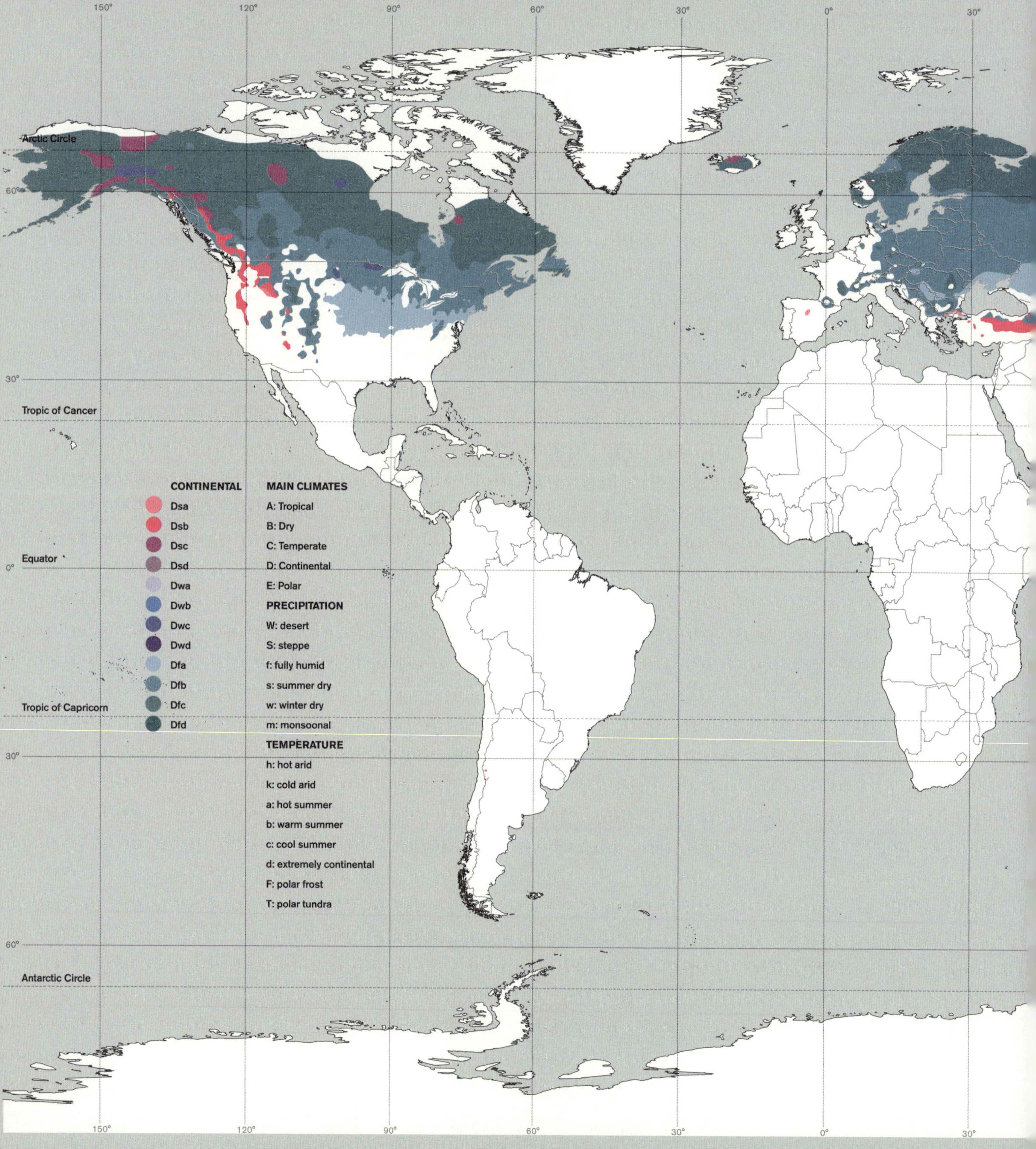

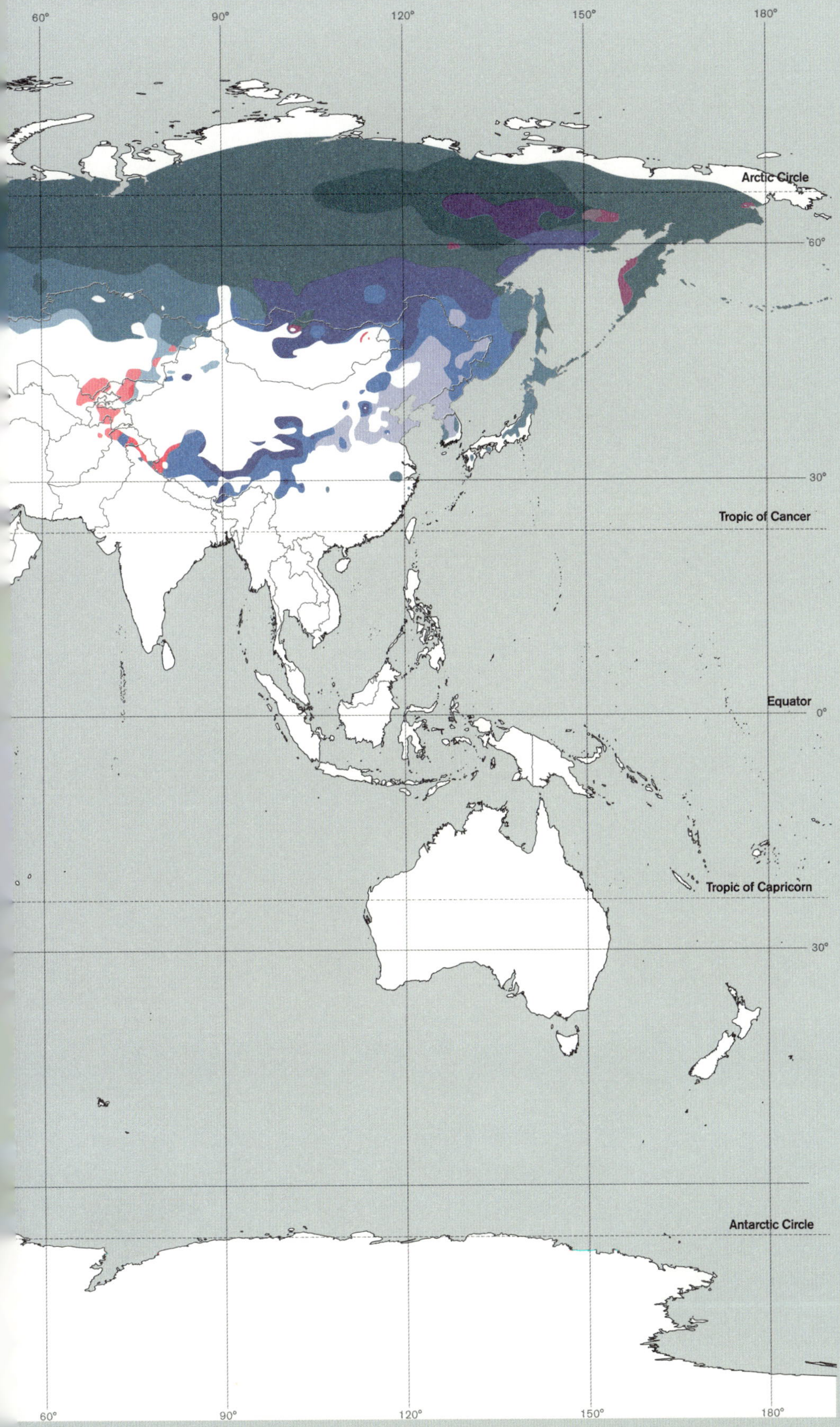

The moist continental climates, type D, are characterized by warm to cool summers and cold winters. The average temperature of the warmest month exceeds 10°C (50°F) and that of the coldest month drops below -3°C (26°F). Winters are severe, with snow, winds and cold temperatures.

These climate regions are controlled by large land masses. Found at latitudes 40–60°, they occur almost exclusively in the northern hemisphere – across much of Canada, Alaska, Scandinavia and Siberia. In the southern hemisphere, the almost complete absence of land at 40–60° means this climate zone exists only in some highland locations. The larger ocean area in this latitudinal band moderates temperatures.

The threshold temperature of -3°C (26°F) marks the southern limit of persistent snow cover in winter; while 10°C (50°F) represents the minimum temperature required for tree growth. These regions therefore experience a great deal of snow that stays on the ground for extended periods, but also have enough summer warmth to support the growth of trees. Forests tend to thrive within this climate zone.

Seasonal temperature contrasts are large. Winters tend to be cold, with very cold or mild spells brought about by periodic intrusions of air from Arctic or tropical areas.

The changeable nature of weather in all seasons is a characteristic feature of the climate. This is especially the case in areas such as the eastern United States and Canada, where there is largely an absence of topographic barriers to limit exchange of air masses between high and low latitudes.

Mean temperatures are typically below freezing from one to several months and the frost-free season varies from less than 150 to 200 days per year. High temperatures in summer typically average between 21 and 22°C (60 and 71°F) during the daytime, while the average temperatures in the coldest month are generally far below -3°C (26°F). Precipitation tends to occur throughout the year. In winter this tends to be derived from frontal storms and, in summer months, also from convective showers when maritime tropical air pushes northward behind the retreating polar front. The winter snow may be associated with high winds from intense storm systems, which can lead to blizzards.

These regions can be subdivided based on annual precipitation – whether humid continental (500–1,000 mm [20–40 in]) or subpolar (less than 500 mm [20 in]), with further distinctions in summer temperatures related to continentality. This has implications for the humidity, length of seasons and the number of frost-free days – all of which have a major impact on vegetation. When winters are severe and summers are short and cool, the climate is classed as subpolar.

Culture and Seasonal Variation in Continental Climates

Continental-climate vernacular architecture is, in essence, a story of timber and the construction of shelters predominantly in forests or agricultural land connected to forests. In ingenious ways, people developed methods of living in and understanding a large area dominated by trees, and learned how best to use the abundant timber and earth resources for construction.

A continental climate requires focus not only on resources adaptation and lifestyles but also on seasonal change. In North American forests the predominant species were cedar and spruce, whereas across the vast terrains of Russia pine, larch and fir were used for building structures and cladding. One building would often use several species for various elements of a single construction. Isolators were mud, bark and turf.

The response to seasonal change has been manifested through temporary structures such as tents and wigwams, connected to fishing and the grazing of animals. Summer houses would have been constructed, at certain times, close to rivers in order to catch a cool breeze, and winter houses were built in the forest in order to benefit from the shelter the trees offered from strong winds. Log construction is a predominant architectural form across the entire continental climate, from the western North American subarctic reaching all the way across to eastern Russia and south to Tasmania. The internal planning of these settlements across regions represented the social and hierarchical structure of their various societies.

The cultural identity of many continental regions manifested itself in ornamentation as well as the use of colour and timber detailing. The Northwest Coast vernacular of North America has fascinating large-scale totem poles, beautifully carved with representations of crest images showing mythic beings; similar patterns were often painted across entire building elevations. Across the Pacific Ocean, thousands of kilometres away, a different ornamentation can be found in New Zealand embracing the identity of Maori cultural storytelling. Scandinavian vernacular, as well as Russian, embraced cultural influences from Europe. In Sweden, Baroque-period stylistic impacts are related to use of vivid colours, whereas Finnish 'Falu red', applied to building elevations, uses red-ochre paint comprised of a natural pigment found in the earth. Ornamentation and the use of colour, as well as refined timber detailing, demonstrated the need for a manifestation of cultural identity. It might be that the isolation of some of these communities enabled, through the centuries, the development of distinct patterns, languages and customs away from foreign cultural influences, and protected their cultural sovereignty.

Several factors impacted on and influenced these indigenous communities' practices and customs. One related to technology transfer and the introduction of various tools for timber cutting – from the axe, handsaw, motor saw and laser cutting to CAD-CAM technologies. Stylistically speaking, mechanization expelled ornamentation; refined, handmade detailing gave a way to mass production, with the loss of timber craftsmanship and knowledge that is now seldom transferred to the younger generation. Industrialization has also impacted on the unique and individual character of indigenous communities across the entire continental-climate region. The import of Westernized solutions brought into question the character of dwellings developed through centuries, and this process manifested itself not only in technology but also in town planning. Finnish 'village and church' traditional urban typologies have, for instance, been replaced by modern town-planning principles and become 'mini-towns', highlighting a global problem of uncontrolled urbanization.

Left Buildings of timber are often found in regions with continental climates, where trees are usually abundant.

Indigenous Dwellings of America's Subarctic and Northwest Coast

Aldona Jonaitis

Geography/Climate

What is architecturally fascinating about North America's subarctic and Northwest Coast is the enormous contrast between how the different peoples of the region lived, and consequently how different their architecture was. This is hardly surprising, since the environments of each area differ so greatly.

The subarctic extends west to east from interior Alaska and British Columbia to Labrador, and between the prairies to the south and the Eskimoan lands to the north. Inhabitants experience short, warm summers and long, often brutally cold winters. It is frequently colder and more snowy in the subarctic than along the Bering Sea and Arctic Ocean coasts.

A range of mountains extending roughly north-northwestward separates the continental subarctic from the more lush and temperate Northwest Coast. This region of southeast Alaska, and all of coastal British Columbia, enjoys a relatively mild climate and abundant rainfall.

Materials

Trees tend to be shorter and more spindly in the subarctic than farther south, limiting their usefulness for building. Therefore, although some log cabins were erected, dwellings often comprised tents and wigwams framed with thin trees and covered with skins and other easily available materials. Seasonally, the subarctic people had to move frequently to obtain game; therefore they needed light, easily transportable housing materials that could be erected quickly.

Forests of cedar (*Cedrus*) and spruce (*Picea*) thrive in the Northwest Coast region, providing plentiful timber for building. Cedar, an easily split wood, was the material of choice for houses except in the northernmost region, where they do not grow; there, spruce was more common. Northwest Coast buildings were large, permanent, often elaborately decorated structures that housed several nuclear families. Unlike the minimalist and functional dwellings of the subarctic, Northwest Coast houses were symbolically rich – embodying social order, economic structure and aesthetics – and represent excellent examples of buildings that express cultural values.

Below Great climatic variation in the North American region shapes equally diverse architectural expression, from the hide huts of Alaskan Inuit families (left) to the timber villages of the Native American Haida with characteristic totem carvings (right).

Opposite The American Northwest Coast provides a lush and materially rich environment to draw on, with thriving forests of cedar and spruce creating an abundant supply of timber for building.

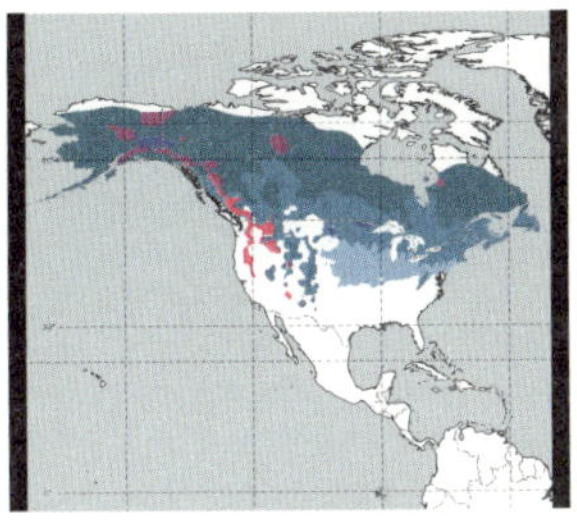

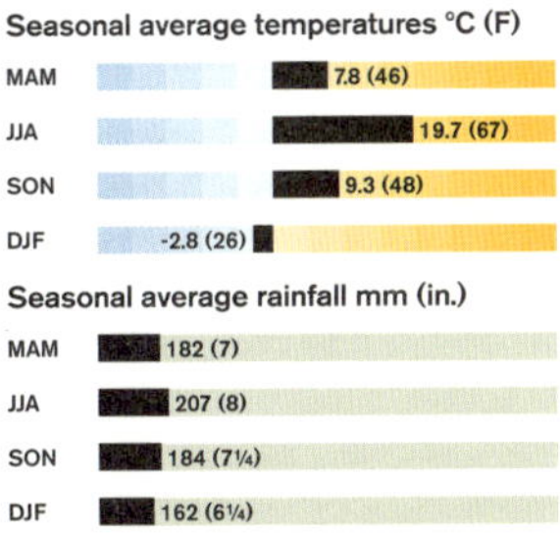

Opposite top Traditional tipis made of hides and supported by a circular or oval arrangement of timber poles are often used by indigenous Indian tribes such as the Cree. These relatively mobile dwellings allow for seasonal relocation.

Opposite bottom Framed with logs and covered with sod, sand and silt, the semi-subterranean houses found near the Bering Sea and Arctic Ocean provide well-insulated interiors, large enough to accommodate up to three families.

Right Slavey peoples created log cabins in a long A-frame shape constructed from thin branches sealed with a variety of materials, such as moss or earth. A central internal fire was used to heat the relatively small space quickly.

Building Plan/Form and Construction Techniques

The Subarctic

Subarctic structures were built to accommodate environment and lifestyle. Aboriginal residents of the subarctic – who fall into two linguistic groups: the Algonquians in the east and the Athabascans in the west – were relatively egalitarian nomadic hunters and fishermen who lived in small bands and, for the most part, had no permanent settlements. They followed seasonal rounds and lived in different places during the summer and winter. Those who exclusively hunted game such as moose, caribou and smaller mammals needed to be the most mobile and therefore had the simplest dwellings – conical and dome-shaped lodges covered with available materials such as hides or bark. In Interior Alaska, spawning salmon swim up rivers from the Pacific Ocean, providing a somewhat more predictable source of food. As a result, some Athabascans of the region maintained a more sedentary lifestyle and built relatively more complex structures. Nevertheless, this food source was not as abundant as those on the Northwest Coast (see below), and needed to be supplemented by game. As a result, even the most permanent Alaskan Athabascan villages were temporary compared with those of the Northwest Coast.

Of central importance to life in this harsh climate was – and still is – keeping warm during the long winters. Many of the subarctic dwellings mentioned here were not large, but they held more than one family, who together created body heat. At the same time, they were sufficiently small that one or two fires could provide adequate warmth. Insulation in the form of furs and skins for the sides of houses, snow banks built half or two-thirds of the way up the outside of structures, and spruce boughs covered with furs on the floors all contributed to the comfort of these dwellings. In some areas, buildings were semi-subterranean, another way of building warmer structures.

Conical lodges, much like tipis, could be sizable – as was the case of those belonging to the Woods Cree, who live from western Manitoba to Alberta. They placed in the ground between thirty and forty poles of 5–6 m (16–19 ft) in length, in a circle or oval, and lashed them at the top. Sewn-together hides of moose or caribou, bark, brush or even pieces of turf covered this framework, leaving a hole for smoke to exit. Depending on the season, the Cree erected these conical lodges in different locations: during the summer they were situated along rivers or lakeshores, which created breezes to keep the mosquitos at bay, while in the winter they were built in the forests for protection against wind.

Some subarctic people made log cabins. For example, the Slavey of the Great Slave Lake region in the Northwest Territories built 6 m (20 ft) long rectangular A-frame structures. They used the thin logs available in the region, which they sealed with brush, snow, mud, earth or moss. The central ridgepole, supported by posts at either end, was about 3 m (10 ft) off the ground. Spruce boughs created a roof with a rectangular opening for a smoke hole. The low ceiling and thorough sealing of spaces between the logs provided an adequately insulated house that could be heated quickly with a central fire.

Residents of villages closer to the Alaskan Eskimoan peoples of the Bering Sea and Arctic Ocean coasts borrowed from them the idea of a semi-subterranean house with a tunnel entrance. During autumn, winter and early spring, the Koyukon of the Upper Yukon and Koyukuk rivers in Alaska lived in rectangular houses measuring 4.5 x 6 m (15 x 20 ft), with floors excavated to the depth of 1 m (3 ft). A tunnel entrance led from ground level down into the living space. The entire structure was framed with logs, covered with moss and sewn pieces of birch bark, and steeply banked with sod, sand and silt. These houses could contain up to three nuclear families. After extensive contact resulting from the fur trade, many subarctic people moved into permanent villages, where most lived in rectangular log cabins with pitched roofs.

Today, as is the case with so many aboriginal people around the world, subarctic groups live in buildings, some of them log cabins, indistinguishable from those of non-natives. But their indigenous architecture is not entirely forgotten. Compared with the situation on the Northwest Coast (see below), subarctic communities have relatively few old-style buildings. One exception to this is Aanischaaukamikw, the Cree Cultural Institute in Ouje-Bougoumou, Quebec. This building was inspired by the Cree indigenous lodge, a transportable structure in which poles placed along each side of a rectangular floor plan joined or crossed each other along a central ridgepole.

Some, such as the prototypes of this wooden building, had curved roofs and rounded ends. Like the conical lodges, these structures were covered with hides or bark.

The Northwest Coast

The Northwest Coast is more temperate than the subarctic, and its abundant salmon runs – far larger than those of the Alaskan Athabascan regions – provide a dependable and easily obtainable source of food. During the summer, families stayed at camps harvesting and preserving the fish that swam upriver in vast numbers to spawn. In the winter, they returned to villages of large plank houses lined up along beaches. These Northwest Coast winter villages were permanent, although sometimes families removed planks from their homes to use at summer fish camps.

Northwest Coast society was hierarchical. Among some groups, villages, and even houses within a village, were ranked, with the highest-ranking structures usually situated centrally. Individuals within houses were also ranked, with the highest-ranking man considered the house chief. The foundation of these hierarchies was wealth-based on both tangible and intangible property, owned corporately by individual houses. Tangible property included fishing streams, berrying lands, hunting areas and the houses themselves. Intangible property took the form of songs, dances, myths, house names and stories explaining the history of clan property. The most visible signifier of wealth was the crest, a mythic being that, in the past, had granted tangible or intangible property to a family ancestor. Crest images appeared on painted screens, carved posts, clothing, ceremonial regalia, and decorated boxes, spoons and dishes.

Northwest Coast architecture was inseparable from wealth and status, for each house embodied the history and prestige of the extended family who lived within. Abundant artworks displaying crest images filled many of these dwellings, and sometimes appeared on their façades to reinforce their meaning. At its completion, the extended family hosted a great potlatch – a splendid several-day affair of feasting, dancing, orating and gift distribution, during which the family's tangible and intangible property was presented and validated.

These rectangular structures held several related nuclear families, and often more than fifty individuals lived in the same house. In the 19th century, houses averaged 15 by 17 m (49 x 55 ft). In the north, pitch-roofed houses dominated. These had four supporting posts, often carved with family crests; an excavated central floor; and one or two tiers ascending from it to ground level. Floors were made of wooden planks covered with woven bark mats. Nuclear families lived on the uppermost wooden platform in cubicles separated by stacks of boxes, screens or mats. In prehistoric times, the entrance to the house was through a relatively small oval opening reached by steps. This arrangement served to protect the inhabitants, since planks set up inside could prevent entrance by enemies (later these were replaced by Western-style doors). In some Tlingit houses in southeast Alaska, a large painted screen at the rear separated the public space from that in which the highest ranking individual and his family lived; access to that space was through an orifice of the crest animal depicted upon the screen.

Exterior decoration of houses differed according to region. In some areas, such as that of the Tlingit, house exteriors were undecorated. In other areas, great attention was paid to presenting crests as publicly as possible. For example, during the 19th century, the Haida of Haida Gwaii, an archipelago previously called the Queen Charlotte Islands, constructed magnificent cedar-plank houses along beaches; some contained poles attached to the façades, with the house entrance through a hole in the lowermost animal or mythic being depicted thereon. Memorial poles and mortuary poles created 'forests of totem poles', which never failed to impress visitors. Further south, on Vancouver Island, the Kwakwaka'wakw vividly

Below The shed-style longhouses of the Salish people on the Northwest Coast drew on ready supplies of timber and their coastal location. Ranging in width from 6 to 18 m (20 to 60 ft) and theoretically able to extend as long as the landscape allowed, the homes gave shared space for multiple families, each separated by a partition.

Opposite top Examples of Haida housing are found at the University of British Columbia's Museum of Anthropology (left) while the best-preserved remaining example of ancient Haida buliding is at Gwaii Haanas, Haida Gwaii (right). This UNESCO World Heritage Site includes elaborately carved totem poles denoting memorial or mortuary markings.

Opposite bottom Abundant, reliable sources of salmon meant settlements of Northwest Coastal people were largely permanent. Plentiful, too, was timber, and the rectangular homes of plank construction, such as the home of Nathan Jackson at Saxman, reflect the widely available building material.

Opposite and below The clans of Northwest Coast societies expressed their strong hierarchy in the arrangement and size of homes – the most important were centrally located and large – as well as through crest motifs. The latter were highly visible and appear on painted screens, carved posts, decorative domestic objects and, most dramatically, the façade of longhouses.

painted their house façades with images of mythic beings associated with the inhabitants.

The Salish people of southern British Columbia and Puget Sound constructed the other type of Northwest Coast architecture: the shed-roof house. Roofs sloped from 5.5 m (18 ft) high in front to 2.75 m (9 ft) at the rear. Instead of a central area around which nuclear families lived, as in the north, in the south, nuclear families lived in sections of the shed-roof houses, separated from each other by plank partitions. These dwellings ranged in width from 6 to 18 m (20 to 60 ft), and were sometimes twice as much in length. In principle, those houses could be built as long as terrain allowed, and held a good number of nuclear families. An early 19th-century explorer, Simon Fraser, described one such house in the region around Vancouver, British Columbia, as being 640 feet long, 60 feet wide and 18 feet high (195 x 18 x 5.5 m). Unlike the ostentatious displays of crests in the north, interior decorations in Salish houses were fewer and tended towards the minimal.

When settlers began arriving on the Northwest Coast in the mid-19th century, they found such communal living appalling. Missionaries, in particular, encouraged native people to live in single-family houses, which, by the late 19th century, most were doing. After the 1960s, Northwest Coast First Nations, like other aboriginal people worldwide, began constructing old-style buildings – in this case, plank houses – for ceremonies and events. In 1963, the Kwakwaka'wakw of Alert Bay, British Columbia, built the first 'Big House' on tribal land; fire destroyed that original building in 1997, and a new structure opened in 1999. This house is used for *potlatches* and other ceremonies, such as the opening of exhibitions at the nearby U'mista Cultural Centre.

Traditional structures also draw tourists. In Saxman Native Village, a few kilometres from Ketchikan, Alaska, visitors can enter a large plank house built in the 1990s, where Tlingit performers sing, dance and explain their culture. Gracing its façade is a painting of the Beaver, the most cherished crest of the chiefly family whose clan house once stood near this site. Tlingit master artist Nathan Jackson painted the façade and carved the two posts that stand in front of the house.

Some communities are even more ambitious in their endeavours to architecturally reconstruct their history. In 2007, the community of Skidegate, British Columbia, with assistance from the provincial and federal governments, opened the Haida Heritage Centre at Kay Llnagaay. Here, several cedar-plank houses line a beach – much as they did 150 years ago before Euro-American settlement disrupted their culture – but instead of being the residence of an extended family, each building serves a different purpose: a greeting house, a museum, a performance space, a restaurant, a canoe house and a carving facility. In this case, and in other places where colonialism eliminated so many traditions, indigenous-style buildings have become important signifiers of contemporary aboriginal and cultural sovereignty.

Turf, Timber and *Skjelter* Construction in Norway

Below and opposite top Buildings formed of logs with roofs of turf capitalize on the resources available in Norway and have recently become more popular thanks to their ecological and thermal benefits.

Opposite bottom Homes and byres would be constructed using logs; less important structures employed post construction – seen in the upper level of this two-storey structure. A particular Nordic variant seen in the building at left is *skjelter*: vertical weatherboards placed in grooved sills and top plates.

Gisle Jakhelln

Geography/Climate

Norway forms the western part of Scandinavia. Its long, rugged coastline is broken by deep fjords and thousands of islands. This coastline faces the North Atlantic Ocean and the Barents Sea.

The Gulf Stream and prevailing westerly winds give Norway higher average temperatures and more precipitation than expected at such northern latitudes. Inland, there is less precipitation than on the coast. The northernmost part of the country has a maritime subarctic climate. Its four seasons are very distinct.

Materials

With its large forests, Norway has a tradition of building in timber, with wood used structurally as well as for cladding. Its vernacular buildings are adapted to the aforementioned weather conditions with a wide variety of building types.

Turf as a roof covering has a long tradition in Norway, reaching back to Neolithic times. It is still a living tradition, although less used now than 100 years ago. However, the use of turf has recently been revived because of the excellent ecological qualities of this material.

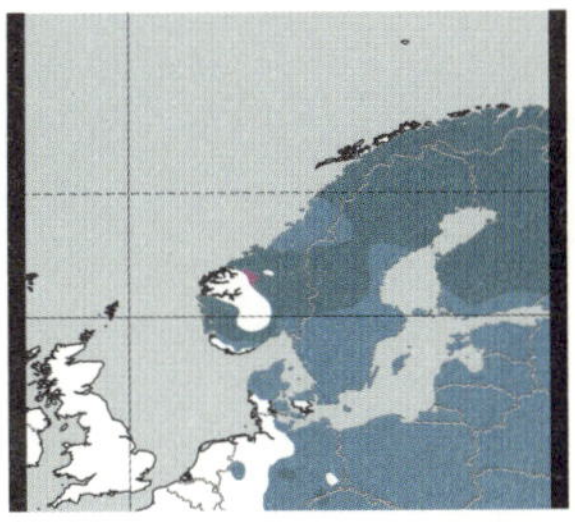

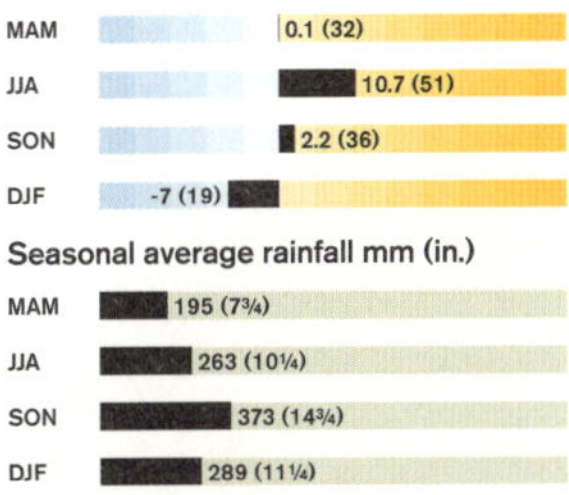

Opposite top Traditional farm dwellings are long, narrow structures that are always oriented west–east to align with the prevailing wind. Determined by the length of timber, the gabled ends dictate the house width. Interiors follow a typical three-room plan.

Opposite bottom Providing excellent thermal insulation but little structural strength, the harvested bog blocks used for turf-roofed houses are supported by a primary construction of timber.

Right Norwegian *gamme* are indigenous dome-shaped structures usually built of birch and clad in turf. Materially and formally, the low-humped abode is well suited to bitter winter temperatures.

Construction Techniques

Log construction gives better thermal insulation than the older post construction with its thin board cladding. The log wall boasts a minimum of 120 mm (5 in) of massive wood – coastal examples normally adding wooden boards as protection against the rain. This construction resists penetrating wind, as the compression produced by the logs' weight yields tight connections. Log construction was used for rooms for living and for the byre, where the cows could keep warm during the nights and through the winter.

Post construction was used where there was no need for a warm room. It affords the possibility of having different types of cladding: impenetrable, or open for cross ventilation. Post construction requires less wood and is a cheaper way of building than log construction.

Building Plan/Form

The Nordland House

The traditional layout of a house in northern Norway is based on a three-room plan with the building's axis running west–east, following the prevailing winds. The house might be extended lengthwise with a repetition of this layout, leading to quite a long structure. The Nordland house is therefore a relatively long, narrow one-and-a-half to two-storey timber construction with the room layout and siting taking into consideration the climatic conditions: sunlight, prevailing winds and snow accumulation. The width of the house is around 5 m (16 ft), the length of a log. The rooms span the width of the house, and have windows on both sides. Smaller rooms are partitioned off from larger ones. The entrance door is never on the gable wall.[1]

The Nordland house demonstrates the ideal of an energy-saving design, in the manner of a 'passive' house: rooms laid out with 'buffer zones' against the chilling winds, windows facing the warmth of the sun and no windows in the gables in order to protect against rain from the west and cold winds from the east. Energy saving was the basis for all these vernacular buildings, for their construction phase as well as for the later stages of maintenance and reuse. Today's designers could learn from these basic points for energy-efficient buildings and sustainability.

The Byre

Among Norwegian farm buildings, the byre might be a separate building or a separate log-constructed room within a larger barn realized in timber post construction.

The Boat Shed

The boat shed (*naust*) is another building type used on the Norwegian coastal farm. Quite often the *naust* is built with *skjelter* construction, a mixture of log and post techniques, with vertical boards. *Skjelter* construction is widely used for storage buildings and boat sheds as it gives good cross ventilation as well as easy access.

Gamme

The traditional Sàmii house is the *goahti* (Norwegian: *gamme*), a small dome-shaped timber structure completely covered with turf. The most common is the *beallje-goahti* (Norwegian: *buesperre-gamme*), in which naturally grown, curved birch (*Betula*) trunks used as wall posts converge as rafters at the top of the roof. A supporting 'purlin' is placed halfway up the wall and thin branches are used as support for the turf cladding, the branches placed vertically for the wall and horizontally for the roof. The dome shape is perfect for energy saving in extreme weather with snow and wind.

Contemporary Norwegian Buildings

Energy saving is the basis for all these vernacular buildings, from construction to maintenance and reuse. The chill factor of the wind, the warmth of the sun and the use of local materials are traditional historical knowledge for application in the future. Contemporary Norwegian architects are in the process of understanding this heritage more deeply and the critical climatic elements it involves.

Swedish Homes of Coniferous and Deciduous Timber

Lena Palmqvist

Materials

Timber has been the basic material in rural house construction in Sweden, and the country's regional differences followed the extension of coniferous and deciduous forests. The knowledge of building a house was transferred from generation to generation by watching and learning.

Construction Techniques

The log cabin has a longstanding tradition in Sweden's coniferous forest regions. The most important part of corner timbering (*knuttimringsteknik*) is the use of notched logs that lock the timber rows together. The external junction formed by alternate notched logs jutting out beyond the corners has varied in shape and design between different areas of the country and over the ages. By studying the shape of the notch, it is possible to make a relatively accurate determination of the cabin's construction date.

Horizontal planking (*skiftesverksteknik*) belongs to the deciduous areas. The system has a supporting structure, using upright posts with crossbeams between the sill at the bottom and the uppermost, binding beam. The walls are filled with planks, placed horizontally between these vertical posts. These planks are loosely set, and will 'sink' as the timber dries. The horizontal-planking technique has been suitable for farm buildings but has also been used for houses, for example on the island of Gotland in the Baltic, where homes built using this technique are known as *bulhus*.

Opposite top Red-hued timber houses have long been a traditional signifier of Sweden's built heritage. Their envelope of horizontal planks covered with vertical boards painted red is predominant in areas of deciduous tree growth.

Opposite bottom left and right and below Coniferous forest regions draw on the vernacular knowledge of log cabin construction. The buildings are held in place by carefully angled notched edges of alternate jutting logs, the pattern of which varies according to locality and chronology.

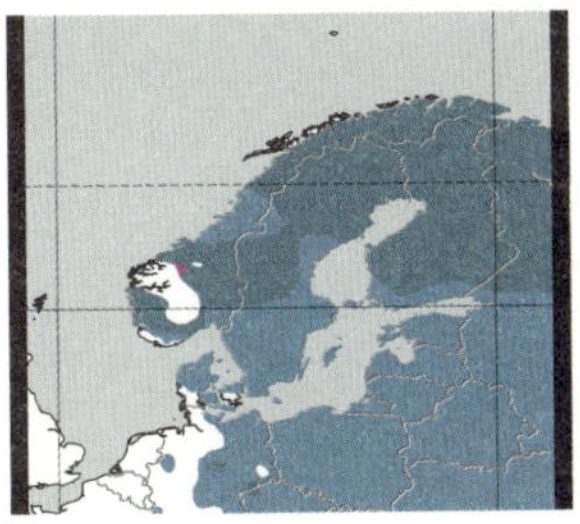

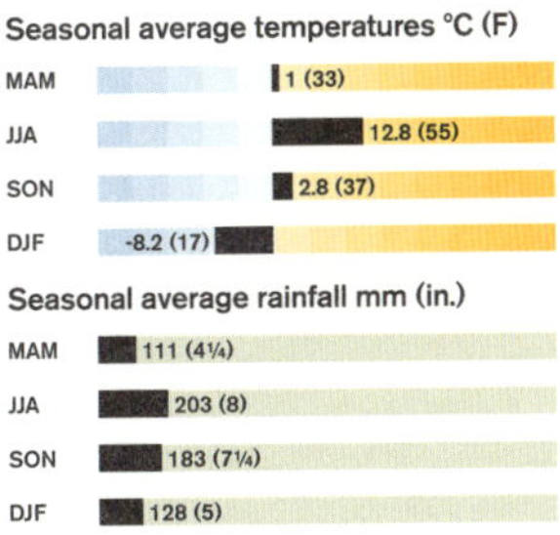

Building Plan/Form

In half-timbered houses (*korsvirkesteknik*), common in South Sweden as well as in Denmark and Germany, the timber framework also serves as supporting structure. The spaces within it are filled with laths and a mud plaster, inside and out – or alternatively with brick.

Local traditions have characterized vernacular building in Sweden as elsewhere, but the house and farm types follow both a topographical and a chronological development from one-room buildings into a four- or six-room planning layout. The single-room cottage (*enkelstuga*) with one large room, and the two-room cottage (*parstuga*), with its symmetrical design of one room on each side of the entrance, were the most significant house types between the late 16th and the early 20th century.

The emblematic Swedish colour scheme, involving red and white, is a Baroque legacy. During the 17th century, manor houses and churches were coloured red – and this was also the case with town houses. But at the beginning of the 19th century, lighter oil paints came to replace the red colour on mansion houses, and red instead gained popularity among vernacular buildings. Single- and two-room cottages have since kept the colour, commonly adorned with white framing around windows and doors.

During the 19th century, new house types were introduced with planning based on four or six rooms. In the latter part of the century, these designs became common in vernacular buildings. These new house types had, in fact, been preceded by intense propaganda stating that the older, long, narrow houses were impractical since erecting them demanded large amounts of timber, and that on top of this they were difficult to heat. The four-room plans with a central chimney stack improved heating facilities and resulted in a more practical house.

At the start of the 20th century, many Swedish dwellings were still built using corner timbering. But at the same time, it became common to cover the houses in wood panels and paint them using light oil colours in the fashion of the 19th-century mansions. That required a smooth timber structure without the protruding notches of *knuttimringsteknik*. Magazines and pattern books of the time presented housing of different sizes and designs, buildings whose façades were covered in detailed wood siding and painted in light colours. The incipient industrialization of vernacular building and the building materials now supplied by the new sawmills were prerequisites of these changes in construction practices.

Below Vernacular timber homes are in themselves usually fairly simple, with symmetrically arranged one- or two-room timber cottages the usual house type until the 19th century. After that, four- to six-room homes became the accepted norm.

Opposite Inheriting an original Baroque palette of red and white, many houses in Sweden continue the decorative tradition, with white framing around windows and doors as seen in these 19th-century farmhouse examples at Hälsingland.

1845

Log Structures and Falu Red of the Finnish Vernacular

Kirsti Kovanen

Geography/Climate

Finland is the northernmost country of the European continent. Its maritime and continental climate is moderated by the warmed air flows of the Atlantic, which means the country experiences higher temperatures than others at this latitude, though winter temperatures are still below freezing, and with abundant snowfall. The country is largely under dense forest cover and this provides a rich source of vernacular building stock.

Materials and Techniques

Historical vernacular buildings in Finland have, through a slow refining process, carried into the present traditions developed over centuries – the oldest being the application of horizontal-log construction techniques and the use of red-ochre paint.

Horizontal-log Construction

One of the oldest and most widespread building techniques in Finland is the horizontal-log structure, adopted two millennia ago from the southern and western coasts of the Baltic Sea. The technique spread with settlers. A settler's yard used to consist of rectangular buildings: rooms for living (called *tupa* or *pirtti*), for bathing (called *sauna*) and for domestic animals or storage. The image of the early Finnish settler is of a man building his house with hand tools – the imported two-pin log vice (*hirsivara*), log screws and axes – from softwood, grey stone and plants abundantly available in the forest. Moss, bark and vegetable fibres were, for example, all used for caulking and insulation.

This technique prevailed for centuries in public buildings and housing, the builders continuously refining it by elaborating the corner joints and improving finishing and decoration. In Finland, the peak of the hand-carving phase was reached around 1850. The finest examples are found among the surviving log churches built by laymen master builders.

The crucial detail of this type of massive timber structure is the corner blocking, of which many variations are known. For instance, the open-air museum of Seurasaari in Helsinki displays twelve basic forms of blocking from different regions of the country. A new tool, the handsaw, was brought into common use during the 19th century, at a time when professional log craftsmen started working, and the motor saw was added to timber builders' toolbox in the 1950s. While making the building process quicker, these saws also reduced the variety of corner details. Nonetheless, Finland's logging industry continues to refine the corner – nowadays, to suit the latest laser-cutting techniques.

Despite such developments, tree-trunk sizes have always regulated the dimensions and forms of construction members and set the dimensions of log buildings: the longest logs, and therefore walls, span a little over 9 m (30 ft). Hand-carving techniques prevailed until the 1930s, when the light timber-frame structure – adopted from western European and North American models, and better suited to mass-production needs – finally won out over the old log construction. The practice of log carving has declined since then, but not vanished – its skills are still practised, and craft masters of horizontal-log construction are still trained. Their skills are used especially for building summer houses and single-family dwellings, as well as in the conservation of historical timber structures.

Red-ochre Paint

Up to the end of 19th century, most Finnish wooden façades – especially in remote rural areas, in the eastern parts of the country and in the archipelago – remained grey, the patina of their many untreated timber surfaces. The practice of painting in red-ochre paste was applied first to public buildings and town houses; in the rural domestic sphere, only the most prominent building of the settler's yard was given this expensive and relatively rare treatment. These major buildings subsequently were the first to adopt the new lighter oil paints, and red eventually became the mark of 'economy buildings'.

Early builders' guidebooks and leaflets advertised it as a cheap 'everyman' finish that would make the landscape clean and the buildings beautiful. Especially active periods for painting in red ochre were the 1920s, when new buildings and building types spread all over the country, and again around 1950, when the advertisements inspired house owners to paint the face of the country 'clean' for the coming Olympic Games. Its use is even connected to Finnish politics. It became the common paint for workers' gathering halls at the turn of the 20th century, and later, in the 1960s, its name, *punamulta*, was adopted to describe the coalition of left-wing parties and the Agrarian Party. The basic, 'technical' ochre was mainly imported from Falun ironworks in Sweden and is now known as 'Falu red'. Finnish equivalents are made of earth pigments.

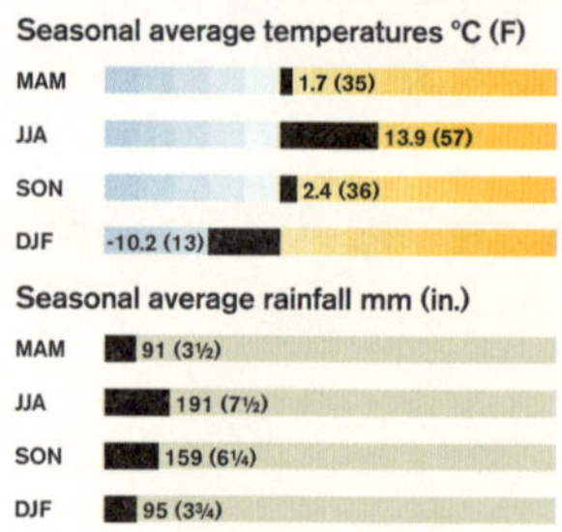

Opposite With an abundance of trees, and forests that cover much of the country, the Finnish built vernacular draws heavily on timber as its primary material source.

Opposite top, middle and bottom right Paint of red ochre now known as 'Falu red' was originally used to beautify timber structures – an expression of the country's pride. The distinctive finish has become embedded in Finland's cultural and built tradition.

Opposite top, middle and bottom left Finnish structures of timber include homes, public buildings and churches. Many of these utilize the traditional horizontal log construction with its distinctive corner-blocking detail that varies in technique across different regions and generations.

Below Buildings of timber continue to dominate Finnish architecture. As represented in these drawings, agricultural threshing barns formed exclusively of logs, and timber boathouses of Mossala on Houtskari Island, are such instances of facilities that are still in active use.

The traditions of preparation and use of red-ochre paste paint remain alive, and their development encompasses both oral and written traditions – resulting in hundreds, maybe thousands, of versions on this common old concept.

Building Plan/Form

Finland's building traditions are also seen in one of the more recent historical settlement types in the country's rural centres: the 'village with a church', whose lifespan covers five to six generations.

The 'Village with a Church'

New centres for Finland's agricultural countryside were formed between five and six generations ago as a result of legislative changes allowing trade outside towns and establishing administration for municipalities. A crossing of roads and waterways situated close to the geographic heart of a new municipality was selected to be the site for its new centre, and its focal point in the open landscape would be a church surrounded by churchyard and cemetery. The village grew next to the stone wall of the churchyard, often in a free-form, linear pattern along a winding road. Public buildings – such as municipal halls, schools and granaries – and houses for the new clergy, merchants, the pharmacist and the police, as well as the small lots and huts of the craftsmen, created a small, diverse and picturesque group of plots and buildings in the landscape.

Rural building practices were barely regulated, and followed the models of local and established traditions. The smiths and other craftsmen would build their dwellings after the pattern of the small cotters' houses, established regulations were used for the vicarage, and the merchants would design their houses to match the fashionable urban villas. Towards the end of the 19th century, handbooks for builders and designers started to be published, and common models for the new houses spread throughout the country. The model of 'villages with a church' had its heyday during the 1950s, when the diversity of services and buildings was at its height.

Regularization and urban planning had already brought signs of urban and modernist building into the villages by the 1930s, especially in the buildings of the cooperative movement. However, from the 1960s onward, new building forms typical of urban areas settled in the villages with the first multi-storeyed, standardized concrete structures. It was no longer self-evident that the church would be the focal point of the village. Soon, the integrity of these villages around the church degraded with the introduction of more large buildings and regulations similar to those of urban planning, and the villages started to resemble miniature towns. However, up until the 21st century this development has been relatively slow, and many Finnish villages have retained their historical layers. More than thirty examples of 'villages with a church' are today listed as historic areas of national importance.

Homesteads of Northern and Central Russia

Anna Yu Mainicheva

Geography/Climate and Culture

The Urals and Siberia contain several climatic zones, changing from tundra to forest steppe when moving north to south, and from mountains to lowlands and plateaus when moving from west to east through the Ural, Altai and Sayan ranges. With an area of more than 10 million sq km (3.8 million sq miles), this vast territory is inhabited by various peoples, who have shaped their own economic and cultural patterns.

Quantitatively, the Eastern Slavs, who settled in both compact and dispersed ways, dominate. The most numerous are the ethnic Russians, followed by the Ukrainians and then the Belorussians. This Eastern Slavic population is divided into two large groups, each having its own peculiar features. These are 'old settlers', the ancestors of whom settled in Siberia from the 17th to the early 19th century (the Chaldon, Kezhmar, Indigirts, and Old Believers, including the Semeyskie and Kerzhak), and 'new settlers', who migrated from the end of the 19th to the beginning of the 20th century. In turn, each group is divided into smaller subgroups. The region's non-Slavic nationalities comprise more than ninety ethnic groups, including the indigenous peoples of Siberia (the Nenets, Mansi, Khanty, Altai, Khakas, Yakuts, Buryats, Siberian Tatars, and so on), and descendants of settlers from the beginning of the 20th century (including Poles, Germans, Czechs, Hungarians, Austrians, Chinese and Jews). Every 'nation' in its locality has its own vernacular architecture – but all are predominantly made of timber.

Materials

Traditionally, timber that grew in the depth of the forest was preferred for construction as its logs were smooth and resinous, with grained wood. Timber growing on the forest edge was avoided; it was gummy and prone to rot. Russian Siberian 'old settlers' knew how to choose good wood, which grew in elevated sunny places, and avoid using trees standing in damp lowlands.

Different kinds of timber were chosen for different applications. The bases of houses and roof structures required moisture resistance – for this reason, larch (*Larix sibirica*), specially treated pine (*Pínus sylvestris*) or fir (*Picea bies* or *Picea obovate*) were used. For covering/cladding, bark of birch (*Betula pendula* Roth.) or of fir (*Abies sibirica*) was adopted. For walls, relatively light timber with ease of handling and resistance to freezing was required – pine or fir was used. Finally, fir, pine or aspen (*Populus tremula*) was employed to furnish the dwelling, because these timbers can be processed easily.

Russian peasants called larch the 'iron tree', for its strength. It was used for underfloor beams and columns at the corners of huts. In larch-rich areas, houses made entirely of this wood were common, and it was held to mask unpleasant odours. But larch can be badly processed; houses built entirely of it, it is said, 'do not breathe'. Tatars, for instance, call larch the 'devil's tree', and did not use it in their buildings.

Pine, on the other hand, was universally used by Siberians. In the hut built of pine logs, so tradition claims,

Below Simple one-room huts or *izba* built of logs were the basis of Siberian peasant dwellings. These structures were usually built of larch, fir or pine, the latter being most popular thanks to its hardy, resinous and 'breathable' qualities.

Opposite Despite encompassing around 75 per cent of Russian territory and dozens of different ethnic groups, the majority of dwellings are made from timber due to the relatively ready wood supply of a variety of species throughout the region.

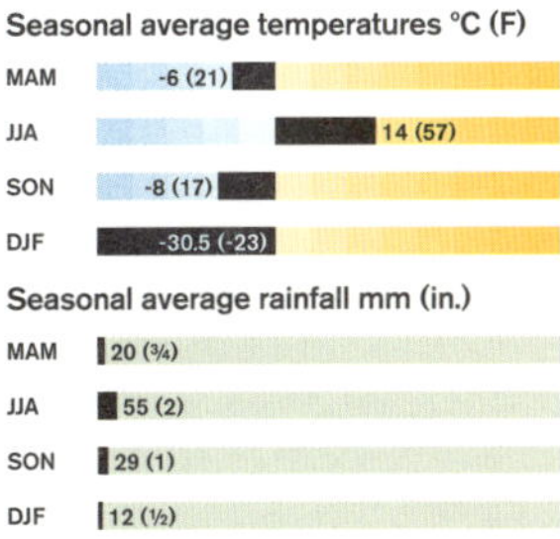

Opposite top left Pine is universally used by Siberians, despite the more than ninety different tribes settled in the area. Though different woods were used for different parts of the building, pine was typically an enduring choice and used to build structures with, as well as to craft furnishings from.

Opposite top right and bottom Elevated huts known as *evenki* built from logs provided safe storage of goods for indigenous groups. These examples built by Nenet people in the Irkutsk region of Siberia illustrate the basic raised structures that are used in nomadic camps of the Forest Nenets.

Right In contrast to 'old settlers', many of the 'new' ethnic groups chose to adapt to sites near lands suitable for hunting, agriculture or fishing. Dugout dwellings near coastal regions, for example, still relied on timber for construction but were primarily covered with turf and provided a permanent winter home for fishing families.

one can breathe easily; pine is strong and, being lighter than larch, is easier to process. Procured in winter, it was used not only for walls but also for floors and roof coverings. Pine buildings typically stand for a long time, reinforced by internal resin; a pine roof might need replacing only every fifty years. Door panels, trim, floors, benches and frames for doors and windows were also made of pine. Its disinfectant properties kept food fresh for long periods, and its odour repelled insects – helping textiles resist moth attack.

Fir was used, but fir logs had to be examined to ensure that they were not hollow. Buildings made of this timber were deemed warm and durable. Fir was considered the best option for roofing, as it would not warp when drying. Fir bark was used to cover outbuildings.

Hardwoods were used less frequently in construction than softwoods, being less durable and more susceptible to decay. Birch was used only for farm buildings and temporary structures. Log cabins built to enclose wells were made of birch, aspen or willow (*Salix alba* L.) blocks, as these did not give the water an unpleasant smell. Aspen was of little constructional use. It was known as a weak type of wood, inferior to conifers' physical and technological properties. Regarded as a 'bitter' tree, it was claimed that it would make 'a bitter house to live in'.

In the early 20th century, the number of *saman* dwellings (built of a mixture of varying proportions of clay, straw and manure) and pit-houses (homes partially buried in the ground) increased owing to the influx of new settlers to the region, who often had to construct their houses with substitute materials. However, peasants continued to build good-quality log houses, which are most suitable for local conditions. (In old settlers' settlements, the number of dwellings made of substitute materials remained insignificant.) The social reforms of the 1917 October Revolution and subsequent collectivization contributed to radical changes in the traditional peasant way of life, affecting the style of both housekeeping and dwelling types. As a result, although the advantages of traditional log-built designs are widely acknowledged despite their primitive sanitation conditions, and they are nowadays achievable with an acceptable level of improvement, they are now available only for elite housing.

Nonetheless, fire danger remains a significant drawback of wooden buildings, and the long-standing regulatory framework designed to combat it in Russia established strict limits on the construction and placement of buildings. In earlier times, an individual's choice of material and the carpentry skills generally known almost from childhood guaranteed the quality of the structure.

Construction Techniques

Accumulated knowledge about the properties of timber and its use functioned mainly on the level of daily routine – hence, the old settlers knew almost intuitively the rules and techniques of wood processing. Being a good carpenter, a peasant old settler could erect both house and household buildings almost by himself, only occasionally inviting in professionals to assist with some specific task.

Nowadays, traditional building techniques are preserved in many places despite the obstacles to timber construction outlined above. The peoples of this region possess vast knowledge about the properties of the different sorts of wood used. To obtain good-quality building materials, they worked out rules for storing and processing. Storing a small amount of wood fitted in with the natural reproduction of resources, but the appearance of sawmills in the 1930s brought a wide-scale, irreversible diminishing of wood resources, which led to poor-quality building materials being adopted.

In the Urals and Siberia, construction techniques extended to a system of building rites, which included acts that symbolically marked the beginning and the end of every stage of the building process. The idea of household spirits was also involved in these rituals. The traditions connected with the erecting and occupying of these houses are ancient and presented a relatively integrated system of prohibitions and permissions. Nowadays, only a very few people follow such traditions.

Building Plan/Form

The types and arrangement of the old settlers' homesteads correspond to agricultural and cattle-breeding patterns, with the rising role of the latter in both the taiga and forest zones. The majority of these buildings served to store and process wheat, as well as to practise handicrafts and trade. The Eastern Slav old-settler homesteads also bore the closest similarity with their Tatar equivalents. Czech homesteads, on the other hand, were smaller and differed considerably from the typical old settlers' homestead. In settlements with mixed Russian, Ukrainian and Mordovian populations, the homesteads have much in common. At the same time, the homesteads of the Mordva (as well as of the Eastern Slavs), who lived in different natural zones, differed in both number and types.

The location of a building in a homestead was dictated by ethnic traditions as much as by natural and climatic conditions. The layout of a homestead and the number of buildings in it depended, to a great extent, on the property status of the owner, poorer owners having few subsidiary buildings. Well-off families possessed developed plots, their homesteads including up to ten buildings.

Ural and Siberian Russian settlements are typified by the following types of dwelling: 'single-chamber', with one living room; 'two-part', with one living room and a porch; 'two-chamber', with two living rooms adjoining each other; 'three-chamber', with two living rooms and a porch with variants; and 'many-chamber', with three or more living rooms along with a porch and other complex forms. These may be further classified by height – from ground-based single-storeyed buildings to two-storeyed structures – and by wall materials: timber dwellings, those made of 'substitute materials', and pit-houses. Most of the wooden dwellings were made of logs. Substitute materials include *saman* and clay in combination with wooden elements. Pit-houses were made of log structures and turf layers. No houses were made of stone or brick, although a few dwellings constructed of timber with brick plinths are known. These were generally owned by wealthy members of society.

The orientation of these houses took into account wind direction and solar penetration, but was also greatly influenced by the overall layout of the settlement. Dwelling alignment was additionally linked to the tradition of forming special window apertures in the walls thanks to which occupants could trace the movement of the sun, accurately telling the hours of the day and (albeit less crucially) the turning points of the seasons. The invention of new ways of time telling – clocks and calendars – resulted in an inevitable loss of such specific knowledge, and, consequently, led to the disappearance of that tradition in the art of central Russian building.

Below Prevalent historically, the timber homes of Ural and Siberian Russian settlement were once carefully orientated in relation to wind and the diurnal path of the sun. Such vernacular homes have since dwindled, replaced by Western-style high-rise blocks.

Opposite Variation in size of Ural and Siberian Russian settlements ranged from single-chamber dwellings with a sole living room to multi-chambered one-storey (top) or two-storey (bottom) houses that include several living spaces as well as porches.

27-07-27

Wooden Folk Architecture in Western Russia

Anna Permilovskaya

Materials

Wooden 'folk' architecture is an abiding feature of Russian traditional culture. Since ancient times, timber was the nation's universal building material. Pine (*Pinus*), fir (*Pinaceae*), larch (*Larix*), cedar (*Cedrus*) and aspen (*Populus*) – each of these species had its own particular properties, colour and texture, and Russian craftsmen knew these particularities well and incorporated them into their work. Not only the timber itself was used, but also the bast, roots and bark of, for example, young birch (*Betula*) trees – in Russian, *beresta*. Although wooden buildings had shorter lives than stone-built structures, they could still stand for more than 400 years. Accordingly, Russia's folk architects valued wood highly as a building material for its abundance and cheapness, its ability to retain heat in a dwelling, its durability and its suitability for erecting structures within a short period of time and practically in any season.

Construction Techniques

Building masters managed a small amount of tools at work, the most basic of which was the axe. A skilled carpenter could make almost everything using an axe; a common saying ran: 'Let a peasant have an axe and he will fix even a clock.' For construction purposes, it was common to use cut instead of sawn wood, although the saw had been known in Russia from ancient times. Sawn boards and logs easily absorb moisture, rapidly swell and decay. With cut boards and logs the situation was quite the opposite: after the axe cuts, the pores of a log became clogged, resulting in a stabler, more inert material. Besides an axe, a decent set of carpentry tools would include a scraper for dressing logs, an adze for grooving, and a chisel and glade for punching logs and bars. Hammers, sledgehammers and line bars (a measurement tool) were also used in construction. Implements used for timber building were well hardened and sharpened. Diverse nail tools and hardware were also used but their cost was relatively high – so Russian peasants preferred building without nails, applying wooden dowels instead or using the minimum possible number of iron nails.

The greatest concentration of this timber architecture can be found in Russia's northern territory: the area comprising the present-day regions of Arkhangelsk, Vologda, Murmansk, Novgorod, Leningrad and Niznegorodskay, and also including the Kareliya and Komi republics in 'eastern European' Russian territory.

Right Based on the plentiful supply of many different kinds of timber – pine, larch, fir, cedar and aspen – the buildings of Russian folk architecture prized wooden construction, which could endure for more than 400 years and usually included elaborate detailing.

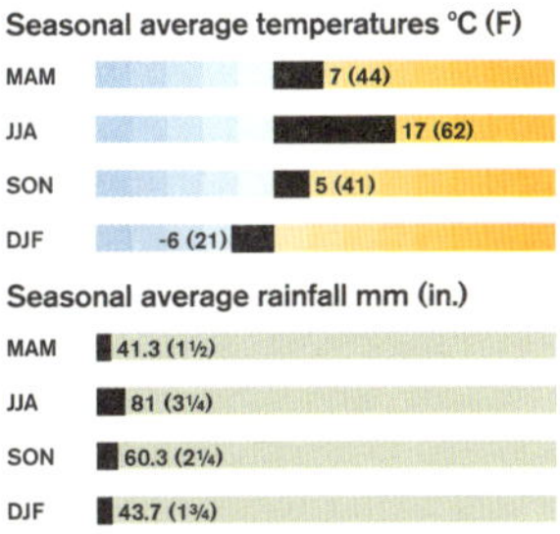

Opposite top and bottom left The ornate forms and skilled craftsmanship of Russian churches reflects the central place of Orthodox religion in the culture. This is expressed architecturally in the variety of wooden churches, such as the multidome style illustrated by the Church of the Intercession of the Mother of God in Karelia.

Opposite bottom right The *kub*-style variation, such as this Ascension wooden church from Kushereka in the Arkhangelsk region, is distinguished by its five cupolas, with duopitched roof.

Right A more ancient, simple variant on the *kub* style, seen here in the Chapel Kenozerovill, has a single centrally placed cupola set atop a duopitched roof on a square-shaped log base.

Not without reason is the Russian North referred to as 'the country of architects': its historically developed reserve of timber architecture is rightly considered the pinnacle of both Russian and world wooden architecture. The forms developed here continually influenced all other branches of Russian art for centuries. The region's Russian folk architecture encompasses residential, commercial, industrial, trade, engineering, defence and religious buildings – in settlements created, for the most part, by unknown artisans and reflecting the mindset of the Russian peasantry, whose leading ideas reflected folk orthodoxy and a mythopoeic world view. This western Russian legacy has also influenced western and eastern Siberian architecture.

Building Plan/Form

Wooden Churches

Church building was the high point of Orthodox national architecture: the church as a generic, semantically rich image of the universe occupied a central place in the Russian concept of sacral space. Wooden churches of several types spread throughout Russia: the 'four-frame type', the 'tent roof' type, the '*kub* style', the 'storeyed type' and the 'multidome'.

Four-frame-type churches are the most ancient of these wooden templates, comprising a standard four-square log structure covered with a duopitched roof. Examples of this type include the Lazarus Murom Church (end of the 14th century) on Kizhi Island in Karelia; the Church of the Deposition of the Robe at Borodava village in the Vologda region (1485); and St George's Church in Uycsovichi village, Leningrad region (1499). Tent-roof churches date from a little later; they include St Nicolas' Church, Lyavya village (1581); St George's Church in Verchina village (1672); and Dmitriy Solunskiy Church in Verhnay Uftuga village (1784) in the Arkhangelsk region. Many *kub*-style churches,' with five cupolas, remain in the Onega River basin, and on the White Sea of Pomorsky and the Karelian coast: Trinity Church, Podporozie village (1757), Transfiguration Church, Turchasovo village (1786), and Ascension Church, Kushereka village (1669) on the Onega River.

In the 17th–18th centuries, multidome temples were constructed, such as the Church of the Intercession at Anhimovo village in the Vologda region (1708, no longer extant) and the Transfiguration Church on Kizhi Island (1714). During this period, a rare, extended variant of the tent-roof church flourished: the 'tent on a cross-like barrel' type. The Odigitriya Church of Kimzha village in the Arkhangelsk region (1709) is a fine example of this model.

Wooden Chapels

These constitute one of the most striking manifestations of Russian folk architecture. Chapels – that is, churches without a sanctuary – were intended to provide a simpler service without liturgy; they served as a place of prayer meetings for people from small villages inhabited by members of a single, patriarchal family. The reasons for founding chapels in particular places were based on their typological characteristics – as places of worship, to pray for the dead, to contain burial vaults, as 'chapels of promise' or as 'ordinary' chapels. A phenomenon of the maritime culture of Pomorye was the construction of 'commercial' chapels in fishing, trapping and forestry areas on the islands of the White and Barents seas. Old Believers' chapels remained the only non-church places of worship accepted by adherents of Russia's 'old religion'. Architecturally, chapels in western Russia shared several typologies with churches of the same region – notably the 'four-frame type', the 'tent roof' type, the '*kub* style' and the 'storeyed type'.

Wooden Crosses

A further important devotional aspect of western Russian folk architecture is the tradition of wooden crosses, which has existed since at least the 11th century. Taking into account their multifunctionality, such crosses are considered monuments of architecture, sculpture, peasant writing and religion – as well as navigation markers for coastal dwellers, which were even recorded in ships' pilot charts. They are classified according to the following groups, with regard to their meaning and role: 'crosses of worship', 'crosses of promise', 'memorial type', 'lighthouse type', 'commemoration type', 'protective type' and 'crosses of thanksgiving'. Pomorye crosses, set on the coast and islands of the White and Barents seas, form a separate group. The cultural meaning of these last-named crosses also reflected Pomorye's firmly maritime culture; they formed the centre of their surrounding spaces, performing a protective and sacred mission. One last variant are the 'eight-finial crosses'. These might be located under a special canopy on columns, or in churches, chapels or chapel-barns.

Wooden Houses

The western Russian peasant's house formed part of a farmstead-based dwelling complex, which constituted one of the main ways of protecting against the environment in this cold climate. It had its own architectural and structural peculiarities, typology and decoration, distinct from those of the region's churches and chapels. The 'northern house' may be classified into three main categories. Those of the first category are distinguished by the way in which they connect the dwelling and the farmstead yard – these are the 'bar', *glagol*, *koshel*, 'T-shaped connection' and 'two-row connection' types. Those of the second category (chiefly log houses) are characterized by the structural planning of their living quarters – these include four-wall and six-wall houses (with such variants as the 'house with crib', the 'twin-house with *zaulok*' and the 'twin-house without *zaulok*'), the five-wall house and the cross house. The final category includes dwellings distinguished by their overall internal layouts. The main living area of the houses in this category has a chimneyless stove. The smoke billowing out of the mouth of this adobe stove rose 3–4 m (10–13 ft) to the high, vaulted ceiling, and then went out through a slit above the stove, which formed a coved smoke escape through the roof.

The outward appearance of the Russian peasant house was characterized by specific 'apparel' features. This definition encompasses both decorative techniques – carving, painting and colouring – and various architectural details, such as porches, balconies, galleries, plat bands and window shutters. The latter category also includes carved boards along the house-roof edge (*pricheliny*), consoles, smoke bonnets and specially carved roof ridges – all of which have a utilitarian purpose and play a decorative role at the same time. The symbols employed by such house decoration included phytomorphic (plant-like), ornithomorphic (bird-like), zoomorphic and anthropomorphic images embodied in carving and painting. A horse or a bird picture in the house decor would, for example, be connected with the sun.

No description of this type of house decoration would be complete without a mention of western Russian house painting. Dwelling paintings both inside and outside form a special group of Russian cultural monuments. Such architectural and decorative elements not only formed the basis for a dwelling design, but also reflected the 'design' of the peasant world view. For this reason, western Russian national 'folk' architecture was, and continues to be, regarded as fundamentally magical and sacred.

Below Architecturally and structurally distinct from wooden churches and chapels, traditional Russian wooden housing was shaped by three distinct categories based on the relationship to the surrounding farmstead, the structural planning of living quarters, and the overall internal layout.

Opposite The external appearance of wooden folk housing varied according to specific utilitarian and decorative features. Alongside the particular details afforded by the log cabin structure, elements such as porches, balconies and shutters reflected architectural adaptations. Carving, painting and colouration of homes – inside and out – gave individuality and referenced sacred motifs.

Traditional Felt Homes of Kazakhstan

Miriam Ho

Geography/Climate and Materials

The traditional *kiiz ui*, meaning 'felt home', supports a way of life attuned to Kazakhstan's harsh climate of hot, arid summers and bitterly cold winters. A circular dwelling with a conical vault, comprising a wooden scaffold with felt coverings, the *kiiz ui* is lightweight and modular; it can be quickly assembled and dismantled for frequent migrations. Pliable woods such as poplar (*Populus*) and white willow (*Salix alba*), or reeds such as meadow grass (*Poa*), are bound together with strips of camel hide to make foldable lattice-wall panels. The nomads' own sheep and camels, breeds that are accustomed to the local climate, moult every spring, producing fleece that is felted (bonded via pressure and shrinkage) to form water-resistant, insulating felts. Wood and wool are organic fibres that have the ability to absorb and give off moisture in balance with the environment. This layered skin of timber and felt allows the *kiiz ui* to ventilate in the summer and insulate in the winter. Nowadays, the transient *kiiz ui* is seldom seen save in the remote mountains, while buildings made of earth, often combined with industrial building materials and modern amenities, make up the rural and informal urban neighbourhoods of contemporary, settled Kazakhstan.

Sedentary life, such as that forced on Kazakh pastoralists by the Soviet collectivization policies of the 1930s, retains elements of this nomadic heritage. To deal with the extreme heat and cold, families rotate between adjacent summer and winter houses, which are made, respectively, of reeds and loess – the latter, an aeolian clay of fine silt, sand and clay particles that can be moulded without any admixtures. Heavy fabric curtains are hung inside the doors and windows of these dwellings, and their floors are lined with felt carpets. Like the layers of the *kiiz ui*, each material contributes to regulating heat and humidity. The summer house is a timber-framed construction with thin walls (roughly 250 mm [10 in] deep) formed by bundles of vertical reeds covered with clay. The winter house has a thicker wall (1–1.5 m deep [3–5 ft]) created by sandwiching reeds between wythes of loess mud brick; it is also plastered with clay for waterproofing. Reeds or straw provide sufficient thermal mass to capture solar heat during the day and release it at night. The winter house's thicker mud-brick walls provide yet greater capacity for diurnal heat storage. Both materials also absorb and release atmospheric moisture, which has cooling effects.

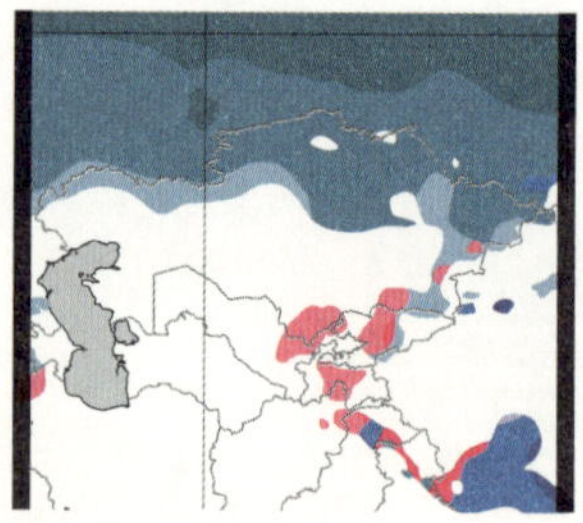

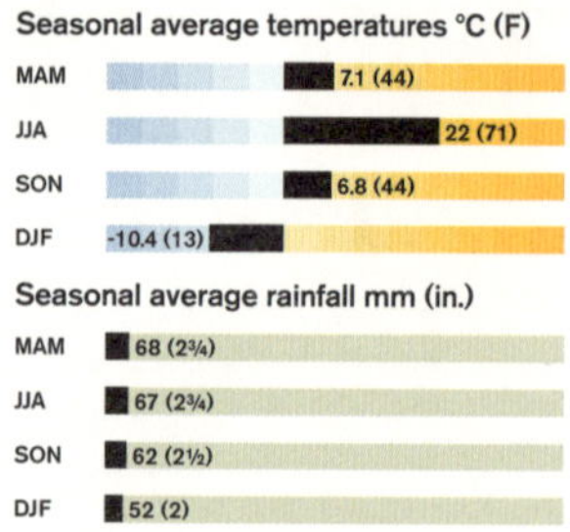

Left Rapid climate change and the desertification of the Aral Sea in the late 20th century has meant that vernacular homes are no longer seen as financially viable or desirable. Instead, an amalgam of concrete, corrugated iron and scrap metal are the usual contemporary building palette.

Opposite Lightweight, modular and easily transported, the traditional felt home or *kiiz ui* is ideally suited to the regular migrations of traditional nomadic Kazak people. The structures are now seen less often, except in remote parts of the country.

Building Plan/Form

Aral'sk: an Evolving Vernacular

The city of Aral'sk is a former Soviet port in southern Kazakhstan that has experienced rapid climate change and accompanying economic shifts with the desertification of the Aral Sea. Houses in Aral'sk are built by individual families and expanded over time, reflecting changes in available materials and technology. A typical home in Aral'sk consists of a walled enclosure containing a summer and a winter house, an outhouse, storage sheds, and possibly a bathhouse, stables and yard space for keeping animals or for conducting various skilled trades. The home evolves with a family's needs: spaces are multifunctional, and new rooms are added for a growing family; an old house may become a stable, or a defunct outhouse may be lined and used as a storeroom.

The Aral Sea rapidly desertified in the 1990s and local industries closed. As the marshlands dwindled, traditional foundations and roofs of reed mats sealed with a layer of waterproofing clay were no longer cost-effective, and the abandoned factories provided low-income Kazakh families with recycled materials to build their homes. Concrete foundations and sheet-metal roofs were adopted while rubble became infill for concrete plinth foundations. Roofs and walls were formed from scrap metal, stripped from abandoned ships or from old oil drums.

Aral'sk now faces renewed growth through regional oil and gas extraction, and building façades reflect the new affluence. Mud houses are traditionally covered in a compacted mixture of clay and straw called *paqsa*, while those who can afford it add more coats for a better finish or may choose an outer layer such as a coat of fine clay and sand, whitewashed plaster, stucco or painted friezes. Newly wealthy families often choose to clad exterior walls in kiln-fired bricks, which are highly regarded aesthetically. Wall cavities continue to be fashioned out of mud and reed or straw.

An adaptation of the indigenous fishermen's hut can be found in a newly revived fishing village near Aral'sk. The *shoshala* is a dugout with a domed roof made of logs and adobe or wattle and daub covered with turf, and is one of the oldest dwelling types found on the Caspian and Aral seas. Recently, a makeshift village of dugouts was built to provide cooling shelters for fishermen on the exposed sandy shore. It used sandbag walls and corrugated metal roofing covered with thick layers of grass and earth to prevent heat gain.

Furnishings and Living Spaces

Kazakh families may own European furniture sets as a status symbol, but the transient furnishings of their nomadic customs are still habitually used. Kazakh nomadic living spaces are traditionally 'created' by taking out and putting away small items of furniture throughout the day. A low table is brought out for meals, and patterned felt rugs are spread around it for seating. The same felt rugs are later unrolled for sleeping. The *tapchan*, an elevated wooden platform built in a dwelling's yard or in any indoor room, can be transformed into dining or sleeping spaces according to the season.

The felt rug (*tekematy*) can be seen as a form of architecture in miniature, which is adapted to the changing seasons: when sleeping in the open on a cool summer's night, it encourages perspiration yet wicks moisture away from the body; in the winter, it is used indoors and retains heat.

Eastern Russia's Yurta, Dugout and *Fanza* Dwellings

Olga V. Maltseva

Geography/Climate and Culture

The territory of eastern Russia, washed by the Arctic and Pacific oceans to the north and east, includes various climatic zones – Arctic, subarctic, northern and southern boreal. Its scope is long, in a north–south direction, and the resulting combination of plots with sharply continental (Siberian) and marine (Pacific coast) climates has led to the development of a variety of building technologies. Three types of settlement can be observed in this region: those typical for Siberia and the northern latitudes, those suited to the Pacific coast, and those combining traditions of the two. The character of housing construction in each of these zones was determined not only by environmental peculiarities (including the local fauna and flora) but also by types of building material, lifestyles (semi-sedentary or nomadic) and local economic traditions.

Indigenous groups of the northeast are united by an existence born of economic circumstances – predominantly taiga-based and marine hunting (the latter of whales, walrus and seals), reindeer herding and fishing – that in turn contributed to the emergence of certain types of housing. The buildings indigenous to the region can be divided into two basic types: the portable, characteristic of nomads; and the semi-stationary, which were used by fishermen and hunters of marine wildlife.

The people of the southern Far East possessed a diversity of structures. This territory is located in the boreal zone with mixed flora and fauna. These include 'northern' nature typical of a subarctic zone – coniferous plants and animals such as taiga reindeer, brown bear and elk – and 'southern' traits, seen in the form of expansive, broadleaved forests including the Amur velvet tree (*Phallodendron amurense*), five-flavour berry plant (*Schisandra chinensis*) and lotus (*Nelumbo*), and home to the Amur tiger, Amur leopard, Manchu hare and Manchu squirrel, which are found in the subtropical zone here as well as in China.

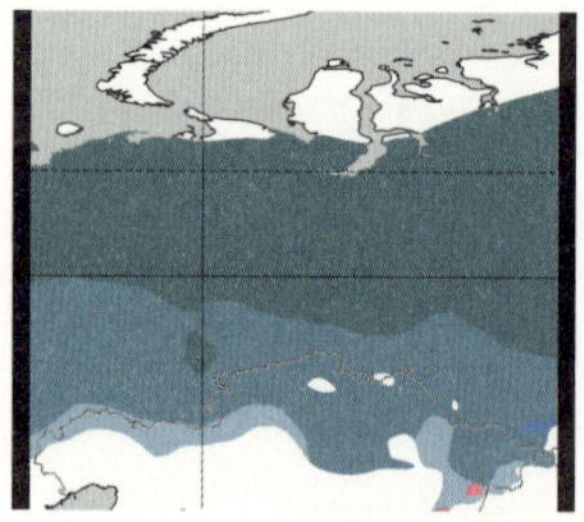

Seasonal average temperatures °C (F)

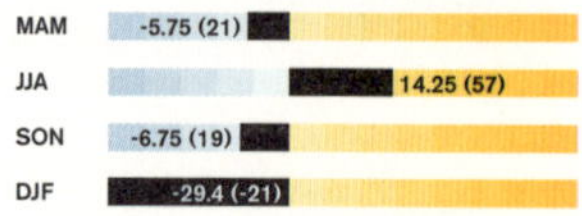

Seasonal average rainfall mm (in.)

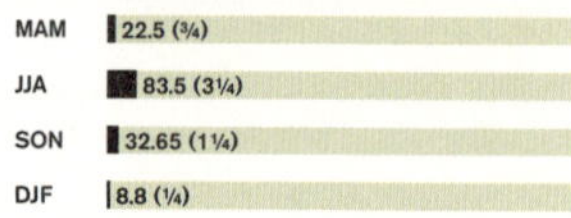

Left and opposite The shape and materials of conical tipi hut frames used in the northeast of Russia are consistent, but cladding materials differ depending on the context: from animal hides of the reindeer tundra to bark from taiga zones. All include a hole at the apex that allows light in and smoke to be released from the enclosure.

Building Plan/Form and Construction Techniques

The Northeast (Siberian) House

Among peoples of these Arctic and subarctic zones, the conical or cylindrical-conical yurta, with its various cladding materials, was a common type of dwelling. On the reindeer tundra, reindeer skin was used; in the taiga zone, birch bark (*Betula*) with a flooring of grass was adopted. The circular bases of the yurta used at the northernmost latitudes enabled the heat obtained from the hearth to be evenly distributed and conserved. This type of home was used as a temporary lodging; it was then dismantled and transported onwards via reindeer sled.

Collective coastal dwellings, in which a few families or family members lived, took the form of dugouts or semi-dugouts, with rectangular or polygonal plans. Externally, their walls were covered with dry grass turf. Inhabitants of the coastal strip, unlike the nomads, had settlements – albeit ones that varied with the seasons. Dugout or semi-dugout dwellings were more permanent winter homes, built in sheltered locations. Timber booths formed temporary summer lodgings, erected during the salmon-fishing period close to the fishing grounds.

The Southeast (Pacific Coast) House

The camps of the indigenous people of the southern Amur Valley, erected on riverbanks or the taiga's edge during their summer salmon-fishing gatherings, contained dwellings fashioned from woven willow (*Salix*) branches and reed huts with canopies made of birch bark. The permanent (winter) settlements of the Nanai people of the Middle Amur Basin included adobe homes (*fanza*) and other household structures – among them warehouses and fish-drying racks. Researchers posit that this tradition of building mud-brick houses was introduced into Nanai territory from Manchuria (northeastern China), and was adapted to the conditions of the Amur Valley. Staves, placed in the earth, formed the rectangular base of these dwellings. Between these were braided branches of willow, and then lumps of clay were hammered into the gaps. The *fanza* walls were then plastered, externally and internally, with clay incorporating grass. Openings were formed in these walls for windows and an entrance door; a roof, with gable ends, was covered with dry grass. Internally, the floors of these dwellings were also made of clay; a clay pipe was laid from the hearth, along the walls at low level, and eventually passed out through the wall of the house. Smoke from the hearth circulated in this pipe and heated the area closest to the floor, which otherwise freezes in winter.

The Nanai people's choice of building material encompassed clay and wood, and their selection was partly related to regional beliefs. In residential buildings, they kept the use of timber to a minimum, the tree having a revered status. (Only sacral objects tended to be made of wood – ritual posts, ancestral tombs, spoons, troughs for ritual 'feeding water' and items associated with bear worship.) However, it is likely that the complexity of timber processing also accounted for the scarcity of its use in the home. Somewhat paradoxically, outbuildings such as barns were often log structures on stilts – but it should be remembered that these held not only hunting or fishing tackle and food stocks but also often shaman equipment, which underlines their ritual significance.

Conclusion

Since the 1930s, with ongoing 'reform' among Russia's Far Eastern aboriginal people and their transfer to a settled way of life, the ecological component of their residential construction has gradually disappeared. During the post-revolutionary collectivization period, the construction of log-built cobble-floored houses with attics and cellars for storing garden harvest was a common practice. According to researchers at the beginning of the 20th century, the introduction of heating furnaces accounted for a weakening of immunity among Russia's aboriginal people.

Below Homes located in the southeast of the region include summer dwellings built of woven willow, as well as winter settlements of adobe homes known as *fanza*. These rectilinear forms were marked out by timber staves and threaded with willow, with clay inserted into the gaps to give thermal insulation.

Opposite The Amur Valley of Russia's southeast region is typified by its abundant rivers and forests, which provide a livelihood through fishing and shape the materials available to build settlements with, such as wood and clay.

Timbered Dwellings of Tasmania

Noni Boyd

Geography/Climate

Tasmania, which has a cool temperate climate, is an island located south of mainland Australia. European explorers documented the construction techniques of the huts erected at seasonal hunting grounds by Aboriginal Tasmanians (Palawa). At Adventure Bay, Bruny Island, curved huts roofed in bark were recorded. In the more inhospitable parts of Tasmania, domes with curved ribs of fire-hardened timber or whalebone, thatched with grass and lined with tea-tree (*Melaleuca alternifolia*) bark, were built. European farming, which restricted access to traditional hunting grounds, and the relocation of the Aboriginal population onto missions soon destroyed their tradition of building seasonal shelters. The ephemeral nature of Palawa shelters has meant that only archaeological evidence survives, as at the Arthur River (near Marrawah, Western Tasmania).

Materials

In 1803, Tasmania became the British penal colony of Van Diemen's Land and a series of isolated prison stations was established across the island. At the Brickendon and Woolmers estates near Longford, rural settlements dating from the 1820s survive that retain vernacular buildings including, at the former, living quarters, barns, a granary, workshops and stables, and at Woolmers the main house, cottages and barn. Assigned convicts cut timbers and made bricks on site. These exceptionally rare vernacular structures have been included on the Australian Convict World Heritage Sites listing. Regular, practical building-conservation training sessions are now held that focus on repairing these buildings.

Tasmanian wood had been used for joinery, furniture and boatbuilding since the discovery of the island's economically useful timbers such as the Huon pine (*Lagarostrobos franklinii*). British Georgian building forms and techniques were adapted to utilize local materials: timber, saplings, reeds, bark, stone and clay.

Right Located south of Australia's mainland, the island of Tasmania has a cool temperate climate with landscapes of woodland and forested valleys, as well as coastal areas.

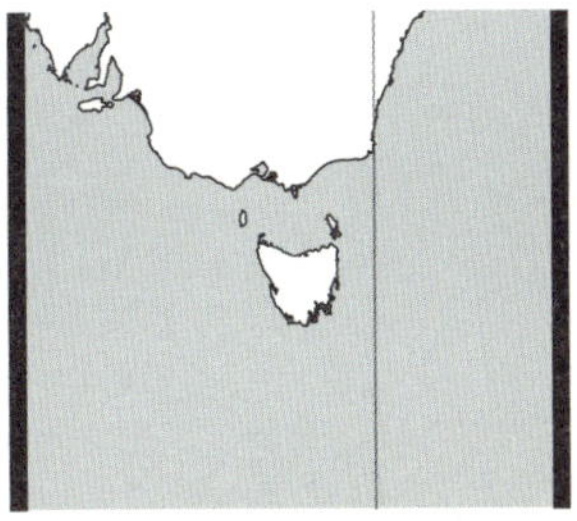

Seasonal average temperatures °C (F)

MAM	13 (55)
JJA	8.4 (47)
SON	12 (53)
DJF	16.2 (61)

Seasonal average rainfall mm (in.)

MAM	46.6 (1¾)
JJA	51.3 (2)
SON	53.7 (2)
DJF	45.6 (1¾)

Opposite top left Vernacular huts in the Tasmanian bush were erected using materials at hand, including whole logs pugged with mud, and bark for the roofs.

Opposite top right Early residences of mud and lath, such as this Risdon Cove example, were photographed by European settlers but have long since vanished.

Opposite middle and bottom Estates at Brickendon (middle) and Woolmers (bottom right) are the best-preserved examples of former Tasmanian penal colonies. Both draw on readily available supplies of timber, such as Huon pine, and adopt weatherboard techniques utilized in rural farm buildings in the South of England

Right Emergency shelter huts built in the high country areas were used by prospectors and later tourists. This example is the Kitchen Hut, erected below the summit of Cradle Mountain. Surviving examples are largely from the 20th century and over time have been altered or rebuilt.

Construction Techniques

Wide hand-split timber slabs erected vertically, logs or panels of wattles or laths pugged (filled) and rendered with clay or mud were used for walling. Acacia trees are still known on the island as 'wattles', indicating their widespread use for hut construction. Split timber shingles soon replaced bark or thatch, creating a more durable (but not fireproof) roof. Once a more permanent house was erected, the initial hut often formed its rear wing – as at Grantham, near Bothwell, dating from 1822.

In an attempt to build weathertight buildings, brick nogging (horizontal weatherboards over a timber frame infilled with bricks), facing brick and stone came to be used. Weatherboards were common in the southeast of England, and the technique had arrived, probably via Sydney, in Tasmania by 1813. Examples include Mount Stuart (commenced 1813), houses built by James Bennell in the 1830s in Launceston, and the Shipwright's Cottage at Port Arthur (1834). English vernacular forms remain evident at Battery Point, Hobart, where cottages dating from the 1840s and 1850s survive. Other building techniques experimented with include pisé (rammed earth) at Wanstead, Campbelltown (commenced 1827) and the Jericho Probation Station (1841).

Building Plan/Form

The term 'bush carpentry' emerged in the mid-19th century, to describe buildings erected by land selectors (small-scale farmers) using materials obtained from their property. A 1860s selector's farm complex built of timber slabs survives at the Woodvine Nature Reserve, near Sorrell. Today, bush carpentry is mainly used for fencing and to repair existing structures – and even these skills are dying out. Post-1900, miners and forestry workers continued to build slab huts, as timber was plentiful and other materials were difficult to transport. The 1930s Depression saw a revival of the slab hut throughout Australia, albeit combined with factory-made joinery. Examples include the Hartzview Fruit Pickers' Huts (1934–43) near Cygnet.

Towards the end of the 19th century, rustic timber 'shelter huts' were erected on Mt Wellington, at the Cascades near Hobart and in the Cataract Gorge, Launceston. Picturesque huts still survive in Cradle Mountain National Park, including Gustav Weindorfer's Waldheim Chalet (1912, rebuilt 1974 after a fire) and his boat shed, and huts built by rangers such as the Kitchen Hut (1939).

Tasmania's surviving vernacular buildings demonstrate a wide range of early Australian building techniques, which have largely vanished in other states. Out of necessity, Old World techniques were adapted to utilize locally available building materials. The Tasmanian Heritage Council now promotes the sensitive alteration of vernacular cottages and barns, encouraging retention of their original materials and forms. Tasmania's indigenous timbers continue to be widely used for building and furniture making.

Settlements and Dwellings of the New Zealand Maori

Deidre Brown

Geography/Climate and Culture

Climate, landscape and culture have been significant influences on the development of Maori architecture in New Zealand from the Polynesian arrival eight centuries ago to the present day. Colonization presented both opportunities and challenges for Maori builders, who have consistently sought to maintain culturally, spiritually and economically sustainable architectural environments.

Materials

Founding Polynesian settlers quickly adapted the architectural knowledge they brought with them from their island homelands to suit a landscape much larger, more densely forested and significantly cooler. The earliest building sites uncovered by archaeologists reveal a settlement pattern based on seasonal occupation of sites close to food and building resources. Waterways and the ocean provided fish, shellfish and eels, and were the 'highways' for travel between distant sites; wetlands were home to waterfowl as well as rushes and *harakeke* (*Phormium tenax*; New Zealand flax), which made ideal thatching material for houses when dried; and forests yielded more birds and great stands of totara (*Podocarpus totara*), kauri (*Agathis australis*) and matai (*Prumnopitys taxiflora*), trees that were felled and dressed for use in building frames.

Construction Techniques

Unable to replicate the open structures of their Polynesian ancestors across a new range of subtropical to alpine conditions, Maori builders responded to the climate by hunkering their buildings into the ground. A reduction in size contained the space for warmth, becoming almost a thatched second skin or cloak for users. The 'top down' gable-building system synonymous with Pacific structures was retained. Extending the ridge pole to create a porch was a uniquely Maori innovation in the oeuvre of Pacific architecture, providing a moderating zone between enclosed interior spaces and the changeable weather conditions. This space came to be the principal occupation zone of the dwelling, where a diverse range of activities took place and to which specific social and spiritual associations were attached.

In time, the Maori moved away from the coasts to gather a wider range of foods from the interior, where some groups eventually settled. Many forests were cleared by burning, and *pa* (fortified settlements) established. *Pa* on volcanoes, islands and ridges required significant landscape modification through terracing and the large-scale mobilization of labour. One can imagine the philosophical shift that must have taken place from living on the land to being *tangata whenua*, a 'people of the land', and having an identity that could not be disentangled from landscape, flora, fauna and climate.

Below The climatic peculiarities of New Zealand required its indigenous Maori population to adapt structures from their Polynesian origins, making lower, smaller buildings that were enclosed and hunkered down into the landscape.

Opposite top Rich natural resources from the ocean, waterways, forests and marshlands gave bountiful materials both for nourishment and for dwellings, including rushes, flax and varieties of wood.

Opposite bottom Fortified settlements, or *pa*, were located at the apex of hills and extinct volcanoes. Though the height gave defensive advantage to the occupying tribe, the steep character also required innovative, large-scale modifications, such as terracing.

Increasing spiritual and social complexity was reflected in architecture through the elaboration of identities and their accompanying stories on the timbers and fibres that constituted communal buildings. A technological breakthrough in the shaping of hardstone for woodworking tools, around the 16th century, generated the production of the beautiful *tiki* (frontal humanoid figure) and *manaia* (profile *tiki* figure) house carvings synonymous with Maori customary art. These ancestral carvings were time-consuming to produce, and were used and reused on the sleeping houses and storehouses of chiefs in order to illustrate their inherited and acquired *mana* (status, prestige).

The arrival of 'Pakeha' (Europeans), especially from the late 18th century onwards, had different impacts on different communities – and, by extension, on their architecture. For Maori in the northern and western North Island and on the South Island, the settlement of the first Pakeha communities heralded conflict and the loss of some indigenous architectural knowledge through depopulation and land alienation. However, the vacuum left by customary architecture was soon filled by the appropriation of Western tools, materials, concepts and formalisms. The resulting buildings were often striking in appearance, and were used for distinctly Maori purposes.

Building Plan/Form

One such building was Hiona, constructed at Maungapohatu in the rugged Urewera region of the central-eastern North Island in 1907. Its name, a transliteration of 'Zion', alludes to its origins and purpose as the main assembly house for a Maori community founded on Old Testament descriptions. The design of Hiona was based on descriptions of Solomon's House and Temple, and a picture of the Dome of the Rock. The Maungapohatu community was drawn together from some of the survivors of two tribes that had suffered significant land confiscations by the colonial government after the late 19th-century New Zealand wars. Stories about the meaning of the bands of painted club and diamond symbols that encircled Hiona related to the redemption prophesied by earlier Maori leaders, and were based on the release from bondage of the Jews as described in the Bible. Hand-sawn palings and roof shingles continued a practice of self-sufficient on-site construction. Hiona illustrates that architectural appropriation was a means of maintaining tribal, religious and political identity rather than being simply a symptom of assimilation.

In other communities, formalisms, practices and aesthetics associated with a continuing ancestral cultural presence were retained. Metal tools traded with, and later purchased from, Pakeha were readily accommodated within the existing carving traditions of the eastern regions of the North Island. They increased the speed of carving production. Meeting houses, built to host large gatherings of chiefs to discuss pressing issues such as Christian conversion and land sales, could be 'fully' decorated with ancestor figures on internal and front external spaces. The oratory developed to explain relationships between the carved ancestors and their legendary deeds continued the tradition of telling important cultural stories inside and around buildings – with the house becoming, in a sense, a mnemonic storybook.

Above top left and bottom row Time-consuming, intricate carvings made from the 16th century onward were used on raised storehouses and chief's houses to confer status. Characterized by figures of *tiki* and *manaia*, they were used and reused as required.

Above top right European colonization of New Zealand impacted on the Maori vernacular in tangential ways. Decorations on Hiona, the main assembly house in the rugged northeastern North Island, show unusual club and diamond patterns – symbols that spoke of Old Testament Jewish redemption.

Opposite With the aid of sophisticated tools introduced by European settlers, Maori could carve more quickly. *Marae*, or meeting houses, came to bear the symbolic, sacred carvings both inside and outside their gabled structures.

Seasonal average temperatures °C (F)

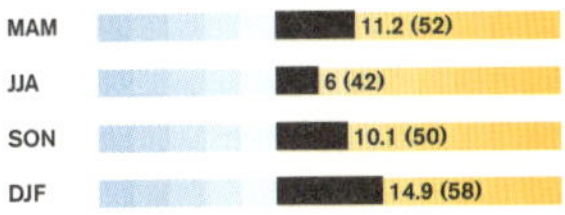

Seasonal average rainfall mm (in.)

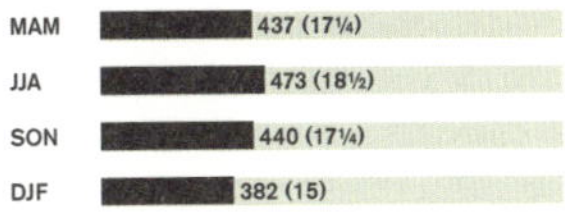

By the mid-20th century, Maori architectural climate responsiveness was increasingly regulated through the national Building Act and the implementation of sanitary codes, which consequently became a means to control and suppress indigenous modes of living and building production. Some traditionalists were able to continue working within these constraints. The School of Maori Arts and Crafts, established in 1926 and based in the central North Island tourist town of Rotorua, reinvigorated carved-house production in the western, central and eastern North Island. These large meeting houses, sometimes constructed with metal frames and concrete foundations, were adorned with ancestral carvings, intricate scroll rafter paintings (*kowhaiwhai*) and lattice panels (*tukutuku*). They were the community halls for Maori land incorporation and farming development programmes, which had been established in order to recover indigenous economic self-sufficiency.

Not all were so fortunate. Sizable rural-to-urban migration after the Second World War shifted the majority of Maori from their home districts to the city. Better educational and employment opportunities were their main purposes for moving. However, discrimination in the rental housing market made it difficult to locate these aspirations in the parts of the city where they could be realized. Extended family modes of living have been retained, albeit within the confines of houses generally designed for nuclear families. A movement is now afoot in the state housing sector to build dwellings that can accommodate up to three generations of permanent occupants and temporary-stay relatives. Maori engineers and architects are exploring the use of sustainably harvested traditional materials, such as *harakeke* (flax), as reinforcing in laboratory- and site-tested modern composite materials, such as rammed earth and concrete block. The importance of using these materials lies not just in their structural integrity and cost-efficiency; they also recall ancestral connections to the land by evoking the experience of the *tangata whenua*.

Colonization rendered the landscape of New Zealand a contested site – ecologically, spiritually and politically. This outcome has been reflected in the Maori architectural response over the last two centuries. A diversity of pressures across the country led to a variety of solutions – some successful, others still to be fully realized. Self-sufficiency through innovative ecological and culturally sustainable building practices is increasingly aligned with self-determination and the will to remain 'the people of the land'.

POLAR

Equirectangular projection. Scale 1: 70 000 000

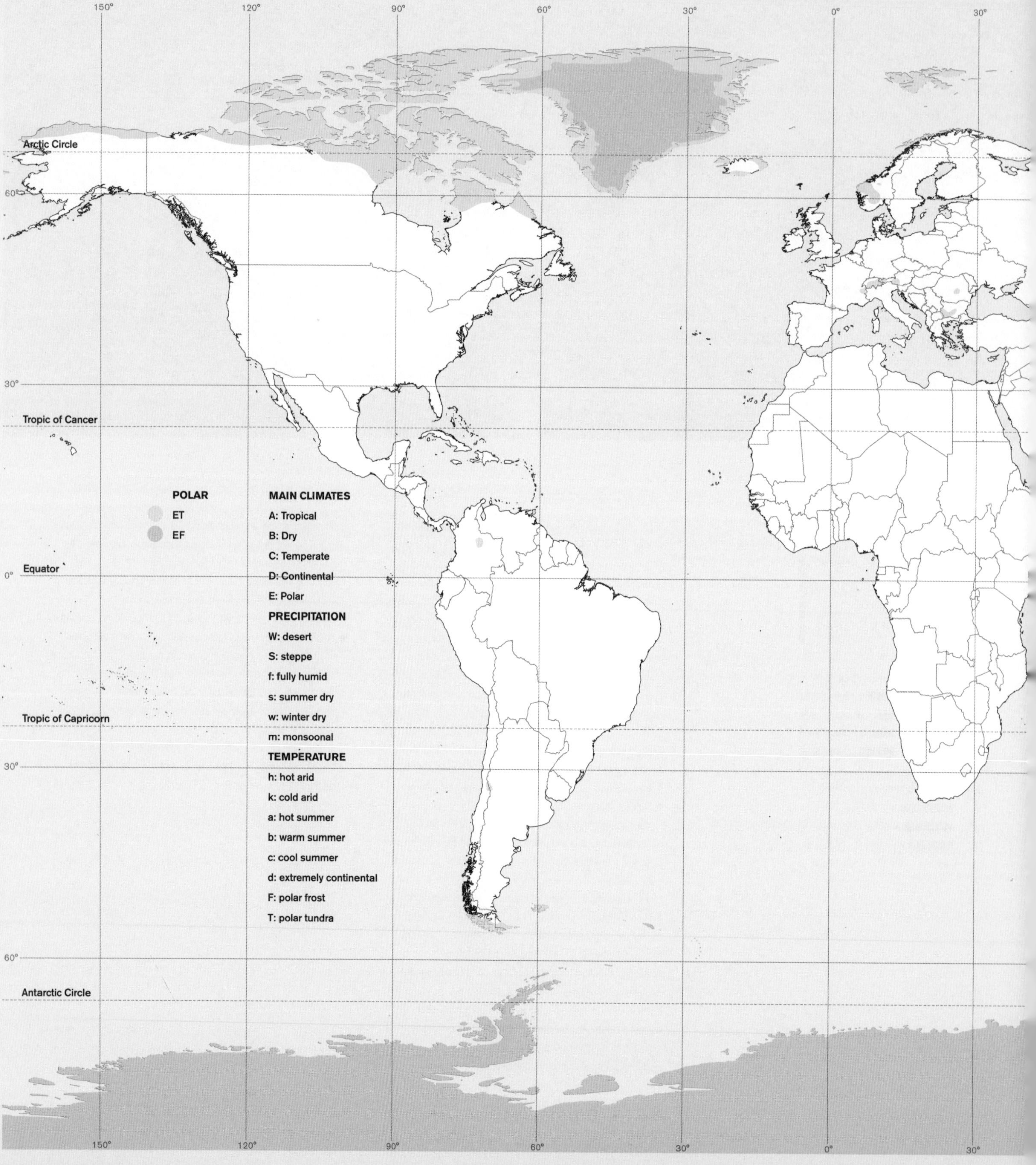

The polar climate regions are characterized by a lack of warm summers. Every month in a polar climate has an average temperature of less than 10°C (50°F). This region extends from northern coastal areas of North America and Eurasia, through Greenland and Antarctica. Regions with a polar climate cover more than 20 per cent of the Earth. A polar climate results in treeless tundra, glaciers, or a permanent or semi-permanent layer of ice.

Many high altitude locations on Earth have a climate where no month has an average temperature of 10°C (50°F) or higher, but as this is due to elevation it is referred to as an alpine climate. Conditions can mimic either tundra (ET) or ice cap climate (EF).

In the polar tundra, the average temperature of the warmest month is below 10°C (50°F) but above freezing. Here, the ground is permanently frozen to depths of hundreds of metres. Summer temperatures cause the uppermost layer of this permafrost, a metre (3 ft) or so, to thaw. Annual precipitation is very low; most stations receive less than 200 mm (7⅞ in) of rainfall. In lower latitudes, this would constitute a desert. But in these latitudes, evaporation and transpiration also are low, and sufficient moisture therefore remains to sustain vegetation growth. Because of the very short growing season, tundra vegetation consists of mosses, lichens, dwarf trees, and scattered, woody vegetation.

In summertime, days are long but the sun is never very high above the horizon, so the intensity of solar radiation remains quite low. Furthermore, snow-covered surfaces are highly reflective, and much of the solar energy that reaches these surfaces is reflected and lost without heating them. Consequently, summers remain quite cool and the extremely cold, long winters produce large annual temperature ranges.

When the average temperature drops below freezing for every month, plant growth is constrained further and the surface is continuously covered by snow and ice. This climatic type is the polar ice cap. It occupies the interior ice sheets of Greenland and Antarctica. Precipitation is also low, mostly occurring during the warmer summer period. Very strong, downslope katabatic winds (that is, caused by a downward motion of cool air) exacerbate the severity of the prevailing climatic conditions.

Snow, Stone and Wooden Adaptations for Polar Regions

Arctic and polar climates have become one of the focal points in the climate-change debate – offering, as they do, scientific evidence about humanity's impact on the global climate. The ingenuity of indigenous people in these regions had to grapple with unforgiving weather patterns and extreme temperatures well below zero. The solutions arrived at for the construction of shelters are mostly extinct today. However, they were closely connected to the availability of natural resources, ranging from stone on the eastern Arctic and snow itself in the central area to timber in the western Arctic. Thermal comfort was secured by building enclosures recessed into the earth and by the construction of thick walls of snow or, in the case of the Icelandic vernacular, turf. Polar houses demonstrate a creative adaptation of limited yet diverse natural materials and their properties to human use by the development of simple technologies that enabled livable conditions for families and communities alike.

The social structure of Arctic Circle families is similar to that of other indigenous groups across the globe, with an inherent relationship between family quarters and the fire – the source of heat and light and forming a gathering point. Sámi vernacular offers an example of settlements adapted to livelihoods focused on reindeer pastoralism and fishing, an existence that is deeply dependent on the seasons and also of a highly temporary character.

The adaptation of vernacular structures to extremes of nature was simple yet inventive and helped them to remain 'part of the landscape', with minimal environmental impact. Common global threats to indigenous cultures remain real, yet one would hope that building with earth could still be an inspiration for technological adaption, in order to meet the contemporary needs of people living in one of the most extreme climatic zones on the planet.

Left In the challenging conditions of polar climates, dwellings are often built from snow, stone, turf or wood, such as these houses in Iceland.

Insulation and Ingenuity of Arctic Dwellings

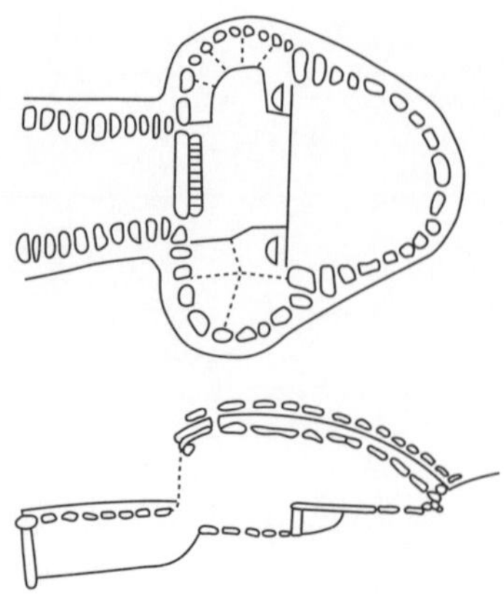

Above Insulated by sods, the straight-sided houses of Greenland and Labrador were built of stone with communal spaces at the front and individual family spaces to the rear.

Below Stilt houses occupied during summers were particular to Bering Strait peoples. Their raised structures differ from most Arctic buildings and were a local adaptation to occupy the steep-sided terrain.

Opposite Limited material choices and the extreme cold of tundra and glacial landscapes shaped the construction of vernacular dwellings in the Arctic. Most of the traditional buildings types have now vanished.

Gregory A. Reinhardt

Geography/Climate and Culture

Eskimo peoples who speak Inuit dialects traditionally ranged from eastern Greenland, across the Arctic Archipelago and northern reaches of continental North America, to coastal and interior Alaska as far west as the Seward Peninsula and the Bering Strait. South of there, Yupik-speaking Eskimos occupied Alaskan coastal areas as far as the Aleutian Peninsula and skipped over to the Gulf of Alaska; they also inhabited easternmost Siberia and islands in the Bering Sea.

Building Plan/Form

Readers should understand that buildings described here are effectively extinct; also, there were dozens of disparate dwelling designs – some used in winter, some year-round and some only in the autumn or summer – as well as ceremonial and other structures.

By and large, Eskimo buildings are divisible into three regions according to wall materials. Eastern Arctic houses used stone (as did those in the Bering Strait islands), central Arctic ones relied on snow, and western Arctic materials were almost universally timber.

Materials and Construction Techniques

Eastern Arctic

Houses in Greenland and Labrador had straight-sided stone walls; flat or gabled roofs; a communal space towards the front; and, at the rear, spaces arranged for individual families – each family's spot defined by a lamp platform (for cooking and light), above which hung a smallish rack for drying clothes and boots. Houses were well insulated beneath sods stacked or draped over every part – roof, sides and entrance tunnel. Gabled roofs required upright posts and crossbeams of wood, an often scarce commodity in parts of the eastern Arctic, and some people insulated the back wall (rear of the sleeping platform) with brush, pegged in place behind sealskins. Northwest Greenlanders had smaller, two-family homes with roofs of cantilevered stone slabs; dwellings farther south tended to be longhouses, in some Greenland sites accommodating several families (each with a partitioning sealskin curtain) or even a whole community. Between body heat and lamps, indoor temperatures rose appreciably once the stone absorbed enough heat to radiate it inwards. Ambient daylight streamed in through animal-membrane windows in the front wall.

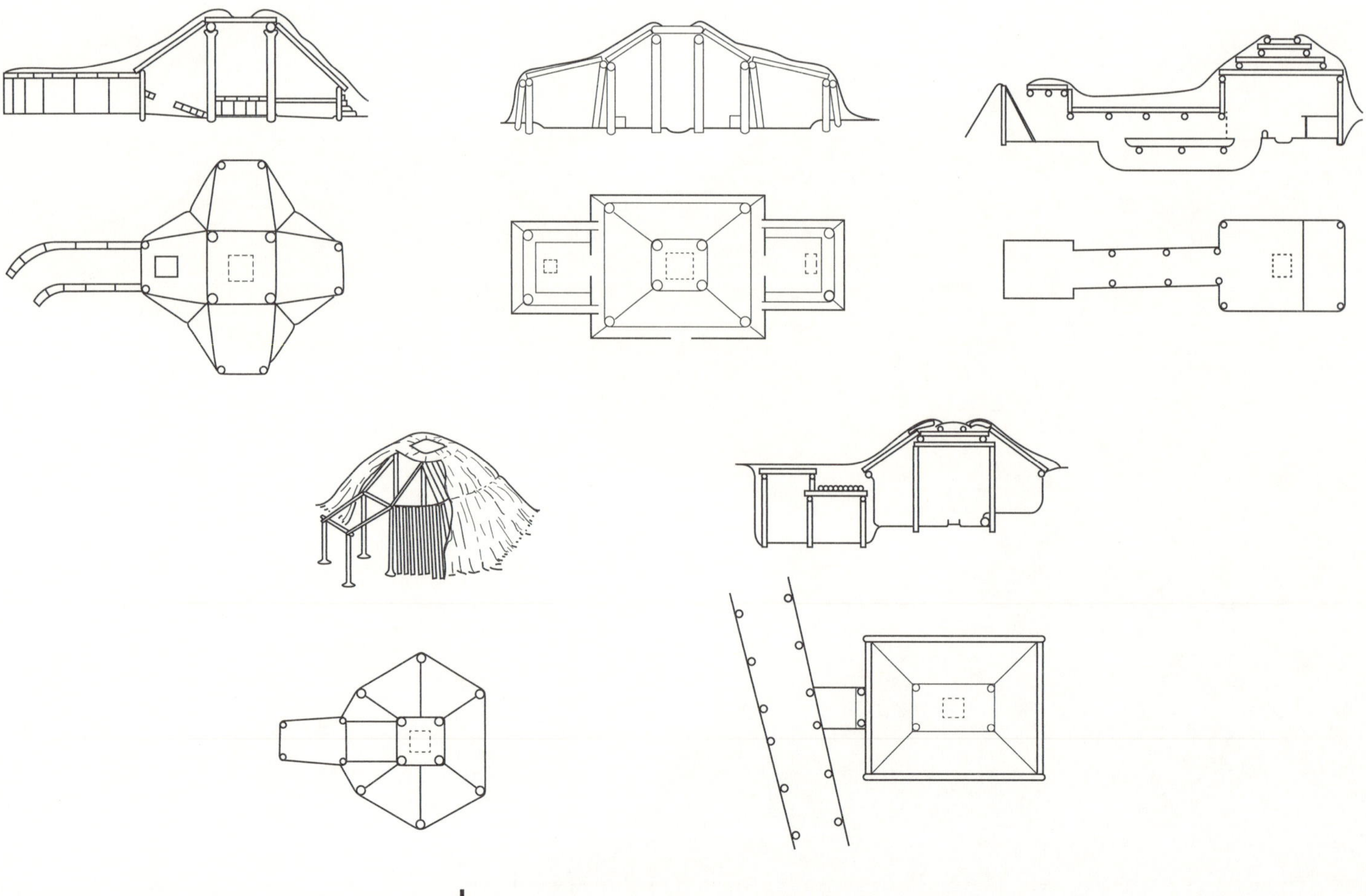

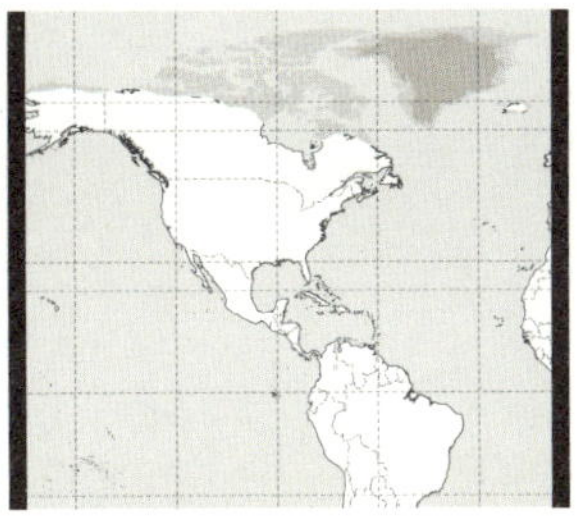

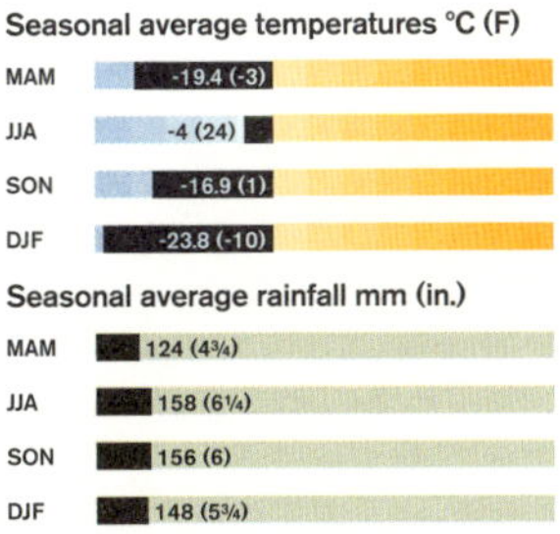

Opposite top Houses built of snow have excellent thermal resistance and allowed for Inuit people to follow the seal population, living atop winter sea ice.

Opposite bottom Known locally as *iglu* – which simply means 'house' – timber dwellings in the Western Arctic displayed many variations, as shown in these drawings. Clockwise from top left (in pairs): Mackenzie Delta Inuit; Koniag of Shelikof Strait; Norton Sound; Nunivak Island; and North Alaska.

Below Built with at least one central chamber with a raised sleeping platform that served as the main living space, houses of the Caribou Inuit style include an entry tunnel that is also used for cooking.

Central Arctic

This region is legendary for its so-called igloos (in Inuit, *iglu* means 'house', regardless of material). These first captured Europe's romantic imagination in the 1820s via the concept of homes made completely of snow, the seeming enemy of cold-climate survival. Snow houses, however, were the perfect adaptation for people who followed the seal and lived amid snowdrifts atop each winter's sea ice.

The characteristic snow house had a main-chamber dome with at least enough headroom for people to sit upright on its raised sleeping platform – lower peak heights conserved more heat (and, therefore, lamp oil). Its floor led to a tunnel, usually with two or more lesser domes leading to the outside, where a wall or angled tunnel deflected wind gusts. Typical main chambers could hold two families, each with their own side to the sleeping platform, as well as a lateral lamp platform. Women regulated heat by monitoring their lamps and punching or blocking holes in the main dome's peak. An ice window, the only part of a snow house transported from place to place, admitted light.

Similar at first glance, the various peoples' snow houses differed in details. Caribou Inuit houses were singular in that the people cooked on a hearth in the tunnel's kitchen rather than over the main chamber's lamp(s). Some sleeping platforms had storage niches built or cut into the front face. Ease of construction with snow blocks allowed domes (small or large) to be added quickly, for example to house equipment, food or dogs in the tunnel; if the exterior doorway had to be shifted away from the wind; or when more families arrived who nonetheless did not need to start an entire new house. In fact, a 19th-century explorer described one snow-house village as a 'beehive', connecting within to every inhabitant's house. The Copper Inuit sometimes built a larger dome in front of the sleeping chamber in order to have more room to dance and celebrate; these people also used straight-walled tunnels and built a wind-buffering external wall around the sleeping chamber. Inside temperatures were low, although Baffin Islanders loosely lined the dome's interior with tent skins, which allowed melt-free warmth.

Western Arctic

Virtually all houses in this region were entirely of wood (using driftwood logs everywhere north of the tree line), layered in sod and often rectangular in floor plan. They varied in size and the number of families who resided therein, but most had a lengthy tunnel, some with a passage above it, one or more sleeping platforms in the main chamber, either a cribbed roof held up by four centre posts or (less often) a gabled roof and a membrane-covered skylight that also vented heat and smoke.

In the Inuit area, Mackenzie Delta houses had four centre posts and a cruciform floor plan – one quadrant containing a hatch to the tunnel, the other three designed as elevated sleeping platforms for one or two families apiece, while the central, lower floor was communal. North Alaska Coast houses were rectangular and intended for one family, but paralleled the Caribou Inuit pattern of cooking in a tunnel side-chamber and using the household lamp principally for light and heat. The people here usually reached their main chamber through a floor hole where the tunnel ended; sometimes adjacent houses shared a tunnel, or two tunnels merged at a single exit. North Alaska Interior dwellings relied on willow poles (rather than driftwood), generally arranged in a hexagonal floor plan with a short, almost porch-like entrance passage.

Yupik peoples had greater access to larger logs, used centralized hearths for heat (hence smaller lamps, only for light), built very enduring houses and often lived in them all year long and for decades. Lodgings around Norton Sound (south of the Seward Peninsula) had a storage antechamber, which was descended into via notched log; a covered floor-level passage for summer; and, beneath that, a subterranean tunnel for winter. Their cribbed roofs needed supporting posts. Further south, Nunivak Island houses required four central posts to hold up a slightly cribbed roof, and had the distinction of sometimes being built in a spoke-like formation, connecting all houses underground by a continuous tunnel. Houses in the Gulf of Alaska were like those of the Mackenzie Delta in that they employed four tall centre posts linked diagonally to four shorter corner posts that together established a spacious common area; however, they were also unique in having separate sleeping chambers.

Summer Dwellings

Caribou- or sealskin-covered tents were the norm except towards the south in Alaska, where most travellers tipped their *umiaks* (large, open skin boats) sideways and sheltered under them. Tents assumed one of four basic shapes – arched, ridged, domed or conical – except in the Bering Strait, where people summered in a stilt house adapted to the steep-sided islands there. Its essence was a rectilinear wooden box, basically shrink-wrapped in sewn-together walrus hides, raised on four deep-set corner stilts, and further stabilized by two lateral, horizontal poles set far into the hillside. Seemingly sturdy, they nonetheless shook violently in high winds. People here spent winters in stone-lined huts built into the slopes.

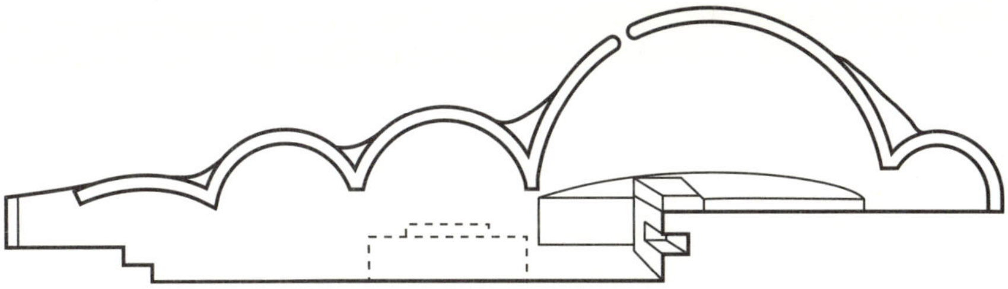

Above Turf is a good building material for cool northern climates because of its high insulating capability and its widespread availability. However, a good source of building turf was also considered a valuable farm resource.

Snidda, Klambra and Kvíahnaus Turf Architecture of Iceland

Sigríður Sigurðardóttir, John M. Steinberg, Douglas J. Bolender

Geography/Climate

Located in the North Atlantic Ocean, the volcanic island of Iceland has a subarctic climate, with cold winters and cool summers. Though the Gulf Stream mediates the full effect of low temperatures to coastal areas that would usually be expected at this latitude, the generally harsh environment forced early settlers to create well-insulated buildings with what materials were available, such as turf, timber and stone.

Materials

The turf-walled houses of Iceland have a complex construction that belies their initial appearance of soil-built structures dug into the earth. Turf is the root mass cut from the upper portion of a bog; once dried, it becomes a light, flexible and durable building material. Turf-walled buildings were probably being erected in Neolithic Europe, and Vikings constructed turf buildings as they expanded across the North Atlantic – the most far-flung example being at L'Anse aux Meadows in Newfoundland.

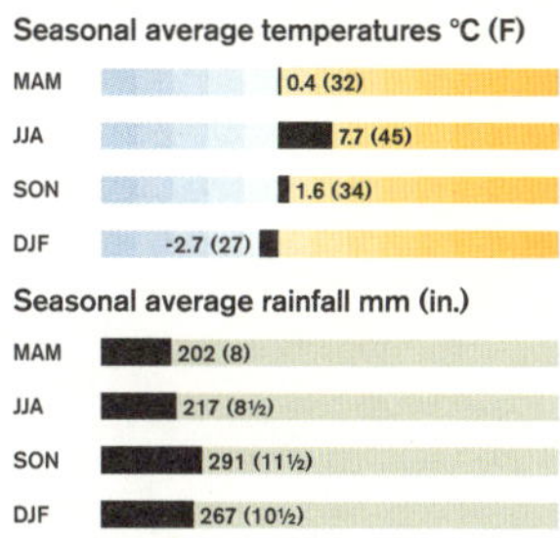

Construction Techniques and Building Plan/Form

Turf houses are an adaptation to subarctic environments, where there is a scarcity of native wood and stone suitable for building freestanding structures. In Iceland, the early Viking Age turf dwellings had the same hall or longhouse shape as those built with timber walls and roofs in mainland Scandinavia. These turf longhouses had gently curving sides and straight ends, sometimes with smaller rooms at either end. Additional barns, smithies, churches and other specialized buildings were separate from the main hall.

Over the centuries, turf-walled houses were elaborated and specialized rooms were attached to the main hall. Farmsteads in Iceland built of turf reached their most complex form between the 17th and 19th centuries. Many of these buildings had wooden gabled façades on one side. At the edges of large farmhouses, but still connected to them, would be rooms containing horse tack; hay storage; and, farthest out, smithies. In the main farmhouse, a central entrance opened on to a long hallway that bisected a warren of kitchens and storage rooms ending in a bedroom, usually with interior driftwood panelling, that bore a resemblance to the original Viking long hall.

Turf, while having good insulating properties, cannot bear very much weight; therefore, driftwood posts supported the lattice of planks framing the roof, which was made of alternating birch, sod and turf layers designed to freeze in the winter and become waterproof. A concentration of rooms allowed for the thick (1–2 m [3–6 ft]) turf walls to be shared between structures. The roofs had chimneys of various types, and sometimes windows, covered with a lining of sheep intestines.

Icelanders cut turf in regular blocks or strips, depending on the type of building that they were constructing. For animal barns, they used long, flat, wide *strengur* (strings) to act as a bonding between layers of stones (cows and sheep will eat turf). For some structures, triangular *snidda* turf blocks were used, while others employed square *kvíahnaus* blocks. The most elegant are the *klambra* turf blocks, which, when interspersed with *strengur*, can create a distinct herringbone-pattern wall. White volcanic ash layers and red iron stains can create beautiful patterns in the turf walls. In northern Iceland, dwelling walls were mostly of turf, sometimes with a single course of foundation rock, while in the south, where it rains more often, they contained a higher proportion of rock.

Traditional turf construction was slowly abandoned in the 20th century, and no Icelanders live in turf houses today. Some contemporary buildings are decorated with turf walls, in characteristic herringbone pattern, for their beauty and connection with the country's heritage. However, old turf buildings still can be found throughout the countryside and at many heritage sites, where they are maintained by a small number of builders who keep these techniques and traditions alive.

Below left The deep turf walls were shared between rooms arranged in close proximity, giving good insulation and maximizing the use of the available materials.

Below and opposite top Though excellent at keeping the cold out, turf is not suited to support heavy structural loads. Posts of driftwood acted as internal columns, supporting an embedded lattice of birch planks upon which the roof was laid. Timber doors and, since 1800, entire driftwood façades, are common fronts for turf buildings, such as the farmhouse at Glaumbær.

Opposite bottom Harvested from the upper layer of bogs, the turf blocks form a light, durable material for building once dry. Turf architecture has several different bonding patterns that utilize distinct turf block shapes and patterns. Most turf blocks are laid grass side down. The long *strengur* and triangular *klambra* blocks can be laid to form an elegant herringbone pattern.

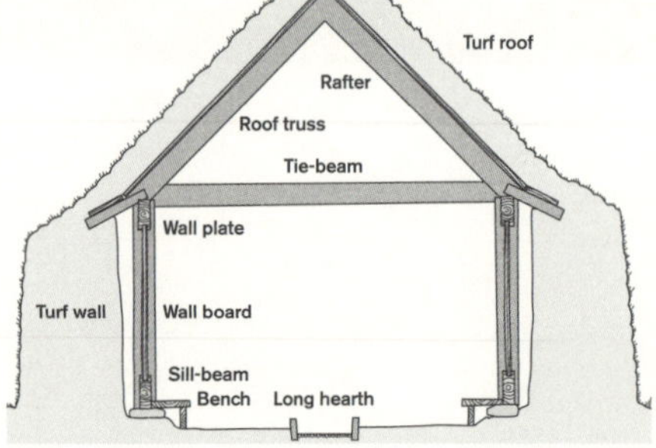

Goahte of the Sámi People

Kjell-Åke Aronsson and Isse Israelsson

Geography/Climate and Culture

The Sámi people are the indigenous population of northern Norway, Sweden, Finland and the Russian Kola Peninsula. For much of their history, they built their homes without the use of a single iron nail. Their knowledge of how to construct from what nature had to offer, in Arctic or subarctic environments, is a remarkable achievement. Traditionally, they relied on hunting, fishing, gathering and reindeer herding – with the last-named forming a migratory activity. Previously, reindeer-herding Sámi and their families moved together with their livestock but today modern vehicles such as snowmobiles or motorcycles are used to reach the herds.

In the Sámi language, a building is called *goahte* and it can assume many forms. Nonetheless, all Sámi building traditions are characterized by ecological adaption to Arctic and subarctic conditions. Their buildings protect against the cold snow-laden winter climate and against wind and rain, but they also need to be comfortable during hot summer days. Many traditional Sámi buildings are still in use today, although there is often no access to roads, electricity or the Internet.

Materials

Materials are taken from what is available in nature. In the boreal forests, pine logs and birch bark are preferred for construction. In the mountains and alongside the Arctic coasts, birch stems, birch bark and grass turf are used. Each of the components forms a stable construction.

Construction Techniques and Building Plan/Form

All types of *goahte* are placed directly on the ground. Twigs from birches are placed on the ground and upon them the hides from reindeer. The fireplace is always located in the middle of the *goahte*, for cooking and warmth.

The most specialized form of Sámi building construction was the portable tent-*goahte*. This comprised a home for an entire family. All its components were brought along during migrations, the only part to be bought or traded being the textile tent cover. The bearing construction consisted of two pairs of curved poles, which ensured that the *goahte* was spacious and stable. Supple timbers, usually spruce, were bent to form the curved structure of the tent-*goahte*. This use of exceptionally sturdy curved poles as supporting construction is unique to Sámi buildings, which were required to resist the forces of strong winds from the tundra. Birch stems with a natural bend were the supporting construction in different types of permanent *goahte* buildings. Portable *goahte* are still used in the mountains, so that the whole family can stay together during the marking of reindeer calves.

Sámi storehouses demonstrate a variation dependent on available building materials. They can be standing on one, two or more poles. House equipment and dried meat is stored in an elevated position guarded against wild animals like wolverines, pine martens and rodents searching for food.

Today, the only remains of migratory Sámi settlements are the stones around the fireplace.

Seasonal average temperatures °C (F)

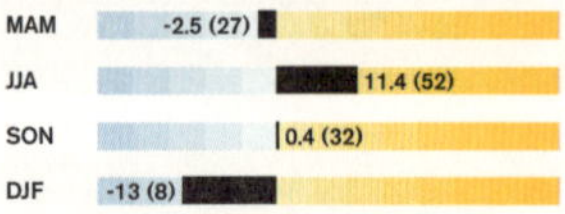

Seasonal average rainfall mm (in.)

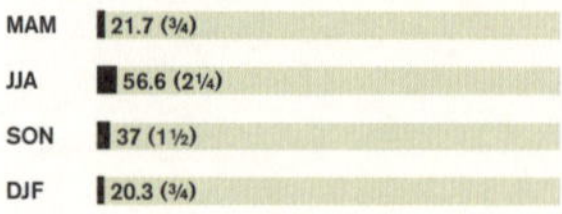

Left The most portable of all the Sámi's structures is the tent-*goahte* – a textile-based home that was supported by curved spruce and birch, which is in continued use today.

Opposite top Giving protection from the tundra gales and bitter winters as well as the hot summer, *goahte* are built from what is readily available. Mountainous and coastal areas usually draw on turf for construction.

Opposite bottom Elevated on four poles, storehouses known as *ajtte* are used to keep food and equipment away from wild animals, such as wolverines and rodents.

Appendix: Contemporary Vernacular

Opposite To create sustainable architecture that is also of its place, we urgently need to consider contemporary vernacular solutions that draw on ancient construction wisdom allied with modern knowledge. Making use of local material resources, the results are buildings, such as Morocco's Technology School of Guelmim, that are appropriate for each region and climate.

Wind and Water Bar

Vo Trong Nghia Architects
Binh Duong, Vietnam
2008

Located within an artificial lake in Vietnam's Binh Duong Province, the Wind and Water Bar is a structure built entirely from bamboo. Designed as a closed dome, the Bar contrasts with the adjacent open linear space of the Wind and Water Café, which is also solely built of bamboo and preceded the bar. As a result, the site has two very different types of building formed from the same material that harmonize with the natural setting in different ways.

The dome is constructed from a structural bamboo arch system that reaches 10 m (33 ft) in height and spans 15 m (50 ft). The main frame is made up of forty-eight prefabricated units, each of which were assembled from various lengths of bamboo then bound together and bent into arches. By dividing the whole dome into several framed units, an accurate structure could be realized that would also meet cost controls. The framed units were assembled on site, allowing for greater flexibility in transporting the structure.

The aim of the design was not merely to build folk handicrafts in local areas but to create green architecture for the modern age. Therefore it was essential to develop a system of production and construction of bamboo architecture.

The building uses the natural energy of wind together with cool water from the lake to create natural air ventilation. A circular opening with a diameter of 1.5 m (5 ft) at the apex of the dome serves to release any hot air generated inside the bar. These passive design methods greatly reduce the energy consumption of the building.

Local workers built the Wind and Water Bar over a three-month period. Projects such as this offer low-cost investment and rapid assembly; they also promise greater likelihood of development among low-income classes because of the reduced energy consumption both during construction and in operation.

Project Credits
Client: Wind and Water Company JSC
Principal Architect: Vo Trong Nghia
Architect: Ritsu Uchiyama
Contractor: Nghiem Dinh Toan and Vo Trong Nghia Architects

Bamboo Courtyard Teahouse

Harmony World Consulting and Design Associates (HWCD)
Shiqiao, Yangzhou, China
2012

Project Credits
Principal Architect: Sun Wei
Design Team: Shi Jun, Peter Dykes, Zhang QianQian

Part of the Shiqiao garden in Yangzhou, a city northwest of Shanghai, the floating Bamboo Courtyard Teahouse is an example of the design philosophy of Harmony World Consulting and Design Associates (HWCD), which emphasizes the idea of 'global interconnectedness' in architecture and design. In their practice, this manifests by bringing together traditional elements with an Asian aesthetic and the language of modern design.

Traditional courtyards in Yangzhou are formed of inward-facing pavilions to create an internal landscape space. Drawing inspiration from this, the floating teahouse's courtyard has a basic square footprint, fragmented into small spaces to create various internal landscaped areas. Each of the spaces is designed to have views to the surrounding lake and garden. The unassuming yet carefully detailed environment is an appropriate setting in which to experience the tea ceremony – one of China's precious cultural heritages that remains popular after thousands of years.

From the exterior, the bamboo courtyard appears as a cubic form made up of solids and voids. Tall rows of bamboo create corridors along the outdoor walkway and are arranged vertically and horizontally. This enhances the changing sense of depth and perspectival effects that visitors experience as they pass through the spaces. The verticality created by the bamboo lengths becomes more apparent at night when the lighting inside the teahouse illuminates the surroundings.

The design embraces the traditional fundamentals of Chinese garden design while blending into the existing environment. Its simple form is built with natural materials of brick as well as the predominant bamboo, which creates a sustainable approach. The pocket of voids created by the corridors improves natural ventilation within the bamboo courtyard while the thick brick wall retains heat in winter, reducing the dependency on mechanical heating and cooling systems.

Modern Education and Training Institute

Project Credits
Client: Dipshikha/METI Bangladesh in cooperation with Partnerschaft Shanti Bangladesch e.V. and the Papal Children's Mission (PMK)
Sponsor: Partnerschaft Shanti Bangladesch e.V. and Kindermissionswerk, Germany
Architects: Anna Heringer, Eike Roswag
Design and Concept: Anna Heringer
Technical Planning: Eike Roswag
Consulting Structural Engineer, Earth Construction: Ziegert Roswag Seiler Architekten Ingenieure Bürogemeinschaft, Berlin; Dr.-Ing. Christof Ziegert, Dipl.-Ing. Uwe Seiler
Consulting, building supervision and training of workers in construction: Emmanuel Heringer (basket weaver and carpenter), Stefanie Haider (blacksmith)
Design Supervision: Professor Roland Gnaiger, Martin Rauch, Peter Kugelstätter

Anna Heringer, Eike Roswag
Rudrapur, Dinajpur District, Bangladesh
2006

The Modern Education and Training Institute (METI) in the rural town of Rudrapur, Bangladesh, aims to promote individual abilities and interests taking into account the different learning speeds of the schoolchildren and trainees, in an open form of learning that is also free. It offers an alternative to the typical approach to teaching lessons from the front of the class. The architecture of the new school reflects this pedagogic principle and provides different kinds of spaces and uses, which support the alternative approach to teaching and learning.

Three classrooms are located on the ground floor, contained within thick earthen walls. Each has its own access point and opens up to an organically shaped system of 'caves' at the rear of the classroom. The soft interiors of these spaces are ideal for tactile exploration, for nestling up against, for retreating into, for exploration or for concentration, whether by individual children or larger groups of pupils.

In contrast, the upper floor is light and open; the apertures in its bamboo walls offer sweeping views across the surroundings, which take in the treetops and distant village pond, while its large interior provides ample space for moving about in. Light and shadows from the bamboo strips play across the earth floor and contrast with the colourful textiles of the saris on the ceiling.

Dipshikha Electrical Skill Improvement Training Centre

Anna Heringer
Rudrapur, Dinajpur District, Bangladesh
2008

The Dipshikha Electrical Skill Improvement (DESI) building in Rudrapur, a town with a population of around 3,000 people in northern Bangladesh, is a vocational school for electrical training that offers a new interpretation of the traditional Bangladeshi homestead.

In rural Bangladesh, all of the various household functions such as eating, sleeping and washing are typically performed in separate structures that are built around a central courtyard. The DESI building, however, attempts to incorporate all of the functions of working and living into a single structure. The design is oriented towards a lifestyle that is no longer linked with agriculture but is still closely linked to the rural context and culture in which it exists.

This change towards rural, educated lifestyles is reflected in the DESI building, which houses two classrooms, two offices and two residences for the school instructors. A separate bathroom for the teachers includes two showers and two toilets, while a bathroom facility with toilets and sinks for the students to use is located on the ground floor.

As well as offering an architectural model with integrated functions, the aim for the project is to renew traditional ecological construction techniques and increase awareness of the opportunities they present. Illustrating the benefit of building with local products that are available with little energy input, as compared to industrially produced alternatives, the DESI building is designed to be instrumental in teaching and disseminating this knowledge to the local community.

Project Credits
Structural Engineering and Technical Supervision: Stefan Neumann
Solar Installations and Electrical Concept: Jakob Schlub
Energy Concept: Oskar Pankratz
Adviser in Earthen Structures: Martin Rauch
Adviser in Bamboo Treatment and Quality Management: Prof. Walter Liese
Supervision of Site: Stefan Neumann, Montu Ram Saw, Shoeb Al Rahe
Project Management: Anna Heringer with Dipshikha

Fale Pasifika, University of Auckland

Project Credits
Principal Architect: Ivan Mercep, JASMAX
Contractors: Ebert Construction

JASMAX
Auckland, New Zealand
2004

The Fale Pasifika located at the University of Auckland, New Zealand, is a contemporary interpretation of customary architecture of the Pacific region, in particular, the *fale* (house/building). The use of durable Western building materials and construction methods is not peculiar only to this Pacific structure, but also applies to other buildings in the main centres of various Pacific Island groups. It could be argued that the aesthetics of some of these customary structures have been changed or replaced through the use of corrugated iron instead of thatching on roofs, and of concrete slab instead of the pebbles that were traditionally used on the *paepae* (front row of seating of a meeting house). Yet despite these transformations, the conceptual basis of the *fale* remains unaltered.

Through processes of colonization and globalization, the 'authentic' is sometimes revalidated by its community to suit another place and time. The Fale Pasifika is one such example, having undergone modern transformations to suit the needs of a new generation of Pacific people living in the diasporic context of New Zealand. It is a hybridized building that represents the Pacific communities of both New Zealand and the ancestral homeland. In this sense, the Fale Pasifika can also be described as a customary and contemporary response to the modern life of Pacific people.

Sabla: The Palm-Leaf Shelters

Project Credits
Client: TCA Abu Dhabi Historic Environment Department
Structural Engineering: BuroHappold Engineering
Fabric: Mehler Texnologies and Ocma Emirates Industries

3 Ideas Limited
Al Ain Oasis, United Arab Emirates
2014

In the Middle East, constructions built of date palm have been in use for around 7,000–8,000 years. Dry date palm leaves, which are an agricultural by-product from harvesting dates, offer huge potential for economic development in desert regions through the development and transfer of historic and modern technologies.

Sabla: The Palm-Leaf Shelters was conceived as a contemporary modular gridshell construction that offers an example of how traditional technologies can be adapted for use today, and scaled up or down to provide for a variety of applications in more than forty-six countries. The project is also a testament of authentic cultural continuity in the UAE.

The Sabla structure is the first modern date palm building in the Middle East and as such it is a case study for how local resilience can be built, whether through the creation of new jobs, the possibility of returning dry palm leaves into economic circulation or the opportunity for further exploration of issues concerning links between rural and urban areas. The project has received several awards internationally and was presented at the United Nations Convention to Combat Desertification, at Habitat III and at the United Nations Framework Convention on Climate Change.

Jeffry's House

Thomas O'Brien (Architect) and Emily Mannion (Artist)
Ards Forest Park, Donegal, Ireland
2014

Jeffrey's House is so named after Jeffry's Lough, over which it commands a view. Though the actual identity of Jeffry is anonymous, his name, and the traces of the lake bearing his name, remains. By remembering Jeffry through this project, the architect Thomas O'Brien and artist Emily Mannion hope to embed the shelter not just in the physical world but also in a more expansive landscape of memory and lore.

When considering the role of sustainability in architecture, O'Brien and Mannion ask: What do we actually mean by sustainability? What is it that we are sustaining? Their response suggests that perhaps the world of 'things' that humans have created, with the central idea that humankind is separate, is not actually worth sustaining. Perhaps instead we should be considering that everything in our universe is intrinsically connected; that matter is only the manifestation of slowed-down energy; and that we are merely accumulations of cosmic dust, like the light breeze of a zephyr. They posit that perhaps it is no longer really useful to use the word 'things' at all; rather better to speak of actors or convergences or portals.

Built from a larch timber frame, thatched in flax, the structure of Jeffry's House is curiously familiar while also appearing strange and un-programmed. Its thatch, in particular, recalls traditional roofs once commonly seen in Ireland and now in decline. The design is intended to be a respite from the elements, as well as from the trials of effort and the everyday. It is imagined as a portal for the irreducible universe of the cosmic.

Project Credits
Commissioners: Donegal County Council in partnership with the Irish Architecture Foundation, Coillte and the Earagail Arts Festival
Design and Construction: Thomas O'Brien, Emily Mannion
Thatch: Ivor KilPatrick

The Enterprise Centre, University of East Anglia

Architype
Norfolk, United Kingdom
2015

The Enterprise Centre is the most recent addition to the University of East Anglia campus in Norfolk. It presents a groundbreaking project that showcases architecture and materiality that is genuinely low-carbon, and that achieves the client's aspiration of Passivhaus standards for thermal comfort through passive measures, a rating of BREEAM Outstanding, as well as a 100-year performance lifecycle.

Where possible, materials for the building were sourced, tested and fabricated within 50 km (30 miles) of the site, with the balance of goods procured from elsewhere in the United Kingdom. Examples of locally harvested materials include the timber-frame construction, for which 70 per cent of the stud work was used, sourced from Thetford Forest, as well as the striking glued-laminated larch beams that support the entrance canopy.

This approach to utilizing local resources introduces an authentic design aesthetic that is genuinely of its place. It reflects the surrounding vernacular and embeds the building in its regional context. Most notably, this is seen in the spectacular and innovative expanse of straw thatched cladding, which was grown in Norfolk and applied by local thatchers.

Project Credits
Client: University of East Anglia and the Adapt Low Carbon Group
Structural Engineer: BDP
M&E Consultant: BDP
Lifecycle Cost Analysis: BSRIA
Landscape Architects: Churchman Landscape Architects
Main Contractor: Morgan Sindall
Project Manager: 3PM

Muir Craig Cottage

MacKay-Lyons Sweetapple Architects
Lower Kingsburg, Nova Scotia, Canada
2013

The Muir Craig Cottage is a prototype for a modest home containing three bedrooms, two bathrooms, a generous study and a large double-height reception room, all housed in 130 sq m (1,400 sq ft) and completed within a modest budget.

The project is a good neighbour: it reinforces the form, scale and siting of adjacent houses and barns. It is an almost invisible type of architecture. Its modest shingled shed creates privacy from the village road; at the same time, its shape and materials are a modest homage to local tradition.

While the form of the house is traditional, the material palette is modern and utilizes corrugated metal cladding that is seen in many local barns. Owing to its 'outsulation' strategy, whereby the structure's insulation is revealed not concealed as would be usual, the wood framing of this modest platform is carefully exposed on the interior. Millwork and finish carpentry are made of affordable Baltic birch plywood.

Every opening is positioned to frame specific landscape features as well as nearby vernacular precedents, which act to further situate the cottage in its physical and cultural context.

Project Credits
Architects: Brian MacKay-Lyons and Peter Broughton
Engineers: Campbell Comeau Engineering Limited
Builder: GR Kilgour Construction

Jianamani Visitor Centre

Atelier TeamMinus
Yushu, Qinghai, China
2013

In China's mountainous Qinghai region, Yushu is a highly regarded religious centre for Tibetans. Its significance mainly comes from the site of Jianamani, the world's largest Tibetan Buddhist cairn with a history that spans more than three centuries. The Jianamani cairn currently bears more than 250 million pieces of Mani stones (rocks inscribed with Buddhist prayer) yet continues to grow, with new pieces added daily by pilgrims.

Alongside its religious importance, the economic impact of Jianamani on the local community is incomparable. For more than 40 per cent of the Yushu population, carving Mani stones is an essential part of life and forms their principal source of income. The loyalty of Yushu's inhabitants to the cairn was illustrated after the 2010 earthquake, when the community immediately set off to repair Jianamani, long before they started repairing their own houses.

The Jianamani Visitor Centre is a site that provides information about Jianamani and its history, which is complemented by viewing spaces over the surrounding historical sites. Designed to serve visitors, pilgrims and the Yushu community, it also provides a post office, a clinic, public toilets and a small research archive that is used by locals.

Consisting of a square building with a central courtyard, the Jianamani Visitor Centre is surrounded by eleven observation decks surrounding it. The central square volume features a typical Tibetan layout. Of the eleven observation decks, two point to Jianamani while the remaining nine point to other sites of historic or religious note that are related to Jianamani. Built mainly using local construction techniques, the stone masonry was completed by local masons, using the same kind of rock from which the Mani stones are carved. The railings around the roof terrace and the observation decks are made of wood, with other elements recycled from usable debris retrieved after the earthquake, creating a distinctive architecture that is rooted in its local context.

Project Credits
Principal Architect: Brian Zhang Li
Construction: Yushu community

China Resources University

Foster + Partners
Shenzhen, China
2016

Xiao Jing Wan is a coastal urban development located to the east of Shenzhen. Part of Foster + Partners' masterplan for the region, this 55,000 sq m (600,000 sq ft) university is located on the top of a hill with exceptional views towards the sea. Teaching rooms and an Innovation Centre flank the central axis, which terminates with a grand building that houses the main auditorium and executive meeting rooms. The library, additional auditoria, students' bar, gym and residences step down the hill, maintaining views and linked by landscaping. The buildings maintain a strong horizontal emphasis, and utilize a restrained materials palette: fair-faced, exposed concrete, bronze-coloured cladding and a specially designed clay brick.

This area of Shenzhen has a history of brick masonry buildings, and the design of the university buildings follow in this tradition by offering a contemporary interpretation of the conventional building block. To accentuate the horizontality of the buildings, the brick extends more than half a metre (20 in) long, with a narrower cross-section. Although machine-pressed, the brick is rough-textured, giving it a crafted, handmade quality. The texture comes from pressing rough stones against the bricks by hand before firing them. The bricks are baked at varying temperatures (1,250–1,290°C [3,280–2,355°F]) to obtain a narrow variation in hue, which closely matches the tones of earth found locally.

Each dimension of the brick is carefully calibrated. Following a general module of 50 mm (2 in), the 42 mm (1⅔ in) height is overlaid with an 8 mm (⅓ in) layer of mortar to align the brickwork with other building elements such as doors, windows and staircases. The colour of the mortar exudes warmth, matching the shade of the fair-faced concrete on the buildings. The different brick-bonding patterns have also been developed in consonance with the horizontal theme of the buildings, with special L-shaped bricks designed to terminate the walls. The result is a precise, well-engineered complex of buildings that obtain their character from the basic building block – the brick – simultaneously reflecting the area's vernacular heritage and the contemporary nature of the university buildings.

Project Credits
Contractor: China Resources Construction
Architectural Design Team: Spencer de Grey, David Nelson, Armstrong Yakubu, David Summerfield, Chris Bubb, Niall Dempsey, Robert Seymour, Rui Pedro Rabaca, Lawrence Wong, Rui Alves, Cheuk Yin (Louise) Yeung, Tandorn Prakobpol, Sunil Rajaratnam, Eva Diu, Vivienne Wong, Lee Hallman, Andy Lister, Benjamin Stevenson
MEP and Structural Design Team: GDI
Façade Consultant: WSP

Shiv Temple of Wadeshwar

Sameep Padora & Associates
Wadeshwar, Maharashtra, India
2010

Project Credits
Design Team: Minal Modak, Vinay Mathias, Viresh Mhatre, Anushka Contractor, Maansi Hathiwala, Prajish Vinaya

The Shiv Temple in Wadeshwar, in the Pune district of India's Maharashtra state, exemplifies how architecture can adhere to the logic of traditional project typologies while also departing from conventional responses. It offers a design process based on an informed response to the site, materials and labour that avoids clichés while constantly engaging with the clients and their needs.

Built with very limited means and with materials available within a radius of 5 km (3 miles), the Shiv temple also highlights the multi-use nature of its architecture. Since the temple is designed to be as much a landscape project as an architectural one, it allows the space to encourage social interaction among the villagers as well as to function in its religious capacities.

Designed in dialogue with the priest and the people from surrounding villages, the architecture of the temple is a collaborative effort. A local basalt stone is used as a primary building block, chosen for its availability from a quarry only 200 m (650 ft) from the temple site; the stone also has a patina that seems to confer age, as if the temple had always existed. The form of the temple was chosen to evoke memories of the shikhara temple silhouette, while adhering to the planning logic of traditional temple architecture. Only embellishments integral to the essence of temple architecture in memory actually appear in the finished temple.

The heavy foliage of the trees along the site's edge demarcates an outdoor room, which becomes the traditional *mandapa* (pillared hall), a room where the trees form the walls and the sky is the roof. The path to the temple winds in between white oak trees to two freestanding basalt stone walls embedded in the landscape, which create a pause as well as directing visitors on to the east–west axis on which the *garbagriha* (inner sanctum) lies. Entry to the sanctum is through an exaggerated threshold space that, in turn, frames the outdoor landscape for those inside. Stepped seating on the site's southern edge negotiates the existing steep contours while transforming a purely religious space into a sociocultural one, which is used for festivals and gatherings.

Maria Grazia Cutuli Primary School

2A + P/A, IaN+ and MaO Architects
Herat, Afghanistan
2011

Following the murder of the Italian journalist Maria Grazia Cutuli in Afghanistan in 2001, her family established the Maria Grazia Cutuli Foundation. Its remit is to assist with social and educational programs for women and children in countries devastated by war or natural disasters, particularly in Afghanistan. This primary school bearing Maria Grazia's name is one such initiative.

As an innovative educational space, one of the school's main points has been to provide an alternative structure to schools usually built in post-war emergencies, as well as to introduce the idea of a 'green classroom' – an outdoor space for learning – and to use local technologies and construction logic as much as possible.

Sited on a dry landscape that is flat and dusty and with few neighbouring buildings, the school is defined by a necessary security border wall and created from a series of interlinked rectilinear structures that contain classrooms and corridors. The only two-storey volume among the low-lying forms is the library, which acts as a symbol of the project for the village. Together, the buildings and walls create a series of solids and voids, interspersed with shaded areas where children can play and relax.

The school is constructed from a frame of reinforced concrete and enclosed by solid bricks; all of the materials were built and sourced according to local use, with Afghan workers adapting designs to their construction processes. The orientation of each classroom and the fenestration of the façades were considered in relation to sun and wind patterns, to gain the optimum balance of daylight and natural ventilation. Coloured a vivid blue, the project has become a visible positive landmark within its arid environment.

Project Credits
Architects: 2A+P/A, Gianfranco Bombaci, Matteo Costanzo; IaN+ – Carmelo Baglivo, Luca Galofaro, Stefania Manna; Ma0 – Massimo Ciuffini, Ketty Di Tardo, Alberto Iacovoni, Luca La Torre with Architect Mario Cutuli
Collaborators: 2A+P/A – Valeria Bartolacci, Antonino Crea, Domenica Fiorini, Maxim Mangold, Valentina Morelli, Consuelo Nunez Ciuffa; IaN+ – Juliette Dubroca, Simone Lapenta; Ma0 – Manfredi Mazziotta, Mario Cutuli, Marco Bordone
Structures: Studio Croci Associati Ing. Federico Croci

Primary School Complex, Gando

Project Credits
Client: Schulbausteine für Gando e.V., Gando Village Community
Principal Architect: Francis Kéré

Kéré Architecture
Gando, Burkina Faso
2001

This project is based on the principles of designing for climatic comfort with low-cost construction to achieve sustainability. Making the most of local materials and the potential of the local community, the approach adapted technology from the industrialized world in a simple way. It was also conceived as a standard model that could be copied within the community and that would raise awareness of the merits of traditional materials.

The building's form and materials are largely determined by climatic considerations. Three classrooms are arranged in a linear fashion, separated by covered outdoor areas that can be used for teaching and play. The structure comprises traditional loadbearing walls made from stabilized and compressed earth blocks. Concrete beams span the width of the ceiling, and steel bars lying across these support a ceiling also made of compressed earth blocks. The corrugated metal roof sits on a steel truss, allowing cool air to flow freely between the roof and the ceiling. The roof's large overhang shades the façades and helps to ensure climatic comfort. Room temperature is additionally moderated by the earthen walls, which absorb heat.

The roof form was dictated by practical considerations: it was not possible to transport large elements to the site from afar, nor economically viable to use lifting machinery such as cranes. Instead, the architect devised a process in which common steel construction bars were used to create lightweight trusses, overlaid with corrugated metal sheeting to form the roof. Local people only needed to learn how to use a handsaw and a small welding machine.

Everyone involved in the project's management was native to the village, and the skills learned here could be applied in further initiatives for the village and elsewhere. The community's organization itself set an example for two neighbouring villages, which subsequently built their own schools as a cooperative effort. Local authorities also recognized the project's worth, providing and paying for the teaching staff, and endeavouring to employ the young people trained onsite in the town's public projects, using the same techniques.

Primary School Library, Gando

Project Credits
Client: Schulbausteine für Gando e.V.
Sponsor: Hevert Arzneimittel GmbH und Co Kg
Design Team: Francis Kéré, Dominique Mayer, Yasmin Bremer
Structural Engineering, Plant Engineering, Construction Supervision, Landscape Design: Kéré Architecture

Kéré Architecture
Gando, Burkina Faso
2012

Completed after the primary school building and its extension (see previous page), the library forms a joint between the two structures, sheltering the schoolyard from dust-carrying easterly winds. The library is open to everybody, not just pupils of the school, and is intended as a place for village elders to pass on knowledge and traditions to younger generations. As in the school buildings, the main construction material is compressed earth block, however the elliptical geometry of the library contrasts with the strictly rectangular school.

The ceiling is an innovative feature that makes good use of local technology. Clay pots, traditionally made by the women of the village, were brought to the site and cut, to be open at both top and bottom. The pots were then cast into the concrete ceiling to create holes for light and ventilation. A rectangular corrugated iron roof sits above this ceiling and extends beyond the library walls to create a separate shaded area for study or relaxation. As the metal roof becomes hotter it draws air from inside the library up and out through the holes in the roof, ensuring a comfortable rate of air circulation. The rectangular area around the library is enclosed by a façade of thin eucalyptus columns.

Eucalyptus is thought of as a weed in Burkina Faso; it dries out the soil and provides little shade from the sun; normally it is burned as firewood. However, this fast-growing, hardy plant is an appropriate building material for such an arid country, which suffers from desertification due to deforestation.

The interior quality of the library and surrounding space is pleasant, cool and airy – ideal conditions for learning, thinking and studying.

Rufisque Women's Centre

Hollmén Reuter Sandman Architects
Rufisque, Senegal
2001

The general African women's way of organizing themselves into groups of various sizes, from tens to hundreds, also occurs in Senegal. Women's organizations seek to ease their members' everyday life amid poverty, to guarantee them a reasonable 'social security', and to improve levels of schooling through independent initiatives and literacy courses. Supplementary income is created by selling homemade food and needlework. They also assist women to adapt to life-changing moves from the countryside to the city. These organizations are a structured version of women's traditional social networks created among family and friends.

The Women's Centre built in a suburb of Rufisque in the Dakar region offers facilities for activities of the various organizations for women. The centre is a collaborative project: its idea, finance, site and spatial programme were born in cooperation with the generosity of the local government and groups, NGOs and various other foundations.

According to West African custom, the building is grouped around an internal courtyard, creating a line between private and public that is clear but flexible. The simplicity of the street façades adapts the building to its surroundings – the corner facing a road crossing, for example, creates a small public square where facilities reserved for trading are located. Painted red, the bright colour gives the house its own identity amid the general grey tones of the neighbouring city blocks.

The choice of materials emphasizes local resources and recycling. Framed by a column-and-beam structure cast in situ, the walls are made of concrete blocks cast in a mould and dried on site. The roof of corrugated metal sheeting is supported by a system of steel beams, with thick woven straw matting to form an insulating ceiling structure. The space in between is ventilated, which guarantees that the air indoors remains pleasantly cool. Wood – a scarce material – was used only in places where no other substitute was possible. In the details, too, the sustainable approach continues: old car wheel rims are used as ventilation holes, and the bottoms of old glass bottles form windows. The reinforcement iron in the concrete is made of recycled material.

Project Credits
Principal Sponsors: Tekniska Föreningen i Finland NGO, Finnish Foreign Ministry, Senegalese-Finnish Association ARC
Architects: Saija Hollmén, Jenni Reuter, Helena Sandman
Structural Engineer: Galaye Niang, Maty Ingenierie Consultant
Consulting Architect: Mbacke Niang
Contractor: Abdourahmane Mbaye

Technology School of Guelmim

Project Credits
Client: Université Ibn Zohr D'Agadir
Architects: Saad El Kabbaj, Driss Kettani, Mohamed Amine Siana
Project Team: Yassine El Aouni, Rachid El Maataoui
Engineering: Bepol Sarl
Contractor: Zerkdi & Fils

Saad El Kabbaj, Driss Kettani, Mohamed Amine Siana
Guelmim, Morocco
2011

The Technology School of Guelmim was constructed as part of the development policy of academic institutions in the southern regions of Morocco. The school includes an amphitheatre, classrooms, workshops, laboratories, administration facilities, a library, teacher's offices and housing for office staff.

The starting point for the project was to provide a strong architectural form that was contemporary but was also inspired by the context in which it occurs. The challenge was to recreate a particular mood and a particular scale that was locally relevant while using a vocabulary and technology that make reference to modern architecture. The result a form that is voluntarily massive and powerful, and explores the contrast between interior and exterior spaces.

Organized along a north–south axis created by a formal pathway that is partly covered, the various buildings are arranged in a series of L-shaped forms or indoor gardens. This arrangement helps the various entities of the project to be readable and clearly articulated while also maintaining structures built at a range of scales that reflect the diversity of the programmes held inside.

Similarly, in order to achieve good thermal quality, the work is oriented in specific directions, with openings protected through overhanging brise-soleil and vegetation cover; this passive conditioning is an embedded part of the project's architectural language and principles.

In addition to the sustainable and contextual criteria shaping the project, its final form assumes a certain theatricality and a degree of gravitas that is appropriate to an educational institution of this type.

Tambabox

Project Credits
Design Team: Iván Juárez and Patricia Meneses
Collaborators: Mamadou Diouf and Amadou Souka Gom
Supported By: Collectif Artistes Plasticiens, Geneva

Iván Juárez and Patricia Meneses
Tambacounda, Senegal
2004

Tambabox is an object-space created from the extraordinarily varied and complex selection of industrial textiles that many Senegalese use to make their own *boubous* (robes). The project consists of an inner space that is enveloped by an assembly of textile canvases and is proposed as a site with open programming in which different art practices, such as dance, music and acting, could occur alongside the poetic experience of the structure itself.

The fabrics that form the architecture are like murals in which people's arms can fit through sleeves embedded in the walls, partly transforming the project and allowing visitors to interact with the cloth. The textiles themselves are part of a complex cultural story that describes the variety of skills and materials of the Senegal landscape and its people, as well as the towns that coexist in their markets and their cities. The project was realized in collaboration with local craftsmen, carpenters and tailors, all of which are fundamental professions in Senegal, with great traditions.

The project behaves like a structure that is interposed between the sunlight and the interior space it encloses. The textile planes become regulators of light and filter natural daylight; during the day, the ambient lighting in the space changes thanks to the different patterns and colours of the different textile panels. The result of Tambabox is a space that brings together architecture, sculpture and movement – a space that people can explore the through their direct and changing experience of the light and the form itself.

The Brighton Waste House

BBM Sustainable Design
Brighton, United Kingdom
2014

The Brighton Waste House is Europe's first permanent public building with 90 per cent of its structure made from discarded material. The project is also 'carbon negative', creating about 25 per cent more energy than it consumes. Constructed by more than 360 design and construction students, the project mines local material flows that are normally overlooked.

Originally conceived as a live research project that would utilize the 20 per cent of material that is most often sent to landfill or for incineration from conventional construction sites, the project became more of a polemic by capturing everyday domestic waste as well. In only four days, 19,800 toothbrushes were collected, along with 4,000 VHS video cassettes, and two tonnes of denim.

All of these unusual materials form part of a wider array that is used in the building to form low-grade wall insulation and will remain until or if someone finds a useful new life for them.

The building accommodates the University of Brighton's Sustainable Design MA programme, as well as being an open studio for local communities to use. Its external fabric is currently being monitored to see how its unusual materials perform thermally. The future intention for the project is that it will be updated by new generations of students, so that one day, for example, the 2,000 carpet tiles currently cladding the exterior may be replaced with another waste material that is also local to the site. The project aims to prove the designers' motto that 'there is no such thing as waste, just stuff in the wrong place'.

Project Credits
Project Managers, Architects, Contract Administrators, Lead Consultants: BBM Sustainable Design
Design Collaboration and Construction: University of Brighton staff and design students, City College Brighton and Hove staff and construction students
Principal Contractors: The Mears Group
Structural Engineers: BBP Consulting Engineers
Environmental Engineers: Robinson Associates
Resource Manager: Cat Fletcher, FREEGLE UK
Facilitators: Brighton & Hove City Council

RATIONING'S
FINE BUT
RECYCLING'S
SUBLIME.
@reAquasystems

MEARS

Notes

INTRODUCTORY ESSAYS

Introduction

1 COP21 Paris Agreement, Preamble.

A Geographical Classification of Earth Materials in Vernacular Buildings

1 See www.fao.org/docrep/003/y1899e/y1899e02.htm (accessed 9 November 2015).

An Anthropological Introduction to Vernacular Architecture

1 Gérard Toffin, 'Ecology and Anthropology of Traditional Dwellings,' *Traditional Dwellings and Settlements Review*, 1994, Vol. 5, No. 2, pp. 9–20.
2 André Singer, *Ethnic Identity in Eastern Iran*, 1976, PhD dissertation, Exeter College, Oxford.
3 Claude Lévi-Strauss, *Anthropologie Structurale* (Paris: Plon, 1958).

The Value of the Vernacular

1 The protection and restoration of old Kabul under the Turquoise Mountain Project or the restoration of Djenné in Mali may be considered good examples of this, although there are numerous others.
2 As has been experienced in China since 1978.
3 As has been the case in the recent desertification in the Sahel region of West Africa.
4 Distributors of cement or corrugated iron in poor countries frequently benefit from economies of scale that locally based builders, using local materials, cannot compete with.

TROPICAL CLIMATE

Chattel Houses and Timber Architecture of the Caribbean

1 This follows UNESCO's definition, and comprises 16 independent sovereign states (Antigua and Barbuda, the Bahamas, Barbados, Belize, Cuba, Dominica, the Dominican Republic, Grenada, Guyana, Haiti, Jamaica, Saint Kitts and Nevis, Saint Lucia, Saint Vincent and the Grenadines, Suriname, and Trinidad and Tobago) and 18 associated overseas territories and dependencies: Guadeloupe, Martinique, Saint Barthélemy and Saint Martin (France), Aruba, Bonaire, Curaçao, Sint Maarten, Sint Eustatius and Saba (the Netherlands), Anguilla, Bermuda, the Cayman Islands, Montserrat, the Turks and Caicos Islands, the British Virgin Islands (United Kingdom), and Puerto Rico and the US Virgin Islands (United States of America).
2 Pieter C. Emmer (ed.), *General History of the Caribbean, Volume II – New Societies: The Caribbean in the long sixteenth century* (Paris: UNESCO Publishing, 1999), pp. 6–7, 33.
3 Peter L. Drewett, *Prehistoric Settlements in the Caribbean* (Barbados: Archetype Publications for the Barbados Museum and Historical Society, 2000), p. 4.
4 CARIMOS, *Monumentos y Sitios del Gran Caribe* (Monuments and Sites of the Greater Caribbean) (Santo Domingo: CARIMOS, 2000), p. 4.
5 Emmer, *General History*, p. 282.
6 R. van Oers, 'Multi-ethnicity and Cultural Significance in Georgetown (Guyana)', in *Partnerships for World Heritage Cities*, World Heritage Papers 9 (Paris: UNESCO, 2004), p. 40.
7 David F. Marley, *Historic Cities of the Americas – An Illustrated Encyclopedia. Volume 1: The Caribbean, Mexico and Central America* (Santa Barbara, CA / Oxford: ABC Clio, 2005), p. 24.
8 Emmer, *General History*, pp. 229–34.
9 *Ibid.*, p. 32; A. Gravette, *Architectural Heritage of the Caribbean* (Kingston: Ian Randle Publishers, 2000), p. 7.
10 Carter et al., *History of the West Indian Peoples – Book III: From Earliest Times to the 17th Century* (Walton-on-Thames, Surrey: Thomas Nelson and Sons, 1959), p. 22.
11 Emmer, *General History*, p. 19; Gravette, *Architectural Heritage*, p. 9.
12 Gravette, *Architectural Heritage*, pp. 14–17.
13 *Ibid.*, p. 117.
14 Steve A. Devonish, 'The use of timber in Barbados: the case of the chattel house', in R. van Oers and S. Haraguchi (eds), *Caribbean Wooden Treasures*, World Heritage Papers 15 (Paris: UNESCO, 2005), p. 48; Alvin O. Thompson, 'Sites of Memory: contributions of enslaved Africans to the built heritage of the Caribbean', in S. Haraguchi and R. van Oers (eds), *Safeguarding Precious Resources for Island Communities*, World Heritage Papers 38 (Paris: UNESCO, 2014), p. 62.
15 Gravette, *Architectural Heritage*, p. 20.
16 Nilson Acosta Reyes, 'Wood: the Cultural Bridge of the Caribbean', in *Caribbean Wooden Treasures*, World Heritage Papers 15 (Paris: UNESCO, 2005), p. 52.
17 *Ibid.* p. 53.
18 Gravette, *Architectural Heritage*, pp. 56–66.
19 S. Gordon, 'The folk architecture of Saint Kitts and Nevis', in Van Oers and Haraguchi, *Wooden Treasures*, p. 69.

Creole, Carbet, Caboclo and Brasileiro-Caribbean Houses of French Guiana and Brazil

1 Patrick Pérez and Olivier Archambeau, *Architectures et Paysages de Saint Georges de l'Oyapock* (Cayenne: OHM CNRS, 2010).

Upper Xingu and Wajãpi Vernacular Of Brazil

1 Michael Heckenberger, *The Ecology of Power: Culture, Place, and Personhood in the Southern Amazon, A.D. 1000–2000* (New York / London: Routledge, 2005), p. 191.

Favelas of Brazil's Urban Periphery

1 The favelados' intention was to demonstrate their eligibility for equal rights and the right to use the land, establishing the People's Assembly (Assembléia do Povo, or AP). This organization used a range of strategies to illustrate that they were not 'idlers, misfits or prostitutes' but rather decent citizens who worked and should have rights. See Evelina Dagnino, 'Civic Driven Change and Political Projects' in Alan Fowler & Kees Biekart (eds), *Civic Driven Change: Citizen's Imagination in Action.* (The Hague: Institute of Social Studies, 2008), pp. 3–5.

Guarani 'Big Houses' of Paraguay

1 J. R. Rengger, *Reise nach Paraguay in den Jahren 1818 bis 1826* (Journey to Paraguay between 1818 and 1826) (Aarau: Verlag H. R. Saverlaender, 1835).

Vernacular Settlements of Côte d'Ivoire, Ghana, Togo, Benin and Cameroon

1 G. T. Stride and C. Ifeka, *Peoples and Empires of West Africa: West Africa in History 1000–1800* (Surrey: Thomas Nelson and Sons Limited, 1986).
2 J. Hockings, 'Built Form and Culture: A theoretical Appraisal Supported by a Case Study of the Dwelling Houses in the Gilbert Islands, West Pacific', *Architecture and Comfort/Architectural Behaviour*, Vol. 3, No. 4 (1987): 281–300; J. B. Webster and A. A. Boahen, *The Growth of West African Civilisation - The Revolutionary Years: West Africa since 1800* (London: Longman Group Limited, 1967).
3 Paul Oliver (ed.), *Encyclopedia of Vernacular Architecture of the World* (Cambridge: Cambridge University Press, 1997).
4 M. Mitchell and A. Bevan, *Culture, Cash and Housing: Community and Tradition in Low-income Building* (London: Intermediate Technology Publication Ltd, 1992), pp. 12–33.
5 *Ibid.*
6 B. Rudofsky, *Architecture without Architects – A Short Introduction to Non-Pedigree Architecture* (Albuquerque, NM: University of New Mexico Press, 1964) – eighth paperback printing, 2003.
7 Mitchell and Bevan, *Culture*; Webster and Boahen, *Growth.*

Vernacular and Colonial Structures in Sri Lanka

1 *CIA World Fact Book.* Available at www.cia.gov/library/publications/resources/the-world-factbook/geos/ce.html (accessed 27 October 2015).
2 Robert Knox, *An Historical Relation of the Island Ceylon in the East-Indies* (London: Richard Chiswell, 1681), p. 87.
3 Ronald Lewcock et al., *The Architecture of an Island* (Colombo: Barefoot, 1988), p. 53.

Southeast Asian Adaptation to Migration, Mobility and Monsoons

1 The principle of 'renewing' buildings is exemplified by the ritual rebuilding of the main building (*shoden*) of the Ise Shrine, Kyoto, dating to the 7th century AD, a structure ceremonially reconstructed anew every 20 years. In Lai Tarung, a ceremonial village in Central Sumba, Indonesia – no longer inhabited, but maintained as a centre for ritual – the houses of the gods are reconstructed periodically, and used only for ceremonies honouring the ancestors.
2 Roxana Waterson, *The living house: An anthropology of architecture in South-East Asia* (New York: Whitney Library of Design, 2008).
3 The Dorothy Pelzer Collection – the National Anthropological Archives, Smithsonian Institution, Washington, DC, and the Institute of Asian Studies, Singapore – comprises an annotated photographic archive of traditional 'built forms' photographed by Pelzer (1961–71) in Brunei, Burma, Cambodia, Hong Kong, Indonesia, Laos, Malaysia, the Philippines, Sarawak (Malaysian Borneo), Singapore, Thailand and Vietnam.
4 Anthony Tung, *Preserving the World's Great Cities: The destruction and renewal of the historic metropolis* (New York: Three Rivers Press, 2002).

Vernacular and Colonial Structures of Singapore

1 Much of the archaeological evidence substantiating the island's early history is the result of research by archaeologist John N. Miksic (National University of Singapore), and scholars Peter Borschberg, Brian Farrell, Kwa Chong Guan, Derek Heng and Tan Tai Yong. Their revised history informs a new school text, *Singapore: The Making of a Nation-State, 1300–1975* (Singapore: Star Publishing, 2014).

Rumah Adat and *Marapu* of Indonesia's Sumbanese Vernacular

1 Fikret Berkes, 'Traditional Ecological Knowledge in Perspective in Inglis', Julian T. Inglis, *Traditional Ecological Knowledge: Concepts and Cases* (Ottawa: Canadian Museum of Nature, 1993), p. 3.
2 Nggodu Tunggul, *Etika dan Moralitas dalam Budaya Sumba* (Jakarta: Pro Millenio Center, 2003), p. 21.
3 *Ibid.* pp. 56–57.
4 *Ibid.* p. 21.
5 World Wildlife Fund information on Southeastern Asia: Island of Sumba in 'Indonesia, Ecoregions', by John Morrison, quoted from *Terrestrial Ecoregions of the Indo-Pacific: A Conservation Assessment* (Washington, DC: Island Press, 2003).
6 Fritjof Capra, quoted in Berkes, *Traditional Ecological Knowledge in Perspective*, p. 1.

Longhouses and Korowai Treehouses of New Guinea

1 Based on uranium/thorium dating and thermoluminescence dates of volcanic ash associated with waisted blades on the Huon Peninsula: P. Kirsch, *On the road of the winds: an archaeological history of the Pacific Islands before European contact* (Berkeley, CA: University of California Press, 2000), p. 63.
2 Frank Hurley, cited in Jim Specht and John Fields (eds), *Frank Hurley in Papua: Photographs of the 1920–1923 Expeditions* (Bathurst: Robert Brown and Associates in association with the Australian Museum Trust, 1984), p. 124.
3 Rupert Stasch, *The Society of Others: Kinship and Mourning in a West Papua Place* (Berkeley, CA: University of California Press, 2009).

Micronesia's *Bai, Ulitao, Pebaye*, Katelu and Stone Constructions

1 S. A. Earle and the National Geographic Society (US), *National Geographic atlas of the ocean: the deep frontier* (Washington, DC: National Geographic Society, 2001).
2 A. P. Sturman and H. P. McGowan, 'Climate', in M. Rapaport (ed.), *The Pacific Islands: Environment & Society* (Honolulu: Bess Press, 1999), pp. 3–18.
3 P. V. Kirch, 'Peopling of the Pacific: a holistic anthropological perspective', *Annual Review of Anthropology*, 39 (2010): 131–48.
4 The current polities of the region are the US Territory of Guam, the Commonwealth of the Northern Mariana Islands, the Republic of Palau, the Federated States of Micronesia (Yap, Chuuk, Pohnpei and Kosrae states), the Republic of the Marshall Islands, Nauru and Kiribati. G. Petersen, *Traditional Micronesian Societies: Adaptation, Integration, and Political Organization* (Honolulu: University of Hawai'i Press, 2009).
5 J. Liston, 'Cultural Chronology of Earthworks in Palau, Western Micronesia', *Archaeology in Oceania*, 44 (2009): 56–73.
6 G. Keate, *An Account of the Pelew Islands, Situated in the Western Part of the Pacific Ocean; Composed from the Journals and Communications of Captain Henry Wilson, and some of his Officers, Who, in August 1783, were there Shipwrecked, in the ANTELOPE, a Packet Belonging to the Honourable East India Company*, 1st edition (London: G. Nichol, 1788).
7 K. L. Nero, 'Keate's *Account of the Pelew Islands*: A View of Koror and Palau', in K. L. Nero and N. Thomas (eds), *An Account of the Pelew Islands: George Keate* (London / New York: Leicester University Press, 2002), pp. 7–25.
8 See the Palau Society of Historians, *Rechuodel: Traditional Culture and Lifeways Long Ago in Palau* (San Francisco: Micronesian Endowment for Historic Preservation, 1997) (English translation by DeVern Reed Smith), pp. 51–3, for an introduction to Palauan carpentry still used today.
9 See G. Fahr-Becker & C. Murray, *The Art of East Asia* (Cologne: Könemann,1999), for images on pp. 320, 323, and especially p. 315 depicting the high-gabled thatched saddle-back roofs found on nearly all Micronesian buildings.
10 G. Fritz, *The Chamorro: A History and Ethnography of the Marianas* (Saipan: Division of Historic Preservation, 1989 [1904]), translated by E. Craddock and edited by S. Russell.
11 A single pillar could reach 6 m (20 ft) long, and weigh 34 tonnes (Eric Metzgar: personal communication with the author, 18 June 2014).
12 E. Metzgar, 'Sacred Space, Taboo Place: Negotiating Roang on Lamotrek Atoll', *Micronesian Journal of the Humanities and Social Sciences*, 3 (1-2) (2004): 3–18.
13 Eric Metzgar: personal communication with the author, 18 June 2014.
14 See *https://whc.unesco.org/en/tentativelists/5652* (accessed 2 November 2015).
15 See W. N. Morgan, 'Prehistoric architecture in Micronesia' (Austin, TX: University of Texas Press, 1988), see provisional site map pp. 66–67.
16 Ayres and Mauricio, 1997.
17 Nancy Pollock: personal communication with the author, 18 June 2014.
18 C. Wilkes, *Narrative of the United States Exploring Expedition during the years 1838, 1839, 1840, 1841, 1842* (Vol. 4) (Philadelphia, PA: Lea and Banchard, 1845): 5, image facing p. 56.

Navala and Lau *Bure* of Fiji

1 Thomas Williams, *Fiji and the Fijians* (New York: D. Appleton, 1858), p. 79.

The 'Big Roof' of the Cook Islands

1 Jeanette Budgett, 'Coral Architecture of the Cook Islands' Master's thesis, University of Auckland, 2007.
2 From Josef Frank, 'Akzidentismus', in M. Bergquist and O. Michelsen (eds), *Josef Frank Architektur* (Basel: Birkhäuser, 1995).
3 Jeremy Treadwell, 'Ventilating the Tropical Modern', proceeding of the audience: 28 Annual Conference of the Society of Architectural Historians, Australia and New Zealand, Brisbane, 7–10 July 2011.

Fare and *Marae* Structures of French Polynesia

1 J. C. Beaglehole (ed.), *The Journals of Captain James Cook on his Voyages of Discovery*, Vol. I: 'The Voyage of the Endeavour, 1786–1771' (Glasgow: Cambridge University Press for the Hakluyt Society, 1955), p. 128.

DRY CLIMATE

Pueblo and Mesa Developments of the American Southwest and Mexico

1 Lisa Heschong and John DeKay, *Thermal Delight in Architecture* (New York: John Wiley & Sons, 2001), p. 8.
2 Amos Rapoport, *House Form and Culture* (New York: Prentice Hall, 1969).
3 Christopher Alexander et al., *A Pattern Language* (New York: Oxford University Press, 1977), p. 911.
4 Marc Treib, *Sanctuaries of Spanish New Mexico* (Berkeley: University of California Press, 1993), p. 23.
5 Alexander, *Pattern Language*, p. 910.
6 G. Z. Brown and Mark DeKay, *Sun, Wind and Light: Architectural Design Strategies* (New York: John Wiley & Sons, 2nd edition, 2001), p. 83.
7 Heschong and DeKay, *Thermal Delight*, p. 7.
8 Brown and DeKay, *Sun, Wind and Light*, p. 136.
9 Amos Rapoport, 'The Nature of the Courtyard House', *Traditional Dwellings and Settlements Review*, Vol. XVII, No. II (Berkeley: University of California, 2007): pp. 57–72.
10 Alexander, *Pattern Language*, p. 581.

Totora and Adobe Homes of Peru

1 John Hemming, 'Peru's Domestic Architecture', unpublished article, 2015.

Defensive *Qsur* of Algeria

1 D. J. Mattingly (ed.), *The Archaeology of Fazzān*, Vol. 1, 'Synthesis' (London: The Society of Libya Studies; Tripoli: Department of Antiquities, 2003), pp. 136–48.
2 This phrase is drawn from the medieval Arabic expression 'land of the blacks', which was used to describe the regions of settled Africa close to the southern Saharan boundary.
3 Ibadism is a distinct sect of Islam that is neither Sunni nor Shia and exists mainly in Oman, East Africa, the Mzab valley of Algeria, the Nafus mountains of Libya, and the island of Jerba in Tunisia. See Professor Valerie J. Hoffman's Introduction to Ibadism at http://islam.uga.edu/ibadis.html (accessed 25 January 2016).

Southern Africa's Vernacular Diversity

1 D. Claude, 'Space and symbols in rural KwaZulu-Natal', *KZNIA Journal* 2/1997: 22; D. Claude, 'Traditional architecture of the Tembe', *Journal of Architecture* 4 (1999), pp. 1–15.
2 B. Biermann, 'Indlu: The domed dwelling of the Zulu', in P. Oliver, *Shelter in Africa* (London: Barrie & Jenkins, 1971); W. Knuffel, *The Construction of the Bantu Grass Hut* (Graz: Akademische Druck-u. Verlangsanstalt, 1975).
3 A. Kuper, 'Symbolic dimensions of the Southern Bantu Homestead', *Africa* 50 (1) (1980): 8–23; T. Evers, 'The recognition of groups in the Iron Age of Southern Africa', PhD (Archaeology) thesis, University of Witwatersrand, 1988.
4 A. Berglund, *Zulu Thought Patterns and Symbolism* (Bloomington, IN: Indiana University Press, 1989), p. 108.
5 R. Harber, 'The American flat in Africa', *SA Architect* (March 2000), pp. 37–40.
6 F. Frescura, 'The South African flat-roofed dwelling: A study in geographical adaptation and cultural tradition' in *South African Journal of Culture and Art History* 3(4) (Johannesburg: South African Association of Art Historians, 1989), pp. 365–387.

Earthen and Date-palm Structures in the Arabian Peninsula

1 See A. Zaid and P.F. de Wet's analysis: http://www.fao.org/docrep/006/y4360e/y4360e06.htm (accessed 25 October 2015).

Architecture of Stone and Clay in Israel and the Levant

1 World Heritage inscription statement
2 Jerusalem Talmud, Tractate Yoma Chapter 5:2.

Throne Villages of Palestine's Central Highlands

1 Suad Amiry and Vera Tamari, *The Palestinian Village Home* (London: British Museum Publications, 1989), p. 24.

Variety, Locality and Western Influence in Iran

1 Lord Curzon, *Persia and the Persian Question* (London: Longman Green & Co., 1982), p. 303.

Chaura, Earth, Timber and Stone Dwellings of Pakistan

1 Paul Oliver, *Encyclopaedia of Vernacular Architecture of the World* (Cambridge: Cambridge University Press, 1997).
2 Hassan Fathy, *Architecture for the Poor: An Experiment in Rural Egypt* (Chicago: University of Chicago Press, 1973).
3 The wide-ranging work carried out by the Heritage Foundation of Pakistan (HF) in communities recovering from 'natural' disasters has demonstrated that vernacular construction techniques are relevant responses to the challenges created by greenhouse gas-based climate change. By incorporating modifications and relevant technical interventions, keeping in view the impact of climate change, HF is promoting the use of vernacular methodologies as least-cost alternatives that are also DRR (Disaster Risk Reduction) compliant (see The Heritage Foundation's 2011 document 'Build Back Safer with Vernacular Methodologies'). For instance, owing to improved vernacular methodologies devised by HF, not a single tree has been felled in the construction of 40,000 zero-carbon-footprint shelters by the International Organization for Migration (IOM). At the same time, the local economy has been regenerated and dormant skills have been revived for poverty alleviation, thus fostering pride in local traditions and culture among marginalized communities.
4 A notable exception is provided by Caroline Denigan's 2002 research paper for the University of Adelaide, 'The Self-Build Housing of Men and Others: Researching Gender and Vernacular Architecture in Australia'.
5 HF's replacement of timber logs with specially designed bamboo joists, and a roof covering finished with a lime/mud render, have resulted in the construction of thousands of flood-resistant sustainable shelters in Sindh province that have withstood three consecutive years of flooding.
6 Randolph Langenbach, *Don't Tear it Down! Preserving the Earthquake Resistant Vernacular Architecture of Kashmir* (New Delhi: UNESCO, 2009).
7 Replacing wood with bamboo to achieve a low ecological footprint, HF has adopted well-anchored and carefully tied *dhajji* construction in flood-prone areas. HF's multiple-bamboo-joist roofs are light and at the same time very strong as they provide refuge from flood waters. They can also be used as roof vegetable gardens for food security, or for sleeping during most of the year. Hundreds of units have been built in Swat (northern Pakistan) and Sindh (southern Pakistan), using stone infill or mud respectively.
8 Yasmeen Lari, *Traditional Architecture of Thatta*, (Karachi: The Heritage Foundation, 1989).
9 By designing technical interventions for flood-resistant sustainable construction and replacing timber with bamboo for supporting frame structures, Yasmeen Lari has promoted the *chaura* form extensively in rural and semi-urban locations in Pakistan.

Turkmenistan's Earthen Structures

1 L. Cooke, *Conservation Approaches to Earthen Architecture in Archaeological Contexts*, British Archaeological Reports International Series S2147 (Oxford: Archaeopress, 2010).
2 L. Cooke, 'Earthen Building Materials and Techniques at Merv, Turkmenistan', in Franz Volhard and Ulrich Röhlen (eds), *Lehm 2004. 4. Internationale Fachtagung für Lehmbau* (Weimar: Dachverband Lehm e.V., 2004), pp. 52–61.

Ger Dwellings of Inner Asian Mongolia

1 The Mongolian terms in parentheses here indicate the Khalkha terminology for the *ger's* constituent parts. Khalkha was the official language of the Mongolian People's Republic.

TEMPERATE CLIMATE

Chickee, Charleston and Shotgun Housing in the American South

1 *Anthony King, Spaces of Global Culture: Architecture, Urbanism, Identity* (London: Routledge, 2004).
2 Bernard Herman, 'The Charleston Single House', in Jonathan Poston, *The Buildings of Charleston: A Guide to the City's Architecture* (Columbia, SC: University of South Carolina Press, 1997). In general, urban lots vary from about 9 to 15 m (30–50 ft) in width and 30 m (100 ft) in depth. Some grand houses occupy much larger lots.
3 Bernard Herman, *Town House: Architecture and Material Life in the Early American City*, 1780–1830 (Chapel Hill, NC: University of North Carolina Press, 2005), pp. 119–54. Herman demonstrates that surveillance was more an aspiration than a reality. The only access to the servants' quarters was generally through the passage beside the house. Alleys behind these houses are not common.
4 The Aiken-Reitt House, built in 1818 and added to in 1833, has thick masonry walls. Its interior remains cool through most of the summer, heating up finally in August and September.
5 James R. Cothran, *Charleston Gardens*, p. 98. Also, see Aitken-Reitt House: recent research suggests a formal garden to the rear of the house past the stables and kitchens.
6 In the early 19th century, New Orleans received a large inward migration from Haiti, including many free black families and white French-speaking masters and their slaves. See: www.inmotionaame.org/migrations/topic.cfm;jsessionid=f8301991401400496736819?migration=5&topic=3&bhcp=1 (accessed 22 November 2015).

Vernacular Responses to Climate across the European Continent

1 Heather Catchpole, 'Roaring forties', *In Depth. ABC Science* (20 September 2007).
2 J. Wenhao, 'A study into the sustainable system between the wind and the villages in Rincón de Ademuz, Spain', PhD thesis, Polytechnic University of Valencia, 2014, pp. 60–70.
3 Toshio Tsukidate, 'Research on the uses of fire in vernacular houses in the Eurasian Continent', in C. Mileto et al. (eds), *Vernacular Architecture. Towards a Sustainable Future* (London: CRC Press/Balkema, Taylor & Francis Group 2015), pp. 719–24.
4 Tsukidate, 'Research', pp. 720–23.
5 Tsukidate, 'Research', p. 724.
6 Martín Almagro-Gorbea and Lucía Moltó, 'Saunas en la Hispania prerromana' (Saunas in pre-Roman Hispania), *Espacio, Tiempo y Forma*, Serie II, Historia Antigua, Vol. V (1992), pp. 67–102.
7 Fernando Vegas and Camilla Mileto, 'Radiant heating underfloor systems: Glorias and trébedes', in M. Correia, L. Dipasquale and S. Mecca (eds), *Versus: Heritage for Tomorrow. Vernacular Knowledge for Sustainable Architecture* (Florence: Firenze University Press, 2014), p. 265.
8 F. Vegas, C. Mileto, J. M. Songel and J. F. Noguera, 'In-between spaces, borderline places' in Correia et al., *Versus*, pp. 186–19.
9 F. Vegas, C. Mileto, L. García Soriano and S. García Sáez, 'Shading and cooling systems', in Correia et al., *Versus*, pp. 244–254.
10 Fernando Vegas and Camilla Mileto, *Lazos de alarife / Entrelacs de bâtisseur* (Interlacing builders) (Málaga: OMAU, 2013), pp. 103–5.
11 Marcel Vellinga, Paul Oliver and Alexander Bridge, *Atlas of Vernacular Architecture of the World* (Oxford/New York: Routledge, 2007), pp. 30–31, 46–47.
12 Camilla Mileto and Fernando Vegas (eds), *La restauración de la tapia en la Península Ibérica. Criterios, técnicas, resultados y perspectivas* (The restoration of rammed earth in the Iberian Peninsula. Criteria, techniques, results and perspectives) (Lisbon/Valencia: Argumentum/TC Ediciones, 2014), p. 12.
13 Zuzana Syrová, and Jan Syrový, 'Rammed earth in Moravia (Czech Republic) in the context of neighboring lands', in Camilla Mileto, Fernando Vegas and Valentina Cristini (eds), *Rammed Earth Conservation* (London: CRC Press/Balkema, Taylor & Francis Group, 2012), pp. 229–35 (especially p. 231).
14 CRAterre-ENSAG (eds), *Terra Incognita: Discovering & Preserving European Earthen Architecture* (Lisbon/Brussels: Argumentum/Culture Lab Éditions, 2008).
15 Mariana Correia, Letizia Dipasquale and Saverio Mecca (eds), *Terra Europae. Earthen Architecture in the European Union* (Pisa: Edizioni ETS, 2011).
16 Vellinga et al., *Atlas*, pp. 50–51.
17 Antonella Mamì, *Il gesso* (Gypsum) (Sant'Arcangelo di Romagna: Maggioli, 2006).
18 David Sanz Arauz, 'Análisis del yeso empleado en revestimientos exteriores mediante técnicas geológicas', PhD thesis, Polytechnic University of Madrid, 2009.
19 Vellinga et al., *Atlas*, pp. 56–57.
20 Carmen-Oliva Menéndez, *Teitos. Cubiertas vegetales de Europa Occidental: de Asturias a Islandia* (Thatched roofs in Western Europe: from Asturias to Iceland) (Oviedo: Colegio Oficial de Aparejadores y Arquitectos Técnicos del Principado de Asturias [Official Association of Quantity Surveyors of Asturias], 2008); Vellinga et al., *Atlas*, pp. 50–51.
21 Saverio Mecca and Letizia Dipasquale (eds), *Earthen Domes and Habitats* (Pisa: Edizioni ETS, 2009).
22 Fernando Vegas, Camilla Mileto and Valentina Cristini, 'Corbelling domes and bridges in Spain and Portugal: a comparative study', in B. Chen and J. Wei (eds), *Arch'10. 6th International Conference on Arch Bridges* (Zagreb: SECON-HDGK, 2010), pp. 297–303.
23 Manfredi Nicoletti, *L'architettura delle caverne* (The Architecture of Caves) (Rome-Bari: Laterza, 1980).
24 F. Vegas, C. Mileto, V. Cristini and J. R. Ruiz Checa, 'Underground cities', in Correia et al., *Versus*, pp. 114–23
25 Sanz Arauz, 'Análisis'.
26 Mamì, *Il gesso*.
27 Sanz Arauz, 'Análisis'.
28 Ivan Lafarge, 'Le plâtre dans la construction en Ile-de-France. Techniques, morphologie et économie avant l'industrialisation. Rapport d'étude' (Gypsum in the buildings of Ile-de-France. Techniques, morphology and economy before industrialization. Study report), PhD thesis, University of Paris 1 – Pantheon Sorbonne, 2013.
29 Gianfranco Caniggia, *Lettura dell'edilizia di base* (Reading of dwellings) (Florence: Alinea Editrice, 2008), p. 135.
30 Caniggia, *Lettura*.
31 Herman Hertzberger, *Lessons for Students of Architecture* (Rotterdam: Uitgeverij 010 Publishers 1991, pp. 48–49)

CONTINENTAL CLIMATE

Turf, Timber and *Skjelter* Construction in Norway

1 Gisle Jakhelln, 'Nordlandshuset. Bakgrunn, definisjon, bruk og ny bruk' (Nordland house. Background, definition, use and reuse), *Fortidsminneforeningen Årbok* (2013), pp. 187–98.

Wooden Folk Architecture in Western Russia

1 As discussed by Evgeny Khodakovsky, the massive superstructure of *kub* churches is formed of a four-sided curving closed roof with an ogival silhouette from each side, resembling an onion dome. The structure allows for the church to be topped by a single central dome, or five smaller domes. See Evgeny Khodakovsky, *Wooden Church Architecture of the Russian North: Regional Schools and Traditions (14th–19th Centuries)*, (London/New York: Routledge, 2015), p. 76.

Bibliography

TROPICAL CLIMATE

CARIBBEAN

CARIMOS, *Monumentos y Sitios del Gran Caribe* (Monuments and Sites of the Greater Caribbean) (Santo Domingo: CARIMOS, 2000).

Carter, E. H., G. W. Digby and R. N. Murray, *History of the West Indian Peoples – Book III: From Earliest Times to the 17th Century* (Walton-on-Thames, Surrey: Thomas Nelson and Sons, 1959).

Devonish, Steve A., 'The use of timber in Barbados: the case of the chattel house', in R. van Oers and S. Haraguchi (eds), *Caribbean Wooden Treasures*, World Heritage Papers 15 (Paris: UNESCO, 2005).

Drewett, Peter L., *Prehistoric Settlements in the Caribbean* (Barbados: Archetype Publications for the Barbados Museum and Historical Society, 2000).

Emmer, Pieter C. (ed.), *General History of the Caribbean, Volume II – New Societies: The Caribbean in the long sixteenth century* (Paris: UNESCO Publishing, 1999).

Gordon, S., 'The folk architecture of Saint Kitts and Nevis', in R. van Oers and S. Haraguchi (eds), *Caribbean Wooden Treasures*, World Heritage Papers 15 (Paris: UNESCO, 2005).

Gravette, A., *Architectural Heritage of the Caribbean* (Kingston: Ian Randle Publishers, 2000).

Marley, David F., *Historic Cities of the Americas – An Illustrated Encyclopedia. Volume 1: The Caribbean, Mexico and Central America* (Santa Barbara, CA / Oxford: ABC Clio, 2005).

Thompson, Alvin O., 'Sites of Memory: contributions of enslaved Africans to the built heritage of the Caribbean', in S. Haraguchi and R. van Oers (eds), *Safeguarding Precious Resources for Island Communities*, World Heritage Papers 38 (Paris: UNESCO, 2014).

Van Oers, R., 'Multi-ethnicity and Cultural Significance in Georgetown (Guyana)', in *Partnerships for World Heritage Cities*, World Heritage Papers 9 (Paris: UNESCO, 2004).

BRAZIL: FRENCH GUIANAS

Pérez, Patrick and Olivier Archambeau, *Architectures et Paysages de Saint Georges de l'Oyapock* (Cayenne: OHM CNRS, 2012).

VENEZUELA

López Villa, Manuel Antonio, *Arquitectura e Historia: Curso de Historia de la Arquitectura* (Architecture and History: Course of History of Architecture) (Caracas: UCV: Consejo de Desarrollo Científico y Humanístico [Council of Scientific and Humanistic Development], 2003).

Pereira Colls, Nory and Nelly Mejía Barrios, 'El uso de la tierra en la vivienda rural venezolana. Diversidad en su tecnología y en su expresión' (The use of the land in Venezuela's rural housing. Diversity in its technology and in its expression'), paper presented to the Universidad de los Andes, Centro de Investigaciones de la Vivienda (Research Centre for Housing) (CINVIV).

BRAZIL: UPPER XINGU AND WAJÃPI

Franchetto, Bruna (ed.), *Documentation of Karib Language of Upper Xingu – Kuikuro*, Program for the Documentation of Endangered Languages (DoBes), 2001–5.

Franchetto, Bruna (ed.), *Alto Xingu: uma sociedade multilíngue* (Upper Xingu: A multilingual society) (Rio de Janeiro: Museu do Índio – FUNAI, 2011).

Gallois, Catherine J. S., *Wajãpi rena: roças, pátios e casas* (Wajãpi: gardens, courtyards and houses) (Rio de Janeiro: Museu do Índio, 2002).

Gallois, Catherine J. S., 'Sentidos e formas do habitar indígena: entre mobilidade e sedentarização. Estudo de caso entre os Wajãpi do Amapá' (Directions and forms of indigenous dwelling: between mobility and sedentarization. Case study among the Amapa Wajãpi) MSc thesis, Rio de Janeiro: IPPUR-UFRJ, 2004.

Gallois, Catherine J. S., *Elementos para um inventário nacional das arquiteturas indígenas brasileiras* (Elements for a national inventory of Brazilian indigenous architectures) IPHAN – Instituto Nacional do Patrimônio Histórico e Artístico Nacional/ COPEDOC – Coordenação Geral de Pesquisa e Documentação. Metodologia de Pesquisa e Multidisciplinaridade no IPHAN: Anais da II Oficina de Pesquisa, Rio de Janeiro: IPHAN/ DAF/COPEDOC, 2010.

Heckenberger, Michael, *The Ecology of Power. Culture, Place, and Personhood in the Southern Amazon, A.D. 1000–2000* (New York / London: Routledge, 2005).

ISA – Instituto Socioambiental, 'Povos Indígenas no Brasil. Quadro Geral dos Povos' Available at http://pib.socioambiental.org/pt/c/quadro-geral (accessed 24 October 2015).

Kalapalo, Nahukua, Matipu, *Ngongoha igei kungatagoho: esta é a terra que nós plantamos* (Belo Horizonte: FALE-UFMG, SECAD-MEC, 2007).

Kuikuro. *Kungatagohoha igei ngongoi: esta é a terra que nós plantamos* (This is the land that we plant), (Belo Horizonte: FALE-UFMG, SECAD-MEC, 2007).

Sá, Cristina, *Observações sobre a habitação em três grupos indígenas brasileiros* (Comments on housing in three Brazilian indigenous groups), in Sylvia Caiuby Novaes (ed.), *Habitações Indígenas* (São Paulo: Nobel / Edusp, 1983).

BRAZIL: FAVELAS

Azevedo, Sérgio and Luiz A. Andrade, *Habitação e Poder. Da Fundação da Casa Popular ao Banco Nacional da Habitação* (Housing and Power. Of the People's House to the National Housing Bank Foundation) (Rio de Janeiro: Zahar, 1982).

Bonduki, Nabil, *Habitat: As práticas bem sucedidas em habitação, meio ambiente e gestão urbana nas cidades brasileiras* (Successful practices in housing, environment and urban management in Brazilian cities) (São Paulo: Studio Nobel, 1996).

Bonduki, Nabil, *Origens da habitação social no Brasil* (Origins of social housing in Brazil) (São Paulo: Estação Liberdade, 1999).

Cardoso, Adauto Lucio, *O Programa Favela-Bairro: Uma avaliação. Anais do Seminário de Avaliação de projetos IPT em habitação e meio ambiente: assentamento urbano precário* (The Favela-Bairro Program: An assessment) (São Paulo: IPT, 2002).

Duarte, Cristiane, Osvaldo Silva and Alice Brasileiro, *Favela, Um Bairro: Propostas Metodológicas para Intervenção Pública em favelas do Rio de Janeiro* (Favela, A Neighborhood: Methodological Proposals for Public Intervention in the Rio de Janeiro slums) (São Paulo: Pro-Editores, 1996).

Maricato, Ermínia, *A Produção Capitalista da Casa*

(e da Cidade) no Brasil Industrial (The Capitalist Production House (and the City) in Industrial Brazil) (São Paulo: Alfa Ômega, 1979).

Maricato, Ermínia *Política Habitacional no Regime Militar: do Milagre Brasileiro à Crise Econômica* (Housing Policy in the Military Regime: Miracle of the Brazilian Economic Crisis) (Rio de Janeiro: Vozes, 1987).

Maricato, Ermínia *Habitação e Cidade* (Housing and City) (São Paulo: Editora Atual, 1997).

Ribeiro, Luiz César Queiróz, *Dos Cortiços aos Condomínios Fechados: As formas de produção de moradia na cidade do Rio de Janeiro* (From Tenements to Closed Charges: The forms of housing production in the city of Rio de Janeiro) (Rio de Janeiro: Civilização Brasileira / IPPUR/ UFRJ, 1997).

Silva, Maria Laís Pereira da, *Favelas cariocas, 1930–1964* (Rio's favelas, 1930–1964) (Rio de Janeiro: Contraponto, 2005).

Zaluar, Alba and Marcos Alvito, *Um Século de Favela* (A Century of Favela) (Rio de Janeiro: FGV, 1998).

PARAGUAY

Rengger, J. R., *Reise nach Paraguay in den Jahren 1818 bis 1826* (Journey to Paraguay Between 1818 and 1826) (Aarau: Verlag H. R. Saverlaender, 1835).

IVORY COAST, GHANA, TOGO, BENIN, CAMEROON

Bradley, K. R., 'On the Roman Slave Supply and Slave Breeding', in Moses Finley (ed.), *Classical Slavery* (London: Cass Publishers, 1987).

Ghana Museums and Monuments Board (GMMB), Asante Traditional Building' prepared within the 'Africa 2009' in situ programme (UNESCO, ICCROM, CRATerre-EAG) with support from the French Embassy in Ghana and the Alliance Française in Kumasi, Ghana, 2009.

Grehan, F., *Wright Houses 1999: The Houses of Frank Lloyd Wright* (New York: Universe Publishing, 1998).

Guthrie, W. K. C., 'Meno', in Edith Hamilton (ed.), *Collected Dialogues of Plato* (Princeton, NJ: Princeton University Press, 1989).

Hockings, J., 'Built Form and Culture: A theoretical appraisal supported by a case study of the dwelling houses in the Gilbert Islands, West Pacific', *Architecture and Comfort/Architectural Behaviour*, Vol. 3, No. 4 (1987), pp. 281–300.

Howard, R. G., 'A Theory of Vernacular Rhetoric: The Case of the "Sinner's Prayer" Online', *Folklore*, 116:2 (2005), pp. 172–88. Access granted via University of Liverpool on 26 August 2009.

Huemer, Michael (ed.), with an introduction by Robert Audi, *Epistemology Contemporary Readings* (London / New York: Routledge Taylor and Francis Group, 2002).

Joffroy, T. and N. Djanguenane, 'KOUTAMMAKOU' le pays des BATAMMARIBA *'ceux qui façonnent la terre'*, (Koutammakou 'the land of Batammaribas' those that shape the earth) (CRATerre-ENSAG with Les Amis du Patrimoine, 2005).

Mitchell, M. and B. Bevan, *Culture, Cash and Housing: Community and Tradition in Low-income Building* (London: Intermediate Technology Publication Ltd, (1992).

Navrongo-Bolgatanga Diocese (N-BD) and Ghana Museums and Monuments Board (GMMB), *Navrongo Cathedral - The merge of two cultures* (Villefontaine: CRATerre-Editions, France, 2004).

Oliver, Paul (ed.), *Encyclopedia of Vernacular Architecture of the World* (Cambridge: Cambridge University Press, 1997).

Rudofsky, B., *Architecture without Architects – A Short Introduction to Non-Pedigree Architecture* (Albuquerque, NM: University of New Mexico Press, 1964) – eighth paperback printing, 2003.

Rudofsky, B., Note on 'Architecture Without Architects' in B. Rudofsky, *The Prodigious Builders – notes toward a natural history of architecture with special regard to those species that are traditionally neglected or downright ignored* (Secker & Warburg, London, 1977).

Schreckenbach, H. and J. G. K. Abankwa, *Construction Technology for a Tropical Developing Country* (Kumasi: Deutsche Gesellschaft fur Technische Zusammenarbeit [GTZ] (German Society for Technical Cooperation) GmbH for the Department of Architecture, University of Science and Technology, Kumasi, Ghana, 1983).

Stride, G. T. and C. Ifeka, *Peoples and Empires of West Africa: West Africa in History 1000–1800* (Surrey: Thomas Nelson and Sons Limited, 1986).

Webster, J. B. and A. A. Boahen, *The Growth of West African Civilisation – The Revolutionary Years: West Africa since 1800* (London: Longman Group Limited, 1967).

NIGERIA

Bascom, W., *The Yoruba of Southwestern Nigeria* (New York: Holt, Reinhart & Winston, 1969).

Dmochowski, Z. R., *An Introduction to Nigerian Traditional Architecture*, Vols 1–3 (Lagos: The National Commission for Museums and Monuments, 1990).

Osasona, C. O., 'Defining the Vernacular', *Legacy*, Vol. 2, No. 2 (Lagos, 2000).

Osasona, C. O., 'The Symbolic Value of Space and Material in Nigerian Traditional Houseforms', *Journal of Environmental Technology*, Vol. 1, No. 2 (2002).

Sa'ad, H. T., 'Between Myth and Reality: The aesthetics of Hausa traditional architecture in Hausaland', PhD thesis, University of Michigan (1981).

Schwedrtfeger, F. W., *Traditional Housing in African Cities: A Comparative Study of Houses in Zaria, Ibadan and Marrakech* (New York: John Wiley and Sons, 1972).

CENTRAL AFRICA: SOUTHERN SUDAN, KENYA, RWANDA, BURUNDI

Acquier, Jean-Louis, *Le Burundi*, Collection: Architectures traditionnelles 3 (Roquevaire: Editions Parenthèses, 1986).

Aradeon, Susan B., 'Moufou Architecture', *African Arts* 14, No. 1 (1980), pp. 58–60, 88.

Arensen, Jonathan E., *Sticks and Straw: Comparative House Forms in Southern Sudan and Northern Kenya*, International Museum of Cultures 13 (Dallas, TX: International Museum of Cultures, 1983).

Beguin, J. P., *L'habitat au Cameroun* (Paris: ORSTOM and Union Française, 1952).

DeLancey, Mark D., 'The Spread of the Sooro: Symbols of Power in the Sokoto Caliphate', Journal of the Society of Architectural Historians 71, No. 2 (2013), pp. 168–85.

Jewsiewicki, Bogumil., 'Peintres de cases, imagiers et savants populaires du Congo, 1900–1960: Un essai d'histoire de l'esthétique indigène' (Painters of earthen houses, picture books and popular scientists of the Congo, 1900–1960: A History essay on the indigenous aesthetic), *Cahiers d'études africaines* 123, Vol. 31, No. 3 (1991): 307–26.

Lyons, Diane, 'Witchcraft, Gender, Power and Intimate Relations in Mura Compounds in Déla, Northern Cameroon', *World Archaeology* 29, No. 3 (1998), pp. 344–62.

Lyons, Diane, 'The Politics of House Shape: Round vs. Rectilinear Domestic Structures in Déla Compounds, Northern Cameroun', *Antiquity* 70, No. 268 (1996), pp. 351–67.

Philippart de Foy, Guy, *Les Pygmées d'Afrique central*, Collection architectures traditionnelles 2 (Roquevaire: Editions Parenthèses, 1984).

Schildkrout, Enid and Curtis A. Keim, *African Reflections: Art from Northeastern Zaire* (Seattle, WA: University of Washington Press and New York: American Museum of Natural History, 1990).

Seignobos, Christian, *Nord Cameroun: montagnes et hautes terres* (North Cameroon: mountains and highlands), Collection: Architectures traditionnelles 1 (Roquevaire: Editions Parenthèses, 1982).

MADAGASCAR

Acquier, Jean-Louis, *Architectures de Madagascar* (Nancy: Berger-Levrault, 1997).

Bird, Randall, *The Majesty of Architecture in Madagascar: Transforming a Kingdom in the Central Highlands* (forthcoming 2015).

La Vaissière, Camille de, *Histoire de Madagascar: ses habitants et ses missionaires* (A History of Madagascar: its inhabitants and its missionaries), 2 volumes (Paris: Librairie Victor Lecoffre, 1884).

Oliver, Samuel Pasfield, *Madagascar and the Malagasy* (London: Day & Sons, 1866).

Ruud, Jorgen, *Taboo: A Study of Malagasy Customs and Beliefs* (Oslo: Oslo University Press, 1960).

Sibree, James, *A Naturalist in Madagascar* (London: Seeley, Service & Co. Limited, 1915).

INDIA

Abrams, Charles, *Man's Struggle for Shelter in an Urbanizing World* (Cambridge, MA: MIT Press, 1964).

Apte, Prakash, 'Dharavi: India's Model Slum', *Planetizen*, 29 September 2008. Available at www.planetizen.com/node/35269 (accessed 27 October 2015).

Apte, Prakash, 'World's most famous slum must be remodeled not redeveloped', *City Mayors Development 16*, 21 June 2011. Available at www.citymayors.com/development/dharavi.html (accessed 27 October 2015).

Baker, Laurie, *Houses: How to Reduce Building Costs* (Trichur: Centre of Science and Technology for Rural Development [COSTFORD], 1986).

Bhatia, Gautam, 'Architecture and Tradition', *World Architecture*, No. 7 (1990).

Cooper, Ilay and Barry Dawson, *Traditional Buildings of India* (London: Thames & Hudson, 1998).

Davis, Mike, *Planet of Slums* (New York: Verso, 2006).

'Dharavi: Mumbai's Shadow City', *National Geographic*, (May 2007).

French, Matthew and Joseph Gardner, 'The Health of Informal Settlements: Illness and the Internal Thermal Conditions of Informal Housing' in S. Rassia and P. Pardalos (eds), *Sustainable Environmental Design in Architecture: Impacts on Health* (New York: Springer, 2012).

Grover, Satish, *Masterpieces of Traditional Indian Architecture* (New Delhi: Roli Books Pvt. Ltd., 2005).

Jenks, Michael and Rod Burgess (eds), *Compact Cities: Sustainable Urban Forms for Developing Countries* (London: E & FN Spon Press, 2000).

Kolkman, René and Stuart Blackburn, *Tribal Architecture in Northeast India* (Leiden / Boston, MA: Brill, 2014).

McDonough, William and Michael Braungart, *Cradle to Cradle: Remaking the Way We Make Things* (New York: [Farrar, Straus and Giroux, 2002).

Mileto, C., F. Vegas, L. García Soriano and V. Cristini (eds), *Vernacular Architecture: Towards a Sustainable Future* (Abingdon: CRC Press/Taylor & Francis Group, 2014).

Oliver, Paul (ed.), *Encyclopedia of Vernacular Architecture of the World* (Cambridge: Cambridge University Press, 1997).

Oliver, Paul, *Dwellings: The Vernacular House Worldwide* (London: Phaidon Press, 2007).

Pandya, Yatin, *Concepts of Space in Traditional Indian Architecture* (Ahmedabad: Mapin Publishing, 2014).

Patidat, Shikha and Brishbhanlali Raghuwanshi, 'Changes in Culture and Architecture from Vernacular to Modern: M.P., India', paper presented to 30th International Passive and Low Energy Architecture Conference, 16–18 December 2014, Centre for Environmental Planning and Technology University, Ahmedabad. Available at brishbhanlali@spabhopal.ac.in http://www.plea2014.in/wp-content/uploads/2014/12/Poster_PB_2762_PR.pdf (accessed 27 October 2015).

Prashad, Deependra and Saswati Chetia, *New Architecture and Urbanism: Development of Indian Traditions* (Newcastle upon Tyne: Cambridge Scholars Publishing, 2010).

Rudofsky, B., *Architecture without Architects* (Albuquerque, NM: University of New Mexico Press, 1987).

Saraswat, Smriti, 'Understanding Courtyard Design through Havelis of Rajasthan', *INSITE* (2011), pp. 18–21.

Subhankar, Nag and Gondane Amol, 'Architecture of North East India: Vernacular Typologies'. Available at www.academia.edu/6055160/Architecture_of_North_East_India_Vernacular_Typologies (accessed 27 October 2015).

Thapar, Bindia, *Introduction to Indian Architecture* (Singapore: Periplus Editions, 2004).

Tipnis, A., *Vernacular Traditions: Contemporary Architecture* (New Delhi: The Energy and Research Institute [TERI] Press, 2012).

United Nations Department of Economic and Social Affairs, 'World Urbanisation Prospects: the 2014 Revision', United Nations, 2014. Available at http://esa.un.org/unpd/wup/Highlights/WUP2014-Highlights.pdf (accessed 27 October 2015).

United Nations Development Programme, 'India: Urban Poverty Report 2009'. Available at www.in.undp.org/content/india/en/home/presscenter/pressreleases/2009/02/03/india-urban-poverty-report-2009.html (accessed 27 October 2015).

United Nations Human Settlements Programme, *The Challenge of Slums: Global Report on Human Settlements* (London: Earthscan Publications, 2003).

SRI LANKA

Knox, Robert, *An Historical Relation of the Island Ceylon in the East-Indies* (London: Richard Chiswell, 1681).

Lewcock, Ronald, Barbara Sansoni and Laki Senanayake, *The Architecture of an Island* (Colombo: Barefoot, 1988).

Robson, David, *Geoffrey Bawa: The Complete Works* (London: Thames & Hudson, 2002).

Robson, David, *Beyond Bawa: Modern masterworks of Monsoon Asia* (London: Thames & Hudson, 2007).

de Silva, K. M., *A History of Sri Lanka* (India: Penguin Books, 2005).

SOUTHEAST ASIA

Alfieri, B. M. and F. Borromeo, *Islamic Architecture of the Indian Subcontinent* (London: Laurence King Publishing, 2000).

Ameen, Farooq (ed), *South Asian Architecture.* Memphis, TN: Books LLC, 2011).

Ameen, Farooq, *Contemporary architecture and City Form: The South Asian Paradigm* (Mumbai: Marg Publications, 1997).

Ashraf, K. K., J. Belluardo and the Architectural League of New York, *An Architecture of Independence: The Making of Modern South Asia: Charles Correa, Balkrishna Doshi, Muzharul Islam, Achyut Kanvinde* (New York: Architectural League of New York, 1998).

Baptiste, Pierre and Thierry Zéphir. *Trésors d'art du Vietnam: la sculpture du Champa, V-XV siècles*, catalogue of the exhibition, Musée Guimet, 12 October 2005–6 February 2006 (France: 2005).

Behrendt, Kurt, 'Pre-Angkor Traditions: The Mekong Delta and Peninsular Thailand', in *Heilbrunn Timeline of Art History* (New York: The Metropolitan Museum of Art, 2000). Available at www.metmuseum.org/toah/hd/pang/hd_pang.htm (accessed 31 October 2015).

Bellew, P., M. Davey and Atelier Ten (firm), *Green House, Green Engineering: Environmental Design at Gardens By the Bay* (Singapore: Oro Editions, 2012).

Bishop, R., J. Phillips and W.-W.Yeo, *Beyond Description: Singapore Space Historicity* (London: Routledge, 2004).

Bloom, Jonathan M. and Sheila S. Blair (eds), *Grove Encyclopedia of Islamic Art and Architecture* (Oxford: Oxford University Press, 2009).

Boyarsky, N. and P. Lang, *Urban Flashes Asia: New Architecture and Urbanism in Asia* (Chichester: Wiley, 2003).

Crouch, D. P. and J. G. Johnson, *Traditions in Architecture: Africa, America, Asia, and Oceania* (New York: Oxford University Press, 2001).

Davidson, C. C., *Legacies for the Future: Contemporary Architecture in Islamic Societies* (New York: Thames & Hudson, 1999).

Dumarçay, J. and M. Smithies, *The House in South-East Asia* (Singapore: Oxford University Press, 1987).

Esposito, J. L., *The Oxford History of Islam* (New York: Oxford University Press, 1999).

Fisher, R. E., *Buddhist Art and Architecture* (New York: Thames & Hudson, 1993).

Frampton, K., *World Architecture 1900–2000: A Critical Mosaic* (Vienna: Springer, 1999).

Patrick Goode (ed.), *The Oxford Companion to Architecture* (Oxford: Oxford University Press, 2009).

Grabar, Oleg, *The Formation of Islamic Art and Architecture* (New Haven, CT: Yale University Press, 1987).

Guy, John, *Lost Kingdoms: Hindu-Buddhist Sculpture of Early Southeast Asia, 5th to 8th Century*, catalogue to the exhibition, Metropolitan Museum of Art, New York, 14 April–27 July 2024 (New York / MMA / New Haven, CT: The Yale University Press, 2014).

Hamzah, T. R. and Ken Yeang, *Bioclimatic Skyscrapers*, Pidgeon Audio Visual (Monica Pidgeon, producer) (London: Sussex Video; New York: Insight Media, 1994).

Hattstein, Markus and Peter Delius, *Islam: Art and Architecture* (Potsdam: h.f. Ullmann, 2004) English edition, 2010.

Hillenbrand, Robert, *Islamic Architecture: Form, Function and Meaning* (New York: Columbia University Press, 1994).

Hyde, R., *Climate Responsive Design: A Study of Buildings in Moderate and Hot Humid Climates* (London: E. & F. N. Spon, 2000).

Ingersoll, R. and S. Kostof, *World Architecture: A Cross-Cultural History* (New York: Oxford University Press, 2013).

Izikowitz, K. and P. Sorensen (eds), *The House in East and Southeast Asia: Anthropological and Architectural Aspects* (London: Curzon, 1982).

Jodidio, P., *Under the Eaves of Architecture: The Aga Khan, Builder and Patron* (Munich: Prestel, 2007).

Kahn, L. I., Y. Futagawa, Y. and K. K. Ashraf, *Louis I. Kahn, National Capital of Bangladesh, Dhaka, Bangladesh, 1962–83* (Tokyo: A.D.A. EDITA Tokyo, 1994).

Katharithamby-Wells, J. and J. Villiers (eds), *The Southeast Asian Port and Polity: Rise and Demise* (Singapore: Singapore University Press, 1990).

Khan, H.-U., *Contemporary Asian Architects* (Cologne: Taschen, 1995).

Khoo, J. C. M. (ed.), *Art & Archaeology of Fu Nan: Pre-Khmer Kingdom of the Lower Mekong Valley* (Bangkok: Orchid Press, 2003).

Knapp, R. G., *Asia's Old Dwellings: Tradition,*

Resilience, and Change (Oxford: Oxford University Press, 2003).
Kostof, S., *A History of Architecture: Settings and Rituals* (New York: Oxford University Press, 1985).
Kronenburg, R., J. Lim and W. Y. Chii, *Transportable Environments 2* (London: Spon Press, 2003).
Kurokawa, K., D. Sharp, C. Slessor and T. Ōhashi, *Kisho Kurokawa: Kuala Lumpur International Airport* (Stuttgart: Edition Axel Menges, 1999).
Kwa Chong Guan, Derek Heng and Tan Tai Yong, *Singapore: A 700-Year History – From Early Emporium To World City* (Singapore: Singapore National Archives, 2009).
Laquian, A. A., V. K. Tewari and L. M. Hanley, *The Inclusive City: Infrastructure and public services for the urban poor in Asia* (Washington, DC: Woodrow Wilson Center Press, 2007).
Lee Kuan Yew, *From Third World to First* (Singapore: Times Editions, 2000).
Lim, Irene, *Sketches in the Straits: Nineteenth Century Watercolours and Manuscript of Singapore, Malacca, Penang and Batavia by Charles Dyce* (Singapore: NUS Museums, 2003).
Lim, W. S. W. and H. B. Tan, *The New Asian Architecture: Vernacular traditions and contemporary style* (Hong Kong: Periplus Editions, 1998).
Lim, W. S. W. and Tan Hock Beng, *Contemporary Vernacular* (Select Books, 1998).
Liu, Gretchen, *Singapore: A Pictorial History 1819–2000* (Singapore: Archipelago Press, 1999).
Malaysia Green Building Confederation (MGBC): www.mgbc.org.my (accessed 31 October 2015).
Mostafavi, M., G. Doherty and Harvard University, *Ecological Urbanism* (Baden: Lars Müller Publishers, 2010).
Nguyen, Ba Dang, Nguyen Vu Phuong and Ta Hoang Van, *Traditional Vietnamese Architecture* (Hanoi: Thế Giới Publishers, 2006).
Nguyen-quang-Nhac and N. D. Nguyen, *Vietnamese Architecture* (Washington, DC: Embassy of Vietnam, 1970).
Nguyen, Van Ku, *Di San Van Hoa Cham: Heritage of Cham Culture* (Hanoi: Thế Giới Publishers, 2007).
Nguyen, Van Ku and Lu'u Hung (introduction by Nguyen Ngoc), *Nha Rong Tay Nguyen: Rong Community Halls in the Central Highlands of Vietnam,* Vietnamese Academy of Social Sciences and Vietnam Association of Photographic Artists (Hanoi: Thế Giới Publishers, 2007).
Norindr, P., *Phantasmatic Indochina: French colonial ideology in architecture, film, and literature* (Durham, NC: Duke University Press, 1996).
Osborne, Milton, *Exploring Southeast Asia* (Sydney, New South Wales: Allen & Unwin, 2002).
Philippine Green Building Council: philgbc.org (accessed 31 October 2015).
Reid, Anthony, 'Southeast Asia: A Region and a Crossroad', *Cultures at Crossroads: Southeast Asian Textiles from the Australian National Gallery*, catalogue to the exhibition, Australian National Gallery, 18 September 1992–17 January 1993, (Canberra: The Australian National Gallery, 1992).
Royal Netherlands Institute of Southeast Asian and Caribbean Studies (KITLV): www.kitlv.nl (accessed 31 October 2015).
Rudofsky, Bernard, *Architecture without Architects* (New York: MoMA / Doubleday, 1965).
Rykwert, Joseph, *On Adam's House in Paradise, The Idea of the Primitive Hut in Architecture*, The Museum of Modern Art Papers on Architecture, The Museum of Modern Art in association with The Graham Foundation for Advanced Studies in the Fine Arts (Chicago / New York: The New York Graphic Society, Ltd., 1972).
Schweyer, Anne-Valérie Schweyer (photography: Paisarn Piemmettawat), *Ancient Vietnam: History, Art and Archaeology* (Bangkok: River Books, 2011).
Scriver, P. and V. Prakash, *Colonial Modernities: Building, dwelling and architecture in British India and Ceylon* (London: Routledge, 2007).
Singapore Green Building Council (SGBC): www.sgbc.sg (accessed 31 October 2015).
Smith, Holly S., *Aceh, Art and Culture*, Images of Asia series (Kuala Lumpur / Oxford / Singapore / New York: Oxford University Press, 1997).
Smitthi, S., E. Moore and M. Freeman, *Palaces of the Gods: Khmer art & architecture in Thailand* (Bangkok: River Books, 1992).
Sterling, E. J., M. M. Hurley and Le Duc Minh, *Vietnam: A Natural History* (New Haven, CT: Yale University Press, 2006).
Tan, Rosario 'Ning' Encarnacion, *100 Things About Building With Bamboo* (Quezon City: TAO-Pilipinas, Inc. 2012).
Tran Ky Phuong and Bruce M. Lockhart (eds), *The Cham of Vietnam: History, Society and Art* (Singapore: NUS Press, 2011).
Tzonis, Alexander, Liane Lefaivre and Bruno Stagno (eds), *Tropical Architecture: Critical Regionalism in the Age of Globalisation*, 2001.
Tung, A. M., *Preserving the World's Great Cities: The destruction and renewal of the historic metropolis* (New York: Three Rivers Press, 2002).
Urban Redevelopment Authority (Singapore), *20 Under 45: A selection of works by under-45 Singapore-registered architects* (Singapore: Urban Redevelopment Authority, 2004).
Vale, L. J., *Architecture, Power, and National Identity* (New Haven: Yale University Press, 1992).
Van, B. G. W., B. O. Van and the Smithsonian Institution. *Glorious Mud! Ancient and contemporary earthen design and construction in North Africa, Western Europe, the Near East, and Southwest Asia* (Washington, DC: Smithsonian Institution Scholarly Press, 2008).
Velayutham, Selvaraj, *Responding to Globalization* (Singapore: Institute of Southeast Asian Studies, 2007).
Vietnam Green Building Council (VGBC): www.vgbc.org.vn (accessed 31 October 2015).
Waterson, R., *The Living House: An anthropology of architecture in South-East Asia* (New York: Whitney Library of Design, 2008).
Wheatley, Paul, *Impressions of the Malay Peninsula in Ancient Times* (Singapore: Eastern Universities Press Ltd, 1964).

THAILAND

Chaichongrak, Ruethai, Somchai Nilathi, Ornsiri Panin and Saowalak Poysanonda (photography: Michael Freeman) *The Thai House: History and Evolution* (Bangkok: Asia Books, 2002).
Jumsai, Sumet, *Naga: Cultural Origins in Siam and the West Pacific* (Bangkok: Chalermnit Press and DD Books, 1997).
Powell, William (photography: Albert Lim Koon Sing), *The Modern Thai House* (Rutland, VT: Tuttle Publishing, 2012).
Srisuro, Wiroj, *Isan Sim: Northeast Buddhist Holy Temples* (Tokyo / Khon Kaen: The Toyota Foundation, n.d.).

CAMBODIA

Grant Ross, Helen and Darryl Leon Collins, *Building Cambodia: 'New Khmer Architecture' 1953–1970* (Bangkok: The Key Publisher Co. Ltd., 2006).
Lindt, Naomi, 'In Cambodia; a House With Legs', *New York Times*, 7 July 2010.
Phuoeng, Sophean, 'La maison khmère', in Ministère de la Culture and Atelier parisien d'urbanisme (Ministry of Culture and Parisian Planning), *Phnom Penh: développement urbain et patrimoine* (Phnom Penh: Ministère de la Culture and Atelier parisien d'urbanisme, 1997).
Tainturier, François (ed.), *Wooden Architecture of Cambodia: A Disappearing Heritage* (Siem Reap: Center for Khmer Studies, 2006).
U, Srei, 'House Building', in Ly Darvuth and Ingrid Muan (eds), *Cultures of Independence: An Introduction to Cambodian Arts and Culture in the 1950s and 1960s* (Phnom Penh: Reyum Publishing, 2001).

PAPUA NEW GUINEA

Kirsch, P., *On the Road of the Winds: An archaeological history of the Pacific Islands before European contact* (Berkeley, CA: University of California Press, 2000).
Hurley, Frank, cited in Jim Specht and John Fields (eds), *Frank Hurley in Papua: photographs of the 1920–1923 expeditions* (Bathurst: Robert Brown and Associates in association with the Australian Museum Trust, 1984).
Stasch, Rupert, *The Society of Others: Kinship and Mourning in a West Papua Place* (Berkeley, CA: University of California Press, 2009).

MICRONESIA

Duperrey, Louis-Isidore, *Voyage autour du monde* (Paris: Arthus Bertrand, 1824).
Earle, S. A. and the National Geographic Society (US), *National Geographic Atlas of the Ocean: The Deep Frontier* (Washington, DC: National Geographic Society, 2001).
Fahr-Becker, G., and C. Murray, *The Art of East Asia: Indonesia, Traditional Houses* (Cologne: Koenemann Verlagsgesellschaft mbH, 1999).
Fritz, G. *The Chamorro: A History and Ethnography of the Marianas* (E. Craddock, trans.; S. Russell ed.) (Saipan: Division of Historic Preservation, 1989 [1904]).
Keate, G., *An Account of the Pelew Islands, Situated in the Western Part of the Pacific Ocean; Composed from the Journals and Communications of Captain Henry Wilson, and some of his Officers, Who, in August 1783, were there Shipwrecked, in the ANTELOPE, a Packet Belonging to the Honourable East India Company* (1st edition) (London: G. Nichol, 1788).

Kirch, P. V., 'Peopling of the Pacific: a holistic anthropological perspective', *Annual Review of Anthropology*, 39 (2010), pp. 131–48.

Liston, J., 'Cultural Chronology of Earthworks in Palau, Western Micronesia', *Archaeology in Oceania*, 44 (2009), pp. 56–73.

Metzgar, E., 'Sacred Space, Taboo Place: Negotiating *Roang* on Lamotrek Atoll', *Micronesian Journal of the Humanities and Social Sciences*, 3 (1-2) (2004), pp. 3–18.

Morgan, W. N., *Prehistoric Architecture in Micronesia* (Austin, TX: University of Texas Press, 1988).

Nero, K. L., 'Keate's *Account of the Pelew Islands*: A View of Koror and Palau', in K. L. Nero and N. Thomas (eds), *An Account of the Pelew Islands: George Keate* (London / New York: Leicester University Press, 2002).

Palau Society of Historians, *Rechuodel: Traditional Culture and Lifeways Long Ago in Palau* (D. R. Smith, trans.) (San Francisco: Micronesian Endowment for Historic Preservation, 1997).

Petersen, G., *Traditional Micronesian Societies: Adaptation, Integration, and Political Organization* (Honolulu: University of Hawai'i Press, 2009).

Roberts, C. R., 'Observations in Micronesia: an architectural review' (Medford, OR: University of Oregon, 1997).

Sturman, A. P. and H. P. McGowan, 'Climate', in M. Rapaport (ed.), *The Pacific Islands: Environment & Society* (Honolulu: Bess Press, 1999).

Wilkes, C., *Narrative of the United States Exploring Expedition during the years 1838, 1839, 1840, 1841, 1842* (Vol. 4) (Philadelphia, PA: Lea and Banchard, 1845).

COOK ISLANDS

Budgett, Jeanette , 'Coral Architecture of the Cook Islands', Master's thesis, University of Auckland, 2007.

Frank, Josef, 'Akzidentismus', in Mikael Bergquist and Olof Michelsen (eds), *Josef Frank Architektur* (Basel: 1995).

Treadwell, Jeremy, 'Ventilating the Tropical Modern', proceeding of the audience: 28th Annual Conference of the Society of Architectural Historians, Australia and New Zealand, Brisbane, 7-10 July 2011.

FRENCH POLYNESIA

Beaglehole, J. C. (ed.), *The Journals of Captain James Cook on His Voyages of Discovery*, Vol. I: 'The Voyage of the Endeavour, 1768–1771' (Glasgow: Cambridge University Press for the Hakluyt Society, 1955).

Emory, Kenneth P., *Stone Remains in the Society Islands*, Bernice P. Bishop Bulletin 116 (Honolulu: Bernice P. Bishop Museum, 1933).

Handy, E. S. Craighill, *Houses, Boats, and Fishing in the Society Islands*, Bernice P. Bishop Bulletin 90 (Honolulu: Bernice P. Bishop Museum, 1932; reprint: New York, Kraus Reprint Co., 1971).

Sharp, Warren D., Jennifer G. Kahn, Christina M. Polita, and Patrick V. Kirch, 'Rapid evolution of ritual architecture in central Polynesia indicated by precise 230Th/U coral dating', *Proceedings of the National Academy of Sciences of the United States of America*, Vol. 107, No. 30 (27 July 2010), pp. 13, 234–39.

DRY

NORTH AMERICA: WESTERN AMERICA AND MEXICO

Alexander, Christopher et al., *A Pattern Language* (New York: Oxford University Press, 1977), p. 911.

Alexander, *Pattern Language*, p. 581.

Alexander, *Pattern Language*, p. 910.

Brown, G. Z and Mark DeKay, *Sun, Wind and Light: Architectural Design Strategies* (New York: John Wiley & Sons, 2nd edition, 2001), p. 83.

Brown and DeKay, *Sun, Wind and Light*, p. 136.

Heschong and DeKay, *Thermal Delight*, p. 7.

Heschong, Lisa and John DeKay, *Thermal Delight in Architecture* (New York: John Wiley & Sons, 2001), p. 8.

Rapoport, Amos, 'The Nature of the Courtyard House', *Traditional Dwellings and Settlements Review*, Vol. XVII, No. II (2007), pp. 57–72.

Rapoport, Amos, *House Form and Culture* (New York: Prentice Hall, 1969).

Treib, Marc, *Sanctuaries of Spanish New Mexico* (Berkeley: University of California Press, 1993), p. 23.

BOLIVIA

Bernabé, A., *Revalorización de sabidurías Uru Chipaya: Experiencias de apoyo* (Revaluation of Uru Chipaya wisdoms) (Cochabamba, Bolivia: Agroecología Universidad Cochabamba, Programa Regional BioAndes, 2010).

Calla, A., 'Vigencia de recursos endógenos en la producción social de la vivienda rural' (Effect of endogenous resources in social production of rural housing), *INVI Journal* No. 60, Vol. 22 (2007), pp. 133–65.

Carrillo, L. and T. Sosa, 'Universo Chipaya' (Chipaya Universe), *Miradas*, No. 19 (2011).

Cerrón-Palomino, R., *El Chipaya o la lengua de los hombres del agua* (The Chipaya or the language of water men) (Lima: Fondo Editorial Pontificia Universidad Católica del Perú, 2006).

Kuno, M. and P. Paicagua, *Diagnóstico de necesidades educativas y Proyecto de Centro de Educación Alternativa para la población Uru-Chipaya* (Diagnosis of educational needs and Alternative Education Center Project for the Uru-Chipaya population), in Serie Estudios con propuestas en educación de personas jóvenes y adultas (Studies Series with proposals on education of young people and adults), No. 10 (La Paz, Bolivia: DVV International, 2010).

Lecoq, P., 'Datos preliminares sobre el periodo formativo en el sur de Potosí, Bolivia' (Preliminary data about the formative period in the south of Potosí, Bolivia), *Boletín de Arqueología PUCP, Norteamérica* (March 2012), pp. 337–52.

Muñoz, C., 'Los Uru-Chipayas en Chile' (The Chipayas-Uru in Chile), *Revista Ciencias Sociales* (Social Sciences Journal), No. 27 (2011), pp. 7–20.

ALGERIA

Ballais, Jean-Louis, 'Des oueds mythiques aux rivières artificielles: l'hydrographie du Bas-Sahara algérien', *Physio-Géo – Géographie Physique et Environnement*, Vol. IV (2010), pp. 107–27.

Barrucand, Marianne, 'Prospection dans le Gourara-Touat, rapport préliminaire', *Colloque international d'archéologie islamique* (Cairo: IFAO, 3–7 February 1993), pp. 183–216.

Echallier, Jean-Claude, *Essai sur l'habitat sédentaire traditionnel au Sahara algérien* (Paris: Université de Paris, Institut d'Urbanisme, 1968).

Echallier, Jean-Claude, *Villages désertés et structures agraires anciennes du Touat- Gourara (Sahara Algérien)* (Paris: Arts et Métiers Graphiques, 1972).

Mattingly, D. J. (ed.), *The Archaeology of Fazzān. Volume 1* Synthesis (London: The Society of Libya Studies; Tripoli: Department of Antiquities, 2003).

Schacht, Joseph, 'Sur la diffusion des formes d'architecture religieuse musulmane à travers le Sahara', *Travaux de l'Institut des Recherches Sahariennes*, No. 11 (1954), pp. 11–27.

Van Staëvel, Jean-Pierre, 'Ḳaṣr', *Encyclopédie de l'Islam* (2nd edition), XII (supplement) (Leiden: Brill, 2002), pp. 519–20.

SAHEL: CHAD to SOMALIA

Denyer, Susan, *African Traditional Architecture: An Historical and Geographical Perspective* (New York: Africana Publishing Company, 1978).

Gebremedhin, Naigzy, 'Some Traditional Types of Housing in Ethiopia,' in Paul Oliver (ed.), *Shelter in Africa* (London: Barrie & Jenkins, 1971), pp. 106–23.

Greenlaw, Jean-Pierre, *The Coral Buildings of Suakin: Islamic Architecture, Planning, Design and Domestic Arrangements in a Red Sea Port* (Stocksfield, London, and Boston: Oriel Press, 1976; London, New York: Kegan Paul International, 1995).

Lambourn, E., 'The Decoration of the Fakhr al-Din Mosque in Mogadishu and Other Pieces of Gujarati Marble Carving on the East African Coast', *Azania* 34, No. 1 (1999), pp. 61–86.

Nelson, Steven, *From Cameroon to Paris: Mousgoum Architecture In and Out of Africa* (Chicago: University of Chicago Press, 2007).

Prussin, Labelle, *African Nomadic Architecture: Space, Place and Gender* (Washington, DC: Smithsonian Institution Press and the National Museum of African Art, 1995).

Verity, Paul, 'Kababish Nomads of Northern Sudan', in Paul Oliver (ed.), *Shelter in Africa* (London: Barrie & Jenkins, 1971), pp. 25–35.

Waltz, Terence, 'House Decoration in Lower Nubia', in Daniel F. McCall and Edna G. Bay (eds), *African Images: Essays in African Iconology*, Boston University Papers on Africa 6 (New York: Africana Publishing Co. for the African Studies, Boston University, 1975), pp. 190–221.

Wenzel, Marian, *House Decoration in Nubia* (Toronto: University of Toronto Press, 1972).

SOUTH AND EAST AFRICA

Argyle, J. and F. Buthelezi, *Zulu Symbolism of right and left in the use of domestic and public space* (University of Durban Westville, South Africa: Association of South African Anthropologists Conference proceedings, 1992).

Berglund, A., *Zulu Thought Patterns and Symbolism* (Bloomington, IN: Indiana University Press, 1989).

Biermann, B., 'Indlu: The domed dwelling of the Zulu', in P. Oliver, *Shelter in Africa* (London: Barrie & Jenkins, 1971).

Claude, D., 'Space and symbols in rural KwaZulu-Natal', *KZNIA Journal* 2 (1997), p. 22.

Claude, D., 'Traditional architecture of the Tembe', *Journal of Architecture* 4 (1999), pp. 1–15.

Evers, T., 'The recognition of groups in the Iron Age of Southern Africa', PhD (Archaeology) thesis, University of Witwatersrand, 1988.

Frescura, F., *Rural shelter in Southern Africa* (Johannesburg: Ravan Press, 1981).

Frescura, F., 'The South African flat-roofed dwelling: A study in geographical adaptation and cultural tradition', *South African Journal of Culture and Art History* 3 (4) (1989), pp. 365–87.

Harber, R., 'The American flat in Africa', *SA Architect* (March 2000), pp. 37–40.

Knuffel, W., *The construction of the Bantu Grass Hut* (Graz: Akademische Druck-u. Verlangsanstalt, 1975).

Krige, E., *The Social System of the Zulus* (Pietermaritzburg: Shuter and Shooter, 1962 [reprint of 1936 original]).

Kuper, A., 'Symbolic dimensions of the Southern Bantu Homestead', *Africa* 50 (1) (1980), pp. 8–23.

Oliver, P., *Encyclopedia of Vernacular Architecture of the World* (Cambridge: Cambridge University Press, 1997).

SYRIA

Aurenche, O., *La maison orientale. L'architecture du Proche Orient Ancien des origins au mileu du Quatrième Millénaire* (Paris: Librairie Orientaliste Paul Geuthner S.A., 1981).

Besenval, R. *Technologie de la vôute dans l'Orient ancienne*, Synthèse n° 15 (Paris: Recherche sur les Civilisations, 1984).

Daker, N., 'Contribution a l'étude de l'evolution de l'habitat bédouin en Syrie', in O. Aurenche (ed.), *Nomades et sedentaires. Perspectives ethnoarchéologiques* (Paris: Recherche sur les Civilisations, 1984).

Ghiyas, Aljundi, *L'architecture traditionnelle en Syrie, Etablissements Humains et environnement socio-culturel* (Paris: UNESCO, 1984).

Mecca, S. and L. Dipasquale, *Earthen Domes and Habitats, Villages of Northern Syria: An architectural tradition shared by East and West* (Pisa: ETS, 2009).

IRAQ MARSH ARABS

Lloyd, Seton, *Twin Rivers* (Bombay: University of Oxford Press [Indian Branch], 1947).

Maxwell, Gavin, *A Reed Shaken by the Wind* (London/New York/Toronto: Longmans, Green and Co., 1957).

Nicholson, Emma and Peter Clark (eds), *The Iraqi Marshlands* (London: Politicos Publishing, 2002).

Salim, S. M., *Marsh Dwellers of the Euphrates Delta* (London: Berg, 1962).

Thesiger, Wilfred, *The Marsh Arabs* (London: E. P. Dutton & Co., 1964).

Young, Gavin, *Return to the Marshes* (London: Collins, 1977).

PALESTINE

Amiry, Suad and Rana Anani, *Throne Village Architecture: Palestinian Rural Mansions in the Eighteenth and Nineteenth Centuries* (Ramallah: Riwaq, 2003).

Amiry, Suad and Vera Tamari, *The Palestinian Village Home* (London: British Museum Publications, 1989).

Mubarak, Ghada, 'The implementation of renewable energy technologies in historic centres of towns in rural Palestine', Master's thesis, University of Nottingham, 2008.

ISRAEL LEVANT

Abu-Lughod, Janet, 'The Islamic City – Historical Myth, Islamic Essence, and Contemporary Relevance', *International Journal of Middle East Studies*, Vol. 19, No. 2 (May, 1987), pp. 155–76.

Can'aan, Tawfiq, *The Palestinian Arab House: Its Architecture and Folklore* (Jerusalem: Syrian Orphanage Press, 1933).

Fathy, Hassan, *Architecture for the Poor: An Experiment in Rural Egypt* (Chicago: University of Chicago Press, 1973).

Iqtait, I., 'An Architectural Survey of Raboud (South of Hebron)', *Web Journal on Cultural Patrimony*, 1 (2006), pp. 35–54.

Lutfallah, Gari, 'A History of the Hima Conservation System', *Environment and History*, 12, No. 2 (2006), pp. 213–28.

Metzger-Szmuk, Nitzah, *Dwelling on the Dunes: Tel Aviv* (Paris: Editions De L'Eclat, 2004).

Nulman, Macy, *The Encyclopedia of Jewish Prayer: Ashkenazic and Sephardic Rites* (Lanham, MD: Rowman & Littlefield, 1993).

Shmueli, A., *Bedouin Settlement in the Judean Desert* (Tel Aviv: Gomeh [Hebrew], 1970).

UNESCO, 'Incense Route – Desert Cities in the Negev', UNESCO World Heritage Centre, 2005. Available at http://whc.unesco.org/en/list/1107 (accessed 12 October 2015).

IRAN

Curzon, Lord, *Persia and the Persian Question* (London: Longman Green & Co., 1982).

PAKISTAN

Lagenbach, R. et al., *Don't Tear it Down! Preserving the Earthquake Resistant Vernacular Architecture of Kashmir* (New Delhi: UNESCO, 2009).

Denigan, Caroline, research paper for the University of Adelaide, 'The Self-Build Housing of Men and Others: Researching Gender and Vernacular Architecture in Australia', 2002.

Fathy, Hassan, *Architecture for the Poor: An Experiment in Rural Egypt* (Chicago: University of Chicago Press, 1973).

Lari, Yasmeen, *Traditional Architecture of Thatta* (Karachi: The Heritage Foundation, 1989).

Oliver, Paul, *Encyclopaedia of Vernacular Architecture of the World* (Cambridge: Cambridge University Press, 1997).

AZERBAIJAN

Mammadova, F. J., *Political history and historical geography of Caucasian Albania (3 century BC – 8 century AD)* (Baku: 'Elm', 1986).

Mammadova, G. H., T. A. Abdullayev, S. X. Hajiyeva and Y. Agamaliyeva, *Architectural monuments of Sheki* (Baku: 'Chashioglu', 2003).

Salamzadeh, A. R., and K. M. Mammadzadeh, *Architectural monuments of Sheki* (Baku: 'Elm', 1987), p. 138.

Useynov, M., L. S. Bretanitskiy and A. V. Salamzadeh, *A History of the Architecture of Azerbaijan* (Moscow. 1963), p. 396.

TURKMENISTAN

Cooke, Louise, *Conservation Approaches to Earthen Architecture in Archaeological Contexts*, British Archaeological Reports International Series S2147 (Oxford: Archaeopress, 2010).

Cooke, Louise, 'Earthen Building Materials and Techniques at Merv, Turkmenistan', in Franz Volhard and Ulrich Röhlen (eds), *Lehm 2004. 4. Internationale Fachtagung für Lehmbau* (Weimar: Dachverband Lehm e.V., 2004), pp. 52–61.

MONGOLIA

Andrews, Peter Alford, *Felt Tents and Pavilions. The Nomadic Tradition and its Interaction with Princely Tentage*, Kölner Ethnologische Mitteilungen, Special Volume, Institut für Völkerkunde (Cologne: University of Cologne, 1999).

Birtalan, Ágnes, *Material Culture (Traditional Mongolian Culture I.). Materielle Kultur (Traditionelle mongolische Kultur I.). A Mongol Nomádok Anyagi Műveltsége (Hagyományos mongol műveltség I.)* (Vienna, Budapest: IVA-ICRA Verlag – ELTE, Belső-ázsiai Tanszék, 2008). (DVD)

Gervers, Michael and Wayne A. Schlepp, 'Felt and "Tent Carts" in *The Secret History of the Mongols*', *Journal of the Royal Asiatic Society,* Third Series 7/1 (1997), pp. 93–116.

Humphrey, Caroline and Christopher Evans, 'The afterlives of the Mongolian yurt: the "archaeology" of a Chinese tourist camp', *Material Culture* 2 (2002), pp. 189–210.

Nandinbilig, G., 'Mongol gerīn belegdel' (Symbolism of the Mongolian Yurt), *Mongol sudlalīn erdem šinilgēnī bičig* (Mongolian Academic Studies) XVI. (160) (2000), pp. 238–44.

Sodnom, B., 'Mongol esgī gerīn ner tomiyō' (Vocabulary of the Mongolian Yurt), *Mongolīn sudlal* (Mongolian Studies) VIII (1971), pp. 243–53.

TEMPERATE CLIMATE

UNITED STATES OF AMERICA: SOUTH

King, A. *Spaces of Global Culture: Architecture, Urbanism, Identity* (London: Routledge, 2004).

Herman, B. 'The Charleston Single House', in Jonathan Poston, *The Buildings of Charleston: A Guide to the City's Architecture* (Columbia, SC: University of South Carolina Press, 1997).

Herman, B. *Town House: Architecture and Material Life in the Early American City, 1780–1830* (Chapel Hill, NC: University of North Carolina Press, 2005).

Cothran, James R., *Charleston Gardens and the Landscape Legacy of Loutrel Briggs* (Colombia, South Carolina: University of South Carolina Press, 2010).

LATIN AMERICA

Ferreiro, A. et al., *Construcción con terrón*, in Seminario Iberoamericano de Arquitectura y Construcción con Tierra (SIACOT) 2013 Congress Proceedings, Chile, 2013.

Jorquera, N., 'Culture costruttive in terra e rischio sismico. Conoscenza delle architecture tradizionali cilene e valutazione della loro vulnerabilità al sisma' (Building cultures in earth and seismic risk. Knowledge of traditional Chilean architecture and assessment of its vulnerability to earthquake)', PhD thesis, University of Florence, 2012.

Nunes, Martins de Lima, L. and E. Nazareno, 'Cultural manifestation in Kalunga territory: The Feast of Nossa Senhora de Aparecida as element of identity (re)affirmation and ethnic Reapprochement', *REMIE: Multidisciplinary Journal of Educational Research*, Vol. 2, Issue 1 (2012), pp. 105–27.

Pfenniger, F., M. Lobos and N. Jorquera, *Sustainability notions in vernacular architecture of Choapa Valley*, in Versus 2014 congress proceedings (Valencia: University of Valencia, 2014).

Ríos, S., 'Arquitecturas tradicionales en el Paraguay', in G. Viñuales (ed.), *Arquitectura vernácula iberoamericana* (Latin American vernacular architecture), Red Avi (Iberian-American Architectural Network), Universidad Pablo Olavide (2013), pp. 83–101.

EUROPE

Almagro-Gorbea, Martín and Lucía Moltó, 'Saunas en la Hispania prerromana' (Saunas in pre-Roman Hispania), *Espacio, Tiempo y Forma*, Serie II, Historia Antigua, Vol. V (1992).

Caniggia, Gianfranco, *Lettura dell'edilizia di base* (Reading of dwellings) (Florence: Alinea Editrice, 2008).

Catchpole, Heather 'Roaring forties', *In Depth. ABC Science* (20 September 2007).

Correia, Mariana, Letizia Dipasquale and Saverio Mecca (eds), *Terra Europae. Earthen Architecture in the European Union* (Pisa: Edizioni ETS, 2011).

CRAterre-ENSAG (eds), *Terra Incognita: Discovering & Preserving European Earthen Architecture* (Lisbon/Brusells: Argumentum/Culture Lab Éditions, 2008).

Lafarge, Ivan, 'Le plâtre dans la construction en Ile-de-France. Techniques, morphologie et économie avant l'industrialisation. Rapport d'etude' (Gypsum in the buildings of Ile-de-France. Techniques, morphology and economy before industrialization. Study report), PhD thesis, University of Paris 1 – Pantheon Sorbonne, 2013.

Mamì, Antonella, *Il gesso* (Sant'Arcangelo di Romagna: Maggioli, 2006).

Mecca, Saverio and Letizia Dipasquale (eds), *Earthen Domes and Habitats* (Pisa: Edizioni ETS, 2009).

Menéndez, Carmen-Oliva, *Teitos. Cubiertas vegetales de Europa Occidental: de Asturias a Islandia* (Thatched roofs in Western Europe: from Asturias to Iceland) (Oviedo: Colegio Oficial de Aparejadores y Arquitectos Técnicos del Principado de Asturias [Official Association of Quantity Surveyors of Asturias], 2008).

Mileto, Camilla and Fernando Vegas (eds), *La restauración de la tapia en la Península Ibérica. Criterios, técnicas, resultados y perspectivas* (The restoration of the wall in the Iberian Peninsula. Criteria, techniques, results and prospects) (Lisbon/Valencia: Argumentum/TC Ediciones, 2014).

Nicoletti, Manfredi, *L'architettura delle caverne* (The Architecture of Caves) (Rome-Bari: Laterza, 1980).

Sanz Arauz, David, 'Análisis del yeso empleado en revestimientos exteriores mediante técnicas geológicas', PhD thesis, Polytechnic University of Madrid, 2009.

Syrová, Zuzana and Jan Syrový, 'Rammed earth in Moravia (Czech Republic) in the context of neighboring lands', in Camilla Mileto, Fernando Vegas and Valentina Cristini (eds), *Rammed Earth Conservation* (London: CRC Press/ Balkema, Taylor & Francis Group, 2012).

Tsukidate, Toshio, 'Research on the uses of fire in vernacular houses in the Eurasian Continent', in C. Mileto et al. (eds), *Vernacular Architecture. Towards a Sustainable Future* (London: CRC Press / Balkema, Taylor & Francis Group 2015).

Vegas, Fernando and Camilla Mileto, 'Radiant heating underfloor systems: Glorias and trébedes', in M. Correia, L. Dipasquale and S. Mecca (eds), *Versus: Heritage for Tomorrow. Vernacular Knowledge for Sustainable Architecture* (Florence: Firenze University Press, 2014).

Vegas, Fernando and Camilla Mileto, *Lazos de alarife / Entrelacs de bâtisseur* (Interlacing builders) (Málaga: OMAU, 2013),

Vegas, Fernando, Camilla Mileto and Valentina Cristini, 'Corbelling domes and bridges in Spain and Portugal: a comparative study', in B. Chen and J. Wei (eds), *Arch'10. 6th International Conference on Arch Bridges* (Zagreb: SECON-HDGK, 2010)

Vellinga, Marcel, Paul Oliver and Alexander Bridge, *Atlas of Vernacular Architecture of the World* (Oxford/New York: Routledge, 2007).

Wenhao, J., 'A study into the sustainable system between the wind and the villages in Rincón de Ademuz, Spain', PhD thesis, Polytechnic University of Valencia, 2014.

CONTINENTAL CLIMATE

NORWAY

Berg, Arne, *Norske gardstun* (Norwegian farm structures) (Universitetsforlaget, Oslo, 1968), p. 277.

Jakhelln, Gisle, 'Nordlandshuset. Bakgrunn, definisjon, bruk og ny bruk' (The Nordland House – the traditional farm house of Northern Norway – Background, tradition, use and new use), *Fortidsminneforeningen Årbok* (2013), pp. 187–98.

FINLAND

Kaila, Panu, Talotohtori, rakentajan pikkujättiläinen (Porvoo: WSOY, 1997).

Kaila, Panu, Kevät toi maalarin, perinteinen ulkomaalaus (Jyväskylä: Multikustannus Oy, 2000).

Lounatvuori, Irma and Lauri Putkonen (eds), Rakennusperintömme, kulttuuriympäristön lukukirja (Hämeenlinna: Rakennustieto oy, 2001).

WESTERN RUSSIA

Khodakovsky, Evgeny, *Wooden Church Architecture of the Russian North: Regional Schools and Traditions (14th–19th Centuries)* (Routledge: London/New York, 2015).

Permilovskaya, A. B., *Cultural Meanings of the Folk Architecture of the Russian North* (Yekaterinburg: Ural Branch, Russian Academy of Sciences, 2013).

TASMANIA

Australian Heritage Commission, *The Heritage of Australia. An Illustrated Register of the National Estate* (Melbourne: Macmillan Australia in association with the Australian Heritage Commission, 1981).

Robertson E. Graeme, *Early Houses of Northern Tasmania* (Melbourne: Georgian House, 1964). *Early Buildings of Southern Tasmania* (Melbourne: Georgian House, 1970).

Memmott, Paul, *Gunyah, Goondie + Wurley, The Aboriginal Architecture of Australia* (Santa Lucia: University of Queensland Press, 2007).

Websites:

Australian Convict Sites (on the World Heritage List): whc.unesco.org/en/list/1306

APT (Association for Preservation Technology) Australasian Chapter, Longford Academy: aptaustralasia.wordpress.com/tag/longford-academy/

Brickendon: brickendon.com.au

Tasmanian Heritage Council: heritage.tas.gov.au

Woolmers Estate: woolmers.com.au

POLAR CLIMATE

ARCTIC

Lee, Molly and Gregory A. Reinhardt, *Eskimo Architecture: Dwelling and Structure in the Early Historic Period* (Fairbanks, AK: University of Alaska Press and University of Alaska Museum, 2003).

ICELAND

Loveday, Roy, 'Where Have all the Neolithic Houses Gone? Turf – an Invisible Component', *Scottish Archaeological Journal* 28 (2006), pp. 81–104.

Mook, Reinhard and Reidar Bertelsen, 'The

Possible Advantage of Living in Turf Houses on Settlement Mounds', *Acta Borealia* 24 (1) (2007), pp. 84–97.

Myhre, Bjørn, Bjarne Stoklund and Per Gjærder, 'Vestnordisk byggeskikk gjennom to tusen år: tradisjon og forandring fra romertid til det 19. århundre (West Nordic building customs from the Roman period to the 19th century)', *AmS-skrifter*, Vol. 7 (1982).

Sigurðardóttir, Sigríður, *Building with Turf* (English version by Nancy Marie Brown), Smart Byggðasafn Skagfirðinga IX (2008).

Steinberg, John M, 'Note on organic content of turf walls in Skagafjörður, Iceland', *Archaeological Islandica* 3 (2004), pp. 61–70.

van Hoof, Joost and Froukje van Dijken, 'The historical turf farms of Iceland: Architecture, building technology and the indoor environment', *Building and Environment* 43(6) (2008), pp. 1,023–30.

Wallace, Birgitta Linderoth, 'The Viking Settlement of L'Anse aux Meadows', in W. W. Fitzhugh and E. I. Ward (eds), *Vikings: The North Atlantic Saga* (Washington, DC: Smithsonian Institution Press, 2000), pp. 208–16.

Wilkinson, Brian, 'A Study of Turf: Historic Rural Settlements in Scotland and Iceland', *Architectural Heritage* 20 (2009), pp. 15–31.

Author Biographies

Tomasz Chruszczow is Former Chair of the Subsidiary Body for Implementation & Subsidiary Body for Scientific and Technological Advice of the UN Framework Convention on Climate Change. Tomasz was also appointed High-Level Climate Champion for COP24.

Dr Sandra Piesik is an award-winning architect, author and researcher specializing in the implementation of global sustainable legislation, nature-based solutions and traditional knowledge adaptation. She is the founder of 3 ideas B.V., an Amsterdam-based consultancy, and a senior consultant to UN-HABITAT on Urban and Rural Linkages at the Global Solutions Division. Dr Piesik is a stakeholder and network member of several UN organizations, including UNFCCC: The Resilience Frontiers, the Nairobi Work Programme (NWP), the Paris Committee on Capacity Building (PCCB) and the Climate and Technology Centre & Network (CTCN). Her written work includes *Arish: Palm-Leaf Architecture*, also published by Thames & Hudson.

The Influence of Climate

Dr Catherine Souch is Head of Research and Higher Education at the Royal Geographical Society. A physical geographer by training, she now provides oversight of the Society's scholarly publications, academic conferences and workshops, grants programme and professional accreditation.

A Geological Classification

Dr Graham Lott has worked as a geologist in the British Geological Survey (BGS) since 1971, specializing principally in the study of sedimentary basins and their rocks and sediments. Since 1996 he applied his varied sedimentological and petrographic experience to the study of the vernacular building stone resources of the UK in support of the work of the UK's many heritage conservation organizations.

Plants in the Built Environment

Dr William Milliken is Head of Tropical American Research at the Royal Botanic Gardens, Kew. He has written numerous books and scientific articles on the traditional use of plants around the world. His field experience includes Brazil, Indonesia, New Guinea, Bolivia, Peru, Venezuela, Sri Lanka, Bhutan and the United Kingdom.

An Anthropological Introduction

Dr André Singer is a documentary film-maker and anthropologist. He is currently CEO of Spring Films Ltd of London and is President of the Royal Anthropological Institute of Great Britain and Ireland. Having studied at Oxford University under Professor Sir E. E. Evans-Pritchard specializing in Iran and Afghanistan for his doctorate, he moved to television in the early 1970s as a researcher, then producer and director for the Disappearing World series at Granada Television.

The Value of the Vernacular

Professor Jim Coleman is Head of Economics at Happold Consulting. An economist specializing in spatial economic development and urban regeneration, Coleman is a visiting professor in the School of Architecture and the Built Environment, University of Westminster, and an honorary senior research associate at the Bartlett School of Planning, University College London. He has acted as an expert adviser to various organizations including the UK Town and Country Planning Association and the UK Commission for Architecture and the Built Environment (CABE).

Henry Fletcher is an associate at Happold Consulting, specializing in infrastructure and planning. An architect by training, he leads teams of engineers, architects and social scientists on projects for the development of new urban settlements and infrastructure systems as well as, increasingly, on interventions in existing cities and 'natural infrastructure' systems. Prior to joining Happold, Fletcher worked on construction and training projects using indigenous building techniques and materials in Mali, Ghana, Burkina Faso, Sri Lanka, Pakistan, Turkmenistan and the United Kingdom.

TROPICAL CLIMATE

Caribbean

Dr Ronald van Oers was an urban planner specializing in urban conservation. His doctoral thesis at Delft University focused on Dutch colonial town planning. Before his appointment as representative of the UNESCO World Heritage Institute of Training and Research for Asia and the Pacific he led the UNESCO Latin American and Caribbean Region unit.

Latin America

Brazil and Guayanas

Dr Patrick Pérez is an ethnologist and architect who lectures at the Social and Human Sciences Department at the National Superior School of Architecture at the University of Toulouse. His research focuses on the anthropology of landscape and architecture.

Venezuela

Alessandro Famiglietti is a practising architect with his own practice, Alessandro Famiglietti y Asociados, based in Caracas, Venezuela. He is a lecturer at the Faculty of Architecture and Urbanism at the Central University of Venezuela.

Adriana Useche is an architect at Alessandro Famiglietti y Asociados.

Angela Rodríguez de Famigliettiis is a restoration architect at Alessandro Famiglietti y Asociados.

Ecuador

Dr Laura Rival is an anthropologist and lectures in the Department of International Relations at the University of Oxford. She has undertaken extensive fieldwork on the Huaorani Indians of Amazonian Ecuador. Rival is a Member of OCTF (Oxford Centre for Tropical Forests) and BIO (Oxford Biodiversity Institute) as well as editor of Tipití (Journal of the Society for the Anthropology Lowland South America, SALSA).

Dr María Gabriela Zurita Benavides is an anthropologist and a researcher at Universidad Regional Amazónica Ikiam, Napo, Ecuador. Her research interests focus on natural resource management and human subsistence strategies. She has undertaken extensive fieldwork in Mexico, the Ecuadorian Andes and the Ecuadorian lowlands.

Brazil Upper Xingu and Wajãpi
Catherine Gallois is an architect with a focus on conservation at the IPHAN Institute of Historical and Artistic National Heritage, Rio de Janeiro, Brazil. She is responsible for drafting conservation regulations and acts as an adviser for architectural conservation and restoration projects.

Brazil Yanomami Yano
Dr William Milliken is Head of Tropical American Research at the Royal Botanic Gardens, Kew. He has written numerous books and scientific articles on the traditional use of plants around the world. His field experience includes Brazil, Indonesia, New Guinea, Bolivia, Peru, Venezuela, Sri Lanka, Bhutan and the United Kingdom.

Brazil and Colombia
Dr John Hemming is an explorer who has published widely on the Incas and indigenous population of the Amazonas since the 1970s. He has served as director of the Royal Geographical Society and was one of the founding members of South American Explorers. His book *Tree of Rivers: The Story of the Amazon* was published by Thames & Hudson in 2008.

Brazil Favelas
Professor Ronaldo de Moraes Brilhante is a graduate of Urban Space Management at the School of Architecture and Urbanism, Universidade Federal Fluminense, where he is a research professor. He is undertaking a PhD in Urban Planning at the Post-Graduate Program in Urban Planning (PROURB) of the Faculty of Architecture and Urbanism, Federal University of Rio de Janeiro (FAU-UFRJ). His current research is devoted to support a way of teaching architecture and urbanism that has been trampled in the fabric of dialogue relations, whereby students are asked to reveal their stories within the urban environment.

Paraguay
Dr Luis Silvio Rios Cabrera teaches at the Department of Architecture at the National University of Asunción, Paraguay. He has published books on construction materials and rural architecture.

Central Africa
Sierra Leone West Africa
Tom Perry is a trained town planner and the International Programme Manager at the Prince's Foundation for Building Community. The foundation works with local NGOs in order to provide training opportunities for students among others in Freetown, Sierra Leone.

Burkina Faso
James Morris is a British photographer of landscape and the built environment, with an interest in the evidence of man's intervention into landscape. In 2003 he published *Butabu*, which records the threatened and vulnerable landscape of West African vernacular architecture. His work is held in the following collections, among others: British Council, Museum of African Art NY, Princeton University, Victoria and Albert Museum, Aga Khan Foundation.

Côte d'Ivoire, Ghana, Togo, Benin, Cameroon
Dr Samuel Amos-Abanyie is a senior lecturer and the director of undergraduate programmes in architecture at Kwame Nkrumah University of Science and Technology, Kumasi, Ghana. His research interests focus on carbon-free architectural design approaches and climate control in tropical architecture.

Professor Rexford Assasie Oppong is a researcher, academic and architect with interest in Human Settlements Planning, Kumasi, Ghana. He is a senior lecturer in the Department of Architecture at Kwame Nkrumah University of Science and Technology.

Nigeria
Peter Zanang-Kazah Barwa is an architect and landscaper interested in sustainable design. He is based in Zaria, Nigeria.

Central Africa
Dr Mark Dike DeLancey teaches the history of African and Islamic art and architecture at the College of Liberal Arts and Social Sciences at DePaul University, Chicago. He specializes in Fulbe art and architecture, architecture of Cameroon, Islamic art and architecture in sub-Saharan Africa as well as arts of the book in Mauritania and Mali.

Madagascar
Dr Randall Bird is a trained architect and lectures in the history of architecture in Africa and the Indian Ocean area at the School of Architecture and Planning at the University of the Witwatersrand, Johannesburg. His forthcoming book *The Majesty of Architecture in Madagascar: Transforming a Kingdom in the Central Highlands, 1820–190<* traces the transformations in architecture and planning of the Merina people, located in Madagascar's central highlands.

India and Sri Lanka
India
Karen Rizvi has a degree in architecture from Yale University. She is currently working as a manager at the Wildlife Conservation Society, Greater New York.

Sri Lanka
Rajiv Wanasundera is an associate architect at Lord Aeck Sargent architecture and design firm and a member of the US Green Building Council.

Southeast Asia
Myanmar
Su Su is Professor and Head in the Department of Architecture, Mandalay Technological University. She has been widely published and given conference papers internationally focusing on her speciality of heritage and urbanism, including significant research about conservation of the last Myanmar Kingdom in Mandalay. She is currently contributes to projects of national importance in Myanmar, including the National Building Code Drafting and collaborations with the Ministry of Culture.

U Win Kyaing is Principal in the Field School of Archaeology, Pyay. He holds a Post Graduate Diploma in Archaeology from the Institute of Archaeology, New Delhi, and has undertaken surveys and excavations at Anyathian sites. He has discovered Mesolithic sites of Central Myanmar, Neolithic sites (2010–11) and the ancient Srikshetra Pyu site.

Daw Yin Nyein Aye is a graduate of Technology University Mandalay, and is currently a tutor at the Field School of Archaeology, Pyay, the Department of Archaeology, National Museum and Library.

Laos
Denise Heywood is an author, lecturer, photographer and journalist. She worked in Cambodia as a journalist for three years and has published a book on the Buddhist temples of Laos, *Ancient Luang Prabang*. Based in London, she is a lecturer for the Art Fund, the School of Oriental and African Studies (University of London) on their post-graduate Asian Art Course, and Madingley Hall (University of Cambridge).

Thailand and Cambodia
Dr William R. Chapman is a trained anthropologist with an interest in architectural recording, the management of historic districts, and materials conservation with a focus on the Asia and Pacific area. He serves on three ICOMOS committees: History and Theory, Historic Towns and Urban Areas, and Vernacular Architecture. Chapman is a member of the UNESCO committee for the Heritage Awards in Asia and the Pacific.

Southeastern Asia
Barbara J. Anello-Adnani is an artist, photographer, art historian and educator who has spend many years teaching and researching in Southeast Asia, most recently as a Fulbright senior researcher on vernacular architecture in Indonesia, Cambodia and Vietnam. She is currently a lecturer at the Pratt Institute in Brooklyn, New York.

Indonesia
Yenny Gunawan is a lecturer in Architecture at the Universitas Katolik Parahyangan in Bandung.

She is an architect and researcher, who holds an MA in International Studies, Vernacular Architecture from Oxford Brookes University, UK, and a BSc in Architecture Engineering from Universitas Katolik Parahyangan, Bandung, Indonesia. Her research interests consider the nature of vernacular architecture, especially in Indonesia, and she has been published in books including *Vocabulary of Architecture: DESIGN* and *Design Fever*.

North and South Pacific

Australia

Dr Timothy O'Rourke is an architect and a lecturer at the School of Architecture, University of Queensland. His research interests focus on building technology and craft traditions, the environmental and socio-cultural context for vernacular architecture, and its actual and potential influence on Indigenous housing. O'Rouke has completed building projects for several Aboriginal communities in the wet tropics region.

New Guinea

Dr Lissant Bolton is a curator for the Department of Africa, Oceania and the Americas at the British Museum. She is a trained anthropologist who specializes in the Pacific, especially on questions of gender in Vanuatu, where she has worked in annually since 1989. She has lead-curated the permanent gallery *Living and Dying* and curated the exhibitions *Power and Taboo: Sacred Objects from the Pacific* and *Baskets and Belonging: Indigenous Australian Histories*, all for the British Museum.

Micronesia

Dr Karen Nero is a senior research fellow at the University of Otago, New Zealand. She has undertaken extensive research in the region with a focus on cultural heritage and its transmission in a museum context.

Fiji and Tonga:

Dr Charmaine 'Ilaiū Talei is an architect and currently a PhD candidate at the Aboriginal Environments Research Centre, School of Architecture at the University of Queensland. Her thesis focuses on the changes of building materials in Tongan domestic *fale* architecture from the 18th century to the present.

Cook Islands

Jeanette Budgett is an academic and a lecturer in the Department of Architecture at UNITEC Institute of Technology, New Zealand. Her Master thesis investigated the history and conservation of coral mission-period architecture of the Cook Islands. Budgett has authored a chapter on the topic published in *Cook Islands*.

Dr Jeremy Treadwell is a senior lecturer in architecture at the University of Auckland, New Zealand. He has published on South Pacific architecture.

French Polynesia

Professor Anne E. Guernsey Allen is a lecturer in the Fine Arts department at the Indiana University Southeast. She is the editor of *Pacific Arts Journal*, which focuses on visual and performing arts.

Hawaii

Dr Alice Spencer Leineweber is an expert on historical architecture. She is chair of the graduate programme and director of the Heritage Centre at Hawaii University with a focus on the history of architecture and heritage studies. She has received multiple awards, including the National AIA Design Honor Award for her work at Hawaii's Plantation Village dedicated to maintaining the cultural identity and authenticity of an ethnic history museum. She co-authored *Hawaiian Modern*, co-published by Yale University Press.

DRY CLIMATE

North America

American Southwest and Mexico

Professor Mark L. Gillem is an architect and a lecturer at the Department of Architecture and Landscape Architecture at the University of Oregon. Through his architectural practice the Urban Collaborative he addresses sustainability, social responsibility and historic preservation.

Latin America

Colombia

Lucia Garzon is a Colombian architect who designs, constructs, researches and teaches using natural and unconventional materials, including earth, wood, stone and bamboo.

Peru

Sophía Rodríguez Larraín is an architect and a lecturer at the Faculty of Architecture at the Pontifical Catholic University of Peru. She is a coordinator of Heritage at the Center of Architectural Investigation at the university and focuses on social responsibility, vernacular architecture and the conservation of heritage buildings.

Professor Marcial Blondet is the director of the Civil Engineering doctoral programme at the Pontifical Catholic University in Peru. He specializes in the development of low-cost solutions to mitigate seismic risk on earthen and masonry dwellings and the conservation of earthen historical monuments in seismic areas.

Chile

Hugo Pereira Gigone is a Chilean architect and a member of ICOMOS-Chile and Protierra Chile. He organized the National Encounter of Architecture in Construction in Chile at the University of Chile, 2014

Bolivia

Dr Natalia J. Silva is an architect and researcher at the Department of Architecture at the University of Chile. Her research interests include the social responsibility of heritage conservation, the environmental aspects of vernacular architecture and traditional construction techniques. She is a member of the International Scientific Committee on Earthen Architectural Heritage (ISCEAH) ICOMOS scientific committee that is concerned with the protection of world heritage built on raw land.

Argentina

Dr Rodolfo Rotondaro is an Argentinian architect whose practice focuses on earthen architecture and construction in Argentina. He has worked intensively in the Argentinian Northwest, particularly in the UNESCO Biosphere Reserve 'Laguna de Pozuelos', in Jujuy and at the World Heritage Site of Ischigualasto Provincial Park.

North Africa

Africa

Suzanne Preston Blier is an art historian and archaeologist and a professor of Fine Arts and of African and African American Studies at Harvard University. Her books *The Royal Arts of Africa* and *Butabu* are both considered seminal in her field.

North Africa (Morocco, Tunisia, Egypt)

Professor James M. Steele is a teacher, author, researcher and architect with an interest in trends in contemporary architecture, especially in the Middle East and Asia. His seminal book *Rasem Badran: A Narrative on People and Place* was published by Thames & Hudson and led to his appointment at the UNESCO Scientific Committee 'Safeguarding of New Gourna Village'. Steele teaches at the Faculty of Architecture at the University of Southern California.

Algeria

Dr Mounia Chekhab-Abudaya is an art historian with a focus on the history and archaeology of Islamic art, especially of the Maghreb and Sahara regions. She has previously worked in the Department of Islamic Art at the Louvre Museum and is currently the Curator for North Africa and Iberia at the Museum of Islamic Art, Doha.

Libya

Dr Beniamino Polimeni is working as a research fellow at Leicester School of Architecture, De Montfort University, UK. His research focuses on the Maghreb region and Southern Asia. He conducted research on the architecture in the Libyan Nafusah mountains as part of his position as research fellow at the Aga Khan Program for Islamic Architecture at the MIT.

North Africa (Sahel)

Mauritania

Dr Mark Dike DeLancey teaches the history of African and Islamic art and architecture at the College of Liberal Arts and Social Sciences at DePaul University, Chicago. He specializes in Fulbe art and architecture, architecture of Cameroon, Islamic art and architecture in sub-Saharan Africa as well as arts of the book in Mauritania and Mali.

Mali and Niger

James Morris is a British photographer of landscape and the built environment, with an interest in the evidence of man's intervention into landscape. In 2003 he published *Butabu*, which records the threatened and vulnerable landscape of West African vernacular architecture. His work is held in the following collections, among others: British Council, Museum of African Art NY, Princeton

University, Victoria and Albert Museum, Aga Khan Foundation.

South Africa

South and East Africa

Dr Debbie Whelan is a lecturer at the Department of Architecture at Durban University of Technology, South Africa. She runs Archaic Consulting, a platform to inform and connect professionals engaged in historical preservation in South Africa.

Dr Walter Peters is a lecturer in the Department of Architecture at the University of the Free State. He focuses on the history of the environment and research methods in architecture.

Arab Peninsula

Arabian Peninsula

Peter Sheehan is an archaeologist who has been working in the Middle East for more than twenty years. He has worked on numerous historic building conservation projects throughout the region since 1989, particularly in Egypt and in the United Arab Emirates. Sheehan has a particular interest in urban formation processes and has published extensively on the Roman fortress of Babylon in Old Cairo. Since 2007 he has been Historic Buildings Manager with Tourism and Culture Authority Abu Dhabi, where he has been involved in the site management, conservation and presentation of historic buildings throughout the emirate.

Yemen

Professor Ronald Lewcock is an architect, conservator and scholar who specializes in Africa and the Middle East. He has worked on several conservation projects in Yemen, Egypt and Uzbekistan for the UN and UNESCO and directed a design studio on architectural practices in the developing world at the Architectural Association, London. He is currently teaching in the Department of Architecture at the University of Queensland.

Western Asia

Israel and the Levant

Professor Michael Turner is the UNESCO Chair in Urban Design and Conservation Studies at the Bezalel Academy of the Arts and Design in Jerusalem and is a practising architect, conservationist and urbanist, with a focus on environmental issues.

Palestine

Fida Touma has been co-director of the RIWAQ Centre for Architectural Conservation since 2011, and a member of RIWAQ since 2000. She is an architect and restoration expert and has supervised a number of restoration projects in Palestine. A member of the National Cultural Heritage Strategies Group in Palestine, she has presented numerous papers on cultural heritage in Palestine.

Jordan

Dr Rami Farouk Daher is a practising architect with his own firm, TURATH: Architecture & Urban Design, and a lecturer in Architecture at the German Jordanian University in Amman. Daher is a heritage and urban regeneration specialist interested in research related to politics and dynamics of public space making and interventions in existing historic settings.

Lebanon

Dr Aram Yeretzian is an assistant professor in the Faculty of Engineering and Architecture at the American University of Beirut and the president of the Lebanon Green Building Council, which promotes sustainable building strategies throughout Lebanon.

Syria

Professor Saverio Mecca teaches in the Department of Architecture at the University of Florence. He specializes in building techniques and process management as well as vernacular and earthen architecture in the Mediterranean region. He is the Director of the Research Centre on Innovation and Local and Indigenous Knowledge Systems at the University of Florence, Italy.

Dr Letizia Dipasquale is a researcher in the Department of Architecture at the University of Florence, Italy.

Turkey

Dr Tammy Gaber teaches architecture design and theory courses at Laurentian University and was recently awarded a Social Sciences and Humanities Research Council Grant from the Federal Government of Canada.

Turkey (South Anatolia)

Dr Hacer Mutlu Danaci is an Associate Professor in the Department of Architecture at Akdeniz University in Antalya. Her research focuses on sustainable development, traditional vernacular architectural practices in Turkey and the influence and possibilities of ecotourism in the region.

Iraq

Dr Subhi Al-Azzawi is a practising architect and an independent scholar who has worked on heritage on preservation projects in the Arabian world for thirty years. Projects include the master plan for Kuwait Old City and the revitalization and conservation of the Citadel of Erbil (Iraq). He is an associate of the Foundation for Science, Technology and Civilisation.

Iraq Marshes

Born in Scotland in 1940, Alexander Maitland studied at the Glasgow School of Architecture and School of Art. He later worked intermittently for architectural practices in London and Edinburgh while continuing to write and paint. He is a Fellow of the Royal Geographical Society and has contributed to newspapers, magazines, and radio and television programmes. He wrote the authorized biography *Wilfred Thesiger.*

Southern Asia

Iran

Nasser Golzari is an architect and academic who is a principal partner at Golzari-NG Architects, London. He is the leader of the Cultural Identity and Globalisation pathway of the Architecture MA at University of Westminster and has previously taught at Central Saint Martins. He is interested in sustainability, environment and cultural identity, with a focus on Europe and the Middle East.

Afghanistan

Professor Bashir A. Kazimee teaches at the School of Design and Construction at the University of Washington. He is a citizen of the United States of the America as well as Afghanistan and has a research interest in traditional Islamic cities and sustainable housing and communities.

Pakistan

Yasmeen Lari was the first female architect to be registered in Pakistan. She has been a Member of the Royal Institute of British Architects since 1963 and was awarded the Sitara-e-Imtiaz (Star of Distinction) by the Pakistani government in recognition of her services to the architectural profession and heritage conservation. She is the co-founder of the Heritage Foundation in Pakistan dedicated to researching and safeguarding Pakistan's cultural heritage. She has worked as an adviser on several UNESCO projects in Pakistan and is the recipient of the UN Recognition Award for the promotion of culture and peace.

Azerbaijan

Professor Sabina Hajiyeva lectures at the Azerbaijan University of Architecture and Construction and specializes in restoration and the preservation of Azerbaijani heritage.

Uzbekistan

Anna Ietswaart is a journalist, author, lecturer and consultant based in the Netherlands. She trained as an archaeologist with a focus on Near Eastern cultures and has travelled widely in Central Asia. Ietswaart's writing has been published widely in journals such as *National Geographic.*

Turkmenistan

Dr Louise Cooke is Associate Lecturer in Conservation in the Department of Archaeology at the University of York. She has worked on projects in the UK, Central Asia and Middle East, undertaking condition assessment and conservation planning for heritage sites. Recent publications reflect research undertaken in Turkmenistan and Central Asia. Cooke is an expert member of the ICOMOS International Scientific Committee on Earthen Architectural Heritage, and a director of Earth Building UK (EBUK).

Tajikistan and Kyrgyzstan

Dr Munzifakhon Babadjanova is the UNESCO Chair of Intercultural Dialogue for the UNITWIN network as well as Secretary-General for the ASPnet Tajikistan National Commission for UNESCO. She is an associate in the Department for Cultural Studies, Pedagogy and Psychology at Russian-Tajik Slavonic University in Dushanbe, Tajikistan.

Mongolia
Dr Ágnes Birtalan is the head of the Inner Asian Studies Department and deputy director of the Institute of Far Eastern Studies at Eötvös Loránd University, Budapest. She teaches on various fields of Mongolian studies (dialects, religions, traditional nomadic culture, folklore), and Korean religions.

TEMPERATE CLIMATE

United States of America
The American South
Larisa Marenco holds a professional Masters degree from Florida International University. She is a practising architect in Miami.

Dr Gray Read teaches history and theory of architecture at Florida International University. Her research focuses on design strategies for urban buildings that contribute to the health, sustainability, and delight of city life.

Latin America
Dr Natalia Jorquera Silva is an architect and a researcher at the Department of Architecture at the University of Chile. Her research interests include the social responsibility of heritage conservation, the environmental aspects of vernacular architecture and traditional construction techniques. She is a member of the International Scientific Committee on Earthen Architectural Heritage (ISCEAH) ICOMOS scientific committee that is concerned with the protection of world heritage built on raw land.

Europe
Camilla Mileto and Fernando Vegas are architects and professors at the Polytechnic University of Valencia, Spain. They have published extensively on traditional architectural technology and its preservation, and have won a number of international awards for their work.

British Isles
Dr Mike Lawrence is a lecturer in Low Carbon Design within the BRE Centre for Innovative Construction Materials in the Department of Architecture and Civil Engineering at the University of Bath. Lawrence's research interests are in natural building materials and in the field of low-carbon design. From 1995–2012 he was the manager of Ham Hill Stone Company, whose quarry has provided building material for the southwest of England since Roman times for the construction of a wide range of buildings, including many Grade 1 and 2* listed buildings.

Georgia
Dr Suzanne Harris-Brandts received her PhD from the Department of Architecture at the University of Waterloo, Cambridge, Canada. She has undertaken research as a resident of the Decolonizing Architecture Art Residency programme in Sahour, Palestine, and written on urbanism and internal displacement in the Republic of Georgia.

Central Asia
Himalayas
Professor Gérard Toffin is an anthropologist and the Director of Research at the Centre for Himalayan Studies, France. He is interested in the material culture, the social organization and the religions of Himalayan populations. Toffin has conducted fieldwork in the Nepalese Kathmandu Valley, the Ganesh Himal range, North Bengal and Gujarat.

Dr Joëlle Smadja is a geographer and researcher at the Centre for Himalayan Studies in France. She is head of the laboratory UPR 299: 'Environments, Societies and Cultures in the Himalayas'. She has conducted extensive fieldwork in Nepal and Northeast India.

Himalayan Tibet
Professor Frederique Darragon is an explorer and producer of *The Secret Towers of the Himalayas*, which chronicled her expedition to the stone towers of Sichuan and Tibet. She is the founder of the Unicorn Foundation and co-founder of the Sichuan University Unicorn Heritage Institute.

Asia
China Central and Eastern
Professor Zhu Tan is an architect and teaches at the Polytechnic University of Milan, Italy. Her research focuses on the adaption of spatial strategies from traditional Chinese courtyard buildings.

China North
Dr Lijun Zhou teaches at the Institute of Technology at the School of Architecture in Harbin, China. His research interests are in traditional housing in Northeast China, their restoration and their adaptability to environmental influences.

China Northwest
Dr Amy Eisenberg is an ethno-ecologist with a background in botany and cultural studies. Her research focuses on sustainable development and the understanding and transmission of indigenous cultural knowledge. She has held several positions in research institutes in China, including at the Research Institute of Anthropology and Ethnology at Jishou University, Hunan.

John Amato is a photographer.

South Korea
Professor Kyung-Rip Park teaches the design and history of architecture at the Department of Architecture at Kangwon National University, South Korea. His research focuses on urban development and town planning. He is a member of the Jeonju Creative City Planning Commission.

Taiwan
Dr Ping-Sheng Wu is an associate professor at the Department of Architecture at National Cheng Kung University, Taiwan. He specializes in the History of Modern Architecture, with a focus on Chinese and Taiwanese architecture, the theory and practice of conserving World Heritage and the architecture of Colonial East Asia. Wu has served as General Secretary at the Society of Architectural Historians in Taiwan and is a member ICOMOS-UK.

Dr Min-Fu Hsu teaches at the Department of Architecture at National Cheng Kung University, Taiwan. His research focuses on urban preservation, regeneration and Taiwan's architectural history.

Japan
Professor Don Choi teaches architectural history at the College of Architecture and Environmental Design at CalPoly, San Diego. He specializes in the development of architecture in Japan since 1800 and the emergence of a particularly Japanese style.

CONTINENTAL CLIMATE

North America
Alaska and Canada
Dr Aldona Jonaitis is an anthropologist and the Director of the University of Alaska Museum of the North. After graduating with a PhD in History of Art from Columbia University she has published widely on Native American art. Publications include *Art of the Northwest Coast* and *The Totem Pole.*

Scandinavia, Russia, Kazakhstan***Norway***
Gisle Jakhelln is senior architect, partner and administrative director of BOARCH arkitekter a.s in Bodö, Northern Norway. He qualified as an architect in 1964 at the Technical University of Norway (NTH), Trondheim. His field of work is general architectural work: all kinds of building types from housing to hospitals, town planning, refurbishing, rehabilitation and reconstruction of historical buildings. He is the Vice Chairman of ICOMOS and president of the CIAV.

Sweden
Lena Palmqvist is Head of Department at the Nordiska Museet, Stockholm. Her research interests include traditional Scandinavian house building techniques and their adaption in different cultural contexts.

Finland
Kirsti Kovanen is the Secretary General of the ICOMOS Board. She is a regional planning architect with a focus on the environment and natural resources for the ELY Centre of Economic Development, Transport and the Environment.

Central Russia
Dr Anna Yu Mainicheva is leading researcher of the Department of Ethnography at the Institute of Archaeology and Ethnography, Siberian Branch, of the Russian Academy of Science in Novosibirsk. Her research focuses on the symbolism of Siberian wood churches such as Ostrog Illm.

West Russia
Dr Anna Permilovskaya is a Senior Researcher at the Institute of Ecological Problems of the North, Russian Academy of Sciences. She is the author of over eighty articles on North Russian traditional

culture and wooden architecture, including *Northern House* and *Peasant Houses in North Russian Culture.*

Kazakhstan

Dr Miriam Ho received her PhD from the Department of Architecture at the University of Waterloo, Cambridge, Canada. Her thesis focuses on the possibilities of preserving water supplies in the context of vernacular architecture in the North Aral Sea area in Kazakhstan.

East Russia

Dr Olga V. Maltseva is a historian with an interest in the Shamanic traditions of the Nanai People in the Lower Amur region. She is a researcher at the Institute of Archaeology and Ethnography, Siberian Branch, of the Russian Academy of Science in Novosibirsk.

South Pacific

Tasmania

Dr Noni Boyd is an architectural historian and heritage specialist. She has a detailed knowledge of building types, including military and prefabricated buildings, and construction methods of the 19th and 20th centuries. She is a member of ICOMOS, DOCOMOMO and the National Trust of Australia, as well as heritage officer for the New South Wales Chapter of the Australian Institute of Architects. Boyd is a member of the Australia ICOMOS Energy and Sustainability Working Group.

New Zealand

Dr Deidre Brown teaches design and history in the School of Architecture at the University of Auckland. Her research is in the fields of Māori and Pacific architectural and art history, and indigenous design. She has written several books, including *Art in Oceania*, and curated exhibitions. She is a governor of the Arts Foundation of New Zealand and a member of the Māori Trademarks Advisory Committee of the Intellectual Property Office of New Zealand.

POLAR CLIMATE

North America

Dr Gregory A. Reinhardt is Director of Archaeology at the University of Indianapolis Archaeology and Forensics Laboratory and Chair of the Department of Anthropology at the University of Indianapolis. He has published widely on topics such as Arctic geoarchaeology; Eskimo archaeology, architecture, art, and ethnology; and visual anthropology of American Indians.

Iceland

Dr Douglas J. Bolender is a Research Assistant Professor in the Department of Anthropology at the University of Massachusetts, Boston. Sigríður Sigurðardóttir is a director of the Skagafjordur Heritage Museum, Iceland.

Dr John M. Steinberg is a research scientist and Director of the Digital Archaeology Laboratory at the Fiske Center for Archaeological Research, University of Massachusetts Boston. He directs the Skagafjordur Archaeological Settlement Survey, a project looking at the formation of social stratification and property rights during the Viking Age in Northern Iceland.

Sámi Vernacular

Dr Kjell-Åke Aronsson is an archaeologist with a focus on the history of Sámi reindeer herding. He is the director of Ájtte, the Swedish Mountain and Sámi Museum in Jokkmokk, Sweden.

Isse Israelsson is curator of cultural history at Ájtte, the Swedish Mountain and Sámi Museum in Jokkmokk, Sweden. Her research interests include Sámi tents and prehistoric eating habits.

Picture Credits

a=above, b=below, l=left, r=right, c=centre

1 © ARCO/W. Dolder/age fotostock **2-3** De Klerk/Alamy **4a** Hemis.fr/SuperStock **4b, 5a** imageBROKER/Alamy **5b** age fotostock © Sergi Reboredo **6a, bl** Royal Geographical Society (with IBG) **6br** ShutterStock G.R. Lambert & Co. **7ar** Private Collection **7cl** Royal Geographical Society (with IBG) **7cr** G.R. Lambert & Co **7b** Royal Geographical Society (with IBG) **8a** © Arthur F. Selbach/Robert Harding **8b** Hemis/AWL images **9a** Christian Kober/AWL images **9b** © F. Neukirchen/age fotostock **15** Rob Pinney/Alamy **16-17** NASA **18al** Ariadne Van Zandbergen/Alamy **18ar** George Steinmetz/National Geographic Creative **18cl** Vario Images GmbH & Co.KG/Alamy **18b** Fadil/Getty Images **19** Ivan Vdovin/Alamy **20** Stuart Black/Alamy **21a** © Anna Letswaart **21b** © Kevin O'Hara/age fotostock **22** © Florian Kopp/imageBROKER/age fotostock **23** © Philippe Michel/age fotostock **24l** © Dr Sandra Piesik **24r** © Edmund Sumner/VIEW Pictures **25** © Emma Smales/VIEW Pictures **26-27** © Eric Baccega/age fotostock **29** Danita Delimont Stock/AWL images **33al** Katrina Brown/SuperStock **33ar** Danita Delimont Stock/AWL images **33bl, br** image BROKER/SuperStock **34al** Alex Robinson/AWL images **34ar** Danita Delimont Stock/AWL images **34cl, cr, br** Nigel Pavitt/AWL images **34bl** Susanna Wyatt/AWL images **35l** Radius/SuperStock **35r** Nigel Pavitt/AWL images **36-37** Ph. Bouysse, Geological Map of the World – Sheet 2. Geology, structure at 1:50 000 000 scale © CCGM-CGMW 2009 **39al** Gaby Wojciech/Westend61/SuperStock **39ar** Robert Harding/SuperStock **39b** Jeremy Pembrey/Alamy **40al** Photo courtesy William Milliken **40ar** © CSP_geargodz/age fotostock **40cr** imageBROKER/Alamy **40b** © S. Sailer/A. Sailer/age fotostock **42-43** Frank Herholdt/Alamy **45** Nikreates/Alamy **47** Jordi Camí/Alamy **48al** Wolfgang Kaehler/SuperStock **48ar** Independent Picture Service/Alamy **48cl** Robert Harding/SuperStock **48cr** Gary Blake/Alamy **48bl** imageBROKER/Alamy **48br** Wayne Hutchinson/Alamy **50** Photography courtesy Turquoise Mountain **51** Amar Grover/AWL images **54-55** George Steinmetz/National Geographic Creative **56l** Private Collection **56r** Miss E. B. Gibbes **57a** © Ellen Rooney/age fotostock **57b** Dr Ronald van Oers **58a** © Christian Kober/Robert Harding **58b** Suzy Bennett/Alamy **59** Pixtal/SuperStock **60-61** © Mel Longhurst/age fotostock **63a** Robert Harding/SuperStock **63b** © easyFotostock/age fotostock **64l** Landrin Valérie/Alamy **64r, 65** Courtesy Patrick Perez **66l** Viviana Morales/VWPics/Alamy **66r** © Gerard Lacz/age fotostock **67a** © Rigamonti **67cl, c, cr** © NBarrios **67bl** © Ricardo Ribas/age fotostock **67br** Mediacolor's/Alamy **68a** © M.G. Zurita-Benavides **68b** © Laura Rival **69** © M.G. Zurita-Benavides **70** Steven Kazlowski/SuperStock **71al, ar** © Danita Delimont Stock/Danita Delimont Agency/age fotostock **71b** Pablo Cozzaglio/AFP/Getty Images **72l** Miss M. L. Moennick **72r** Commander G. M. Dyott **73** © Jacques Jangoux/age fotostock **74a** Tom Koene/Alamy **74b** Sue Cunningham Photographic/Alamy **74-75a** © Picture Contact Bv/age fotostock **77** Photography Catherine Gallois **78, 79a** Copyright William Milliken/RBG Kew **79b** © Robin Hanbury Tenison/Robert Harding **80al, bl** Copyright William Milliken/RBG Kew **80r** © Environmental Images/Universal Images Group/age fotostock **81l** © Zoonar/Jens Nieswand/ Zoonar GmbH RF/age fotostock **81r** Copyright William Milliken/RBG Kew **82bl** Eye Ubiquitous/Alamy **82r** Eye Ubiquitous/REX/ShutterStock **83a** © Eye Ubiquitous/age fotostock **83b** © Cosmoguias/age fotostock **85** © Neil Emmerson/age fotostock **87** Courtesy Dr Silvio Rios Cabrera **88** Jake Lyell/Alamy **89** Lee Karen Stow/Alamy **90** Photononstop/SuperStock **91al, cl, r** © Tom Perry **91b** Fabian von Poser/imageBROKER/SuperStock **92-95** © James Morris **96** age fotostock/SuperStock **97l** Eric Lafforgue/age fotostock/SuperStock **97r** age fotostock/SuperStock **98** Raquel Carbonell/age fotostock/SuperStock **99a** © Godong/Universal Images Group/age fotostock **99b** © Christian Goupi/age fotostock **101a** Iconotec/Alamy **101cl** G.I. Jones. N.13221.GIJ. Museum of Archaeology and Anthropology, Cambridge **101c** Eye Ubiquitous/Alamy **101cr** Nationaal Museum van Wereldculturen, Amsterdam. Object number TM-20016872 **101bl** Royal Geographical Society (with IBG) **101br** © Patrick Wass/age fotostock **102** © C. Sappa/De Agostini Editore/age fotostock **103l** imageBROKER/Alamy **103r** Photo Mark D. DeLancey, 1999 **104l** INTERFOTO/Alamy **104r** Nationaal Museum van Wereldculturen, Amsterdam. Object number TM-60033962 **105a** Robert Harding/SuperStock **105bl** David Wall/Alamy **105br** Jacques Jangoux/Alamy **107a** Cyril Ruoso/Minden Pictures/SuperStock **107b** Photo Joan Riera, 2013 **108a** Photononstop/SuperStock **108b** © W. Dolder/age fotostock **109al** Hemis/Alamy **109ar** © Willi Dolder/age fotostock **109bl** © W. Dolder/age fotostock **109br** Wolfgang Kaehler/SuperStock **110l** Bibliothèque Nationale de France/Société de Géographie, Paris **110r** Chris Hellier/Alamy **111** Bernd Bieder/imageBROKER/SuperStock **112-113a** © Chinch Gryniewicz/Bridgeman Images **113bl** Samuel Bourne/Private Collection/Bridgeman Images **113br** Dinodia/Bridgeman Images **114** Peter Schickert/imageBROKER/SuperStock **115al** age fotostock/SuperStock **115ar** Robert Harding/Alamy **115bl** Galit Seligmann/Alamy **115br** Robert Harding/SuperStock **116a** © David Beatty/age fotostock **116b** Christine Osborne Pictures/Alamy **117l** Private Collection **117r** Andree/National Geographic Creative **118a** Tony French/Alamy **118c** Private Collection/Bridgeman Images **118b** Courtesy C. Anjalendran **119** Hemis/AWL images **120-121** Majority World/UIG/Bridgeman Images **122-123** © Prof Su Su **124l** Nationaal Museum van Wereldculturen, Amsterdam. Object number TM-20000759 **124r** Royal Geographical Society (with IBG) **125al** W. & H. Meyer **125ar** © Dinodia Photo/age fotostock **125cla** © CSP_cristi180884/Fotosearch LBRF/age fotostock **125ca** © CSP_erikdegraaf/Fotosearch LBRF/age fotostock **125cra** © CSP_rakijung/Fotosearch LBRF/age fotostock **125clb** © Meazza/IML/Icarus/age fotostock **125cb** © CSP_GeorgeDolgikh/Fotosearch LBRF/age fotostock **125crb** © CSP_Reeed/Fotosearch LBRF/age fotostock **125bl**© CSP_pazham/Fotosearch LBRF/age fotostock **125br** © David Clegg/age fotostock **126-127** Barbara Anello-Adnani **128a** © Brandon Seidel/age fotostock **128-129b** Hemis/AWL images **129al** © CSP_slickspics/Fotosearch LBRF/age fotostock **129ar** Nigel Pavitt/AWL images **130-131** © Stefan Auth/age fotostock **132** Pictures from History/Bridgeman Images **133a** © Michael Zegers/age fotostock **133b, 134a** Isarachai Buranaut **134b** Pictures from History/Bridgeman Images **135** National Archives of Thailand, Bangkok **137a** Zoonar GmbH/Alamy **137b** Cam42 shared via CC BY-SA 3.0 https://en.wikipedia.org/wiki/Rural_Khmer_house Re-drawn by Drazen Tomic **138l** © Jose Fuste Raga/ age fotostock **138r** Barbara Anello-Adnani **139al** © JTB Photo/Universal Images Group/age fotostock **139ar** Hemis/AWLimages **139b** © René Mattes/age fotostock **140** © Hoberman/age fotostock **141a** SvetlanaSF/ShutterStock **141b** Neil Setchfield/ Alamy **142a, c, b** Royal Commonwealth Society Library **142-143** Shaun Higson/age fotostock/ SuperStock **144-145** Alexander Scheible/Alamy **146a** Thomas Cockrem/Alamy **146b** JTB Media Creation, Inc./Alamy **147l** Charles Martin/National Geographic Creative **147r** akg-images/Pictures From History **148-151** Justin Coupertino Umbu, January 2014 **153cl** Timothy O'Rourke **153ar** © Gerhard Zwerger-Schoner/age fotostock **153b** © Konrad Wothe/age fotostock **154l** Frank Hurley. nla.obj-149364541. National Library of Australia, Canberra **154r** Private Collection **155a** Private Collection **155bl** Marc Dozier/Getty Images **155br** © Luca Invernizzi Tettoni/age fotostock **156-157** George Steinmetz/National Geographic Creative **159al** National Geographic Creative/Bridgeman Images **159ar** Travel Library Limited/SuperStock **159b** Robert Harding/SuperStock **160al** akg-images/ De Agostini Picture Library/M. Leigheb **160ar** Travel Library Limited/SuperStock **160-161b** Michael Runkel/Robert Harding /SuperStock **161al** agf photo/SuperStock **161ar** Wolfgang Kaehler/ SuperStock **162-163a** © Michael Runkel/age fotostock **162bl** Junius B. Wood/National Geographic Creative **162br** © Philip Game/age fotostock **163** W. Robert Moore/National Geographic Creative **164-165b** © CSP_donyanedomam/ Fotosearch LBRF/age fotostock **165al** Charmaine 'Ilaiū Talei **165ar** © Don Mammoser/age fotostock **166** Luis Marden/National Geographic Creative **167** Charmaine 'Ilaiū Talei **168l** Photograph Alfred Burton, 1884, Tonga, purchased 1943, C.017627. Museum of New Zealand Te Papa Tongarewa, Wellington **168r** Photograph Alfred Burton, 1884, Tonga, purchased 1943, C.017628. Museum of New Zealand Te Papa Tongarewa, Wellington **169a** Drawing Charmaine 'Ilaiū Talei **169b** Charmaine 'Ilaiū Talei **170al** J. Budgett 2005 **170ar** Stock connection/SuperStock **170cl** age fotostock/SuperStock **170b** J. Budgett 2005 **172c** Seaphotoart/Alamy **172bl** Prisma Bildagentur AG/ Alamy **172br** © Mimi Forsyth/age fotostock **175al, ar** © Hawaiian Legacy Archive/age fotostock **175b** Danita Delimont Stock/AWL images **178-179** SuperStock/Alamy **180l** Private Collection/Peter Newark American Pictures/Bridgeman Images **180r** Private Collection **181** Sam Dao/Alamy **182a** © De Agostini Picture Library/G. Cappelli/Bridgeman Images **182b** Robert Harding/SuperStock **183** © Stuart McCall/age fotostock **184** © Witold Skrypczak/age fotostock **185a** © Universal Images Group/age fotostock **185bl, c, cr** Danita Delimont Stock/AWL Images **185br** © Donyanedomam/ Dreamstime.com **186** Photograph Harmon Parkhurst. Collections in the Museum of New Mexico, Sante Fe **187a** Antony Souter/Alamy **187b** Robert Harding/ Alamy **188** © De Agostini Editore/age fotostock **189a, cl, c, cr, br** Julian Castro **189bl** © Gabriel Cusmir/age fotostock **190-191a** Olga Kolos/Alamy **190bl,br, 191b** Lucia Garzon **192al** © José Enrique Molina/age fotostock **192ar** © Picture Contact BV/ Horizons WWP/age fotostock **192bl** © Keith Levit/ age fotostock **192br** © Christopher Rennie/age fotostock **193-195** Marcial Blondet and Sofía Rodríguez-Larrain **197a** Peter Langer/Design Pics/ SuperStock **197cl** Walter Bibikow/AWL Images **197c, cr, bl, br** Photograph Pablo González A **198** Concept Nicole Albornoz, Vania Celpa Valentina Contreras, Fabián Figueroa, Fernanda Muñoz. Re-drawn by Drazen Tomic **199** Photographs Arch. Amanda Riverá **201** © Mónica Ferrari **202** © Michel Renaudeau/age fotostock **204** Private Collection **205a** Reda & Co srl/Alamy **205b** © CSP_mathes/ Fotosearch LBRF/age fotostock **206al** © CSP_ zhuzhu/Fotosearch LBRF/age fotostock **206bl** © Stefano Cellai/age fotostock **206r** © Digfoto/age fotostock **207** Aga Khan Award for Architecture **208-209a** © De Agostini/Archivio J. Lange/age fotostock **209bl** Donald Mac Leish/National Geographic Creative **209br** Philippe Joudiou/ akg-images **210** © Raga Jose Fuste/age fotostock **211a** © De Agostini/age fotostock **211b** © Gounot/ age fotostock **212-215** Beniamino Polimeni **217a** © Peter Giovannini/age fotostock **217b** Photononstop/ SuperStock **218-221** © James Morris **223a** David Evans/Getty Images **223c, br** © C. Sappa/age fotostock **223bl** © Alvaro Leiva/age fotostock **224a, cr, bl** © Eric Lafforgue/age fotostock **224br** Photograph Adam Stones, 2013 **225** © DEA/A. Tessore/age fotostock **226-227** © Ian Trower/Robert Harding **228al** V.C. Scott O'Connor **228ar** Debbie Whelan 1999 **228cla** A.C. Britton **228clb** Royal Geographical Society (with IBG) **228bl** Images of Africa Photobank/Alamy **228br, 229** Sabena Jane Blackbird/Alamy **230** Dick Durrance II/National Geographic Creative **231al** De Klerk/Alamy **231ar** Ariadne Van Zandbergen/Getty Images **231cla** Photononstop/SuperStock **231cra** Photononstop/ SuperStock **231clb** Ariadne Van Zandbergen/Alamy **231crb** Travelpix/Alamy **231bl** Ariadne Van Zandbergen/Alamy **231br** Hemis/Alamy **232a** © Blaine Harrington/age fotostock **232c** image BROKER/SuperStock **232cl, cr, bl, br** Debbie Whelan 2001 **234l** © Joseph Sohm/age fotostock **234r** Walter Peters **235a** Ariadne Van Zandbergen/ Alamy **235b** © Oliver Gerhard/age fotostock **237al** British Airways Archive **237ar** English Heritage **237cl, cr, b, 238** Peter Sheehan **239al, ar** © Bandar El Malaq **239b** Peter Sheehan **240-241** © Dr Sandra Piesik **242a** Ronald Lewcock **242b** Philippe Marion/ Getty Images **243** Ronald Lewcock **244l** © Duby Tal/ age fotostock **244r** © Walter Bibikow/age fotostock **245a** © CSP_SeanPavonePhoto/Fotosearch LBRF/ age fotostock **245b** © Fabian von Poser/age fotostock **246** Ron Havilio **247r** UNESCO **248** Suad Amiry. Redrawn by Drazen Tomic **249al** © Riwaq Photo Archive, Photo by David Landis **249ar, cl, cr** © Riwaq Photo Archive, Photo Mia Grondahl **249c** © Riwaq Photo Archive **249bc, b** © Riwaq Photo Archive, Photo by David Landis **251al** © Tom Koene/ age fotostock **251ar, cr** Rami Daher **251b** © Tom Pepeira/Iconotec/age fotostock **253** Paul Doyle/ Alamy **254-257** Saverio Mecca **258l** © Antonello Perissinotto **258r** akg-images **259a** © José Fuste Raga/age fotostock **259b** Tammy Gaber **260-261** Robert Harding/Alamy **262-263** Hacer Mutlu Danaci **264l** R.A.F. **264r** A. Davis **265a** © Underwood Archives/age fotostock **265b** Ahmad Al-Rubaye/ AFP/Getty Images **267a** Copyright Subhi Al-Azzawi. Redrawn by Drazen Tomic **267c, bl** Nik Wheeler/ Alamy **267cl** Ali Yussef/AFP/Getty Images **267br** © Eric Lafforgue/age fotostock **268** Peter Kohler **269l** © Pitt Rivers Museum, University of Oxford (2004.130.16808.1) **269r** © Pitt Rivers Museum, University of Oxford (2004.130.29534.1) **270** © Pitt Rivers Museum, University of Oxford (2004.130.23206.1) **271a** © Pitt Rivers Museum, University of Oxford (2004.130.13672.1) **271cl** © Pitt Rivers Museum, University of Oxford (2004.130.10541.1) **271cr** © Pitt Rivers Museum, University of Oxford (2004.130.10467.1) **271bl** © Pitt Rivers Museum, University of Oxford (2004.130.774.1) **271br** © Pitt Rivers Museum, University of Oxford (2004.130.16986.1) **272-273** © Nicol Faridani/age fotostock **274** © Egmont Strigl/age fotostock **275al** © Egmont Strigl/ age fotostock **275ar** © Ivan Vdovin/age fotostock **275c** © Jack Malipan/age fotostock **275bl** © Massimo Pizzotti/age fotostock **275br** © Richard Ashworth/age fotostock **276l** R. Byron **276r** W.R. Rickmers **277** Roland and Sabrina Michaud/akg-images **278-279** © Xavier Fournier **280-281** © Martin Puddy/age fotostock **282al, cl, cr, br** Yasmeen Lari **282ar** © Shehzad Noorani/age fotostock **282bl** Neil Cooper/Alamy **285al** akg-images/Sputnik **285ar, b** Saverio Mecca and Sabine Hajiyeva **287-289** © Anna Letswaart **289a** Anna Letswaart. Redrawn by Drazen Tomic **290-291** © Chris Bradley/ age fotostock **292** W.R. Rickmers **293al** © Ton Koene/age fotostock **293ar** © Michael Runkel/age fotostock **293cl** © Image source/age fotostock **293b** © Joerg Reuther/age fotostock **295al** Aurora Photos/Alamy **295ar** gotravel/Alamy **294-295b** © Daniel Kreher/age fotostock **297al, ar, cl, b** Agnes Birtalan **297cr** © CSP_afhunta/Fotosearch LBRF/ age fotostock **298-299** © Philippe Michel/age fotostock **302-303** Paul Street/Alamy **304** Courtesy the State Archives of Florida **305al** Eye Ubiquitous/ SuperStock **305ar** Gray Read and Larisa Marenco **305b** Photo by Willard R. Culver/National Geographic/Getty Images **306a** Stephen Saks Photography/Alamy **306b** Charles O. Cecil/Alamy **307** © John Wollwerth/easyFotostock/age fotostock **308al** Michele Falzone/Alamy **308ar** Cienpies Design/Alamy **308bl** imageBROKER/Alamy **308br** Krys Bailey/Alamy **309** Arch. Natalia Jorquera **311al** Arch. Helena Gallardo **311ar** Arch. Alejandro Ferreiro **311cla** Arch. Natalia Jorquera **311cra** isabela66 **322clb** Arch. Natalia Jorquera **311crb** imageBROKER/SuperStock **311bl** BrazilPhotos. com/Alamy **311br** BrazilPhotos.com/Alamy **312** Photo © Hugh Palmer. From *The Most Beautiful Villages of Spain* by Hugh Palmer, Thames & Hudson, London and New York **313** akg-images/Imagno/ Austrian Archives **314l** © Justforever/Dreamstime. com **314r** Charles Bowman/Alamy **315a** Shirley Kilpatrick/Alamy **315b** Hemis/Alamy **316al** Photograph Fernando Vegas and Camilla Mileto **316ar** Kirsty McLaren/Alamy **316bl** © Justforever/ Dreamstime.com **316br, 317, 318, 319a** Photographs Fernando Vegas and Camilla Mileto **319b** Westend61/SuperStock **320al** Peter Noyce/Alamy

320ar incamerastock/Alamy **320cla, ca, cra** Photographs Fernando Vegas and Camilla Mileto **320clb, cb** Photograph Fernando Vegas and Camilla Mileto **320crb** Trond Hillestad/Mauritius/SuperStock **320bl** Photograph Fernando Vegas and Camilla Mileto **320br** © Robert Zehetmayer/Dreamstime.com **322al, ar** Photograph Fernando Vegas and Camilla Mileto **322cr** Kathy deWitt/Alamy **322bl** © CSP_lachris77/Fotosearch LBRF/age fotostock **322br** westend61/SuperStock **323** Blendimages/SuperStock **325al, ar** Photo © Hugh Palmer. From *The Most Beautiful Villages of Spain* by James Bentley, Thames & Hudson, London and New York **325cla** © ICP/age fotostock **325clr** Photo © Hugh Palmer. From *The Most Beautiful Villages of Spain* by James Bentley, Thames & Hudson, London and New York **325clb** © Olaf Protze/age fotostock **325crb** © Lluís Real/age fotostock **325bl** © Jürgen Schwarz/age fotostock **325br** Photo © Hugh Palmer. From *The Most Beautiful Villages of Spain* by Hugh Palmer, Thames & Hudson, London and New York **326al** © Chris Mattison/age fotostock **326ar** © John Short/age fotostock **326cl, c** Photo © Hugh Palmer. From *The Most Beautiful Villages of England* by James Bentley, Thames & Hudson, London and New York **326ca** © Vladdeep/Dreamstime.com **326cr** © Ron Zmiri/age fotostock **326bl** Chris Hammond/Alamy **326br** Robert Harding/SuperStock **329al** Suzanne Harris-Brandts **329ar** SFM Titti Soldati/Alamy **329cl** © CSP_atasitseli/Fotosearch LBRF/age fotostock **329c, cr** Suzanne Harris-Brandts **329b** © Konrad Zelazowski/age fotostock **330-331b** © Zoonar/Uwe Bauch/age fotostock **331a** © Jo Deleker/age fotostock **332-333** Courtesy J.Smadja **334- 337** F. Darragon **338** © Yongsky/Dreamstime.com **339** © Leonid Andronov/iStock **340a** John Warburton-Lee Photography/Alamy **340b** © Arvinshen/Dreamstime.com **341l** © Shulin Meng **341r** Photograph Zengzong Ma **342** Photograph Zhu Tan **343al** © The Ivy Press Ltd/Coral Mula **343ar** Photograph Yuanhang Luo **343c** Photograph Yuanhang Luo **343b** © Wxin/Dreamstime.com **345** Michael S. Yamashita/Getty Images **346** © Eastphoto RF/age fotostock **347-349** John Amato **350** © JTB Photo/Universal Images Group/age fotostock **351, 352a, bl** Courtesy Professor Kyung-Rip Park **352br** © Im Boohyun/age fotostock **353** Private Collection **354-355b** Photograph courtesy Dr. Yi-Jeng Tseng **355al, ar** Drawn by Chun-Sze Lin **356r** Private Collection **357-358, 359al, ar, c, bl** Photographs courtesy Professor Don Choi **359br** JTB Media Creation, Inc./Alamy **360a, bl** Photograph courtesy Professor Don Choi **360br** MacDuff Everton/National Geographic Creative **364-365** Danita Delimont Stock/AWL Images **366l** akg-images **366r** akg-images/De Agostini Picture Library **367** © Melissa Mercier/age fotostock **368a** © Abbie Enock/age fotostock **368b** © John Greim/age fotostock **369** Vincent Marie Langlois, *Settlement at Lituya Bay*, 1786. Bibliothèque Nationale, Paris. Photo akg- images **370** Image D-00692. Courtesy the Royal BC Museum and Archives, Victoria, Canada **371al** Michael Wheatley/All Canada Photos/SuperStock **371ar** John E. Marriott/All Canada Photos/SuperStock **371b** © Aldona Jonaitis **372a** David Leadbitter/Alamy **372b** Cordier Sylvain/Hemis/SuperStock **373** Gunter Marx/NA/Alamy **374** Gazel Genevieve/Alamy **375a** © Hartmut Pöstges/age fotostock **375b** Gisle Jakhelln **376a** Robert Harding/Alamy **376b** © CSP_aaalesja/Fotosearch LBRF/age fotostock **377** Gisle Jakhelln **378a** © Johnny Franzn/age fotostock **378cl** Arterra Picture Library/Alamy **378bl** Volodymyr Melnyk/Alamy **378br** Johner Images/Alamy **379l** Lars-Ove Jonsson/Alamy **379r** Kunst and Scheidulin/Alamy **380** FocusEurope/Alamy **381** Photographs Lena Palmqvist **383** Doug Pearson/AWL images **384al** Maurice Savage/Alamy **384ar** RJH_RF/Alamy **384cl** Tatiana Savvateeva www.123rf.com **384bl** FinPics/Alamy **384cr** © Kirsti Kovanen **384br** © Peter Erik Forsberg/age fotostock **385a** Measure drawing of Iso-Niemi by Markku Mattila **385b** Measure drawing by Pekka Huima from Measure drawings archive at Technical University of Helsinki. Photograph Kirsti Kovanen **386l** Private Collection **386r** © Sovfoto/Universal Images Group/age fotostock **387** Zoonar GmbH/Alamy **388al** Andrey Kekyalyaynen/Alamy **388ar** Andrey Nekrasov/Alamy **388b** © Nikolay Gyngazov/age fotostock **389** A. Mainicheva **390** Photograph Dean Conger/Corbis via Getty Images **391a** A. Mainicheva **391b** Corentin Le Gall/Alamy **392-393** © V. Vladimir/age fotostock **394a** age fotostock/SuperStock **394bl** Kent Kobersteen/National Geographic Creative **394br** Ivan Vdovin/Alamy **395, 396, 397al** © Anna Permilovskaya **397ar** VPC Travel Photo/Alamy **397cl** © Anna Permilovskaya **397b** Artem Konovalov/Alamy **398** © Dchulov/Dreamstime.com **399** © G. Pohl/age fotostock **400** © A. Мальцев, 2008 **401** © CSP_afhunta/Fotosearch LBRF/age fotostock **402** © O. Мальцева, 2009 **403** Zoonar GmbH/Alamy **404-405** Westend/SuperStock **406al, ar** E. R. Pretyman Collection. Courtesy the Tasmanian Archive & Heritage Office, Tasmania. **406c** Courtesy Anthony Mitchell **406bl** © Andrew Harris/age fotostock **406br** David Wall/Alamy **407** © Christian Handl/age fotostock **408l** Augustus Earle, *A tabood store-house at Range-hue (Rangihoua)*, Bay of Islands, New Zealand, 1827. Rex Nan Kivell Collection NK12/69. National Library of Australia, Canberra **408r** John Webber, *View of a Hippah or Fortified Village*, 1777. Photograph © BL/Robana Picture Library/age fotostock **409a** Fabien Astre/Alamy **409b** David Wall/Alamy **410al** © M. Fantin/age fotostock **410ar** Rua Kenana Hepetipa's wooden circular courthouse and meeting house at Maungapohatu, c. 1908. A. P. Godber Collection. Alexander Turnbull Library, New Zealand **410bl** © Werner Forman Archive/age fotostock **410br** Burton Brothers **411** © Horst Mahr/age fotostock **414-415** Norbert Eisele-Hein/ AWL images **416** akg-images/Universal Images Group/Universal History Archive **417a** © M Lohmann/age fotostock **417b** © Andoni Canela/age fotostock **418a** © Alaska Stock Images/age fotostock **418b, 419** Gregory A. Reinhardt. Redrawn by Drazen Tomic **420-421** Sebastian Wasek/Alamy **422l** © Javier Larrea/age fotostock **422r** Drawing Drazen Tomic © Thames & Hudson Ltd, London **423a** JB-Fotografie/F1 Online/SuperStock **423cl** © Olaf Krüger/age fotostock **423bl, br** Sigríður Sigurðardóttir, John M. Steinberg & Douglas J. Bolender **424** World History Archive/Alamy **425a** Arterra Picture Library/Alamy **425b** Kjell-Åke Aronsson **427** Photograph Fernando Guerra – FG+SG **429** Photos Hiroyuki Oki, Courtesy Vo Trong Nghia Architects **431** Photos T+E **432-433** Anne Heringer and Eike Roswag **435** Anna Heringer **436a, bl, br** Lama Tone **436cr** Godfey Boehnke. Courtesy University of Auckland, New Zealand **438-439** © Dr Sandra Piesik **440-441** Emily Mannion and Thomas O Brien **442-443** Photographs Darren Carter, Morgan Sindall **444-445** Photographs Will Green **446-447** Atelier TeamMinus **448-449** © John Butlin **453a, cl, cr, bl** AKAA/Nazes Afroz **453br** AKAA/Maria Grazia Cutuli Foundation **454-455** Erik Jan Ouwerkerk, 2009 **456-457** Francis Kéré **459a** Hollmén Reuter Sandman Architects **459b 460-461** Photography Fernando Guerra – FG+SG **462** Photos Ivan Juarez **465 endpapers AfriPics.com/Alamy**

Index

Page numbers for illustrations are indicated in *italic*

Acknowledgments

I dedicate this book to my mother.

Following my lecture to launch *Arish: Palm-Leaf Architecture* for Thames & Hudson in spring 2012, my commissioning editor Lucas Dietrich asked 'Would you like to review the entire world?' My answer was 'Yes!' Little did I know what this commitment would entail. At the time I was exploring the extinction of indigenous knowledge in the United Arab Emirates, and I was emphasizing the climatic differences between dry and temperate climate zones to a predominately London-based audience. Expanding this research to include all five of the world's climate zones would require an enormous collaborative endeavour.

I would like to acknowledge Lucas Dietrich for his invitation to be the general editor of *Habitat* and for all the support I received during its preparation. Thanks go to the entire Thames & Hudson team behind the publication, especially Rebecca Roke, and to the international publishers that have also supported the book.

I knew that I could not undertake the research for *Habitat* on my own and I am thankful to the Almighty for allowing me to find over 100 international contributors. Their contributions are so important because they capture the origins of sustainable development around the world, as well as offering invaluable information about global climate change action today. To all of the contributors who responded to my request and agreed to take part in the book, thank you. Your dedication and efforts are much appreciated. And for those who could not contribute, but who directed me to people that could help, I also extend my thanks.

Thank you to my proofreaders Susan Dinor, Sr Ursula Horan OP, Fr Nicholas Crowe OP, Anne Clarke and Rebecca Roke. A personal thank you goes to my family and friends, especially my mother, Patricia Crinnion and Patricia Davey.

Habitat's mission aligns with the implementation of the UNFCCC's Paris Agreement and the Sustainable Development Goals, and this mission does not end with its publication.

Sandra Piesik

Images on the cover are from pages 79a, 109bl, 130–131, 160–161b, 220a, 235b, 360a, 432al and 454, with the exception of: front cover, above left: Morocco's Technology School of Guelmim. Photography Fernando Guerra – FG+SG; centre left: Mudhif belonging to Zair Hashim Bidin, Iraq, from the Thesiger Collection © Pitt Rivers Museum, University of Oxford (2004.130.10541.1); centre right: Wooden shingles. Westend 61/Superstock; below left: Bamboo houses in Manizales, Colombia. Jeremy Horner/Alamy Stock Photo; back cover, centre left: Houses in Qeqertarsuaq, Iceland © Norbert Eisele-Hein imageBROKER/Alamy Stock Photo.

First published in the United Kingdom in 2017 as *Habitat: Vernacular Architecture for a Changing Planet* by Thames & Hudson Ltd, 181A High Holborn, London WC1V 7QX

This compact hardback edition published in 2023

Habitat: Vernacular Architecture for a Changing Climate
© 2017 and 2023 Thames & Hudson Ltd, London

Text © 2017 the authors

Project managed and edited by Rebecca Roke, corvo-uk.com
Book design and layout by Peter Dawson, gradedesign.com

Maps by JP Map Graphics Ltd
Copy editing by Ian McDonald
'Building with Bamboo' translated from the Japanese by Helena Simmonds

All Rights Reserved. No part of this publication may be reproduced or transmitted in any form or by any means, electronic or mechanical, including photocopy, recording or any other information storage and retrieval system, without prior permission in writing from the publisher.

British Library Cataloguing-in-Publication Data
A catalogue for this book is available from the British Library

ISBN 978-0-500-34376-0

Printed in Hong Kong

FSC www.fsc.org MIX Paper from responsible sources FSC® C144853

Be the first to know about our new releases, exclusive content and author events by visiting
thamesandhudson.com
thamesandhudsonusa.com
thamesandhudson.com.au